ASAF A. A. FYZEE

Cases in the Muhammadan Law of India, Pakistan and Bangladesh

ASAF A. A. FYZEE

Cases in the Muhammadan Law of India, Pakistan and Bangladesh

Second Edition

Edited and revised by

Tahir Mahmood

OXFORD
UNIVERSITY PRESS

OXFORD
UNIVERSITY PRESS

YMCA Library Building, Jai Singh Road, New Delhi 110 001

Oxford University Press is a department of the University of Oxford. It furthers the University's objective of excellence in research, scholarship, and education by publishing worldwide in

Oxford New York

Auckland Cape Town Dar es Salaam Hong Kong Karachi Kuala Lumpur Madrid Melbourne Mexico City Nairobi New Delhi Shanghai Taipei Toronto

With offices in

Argentina Austria Brazil Chile Czech Republic France Greece Guatemala Hungary Italy Japan Poland Portugal Singapore South Korea Switzerland Thailand Turkey Ukraine Vietnam

Oxford is a registered trade mark of Oxford University Press in the UK and in certain other countries

Revised and reprinted in India by Oxford University Press, New Delhi by arrangement with Oxford University Press, Oxford

First published in 1965
Second Edition 2005

ISBN 13: 978-0-19-565450-9
ISBN 10: 0-19-565450-1

Typeset in Times New Roman in 10/12
by Excellent Laser Typesetters, Pitampura, Delhi 110 034
Printed in India at Pauls Press, New Delhi 110 020
and published by Manzar Khan, Oxford University Press,
YMCA Library Building, Jai Singh Road, New Delhi 110 001

To the Memory of

JUSTICE SYED MAHMOOD

Master of Law

and

Master of Language

Abū Ḥanīfa said:
No one should be permitted to act as a
judge for more than a year.

It would be proper for the King to look into the affairs of this official and when a year elapses, the King should say: There is nothing wrong with you, but I fear that you will forget the law. So, return and study the law and come back to us. Then, we shall appoint you for a second term (*Al-Nihāya*).

Fatāwā 'Ālamgīrī (Būlāq), III : 317

Preface to the Second Edition

Professor Asaf Ali Asghar Fyzee was one of the most distinguished scholars of Muslim law in modern India. He and I had a very special teacher-taught relationship, though formally I had never been his student. In Delhi's Gymkhana Club where he stayed on his visits to the town we used to have long academic discussions. We had difference of opinion on certain points of law and yet respected each other's views. In 1974 he honoured me by citing my works in the fourth edition of his *Outlines of Muhammadan Law*. On the eve of his birthday the following year a group of his admirers gave me the privilege of editing a festschrift for him. Titled *Family Law and Social Change*,[1] the book had among its contributors many great law brains including Justice Mohammad Hidayatullah. In his foreword to the book eminent jurist Nani Palkhivala had observed about Fyzee that 'he is vastly knowledgeable and vastly lovable' and his 'cheerful, debonair disposition is infectious'. The memory of my association with these great men of the past today makes me sad, as all three are no more amidst us. May their noble souls rest in peace.

Son of one of the daughters of the great nationalist leader and judge Badruddin Tyabji, Fyzee belonged to the Sulaimani Bohora sect of the Isma'ili school of Islamic law, which has a rather microscopic presence in the global Muslim community. He was, however, destined to become a great scholar of Islamic law in its entirety which he studied in its original Arabic sources after having mastered the language in Cambridge. A prolific legal author, he wrote a lot on the Sunni and the Shi'a schools of Islamic law and through a monumental work introduced to the English-speaking world the greatest Isma'ili authority, Qadi al-Nu'man's *Da'aim al-Islam*. Having made an analytical approach to all laws and their sources, he presented these to his readers with a reformist's perception. Writing his 'credo' in his work *A Modern Approach to Islam* (1963), he had observed:

> I do revere the great interpreters of Islam, but I crave their indulgence if I cannot share their beliefs, for belief is at bottom a matter of individual conscience. I cannot agree that they are the keepers of my

1 Tripathi, Bombay, 1975.

conscience. It is the duty of the scholars of each age to interpret the faith of Islam in their own times.

For over half a century Fyzee has been a household name for the English-speaking students of Muslim law. The learned scholar's *Outlines of Muhammadan Law* was first published in 1949. Fifteen years later, while preparing its third edition, he had conceived a case-book on the subject as a 'companion volume'. Titled *Cases on the Muhammadan Law of India and Pakistan*, it was published in 1965.

In his preface to the fourth edition of the *Outlines*, dated 15 November 1971, the author had observed:

> The book was written some twenty years ago; probably a new book should now be attempted, or at least a fresh mind entrusted with the task of editing it.

Very unfortunately his wish could not be fulfilled for thirty-five long years. It is gratifying that the OUP is now bringing out a new edition of the *Cases*, and I deem it a privilege to have been asked to prepare it. Let us hope his *Outlines* will also be published soon in a fresh edition.

Momentous developments have taken place in the area of Muslim law across the world during the last three decades of the twentieth century and in these early years of the new millennium. There have been massive legislation and indeed a spate of judicial decisions all around. It is just not possible to update an old text so as to accommodate all these new trends and changes. Yet, I have done my best to edit and revise Fyzee's forty-year old *Cases* to give the readers a fair idea of where its original contents now stand.

First, a word about the title of the book. While signing the preface to the first edition of his *Outlines* in 1948, Fyzee had forcefully defended his use of the expression 'Muhammadan law' and later repeated the expression in the title of this 'companion volume'—the *Cases*. The term, howsoever it may be spelt, is now considered a misnomer and stands abandoned in the legal circles worldwide. The scholars of law even in Britain, where this expression was born, do not use it any more. In 1968 a learned Muslim Chief Justice of India, Mohammad Hidayatullah, had so denounced it in his preface to the 16th edition of Mulla's *Mahomedan Law*:

> The name of the book has been retained, but I may say that this expression was coined by the English. Islamic law was not Mohammad's law. The expressions 'Mahomedan' and 'Mahomedanism' are not correct and, in any sense, are even objectionable. The proper expressions are Islamic law and Muslim law.

In agreement with the great judge, in early 1970s I had managed to get the rather obnoxious term 'Mohammedan law' replaced with 'Muslim law' in all publications of the Indian Law Institute and also in the *All India Reporter*. Titles of legal classics, however, cannot be changed and so Muslim law had remained 'Mahommadan law' in DF Mulla's book when edited by Justice Hidayatullah. For the same reason it remains 'Muhammadan law' in this new edition of Fyzee's *Cases*. However, since the 'India and Pakistan' of 1965 are now India, Pakistan and Bangladesh, the name of the subcontinent's third country has been added to the title.

The illustrious author of this book had picked up forty-three judicial decisions, which he considered important, and arranged these under nineteen different chapters, offering his own introductory remarks about each case prefixed to the texts of or extracts from their judgments. Most of these decisions are now quite old, handed down in the nineteenth or the early twentieth century. In preparing this second edition, on account of my profound respect for the distinguished author I have neither disturbed his selection and arrangement of cases nor commented on any of his prefatory statements. Instead, at the end of each of his nineteen chapters I have added brief updates indicating the later developments—both statutory and judicial—in respect of the cases covered therein and the current legal position of their subject matters.[2]

To manage the space required for my updates I have taken the liberty of trimming the texts of some old judgments which are now of less relevance in the entire subcontinent due to the impact of the fast-developing constitutions, ever-increasing legislation, and the growing case law in all its three countries. Further, I have omitted the original Arabic texts of extracts from classical Islamic legal texts found in some chapters of the old edition. While deleting these texts, which are not of any great use now for the general readers, I have provided their full references which may be looked up by the interested researchers.

The present edition refers to many new statutes and more than a hundred new cases over and above those referred to in the first edition.

I hope the legal fraternity will find this new edition of Fyzee's *Cases* useful. Interested readers may also make reference to my book *Islamic Law in the Indian Courts since Independence: Fifty Years of Judicial Interpretation*,[3] which incorporates comments by different critics on

[2] In all the updates the references in the parentheses are to the forty-three cases included in the original book, whose serial numbers have been retained in this new edition.

[3] Qazi Publishers, New Delhi, 1997.

almost all the cases in the area of Muslim law decided in India from 1948 to 1996.

Planned about three years ago, this new edition of Fyzee's casebook is being published quite beyond the original schedule, due to some unavoidable reasons. As the proverbial 'blessing in disguise', this delay has enabled me to include in it some very recent Indian rulings.

Fyzee's Sahab had breathed his last in Bombay on 23rd October 1981. By a coincidence I am signing this preface to the new edition of his book on his 23rd death anniversary.

23 October 2004 — Tahir Mahmood

Preface to the First Edition

This is a companion volume to the *Outlines of Muhammadan Law* (3rd ed., 1964) and is intended for students and teachers. The significance of Muhammadan law can be estimated from the fact that it is applicable to 425 million in some twenty countries of Asia, Africa, and Europe.[1] And of these, there is a compact group of 110 million in India and Pakistan, following the Hanafi school of Sunnite law, united to a considerable extent by ties of language, custom, race, and religion. Islam professes to be a message to humanity, and not to any particular country or people. European studies suffer from exclusive preoccupation with the Arabic-speaking countries and with the problems of the cradle of Islam. Thus the Muslims of the Indo-Pakistan subcontinent offer an exceptional field for the study of Hanafi law, as it is actually administered in the courts.

Secondly, Islamic law (*Sharī'at, fiqh*) has come under the influence of common law and equity in India and Pakistan. In so far as the rules applicable have been modified to suit the requirements of a changing society, and to satisfy modem concepts of social justice, Muhammadan law as received in the subcontinent is also of interest to students of comparative law.

Thirdly, the rules of law have been laid down in reported cases and statutes. The language of the judiciary and the legislature has been English for the last 150 years or so; and English continues to be the language of the Supreme Courts and of the High Courts, of India and of Pakistan, even after the achievement of independence in 1947.

As English is now a world language, widely used even in Africa, no less than in the Commonwealth, its correct use by judge and practitioner, teacher and student, becomes a matter of practical necessity. A loose expression or confused thinking would lead to serious consequences to litigants. It is an unfortunate fact that in certain courts of record greater attention is not paid to the use of simple words, the avoidance of cliches, and to accuracy in grammar, spelling and idiom. Americanisms are occasionally affected by non-Americans without justification; prepositions not acceptable to the

[1] The writer's article 'The Relevance of Muhammadan Law in the Twentieth Century' *Cambridge Law Journal*, 1963, 261–9, may be consulted.

Dictionary, and loose spellings of the mid-nineteenth century, are allowed to appear in judgments. It is my hope that the opinions in this volume will afford ample illustrations of that simplicity of language, lucidity of style, and cogency of argument which are the especial marks of the jurists whose judgments have been selected by me. The best advice that can be given to the beginner is, as Victor Hugo stated, to aim at

Concision in style;
Precision in thought;
Decision in life.

Fourthly, many of the volumes cited in this book are not now easily available to the student. A complete set of Indian Appeals is a rare and precious possession. The Indian reprint unfortunately contains mistakes both of spelling and of punctuation, and implicit reliance cannot be placed upon it. And several volumes of the official series of the High Court reports are no longer in print and are not available even second-hand, except rarely. Hence a handy volume containing the most cited cases relating to the Hanafi school would seem to be a desirable textbook and reference work for use by teachers and students, and it may prove useful to practitioners and judges as well.

Fifthly and lastly, these cases are of interest for the social history of the subcontinent during the last two centuries. The influence of custom (*The Aga Khan Case,* 1866); the commixture of races (*Abraham* v. *Abraham; Bhaiya Sher Bahadur* v. *Bhaiya Ganga Bakhsh*); the displacement of Islamic law by treaty between sovereigns (*Nawab Sultan Mariam Begum* v. *Nawab Saheb Mirza*); polygamy, concubinage, cruelty (*Moonshee Buzul-ul-Raheem* v. *Luteefut-oon-Nissa; Sayeeda Khanam* v. *Muhammad Sami; Itwari* v. *Asghari*); the frauds perpetrated upon *pardanashīn* women (*Mahomed Buksh* v. *Hosseini Bibi*)—these will probably interest the social historian as much as the lawyer.

I have tried to avoid the needless excision of judgments in the so-called interest of the student, believing that it is not possible to compress adequately in three pages what Lord Sumner or Justice Mahmood has to say in fifteen or twenty. Law and fact, according to English and Indian law, are closely interrelated; and often a cutting down of the judgment is like the pruning of a vine by an inexpert hand which, instead of producing a healthy crop, leaves us with a truncated cadaver. From this vain form of economy I have endeavoured to keep aloof. Nevertheless, in accordance with the wish of the publishers and the obvious need for economy, some careful pruning has been attempted in order to make the book easy to handle and moderate in price.

The headnotes provided are not by any means a substitute for what the student, with the help of the teacher, could do for himself. They must never be mistaken for the law; the law is to be found in the judgment, and it is strictly and logically related to the particular facts of the case. The note is a brief, rough, and imperfect aid to acquire a knowledge of the law.

I am indebted to Mr Motilal C. Setalvad, formerly Attorney-General of India, for reading the Introduction in typescript and making some valuable suggestions. I read in the chambers of Setalvad for four happy years, learning at close quarters the secret that goes to the making of a great advocate: sobriety, profundity, wisdom, independence.

The cases were selected and notes prepared in the Squire Law Library, Cambridge, while I was holding a Commonwealth Fellowship at St John's College, during the academic year 1962–3. Photocopies of the cases were very kindly prepared by a member of the staff, and I should like to offer my sincere thanks to the Librarian and staff for their kindness and invariable courtesy.

Similarly my thanks are due to Mrs S. Bhiwandkar, Librarian, Government Law College, Bombay, who helped me in a variety of ways when I was revising the notes and preparing the manuscript for the press.

Although most of the judges cited in this book are responsible for one decision only, it is of interest to examine the names of those who appear more than once: Lord Hobhouse 2 (8, 32), Lord Kingsdown 2 (4, 15), Lord Macnaghten 2 (6, 26), Arthur Wilson 2 (2, 43), Ameer Ali 3 (22, 31, 33), Lord Atkinson 3 (7, 14, 19), Syed Mahmood 5 (10, 18, 34, 36, 37).

And to the memory of Mahmood, J., I dedicate this volume.

Bombay A. A. A. F.
29 February 1964

Contents

Introduction

I. Islamic Law Proper

Islamic law (*Sharī'at, fiqh*) was introduced into India soon after the conquest of Sind by Muḥammad b. Qāsim in AD 712; but it was firmly established only after Sulṭān Quṭbu'd-dīn Aybak early in the thirteenth century. The history of its introduction, establishment, and development during seven centuries till the advent of the British has not yet been treated adequately, although materials for it have been collected by M. B. Ahmad[1] and others.[2] The early history of the law is not germane to our purpose, and we shall therefore confine our attention mainly to the British period, 1857–1947, and after.[3]

Although the administration of India was taken over by the Crown in 1857, the British judicial influence really began in the seventeenth century. The exercise of judicial powers by the East India Company commenced with the Charter of Charles II in 1661; but responsibility for the administration of justice was confined, until 1765, to the factories belonging to them. Later, with the establishment of the three High Courts in 1861,[4] a new chapter commenced and British law, including the principles of equity, became a part of the law of the land, and continues so to some extent even to this day.[5]

Muhammadan law was applied to Muslims as a matter of policy. The policy was to let Muslims be governed by their own personal laws in certain matters. Personal laws were based upon religion. The application of such laws was prescribed mostly by statutes; and the earliest trace of the statutory

1 *Administration of Justice in Medieval India*, Aligarh, 1941.

2 A fuller treatment of this part of the Introduction will be found in my article, 'Muhammadan law in India', *Comparative Studies in Society and History* (Ann Arbor, Mich.), v, 1963, 401–15, and therefore detailed references have been avoided. This article has been reprinted in (1964) 66 *Bombay Law Reporter*, Journal, 1–11.

3 A brief historical account will be found in M. C. Setalvad, *The Common Law in India* (Hamlyn Lectures, 12th ser.), London, 1960.

4 Ibid, 29 seqq.

5 Constitution of India, Article 372 (I); *Bank of India* v. *Bowman* (1955) 57 *Bombay Law Reporter* 345; *Outlines of Muhammadan Law*, 55.

application of Muhammadan law to the natives of India is to be found in the Charter of George II granted in 1753, whereby the Muslims could obtain exemption from the Mayor's Courts and have their cases adjudicated on the basis of their own religious personal laws. To implement this policy effectively it was laid down in 1772 that *muftīs* were to attend courts of justice as jurisconsults, to assist the courts in discovering the specific rule of law applicable. Sir Erskine Perry rightly observes:

A jurist *qua* jurist has only to deal with human laws: he recognizes the existence of divine laws, and their validity *in foro conscientiae* with those to whom they are addressed, or who believe in the revelation containing them; but he does not recognize them as enforceable in Courts of Justice any further than the secular power has ordained.[6]

The policy of applying the personal law in accordance with the religion of the party concerned was inherited by the British rulers from the Moghul administration; and it is well to remember that the principle of Indian law that Hindu law (*Dharmashāstra*) is to be applied to Hindus, and Muhammadan law (*fiqh*, *Sharī'at*) to Muslims is not a British innovation. It had its origin in earlier times when the Muslim rulers of India came to realize that it was not just or equitable to force their own notions of law on the people, and to accept the principle that each religious community was entitled to profess its own religion and to obey its own laws. The Hanafi authority, *Hedaya*, lays down:

We are commanded to leave them (*dhimmīs,* persons protected under a covenant) at liberty, in all things which may be deemed by them to be proper, according to the precepts of their own faith.[7]

The *Mufassal*[8] Regulation of 1772, promulgated during the time of Warren Hastings, and later enacted as Section 27 of the Regulation of 1780, provides:

In all suits regarding inheritance, marriage and caste, and other religious usages and institutions, the laws of the Koran with respect to Mahomedans, and those of the

6 Per Perry C. J. in *Kojas and Memons Case, Cases Illustrative of Oriental Life and the Application of English Law to India decided in H. M. Supreme Court at Bombay* (London, 1853). Known and cited as Perry's Oriental Cases 110, 122.

7 Hamilton's *Hedaya* (2nd ed., 1870), 57. Cited by Tyabji, 28.

8 Often misspelt *mofussil*. The regular and established mispronunciation in Bombay is as in *fuse*. An Arabic word, meaning 'cut off', that is from the mainstream of life and power, and therefore the 'country' or 'province' as distinct from the *ṣadr* (literally breast, front, chief), the town or capital, H. H. Wilson, *Glossary of Judicial and Revenue Terms*, edited by A. C. Ganguly and N. D. Basu (Eastern Law House, Calcutta, 1940), s.v. 'Mufassal'.

Shaster with respect to Gentoos,[9] and where only one of the parties shall be a Mahomedan or Gentoo, the laws and usages of the defendant shall invariably be adhered to.

In Islamic countries the rule of the *Sharī'at* is that the school or sub-school of a Muslim litigant is not taken into consideration; the *qazi*[10] follows his own rite. But in India, contrary to the invariable practice in Islam, the law of the individual concerned is ascertained and applied; and in cases of conflict, the law of the defendant prevails.

The general rules of the applicability of Muhammadan law, as laid down by the courts today, may be summarized as follows:

1. Where both the parties to the suit are Muslims belonging to the same school, the law of that school will apply;
2. Where the parties differ in religion, or do not belong to the same school of law, the law of the defendant will apply;
3. Where a person changes his religion, or his school of law within the fold of Islam, in good faith, the personal law ordinarily changes with immediate effect.
4. Where a person is converted to, or becomes a renegade from, Islam and then dies, the law of succession applicable to the estate of the deceased will be the law of the religion which he professed at the time of his death. The same rule obtains where a Sunnite Muslim adopts the Shiite faith, or vice versa.[11]

As the courts of the Company gave place to those of the Crown, and the English lawyers began to preside over the courts and to practise in them, it was found occasionally that there was no rule of law applicable, or that the 'native' law was in conflict with the common law, or that the indigenous rule was so old and unsuited to the needs of a rapidly developing society that some principle for doing substantial justice had to be enunciated. The first step was taken as early as 1726, when the Letters Patent issued during the reign of George I enabled the courts to decide 'according to justice and right';[12] this appears to be the earliest use of a phrase the meaning of which was not defined with precision. In course of time this was interpreted to mean British notions of justice and right, as understood by lawyers trained in the

9 Derived from Portuguese *gentio*, a gentile or heathen, and therefore a Hindu native of India, Wilson, *Glossary*.

10 Strictly *qāḍī*; in India, *kazi*. *Outlines of Muhammadan Law*, 319.

11 *Outlines of Muhammadan Law*, 76–7.

12 Setalvad, *Common Law*, 12.

British system. Thus the judicial officers very naturally drew upon the rich, though somewhat baffling, treasures of the common law of England.

Later, in 1832, came the direction that where no specific rules were laid down the judges were to act 'according to justice, equity and good conscience'.[13] A study of the older enactments and their chronology will show how the statutory provisions differed from province to province, and from year to year. As the case law increased and a variety of courts began to function, doubts began to be expressed as to the exact meaning of the magic formula, and it was left to Lord Hobhouse to give the classical elucidation in *Waghela* v. *Sheikh Masludin* (1887) 14 IA 89, 96, when he said:

> In point of fact, the matter must be decided by equity and good conscience, generally interpreted to mean the rules of English law if found applicable to Indian society and circumstances.[14]

Stephen, in presenting a report of the Law Commission on 31 March 1871, criticized the words of this phrase as an 'imperfect understanding of imperfect collections of not very recent editions of English textbooks'. And it is necessary now to urge a further consideration. In view of the fact that India has become a democratic republic, its continued dependence on the rules of English law will in time probably decrease. The principles of other European and American systems will have to be considered. The study of Islamic jurisprudence, governing 425 million in more than twenty countries, and particularly a critical and historical investigation into the *adab al-qāḍī* (duties and qualifications of the judges), may disclose other rules of natural justice for examination and adoption. It is by no means certain that the rules of common law and of equity will be deemed to be of primary importance, where no specific rule exists.

Nevertheless there can be no doubt that recourse to principles of common law and equity, in most instances, despite some understandable failures, removed the angularities of the law of Islam according to the Hanafi school, as interpreted and applied in India. By and large, the import of judicial principles brought this system in line with modern notions of social justice. To take a few obvious instances, we have: the law relating to *pardanashin*

13 Wilson, *Glossary*, 29 seqq.: Wilson's Introduction is valuable for the history of early enactments, and Tyabji has a comprehensive chart giving the variations in the wording of the enactments and their chronology (Tyabji, op. cit. 28). J. Duncan Derrett gives an account of the history of the term drawn from the writings of the schoolmen in his article 'Justice, Equity and Good Conscience' in *Changing Law in Developing Countries,* ed. J. N. D. Anderson (London, 1963), 114–53.

14 Tyabji, § 12; Setalvad, *Common Law*, 12; *Outlines of Muhammadan Law*, 55 and Index.

women,[15] particularly in reference to gifts and wills; the law of guardianship; the law of marriage, divorce, and cruelty; the rule that 'there is no magic in words' and that the 'pith and substance' of a transaction must be considered as of prime importance;[16] that the use of technical expressions imperfectly understood must not be allowed to prevail over the clear and explicit intention of a settlor.[17] It will thus appear that during the two centuries of British rule the law has in the main remained static and stationary, but for two salutary influences: legislation and the introduction of principles drawn from the common law of England and from Equity, as understood in the Courts of Chancery. Thus the system known as 'Muhammadan law' in India and Pakistan is the *Sharī'at* as modified by English law, both common and statutory, and Equity, in the varying social and cultural conditions of the subcontinent. While in essence the sources of Muhammadan law are the same as those of Islamic countries all over the world, in India and Pakistan Muhammadan law has tended to become a discrete system, somewhat at variance with its original formulations.[18]

It is here that a word may be said as to nomenclature, and to distinguish between 'Islamic law' and 'Muhammadan law'. The purists always insist on the use of the word 'Muslim' or 'Islamic'. This to my mind is needlessly pedantic and slightly inaccurate. The word *Muslim* is in Arabic a noun of action, derived from the verb *aslama*, and means 'one who accepts Islam as a religion'. Strictly speaking it cannot be applied to any thing or concept except a rational human being, capable of making a decision about his faith. Such terms as Muslim law, philosophy, science, art, culture, although in common use, are all unsatisfactory, for the analogy of the terms Buddhist, Christian, or Zoroastrian is hardly applicable. A less objectionable expression is 'Islamic law', a law which derives from or pertains to Islam. By Islamic law is meant the *Sharī'at* or *fiqh* in its pristine purity. Now it is well known that *Sharī'at* in its pure and undiluted form has never been enforced as law in India and Pakistan, and it is doubtful if it can be administered as law in the twentieth century. Muhammadan law, an expression introduced by European scholars and lawyers, is therefore a convenient expression for

15 A *pardanashīn* (or *-nishīn*) is a woman who habitually sits behind a *parda*, curtain. The compound is a Persian word, the suffix *nashīn* meaning 'sitting'. It is applied to a respectable female, Hindu or Muslim, who observes the rules of seclusion, and who on that account is excused from personal appearance in a court of justice (Wilson, *Glossary*).

16 Tyabji, 556, citing Lord Cairns.

17 For instance the observations of Wazir Hasan A. J. C. in *Amjad Khan* v. *Ashraf Khan* (1929) 4 Luck 305, 318.

18 J. Schacht, *An Introduction to Islamic Law* (Clarendon Press, 1964), 94 seqq.

that portion of the Islamic civil law which is applied in the subcontinent to the adherents of Islam as a personal law.

The distinction is clear; and for this reason an attempt has been made not to confuse the parent system, Islamic law (*Sharī'at, fiqh*) with its offshoot, the Muhammadan law of India and Pakistan.

II. Islamic Law in India

In this part of the Introduction it is proposed, first, briefly to mention the chief alterations introduced by the British; and second, with reference mainly to Privy Council decisions, to see how English law and equity influenced Muhammadan law in India.[19] An exhaustive enumeration of all the changes introduced by the British would necessarily embrace matters that are strictly outside the scope of this book. It would necessitate an inquiry into state policy, including legislation; constitutional law, in so far as it defines legislative and other functions; administration, including the establishment of the courts and the appointment of judges; procedure, civil as well as criminal; and a variety of other relevant questions. We shall therefore confine our attention to the most striking changes introduced by the British rulers affecting the application of Muhammadan law to Muslims, and even to non-Muslims (for example the law of pre-emption) in this subcontinent.

1. Slavery was abolished in 1843 (Act V of 1843), *Tyabji*, § 5E; *Wilson*, Glossary 162, 298.

2. The loss of civil rights on apostasy was abrogated. Caste Disabilities Removal Act (XXI of 1850); *Mitar Sen* v. *Maqbul Hasan* (1930) 57 IA 313: Case 41 below.

3. The outdated Islamic criminal law was abolished and replaced by a general law of crimes, the Indian Penal Code 1860.

4. A general law of Evidence, based upon English principles, was introduced by the Indian Evidence Act 1872; this rendered the Islamic rules obsolete.

5. A High Court of Judicature was established in each of the three provinces, Bombay, Calcutta, and Madras in 1861; and later other High Courts were also established by the Indian High Courts Act 1861.

19 For a fuller treatment of the cases, reference may be made to my article 'The Impact of English Law on the *Shariat* in India', *Revue Egyptienne de Droit International*, xviii, 1962, 1–27. Reprinted (1964) 66 *Bombay Law Reporter*, Journal, 107 seq., and 121 seq.

6. The law of pre-emption, applicable in a number of provinces by custom, was not considered to be consonant with 'justice, equity and good conscience' in Madras: *Ibrahim Saib* v. *Mun Mir* (1870) 6 Mad HCR 26, although it was applied even to non-Muslims in other parts of India.

7. The selective use of precedents was laid down by Sir Arthur Wilson in *Baker Ali Khan* v. *Anjuman Ara Begum* (1903) 30 IA 94, 112–13, adopting a dictum of Lord Hobhouse in *Abul Fata* v. *Russomoy* (1894) 22 IA 76, 86 seq.; Setalvád, *Common Law*, 47 seqq.; *Outlines of Muhammadan Law*, 49.

It is now proposed to consider the impact of British law on the applications of the *Sharī'at* in India; and for this it is desirable to restrict our inquiry mainly to the decisions of the Judicial Committee of the Privy Council reported in the series known as Indian Appeals. A few cases have also been taken from the earlier reports, *Moore's Indian Appeals*. The material for an exhaustive examination of this character is vast and would take a substantial volume by itself. Apart from the older reports, such as the Sadar Diwani Adalat Reports, the Bombay and other High Court Reports, and individual volumes such as Perry's *Oriental Cases*, there are hundreds of volumes embodying non-official reports in each of the High Courts, the most important of which seems to be the *All India Reporter*. The influence of British law has been felt in a variety of ways: sometimes there is the conscious adoption of a principle or of nomenclature or of a process of reasoning; in other cases there is an unconscious bias towards a common law doctrine, which in those times seemed to the British-trained judges to be more in accord with justice than the letter of the *Sharī'at*. This is to be seen in cases such as *Abul Fata* v. *Russomoy*,[20] where their Lordships of the Privy Council were so convinced of the pernicious effects of a gift in perpetuity that the Islamic doctrine—whatever its practical value—based as it was on a Tradition of the Prophet and accepted unanimously by all schools in Islam, was not appreciated by them and overruled.

The cases may be classified in four groups, as those where:

A. Muhammadan law is the same as English law but English terms, phraseology, and doctrines are employed;

B. Muhammadan law is modified by doctrines of the common law or of equity;

C. Muhammadan law is varied by custom; and

D. Muhammadan law is abolished or modified by statutory law.

20 See Case no. 32, infra.

A. Cases where Muhammadan Law is the Same as English Law but English Terms, Phraseology, and Doctrines are Employed

1. *Bona fide purchaser for value without notice*

The Privy Council in *Syud Bazayet Hossein* v. *Dooli Chund* (1878) 5 IA 211 laid down that a creditor of a deceased Muslim, whether in respect of dower or otherwise, cannot follow his estate into the hands of a bona fide purchaser for value, without notice to whom it had been alienated, whether by sale or mortgage. The rule of the Muhammadan was identical with that of the English statute. This is an excellent illustration of the use of English textbooks, cases, and statutes for deciding a point in which the two systems appear to be identical.

2. *A 'covinous' instrument*[21]

A gift made by a 'covinous' instrument for the purpose of defeating the creditors is bad; *Abdool Hye* v. *Mir Mohamed* (1883) 11 IA 10.

3. *Immoral custom*

Prostitution is considered immoral both by the law of Islam, and by British law following the ethical precepts of Christianity; hence certain customs followed by the Kanchans, a Muslim community of prostitutes in the Punjab, are contrary to Islam, immoral, and unenforceable: *Ghasiti* v. *Umrao Jan* (1893) 20 IA 193 (Case 8).

4. Wakf *and trust distinguished*

Hindu and Muhammadan endowments (*maths, wakfs*) are to be distinguished from English charitable foundations. The idea of 'trust' *(amāna* in Arabic) is known both to English law and Islamic law, but *wakf* is a distinct institution, and a *mutawallī* is not a trustee, but merely a manager or procurator: *Muhammad Rustam Ali* v. *Mushtaq Husain* (1920) 47 IA 224 and *Vidya Varuthi* v. *Balusami Ayyar* (1921) 48 IA 302; see Case 31 in this volume.

5. *Graveyard* wakf *designated as 'God's Acre'*

Deciding that a suit to recover property belonging to a *wakf*, dedicated as a cemetery, was not barred by limitation, Lord Sumner designated the graveyard as 'God's Acre'[22] (where the faithful are sown), and he held that the land was inalienable: *Abdur Rahim* v. *Narayan Das* (1922) 50 IA 84, 90.

21 *Covin* is old French for deceit, collusion. And *covinous* is used in the Statute, 13 Eliz. c. 5; *OED,* s.v. 'covin'.

22 *OED*; Ballentine, *Law Dictionary*, 553–4; Renton, *Encyclopaedia of the Laws of England*, vi. 79.

6. *Indictment, action*

Occasionally the courts in their inordinate zeal imported notions drawn exclusively from English law which were not suited to Indian conditions. Thus in *Manzur Hasan* v. *Muhammad Zaman* (1924) 52 IA 61, Lord Dunedin, delivering the judgment of the board, said that the method employed by the court below, in deciding the case and importing the distinction between 'indictment' and 'action' known to the common law, was wrong.

7. *Res judicata*

The English doctrine of *res judicata* has found a firm foothold in India, even in respect of a suit relating to a religious endowment such as *wakf*: *Abdur Rahim* v. *Barkat Ali* (1927) 55 IA 96.

B. Cases where Muhammadan Law is Modified by English Law

1. *Pre-emption in Madras*

The Muhammadan law of pre-emption was declared by the Madras High Court to be opposed to 'justice, equity and good conscience', as being one of the 'most unreasonable restraints upon the right of alienation': *Ibrahim Saib* v. *Muni Mir* (1870) 6 Mad HCR 26. In most of the other states of India it is at present applicable not only to Muslims but also to non-Muslims, on the grounds of 'justice, equity and good conscience'. The Chancellor's foot, still active in England, has crossed the seas and put in its appearance six thousand miles away from its original home.

2. *Family arrangements*

A lady of the Ithnā 'Asharī Shiite persuasion received certain property by a family arrangement on condition that she had no power to alienate it outside the family. This was urged to be an illegal clog, and contrary to the principles of Muhammadan law. It was held, citing two English cases, that she was not free to transfer the property, for the restriction was valid in such cases, and the sale to the outsider void: *Muhammad Raza* v. *Abbas Bandi* (1932) 59 IA 236.

3. *Pardanashīn women*

This is a most interesting subject, as it deals with a class of women who, being completely secluded from the normal life of the community and prevented from meeting persons of the opposite sex, are supposed to need the special protection of the courts, a protection that in England used to be extended in equity to married women, infants, and lunatics. A few selected cases will show how the English judges dealt with the problem.

(*a*) *Needless suspicion*. In *Mahomed Buksh* v. *Hosseini Bibi* (1888) 15 IA 81 Lord Macnaghten said that, while 'Their Lordships do not say a word which could interfere with the settled principles on which the court acts in considering the deeds of *pardanashīn* ladies' and the High Court below had entertained needless suspicion in arriving at its decision: 'Their Lordships cannot consider the judgment of the High Court satisfactory. The learned judges suspect everybody; they suspect everything'. Accordingly, they sustained the lady's deed of gift.

(*b*) *Independent advice*. There is no absolute rule that a deed of gift by a *pardanashīn* lady is invalid in the absence of proof of independent advice; and in upholding the lady's deed, the Board said, 'Much as their Lordships support and approve the protection given by law to a *pardanashīn* lady, they cannot transmute such a legal protection into a legal disability': *Kali Baksh* v. *Ram Gopal* (1913) 41 IA 23, 31–2.

(*c*) *Quantum of proof requisite*. The leading case on the subject, an exhaustive statement of the law, will be found in *Farid-un-Nisa* v. *Mukhtar Ahmad* (1925) 52 IA 342. An illiterate *pardanashīn* woman executed a deed whereby she settled the whole of her property by way of *wakf*, reserving a small monthly stipend to herself and her husband who was an invalid, and also the right for her life to use a house, the *mutawallīs* agreeing to pay the stipends and to keep the house in repair. In a suit to cancel the deed and recover possession of the house their Lordships held that the *mutawallīs* had not discharged the burden. Lord Sumner's judgment is considered the *locus classicus* on the kind of proof required in such cases. See Case 27, here.

4. *Treaty between sovereigns*

The effect of a treaty between two sovereign powers is a vital matter, as it may have the effect of abrogating the personal law of the parties. An endowment was made in 1842 by a King of Oudh (strictly, Awadh) in favour of his wife and descendants. This created a perpetuity and a line of succession unknown to Shiite law, which was applicable to the Nawab's family. Their Lordships, however, held that the arrangement of 1842 took effect as a contract or treaty between two sovereign powers; and in such cases the personal law of the parties was displaced by the arrangement arrived at between the high contracting parties: *Nawab Sultan Mariam Begum* v. *Nawab Saheb Mirza* (1889) 16 IA 175, 182; see Case no. 40, in this volume.

This case establishes that a treaty between two sovereigns may have the effect of abrogating the Quranic law of succession and establishing a mode of succession *dehors* the Muhammadan law.

5. *Perpetuity and Aggrandizement of the settlor's family*

The leading case on the subject is *Abul Fata* v. *Russomoy* (1894) 22 IA 76, Case no. 32, here, followed in *Fatuma binti Mohamed* v. *Mohamed bin Salim* [1952] AC I, an appeal from Kenya. This case is fully discussed in the *Outlines of Muhammadan Law*, 240 seqq.

6. *Interest when payable*

The Qur'an forbids the taking of interest on capital lent (III. 130), and it is therefore significant that in India interest at 6 per cent per annum was ordered to be paid to a Muslim widow on the amount of her dower debt (*mahr*), which had remained unpaid: *Hamira Bibi* v. *Zubaida Bibi* (1916) 43 IA 294. Lord Parker of Waddington justifies this on the grounds that such an order would be consistent with the *adab al-qādi*, rules which are allied to equity in English law.

With great respect to his Lordship, although the decision may be deemed to be just and equitable in the circumstances of the case, the reasoning is open to doubt. The argument would have been unassailable if the *adab al-qāḍi* had not been mentioned. For no rule of equity or *adab* can go counter to a plain *naṣṣ* of the Qur'an.[23]

7. *Lost grant*

Where certain persons have for long peaceably enjoyed rights over landed property as tenants, the facts that the lands once belonged to a *wakf* and that the necessary permission of the court to alienate them is not forthcoming, are not sufficient to displace the tenants' rights. Although the expression 'Lost Grant' was not used by Lord Sumner, his argument is closely analogous to the English doctrine of a lost grant: *Mahammad Mazaffar* v. *Jabeda Khatun* (1930) 57 IA 125.[24]

8. *Common calamity*

When two persons perish in a common calamity—in this case an earthquake—there is in India, in the absence of evidence, no presumption that the younger survived the elder. Section 184 of the English Law of Property Act, 1925, whereby survivorship of the younger of the two should be considered by the court as an element in the case, was not applicable. Thus the Board followed an English case, *Wing* v. *Angrave* (1860) 8 HLC 183, 198, and held that such a case was a pure question of fact, the onus of proof

23 In Islamic law, the term *naṣṣ* is applied to a binding rule of law derived from an express injunction of the Qur'an or a reliable Tradition of the Prophet. See my article. 'The *Adab al-Qāḍī* in Islamic Law', 1964, 5 *Malaya Law Review,* 406, 415–16.

24 *Halsbury*, 2nd ed., xi, paras. 541 seqq.

lying on the party who asserts it: *K. S. Agha Mir Ahmad* v. *Mir Mudassir* (1944) 71 IA 171. It may be pointed out that there are definite rules in Muhammadan law governing such cases, and it is submitted that, in conformity with the decision of the Privy Council these rules should apply (*Outlines of Muhammadan Law*, 431).

C. Cases where Muhammadan Law is Modified by Custom

Before the Shariat Act 1937, it was well established in India that custom, if proved according to law, could vary a definite rule of *Sharī'at*. Such for instance were the customs of the Khojas and Memons (western India); the customs of the Punjabi Muslims; the customary law of the Mapillas (Moplahs) in Malabar; and the exclusion of females from inheritance in certain cases in the valley of Kashmir. The application of customary law was, however, largely abolished by the Shariat Act 1937, with a few salutary exceptions.

It will therefore be observed that the cases dealt with here are matters of past history.

1. *Khojas and Memons*

The earliest reported case that established the validity of custom among the Khojas and Memons is the decision of Sir Erskine Perry, Chief Justice of Bombay, in the *Kojas and Memons Case*.[25] Later came *Hirbai* v. *Gorbai* (1875) 12 Bombay HCR 294, and the *Aga Khan Case*, a decision of Arnould J., Case no. 41, in this volume.

These cases established that prior to the Shariat Act 1937, in the absence of satisfactory proof of a custom to the contrary, the courts, especially of the Bombay Presidency, would apply, to the Khojas and Memons, the Hindu and not the Muhammadan law of succession: *Tyabji*, §§ 6A, 10; *Mulla*, § 22; *Outlines of Muhammadan Law*, 66 seqq.[26]

In the *Kojas and Memons Case*, the Quranic basis of the law of inheritance is not discussed;[27] the whole judgment proceeds on the processes of reasoning known to the common law; thus rules of succession are generally founded upon custom; some English rules are arbitrary;

25 Perry's Oriental Cases, 110–29.

26 For Khojas, generally, see *Outlines of Muhammadan Law*, 37 seqq. and 66 seqq. For Memons, ibid., 72 seqq.

27 Historically it would be more accurate to say that these communities have retained their original Hindu customs even after their conversion to Islam and absorption into the Muslim community.

Blackstone and Roman law are cited; Thibaut. Blackstone, and Austin quoted; the custom would be valid under Roman law; English law is related to the validity of custom.

On public policy the words of Sir Erskine Perry are memorable:

Accordingly it has been stoutly argued, that this Hindu custom of disinheriting daughters, which has been adopted by these Mahommedan sectarians,[28] is most unreasonable, and that public policy would dictate the adoption of the wiser rule laid down by the Koran, by which daughters are allowed a defined share in the succession. A contrast is then drawn between the relative positions which females hold in the Hindu and Mussulman systems, and it is argued that the policy of the latter is so much more enlarged and beneficial that it is the duty of the court to give it effect when the two come into collision. But I have often disclaimed in this court any desire to decide private rights with reference to political results. 'Public Policy' in the words of Mr Justice Burroughs, 'is an unruly horse, and if a judge gets upon it he is very apt to be run away with.' Where public policy accords with the well-recognized track of morality, it is the duty of the Judge to make every decision conform to it, if the letter of the law permits; but whenever public policy is a matter of controversy, a lawyer should be the last to express any opinion upon it: and I hardly know any question connected with the East on which so much might be said on either side as on the different characteristics of the marriage state between Hindus and Mussulmans, and on the status in life and influence in domestic circles which Hindu and Mussalman females respectively enjoy. It is sufficient, however, to say that a custom for females to take no share in the inheritance is not unreasonable in the eyes of the English law; for it accords in great part with the universal custom as to real estates where there are any male issue, and entirely with some local customs mentioned in Blackstone, by which, in certain manors, females are excluded in all cases.[29]

Then follow the incidents of a valid custom, and how customary law conflicts with the Qur'an. The Chief Justice then deals with divine law:

A jurist *qua* jurist has only to deal with human laws: he recognizes the existence of divine laws, and their validity *in foro conscientiae* with those to whom they are addressed, or those who believe in the revelation containing them; but he does not recognize them as enforceable in courts of justice any further than the secular power has ordained. Under a government such as that of England, which has established the principle of universal toleration as to religious belief, it is no doubt the duty of a secular judge to pay the utmost respect to the religious opinions of every suitor who comes before the court; and his judicial impartiality should be preserved within such inflexible limits, that on every controversy which is capable of arising within the bosom of society, the opinion should be universally diffused that a calm and just decision between the litigant parties would as surely issue from the judgment-seat

28 Wilson, *Glossary* 500, 504, 507, 508.
29 Perry's *Oriental Cases* 110, 120.

as if it were occupied by a Judge of their own creed and colour. But the question on every such occasion for the Judge would be, what the law was which had been delivered to him for administration by his Sovereign.[30]

There follow: personal laws how secured to Hindus and Muslims; the Gothic conquerors preserve the laws of the Romans; ancient usages to prevail over the text of the Qur'an; European doctrine of *lex loci* suitable for Christians, but not applicable to Asiatics; Selden cited.

This case has been dealt with so fully not only because it is the leading case relating to the inheritance of Khojas and Memons, but also because it lays down certain fundamental principles for the administration of justice which are accepted universally in our courts to this day.

An interesting case of customary law in the Punjab is *Mian Saleh Mohammad* v. *Sayyad Zawwar Hussain* (1943) 71 IA 14.

As regards Memons, the Privy Council has held that when they migrate and settle among Muslims outside India (in this case Mombasa) the presumption that they have adopted the original rules of Quranic law, in conformity with their own faith, should be made readily, and their estates should be distributed according to the Muhammadan and not the Hindu law of succession: *Abdurahim* v. *Halimabai* (1915) 43 IA 35.

The Moplahs (strictly Mapillahs) of Malabar were also governed by the customary law prior to 1947, and their customs have been dealt with fully by Dr Hamid Ali in his *Custom and Law in Anglo-Muhammadan Jurisprudence*.[31] Rattigan's *Digest* was the leading textbook in the Punjab,[32] the stronghold of custom amongst Muslims in the subcontinent. The Muslims of Kashmir also have their customary law, which in some respects contradicts the plain provisions of Muhammadan law.

In *Murtuza Husain* v. *Mahomed Yasin* (1916) 43 IA 269 it was laid down that once the custom of primogeniture was proved as respects *taluqdārī*[33] property, the non-*taluqdārī* property would also be heritable by customary

30 Ibid., 122.

31 Thacker, Spink, Calcutta, 1938. 127 pp.

32 The only edition available to me in Bombay is the 12th, W. H. Rattigan, *A Digest of Civil Law for the Punjab chiefly based on the Customary Law* (known as *riwāj-i 'am*), 12th ed., by K. J. Rustomji, Lahore, 1938.

33 From *ta'alluq*, Arabic, connexion, dependence, and therefore sometimes, possession. An estate, usually in Oudh, similar to *zamīndārī* in Bengal, originally granted by the Moghul government at a favourable assessment as a mark of favour, and held at a fixed amount of revenue. It was hereditary and transferable, so long as the revenue was paid, and subject usually to loyalty. Variations of the original forms of grant are to be found in the South of India and in the West, in such types of tenancies as *ināms* and *saranjāms*. Since 1947 *zamīndarīs* and *taluqdārīs* have been gradually abolished in most parts of India (Wilson's *Glossary*).

law, unless the retention of the personal law governing the parties was proved to the satisfaction of the court.

In cases where a custom is alleged it is often necessary to be clear whether there is proof sufficient to satisfy the court. *Abdul Hussein* v. *Bibi Sona Dero* (1917) 45 IA 10 is the leading case on the kind of proof necessary to establish a family custom.[34] The question of proof was further considered by Mr M. R. Jayakar in *Musammat Subhani* v. *Nawab* (1940) 68 IA 1, and the value of judicial decisions, for establishing the custom put forward, was assessed. It was held that the English rule that a custom, in order to be legal and binding, must have been followed for 'so long that the memory of man knoweth not to the contrary' (Blackstone), is neither apposite nor useful in India. All that is required in this subcontinent is the proof that 'the usage has been acted upon for such a long period and such invariability as to show that by consent it was the governing rule of a particular district'. A feature of this case is the full review of the previous case law by Mr Jayakar. Ordinarily, this is not the practice; only the salient facts, and the most important cases, are briefly discussed.

D Cases Where Muhammadan Law is Modified or Repealed by Statutes

The following are the most important statutes that have modified or repealed the law according to the letter of the *Sharī'at*:

(i) The Slavery Act, V of 1843: An interesting case is *Sayad Mir Ujmuddin* v. *Zia-ul-Nissa Begum* (1879) 6 IA 137. In this case, which gives a graphic description of life lived by the aristocracy in the days when slavery was a common feature of the social structure of Islam, their Lordships of the Privy Council gave a very wide interpretation to the statute.[35]

(ii) The Caste Disabilities Removal Act XXI of 1850: See *Mitar Sen* v. *Maqbul Hasan* (1930) 57 IA 313, Case no. 43, here. On conversion and hybridization, the father being a Hindu and the mother a Muslim, *Bhaiya Sher Bahadur* v. *Bhaiya Ganga Bakhsh* (1913), 41 IA 1 is of great human and social interest (Case no. 7, here).[36]

(iii) The Indian Penal Code 1860, repealed the criminal law of Islam so far as it was administered in India, and imported English principles of

[34] See Case no. 9, in this volume; Tyabji, § 1OA; *Outlines of Muhammadan Law*, 64 seq.

[35] For details see *Revue Egyptience de Droit International*, xviii, 1962, 1, 31.

[36] Ibid., 24–7.

criminal law into the country. The inspiration of the code was obviously drawn from the springs of British jurisprudence; and it was Macaulay, the skilful draftsman, who shaped the rules that had grown from it on the Indian soil, and gave us a Code which, for a century and over, has provided India with a practical code of penal law.[37]

(iv) *Administration of Estates*: Strictly speaking, administration as understood in modern legal systems is foreign to Islamic jurisprudence. It was introduced into the fabric of Muhammadan law by the reception of the English concept of the administration of estates, and later by the enabling provisions of the Probate and Administration Acts. The leading case on the subject is *Jafri Begum* v. *Amir Muhammad Khan* (1885) 7 Allahabad 822, Case 37, here. The early history of the law of representation will be found in the judgment of Sir Arthur Wilson in *Mirza Kurratulain* v. *Nawab Nuzhat-ud-Dowla* (1905) 32 IA 244, esp. 257 seq.; see Case 42, here.[38]

(v) *Evidence*: It is generally thought that the rules of *Sharī'at* regarding evidence have been replaced by the Indian Evidence Act 1872.[39] One of the earliest decisions, raising a question whether Section 112, Indian Evidence Act, supersedes the Muhammadan law, was the opinion of Mahmood J. in *Muhammad Allahdad* v. *Muhammad Ismail* (1888) 10 All 289, 339 (Case no. 18, in this volume). The question was left open by that great judge; but later the trend of modern decisions has been to regard this as a question of the law of evidence, pure and simple, governed exclusively by the Act.[40]

(vi) *Assignment of Insurance Policies*: Prior to 1938, if a conditional assignment was made by a Muslim it would have been considered a contingent gift, the gift being absolute and the condition void: *In re Khyrunnissa Begum* AIR (1955) Madras 459. To do away with this hardship suffered by Muslims, the Insurance Act 1938, sec. 38 (7) lays down.

> Notwithstanding any law or custom having the force of law to the contrary, an assignment in favour of a person made with the condition that it shall be inoperative or that the interest shall pass to some other person on the happening of a specified

[37] T. K. Banerjee, *Background to Indian Criminal Law*, Calcutta, 1963, chap. ii.

[38] I. Mahmud (*Muslim Law of Succession and Administration*, Karachi, 1958), has criticized the decision of Mahmood J., a decision which is the foundation of the Indian law on the subject, with reference to original texts. His learning is commendable, but he has not offered any satisfactory alternative to the present law.

[39] Wilson, *Glossary* 31.

[40] *Tyabji*, 259 seq.; *Outlines of Muhammadan Law*, 182.

event during the lifetime of the person whose life is insured, and an assignment in favour of the survivor or survivors of a number of persons, shall be valid.

Thus a husband assigned insurance policies to his wife by a valid endorsement on the condition 'that in the event of my said wife predeceasing me, this assignment shall become null and void', and it was held that under the Act such an assignment was perfectly valid: *Sadiq Ali* v. *Zahida Begum* AIR 1939 All 957; *Outlines of Muhammadan Law*, 213–15.

This statutory modification of Muhammadan law, as it then existed, has proved to be beneficial to the community.

(vii) *Changes in the Law of Inheritance by Registration of Marriage*: One of the most striking changes in the laws of Islam has been made by the Special Marriage Act 1954. If an existing marriage between two Muslims, for instance a *nikāh*, duly performed in accordance with the *Sharī'at,* is registered under the provisions of the Special Marriage Act, the personal law of succession and inheritance is ousted and the provisions of the Indian Succession Act apply.[41] This permissive use of legal machinery for a salutary change in the personal, substantive law of the parties is hailed as a reform in the true direction. The law has been fully discussed in my *Outlines of Muhammadan Law*, 97 and 356 seq. The relevant provisions of the Act will be found in Appendix C, pp. 469 seq.

(viii) *Muslim Wife's Right to Dissolve Her Marriage by Legal Process—Dissolution of Muslim Marriages Act 1939*: According to Hanafi law, prior to 1939, a wife had no right to sue for divorce even though she was treated with cruelty, or had good cause for seeking a dissolution of her marriage. In this respect, the Mālikī school was most favourable to women; the Shāfi'ī and Ḥanbalī schools took up a middle position; and the Hanafi, Ithnā 'Asharī, and Fatimid schools (the two last being Shiite) were the most unfavourable. The Muslim community, largely Hanafi, being dissatisfied, a private bill was introduced whereby the Mālikī rule was sought to be applied to all Muslims regardless of their religious variations. The bill was passed and became the Dissolution of Muslim Marriages Act 1939. This statute has ameliorated the position of Muslim women greatly; and in India, if one of the eight causes mentioned in section 2 is proved, divorce is easily obtained.[42]

41 Special Marriage Act, 1954, sec. 21. See *India Code*, 1958, vol. vi, pt. ix, p. 22.

42 For a fuller discussion of the topic, see my article 'The Muslim Wife's Right of Dissolving her Marriage' (1936) 38 *Bombay Law Reporter*, Journal, 113. This article was cited with approval by a Division Bench in *Kunju Ismail* v. *Kadeja Umma* AIR (1959) Ker 151, 153. *Outlines of Muhammadan Law*, 160 seq.; the text of the Act will be found on p. 463 seq.

The general policy followed during the British period, as it emerges from a study of the decisions, chiefly of the Privy Council, may be summarized as follows:

A. The British courts studiously avoided any interference with local customs and faiths.

B. The angularities of the indigenous systems, *Dharma* and *Sharī'at*, were smoothed out by the principles of justice and equity, as understood by British lawyers.

C. Where the local rules, whether of substantive law or of usage having the force of law, were outworn and did not conduce to substantial justice, they were abrogated or modified by statutory law.

This concludes our brief survey of the impact of the common law and equity on the Muhammadan law in India and Pakistan. A careful consideration of the field of study will show that this is only a preliminary inquiry; it does not profess to be exhaustive. Much greater research and investigation would be needed for a complete examination of the question.[43]

43 A useful Table of Enactments relating to Muhammadan law will be found in Wilson, *Glossary*, pp. xxxv–xxxviii.

References and Abbreviations

Qur'ān — Translation: *The Meaning of the Glorious Koran* by Marmaduke Pickthall. Allen & Unwin, London, 1930

Ameer Ali — Syed Ameer Ali, *Mahommedan Law.* Tagore Law Lectures, 1884, Calcutta: vol. i, 4th ed., 1912; vol. ii, 5th ed., 1929. [reprinted in Delhi in 1985 with an introduction and update by Tahir Mahmood]

Baillie — Neil B. E. Baillie, *Digest of Moohummudan Law:*

Part I (Hanafi Law, Sunnite), 2nd ed., London, 1875, based upon the *Fatāwā ʻĀlamgīrī*. Arabic Text: 6 volumes, Būlāq, Cairo, AH 1310.

Urdu Translation: by Mawlānā Amīr ʻAlī, 10 vols, Nawalkishore, Lucknow, 1932

Part II (Ithnā ʻAsharī Law Shiite), 1st ed., London, 1896, based upon *Sharāiʻ al-Islām* (*Sharaya-ool-Islam*) of Abū'l-Qāsim Najmu'd-dīn al-Hillī. Arabic Text: Calcutta 1839. Also, ed., Shaykh Muḥammad Jawād Mughniyya, Maktaba al-Ḥayāt, Beirut, 1930. French Translation: *Droit Musulman* par A. Querry. Paris, 1871–2, 2 vols.

Daʻāim — *Daʻā'im al-Islām* (Pillars of Islam) of Cadi Abū Ḥanīfa an-Nuʻmān b. Muḥammad. *Arabic Text:* ed., Āṣaf ʻAlī Aṣghar Fyzee, Dar El Maaref, Cairo: vol. i, 1951 (reprinted, 1963); vol. ii, 1961 [English translation, OUP, 2002]

Hedaya — The *Hedaya* (strictly *Hidāya*) of Burhān ad-dīn al-Marghīnanī. Translated into English from a Persian rendering by Charles Hamilton, 2nd ed., by S. C. Grady, London, 1870 *Arabic Text:* Mujtabā'i Press, Delhi, 1915–25, 4 vols, with an introduction and appendixes by Abū'l-Ḥasanāt ʻAbd al-Ḥayy al-Anṣārī al-Lakhnawī

Persian Translation: by Muḥammad Aʻẓam Ḥusayn, 4 vols, Nawalkishore, Lucknow, 1916

Macnaghten	William H. Macnaghten, *Principles and Precedents of Moohummudan Law*, Calcutta, 1825
Mulla	Dinshah Fardunji Mulla, *Principles of Mahomedan Law*, 19th ed., 1990 [Urdu translation by Tahir Mahmood & S. Saif Mahmood, Butterworths, 2001]
Outlines	Asaf A. A. Fyzee, *Outlines of Muhammadan Law*, 3rd ed., Oxford University Press, Bombay, 1964 [Reprinted 2001]
Tyabji	Faiz Badruddin Tyabji, *Muhammadan Law: The Personal Law of Muslims*, 3rd ed., Bombay, 1940
Wilson	Ronald K. Wilson, *Anglo-Muhammadan Law*, 6th ed., London, 1930.

The original edition of Asaf A. A. Fyzee, *Cases in Muhammadan Law of India and Pakistan*, OUP, 1965, has been referred to in the present edition by the abbreviation cases [followed by page numbers].

I. Interpretation of Texts

1. Aga Mahomed v. Koolsom Bee Bee
(1897) 24 IA 196

Shiite law—wills—Rights of widow regarding maintenance—Childless widow—interpretation of the Qur'an

1. Where power is given to an executor to charge a commission on the proceeds of his real and personal property and cash, it creates not a debt but a legacy payable only out of the bequeathable third.

2. A Muslim widow is not entitled to maintenance out of her husband's estate in addition to what she is entitled by inheritance or under the will.

3. When ancient commentators of great authority have commented on a text of the Qur'an, it would be wrong for the courts to put their own construction on the Qur'an in opposition to their express ruling. *Tyabji*, § 11; *Outlines of Muhammadan Law*, 78–80.

4. A childless widow in Shiite Ithnā 'Asharī law is not entitled to a share in the land forming the site of the buildings. For a similar rule in Fatimid law see *Outlines of Muhammadan Law*, 438; *Da'aim*, II, §§ 1341–3.

Consolidated appeal and cross-appeal from a final decree of the Recorder [of Rangoon] (14 September 1893) involving the correctness of various interlocutory judgments passed in the suit.

The suit was an administration suit, brought originally by one Abdool Razack, but continued by Koolsom Bee Bee, as plaintiff against Aga Mahomed Jaffer Bindaneem, nephew and executor of the will of Hadji Hoosain Bindaneem.

On 14 September 1892, the executor filed his accounts, and on 8 November Koolsom Bee Bee filed a petition stating her objections thereto. On 5 December she filed a written statement in which she alleged that the deceased was a Shiah; that his will, so far as it purported to dispose of certain shares of his property, was invalid except in regard to one-third of his estate. She claimed to have her fourth share as the widow assessed upon the land on which certain houses left by the testator were built, as well as on the houses themselves. She also claimed maintenance for one year from the death of the testator and a right to live rent-free in the testator's house, and asserted her right to certain fixed deposits in the bank of Bengal as having been assigned to her by the testator by way of gift.

On 21 November 1892 the Recorder of Rangoon decided that Koolsom Bee Bee, as being the childless widow of a Shiah, was not entitled to any share of his land. His judgment was as follows:

The plaintiff in this case is the childless widow of a Mahommedan belonging to the Shiah sect, and I have to decide now whether she is entitled to a share in the land on which certain houses belonging to her husband's estate are built. It is admitted that she is entitled to one-fourth of the pure personalty and to one-fourth of the value of the houses apart from the land. The authorities seem to me to make it perfectly clear that she is not entitled to share in the land. The law is thus stated by Baillie, *Imameea*, p. 295:

> 'When the wife has had a child by the deceased she inherits out of all that he has left: and if there was no child she takes nothing out of the deceased's land, but her share of the value of the household effects and buildings is to be given to her. It has been said, however, that she is to be excluded from nothing except the mansions and dwellings; while Moortuza (may God be pleased with him) has expressed a third opinion to the effect that the land should be valued and her share of the value assigned to her. But the first opinion is that which appears to be best founded on traditional authority.'

The correctness of this translation was impeached in *Mussamut Asloo* v. *Mussamut Umdutoonnissa*,[1] and another translation was made by the court interpreter, the material portion of which is this: 'if there be no child she inherits nothing of the land, but her share of the value of goods and buildings will be given to her.' Ameer Ali, J., in the *Personal Law of the Mahomedans*, says (p. 91): 'But when she has no child, or when a child was born to her, but died before the decease of her husband, then she is entitled to a fourth share in the personal estate only including household effects, trees, buildings, & c.' She takes no interest in the real estate; and in the Tagore Lectures, 1874, p. 260, the rule is thus stated: 'if there is no such child she takes nothing out of the deceased's land (*arz*), but her share of the household effects (*àlàt*) and buildings is to be given to her.' I think therefore, that the widow is not entitled to share in the land.

On 24 January 1893, he pronounced a further judgment upon certain issues which had been recorded as arising out of the written statement of Koolsom Bee Bee; these findings, so far as they are material, were:

1. That the directions in the will that the executor shall be allowed to charge 3 per cent for commission, and that he should deduct one-fifth for

[1] (1873) 20 Suth. WR 297.

khooms or gifts for religious purposes, were only valid as bequests out of one-third of the testator's estate.

2. That the widow was entitled to one year's maintenance in addition to her share. He cited Ameer Ali's *Personal Law of the Mahomedans*, ch. x, s. 1, p. 369; *Baillie*, *Imameea*, p. 171.

3. That she was not properly chargeable for use and occupation of her late husband's house after his death, and before sale under the will.

On 2 March 1893, he pronounced a further judgment in which he rejected the alleged gift to Koolsom Bee Bee of the bank deposits, both because he disbelieved the evidence, and because he held that the gift, if made, would be invalid in law as not being followed by sufficient possession. On the same day he gave a decree for an account, laying down as the principles on which it was to be taken the findings which he had recorded in the previous judgments. On 10 July 1893, the executor filed an account showing the share of Koolsom Bee Bee as made up in accordance with the decree. On 24 July 1893, Koolsom Bee Bee filed her objections to this account, upon which a further judgment was delivered on 16 August, when the Recorder held:

> [T]he only way of ascertaining the share of the rents is by ascertaining the value of the land and the houses separately, and apportioning the amount received as rent, and this has been done. As regards the moneys invested, it is admitted that Koolsom Bee Bee would not have been entitled to share in the immovable properties if they had remained unsold, and I do not think she can be allowed to share in the proceeds.

On 14 September the court pronounced its final decree in accordance with all the above findings. Against this decree both parties appealed.

Judgment [Davey J.][2]

Their Lordships also agree with the learned Recorder that the executor's commission can be paid only out of the one-third part of the testator's estate which passed by his will. It is given, no doubt, by way of remuneration, but it is a gratuitous bequest, and nothing more than a legacy to the executor, and certainly not in any sense a debt.

The learned Recorder has decided that the widow is entitled to maintenance at the rate of Rs 150 per mensem for one year after the testator's death, and he has done so on the authority of a passage of the Qur'an quoted by Ameer Ali J. in his work on the *Personal Law of Mahomedans*, on which the text-writer makes the observation that several jurists have held that a wife has a right to be maintained out of her husband's estate for a year,

[2] With Watson & Richard Couch, JJ.

independently of any share she may obtain in the property left by him. Unfortunately the writer does not give any references in support of his statement, and counsel have not been able to furnish their Lordships with any. On the other hand, the *Hedaya* (Book IV, Ch. xv, S. 3) says expressly, 'Maintenance is not due to a woman after her husband's decease,' and gives reasons for so holding. The *Imameea* (Baillie, p. 171), after saying that it would seem that, after the death of her husband, the widow has no right to a residence except in the single case of her being pregnant, says: 'A widow has no right to maintenance even though she be pregnant.'

Their Lordships on these authorities must hold that a Mahomedan widow is not entitled to maintenance out of her husband's estate in addition to what she is entitled to by inheritance or under his will. They do not care to speculate on the mode in which the text quoted from the Qur'an, which is to be found *Sura* II, VV. 241–2, is to be reconciled with the law as laid down in the *Hedaya* and by the author of the passage quoted from Baillie's *Imameea*. But it would be wrong for the court on a point of this kind to attempt to put their own construction on the Qur'an in opposition to the express ruling of commentators of such great antiquity and high authority.

2. BAKER ALI KHAN V. ANJUMAN ARA
(1903) 30 IA 94

Shiite law—Creation of testamentary wakf—Issue as to legitimacy—Admissibility of statements recorded in the wasika office—Interpretation of the Traditions of the Prophet by classical jurists—Logical inferences from undisputed texts made by modern judges

1. Under Shiite, as well as under Sunnite law, a wakf can be created by will. *Agha Ali Khan* v. *Altaf Hasan Khan* (1892) 14 All 429 (Mahmood J., Full Bench) overruled. This is the present law, *Outlines of Muhammadan Law*, 272–3; Mulla, *Principles* §§ 184–5.

2. The testatrix having been in receipt of a pension from government known as *wasika*,[3] made a series of statements to the Wasika Office, as to who were her heirs during the period 1860–9. *Held* that these being authenticated statements coming from a public office, containing statements of one who had the best means of knowledge before any controversy had

3 Strictly, Arabic, *wathiqa,* 'binding agreement'. These were stipends paid by the Indian government, as successors of the East India Company, that had by treaties entered into certain agreements with the Rulers of Oudh regarding payments to be made to the descendants of the Nawabs from generation to generation.

arisen, were rightly admitted in evidence, and were conclusive on an issue as to legitimacy.

3. When the ancient jurists have themselves drawn certain definite conclusions from ancient texts and precepts of the Prophet, 'it would be extremely dangerous to accept as a general principle that new rules of law are to be introduced' by modern jurists. See the discussion in *Outlines of Muhammadan Law*, 78 seqq.

Consolidated separate appeals by each of the two defendants from a decree of the Judicial Commissioner of Oudh (24 February 1899) reversing a judgment of the Additional Civil Judge of Lucknow (15 July 1897).

The main questions decided in this case relate to the validity and effect of a will executed on 10 July 1890, by Mussamat Zaibunnissa, alias Haji Begam, and to the respondents' claim to succeed on an intestacy to her estate as her heirs. Haji Begam died on 19 January 1894. In case of intestacy the plaintiffs, Anjuman Ara Begam and Wasi Ali Khan, were admittedly entitled, if legitimate, to succeed to two-thirds of her estate, and the defendant Baker Ali Khan was entitled by inheritance to the remaining third.

By her will Haji Begam bequeathed to Sadik Ali and Baker Ali Khan, mainly for religious and charitable purposes, government promissory notes, forming a portion of her estate not exceeding one-third, a devise in excess of one-third being void under Mahommedan law. Probate thereof was granted to Sadik Ali alone as executor in consequence of the minority of Baker Ali Khan. Sadik Ali and Baker Ali Khan obtained possession of the property bequeathed, which was in the possession of Haji Begam on her death.

The two plaintiffs above named accordingly sued Sadik Ali and Baker Ali Khan to recover possession from them of two-thirds of Haji Begam's estate, and thereby prayed that the will should be set aside on the ground of mental incapacity of the testatrix, fraud and undue influence on the part of Sadik Ali, and its invalidity as being *wakf-bil-wasiat*, or endowment by will.

The written statement of the first defendant asserted that the will was valid, as it did not dispose of more than one-third of the property of the deceased. The statement of the second defendant asserted that Haidri and Jafri, the mothers of the plaintiffs, were illegitimate, and that they were not entitled as heirs of Haji Begam.

This question of legitimacy depended upon proof of actual marriage of the plaintiffs' mothers, Haidri and Jafri, to Zaka-ud-daulah. No acknowledgment by the father creating legitimacy was alleged. But Haji Begam, as daughter of the King of Oudh, and apparently as interested in one of the various loans made to the East India Company by that dynasty, was a *wasikadar*, or holder of a pension from Government. It appears that it is and was the practice of the Wasika Officer at Lucknow to require *wasikadars* to file in his office from time to time declarations stating the names of the persons who were their heirs. A declaration of this kind is usually called a *wirasat-nama*. A series of these, extending from 1860 to 1890, and proceeding from Haji Begam, had been produced from the Wasika Office, and had been found by both courts to be genuine.

The judge of the first court held that, having regard to the rest of the plaintiffs' evidence, which he examined at considerable length, these documents were not sufficient to establish the marriages, and therefore found that the plaintiffs had failed to prove that they were the heirs of Haji Begam. With regard to the will, he decided that it was not executed under undue influence, and that it disposed of less than one-third of Haji Begam's estate, and was to this extent valid. He, however, was of the opinion that the document in question was not a will, properly so speaking, but a document by which Haji Begam created a *wakf* to take effect after her death, and thus being a *wakf-bil-wasiat*, i.e. the creation of a wakf by means of a will, was invalid. In the result he dismissed the suit with costs.

The Judicial Commissioners found on the evidence that Haidri and Jafri were married to Zaka-ud-daulah in the *muta'i* form, and held that under Shiah law an acknowledgment by the father was not necessary to the legitimacy of the children. They further held that the document dated 10 July 1890, was not a will, but a *wakf-bil-wasiat*, and was invalid by Mahommedan law. The material passage of their judgment upon this latter point is as follows:

> The deed begins in manner following: 'According to the text, "every person is to taste of death," every person has one day to taste the cup of death, and to leave this transient world, and no one knows the time fixed for it; therefore, as a matter of precaution, one is bound to make arrangements in respect of his property during his lifetime in order that the mutual disputes may be prevented. For this reason, as prudence and expediency require it, it seems proper that I should dispose of by will a third part of my movable and immovable property and cash in the way of God for ever, in order to improve my condition in the next world and make arrangements for it in my life-time, that no sort of quarrel may arise after my death.' The deed then goes on to state that the executant makes the following will in respect of the one-third of her property specified below, amounting to Rs 54,100, which has been set apart for the expenses of the *Imambara*, having appointed two executors and *mutawallis*, namely, Sadik Ali Khan and Baker Ali Khan. By the 1st clause the executant 'places' the *Imambara* and its appurtenances, together with the furniture and other things in the *Imambara*, 'under the mutawalliship of the said *mutawallis*, and 'appropriates' for the expenses of the *Imambara* 'for ever' four Government promissory notes amounting to Rs 54,100, of which she gives the particulars, the annual interest of which amounted to Rs 2164. By the 2nd clause the executant

provides for the expenditure of Rs 2164 in connection with the *Imambara*, directs that the said executors 'shall not have at any time the power to reduce or increase the days of *majlises* of the sacred month of *Moharram* till the fortieth day,' and empowers them to dismiss and appoint the servants connected with the *Imambara*. By the 3rd clause the executant provides that Baker Ali Khan, when he attained his age of majority, shall 'superintend and manage the business of the *Imambara*' in conjunction with Sadik Ali Khan, and directs that the pay fixed for him shall, while he is a minor, be kept as 'trust property,' or shall be paid to his guardian. By the 4th clause the executant provides for the appointment of the descendants of old servants attached to the *Imambara* who may die to the posts occupied by such deceased persons, if such descendants are fit persons, and empowers the 'executors,' where such descendants are not fit persons, to appoint other persons, and also to dismiss any servant who may misconduct himself. By the 5th clause the executant provides that Sadik Ali Khan and Baker Ali Khan shall be '*mutawallis* and managers' for their lives, and that their descendants' 'generation after generation,' shall succeed them. By the same clause the executant provides for the appointment of *mutawallis* by the 'English ruler of the time being' and the '*Mujtahid* of the day' in case any of the descendants of Sadik Ali Khan and Baker Ali Khan are not able persons or are not of good character. By the same clause the executant also empowers a *mutawalli* to relinquish his office and to appoint another *mutawalli* in his place. By the 6th clause the executant directs that Mir Husain, *mukhtar*, is to draw the interest of the government notes and to manage the *Imambara* for life in subordination to the *mutawallis*. By the 7th clause the executant provides that the balance of the income derived from the houses and shops attached to the *Imambara*, after payment of the 'miscellaneous expenses' of the *Imambara*, shall be given to *Saiyeds* who are true believers. By the 8th clause the executant provides for the removal of the *mutawallis*, and the appointment of new *mutawallis* in their place by the 'district officer' in case the *mutawallis* are guilty of misappropriation, & c. By the 9th clause the executant forbids any kind of transfer by the 'executors' of the Government promissory notes. By the 10th clause the executant empowers the said *mutawallis* to indorse the notes in execution of their office after her death. By the same clause she declares that she is the owner of all the property; while she is alive, and provides for certain other matters. By the 11th clause the executant provides for the removal of her body to Karbala. By the 12th clause she authorizes the *mutawallis* to permit persons to be buried in the *Imambara*. By the 13th clause she covenants not to make another will. 'According to the law governing the Shia sect of Mahommedans, 'to bequeath is to confer a right to the substance or the usufruct of a thing after death': Baillie's *Imameea Law*, 229; Ameer Ali's *Mahommedan Law*, vol. i. p. 460. A will 'may be constituted by the use of any expression that sufficiently indicates the intention of the testator; so long as it is apparent that the intention of the testator is to make a disposition operative on his death, it will be regarded as a wasiat. The devise may be either to the legatee beneficially or in trust for some purpose or object': Ameer Ali's *Mahommedan Law*, vol. i. p. 460. It appears, therefore, that to constitute a will there must be a devise to some person either beneficially or in trust for some purpose or object. 'It is contended for the appellants that the deed contains bequests for religious and meritorious purposes. It seems to me that there is no devise of any property by the deed. The executant does not devise the Government promissory notes to Sadik Ali Khan and Baker Ali Khan in trust to pay the expenses of the *Imambara* out of the interest. She 'sets apart' and 'appropriates for ever' the notes for the expenses of the *Imambara*, and 'places' the *Imambara* under the superintendentship of Sadik Ali Khan and Baker Ali Khan.

Waqf, according to the Shia doctrines, is a religious act, the effect of which is to tie up the corpus or substance of a thing and to leave its usufruct free: Ameer Ali's *Mahommedan Law*, vol. i. p. 390. 'According to the *Jawahir-ul-Kalam*, the object of a waqf is the continuance in perpetuity of a benefaction in the service of the deity, and it is an act of worship. The express word by which it may be created is waqf, i.e., 'I have dedicated': Ameer Ali's *Mahommedan Law*, vol. i. p. 390.

It is contended for the respondents, with reference to the case of *Agha Ali Khan* v. *Altaf Husain Khan*[4] that the use of formal technical expressions is an essential condition, and without it waqf is not established. In that case the *Jami-ul-Shattat* is cited as authority for this proposition. It is apparently based upon the *Sharaya-ul-Islam*. But the opinion expressed in the *Sharaya* is explained in *Jawahir-ul-Kalam*. According to that work, which is an authoritative commentary on the *Sharaya* there is nothing in the law to debar the creation of a waqf by the use of any other expression besides waqf—that is to say, when the intention of the grantor is clearly to create a waqf, whatever expression he may have used, the dedication will take effect, but where the term waqf itself is used, the dedication will take effect as such without questions: Ameer Ali's *Mahommedan Law*, vol. i. pp. 390, 394–5.

The intention of Haji Begam was clearly to set apart the notes for pious purposes. If a man were to say, 'I have tied up this property and given its profits in the way of God,' it would be a *waqf:* Ameer Ali's *Mahommedan Law*, vol. i. p. 390. This is what Haji Begam has done as to the notes. She has disposed of them, according to her own words, 'in the way of God for ever,' and 'appropriated' them 'for ever' for the expenses of the *Imambara*. It seems to me that there was a valid dedication of the property. I am of opinion that the deed is not a *wasiat* or will, but a *waqf-bil-wasiat*, and that it is therefore invalid.

Judgment [Arthur Wilson][5]

The suit out of which these consolidated appeals arise relates to the devolution of a part of the property of Haji Begam, a Mahommedan lady who died at a very advanced age on 19 January 1894. She was a daughter of a former King of Oudh, and the family to which she belonged are Shiahs and governed by the Shiah law. Haji Begam was married to Ikhtidar-ud-daulah, who died in 1883, and the issue of that marriage was a son, Zaka-ud-daulah, who died about forty years ago, leaving issue by three different mothers,

4 Ind. LR 14 All 429.
5 With Macnaghten, Lindley, Andrew Scoble & John Bonser, JJ.

Farzana, Haidri, and Jafri. By Farzana he left a son, Fazl Ali, who is dead without issue, and a daughter, Najmunnissa, who died leaving a son Baker Ali, the first appellant. By Haidri, Zaka-ud-daulah left a daughter, Shazada, since deceased, whose daughter is the first respondent. By Jafri he had a daughter, Wilayeti, who died leaving a son, the second respondent.

On 10 July 1890, Haji Begam executed a document, the legal effect of which is in controversy, under which it is contended by the appellants that certain portions of Haji Begam's estate have become *waqf* devoted to religious purposes. Under this document Sadik Ali the second and Baker Ali the first appellant were to be executors and *mutawallis*; and on 21 January 1895, Sadik Ali alone obtained probate of the document as a will, Baker Ali being a minor.

On 8 June 1895, the now respondents filed the present suit against the appellants in the Court of the Additional Civil Judge of Lucknow. They alleged that they were entitled as heirs of Haji Begam to two-thirds of the property which should pass to her heirs, while they admitted that the other third passed to the first appellant, Baker Ali, as their co-heir. And they claimed to have it established that the alleged will of 10 July 1890, was invalid as against them as heirs, and to recover two-thirds of the property affected by it.

The Additional Civil Judge who heard the case held that the plaintiffs, the now respondents, had failed to prove that they were heirs of Haji Begam. As to the second question, he held that the will was not valid against heirs; but as he had found that the respondents were not heirs, he dismissed their suit with costs. Against this decision an appeal was brought to the Court of the Judicial Commissioner of Oudh. The two Additional Judicial Commissioners who heard the appeal differed from the first court on the first question, and held that the now respondents were heirs of Haji Begam, while they agreed with the first court as to the effect of the will; and they accordingly reversed the decree of the first court, and made a decree in favour of the now respondents on all points. Against that decree the present appeals have been brought.

With regard to the question whether the respondents are heirs of Haji Begam, their case is that their mothers Shazada and Wilayeti were the legitimate children of Zaka-ud-daulah, inasmuch as the respective mothers of those ladies, Haidri and Jafri, were his wives, married to him in the *muta'i* or temporary form, which is accepted as valid by the Shiah law.

On the other side it was alleged that Haidri and Jafri were both sisters of Farzana, the first wife of Zaka-ud-daulah, and that Farzana was living at the time of the supposed marriages with Haidri and Jafri, so that there could have been no lawful marriages with them. Both courts in India have found that the facts necessary to support this contention are not proved; and their Lordships were not asked to review these findings.

It was also urged in India as matter of law that a child of a *mutai* marriage is not legitimate without proof of acknowledgment by the father; but this contention was abandoned before their Lordships.

The case that remains on behalf of the appellants is that neither Haidri nor Jafri was married to Zaka-ud-daulah, that they were mere slave girls, and that their children by Zaka-ud-daulah were the fruit of illicit intercourse with him. The issue thus raised, which is one purely of fact, is the one upon which the courts in India have differed.

There is no direct evidence of either marriage—a point upon which the courts in India have not laid much stress, and under the circumstances their Lordships think rightly. There is no evidence of acknowledgment of the children by their father—a point which is of less importance than it might otherwise have been by reason of the fact that, when he died, the two children whose status might have been affected were very young.

But marriage and legitimacy may of course be proved in such cases by other means. In the present case the most important evidence in favour of legitimacy consists of a series of statements made by Haji Begam herself which were admitted as evidence by the courts in India, and their Lordships think rightly. It appears that Haji Begam was in receipt of a pension from Government known as a '*wasika*'; and according to the practice in force such pensioners were from time to time called upon to make statements to the Wasika Office, a department under Government, as to who were their heirs. A series of such statements by Haji Begam extending from 1860 to 1890 is in evidence. It also appears that from time to time Haji Begam was asked by the wasika officers to furnish explanations of the statements submitted by her, and several letters in reply to such inquiries have been produced. In these documents, beginning with that of 1860 down to and including that of 1885, Haji Begam speaks of the line of Haidri and that of Jafri as heirs in exactly the same terms as of the line of Farzana, whose legitimacy is not questioned; she speaks of Shazada and Wilayeti as her granddaughters, and as daughters of Zaka-ud-daulah; she speaks of Shazada at a time before Wilayeti was born, as daughter of a *muta'i* wife, coupling her as such with Najmunnissa; and she speaks of Jafri as a *muta'i* wife still alive. In her statement of 1890, it is true, she omitted the respondents from her list of heirs. In her letter of explanation she gave her reasons for this, which do not seem to be inconsistent with her previous statements of fact, but which were not accepted as satisfactory.

Their Lordships think that the appellate court was right in giving great weight to these documents. They come from a public office and bear indorsements which exclude all doubt of their genuineness; they contain the statements of one who had the best means of knowledge, made at times when no such controversy as the present can well have been in contemplation; and the statements are such that, if true, they seem to conclude this part of the case.

Ikhtidar-ud-daulah, Haji Begam's husband, who died in 1883, also appears to have been in receipt of a *wasika*, and when he died a question arose as to who should succeed to it. A petition was presented jointly by Fazl Ali, Shazada, and Wilayeti describing the deceased as their grandfather and asking that his pension should be allotted to them. This petition their Lordships think has been duly proved, and it seems to be by necessary inference a statement by Fazl Ali, and a statement against his own interest, that the title of his two cousins was as good as his own. And so far it confirms the far more important statements of their grandmother.

On the same occasion inquiry was made from the Wasika Office of a number of persons as to the heirs of the deceased man; and the answers then obtained from them with the evidence of the same persons at the trial have been received. This evidence, however, is of very inferior value to that previously referred to, for it consists at best of hearsay reports of statements said to have been made by members of the family. The learned judges who heard the appeal in India do not appear to have attributed much importance to it, and their Lordships do not rely upon it for the conclusions at which they have arrived.

In support of the respondents' case reliance was further placed upon the treatment of Haidri, Jafri, and the descendants of each in Haji Begam's family, which, it was argued, was inconsistent with illegitimacy. In dealing with this branch of evidence their Lordships will only notice those matters as to which there is no controversy of fact.

Haidri and Jafri and their children and grandchildren were always treated as members of Haji Begam's family. Haji Begam made an allowance to each of those ladies for the maintenance of herself and her children. Haji Begam provided for the marriages of the children, and such marriages took place with members of the family: thus the second respondent, Wasi Ali, is married to the daughter of the second appellant, Sadik Ali, who is himself a sister's son of Haji Begam. Lastly, in the will of Haji Begam, the effect of which will have to be considered in another connection, when making provision for the anniversary religious ceremonies in commemoration of the deaths of certain ladies, the testatrix places Shazada in the same list, not only with Najmunnissa, but with the testatrix herself and her mother, and provides alike for all.

To meet the case of the respondents, reliance has been placed upon two lines of defence. First, the learned counsel for the appellants has sought to impugn each piece of evidence in detail, and in particular has examined and criticized every document relied upon, with the object of shaking its credit and minimising its effect. Their Lordships have given full weight to these criticisms, but they have failed to create any doubt in their Lordships' minds as to the trustworthiness or as to the meaning and effect of the documents to which, as already indicated, they attach importance.

The appellants relied secondly upon evidence given at the trial, by witnesses of each side, the effect of which is said to have been to show that in the family to which Haji Begam belonged very lax views as to sexual relations prevailed, and that, for social purposes at least, legitimate and illegitimate children were treated alike. This evidence seems to have had great weight with the court of first instance.

It is unnecessary to consider what effect ought to have been given to this evidence if the case of the respondents had rested only on evidence of treatment in the family, for this is not the case. The statements and letters of Haji Begam and the petition to which Fazl Ali was a party related not to social status or family recognition, but to rights of inheritance. And the evidence in question can have no bearing upon statements on that subject. Certainly, too, it can have no tendency to neutralize the express assertions of Haji Begam that Shazada was the daughter of a *muta'i* wife, and that Afri was a *muta'i* wife.

For these reasons their Lordships are of opinion that the Additional Judicial Commissioners were right in holding that the respondents are co-heirs with Baker Ali of Haji Begam, and are as such entitled to two-thirds of the property descending to her heirs.

The second inquiry involved in these appeals is as to the validity and effect of the alleged will of 10 July 1890. That document commences with the usual invocation and reference to the uncertainty of life, and proceeds:

> 'I deem it proper to dispose of by will a third part of my movable and immovable property and that of cash in the way of God for ever, in order to improve my condition in the next world, and to make arrangements thereof in my lifetime that there may arise no quarrel and dispute after my demise, I... do hereby set apart out of my entire property a third part as detailed below, valuing this date Rs 54,100 Queen's coin, for the expenses of *Imambara*, &c., and having appointed two executors and *mutawallis* (superintendents) named Nawab Sadik Ali Khan and Nawab Baker Ali Khan, make my will with the following provisos.'

Their Lordships think it clear that this document is a will, and that its expressed intention is to convey the property with which it deals, on the death of the testatrix, to the *mutawallis*, the appellants, as wakf for the purposes specified; and effect must of course be given to that intention if the law admits of it.

It was held, however, by both the courts in India that under the Shiah law, unlike the Sunni law, a waqf cannot be created by will. And though it is not so stated, there can be little doubt that the courts in so holding acted out of deference to the decision of a Full Bench of the High Court of the North-Western Provinces in 1892 in the case of *Agha Ali Khan* v. *Altaf Hasan Khan*,[6] in which the law appears to have been so laid down. Their Lordships have therefore to consider whether the High Court, whose reasons were most fully expressed by Mahmood J., were right in deciding, as they seem to have done, in that case that under Shiah law a waqf cannot be created by will, though the result can be secured indirectly by making a gift of property with a direction to the donee to create the wakf desired.

In considering this question their Lordships must start with certain propositions as to which there is no doubt. A Shiah can make a gift. He can make a gift of the kind known as a wakf. He can make a will and can, speaking generally, give a gift by will. It would seem to follow as a logical inference that he can make a wakf by will, as can a Sunni. And in substance and effect it is admitted that he can indirectly do so. It is admitted that he can make a gift of property by will and require the donee to apply it as waqf; the contention is that the testator, though he can do this, cannot himself directly create the waqf by his will. The distinction which has been taken is thus one of form, not of substance; and it is one which has little to commend it unless their Lordships are constrained by authority to accept it.

The only judicial authority prior to 1892 on the present point cited in argument is the case, in 1836, of *Wasiq Ali Khan* v. *Government*,[7] mentioned by Mahmood J. at p. 449 of his judgment, in which effect was given to a testamentary waqf of a Shiah. Mahmood, J. suggests that the Sudder Court wrongly applied Sunni law to the case, and it may be so; but it may equally well be that it was not then thought that there was any difference on this point between the two schools of Mahommedan law. The learned judge suggests also that until the case before this Committee in 1841, *Rajah Deedar Hossein* v. *Ranee Zuhoor-oon Nissa*,[8] Shiah law was not consistently applied to Shiah cases. And again he may be right, though the language used in the case just cited[9] hardly supports him in this view. The case before the Sudder Court is not a strong authority, but so far as it goes it lends support to the more liberal view upon the question under consideration. The case of *Prince Suleman Kadr* v. *Darab Ali Khan*,[10] decided in

6 ILR 14 All 429.
7 SDA 110.
8 (1841) 2 Moore's IA Cal 441.
9 Moore's IA Cal, pp. 477, 478.
10 (1881) LR 8 IA 117.

1881, shows at least that in the same family to which Haji Begam belonged a testamentary *waqf* was created and apparently went unquestioned. On the other hand, the only support for the doctrine that a Shiah cannot directly make a waqf by will is to be found, not in any positive statement by any of the recognized authorities on Shiah law, but in the reasoning of Mahmood, J. upon a number of more or less ambiguous texts, which their Lordships have considered with all the respect due both to the opinion of so eminent a Mahomedan lawyer and to the concurrence of his colleagues in the Full Bench in his views.

In the earlier and more important part of his judgment the learned judge deals with texts, many of them of undoubted authority, which purport to lay down the essentials of a waqf under Shiah law, namely, that a wakf is by definition a contract involving offer and acceptance, that as essential conditions there must be delivery of seisin, that the gift must be unconditional, and that nothing must be reserved for the settlor.

The last two conditions may, their Lordships think, be disregarded for the present purpose. If a *waqf* may be made by will speaking from the death, there is no condition and no reservation in such a case as the present. Mahmood J.'s reasoning turns on the definition and the first condition; he thinks his conclusion necessarily follows from them, and this is the really important part of his reasoning on which the whole depends. The argument of the learned counsel for the respondents was the same: he contended that if you accept the texts, as you must do, you are bound to accept their logical consequences.

In *Abul Fata v. Russomoy Dhur Chowdhry,*[11] in the judgment of this Committee delivered by Lord Hobhouse, the danger was pointed out of relying upon ancient texts of the Mahomedan law, and even precepts of the Prophet himself, of taking them literally, and deducing from them new rules of law, especially when such proposed rules do not conduce to substantial justice. That danger is equally great whether reliance be placed upon fresh texts newly brought to light, or upon fresh logical inferences newly drawn from old and undisputed texts. Their Lordships think it would be extremely dangerous to accept as a general principle that new rules of law are to be introduced because they seem to lawyers of the present day to follow logically from ancient texts however authoritative, when the ancient doctors of the law have not themselves drawn those conclusions.

There are, moreover, special difficulties in the way of accepting the inference drawn by Mahmood J. from the definition and conditions of a *waqf* as laid down in the ancient Shiah texts. The more important of those texts

11 (1894) LR IA, pp. 86–7.

have long been accessible to all lawyers. In none of them does the author himself draw the conclusion that the creation of a wakf by will is excluded. Nor has that conclusion been drawn by any modern writers who have collected and translated such texts, though in other respects the difference between the Shiah and the Sunni law of waqf has been pointed out.

And beyond these negative indications their Lordships find an important guide for determining the light in which the definition and condition in question should be regarded, as bearing upon the testamentary creation of a waqf, in the closely analogous case of a gift. A gift like a wakf is defined as a contract requiring offer and acceptance, and delivery of seisin is a condition of the validity of a gift as of a waqf. Yet from the time of the earliest Shiah authorities until now it has always been clear that a Shiah can make a gift by will. The most authoritative work of that school (the one translated by Baillie) contains a chapter on wills. This Committee in *Nawab Amin-ood-Dowlah* v. *Syud Roshun Ali Khan*[12] affirmed their validity. And the distinction drawn by Mahmood J. is itself based on the legal efficacy of a gift by will. Their Lordships think that, in applying the same definition and condition to the case of a waqf, it is safer to follow this analogy than to draw the logical conclusions which may seem to an acute modern dialectician to follow from the words of the old texts.

Another part of the judgment of Mahmood J. deals with texts which seem to have little bearing upon the present question. They discuss the consequences of the death of a settlor before delivery of seisin, and they relate apparently, not to wills, but to cases in which a man has made a deed of waqf intended to operate inter vivos, but has died before he could complete the transaction by delivery.

The last part of the judgment of the learned judge cites texts bearing somewhat more closely upon the present question. But there is no unanimity among them; the learned judge has to choose between texts which he thinks are of various degrees of authority, and it is to reconcile those which he accepts that he adopts his distinction between the direct and indirect creation of a waqf by will. Their Lordships doubt whether the learned judge would himself have relied upon such texts as sufficient to support his conclusion had he not already been satisfied of its correctness by the reasoning of the earlier part of his judgment, in which their Lordships are unable to concur.

For the foregoing reasons their Lordships are of opinion that the rule of law laid down by the Allahabad High Court, and followed by both the courts in India in the present case, to the effect that a Shiah cannot create a waqf by will, is unsound.

12 (1851) 5 Moore's IA Cal 199.

Their Lordships thus differ from the first court upon both the broad issues raised in the case, while they agree with the Appellate Court upon the first and differ upon the second. But the result is that the suit of the plaintiffs, the present respondents, fails and was rightly dismissed by the first court, though not upon the right grounds.

Their Lordships will humbly advise His Majesty that the decree of the Judicial Commissioner's Court should be set aside with costs, and that of the Additional Civil Judge of Lucknow affirmed. The respondents will pay the costs of these appeals.

3. Anis Begum v. Muhammad Istafa
(1933) 55 ILR All 743

Muhammadan law—restitution of conjugal rights—prompt dower remaining unpaid after cohabitation—suit for restitution not defeated thereby—conditional decree—power to impose condition of payment or other equitable or necessary conditions—legal cruelty of husband—discretion of court—interpretation of Muhammadan law—divergent texts

1. The absolute right of the wife to insist on the payment of the whole of the prompt portion of the *mahr* before restitution of conjugal rights is lost after the consummation of the marriage, unless consummation took place when she was a minor or of insane mind so as to be incapable of giving consent. Discussed in *Outlines,* § 18.

2. The husband has no absolute right to claim restitution. The suit is in the nature of a suit for specific performance in equity; and the court can impose conditions, such as the payment of dower, before the suit is decreed.

3. And where the husband had been keeping a mistress in the same house with the wife, and quarrels had ensued, leading to cruelty on the part of the husband, the court could lawfully impose the conditions (*a*) that a separate residence be provided for the wife, and (*b*) that two servants be employed for her safety.

4. (i) Where the earlier jurists of authority differ, and the leading doctors of later centuries have unanimously adopted a particular interpretation, it would not be proper now to go behind such a consensus of opinion and decide a point contrary to it.

(ii) But if the later jurists are still divided in opinion, and general consensus is wanting, it is open to the court to choose whichever opinion appears to be sounder and better adapted to the needs and conditions of the times.

Fully discussed in *Outlines*, 83 seq.

Judgment [Sulaiman, CJ]

This is a defendants' appeal arising out of a suit for restitution of conjugal rights. The plaintiff alleged that the parties were married in 1923 and the defendant No. 1 was sent to the plaintiff's house in October, 1926, and began to live with him as his wife and gave birth to a daughter; but that about two years ago the other defendants took her away from the plaintiff's house to their own house for a week under the pretext of attending a ceremony; that, when after the expiry of the week, the plaintiff went to bring his wife, the defendants made excuses and ultimately refused to send her, although they sent the plaintiff's daughter to the plaintiff's house. He accordingly prayed that the defendant should be ordered to come to the plaintiff's house and that a perpetual injunction should be granted against the other defendants from interfering with the defendant No. 1's returning to the plaintiff's house.

The defendant No. 1 in her written statement asserted that the plaintiff became immoral and contracted illicit connection with one Mst Hibia who was kept in the same house and at her instigation the plaintiff began to ill-treat the defendant and ultimately turned her out of his house. She did not admit the paragraph containing the allegation that the daughter was sent to the plaintiff's house afterwards. She pleaded that when the plaintiff neglected her and did not pay her dower debt, she was obliged to file a suit to recover Rs 15,000 as her prompt dower and that the plaintiff's suit was filed by way of reply to her suit. She pleaded that so long as the plaintiff does not pay the prompt dower due to the defendant, he is not competent to maintain the suit, and she also urged that the suit should be dismissed on the ground of the plaintiff's cruel acts in ill-treating her and in contracting illicit connection with Mst Hibia, and that the defendant's refusal to go to his house is through fear of life and honour. She admitted that she was staying away from the plaintiff's house at her own instance and no other defendant is exercising any influence over her. The other defendants denied that they were in any way preventing the defendant from going to the plaintiff's house.

The learned Subordinate Judge framed four issues: (1) Whether the plaintiff had been guilty of cruelty towards the defendant? (2) Whether any prompt dower was due to the defendant, and if so, can the plaintiff get a decree without paying it? (3) Whether the plaintiff has any cause of action against the other defendants? (4) To what relief was the plaintiff entitled and against whom? He decided all the issues in favour of the plaintiff and against the defendants and decreed the claim. All the defendants have accordingly appealed.

It may be here stated that the suit for dower brought by the defendant against the plaintiff succeeded in the court below and the defendant, in spite of contest, obtained a decree for Rs 15,000, which decree has become final. Thus neither the amount of the dower debt due to the defendant nor the fact that it has not been paid is now in question.

The learned Subordinate Judge, relying very properly on certain reported rulings of this court, has held that after the consummation of her marriage the defendant's right to resist the claim for restitution of conjugal rights was destroyed. Finding that legal cruelty was not established, he has decreed the suit. He does not appear to have considered whether apart from legal cruelty there are any circumstances justifying the passing of a decree conditional on the payment of the dower debt.

I propose to consider first of all the question whether under the Muhammadan law the right of a wife to insist on the payment of the prompt portion of her dower subsists even after consummation of marriage.

The leading case of this court is undoubtedly that of *Abdul Kadir* v. *Salima.*[13] The judgment of Mahmood, J., was adopted by the Full Bench. It has since been regarded as a detailed survey of the Muhammadan law with particular reference to the points noted on page 154, viz., (1) the exact nature and effect of marriage upon the contracting parties; (2) the exact nature of the liability of the husband to pay the dower; (3) the matrimonial rights of the parties as to conjugal cohabitation; and (4) the rules of general law as to the decree of the court in such cases. But the only point that had been referred to the Full Bench for an answer was 'Whether under the circumstances of the case the plaintiff had the right to maintain the suit.' In that case the dower debt had not been paid before the suit for restitution of conjugal rights, though the marriage had been consummated, but the amount was tendered in the trial court. That court held that the plaintiff was entitled to succeed in his claim for bringing his wife to his house. On appeal, the District Judge accepted the defendant's contention that the payment into court after the institution of the suit was insufficient because the husband had no cause of action when he brought the suit, and it was on this ground that he dismissed the suit *in toto.* The main point which was for consideration before the Full Bench was, therefore, whether the non-payment of the dower before the institution of the suit was fatal to the suit because without such payment there was no cause of action for suing for restitution of conjugal rights. The opinion of the court was that it is not correct to say that there was no cause of action and that non-payment of the dower before the suit was not a fatal defect. That opinion is binding upon us. I am not aware that this view has ever been questioned in any other court.

13 (1886) ILR 8 All 149.

But although we are bound to respect the expression of opinion on the other points mentioned in the judgment of that learned Judge, some of the observations made by him are obviously in the nature of *obiter dicta* which he had to make when surveying the whole law. It is, therefore, not possible for one to hold oneself bound by all the observations that have been made or all the opinions expressed in connection with all the four fields of inquiry enumerated by the learned Judge at the outset. Nor would it be convenient to refer to a Full Bench of five or more judges whenever any observation made therein is called into question. Much less would such a course be necessary if the observation of the learned Judge is followed, though the reasoning on which it is based is not accepted.

Now at page 166 it was observed:

> I take it as a general rule of interpreting that law, that whenever there is a difference of opinion, the opinion of the two (out of the three Masters, namely, Imam Abu Hanifa and his two disciples) will prevail against the opinion of the third.

A similar observation was made by the same learned Judge in *Agha Ali Khan* v. *Altaf Hasan Khan.*[14] I do not think that the learned Judge meant to lay down any inflexible rule which would have universal application. Presumably, what he meant was that ordinarily the opinion of the majority has been accepted. But it would be easy to cite instances in which the opinion of Imam Abu Hanifa alone has prevailed, particularly in matters of prayer and ritual, or of Imam Yusuf in matters of worldly affairs, or of Imam Muhammad in matters of inheritance. There appears to be no such invariable rule which would make the decision depend on the majority of votes only.

Mr Ameer Ali in his *Mahommedan Law*, volume II, 5th edition, chapter XII, section III, page 460 has pointed out that there is no such fixed rule, as over and over again the opinion of only one has been adopted *fatwas* and decrees. In volume I, at pages 16–17, he has quoted *Hamadia, Jami'-ul Fuselain* and *Kazi Khan* for the proposition that the joint opinion of the two disciples can be preferred to that of Imam Abu Hanifa if the difference is due to a change of circumstances and alterations in the conditions of mankind.

The learned advocate for the appellants has adopted as part of his argument a well known judgment of 1891 delivered by Maulvi Sami Ullah, District Judge of Rae Bareli, in which original authorities were quoted to challenge the opinion of Mahmood, J., both as regards this rule of preference and also the distinction of the right of the wife whose prompt dower

14 (1892) ILR 14 All 429 (448).

remains unpaid to resist restitution of conjugal rights even after consummation. This judgment has been referred to by Mr Ameer Ali as well as Sir Roland Wilson in their learned treatises. These authorities were subsequently incorporated in the judgment of an Oudh Bench in *Wajid Ali Khan* v. *Sakhawat Ali Khan.*[15] On pages 144–7 of the report in that case some of the texts have been reproduced to show that, even in the case of a difference, the opinion of Imam Abu Hanifa is to be preferred. Of course, there is no such general rule either. As a matter of fact, there does not appear to be any fixed rule: See *Irfan Ali* v. *Bhagwant Kishore.*[16] Different doctors have followed different rules of preference. Those who were more orthodox and, generally speaking, more ancient, in many cases preferred the solitary opinion of Abu Hanifa to even the joint opinion of his disciples. There are later text-book writers who have preferred the opinion of two as against that of one. But such rules are helpful only when there is no clear consensus. In the early days when new points arose and the decision had to depend on an inference drawn from other *fatwas* or from analogy, it was open to the learned doctors to prefer one opinion over the other which they considered more correct and consonant with the other principles, inasmuch as the three Imams were not law-givers but merely interpreters of the law. But if one finds a question well threshed out and in later centuries a particular interpretation adopted by the leading doctors and text-book writers, it would not be proper for us in the twentieth century to go behind such a consensus of opinion and decide a point contrary to such opinion, on the ground that the majority of the three Imams favoured that view in the earlier centuries. Such a course of action would unsettle the Muhammadan law. Rules of preference were for the guidance of ancient jurists, and they are of no help when there is a clear preponderance of authority in support of one view. It would be too late now to resort to such rules in support of a new conception as to how a point ought to have been decided, though contrary to accepted opinion. Maulvi Abdul Hai of Lucknow, the most renowned and learned Hanafi jurist of his time, has in his Introduction to *Sharah Wiqayah* dealt with this matter at considerable length. A good deal of that matter is to be found in *Radd-ul-Muhtar* summarized in Sir Abdur Rahim's *Muhammadan Jurisprudence* at pages 187–8, which can be conveniently referred to. He has rightly pointed out that there is no accepted rule that, when there is a difference of opinion amongst the founders of schools and their disciples, opinion or ruling of a lawyer ought to be given according to the opinion of Abu Hanifa, even if all his disciples differ from

15 (1912) 15 Oudh Cases 127.
16 AIR 1929 All 180 (187).

him; and in the absence of any dictum of his in accordance with the opinion of Abu Yusuf, then Muhammad, then Zufar and then Hasan Ibn Ziyad. If the authorities were examined it will generally be found that in some matters the solitary view of Abu Hanifa has been preferred whereas in other matters the view of Abu Yusuf, Muhammad or Zufar has been followed. According to *Al-Hawi* the correct rule was that in cases of difference of opinion regard should be had to the authority and reasons in support of each view and the one which has the strongest support should be followed.

'But according to the modern interpretation of *Taqlid* as above stated a lawyer of the present day should, in such cases, accept the view which according to the jurists of the fourth, fifth, and sixth degrees is correct and has been acted upon. But if in any case the later doctors have not adopted in clear language anyone of the conflicting opinions, the law is to be ascertained by proceeding on the view which is most in accord with the habits and affairs of men.' [p. 188]

The *Radd-ul-Muhtar*, [*Shami*] volume I, page 73, states that if on any matter no clear answer from anyone of the early jurists were to exist, and the later doctors have one opinion, then that should be adopted; but if they differ, then the view of the majority of those on whom well known doctors like Abu Hafs, Abu Jafar, Abul Lais, Tahawi and others have relied should be accepted. And if a clear answer were not to exist from any one of these later jurists, then the Mufti should consider the question carefully and try his best to arrive at a correct conclusion so that he may be relieved of the charge of not having considered it fully. [Arabic text: Cases, 24]

It would follow that if jurists of the first rank have differed among themselves but the jurists of the second, third and fourth ranks have followed the opinion of one of them, it would not be proper in later times to go behind the opinion of these later jurists and prefer the opinion of the majority of the jurists of the first rank which has been discarded by those of subsequent periods.

The proper course undoubtedly is to abide by the opinions which have been adhered to in the commentaries which are of recognized authority in India and not to decide the point on any general rule of interpretation based on the majority of votes of the ancient jurists.

Their Lordships of the Privy Council in the case of *Aga Mahomed Jaffer Bindanim* v. *Koolsom Bee Bee*,[17] remarked:

'But it would be wrong for the courts on a point of this kind' (the right of the widow: to inherit) 'to attempt to put their own construction on the Koran in opposition to the express ruling of commentators of such great antiquity and high authority

17 (1897) ILR 25 Cal 9 (18).

(as the *Hedaya* and the *Fatawa Alamgiri*). It is the practice of the great commentators to state the difference of opinion which at one time prevailed on a particular point and then to add on which view is the *fatwa*, or which is the more correct or stronger view, or to use other expressions of like import. But where the learned commentators content themselves with a mere statement of the conflict of opinion without expressing any definite opinion of their own in favour of one or the other view and without saying anything about the consensus of opinion or the *fatwa* being in accordance with a particular view, they imply that the conflict of opinion was still continuing and that no unanimity or general concurrence had till then been obtained. This would have the effect of leaving the question open. The Qazi would then be free to choose whichever of the two opinions appears to him to be the sounder and better adapted to the conditions and the needs of the times.'

The *Radd-ul-Muhtar*, [*Shami*] volume I, page 80, when reproducing the text of the *Durr-ul-Mukhtar* has quoted from *Quduri* as follows:

And if you said that they (jurists) have sometimes quoted several opinions without giving preference and have differed as to their correctness: Then I would say that we should act as they, having regard to the change in the habits and conditions of men, did what was more convenient, practicable and better. And people who can discriminate are not extinct. This is a fact and not an imagination. But those who cannot discriminate should refer to those who can, so that they will be free from responsibility. [Arabic text: *Cases*, 25]

Now before Mahmood, J., in the case of *Abdul Kadir* v. *Salima*,[18] no texts other than those of *Durr-ul-Muhktar*, *Fatawa Alamgiri* (and possibly *Hedaya*) which all state the conflict of opinion, without saying which view should be preferred, were cited. The learned Judge accordingly felt compelled to make a deduction from certain principles governing sale of goods, and applying them to the contract of marriage observed, at page 167 of the judgment in *Abdul Kadir's* case, 'after consummation of marriage, non-payment of dower, even though exigible, cannot be pleaded in defence of an action for restitution of conjugal rights; the rule so laid down having, of course no effect upon the right of the wife to claim her dower in a separate action.'

If the observation was intended to mean that the plea of non-payment of dower would not result in the dismissal of the suit, it has never been questioned. If it was intended to lay down that under the Muhammadan law the right to demand payment of dower before restitution of conjugal rights is destroyed completely after the marriage has once been consummated, then it was an *obiter dictum* in that case and though it must be treated with all respect it may not be of binding authority. That it was an *obiter dictum* is apparent from the very next sentence which is to the effect: 'But the rule

18 (1886), ILR 8 All 149.

enunciated by me need not be applied in its fullest extent to the present case, because, etc.' The line of reasoning based on the analogy of sale has naturally been very severely criticized at pages 148–9 in *Wajid Ali Khan's Case*[19] by the Oudh Bench, and so also by Mr Ameer Ali in his *Mahommedan Law*, volume II, pages 459–60. No doubt the Muslim commentators have, by way of illustration, applied certain principles governing a contract of sale of goods to the contract of marriage, but that was by way of analogy only. The similarity cannot be pushed too far, nor can the principles governing the sale of goods be applied in all their details. Indeed, if one were to pursue the analogy far enough there would be a *reductio ad absurdum*. The contract of sale of goods can be cancelled if a portion of the price has not been paid. Even if the goods have been once delivered they may in such an event be returned. But if consummation of marriage has taken place and a part of the dower remains unpaid, it would be absurd to suppose that the marriage could be cancelled by the wife at her will. Similarly, I do not think that the learned Judge, when he referred to the right of stoppage *in transitu* at page 166 at all intended to apply that rule to the restitution of conjugal rights. Such a right is exercised when the goods are in the possession of a carrier or agent and are in the course of transit, when the original owner of the goods has only a constructive and not actual possession. That doctrine can, by no stretch of the imagination, be applied to the refusal of the wife to go to her husband, as there can be no question of transit or carrier at all.

It is quite obvious that the analogy of sales cannot be carried too far. The marriage cannot be regarded as purely a sale of the person by the wife in consideration for the payment of dower and even if such a grotesque analogy were to be carried to its fullest extent, it would not necessarily result in support of the observation made in *Abdul Kadir's Case*. The answer will depend on whether the dower is the consideration for the first consummation of marriage only or whether it is the consideration for the society of the life during the married life. The mere fact that the whole dower becomes due after consummation is no conclusive ground for holding that the dower is consideration only for the first consummation. The lien on goods sold may be lost when possession is lost, but that lien is revived when possession is again recovered. Again, if part of the goods have been delivered and part of it is still retained, the lien on the part retained continues. It may therefore be well argued that if the wife after the consummation returns to her own house she can still resist restitution of conjugal rights so long as her dower is not paid, because her right has been revived after the cohabitation ceased. It may also be pointed out that a prompt dower does not become payable

19 (1912) 15 Oudh Cases 127.

unless a demand is made. Prompt dower is dower payable on demand. It follows that no demand might have been made, and in most cases it is not made before the consummation of marriage. The consent of the wife before her dower became due should logically not destroy her right to recover her dower after it has become due, though previous to it consummation had taken place. She should have the right to insist upon its payment before further cohabitation. I have not mentioned these points in order to base any conclusion on the analogy of sales, but merely to emphasize that the analogy cannot be carried too far, and even if carried very far, it does not necessarily clinch the matter. It may not be out of place to mention here that Maulvi Samiullah collected some authorities showing that a marriage is not regarded as a mere civil contract, but as a religious sacrament.

The original authorities on the main question before us may be grouped under three heads. For the sake of brevity I am not quoting the original texts or their translations if they have already appeared in the reported judgment of *Wajid Ali Khan* v. *Sakhawat Ali Khan*.[20]

Under the first head come some of the ancient textbooks called *Matan*. These are very terse and concise and generally state the opinion of Imam Abu Hanifa on this point without even mentioning the difference of opinion between him and his two disciples and consequently without saying which opinion is to be preferred. These are (1) The *Bedaya*, (2) The *Tanvir-ul-Absar*, (3) The *Kanz-ud-Dakaik* and (4) The *Waqayat-ur-Rewaya*. These are all quoted in *Wajid Ali Khan's Case*. No doubt in the early days there was a recognized rule that the texts should be preferred to commentaries and that commentaries should be preferred to collections of *fatwas*; but when centuries passed, the consensus of opinion of jurists and doctors was often found to be contrary to some of the ancient texts. Accordingly the commentaries which stated both the opinions and then preferred one over the other on the strength either of reason or *ijma* gained greater strength. So much so that in later centuries the ancient text-books or *matan* came to be regarded as elementary treatises in which the law is only concisely and tersely laid down and the statement of the law contained therein required further explanation. The *Kanz-ud-Dakaik* (though of much later date) is particularly a book of this description, as it is extremely concise. This matter is discussed at length in *Radd-ul-Muhtar*, a reference to which is also found in Sir Abdur Rahim's *Muhammadan Jurisprudence* on pages 189–90. The author of *Radd-ul-Muhtar* goes so far as to suggest that even the *Durr-ul-Mukhtar* on which he was writing his commentary should not be readily accepted on account of its brevity.

20 Ibid.

Under the second group may be put the great commentaries which discuss the law, state the difference of opinion and do not clearly indicate a preference for one view and so in a way leave the point open.

(1) The *Hedaya*, which is the commentary on the *Bedaya* by the same author, first quotes the text of the *Bedaya* and then notes the difference of opinion between the Imam and his disciples, but omits to say which of the two should be preferred. (Hamilton's Translation, volume I, book II, chapter III, page 52).

(2) The *Durr-ul-Mukhtar* which is the commentary on the *Tanvir-ul-Absar* quotes the text of *Tanvir-ul-Absar* and comments on it, giving some reasons. It does not in express terms state its own opinion as to what is to happen if consummation has taken place, but by implication it adopts the text, particularly as it does not even mention the difference of opinion between the Imam and the disciples.

In *Wajid Ali Khan's Case*[21] the text of *Tanvir-ul-Absar* has been correctly quoted, but there has been a little confusion in quoting the text of the *Durr-ul-Mukhtar*. What has been quoted includes again the words of the text of *Tanvir-ul-Absar* interspersed with the comments of the author of the *Durr-ul-Mukhtar*. The author merely attempts to explain the obscure words. He does not purport to discuss them.

(3) The *Bahr-ur-Raik* which is an elaborate commentary on the *Kanz-ud-Dakaik* (volume 3, at page 191, Egyptian edition) quotes the difference of opinion, but does not clearly express the view that the opinion of the disciple is to be preferred. But on page 192 it quotes Bazdavi, who attained the position of a *mujtahid* of the third rank (Sir Abdur Rahim's *Muhammadan Jurisprudence*, page 183), to the effect that Abul Qasim Saffar gave *fatwa* against the right of the wife to resist restitution after consummation and says that Bazdavi considered that opinion to be good. [Arabic text: *Cases*, 29]

(4) The *Sharh Waqaya*, which is a commentary on the *Waqayat-ur-Rewaya*, quotes the text on which it comments, and then just mentions the difference of opinion, but omits to express any preference of its own.

(5) The author of *Fath-ul-Qadir*, which in turn is a great commentary on the *Hedaya*, also states the difference of opinion, but omits to give his own opinion as to which view should be preferred. Although it is an exhaustive commentary, it deals with this point rather briefly, and does not even refer to Saffar or Bazdavi.

(6) *Tahtawi*, a great commentary on the *Durr-ul-Mukhtar*, also quotes the difference of opinion and refers to the *fatwa* of Saffar, and says that

21 (1912) 15 Oudh Cases 127.

Bazdavi considered it better, but does not express its own preference (Book on Marriage, chapter on Dower, page 99, Calcutta edition). [Arabic text: *Cases*, 30]

(7) The author of the *Radd-ul-Muhtar* (more commonly known after its author Shami), another and more exhaustive commentary on the *Durr-ul-Mukhtar*, curiously enough deals with the matter briefly, gives the difference of opinion between the Imam and the disciples without mentioning Saffar or Bazdavi. He does not state his own conclusion as to which of the two opinions should be preferred.

(8) Under this category I may also mention the following *fatwas* in particular: (i) *Fatawa Kazi Khan*. It quotes the difference of opinion, but omits to express any preference (15 Oudh Cases, at page 134); (ii) *Fatawa Alamgiri*. Baillie's *Muhammadan Law*, volume I, page 125 gives a correct translation of the relevant passage in the *fatwa* except perhaps the last sentence in which the original word *ba'z* has been translated as 'several', though it would be more correct to say 'some'; but here, too, after quoting the practice of Shaik-us-Saffar, the compilers omit to add on which view the *fatawa* should be given.

Other ancient textbooks like *Qaduri* do not refer to the difference of opinion at all.

In the third group may be placed some books which prefer the opinion of the disciples. I am not quoting them as books of overriding authority but merely to point out that the *fatawas* have not been all one way.

(1) *Fatawa Ghiyasia* (chapter on Marriage, page 65, line 19, Egyptian edition) says:

If a wife were to submit her person without obtaining her dower and then wish to refuse to cohabit with him until she recover her dower when he has cohabited with her, then in this there is a well known difference. But the opinion to be adopted is that she has not this right, but she can demand from her husband the prompt dower. [Arabic text: *Cases*, 31]

(2) The *Jami-ul-Rumuz* which is a commentary on *Mukhtasar-ul-Waqayah* by *Sadr-us-Sharaya*, says (volume II, page 211, Nawal Kishore edition):

And Abul Qasim-us-Saffar gave *fatwa* on the absence of the right to refuse cohabitation, and according to his (Imam's) opinion on the right to refuse to go out on journey, and on this is the *fatwa* as is mentioned in the *Haqaiq*. [Arabic text: *Cases*, 31]

It is possible to urge that the language of the text is capable of the interpretation that 'this' refers only to the refusal to go out on journey.

(3) *Fatawa Himadya* quotes *Umdat-ul-Fatawa* which does not refer to the case of consummation. Similarly, the quotation from *Fatawa Mufti* has no reference to consummation (see 15 Oudh Cases 135). The learned judges of Oudh thought that *Himadya* quotes a passage from *Tahzib* which states that 'although she has once cohabited willingly with her husband, she has a right of refusal contrary to the view of the *Sahabain*'. But the learned judges seem to have overlooked that the passage goes on to refer to the opinion of Qasim Saffar and then the opinion of the author of *Tahzib* is stated in the following terms:

The approved view according to me is that the wife possesses the right of refusal if there has been ill-treatment on the part of the husband, and if it be the fault of the wife, then she has no such right.

It would, therefore, follow that the *Tahzib* is against there being any absolute right of refusal in the wife. On the other hand, she is given that right only when the husband has been ill-treating her. This might be a very commonsense view to take, but there does not appear to be any further support for it. But in any case *Tahzib* cannot be cited as an authority in favour of the wife's right. If anything, it is an authority against such right.

(4) In this connection I ought to mention *Fatawa Maulana Abdul Hai*, who was undoubtedly the most learned Hanafi doctor in India in his time. His *fatawa* cannot be put on a par with the recognized commentaries or *fatawa*. I propose to cite his *fatawa* in order to show the trend of opinion that has prevailed in this country. His *fatawa* are even now freely referred to and relied upon by *Maulvis* when easy access to the original authorities in Arabic is not to be had.

Fatwa No. 197 (1296 AH corresponding to 1878) volume I, page 240, is particularly important. It may be briefly summarized as follows:

A Sunni woman, Hinda, was married to a Shia husband, Zaid, and the marriage was performed according to the Shia form. After having cohabited and lived with her husband for some days, Hinda returned to her mother's house with her husband's permission and then remained there demanding her prompt dower. Zaid feared that she might become immoral. The question put to the Maulana was whether Zaid could, according to his religion, bring her to his house without payment of prompt dower in accordance with the opinion expressed in the Shia text-book, *Sharaya-ul-Islam*, although according to the *Hedaya* there appeared to be some difference of opinion. The answer was that the husband can take away the wife without payment of her dower debt, and for authority *Bahr-ur-Raiq* was cited which quotes the opinion of Bazdavi who referred to the *fatwa* of Abul Qasim Saffar.

It thus appears that the older text-books no doubt preferred the opinion of Abu Hanifa as against those of his disciples, so much so that they did not even care to mention the difference of opinion; but the later commentators pointed out that the disciples had differed from the opinion and also noticed that jurists like Bazdavi and Saffar had not followed Abu Hanifa strictly; but these commentators omitted to express their own definite opinion as to which view should be preferred. On the other hand there are, at any rate, some authorities which definitely preferred the opinion of the disciples to that of Imam Abu Hanifa. It is obvious that though in the earlier centuries the view of Abu Hanifa was generally accepted, the divergence from it became more pronounced in later times. Even down to the time of Aurangzeb in India, when the *Fatawa Alamgiri* was compiled, the conflict of opinion continued and no definite consensus of opinion seems to have been reached, otherwise it was most probable that the approved opinion would have been mentioned.

This being the state of the authorities, the question is whether the *obiter dictum* of Mahmood, J., which has been accepted by so many other High Courts, is to be followed.

Had I been sitting as a Judge in the times of the East India Company, I might then possibly have been inclined to prefer the opinion of Imam Abu Hanifa, because although a conflict ensued afterwards no eminent commentator expressly dissented from that view. But if another Judge had been prepared to take the contrary view, I would not have been in a position to say that he was necessarily wrong. The two considerations which might well justify the acceptance of the view of the disciples in India are: First, that owing to the prevalent practice, the amounts of dower fixed in this country are often unduly high and beyond the means of the husband. To allow to the wife the right of refusing to live with her husband, even after consummation, so long as any part of the prompt dower remains unpaid would, in many cases, where the husband and wife quarrel, amount to an absolute option to the wife to refuse to live with her husband and yet demand a maintenance allowance. This would dislocate domestic life. Secondly, as will be shown hereinafter, under the Anglo-Muhammadan law as administered in this country a suit for restitution of conjugal rights, though brought for the enforcement of a right under the Muhammadan law, is in the nature of a suit for specific performance, and there is accordingly a certain amount of discretion in the courts of justice which can impose a condition of previous payment of the dower debt, or, at any rate, a portion of it, in the decree.

And now the position is still stronger. For nearly 40 years the observation of Mahmood, J., even though an *obiter dictum*, has been accepted in this Court, and indeed it has been followed by all the other High Courts excepting Oudh: *Kunhi* v. *Moidin;*[22] *Hamidunnessta Bibi* v. *Zohiruddin*

22 (1888) ILR 11 Mad 327.

Sheikh[23] *Bai Hansa* v. *Abdulla Mustafa*;[24] *Ashia Khatoon* v. *Abdul Hakim Maistry*[25] and *Mst Saleh Bibi* v. *Rafiuddin*.[26]

In the case of *Abdul Karim Khan* v. *Mst Chhoti*[27] a learned judge of this court followed an earlier decision in the case of *Wilayat Husain* v. *Allah Rakhi* [28] which had been overruled by the Full Bench. But apparently the attention of the learned Judge was not drawn to the observation in the Full Bench case as there is no reference to it in his judgment. On the other hand, a Division Bench of this Court in the case of *Hijaban* v. *Ali Sher Khan*[29] adhered to the view expressed in *Abdul Kadir's Case*.

Numerous cases must have been decided, though not reported, on the assumption that the view of the disciples is to be preferred. When the law has been interpreted in a particular way, it may well be that in some cases the law governing the rights of the parties to a marriage was implied as a part of the terms of the contract of marriage.

No doubt, in Oudh, a Bench of that court has taken a contrary view, but the Oudh Court was not bound to follow the opinion expressed by the Full Bench of this Court; and further, in Oudh, the difficulty of a wife insisting on the previous payment of an unreasonably high dower, which is beyond the means of her husband, does not at all arise, for under section 5 of the Oudh Laws Act the courts of Oudh have power to reduce the amount of the dower debt if it is 'excessive with reference to the means of the husband', though in fact agreed upon. It also appears that the authorities placed before the Oudh Court were those quoted in the judgment of Maulvi Sami Ullah and were all one way. The authorities in support of the contrary view were apparently not cited before them. Nor is it clear that the effect of the point having been left open in the later commentaries was put prominently before the learned Judges.

It is true that in the other High Courts the question has not been re-examined in the light of the original authorities, but the observation of Mahmood, J., has been simply followed. It is also true that a Bench of the Calcutta High Court in *Hamidunnessa Bibi's Case*,[30] one member of which, Petheram, C. J., had been a party to the Full Bench of Allahabad in *Abdul Kadir's* Case, thought that according to the *Fatawa Alamgiri* the practice

23 (1890) 1LR 17 Cal 670.
24 (1905) ILR 30 Bom 122.
25 AIR 1929 Rang 189.
26 (1889) Punj. Rec No. 164.
27 *Weekly Notes*, 1906, p. 136.
28 (1880) ILR 2 All 831.
29 (1921) 19 ALJ 880.
30 (1890) ILR 17 Cal 670.

of the later jurists was to follow the two disciples; whereas, in point of fact, the *Fatawa Alamgiri* also in one sense leaves the matter open. But the fact remains that throughout India, excluding Oudh, the same view has prevailed for several decades.

I therefore consider that it would now be dangerous to go back upon this course of decisions and not to adhere to the well recognized principle of *stare decisis*, particularly when at the time when Mahmood, J., made his observation it was to some extent open to him to prefer the view of the disciples.

In this view of the matter, I hold that the rule laid down in *Abdul Kadir's* Case,[31] though an *obiter dictum,* must be followed even though the analogy of sale may not be accepted. It may be re-stated as follows:

The absolute right of a wife to insist on the payment of the whole of the prompt portion of her dower before restitution of conjugal rights (except when the husband wants to take her out on a journey to another town) is lost after the consummation of the marriage, unless the consummation took place when she was a minor or of insane mind so as to be incapable of giving consent.

Just as we respect the observation made as regards the loss of the right of the wife on consummation, even though it be an *obiter dictum,* we must in the same way respect the other observation—though an equal *obiter dictum-made* in *Abdul Kadir's* Case that 'courts of justice in India, in the exercise of their mixed jurisdiction as courts of equity and law, are at full liberty to pass conditional decrees to suit the exigencies of each particular case' (page 169). Mahmood, J., undoubtedly held that the loss of the absolute right of the wife to resist the claim for restitution of conjugal rights did not prevent the court from making the previous payment of the dower debt a condition precedent to the execution of the decree for restitution of conjugal rights. At page 157 it was observed: 'That the latter right' (the right of dower) 'may modify and affect the former' (right of cohabitation) 'cannot be doubted: how it affects and modifies it is the main subject of the reference.' The observation at page 160 shows that the contention for the wife was that the right of cohabitation does not accrue to the husband at all until he has paid the prompt dower. The observation at page 160 has already been quoted. At page 170 it was stated:

> It is one thing to say that such a defence may be set up under certain conditions; it is a totally different thing to say that until the dower was paid no cause of action could accrue to the plaintiff. The payment of dower not being a condition precedent to the vesting of the right of cohabitation, a suit for restitution of conjugal rights,

31 (1886) ILR 8 All 149.

whether by the husband or by the wife, would be maintainable upon refusal by the other to cohabit with him or her; and in the case of a suit by the husband, the defence of payment of dower could, at its best, operate in modification of the decree for restitution of conjugal rights by rendering the enforcement of it, conditional upon payment of so much of the dower as may be regarded to be prompt.

Similarly at page 171 the conclusion was:

So that, pushing the analogy of the law of sale to its fullest extent, the right of a Muhammadan wife to her dower is at best a lien upon his right to claim cohabitation, and I am unaware of any rule of Muhammadan law which would render such lien capable of being pleaded so as to defeat altogether the suit for restitution of conjugal rights.

It is thus clear that the learned Judge was prepared to make the decree for restitution of conjugal rights conditional upon the payment of the dower debt. This, for all practical purposes, would amount to upholding the right of the widow to claim her dower, even though consummation of marriage has taken place, the only difference being that the power of the court to impose such terms is held to be based on the general rules of justice, equity and good conscience and not on the strict principles of the Muhammadan law as now interpreted.

This view was accepted by the Punjab Chief Court in the case of *Mst Saleh Bibi* v. *Raft Uddin*;[32] and the passing of a conditional decree was approved by a Bench of this court in the case of *Hijaban* v. *Ali Sher Khan*.[33] No doubt no conditional decree was passed in the case of *Kunhi* v. *Moidin*[34] nor in the case of *Hamidunnessa Bibi* v. *Zohiruddin Sheik*.[35] But the point does not appear to have been raised in those cases. *Nawab Wazir Jahan Begam* v. *Nawab Haidar Raza Khan*[36] was apparently a Shia case…

It is argued on behalf of the respondent that the husband has a substantive right to claim restitution of conjugal rights after consummation, even though the dower has not been paid. It is said that this right is not a matter of mere procedure but is a substantive right under the Muhammadan law which the court has no discretion to refuse. Their Lordships of the Privy Council in the case of *Moonshee Buzloor Ruheem* v. *Shumsoonnissa Begam*[37] observed

32 (1889) Punj. Rec. No. 164.
33 (1921) 19 ALJ 880.
34 (1888) ILR 11 Mad 327.
35 (1890) ILR 17 Cal 670.
36 (1905) 10 Oudh Cases 11.
37 (1867) 11 Moo IA 551.

that a suit for restitution of conjugal rights, though in the nature of a suit for specific performance is in reality a suit to enforce a right under the Muhammadan law and the courts should have regard to the principles of Muhammadan law. The observation of their Lordships was directed to emphasizing the point that courts should not exercise their discretion in complete supersession of the Muhammadan law, but that in exercise of their discretion they should refer to that law. But the principle was fully recognized that in passing a decree for the restitution of conjugal rights the court has power to take into account all the circumstances of the case and impose terms which it considers to be fair and reasonable.

The rule may, therefore, be re-stated as follows:

> There is no absolute right in a husband to claim restitution of conjugal rights against his wife unconditionally; the courts have a discretion to make the decree conditional on the payment of her unpaid dower debt or to impose other suitable conditions considered just, fair and necessary in the circumstances of each case.

Applying these principles to the case before us I would hold that the condition of the previous payment of the dower debt should be imposed on the decree for restitution of conjugal rights, if passed[....]

The next question is whether the defendant succeeded in establishing legal cruelty which would disentitle the plaintiff from claiming restitution of conjugal rights. That question is one of fact and depends mainly on oral evidence[....]

In view of all these circumstances I am compelled to hold that the learned Subordinate Judge has not appreciated the seriousness of the evidence that was laid before him and has been led away by unjustifiable considerations to think that the defendant's story was grossly exaggerated and there was no case of legal cruelty.

In fairness to him it must be pointed out that there is certainly a possibility that the story told by the defendant that she was beaten with *lathis*[38] and shoes might not be true, but I have no hesitation in holding that the fact that Mst Hibia, a mistress, was kept in the same house with the wife is fully established and I do not believe the denial made by the husband nor do I accept the statements of his two brothers, who, admitting the presence of Mst Hibia in the house, tried to explain it away by saying that she was a mere maid-servant of the insane mother. These brothers do not live in the same part of the house, and are therefore not in a position to know about the relations between the husband and Mst Hibia to the same extent as the wife living under the same roof would be able to see for herself. Further,

38 *Lathi*, Hindustani for a staff (used by shepherds and villagers).

I think that in view of the claim for dower brought by the wife these brothers are supporting the plaintiff. I have no hesitation in holding that the husband misbehaved in this way that he kept a mistress in his house along with his wife and caused mental pain to her in consequence and that he must have, when quarrels ensued, treated his wife cruelly; and that as the quarrels were not and could not be patched up, so long as Mst Hibia remained in the house, the defendant No. I had reasonable apprehension of injury to her person.

I think that the wife is fully justified in refusing to go and live with her husband so long as there is no undertaking not to keep any mistress in the house; she can go to live with him only if a separate house is given to her. Further, I think that in order to protect her safety it is necessary that she should have the option of keeping one female servant and one male servant, according to her choice, in the house....

I would accordingly allow the appeal in part and impose conditions on the decree for the restitution of conjugal rights.

◊ UPDATE ◊

1. *Trends in India*

The caution given by the Privy Council in the cases of *Aga Mahomed* and *Baker Ali Khan* [Cases 1 & 2] against directly relying on and re-interpreting the Holy Qur'an and *Sunnah* has generally been followed in India.

Of course, at times the courts have directly relied on some Quranic verses and the Prophet's Traditions to draw a point. The Assam High Court judgment in *Jiauddin Ahmad* v. *Anwara Begum* 1981 GLR 358, for instance, profusely quoted the Quranic verses on *talaq*. In *Ibrahim Fathima* v. *Saleem* AIR 1980 Mad 82 the High Court based its decision on the father's liability to provide maintenance to his children directly on a Tradition of the Prophet. The Supreme Court of India in its celebrated decision in *Mohammad Ahmad Khan* v. *Shah Bano Begum* AIR 1985 SC 985 also made elaborate references to the Holy Book of Islam in support of its viewpoint.

No court has, however, specifically claimed an authority to re-interpret the Quranic verses or the Prophet's Traditions on law. On the contrary in *Usman Khan Bahmani* v. *Fathimunisa* AIR 1990 AP 225, the Andhra Pradesh High Court reiterated the Privy Council dicta from *Aga Mahomed* and *Baker Ali Khan* [Cases 1 & 2] and, drawing attention to the 'inherent danger' in attempting direct reinterpretation of the Qur'an, observed:

The interpretation which has been put to such verses by the established authorities is to be taken as authoritative pronouncements which cannot be deviated from.[39]

The courts in India are, of course, fully aware of the utmost sanctity the Holy Qur'an as the only revealed book of Islam. In *Chandanmal Chopra* v. *State of West Bengal* AIR 1986 Cal 104, dismissing a petition attacking the Qur'an for the literal meaning of some of its verses, the High Court of Calcutta so explained the importance of the Holy Book of Islam:[40]

For the Muslims the Qur'an is *ipsissima verba* of God Himself. It is God speaking to man not merely in 7th century Arabia to Arabs but eternally to every man throughout the world. The Qur'an is *al-Furqan*, showing truth from falsehood... Muslim religion cannot exist without Qur'an.

2. *Trends in Pakistan and Bangladesh*

The trends in Pakistan and Bangladesh, both of which officially owe allegiance to Islam and are Muslim-majority countries, have been very different from India. In Pakistan, in the case of *Rashida Begum* v. *Shahan Din* PLD 1960 Lah 1142 the High Court of Lahore had observed:

If the interpretation of the Holy Qur'an by the commentators who lived thirteen or twelve hundred years ago is considered as the last word on the subject then the whole Islamic society will be shut up in an iron cage and not allowed to develop along with the time.

In a later case two judges of the Lahore High Court expressed conflicting views on the subject. While one of them referred to the two PC rulings, *Aga Mahomed* and *Baker Ali Khan* [Cases 1 & 2], and held 'I am not inclined to depart from the view taken by the Privy Council', the other observed 'the courts must be given the right to interpret for themselves the Qur'an and the *Sunnah*'—Wahiduddin and Anwarul Haq, JJ in *Khurshid Jan's* case PLD 1964 Lah 558.

The views about difference of juristic opinions within particular schools of Muslim law, expressed in the old Allahabad decision of 1933 in *Anis Begum* [Case 3], are no more shared by the courts in Pakistan which do not consider themselves bound by any of those old opinions. In *Khurshid Bibi* v. *Mohammad Amin* PLD 1967 SC 1967 the Supreme Court of Pakistan observed:

39 The High Court in this case cited my article on the *Shah Bano* case from the *Islamic and Comparative Law Quarterly*, V: 1985, pp. 110–20.

40 Full details of this case may be seen in my article 'Validity of the Holy Qur'an by Indian Legal Standards', *Islamic and Comparative Law Quarterly*, V: 1985, pp. 93–109.

The opinions of jurists and commentators stand on no higher footing than that of reasoning of men falling in the category of secondary sources of Muslim law and, cannot, therefore, compare in weight or authority with, nor alter, the Quranic law or the *ahadith*. If the opinions of the jurists conflict with the Qur'an and the *Sunnah*, they are not binding on courts and it is our duty as true Muslims to obey the word of God and the Holy Prophet.

By an amendment of the Constitution, a Federal Shariat Court was established in Pakistan in 1979, with powers to adapt the national laws to the principles of the Qur'an and *Sunnah.* Article 302-D so laid down the power of the court:

The court may, either on its motion or on the petition of a citizen of Pakistan, or the Federal Government or a Provincial Government, examine and decide the question whether or not any law or provision of law is repugnant to the injunctions of Islam as laid down in the Holy Qur'an and the *Sunnah* of the Holy Prophet.

In *Muhammad Riaz* v. *Federal Government* PLD 1980 FSC 1 the Federal Shariat Court clarified that the new Constitutional provision aimed at adapting the law to the express provisions of the Qur'an and *Sunnah* only, and not to their established interpretation according to any of the classical schools of Islamic law:

The principle under which the repugnance of a particular law to the injunctions of Islam is to be judged is limited to the consideration of the question whether the laws sought to be challenged before this court are in conformity with the injunctions of Islam as laid down in the Holy Qur'an and the *Sunnah* of the Prophet. It would, therefore, be clear that the language of the Constitution does not warrant any attempts at harmonizing the laws with any particular jurisprudence (*fiqh*) or jurisprudence of any particular school of thought or sect. On the other hand it appears that reference to any particular doctrinal approach (*fiqh*) has been eliminated deliberately so as to enable the courts to test the validity of a law only on the criteria of commandments laid down in the Holy Qur'an or the *Sunnah* of the Prophet.

In Bangladesh, in *Md Hafzur Rahman* v. *Shamsun Nahar Begum* 47 (1995) Dhaka Law Report 54, the court referred to the Privy Council decision in *Aga Mohammad* [Case 1] and observed:

A civil court has the jurisdiction to follow the law as in the Qur'an disregarding any other law on the subject if contrary thereto even if laid down by the earlier jurists or commentators, may be of great antiquity and high authority and though followed for a considerable period.

II. Who is a Muslim?

4. Abraham v. Abraham

(1863) 9 MIA 195

Conversion—Hindus to Christianity—law applicable—'native Christians'—'East Indians'

Upon the conversion of a Hindu to Christianity the Hindu law ceases to have any continuing obligatory force upon the convert. He may (1) renounce the old law by which he was bound, as he has renounced his religion, or (2) if he thinks fit, he may abide by the law notwithstanding that he has renounced his old religion. In India, however, Hindu law applies to Hindus and Muhammadan law to Muslims. Whence, normally, upon conversion to Islam, Muhammadan law applies immediately.

See case 43, below; *Tyabji*, esp. 50; *Mulla*, § 21; *Outlines*, 59, 62 seqq., 77, especially (iii) and (iv).

This is a leading case and lays down several important rules. But, strictly speaking, we are not concerned with them, except as stated above.

The principal question involved in this appeal was as to the law which governed the succession to the property of the late Matthew Abraham, a Protestant native of India, resident in the Madras Presidency, who died intestate in the year 1842. The ancestors of Matthew Abraham for several generations had been Christians; and Matthew Abraham, who had been baptized in infancy in the Roman Catholic faith but afterwards became a convert to the Protestant religion, married a European wife in the year 1820, and with her and the children of the marriage conformed in all respects to the language, dress, manners, and habits of English persons up to the time of his death. The Sudder Court at Madras held that the property should be distributed in accordance with the Hindu law.

Judgment [Lord Kingsdown][1]

[....]

The first and most important question raised by this appeal is, by what

[1] With Bruce, Turner & Coleridge, JJ; Assessors: L. Peal & J.W. Colvile.

law the rights of the parties ought to be determined. In considering this question it is material in the first place to observe what was the real point in issue in the cause. Laying out of consideration the objection raised by the answer, that the Plaintiff, Charlotte Abraham, as widow, could not sue jointly with the other Plaintiffs, her sons, an objection of misjoinder of parties which, in their Lordships' opinion, was properly answered by the replication, and properly disposed of by the Sudder Court when the case was first brought before it by appeal, the true question a tissue in this case is, not who was the heir of the late Matthew Abraham, but whether he and the Respondent formed an undivided family in the sense which those words bear in the Hindoo law with reference to the acquisition, improvement, enjoyment, disposition, and devolution of property. It is a question of parcenership, and not of heirship. Heirship may be governed by the Hindoo law, or by any other law to which the ancestor may be subject; but parcenership, understood in the sense in which their Lordships here use the term, as expressing the rights and obligations growing out of the status of an undivided family, is the creature of, and must be governed by, the Hindoo law. Considering the case, then, with reference to parcenership, what is the position of a member of a Hindoo family who has become a convert to Christianity? He becomes, as their Lordships apprehend, at once severed from the family, and regarded by them as an outcast. The tie which bound the family together is, so far as he is concerned, not only loosened, but dissolved. The obligations consequent upon and connected with the tie must, as it seems to their Lordships, be dissolved with it. Parcenership may be put an end to by a severance effected by partition; it must, as their Lordships think, equally be put an end to by severance which the Hindoo law recognizes and creates. Their Lordships, therefore, are of opinion, that upon the conversion of a Hindoo to Christianity the Hindoo law ceases to have any continuing obligatory force upon the convert. He may renounce the old law by which he was bound, as he has renounced his old religion, or, if he thinks fit, he may abide by the old law, notwithstanding he has renounced the old religion.

It appears, indeed, both from the pleadings and from the points before referred to, that neither side contended for the continuing obligatory force of Hindoo law on a convert to Christianity from that persuasion. The custom and usages of families are alone appealed to, with a reference also to the usages of this particular family; a reference which implies that the general custom of a class is not imperatively obligatory on new converts to Christianity. The conclusion at which their Lordships have arrived on this point, appears also to be supported by authority; for the opinion expressed as to the Hindoo law by the Judge of the Civil Court at Bellary seems to coincide entirely with the opinions of Pundits reported in W. H. Macnaghten's

Hindu Law, Vol. II. pp. 131–2. It is there stated, that on the death of an apostate from the Hindoo faith, his heirs, according to Hindoo law, will take all the property which he had at the time of his conversion; and the marginal note states, that his subsequently acquired property would be governed as to its devolution by the law of his new religion. The religion embraced in that case was the Mahommedan, which regulated the devolution of property. The Pundits, therefore, in their reply, naturally connected religion with the rules of descent of property as an adjunct, but the important point which they declare is the separation of the convert from the binding force of Hindoo law, as to his subsequent acquisitions.

Such, then, being the state of the case, so far as the Hindoo law is concerned, we must next consider whether there is any other law which determines the rights over the property of a Hindoo becoming a convert to Christianity. The *lex loci* Act clearly does not apply, the parties having ceased to be Hindoo in religion; and looking to the Regulations, their Lordships think that so far as they prescribe that the Hindoo law shall be applied to Hindoos and the Mahommedan law to Mahommedans, they must be understood to refer to Hindoos and Mahommedans not by birth merely, but by religion also. They think, therefore, that this case fell to be decided according to the Regulation which prescribes that the decision shall be according to equity and good conscience. Applying, then, this rule to the decision of the case, it seems to their Lordships that the course which appears to have been pursued in India in these cases, and to have been adopted in the present case, of referring the decision to the usages of the class to which the convert may have attached himself, and of the family to which he may have belonged, has been most consonant both to equity and good conscience. The profession of Christianity releases the convert from the trammels of the Hindoo law, but it does not of necessity involve any change of the rights or relations of the convert in matters with which Christianity has no concern, such as his rights and interests in, and his powers over, property. The convert, though not bound as to such matters, either by the Hindoo law or by any other positive law, may by his course of conduct after his conversion have shown by what law he intended to be governed as to these matters. He may have done so either by attaching himself to a class which as to these matters has adopted and acted upon some particular law, or by having himself observed some family usage or custom; and nothing can surely be more just than that the right and interests in his property, and his powers over it, should be governed by the law which he has adopted, or the rules which he has observed.

Their Lordships have thought it right thus to state their opinion on this point, as this is the first case in which the question has been brought under their consideration. They consider the decision referred to in the judgment of the Sudder Dewanny Adawlut in the case of a succession to one of the class of East Indians to be an instance of a just and proper exercise of the discretion entrusted to these courts. The English law, as such, is not the law of those courts. They have, properly speaking, no obligatory law of the forum, as the Supreme Courts had. The East Indians could not claim the English law as of right; but they were a class most nearly resembling the English, they conformed to them in religion, manners, and customs, and the English law as to the succession of movables was applied by the courts in the Mofussil to the succession of the property of this class.

Such, then, being their Lordships' opinion as to the law by which they ought to be guided in the decision of this case, it becomes necessary to see how the case stands upon the evidence.

Their Lordships collect from the evidence that the class known in India as 'native Christians', using that term in its wide and extended sense as embracing all natives converted to Christianity, has subordinate divisions forming again distinct classes, of which some adhere to the Hindoo customs and usages as to property; others retain those customs and usages in a modified form; and others again have wholly abandoned those customs and usages, and adopted different rules and laws as to their property.

Of this latter class are the 'East Indians', a class well defined in India, the members of which follow in all things the usages and customs of the English resident there, and though they cannot claim the exemption from jurisdiction, nor the privilege of a personal law, which the British subjects, in the limited sense of the terms of the jurisdiction of the Charters of the Supreme Courts, enjoy, in other respects, in the common bond of union in religion, customs, and manners, approach the class of British subjects.

Reverting again to the evidence, their Lordships think that it is to be collected from it that the family from which both the late Matthew Abraham and the Respondent descended was of that class of native Christians which commonly retains native usages and customs, and they consider it probable, therefore, that had the family possessed property they would, so long as those usages and customs were retained, have enjoyed it in common according to Hindoo custom; but their Lordships are perfectly satisfied upon the evidence that the late Matthew Abraham and the Respondent had no ancestral property, and that the property which the late Matthew Abraham had was acquired by him by his own sole unaided exertions, and without any use whatever of any common stock. They fully concur in the finding of both the courts in India upon this point. They are also quite satisfied upon the evidence that from the time of the late Matthew Abraham's marriage he and the Appellant, Charlotte, his wife, and their children adhered in all respects to the religion, manners, and habits of the East Indians, the class to which the Appellant, Charlotte Abraham, belonged.

Previously to the marriage some doubt appears to have been entertained whether the East Indians, the class to which the lady belonged, would receive Matthew Abraham into their society and treat him as one of themselves. The evidence on this point of the Appellant, Charlotte Abraham, the first Plaintiff, is corroborated by that of a very respectable witness, on whose veracity no doubt can rest. Before this time Mr Matthew Abraham had assumed the English dress, and had outwardly conformed to all the habits of the English. Assurances were given that the East Indians of Bellary would recognize her husband as one of their body, and the marriage took place. On one important public occasion when a jury was summoned of East Indians, Matthew sat as one of them, and acted as their foreman.

The evidence on this part of the case appears to their Lordships to be clear beyond all doubt. They proceed, then, to consider its effect. That it is not competent to parties to create, as to property, any new law to regulate the succession to it *ab intestato*, their Lordships entertain no doubt; but that is not the question on which this case depends. The question is, whether, when there are different laws as to property applying to different classes, parties ought not be considered to have adopted the law as to property, whether in respect of succession *ab intestato* or in other respects, of the class to which they belong. In this particular case the question is, whether the property was bound by the Hindoo law of parcenership.

Now, Matthew Abraham acquired the nucleus of his property himself. No law imposed any fetter upon him as to his mode of dealing with it. It is not even shown, as a fact, how his ancestors after their conversion dealt with such property, as to the use and enjoyment of it. It is plain that no rule as to such use and enjoyment, which the ancestors may voluntarily have imposed on themselves, could be of compulsory obligation on a descendant of theirs acquiring his own wealth. If a Hindoo in an undivided family may keep his own sole acquisitions separate, as he undoubtedly may, *a fortiori* a Christian may do the same. Customs and usages as to dealing with property, unless their continuance be enjoined by law, as they are adopted voluntarily, so they may be changed, or lost by desuetude. It was well observed by Mr Melvill, that custom implies continuance. If a family of converts retain the customs in part of their unconverted predecessors, is that election of theirs invariable and inflexible? Can neither they nor their descendants change things in their very nature variable, as dependent on the changeful inclinations, feelings, and obligations of successive generations of men? If the spirit of an adopted religion improves those who become converts to it, and they reject, from conscience, customs to which their first converted ancestors adhered, must the abandoned usages be treated by a sort of *fictio juris* as still the enduring customs of the family? If it be not so as to things which belong to the jurisdiction of conscience, is it so as to things of convenience or interest? Surely, in things indifferent in themselves, the Tribunals which have a discretion and have no positive *lex fori* imposed on them should rather proceed on what actually exists than on what has existed, and in forming their own presumptions have regard rather to a man's own way of life than to that of his predecessors. Though race and blood are independent of volition, usage is not.

The law has not, so far as their Lordships can see, prohibited a Christian convert from changing his class. The inconvenience resulting from a change of succession consequent on a change of class is no greater than that which often results from a change of domicile. The *argumentum ab inconvenienti* cannot, therefore, be used against the legality of such a change. If such change takes place in fact, why should it be regarded as non-existing in law? Their Lordships are of opinion, that it was competent to Matthew Abraham, though himself both by origin and actually in his youth a 'Native Christian,' following the Hindoo laws and customs on matters relating to property, to change his class of Christian, and become of the Christian class to which his wife belonged. This was no light and inconsiderate step, taken up on a whim, and to be as lightly laid aside. We find in the evidence that there was on one side an exhibition of preliminary caution. The change was deliberate, it was publicly acted upon, and endured through his life for twenty years or more. His family was managed and lived in all respects like an East Indian family. In such a family the undivided family union in the sense before-mentioned is unknown. How, then, can it be imposed on that family of which Matthew Abraham formed the head as father? Not by consent, for there was none; not by force of obligatory law, for there was none; not by adoption, for they had not adopted any Hindoo customs, but, on the contrary, had rejected them all. It could only be imposed, as it seems to their Lordships, by passing over the actual family springing from the marriage, and by absorbing all its members in the original family of which the two brothers were members; by passing over all actual usages, customs, and ways of living; and by supposing, contrary to fact, the prevalence of Hindoo customs which had been deliberately abandoned. Their Lordships, therefore, are of opinion, that the undivided family on which the Defendant relies in his answer did not exist in any sense which is material to or assists the decision of the case.

There being then, in their Lordships' opinion, no such undivided family, and the case not being, in their judgment, governed by the Hindoo law, it is unnecessary to discuss the opinion given by the *Pundits* upon the operation of that law, or to enter into the question, so much discussed at the Bar, whether the late Matthew Abraham's acquisitions ought, or ought not, according to that law, to have been deemed to be his separate estate. It is sufficient, with reference to the opinion of the Pundits, to say, that the case stated for their opinion proceeds upon an assumption which, in their Lordships' judgment, was not warranted by the facts. Their Lordships, however, think it right to add, for the guidance of the Courts in India in future cases, that whenever the opinion of Pundits is required, and there are any special circumstances which may bear upon the question to be submitted for their opinion, those special circumstances ought to be set forth in the case submitted to them. Their Lordships make this observation with reference to the broad and general statements contained in the case which, in this instance, was laid before the Pundits; 'that the brothers lived together, and that the eldest acquired some property,' unaccompanied as those statements were by any specification of the mode in which, and the circumstances under which, the brothers so lived, and the property was so acquired—circumstances which, to say the least, were important to be considered in forming an opinion upon the point submitted for consideration.

[....]

Their Lordships, therefore, will humbly recommend Her Majesty to reverse the decree of the Sudder Court, and to restore the decree of the Civil Court of Bellary, modified as above pointed out.[2]

5. Narantakath v. Parakkal (1922) 45 Mad 986

Indian Penal Code, Sections 79, 494—*bigamy—creed of Islam—husband converted to Ahmadiya school—whether amounts to apostasy—wife's marriage to another—whether bigamy committed—good faith—mistake of law*

The essential creed of Islam is that there is only one God *(Allah)* and that Muhammad is His Prophet. The Ahmadis who also subscribe to this dogma are one of the schools of Islam, although they differ from the generality of Muslims in certain respects. Hence a Muslim who becomes an Aḥmadī does not commit apostasy, and his wife is guilty of bigamy if she marries another man during her husband's lifetime.

The modern law of apostasy and conversion is discussed in *Outlines*, § 2, and for its effects on the status of marriage see *Outlines*, § 26 and *Tyabji*, § 9.

2 See *Varden Seth Sam* v. *Luckpathy Royjee Lallah*, *post*, 303.

Judgment-I [Oldfield, J.][3]

We are asked to revise the acquittal of the fifth respondent on a charge of bigamy punishable under section 494, Indian Penal Code, and of the other respondents on subsidiary charges. The petitioner is the complainant who prosecuted as fifth respondent's husband; and the Public Prosecutor who has had notice, has under instructions taken no part in the proceedings. We should not ordinarily proceed at the instance of a private party in revision of an acquittal; and we do so here only because we are satisfied that a question of public importance relating to the personal status of a substantial part of the Muslim community is raised.

The question is whether petitioner's adherence to Ahmediyan tenets made him a *murtad* or apostate from Muhammadanism. If it did, it had, it is not disputed, the effect of dissolving his admitted marriage with fifth respondent; and such dissolution prior to her remarriage with third respondent is her first and principal defence to the charge. The reply attempted is that Ahmediyas are merely a sect of Muhammadans, their divergences from ordinary Muhammadanism not involving abandonment of that creed or making them schismatics. Some objection has been taken to our entering on this controversy in revision, by petitioner on the ground that it is purely one of fact since only his religious views and their orthodoxy are in question, and by respondents on the ground that it relates only to degrees of orthodoxy which the court has no business to estimate. But although I feel the difficulty involved in an attempt to deal with matters, with which I am necessarily unfamiliar and although I appreciate the improbability that our decision can commend itself to those with whom personal associations and devotional sentiment must weigh more than the materials on which we have to proceed, the issue cannot be avoided. For it is one of mixed law and fact inasmuch as it relates substantially and ultimately to the personal status, which petitioner's religious views determine and to say that only degrees of orthodoxy are in dispute is to beg the question whether the Ahmediyans' deviation from Islam is such as entails abandonment of any essential thereof.

The lower court has attempted very little by way of direct ascertainment whether that deviation does so, its conclusion appearing really to rest on the finding that the Ahmediyas are regarded as apostates by orthodox Muhammadans and the principle that—

> [W]hat the doctrine and faith preached in the Koran are is to be decided, not according to the interpretation put on it by individual persons, but according to the interpretation generally accepted and adopted by Mussalmans as a whole.

3 Oldfield and Krishnan, JJ.

And this test, *securus judicat orbis,* may in appropriate circumstances have its value. But to apply it fairly, we must make sure that the judgment relied on is really general and had been reached by the community as a whole and that it has been reached after due deliberation and the passing of sufficient time for the disappearance of the prejudice which new beliefs must always incur. Ahmed, whom the Ahmediyans follow, died, we were told, in the Punjab in 1908; and in the fifteen years, which have passed, it is difficult to suppose that Islam or even Islam in India can have come to any mature conclusion on his teachings. In fact it has not been shown that it has done so. For, of 4th, 6th and 7th defence witnesses whose evidence alone is relied on, the first is the son of the Government Kazi of Madras, who was formerly an Assistant Kazi and Arabic Professor in a private Madrassa in this city and describes himself as now chief priest in a district in the Nizam's Dominions, whilst the other two are a *kazi* and a *musaliar* or religious leader in Malabar. The evidence of the second attracts suspicion to the extent of his acquaintance with Ahmed's writings and the third said that there was 'no one in the Muhammadan world, whose opinion on religious matters was binding on the conscience of Mussalmans.' These persons are not shown and do not appear to have more than a local influence and reputation; and there is nothing before us except their assertions, in some instances of doubtful value. In the question propounded to the father of D. W. 4 in the *fatwa* Exhibit I, 'Religious decrees of learned men of Arabia and India' declaring Ahmed and his followers apostates, are referred to; but none is specified either in the question or answer, and none was produced at the trial. In these circumstances it has not been established that the Muslim community either generally or in India has reached any decision which we can regard as conclusive.

This failing, discussion has turned on the character of the divergences between the teaching of Ahmed and the orthodox creed. The former are enumerated, it is not disputed, correctly by the lower court. But as regards the latter the parties are at variance, petitioner contending that the formula 'There is one God and Muhammad is His Prophet' is exhaustive; respondents contending that we must take account of other doctrines sanctioned by the Koran or other authorities. Petitioner in support of his contention relies on the judgment of Mahmood, J., in *Queen-Empress* v. *Ramzan*,[4] those of Edge, C. J., and Mahmood, J. in *Ata-Ullah* v. *Azim-Ullah,*[5] and on *Maula Baksh* v. *Amir-ud-din*[6] as showing that monotheism and belief in Muhammad as God's prophet are the only essentials. But it

4 (1885) ILR 7 All 461 (FB).
5 (1920) ILR 1 Lahore 317.
6 (1890) ILR 12 All 494.

is clear that the question in those cases was only between one sect and another or the general body of Muhammadans as to the right to worship in a mosque or the validity of a wakf, not as it is here, between orthodoxy and alleged schism. To decide between them, something more is evidently required than the bare formula referred to above. For, the latter portion of it cannot be taken as requiring a belief only in the history or legend of Muhammad without reference to the acceptance of his message and ascertainment of its terms and of the legitimacy of the constructions placed on them later, of which in fact, in the case of the Ahmediyas, respondents complain. The materials for a conclusion which the parties have provided are the evidence of the witnesses already mentioned, the *fatwa* Exhibit I, a book MOI, 'The claims and teachings of Ahmed' and a pamphlet MOV, 'What distinguishes Ahamedees from non-Ahamedees.' No reliance was placed before us on the works exhibited as MOs II, III, IV.

It is first to be observed that the Ahmediyas, statedly at least, emphasize their adherence to the Islamic formula. In MOV, Ahmed's principles are stated in his own words, beginning:

We are Muslims by the Grace of God; Mustafa, the Holy Prophet of Arabia is our leader and guide. The wine of our spiritual knowledge is from the cup of the Book of God, which is called the Koran. Every Prophethood has found its culmination in that Messenger of God, whose name is Muhammad. The revelation and inspiration that we receive have not been granted to us independently, but it is through him that we have received this gift.

The pamphlet goes on like the manifestations of other religious developments, to state the distinctive features of Ahmed's teaching as a return to the early fervour of the recipients of the original revelation, an abandonment of worldly affairs and political greatness for the earlier and more spiritual methods of propagating the faith, and an eradication of the errors, into which Moslems from time to time have fallen. And similarly in MOI, the first chapter maintains Monotheism and the supremacy of the Koran and there are (page 106), extracts from the latter under headings:

'The Almighty God declares that Islam is the perfect and chosen religion.' 'The Almighty God commands every soul to follow no other religion than Islam'; and 'Muhammad is the Prophet of God for all the nations of the world'.

The form moreover to be signed on initiation (page 104) runs:

'I bear witness that there is no God but Allah. He is one, having no partner, and Muhammad is the servant and Messenger of God.'

All this would seem to involve a plenary acceptance of Muhammadanism and in fact the respondents' objection is to the Ahmediyan additions to it and their alleged inconsistency with it. But I have in my opinion been shown no distinct authority as to which doctrines of Islam are regarded as fundamental or the extent to which additions to them, deviations from them, or inconsistencies with them, are permitted. Seventh defence witness no doubt said generally that any Mussalman who took away from, added to, or tampered with the Koran was a *murtad* and 4th defence witness, that among sects the differences were not in matters of faith, but in ritual; and there is also the judgment of Mahmood, J., in *Queen-Empress* v. *Ramzan*,[7] in this sense. But 4th defence witness also explained his description of some sects as *murtads* on the ground that their deviations from the teaching of the Koran were on fundamental points, refusing however to regard the Shiyas' disbelief in the first three Caliphs as a deviation from the faith at all. That private judgment and analogical deduction are in appropriate circumstances and to a greater or less extent, legitimate methods of ascertaining the law is recognized in the text books; (Ameer Ali's *Mahommedan Law*, Vol. II, pages 11 to 14, Abdur Rahim's *Muhammadan Jurisprudence* 25); and we have not been shown how they are not also legitimate in theology so long as fundamental principles are maintained and the question is only of the development, to which every creed must be subject, so long as it retains life and growth and adapts itself to altered conditions. This in fact is enough to justify the Ahmediyans in their faith in the six alleged deviations from orthodoxy as enumerated by the lower court. For their abandonment of the sword for peaceful argument as the method of propagation of Islam has been inevitable since the cessation of militant conditions and the permeation by Muhammadans of countries to whose law they owe allegiance; and their refusal to acknowledge the spiritual supremacy of the Sultan of Turkey cannot, if only for chronological reasons, be fundamental.

The remaining four points of divergence referred to by the lower court are set out in its judgment, the evidence and Exhibit I, unfortunately in very general language, which was not made more specific before us. But they amount, as I understand them, to assertions that Muhammad and other earlier recognized prophets, for instance Jesus Christ, have not been the sole channels of communication between God and Man; that others, for instance Buddha, Rama and Krishna have been bearers of the divine message; and that the last of such messengers was Ahmed himself who is to be identified with the prophet 'who will come after me and whose name will be Ahmed' referred to in Koranic verse quoted in Exhibit I; and there is also imputed to the Ahmediyans a novel doctrine that Jesus Christ is still

7 (1885) ILR 7 All 461 (FB).

dead and buried and not in heaven. As regards this doctrine it is sufficient that it is presented in Exhibit V (page 49) the only source of information available, as founded on the interpretation of the Koran and tradition and that it has not been shown how rejection of any dogma, which is fundamental or affects the position and supremacy of Muhammad or has been defined by any final or general authority is involved. As regards the remaining points, it is obvious and the references in the latter part of 4th defence witness's evidence indicate that much must depend on the sense, in which the expressions used by Ahmed are understood and the significance of his teaching as a whole. If, for instance, he did (and we have not been referred to any particular passage) speak of Krishna and Rama as heavenly messengers or *avatars*, the corrective is given in the far less definite claim at page 160 in Exhibit V:

I do not say it to please anybody, but God has revealed to me that Krishna and Rama were also righteous servants of God and had true connexion with Him.

and if he did identify himself with the Promised Messiah, he explained at page 143 that:

The perfect follower of God's revelation cannot be called an independent prophet, for this is a disrespect towards the prophethood of Muhammad.

and in the note on page 144 that:

No prophet, who is also a law-giver, can appear after the Holy Prophet, even from among his followers. For this door is completely closed.

That Ahmed identified himself with the Ahmed whose advent is foretold in the verse above referred to, can involve no unorthodoxy, much less rejection of any fundamental tenet, unless what we have not been shown, all speculation as to the fulfilment of Koranic prophecy is forbidden; and the quotation in Exhibit I from the *Fatawa Alamgiri* must be inconclusive in the absence of information as to its context or the method, by which its author would have reconciled it with the Koranic text. Reference has been made to the extent to which Ahmed statedly accepted and proceeded from the fundamental tenets of Islam. It was then for respondents to show that his additions to and divergences from them involve their abandonment; and it is not possible on the materials before us to hold that they do so. It is satisfactory that a similar conclusion was reached in *Hakim Khalil Ahmad* v. *Malik Israfi* and *Malik Israfil* v. *Hakim Khalil Ahmad*.[8] It follows that petitioner is not a *murtad* and his marriage with 5th respondent is subsisting.

[8] (1917) 2 Pat LJ 108.

This conclusion makes it necessary to consider the further defence accepted in the alternative by the lower court that the respondents are entitled to acquittal, because they acted without *mens rea* and in the honest belief that the marriage was dissolved. This is unsustainable. For there is not really any question here of the doctrine of *mens rea* or of the application of section 79, Indian Penal Code, since the respondents acted under a mistake of law or under a mistake of mixed law and facts; *The Queen* v. *Tolson*[9] being distinguishable on that ground. I am with all respect unable to follow the authority relied on by the lower court, the judgment of Holmwood, J. in *Abdul Ghani* v. *Azizul Huq*,[10] and must hold that, whatever weight the good faith of respondents might deserve, if the proper sentence to impose were in question, it is irrelevant to their liability to conviction.

The case however is before us in revision and with reference to the last clause of s. 439, Criminal Procedure Code, the only course open to us is to order a retrial. Mr Zafrullah Khan for petitioner does not ask us to take this course, since he desires only to obtain an authoritative settlement of the questions argued. Further proceedings are in my opinion unnecessary since respondents acted in a mistaken but honest belief as to the law and only nominal sentences would be the result. In these circumstances and for this reason the petition is dismissed.

Judgment II [Krishnan, J.]

[. . . .]

Turning now to the question of apostasy raised, it is undoubtedly a question of Muhammadan theology to say that deviation from the recognized doctrines of Muhammadanism would amount to apostasy; but as civil rights and legal status of parties are based on its decision, we must decide it ourselves. The accused has called three witnesses of the orthodox party who assert themselves to be men learned in Muhammadan theology and who say that the adoption by a Muhammadan of the tenets of Gulam Ahmed Mirza the founder of the sect of Ahmediyans amounts to apostasy under that law; but we cannot accept their opinion as settling the question as argued for the accused, particularly as they are interested as orthodox Muhammadans in denouncing the members of the new sect as unbelievers and as they have not given satisfactory reasons for their opinions. As pointed out by Sir Abdur Rahim in his *Muhammadan Jurisprudence*, page 250, some people are too prone to charge others with unbelief and treat them as heretics. But the correct law is that when heretical doctrines are opposed to clear and

9 (1889) 23 QBD 168.
10 (1912) ILR 39 Cal 409.

indisputable texts they would amount to unbelief and not otherwise. Consensus of opinion as a source of law or the doctrine of *Ijma* is not universally recognized among Muhammadans; but even if we take consensus of opinion as a proper source of law there has not been, as pointed out by my learned brother, such a lapse of time since the founding of the new sect of Ahmediyans as to have developed any such general consensus of opinion regarding the status of its members. We must therefore consider the doctrines of Ahmediyans and see whether their adoption by Muhammadans would amount to heresy and make them apostates or *murtads* and put them outside the pale of Muhammadanism. It may be observed that in doing this we must take the doctrines as propounded by Ahmed himself and accepted by his followers and not the distorted version of them as given by their opponents. It is accepted by the complainant that the Ahmediya doctrines are correctly stated in a small pamphlet by Mr Sher Ali, BA, and published by Sadr Anjuman Ahmediyya of Qadian, Punjab, entitled 'What distinguishes Ahmadees from non-Ahmadees' filed as an exhibit in this case. MO 5. The creed of Ahmed is set out in it on pages 2 and 3. It begins by saying:

> We are Muslims by the Grace of God; Mustafa (the Holy Prophet of Arabia) is our leader and guide. The wine of our spiritual knowledge is from the cup of the Book of God which is called the Quran.

A perusal of what is stated in the pamphlet shows clearly that the Ahmediyans subscribe to the *Kalima* that there is no God but one God and Muhammad is His Prophet, and unreservedly accept the prophethood of Muhammad and the supreme authority of the Qur'an. In fact it would seem that they differ from the orthodox Muhammadans only in some six points which are set out in the pamphlet and also by the learned Judge in his judgment. They are briefly stated as follows:

1. While both parties believe that God has been speaking to his prophets in the past, the non-Ahmadees hold that Muhammad was the last prophet with whom God spoke and since then He has not spoken to and will not speak to any until the end of time. The Ahmadees on the other hand believe that God continues to hold communion with His holy servants now as in the past.

2. While both sides accept that Muhammad was *Khatam-un-Nabiyyin* (the seal of the Prophets) they differ as to its interpretation. Ahmadees say that it means that no new prophet can arise except as a follower of Muhammad and bearing his seal and not that no new prophet can arise at all as the non-Ahmadees hold.

3. Ahmadees admit into the list of prophets before Muhammad world-teachers such as Zoroaster, Buddha, Krishna and Ramachandra and this they say is according

to the Koran but non-Ahmadees refuse to acknowledge them as prophets. Of course the Ahmadees hold that Ahmed was himself a prophet of God but, unlike the earlier prophets, he got his prophethood through Muhammad who was made a prophet-maker by God.

4. Ahmadees believe that Jesus Christ was actually crucified, but he did not die on the cross. He came out alive and went to Kashmir and died and is buried there. Whereas the non-Ahmadees hold that Jesus was bodily carried away to heaven by God before crucifixion. The Ahmadees think that the prophecy of the second advent of Jesus is to be fulfilled not by Jesus coming back in person but by his spirit entering another man and they believe this has been fulfilled by the advent of Ahmed himself.

5. While the non-Ahmadees believe that the promised *Mahdi* will carry on a holy war or *Jihad* and spread Islam by the sword, Ahmadees repudiate this doctrine and hold that the promised *Mahdi* and the Messiah are the same and that he will spread Islam by arguments and heavenly signs and not by violence. They accept Ahmed as that Messiah.

6. Ahmadees deny the claim of the Sultan of Turkey to the Caliphate and hold that every Muslim is bound to remain loyal to the Government under which he lives and which protects him.

These are said to be the main differences. I agree with my learned brother in thinking that these differences are not sufficient to justify us in holding that the Ahmadees are not Muhammadans but apostates. As already stated they accept the *Kalima,* the prophethood of Muhammad and the authority of the Qur'an. These undoubtedly are the essential conditions for a person to be a Muhammadan and they are complied with by the Ahmedees; that would seem to make them Moslems governed by the Muhammadan law. Sir Ameer Ali says in his book on *Mahommedan Law*, 4th Edition, Vol. II, page 36, that:

Any person who professes the religion of Islam, in other words accepts the unity of God and the Prophetic character of Muhammad, is a Moslem and is subject to the Mussalman Law. So long as the individual pronounces the *Kalima* of *Tauhid*, the credo of Islam, it is not necessary for him or her to observe any of the rites and ceremonies or to believe in particular doctrines which imply *Iman* or belief.

And again on page 112:

Every person who acknowledges the Divine Unity and the messengership of the Arabian Prophet is regarded as within the pale of Islam; nothing more is required.

To the same effect is the opinion of Sir Abdur Rahim in his *Muhammadan Jurisprudence*, page 249, where he says that the Islamic faith consists in acknowledging the authority of one God the Law-giver and the truth of Muhammad's mission as His prophet. Similar expressions of opinion are found in the judgment of Mahmood, J., in *Queen-Empress* v. *Ramzan*,[11] and in *Ata-Ullah* v. *Azim-Ullah*,[12] which was a case relating to the sect of Wahabis; though the decisions in those cases referred to worship in a mosque, they are of value to show how eminent Muhammadan lawyers have looked upon the question as to who are Muhammadans. Besides these cases the learned counsel for the petitioner has brought to our notice one recent decision in which the very question raised before us as to the status of Ahmadees seems to have been raised, viz., the case of *Hakim Khalil Ahmad* v. *Malik Israfi* and *Malik Israfi* v. *Hakim Khalil Ahmad*.[13] It was expressly ruled there that the sect known as Ahmadees are Muhammadans notwithstanding their pronounced dissent on several important matters of doctrine from the orthodox Muhammadan faith. In view of these authorities which I accept, it follows that a Muhammadan does not become an apostate by merely accepting the doctrines of Ahmadees. The Ahmediyans are in my view only a reformed sect of Muhammadans.

If we examine the six points of difference set out above between the Ahmadees and the non-Ahmadees none of them seems to refer to any essential principles of Muhammadanism or to conflict with the Qur'an. The point that has been most pressed before us is that Ahmed having set himself up as a prophet has by that very act become an apostate and his followers as followers of an apostate are also apostates. No authority has been cited for this contention. We cannot act on what D. W. 4 says in his answer (Exhibit I) is stated in the *Fatawa Alamgiri*. The original passage has not been shown to us nor has it been shown that it applies to a case like the present where the prophethood of Muhammad is unreservedly accepted.

For the above reasons I have come to the conclusion that the complainant never became an apostate and that his marriage with the 5th accused was subsisting at the time of her second marriage.

[. . . .]

11 (1885) ILR 7 All 461 (FB).
12 (1890) ILR 12 All 494 (FB).
13 (1917) 2 Pat LJ 108.

◊ UPDATE ◊

1. *Monotheism*

As regards the basic beliefs of the Islamic religion, in the Indian case of *Shihabuddin Thangal* v. *Ahamad Koya* AIR 1971 Ker 206 Justice VR Krishna Iyer had observed:

> Belief in oneness of God is indubitably the first fundamental belief an unquestioning embrace of which makes one a Muslim. Nothing is more obnoxious to Islam than non-acceptance of the unity of God.

In Pakistan, Article 260 (3) (a) of the Constitution of 1973, as amended in 1974, defines the word 'Muslim' as occurring in its provisions as follows:

> 'Muslim' means a person who believes in the unity and oneness of Almighty Allah, in the absolute and unqualified finality of the Prophethood of Muhammad (peace be upon him), the last of the Prophets, and does not believe in or recognize any person who claimed or claims to be a prophet, in any sense of the word or of any description whatsoever, after Muhammad (peace be upon him).

2. *Status of Ahmadis*

In India the ruling in the case of *Narantakath* v. *Parakkal* [Case 5] relating to the status of Ahmadis has been re-affirmed by the Kerala High Court in *Shihabuddin Thangal* v. *Ahamad Koya* AIR 1971 Ker 206:

> In major religions monopoly of spiritual finality is not infrequently claimed by each for the truth as revealed or illumined through its prophet or founder, and acceptance of this truth constitutes the faith…Every departure from orthodoxy is not apostasy, although witch-hunt is not the monopoly of any particular religion when polemics appear and libertarian trends assert themselves…Looking at the issue devoid of sentiments and in the cold light of the law I hold that Ahmadiya sect is of Islam and not alien.

In Pakistan the Ahmadis, both of the Qadiani and the Lahori groups, are now regarded by the law as 'non-Muslims'. Article 260(3) (b) of the Constitution, as amended by the Constitution (Second Amendment) Act 1974 and PO No. 24 of 1985, says:

> 'Non-Muslim' means a person who is not a Muslim and includes a person belonging to the Christian, Hindu, Sikh, Buddhist or Parsi community, a person of the Qadiani group or the Lahori group (who call themselves 'Ahmadis' or by any other name), or a Bahai, and a person belonging to any of the scheduled castes.

3. *Law for converts to Islam*

The dictum of the old case of *Abraham v Abraham* [Case 4] remains the general law in India. However, in specific matters application of Muslim law to a convert to Islam may be ousted by virtue of statutory provisions or judicial decisions to that effect.

In India, a non-Muslim married under the Special Marriage Act 1954 or the Foreign Marriage Act 1969 will, on conversion to Islam continue to be governed by their provisions—the Muslim matrimonial law will not become applicable to him or her even if a *nikah* ceremony follows.

Under the law as now settled by the Supreme Court of India, a married non-Muslim on conversion to Islam cannot claim instant application of the Muslim law on bigamy as traditionally understood. In *Sarla Mudgal* v. *Union of India* AIR 1995 SC 1531 the Supreme Court has held:

> A second marriage by an apostate under the shelter of conversion to Islam would nevertheless be a marriage in violation of the [Hindu Marriage] Act [1955] by which he would be continuing to be governed so far as his marriage under the Act is concerned despite his conversion to Islam.[14]

The dictum of *Sarla Mudgal* case was reaffirmed in *Lily Thomas* v. *Union of India* (2000) 6 SCC 224.

14 An in-depth study of this case is found in my book *Uniform Civil Code: Fictions and Facts*, IIRC, Delhi, 1995.

III. Hybrids

6. Abdool Razack v. Aga Mahomed
(1894) 21 IA 56

Marriage with unbeliever—presumption—acknowledgement of legitimacy

In this case it was held upon evidence that an alleged marriage between a Mahommedan and a Buddhist woman was disproved.

Quaere, whether Buddhists come under the same category as Jews and Christians, with whom Mahommedans may intermarry.

Semble, in all cases where, according to Mahommedan law, unbelief or difference of creed is a bar to marriage with a true believer, such marriage will be valid if the alien in religion embraces the Mahommedan faith. Profession of such faith, whether with or without conversion, is necessary and sufficient to remove the disability.

The presumption which ought to be made in favour of marriage, where there has been a lengthened cohabitation, is rebutted by showing that the conduct of the parties is inconsistent with the relation of husband and wife.

The Mahommedan doctrine of legitimacy by acknowledgment does not apply to every case of admission of paternity; an intention to confer the status of legitimacy must be proved or presumed.

Ashrufood Dowlah Ahmed Hossein Khan v. *Hyder Hossein Khan*[1] followed.

How far a Muslim, man or woman, may marry a non-Muslim is discussed in *Outlines,* § 9 (2), Disabilities due to religious differences.

Appeal from a decree of the Recorder of Rangoon (5 February 1892), dismissing the suit of the Appellant against the Respondent, as executor of the will of Hadjee Hoosain Bindaneem....

The Appellant claimed as brother's son to the testator, and therefore, by the law of inheritance, entitled to his estate, after deducting the share of the widow and such legacies as the testator was, by the Shiah law, entitled to give. The name of the testator's brother was Abdul Hadee. The material portion of the Recorder's judgment was as follows:

1 11 MIA 113.

The first point to consider is whether there was a marriage between Mah Thai and Abdul Hadee. It is not disputed that before there can be a valid marriage between a Mahommedan and a woman who is not a '*Kitabi*', the woman must be converted to Mahommedanism (see Tagore Lect. 1873, p. 305). *Mah Thai's* evidence as to the marriage is that she was in an inner room, that she heard voices in the outer room, and some one asked her if she loved Abdul Hadee, and consented to the marriage? Then she was asked 'Was anything said about religion?' and she replied, 'My husband said something which I did not understand. Abdul Hadee said he would marry me according to Kala custom. I agreed.' Then, in cross-examination, she said: 'I said he would have to give dower according to custom among Kalas. I did not understand; but it was said it must be according to Kala custom, and so I said he must give dower according to Kala custom. I know nothing about the Mahommedan religion. I have all my life lived and worshipped as a Burman. While cohabiting with Abdul Hadee I worshipped as he did. As a long time has elapsed, I have forgotten. I could repeat after him; but have forgotten now. He repeated his prayers in some Kala language; I don't know that language. I repeated in the language he used; I did not understand the meaning of a single word. . . I know there is a Mahommedan mosque here. I wasn't allowed to go to it; I had to stay at home. I knew that wives of Moguls go to the mosque; I didn't go, because Abdul Hadee would not allow me to go. I said I wanted to go; but he wouldn't allow me.' Then, in re-examination, she said that she ceased to be a Buddhist during her cohabitation with Abdul Hadee from the time of her marriage; and that, being the wife of a Kala, she followed the Kala religion. This is all the evidence as to conversion, and I do not see how, on such evidence, it can be held that Mah Thai was converted to Mahommedanism. It would, it seems to me, be a mere mockery of the Mahommedan religion to say that there was a conversion, when there was not even a semblance of discussion on the subject, when no priest intervened, and when the utmost the alleged convert can say is, that she repeated prayers in a language she did not understand. This alone would be sufficient to show that no valid marriage could have taken place. But the other evidence goes to show that Mah Thai could not have been married to Abdul Hadee.

I think then that the plaintiff Abdul Razack has not succeeded in proving that his mother, Mah Thai, was converted to the Mahommedan religion at the time of the alleged marriage, and that, as she was not a '*Kitabi*', no valid marriage could have taken place between her and Abdul Hadee; not only this, but Mah Thai admittedly had, before going to live with Abdul Hadee, been married according to Burmese law, and the evidence that she was ever divorced rests only on her unsupported statement. However, 1 do not lay much stress upon this, but go on this ground—that, assuming for the sake of argument that Mah Thai did live with Abdul Hadee at the time she says she did, and that the Plaintiff is her son by Abdul Hadee, yet that, not having been converted to Mahommedanism, she could not have been legally married to Abdul Hadee. If I am right in this view, then it follows, according to the decision of the Allahabad Court in *Muhammad Allahdad Khan* v. *Muhammad Ismail Khan* that no acknowledgment on the part of the father could legitimize the offspring of such union. Mahmood, J., points out that, according to Mahommedan law, so far as inheritance from males or through males is concerned, the existence of legitimacy of descent or consanguinity is a condition precedent to the right of inheritance, and that such legitimacy depends upon a valid marriage or connection between the parents of the inheritor. Further, that in no case can an illegitimate child inherit, and that where a marriage is not possible between the parents, acknowledgments cannot make the offspring of the union legitimate. He also points out that the Mahommedan law of acknowledgment of parentage with its legitimating effect, has no reference whatever to cases in which the illegitimacy of the child is proved and established, either by reason of a lawful union between the parents of the child being impossible, as, in my opinion, is the case here, or, by reasons of marriage necessary to render the child legitimate being disproved. Further, that the doctrine relates only to cases where either the fact of the marriage itself, or the exact time of its occurrence with reference to the legitimacy of the acknowledged child is not proved, in the sense of the law, as distinguished from disproved—in other words, that the doctrine only applies to cases of uncertainty as the legitimacy when acknowledgment has its effect, but that that effect always proceeds upon the assumption of a lawful union between the parents of the acknowledged child.

This view, if I may say so, appears to me to be clearly right. Otherwise if the proposition that acknowledgment alone is sufficient to establish legitimacy is correct, these results must necessarily follow: that a Mahommedan may legitimatize the offspring of adulterous or incestuous intercourse, or even a person of whom he could not possibly have been the father—for example, to put an extreme case, a person older than himself. And this result would also follow in the present case. The parents of the plaintiff, Abdul Razack, could not, according to Mahommedan law, contract a legal marriage; the offspring of their intercourse must therefore be illegitimate. But Abdul Hadee acknowledged the child; therefore he is legitimate.

In the view, then, that I take of the case, it is unnecessary to consider the evidence as to the acknowledgment and as to the will, for, assuming the whole of it to be true, the Plaintiff, Abdul Razack, cannot be the legitimate son of Abdul Hadee; so far as he is concerned, the suit must be dismissed with costs.

Judgment [Macnaghten, J.][2]

Hadjee Hoosain, who was a member of a Mahommedan family belonging to the Shiah sect and settled in Calcutta, traded as a merchant in Rangoon, made a fortune, and died there, married but without issue, in February, 1890. He left a will by which he purported to dispose of all his property. Hadjee Hoosain had an only brother of the full blood called Abdul Hadee, who died before him in March, 1886. He, too, was engaged in business in Rangoon for many years, but his career was less prosperous, and he returned to Calcutta a poor man some time before his death. The Appellant claims to be the lawful son of Abdul Hadee by a Burmese woman, and as such to be the heir or one of the heirs of Hadjee Hoosain, and entitled, therefore, to a

2 With Morris & Richard Couch, JJ.

share in so much of his estate as he could not dispose of by will according to Mahommedan law. For the purpose of the present case it is conceded that the Appellant's claim is well founded, provided he can make out that he either is or is entitled to be treated as the lawful son of Abdul Hadee. And the only questions on this appeal are these: (1) Has it been established that a valid marriage took place between *Abdul Hadee* and the Appellant's mother, Mah Thai, who was undoubtedly a Buddhist when she met her alleged husband? (2) If proof of legitimacy is wanting, is there sufficient evidence of the legitimation of the Appellant by acknowledgment?

The learned Recorder found that there was no marriage, holding upon the evidence that Mah Thai was not a convert to Mahommedanism. 'It would, it seems to me,' he observed, 'be a mere mockery of the Mahommedan religion to say that there was a conversion, when there was not even a semblance of discussion on the subject, when no priest intervened, and when the utmost the alleged convert can say is, that she repeated prayers in a language she did not understand.' Taking this view, he thought it unnecessary to consider the evidence as to acknowledgment. No acknowledgment in his opinion could confer the status of legitimacy upon the offspring of a Mahommedan and an unconverted Buddhist.

The learned counsel for the Appellant took exception to the proposition upon which the Recorder's ruling seems to be based. It was a mistake, they said, to talk of conversion. No court can test or gauge the sincerity of religious belief. In all cases where, according to Mahommedan law, unbelief or difference of creed is a bar to marriage with a true believer, it is enough if the alien in religion embraces the Mahommedan faith. Profession with or without conversion is necessary and sufficient to remove the disability.

This criticism seems to be well founded. But the correction does not mend the Appellant's case. There is nothing in the evidence tending to show that Mah Thai made any profession of the Mahommedan faith before or at the time of the ceremony which is said to have constituted marriage. Mah Thai was a witness for the Appellant. She said that she knew nothing about the Mahommedan religion; all her life she lived and worshipped as a Burmese. While cohabiting with Abdul Hadee she worshipped as he did; she repeated his prayers. But she added that she did not understand the meaning of a single word. In re-examination she said that she ceased to be a Buddhist during her cohabitation with Abdul Hadee from the time of her marriage.

The learned counsel for the Appellant then invited their Lordships to embark on a wider inquiry. They proposed to examine and discuss the tenets of Buddhism with the view of showing that Buddhists come under the same category as Jews and Christians, with whom undoubtedly Mahommedans may inter-marry. But it was obviously impossible for their Lordships to entertain the question in the present case. In the court below it was common ground that such a marriage would be invalid, and there was therefore no evidence before the court directed to the point.

In the next place, it was urged that every presumption ought to be made in favour of marriage when there had been a lengthened cohabitation, especially in a case where the alleged marriage took place so long ago that it must be difficult if not impossible to obtain a trustworthy account of what really occurred. There would be much force in this argument—indeed, it would be almost irresistible—if the conduct of the parties were shown to be compatible with the existence of the relation of husband and wife. In cases like the present, conduct is a very good test, and a safer guide than the recollection or imagination of interested or biased witnesses.

Mah Thai's own account of the way in which she was treated may be accepted as a fairly truthful story, considering her relationship to the claimant, and the fact that she is speaking of what occurred many years ago. The alleged marriage took place somewhere about the year 1854. If the date is correct the connection between her and her alleged husband ceased in 1856, though Abdul Hadee did not leave Rangoon for good until more than twenty years afterwards. The marriage was proposed to her, she says, by a married sister of hers who was living in Rangoon, and who sent for her from her native village—a place called Mangi, about half a day's journey off. She had already been married once, but that marriage was dissolved by mutual consent. Abdul Hadee was brought for her to see. She asked him if he would look after her and cohabit with her for a long time, and he said he would. He came four or five times before the marriage. He said he would invite his male relatives, but he was not going to invite his female relatives. At the marriage some money and a ring were put into her hands as dower; with that part of the ceremony she seems to have been previously acquainted, and to have been careful to insist upon it; and her consent to the union appears to have been given in due form. Then we have a picture of her married life. After the marriage she was not allowed to go out. She never saw any of her husband's female relatives. She did not know why they did not come to see her. She was not allowed to go to the mosque. She knew that wives of Mahommedans go to the mosque. She did not go because Abdul Hadee would not allow her. None of the female members of the Mahommedan community visited her, nor did she visit them. She never saw Hadjee Hoosain or any of Abdul Hadee's male relatives. At the end of about a year and a half, when she was far gone in pregnancy, she went back to her mother's home in Mangi. She was confined there of a boy, whom she identifies as the present Appellant. When the child was born she sent a message to Abdul Hadee to tell him of the birth. His answer was that he was busy and could not come. He sent, however, money for expenses, and he sent a message to her parents to look after her. On two occasions afterwards he went to Mangi to visit her, returning to Rangoon in the evening. The first visit was about six months, the second about twelve months, after the birth or the child. On the first occasion Mah Thai says she saw Abdul Hadee alone, but nothing in particular was said. He wrote on a piece of paper a Mahommedan name for the child. Afterwards, for fear it would be lost, it was copied on a palm leaf. The name was never used. The paper and the palm leaf have disappeared. But Mah Thai says the name was Abdool Razack, and that name has been reproduced or adopted in connection with this claim. On the second occasion, according to Mah Thai's statement, Abdul Hadee wanted to take the child to Rangoon, and wanted her to go with him. She said she was not well yet and that the child was not old enough. That was the last occasion on which Mah Thai saw Abdul Hadee. So far as appears she never even heard from him or of him afterwards. He was at that time apparently in prosperous circumstances, but he made no provision for her or for the child, and he left the child to be brought up as an unbeliever without so much as performing the primary rite of his religion. Mah Thai was very badly off, but she never applied to her alleged husband for assistance, nor did she make any attempt to see him, though she knew where he lived, and he had, she said, been kind to her while they cohabited together, and she liked her life with him. At the end of two years, or four years as she says in one place, she married a Burman by whom she had seven children. Then she divorced him, and at the time of the trial she appeared as the wife or partner of a fourth consort.

Abdul Hadee continued to reside in Rangoon for a good many years, paying occasional visits to Calcutta. After a time he met with reverses and left Rangoon altogether. The last years of his life he spent at Calcutta, living as a pensioner on the bounty of his brother, Hadjee Hoosain.

The child was brought up by Mah Thai's parents, who were in humble circumstances. As Moung Hpay, which was the name they gave him, he lived till he was about thirty-five, with no higher aims or aspirations than those of an ordinary Burmese peasant. When the heirs of Hadjee Hoosain were wanted, he was discovered in the jungle at Mangi by some enterprising gentlemen at Calcutta who took the matter up as speculation. They put him forward as the missing heir, and Moung Hpay has become an *alias* for Abdool Razack. Their interest in the success of the claim is at least a guarantee that no stone has been left unturned to enable the case to be presented in as favourable an aspect as possible.

In the course of the argument Mr Wheeler, the Judicial Clerk of the Privy Council, referred their Lordships to a case decided by the Special Court of

British Burma in 1875. It is to be found at page 75 of Mr Christopher's *Collection of Circular Orders and Judgments*, published under the authority of the Judicial Commissioner in 1881. The opinion delivered by the court throws so much light on the practice relating to mixed marriages in Burma, and the position held by the wife and children when there is a lawful marriage, that it will not be out of place to quote a passage from it. After stating as a matter apparently not open to controversy that, in order to constitute a valid marriage between a Mussulman and a Burmese woman, the woman must first apostatize and embrace Islam, the judgment proceeds as follows:

In a country like this, where a large number of Mahommedans from other countries have taken up their residence, and in very many cases their permanent abode, and when the natives have no race prejudices against alliances with foreigners, and whose religion offers no impediment to such, we find these mixed marriages everywhere existing among them, which have been duly celebrated according to Mahommedan rites; the wife having previously renounced her own religion and embraced that of her husband. Such an alliance is not regarded by either party as one of a temporary character, or in any way partaking of concubinage such as the *liaisons* which at one time prevailed here between Europeans and the women of the country, but as a formal and a binding marriage. It only requires a short experience of this country to know that these marriages are regarded amongst the Mahommedan community as being of as binding a character, and as conferring on the wife as honorable a position in the family as if she had been of Mahommedan descent for she holds the same position as the husband's other wife does, if he happens to have another. The offspring likewise of these marriages are brought up in the Mahommedan faith, and are acknowledged by their father as his legitimate children, and at his death share in his property as such. The Burmese wife also takes the wife's share, if she is the only one, or divides it with the other or others as the case may be; and these rights both as regards the children and the wife are recognized by our courts.

If this be a correct description of the position of a Burmese woman lawfully married to a Mahommedan settler in Rangoon it certainly would require a very violent presumption in favour of marriage to enable the court to hold that Mah Thai was lawfully wedded to Abdul Hadee. It is tolerably obvious that neither Abdul Hadee nor Mah Thai regarded the ceremony which preceded their cohabitation in the light of a lawful and binding marriage. On this point their Lordships are glad to find themselves entirely in accord with the court below.

The only question remaining for consideration is the question of acknowledgment, with which the learned Recorder dealt in rather a summary way. The learned counsel for the Respondent did not deny that Abdul Hadee might have married Mah Thai, as no doubt he might have done if she had embraced Islam, nor did they contend that the intercourse between Abdul

Hadee and Mah Thai was of such a character as to prevent the possible legitimation of the offspring. Their contention was that there was no acknowledgment in the legal and proper sense of the word, although there may have been an admission of paternity.

The learned counsel for the Appellant cited various texts, which taken apart from the context would seem to show that any admission of paternity, though made casually and not intended to have a serious effect, would be sufficient to confer the status of legitimacy. It is not in their Lordships' opinion necessary to examine these ancient authorities, or to inquire how far they are applicable to a state of society very different from that which existed at the time when they were promulgated. Their Lordships are bound by the decision of this Board, which is clear upon the point. The question arose in the case of *Ashrufood Dowlah Ahmed Hossein Khan* v. *Hyder Hossein Khan*.[3] There it was contended that the claimant, who was defendant in the suit and respondent on the appeal, had been acknowledged by his putative father. The fact of acknowledgment was denied by the appellant. And a deed of repudiation was set up, in which the father expressly repudiated the claimant as his son. An issue was framed in these terms: 'Has the deed of repudiation the effect of cancelling previous acknowledgment of defendant's legitimacy, if such were made?' In the course of their judgment (p. 104) their Lordships comment upon that issue. It was, they said, 'very correctly framed. It substitutes for the ambiguous word 'sonship', which might include an illegitimate son, the word 'legitimacy', and uses the word 'acknowledgment' in its legal sense, under the Mahommedan law, of acknowledgment of antecedent right established by the acknowledgment on the acknowledger, that is, in the sense of a recognition, not simply of sonship, but of legitimacy as a son.' It is clear that it is in that sense that the term 'acknowledgment' is used in a later passage of the judgment which has often been cited, where their Lordships say, 'a child born out of wedlock is illegitimate; if acknowledged, he acquires the status of legitimacy. When, therefore, a child really illegitimate by birth becomes legitimated, it is by force of an acknowledgment expressed or implied, directly proved or presumed.'

It cannot be contended that there was any acknowledgment of legitimacy in the present case. The so-called acknowledgment, even if the evidence on the part of the Appellant is accepted as true in every particular, comes to nothing more than an admission of paternity which was not intended to have the serious effect of conferring the status of legitimacy. A witness is produced who says he accompanied Abdul Hadee on his second visit to Mangi, and that Abdul Hadee told him that he was going to see his son.

3 1 Moore's IA 113.

And there is some other evidence to the like effect. Then there is some evidence that Abdul Hadee, though he had no property, left a will, bequeathing everything to his brother Hadjee Hoosain, in which he mentioned that he had offspring in Burma. According to one witness he named the offspring as 'Abdool Razack', and expressed a wish that his brother should give him 'something'. The will, it seems, was sent to Hadjee Hoosain, but it is not forthcoming, nor was it acted upon. Assuming, however, every word that is said about it to be perfectly true, the evidence falls very far short of such an acknowledgment as would confer the *status* of legitimacy upon an illegitimate child.

Their Lordships therefore in the result agree with the learned Recorder in thinking that the Appellant's claim fails, and they will humbly advise Her Majesty that the appeal must be dismissed with costs.

7. Bhaiya Sher Bahadur v. Bhaiya Ganga Bakhsh (1913) 41 IA 1

Will of Hindu—construction—intention—natural son of Hindu father and Muslim mother, brought up as Hindu—validity of marriage with Hindu—aulād—khāndān

The Maharajah of B., a Hindu of the Junwar Kshatriya caste, had an illegitimate son by a Muslim woman. He brought up this son J. B., as a Hindu and procured for him a marriage with a Hindu lady of the Kshatriya caste. The first respondent, born in 1871, was the only issue of this marriage. J. B. also had four illegitimate sons by a Muslim mistress, the eldest, born before 1871, being the appellant. The Maharajah died in 1882, having, by a codicil to his will made in 1878, provided that Rs 48,000 per annum should be paid to J. B. 'and his issue (*aulād*) for generation after generation so long as the family (*khāndān*) of J. B. and his issue (*aulād*) remain in existence.' It further provided that after the death of J. B. 'from among his issue (*aulād*) one person, to whom the right may go, shall be considered the proprietor of this maintenance allowance, without division, as a *rais*.' The codicil allocated certain villages to meet those payments and provided that J. B. and his family descendants should hold possession of them in perpetuity. In 1899 J. B. died, and the first respondent took possession of the villages and all other movable and immovable property left by his father. The appellant brought a suit against the first respondent and his younger brothers claiming to recover the property, or alternatively the share to which he was entitled.

Held, that it was not necessary to decide whether J. B. could contract a valid marriage with a Hindu of the Kshatriya caste so as to render the first respondent legitimate, for the intention of the testator, as shown by the language of the codicil in conjunction with the surrounding circumstances, was to treat the marriage as valid; that the first respondent was therefore entitled to the property, and that the suit should be dismissed. Though there may be some cases which the word *aulād* includes illegitimate children, *prima facie* that word and the word *khāndān* includes only legitimate offspring.

This case is of great importance as indicating that, in spite of the law, marriages did take place between Hindus and Muslims during the centuries since the Muslims first came to India. The distinction that may be observed is that in case of marriages where there was a Muslim father, as in the case of the Mughal Emperors, the issue was deemed to be legitimate, and the son entitled to succeed to the throne. But where the father was a high caste Hindu, the issue of the marriage was considered as outside the caste, and not legitimate. Details of such marriages will be found in abundance in historical works relating to the Muslim period.

For the purely legal aspects, see Ameer Ali, II. 154, 281 seqq., 342, 351; and *Outlines,* §§ 2, 3, 26.

Judgment [Atkinson, J.][4]

This is an appeal from a judgment and decree dated 26 February 1906, of the Court of the Judicial Commissioner of Oudh, which affirmed a judgment and decree dated 3 January 1905, of the Court of the Subordinate Judge of Gonda, dismissing the plaintiff's suit.

The action out of which the appeal arises was instituted on 3 April 1902, by the plaintiff as eldest son and heir of his father, Jang Bahadur Singh, by a Mahommedan woman, claiming to recover the possession of the several villages mentioned in the schedule annexed to the statement of claim. These villages formed part of an estate called the Balrampur estate which had been bequeathed to the plaintiff's father by his (the plaintiff's) paternal grandfather, the Maharajah of Balrampur, by a codicil dated 15 March 1878, to the last will of the Maharajah. Possession of these villages had been taken in the year 1899 by the first defendant, and has since been retained by him. Mesne profits were claimed in respect of this possession, and a claim was added to recover possession of the movable and immovable property mentioned in schedules B and C, also annexed to the statement of claim, or in the alternative the plaintiff's legal share thereof, on the ground that the same was property acquired by the plaintiff's said father, with an additional claim for further relief.

4 With Shaw, John Edge and Syed Ameer Ali.

The first defendant, Bhaiya Ganga Bakhsh Singh, filed a written statement alleging that the plaintiff was the issue of a Mahommedan woman with whom his (the said defendant's) father, Jang Bahadur Singh, had had illegal intercourse, as were also the defendants numbered 2, 3, and 4, and that her nikah had never taken place; that his father followed the Hindu religion bigotedly, and was a Hindu from his boyhood up to his death; that he married for the first time a Hindu lady of a Surajbansi Kshatriya family; that he (the first defendant) was the only child of that marriage, is the only legitimate son and heir-at-law of his father, and is consequently under the provision of the said codicil entitled to the allowance therein mentioned.

The plaintiff replied traversing the several allegations contained in this and the other written statements filed by other defendants, and upon these pleadings eight issues were formulated. A vast body of evidence was given bearing upon each of these issues. Many of them are no longer of importance on this appeal, which is the ultimate stage of the litigation. The real questions now in dispute are, first, the proper construction of the language of the codicil of 15 March 1878, and second, the actual intention which the Maharajah desired to effect in executing it.

The facts so far as material to the decision of these questions are as follows. The plaintiff is the firstborn son of his father, and the second, third, and fourth defendants are his brothers, sons of Jang Bahadur Singh by the Mahommedan woman already mentioned. It has been found as a fact by both the courts before which this case has come that no ceremony of marriage was ever gone through between Jang Bahadur Singh and this woman, that she was his mistress not his wife, and that, consequently, the plaintiff and his brothers are illegitimate. The appellant accepts this finding as conclusive on this point. The first defendant is the son of Jang Bahadur by a Hindu lady of the Kshatriya caste with whom he had, admittedly, gone through the ceremony of marriage according to the strict Hindu rite.

The validity of this marriage is impeached by the plaintiff upon the ground that at the time it was celebrated Jang Bahadur was neither a Hindu nor a member of the Kshatriya caste, and that consequently the first defendant is, like the plaintiff and his brothers, illegitimate. The issue thus raised necessitated a somewhat lengthy examination of the life history of Jang Bahadur. He was, as already mentioned, the son, born in the year 1846, of a rather distinguished man, a Hindu by religion of the Junwar Kshatriya caste, Sir Digbijai Singh, Maharajah of Balrampur, by a Mahommedan mistress named Imam Bandi, and was therefore, as held by both the courts above mentioned, a Mahommedan by birth. This decision is also accepted by the appellant.

The Subordinate Judge found that 'Jang Bahadur was brought up, not as a Mahomedan under the influence of his Mahommedan mother, but by his Hindu father in the religion of Hindus.' He also found that 'he never professed the Mahommedan religion and was never a Mahommedan in fact; that after he was able to make a choice he did not choose the religion of Islam but on the other hand lived and died in the faith of Hinduism... that he was throughout his life a follower of the popular idolatrous form of Hinduism, a form directly antagonistic to the cardinal principles upon which the religion of Islam is founded.' The Subordinate Judge came to the conclusion that 'as Jang Bahadur was never throughout his life a Mahommedan, the Mahommedan law did not regulate the succession to his estate and as he was not a Hindu by birth neither did the Hindu law regulate it; that neither of these laws nor yet the Indian Succession Act governed him at his death, and that according to the principles of justice, equity, and good conscience, and by the application of so much of the Hindu law as was applicable to the case, Ganga Bakhsh Singh, the first defendant, was his father's legitimate son and sole heir.'

The Court of the Judicial Commissioner, whilst abstaining from pronouncing any definite opinion on the legitimacy of the first defendant, gave in the following passage of their judgment a sketch of the status, life, and character of Jang Bahadur Singh, which, though it differs to some extent from that of the Subordinate Judge, is, in their Lordships' view of the evidence, fairly accurate. It runs thus: 'Jang Bahadur belonged to no caste, and even if the issue of his marriage with Hansraj Kunwar should be held to be legitimate, a point on which I express no opinion, it is clear that the Hindu community at Balrampur treated the validity of the marriage as open to question. The Subordinate Judge has cited several authorities to show that the Hindu religion admits proselytes of all kinds. The truth of this is indisputable, but it is equally true that the admission of a proselyte and his descendants into the society of orthodox Hindus is a very slow process. The defendant's witnesses hit off the position exactly when they say that they might eat with Jang Bahadur's family if they persevered in their Hindu habits and maintained their character for several generations. In two parts of one and the same house Jang Bahadur had a Mahommedan and a Hindu family and seems to have been on equally affectionate terms with both. He ate food in English hotels and railway refreshment rooms, drank gin and kept fowls and pigs. It is evident that he was neither an orthodox Hindu nor an orthodox Mahommedan. It appears to be that he led a double life as was almost inevitable under the circumstances. He no doubt called himself a Hindu, and if he had any religion it was, as the Subordinate Judge says, the popular idolatrous form of Hinduism, but he is not proved to have been an orthodox Hindu, and therefore it seems to me that if the plaintiff were found to be of legitimate birth the circumstance that his father became a Hindu to the extent shown by the evidence would be no reason for passing over the plaintiff and giving the property to the first defendant.'

It has been urged on behalf of the respondents that the court of the Judicial Commissioner was mistaken in supposing that Jang Bahadur kept his two families in two sides of the same house, that, in truth and fact, he kept them in two different houses. This is really a small matter and does not affect the general accuracy of the passage.

A vast body of evidence was given describing in great detail the participation of Jang Bahadur Singh on many occasions in the most solemn rites and ceremonies of the Hindu religion. It was proved by many witnesses that he wore, somewhat ostentatiously, the Hindu *tilak* on his forehead, that he was invested by his father with the sacred thread, that he kept a Hindu cook to cook his food. The fair result of the evidence in their Lordships' opinion is that Jang Bahadur did his utmost to become an orthodox Hindu, and to pass as such in the society in which he lived; that his father, from the boy's youth upwards, aided and encouraged him in those efforts; and, finally, when he was only fifteen years of age, procured a marriage to be celebrated with great pomp and rejoicing according to the strict Hindu rite between him and the already mentioned Hindu lady of the Kshatriya caste, Hansraj Kunwar.

This lady's family were apparently not well off, and it was stated in evidence that the Maharajah gave to her brother Sheo Dial a village to induce him to consent to the union. This, however, only proves the anxiety of the Maharajah to bring about the marriage. No doubt the Maharajah did not attend the ceremony himself. He allowed certain priests to perform for him those ceremonies properly performable on such occasions by a father, but the marriage cannot but be regarded as a somewhat bold attempt to force, as far as possible, the son's entrance into the ranks of a high (twice born) caste, and it might well be that the father, as the Subordinate Judge thought, may have absented himself from the ceremony from motives of prudence. On the other hand it is difficult to believe that all the parties concerned, Sheo Dial, with his own sons, and his daughters to get married, the Maharajah with his position and distinction, the priests with their duties to their religion and office, and all those who assisted at the ceremony with their notions of what was due to their creed, would have promoted, or taken part in, an elaborate public function if they knew that it could at best create only a relation of permanent concubinage, without hope or prospect of elevation into a worthier and more respected state. The evidence of Sheo Dial is important in this connection. He said he went with two pandits to visit the Maharajah; that he had learned that Jang Bahadur was a Mahommedan woman's son;

that on his expressing his scruples about the contemplated marriage owing to this fact the Maharajah assured him that Jang Bahadur was a Hindu; that he (the Maharajah) held him (Sheo Dial) by the arm and said: 'From childhood I have got him suckled by a Brahmin woman. He eats with me. He does *puja*, and his ways are the ways of a Hindu.' Sheo Dial further says that Jang Bahadur Singh wore a *tilak* of *chandan*, that his cook was a Hindu, that he saw him sitting near the Maharajah at dinner, and that hearing and seeing this he, Sheo Dial, consented to the marriage of his sister with Jang Bahadur. No doubt it is stated by another witness that the Maharajah did not sit at meals with this son, but unless this evidence of Sheo Dial be an entire fabrication it bears additional testimony to the anxiety of the Maharajah to have his son accepted and treated as a Hindu. Hansraj Kunwar died in the Maharajah's lifetime. Jang Bahadur performed all the obsequies proper to be performed according to the Hindu religion by a surviving Hindu husband. His father, in the year 1872, got him, then about twenty-four years of age, again married to another Hindu lady, a member of the same Kshatriya caste, Raj Kali Kunwar, who survived him, and is the fifth defendant in this suit. There was the same publicity and pomp as on the occasion of the first marriage, the same religious ceremonial. The Maharajah on this occasion, as on the former, absented himself and got his duties performed vicariously in the same way. The sole issue of this second marriage was a girl. Both she and Bhaiya Ganga Bakhsh Singh married members of the Kshatriya caste. Sir Robert Finlay insists that the law for many centuries has been that a Hindu must be born not made, and he cited several authorities in support of that proposition. On the other hand, the treatises referred to by the Subordinate Judge in his judgment appear to tend in an opposite direction, and the facts of this case show that in this matter of marriage the rules, both of Hinduism and of caste were not, in this instance at all events, strictly applied. In the view their Lordships take it is unnecessary to express any opinion on the point. The matter for decision in this case being the construction of a codicil to the Maharajah's will, the point is not what is the strict rule of the Hindu religion, or the strict rule of the Kshatriya caste, but this, namely, what were the wishes and intentions of the testator as revealed by the language of that instrument, viewed through the light of the circumstances which surrounded him at the time he made it.

It would be strange indeed if the man who had made it his special care to rear this son of his as a Hindu, and had succeeded in marrying him to two high caste Hindu women, should intend or desire, whatever might be the strict letter of the law, to place the offspring of these unions on the same level as the illegitimate children of his son's Mahommedan mistress and make them all equally the objects of his bounty.

Much reliance was placed by the appellant upon the evidence of several witnesses, members of the Kshatriya caste, which was directed to show that they would not eat with Jang Bahadur Singh, take betel leaves from him, or recognize him as a member of that caste, or of the Hindu religion, and it was contended that the Subordinate Judge had not paid sufficient attention to this evidence, or given it its due weight. He has no doubt not commented upon it at any great length, but it would be quite unreasonable because of this to conclude that he had not fully considered it. When the evidence is examined it will be found that the objection of many, if not most, of these witnesses to eat with Jang Bahadur or to give him betel leaves, &c., was due to the well-known and undisputed fact that he was the illegitimate son of a Mahommedan mistress, rather than to the fact that he was not a genuine Hindu. This is notably so in the case of the witnesses Kali Parshad and Jagdeo Singh. The former said 'I did not eat with Jang Bahadur because he was Imam Bandi's son,' and again, 'I won't eat kutcha food touched by Ganga Bakhsh. I won't drink water from his hand because his grandmother was a Mahommedan,' and the latter said 'I cannot eat food cooked by Raj Kali Kunwar because she was Jang Bahadur's wife,' but he proceeded to say that he would have no objection to eat with Jang Bahadur Singh if the Maharajah had asked him to do so, and then he added the important statement: 'Jang Bahadur had offended the Maharajah by keeping a Mahommedan woman, that woman had four sons, she lived with Bandi as Jang Bahadur's mistress for twelve or thirteen years until her death.' Babu Basudeo Lal, an educated man and an advocate, says 'Jang Bahadur took particular care to put on the tilak more than a born Hindu would take because he was anxious to appear a Hindu; that from the orthodox point of view he (the witness) did not consider him a Hindu, but he could not say he was a Mahommedan, because he professed to be a Hindu,' yet he gave not this fact but the fact that Jang Bahadur was of illegitimate birth as the reason for his unwillingness to take water from his hands. Hanwant Singh gives remarkable evidence to the same effect. He said: 'I consider Jang Bahadur a Hindu. He worshipped like a Hindu. He did pilgrimages like a Hindu. He gave *dans* to Brahmins like a Hindu. His ways were those of a Hindu. I saw him doing *puja* in the temple for the first time thirty years ago, and three times altogether I saw him feeding Brahmins at the temple.' Yet despite what he saw, and his opinions on Jang Bahadur's religion, he says on the next page he would not eat with him because he was born of Imam Bandi, nor would he eat with Ganga Bakhsh, because presumably he was his father's son, though he admits that if the latter 'persevered in his Hindu habits for two generations he would be taken into the *biradri*.'

These witnesses are fair specimens of those examined on this point. Their evidence might be of importance if it was necessary for their Lordships to determine whether or not the first defendant was the legitimate son and heir-at-law of Jang Bahadur. The Subordinate Judge has determined that question in the affirmative. Their Lordships concur with the Court of the Judicial Commissioner in thinking that it is not necessary to determine it one way or the other for the purposes of the decision of this appeal, and they therefore abstain from expressing any opinion upon it. What is of importance, when one has to construe this codicil, and determine what was the testator's intention in making it, is to ascertain in what light he regarded his son, the marriages he helped that son to contract, and the issue that sprung from them.

Their Lordships are of opinion that the reasonable conclusion to be drawn from the evidence is that the Maharajah treated this son of his as a Hindu in religion, and desired that others should so treat him; that he treated his marriages with the two Kshatriya ladies as lawful marriages and desired that others should so treat them, and consequently resolved to regard and treat the offspring of these unions as legitimate, and desired they should be so treated and regarded by others; and that it was in this frame of mind he made the testamentary disposition which is in dispute. It is lengthy, and in its material parts runs thus:

Whereas I have a son, named Jang Bahadur Singh, born of an unmarried mahal, and whereas he is not born of khas mahal, and it is against the usage of the family and against religion according to the Hindu *Shastras*, so he is not considered capable of *gaddinashini* and the proprietorship of the riasat. But he also being born of my loins, it is incumbent on me that such means be provided for support as would enable him and his (*aulad*) issues to support themselves well and with respect. Accordingly ever since the date of his birth till this day whenever proper opportunity presented, grant was made for his support; and during my lifetime I shall make grants according to my will whenever I shall deem it expedient to do so. But with a view to clearly make a provision beforehand in order that there may not remain any co-ownership and dispute relating to a part or the whole of my movable and immovable property, a property should be determined for Jang Bahadur Singh and his (*aulad*) issues for generation after generation in order that the conditions of the deed may remain binding in perpetuity. Accordingly the settlement is made as follows. It is this: Rs 4000 per mensem or Rs 48,000 per annum shall be continued to be paid by the proprietor of the riasat, the *locum tenens* of the *gaddinashin* for the time being; and that amount shall be paid to Jang Bahadur Singh and his (*aulad*) issues for generation after generation as long as the (*khandan*) family of Jang Bahadur Singh and his (*aulad*) issues remain in existence.

Details of Conditions

1. He shall not directly or indirectly take part in running the *riasat*, and shall also remain a well-wisher of the *riasat*. 2. He shall not transfer his maintenance allowance to a stranger by sale, mortgage or otherwise.… (details of the dispositions.)

The testator died on 27 May 1882. In or about January, 1894, Jang Bahadur Singh became insane. He so continued for several years, and died on 1 October 1899, leaving as his own the movable and immovable property mentioned in schedules B and C attached to the statement of claim. The first defendant, as already mentioned, immediately went into possession of the property mentioned in schedule A and has since retained it.

Jang Bahadur Singh was created by the codicil ancestor or first proprietor of the estate. Maintenance allowances, somewhat resembling rent-charges, were charged upon it. It was to be perpetual, impartible, indivisible, and incapable of being otherwise charged or incumbered, and it was not to be the subject of any co-ownership. On the death of Jang Bahadur a person, styled the representative of the former, was to succeed him as proprietor of this maintenance allowance, without 'division,' as a rais. This proprietor was to be one of the issue of Bahadur Singh, the other issue (*aulād*) of the family (*khāndān*) of Jang Badahur Singh being only entitled to get food and raiment out of the allowance. In addition the marriage and funeral expenses of the male and female children of the family of Jang Badahur Singh were to be paid. The only indication given as to how the particular individual, one of the issue of Jang Bahadur, who was to succeed him as proprietor of the allowance was to be ascertained is that contained in the words 'on whom the right may go.' The testator must have had in mind some law or rule which would apply to fix the succession. What law could this high caste Hindu possibly have had in mind for such a purpose other than the Hindu law? That law, however, in the matter of succession to property, takes no account, in the three higher classes, of illegitimate descendants. Sir Robert Finlay, as their Lordships understood, admitted this contention—at, least to this extent, that if when a successor came to be ascertained the class of beneficiaries contained both legitimate and illegitimate members, the eldest legitimate male would by the Hindu law succeed; but where, as in the present case, as he contended, all the children are illegitimate, the eldest male amongst them should succeed. But by what law or rule he did not indicate. It is difficult to suppose that if the testator intended all his grandchildren to be put upon the same level he would not have indicated some method by which the successor to his son should be selected. If he relied at all upon the Hindu law to select that successor it could only be because he wished it to be assumed that that law applied to some of the issue of his son, and that could only be the case if those members of the issue were to be taken to be legitimate.

At the date of this codicil Jang Bahadur was only about thirty years of age. He had already had one son by his deceased Kshatriya wife. He had been married for some time to another Kshatriya wife, by whom it was quite possible he might have had male issue, and it would have been quite in conflict with the whole tenor of the Maharajah's treatment of and conduct towards his son Jang Bahadur to deprive by this codicil these marriages and the issue springing from them of the character and status he had striven to secure for them. The Court of the Judicial Commissioner came to the conclusion that the Maharajah thought these marriages of his son were valid, and the issue of them legitimate. However that may be, it is clear, their Lordships think, upon the whole of the evidence that he wished them to be so regarded by others. Nothing would more surely have defeated that desire than that he should by this testamentary instrument show that he himself regarded them in a wholly different light, and placed the children of these marriages on an equality with those of a Mahommedan concubine. The Maharajah has used the word '*aulād*' throughout this codicil to describe the issue of his son Jang Bahadur. The Court of the Judicial Commissioner has laid it down that this word prima facie means legitimate issue. This case is not one where a gift is made by will of the corpus of a fund, or a life interest in a fund, to the 'children' of the testator or of another as a class. There may be good reason in some such cases for holding that in India the word 'children' includes illegitimate children, but here a succession of life interests from generation to generation is intended to be set up, the successor or 'proprietor' in each instance being vested with absolute control of the income, subject only to the duty of maintaining the issue (*aulad*) of the family (*khāndān*) of the first proprietor, Jang Bahadur Singh. There is nothing on the face of the will to suggest that a meaning should be given to the word '*aulād*' different from its prima facie meaning; but if it is to be read as including illegitimate issue, then it follows that the testator intended to bring into the line of succession not only his illegitimate grandchildren but their illegitimate issue from generation to generation. Such a construction would render rather unnecessary the provision that if no descendants of the family of Jang Bahadur remained, the monthly allowance should fall into the possession of the *gaddinishin*, and would also seem to defeat the whole purpose and object of the testator in establishing this succession of life interests. Nor do their Lordships see any reason for extending in this instance the meaning of the word '*khāndān*,' which ordinarily refers to the group of descendants who constitute the family of the progenitor, so as to include illegitimate offspring who from the necessities of the case cannot share in the family life or its worship or ceremonials.

It has been strenuously urged by Sir Robert Finlay on behalf of the appellant: first, that there would have been nothing easier for the testator, if he desired to exclude his illegitimate grandchildren from all benefit under this codicil, than to have said so. The question is, has he not done so by the use of the word 'aulad'? But even if this be not so, it was quite as easy for him to include them in the class described by the word 'issue' as to exclude them from it, so that the argument cuts both ways. It was in the second place contended that, having regard to his interest in these children, he never could have intended to leave them unprovided for. He undoubtedly did show some interest in them, but not a very keen interest, and it is by no means clear that he did not intend them to be provided for in the way they have been provided for, namely, by being maintained by their grandmother Imam Bandi during her life, out of the income left to her by the codicil. He enabled her by the exercise of the testamentary power over this income conferred upon her so to provide for them after her death. The income was large, Rs 1000 per mensem. She was a woman who at the date of the codicil must have been at least forty-five years of age, her son Jang Bahadur being then thirty years of age. The son's mistress and her children lived with her. She, according to the evidence, helped to rear them. It was scarcely conceivable that she should require Rs 12,000 per annum for her personal expenses alone. The power of disposing of this income by will clearly showed that the testator had some object in view beyond providing adequately for her maintenance. What more natural than that this income, handsome in amount, and disposable by her will, should have been given to enable her to provide for her grandchildren? Their Lordships are therefore of opinion that, having regard to all the evidence in the case and the provisions of the codicil itself, the intention of the testator plainly was to treat the marriages of Jang Bahadur with the two Kshatriya women already mentioned as valid marriages, and the issue of those marriages as legitimate issue. They think that the judgment appealed from was right, and that this appeal should be dismissed with costs, and they will humbly advise His Majesty accordingly.

◊ UPDATE ◊

1. *Children of inter-religious marriages*

The use of the term 'hybrid' for children of parents professing different religions now seems rather inappropriate. Legislation in India now facilitates inter-religious marriages both between Indian citizens and between Indians and foreigners. See the Special Marriage Act 1954 and the Foreign Marriage Act 1969. Children born to parents lawfully marrying under either of these laws will be legitimate under the law of India.[5]

5 A study of the Special Marriage Act 1954 and its working in found in my book *Civil Marriage Law: Perspectives and Prospects*, ILI, Delhi, 1978.

In *Abdur Rahim* v. *Padma* AIR 1982 Bom 341 the High Court of Bombay has held:

It can safely be said that the Special Marriage Act is in reality an Indian Marriage Act which applies to all Indian communities irrespective of caste, creed or religion… So far as secular marriages are concerned, the said law will become *lex domicile* of India for the purposes of matrimonial reliefs.[6]

2. *Presumption of marriage*

The two old cases of *Abdool Razack* and *Bhaiya Sher Bahadur* [Cases 6 & 7] establish the legal position that where a marriage is not permissible by law, there is no room either for a presumption of marriage due to long cohabitation or for giving effect to the father's acknowledgement of a child's paternity and legitimacy under Muslim law.

Some recent Indian cases reaffirming these points are *Syed Amanullah* v. *Rajammal* AIR 1977 AP 152 and *Mohamed Khan* v. *Ali Khan* AIR 1981 Mad 209. In the latter case the court observed:

A child born of *zina* cannot be made legitimate by acknowledgement. Similarly, the defendants who were born before the date of marriage of their mother with the plaintiff's father cannot be held to be legitimate sons of the plaintiff's father by relying on the doctrine of acknowledgement.

3. *Children brought up as Hindu*

As regards children of inter-religious marriages, the Hindu Marriage Act 1955, Section 2 (1), Explanation, provides as follows:

The following persons are Hindu, Buddhist, Jain or Sikh by religion, as the case may be:

(a) any child, legitimate or illegitimate, both of whose parents are Hindu, Buddhist, Jain or Sikh, by religion;

(b) any child, legitimate or illegitimate, one of whose parents is a Hindu, Buddhist, Jain or Sikh, by religion and who is brought up as a member of the tribe, community, group or family to which such parent belongs or belonged; and

(c) any person who is a convert or reconvert to the Hindu, Buddhist, Jain or Sikh religion.

6 The Judgment quotes my viewpoint with approval from my book *The Muslim Law of India* (1st. ed., Allahabad, 1980)—TM.

IV. Custom

8. Ghasiti v. Umrao Jan
(1893) 20 IA 193

Custom of the tribe of Kanchans—prostitution as family business—property held in common—adoption—succession

Customs which aim at the continuance of prostitution as a family business are contrary to Muhammadan law, immoral and not enforceable. A Muslim woman who is adopted according to family custom into a Kanchan brothel is not thereby severed from her own family. And her own property, however acquired, will at her death devolve according to Muhammadan law.

Adoption is not known to the general law of Islam. On custom and its validity, see the next case; *Outlines*, 62 seqq.; *Tyabji*, 47 seqq.

Judgment [Hobhouse, J.][1]

These suits relate to the inheritance of a woman named Bando Jan, who died in August, 1879, leaving a substantial property. Her father, Ali Bakhsh, and his children professed the Mahommedan religion. She had no issue, and she survived her parents. Her heirs, according to Mahommedan law, were her two brothers, Jaggu and Sannu, who are Respondents in the second appeal, and her four sisters, Amir Jan (now represented by Umrao Jan) and Ilahi Jan, who are Respondents in the first appeal, Nanhi Jan, who is one of the Appellants in both appeals, and Banno Jan; and as between them the inheritance would be divided into eight shares, each brother taking two shares and each sister one.

Banno brought a suit and obtained a decree in February, 1880, for one-eighth share; and she is no party to the present litigation.

In the year 1882 the two brothers, Jaggu and Sannu, the two sisters, Amir and Ilahi, and a woman called Imaman, sued the remaining sister, Nanhi, who had got into possession of the property. They alleged that, Banno being satisfied, the remaining property was divisible into six shares, of which Nanhi was entitled to one, and each of the five Plaintiffs to one. They made out their claim as follows: All the parties to the dispute belong to the people

[1] With Macnaghten and Richard Couch, JJ.

(in the translated plaint it is called the tribe) of Kanchans. In that tribe the business of brothel-keeping and prostitution is carried on by families or communities who are recruited by adoption. Bando left her own family to be adopted by one Dildara, who was the head of another establishment of the same kind. She succeeded to Dildara's property; and as Dildara was dead and her brothel had ceased to have any members except Bando herself, on Bando's death her estate was distributable according to the custom of the Kanchans, which, it was alleged, would carry it to the family heirs of Bando, and to Imaman, the sister of Dildara, in equal shares. It is obvious that such a claim is full of difficulty and apparent inconsistencies in itself, but it was made.

After a while the brothers reconsidered their position. They determined to assert a claim under the common law of Mahommedans by which they would take larger shares than under the custom of Kanchans. Thus their interests became adverse to those of their sisters, and they could no longer be co-Plaintiffs. They procured orders under which they were made Defendants instead of Plaintiffs. And they instituted a suit of their own to enforce their claim against their three sisters. That is the second suit in which an appeal is brought. These matters of procedure have no importance except for the reason that the institution of the brothers' suit is objected to as irregular. The Chief Court has held it to be regular, and their Lordships have declined to hear the appeal on this point argued. The decree complained of can be made as properly in the suit where the brothers are Defendants as in that where they are Plaintiffs, and the objection is based on a technicality without any practical bearing.

The substantial defences of Nanhi were, first, that Ghasiti was the adopted daughter, and also the legatee of Bando; and, secondly, that as Bando had been adopted by Dildara, no right of inheritance could devolve on the Plaintiffs either by Mahommedan law or by custom. The allegations respecting Ghasiti were negatived by both courts; so that the only questions which remained for them were whether the Plaintiffs could claim any inheritance, and if so in what shares. Imaman was discharged from the suit, and died before the hearing. The contest, therefore, was between the two sisters claiming customary shares, the two brothers claiming shares by common law, and the third sister contending that none of her father's family had any claim at all.

It is quite clear that there was no adoption under any general Indian law. Adoption is not known to the general law of Mahommedans, and adoption of girls is not known to the general law of Hindus. If there was adoption, it could only have been under some local, tribal, or family custom, which must be proved by those who allege it. Accordingly a great deal of evidence was given to prove the customs of the Kanchans. The two courts are in accord as to the result, a portion of which their Lordships will now re-state.

It appears that each family or community live a caenobitical, quasi-corporate life in what the learned Judges call the family brothels. All the members, including males, are entitled to food and raiment from the business, the males living a life of idleness at the expense of the females. There is no such thing as separate or individual succession upon death. All the members succeed jointly. No division or partition is allowed, for that would break up the establishments, and the witnesses say that the lamp should be kept burning in the house. A member of a family brothel who leaves it does so with only her clothes on her back and nothing more. The body is recruited by adoption. A girl is brought in as the adopted daughter of a female member of the institution, and the girl thus adopted is regarded as having ceased to belong to her own family.

That Bando was adopted by Dildara according to the custom there seems to be no doubt, if indeed there was any dispute. Whether she thereby acquired a right of inheritance according to the custom is a question which does not arise in this suit. She joined Dildara's establishment, and on Dildara's death became its head, took the property there, and increased it by her own earnings. But the suit relates entirely to the succession from Bando; it raises no question as to the succession from Dildara to Bando, nor has anybody made any claim adverse to Bando in respect of property belonging to Dildara, or in respect of any property possessed by Bando at her death. The question is how that property is to devolve, and how Bando got it is immaterial.

The two Plaintiff sisters contend that Bando held the property as head of the brothel into which she had been adopted. By what process they claim that it passed to them and the other Plaintiffs is, as above intimated, not easy to understand. The Defendant sister is more logical. Agreeing that Bando was adopted by Dildara, she says that the adoption severed Bando completely from her own natural family. That certainly is the effect of adoption by Hindu law, and the evidence shows that it is the same according to Kanchan custom. A distinct issue on the point was settled and decided by the first court.

On this issue the District Judge found as follows: 'Upon the custom as above stated no question can arise as to Mussammat Bando Jan having ceased to be a member of her natural family by being adopted by Mussammat Dildara. The adoption (if proved) really was for the purpose of succession to Dildara's family brothel, and in this way Mussammat Bando Jan ceased to be a member of the brothel of her natural family, and ceased to have any claim therein.' But he stated his view of the law to be that all these rules and customs of the Kanchans aim at the continuance of prostitution as a family business, that they have a distinctly immoral tendency, and should not be enforced in courts of justice. He therefore held that the whole transaction was null and void, that there was no severance of *Bando* from her family, and that her property must be distributed according to Mahommedan law.

The Chief Court expressly abstain from pronouncing any opinion on the question whether the adoption of a girl by a prostitute at the head of a brothel gives that girl any legal rights in the property of the institution. They sum up the case thus: 'As to the custom of inheritance, there is none applicable. It is clear that Mussammat Bando Jan left the family brothel of Ali Bakhsh, and no question arises as to succession to Mussammat Bando Jan as a member of that institution. She was the last survivor of the brothel of which she became a member under Mussammat Dildara, and no question arises of succession to her as a member of that brothel.'

Their Lordships are disposed to think that is a sound conclusion; and if so, it would suffice to settle the controversy between the Plaintiff sisters and their brothers. But it does not cover the whole ground. If the custom is valid, what answer is there to the Defendant sister's contention that Bando's natural family could not inherit from her after her adoption by Dildara?

Their Lordships have no hesitation in affirming the law as laid down by the District Judge. In the case of Hindus there are stronger grounds for maintaining that practices of prostitution are related to worship in the temples and meet with countenance from the law. But even in the case of Hindus great difficulties have been felt by courts of justice in admitting the validity of transactions intended for the furtherance of prostitution. See the case of *Mathura Naikin* v. *Esu Naikin*,[2] and the authorities there referred to. And as regards Mahomedans, prostitution is not looked on by their religion or their laws with any more favourable eye than by the Christian religion and laws.

Mr Baillie's valuable *Digest of Mahomedan Law* opens thus:

> The intercourse of a man with a woman who is neither his wife nor his slave is unlawful, and prohibited absolutely. When there is neither the reality nor the semblance of either of these relations between the parties, their intercourse is termed *zina*, and subjects them both to *hadd*, or a specific punishment for violating the laws of Almighty God.

The statement is quite justified by the authority of the *Hedaya*, Lib. VII, sec. 1, 2, and 3, according to which the practice of *zina* is held up to

2 ILR 4 Bom 545.

reprobation, and is punishable in ways which would now be considered as savage and cruel. Indeed, the most venerable of all authorities, the Koran itself, though not going so much into detail as the *Hedaya*, forbids harlotry under severe penalties, see caps. 4 and 24 of Sale's Translation. It seems to their Lordships impossible to say that such customs as are proved in this case to exist among the Kanchans are not contrary to the policy of the great religious community to which the courts have found that all the parties belong.

A minor point in the case relates to certain moveable property which appears to have been stolen after the commencement of litigation by Banno. The courts below have concurred in thinking that Nanhi had the property in her possession, and therefore is responsible for the loss, and their Lordships consider that it would not be proper to disturb concurrent decisions on such a point. The result is that both appeals should be dismissed, and their Lordships will humbly advise Her Majesty to this effect.

9. Abdul Hussein v. Bibi Sona Dero (1917) 45 IA 10

Custom of family—inheritance—evidence of custom—instances—Bombay Regulation IV of 1827, s. 26

A Shiite Muslim belonging to a family resident in Sind for many generations died intestate, and an administration suit was filed. The Appellant alleged that by a custom of the family, contrary to the general rule of Muhammadan law, the sister of the intestate was excluded as a female in favour of male collaterals.

The Board held that the evidence did not establish the custom put forward, and dealt with the weight to be attached to the different kinds of evidence adduced and the presumptions that arise in such cases.

This leading case is discussed in *Tyabji*, §§ 10, 10A, *Outlines*, 64 seq.

Appeal from a judgment and decree of the Court of the Judicial Commissioner of Sind (9 January 1912) reversing the decree of the District Court (31 May 1910).

Judgment [Buckmaster J.][3]

On 30 January 1907, Mir Hussein Ali Khan of Talpur died intestate, leaving neither widow nor child. His nearest surviving relations were the plaintiff, Abdul Hussein, the son of his brother by the half-blood, one sister, the first defendant upon the record, and his sister's son, who is the second defendant.

3 With Buckmaster, John Edge, Syed Ameer Ali and Walter Phillimore, JJ.

His estate, consisting exclusively of personal property, and largely of what we should call personal effects, is of great value, and doubtless also, from the character of many of the articles, of great personal interest to his relations. It is a dispute about the inheritance of this property that has given rise to the present appeal. The deceased was a member of the family of Talpur Mirs of Sind, who were a branch of the large Baluchi tribe. He was a Mahommedan, and, if Mahommedan law governed the question, the rights of the parties would vary accordingly whether the deceased was a member of the Shia or of the Sunni sect. If the former, the sister would inherit the whole estate; if the latter, the plaintiff would be entitled to a half. The plaintiff alleges, however, that the rights of inheritance are not to be determined according to Mahommedan law, but that they are regulated by a custom well known and distinctly ascertained, by which, notwithstanding the provisions of the Koran, women are excluded from any share in the inheritance of a paternal relation. He further alleges that, if this contention does not prevail, the deceased was a Sunni and not a Shia, and that he is therefore entitled to the more limited rights to which reference has been made. Their Lordships think it is convenient to dispose of the latter contention first.

Although the holding of religious opinion is a matter of personal faith, and ordinarily it may not be easy to determine what the nature of that faith may be, yet in a case like the present, where the question lies between two sects so sharply divided in ritual and observances, performance of prayers, and public declarations of faith as the Sunni and the Shia, it is readily capable of being determined by definite evidence of action, conduct, and observance. For reasons which their Lordships consider as conclusive, both the Judicial Commissioner, before whom the case was first tried, sitting as District Judge, and the Court of the Judicial Commissioner of Sind, before whom the appeal was heard, have decided that the deceased was of the Shia persuasion, and with this finding their Lordships see no reason to interfere.

There remains, therefore, for consideration only the question of custom, and upon this the Court of first instance and the court of appeal have differed, the District Court holding that the custom was established, and the Court of the Judicial Commissioner of Sind deciding that it was not. It is from this latter decision that the present appeal proceeds.

Before proceeding to investigate the facts and circumstances that have influenced the two judgments already mentioned, it is desirable to make plain what is the position of a person like the plaintiff, who asserts that custom, and not Mahommedan law, gives him the rights he claims. The appellant alleges that, by s. 26 of Bombay Regulation IV of 1827, which has by notice been extended to the district of Sind, a presumption ought to be made in favour of the existence of a usage or custom where it is known that that usage or custom is prevalent. He bases this argument upon the words of the Regulation, which are as follows:

> The law to be observed in the trial of suits shall be Acts of Parliament and Regulations of Government applicable to the case; in the absence of such Acts and Regulations, the usage of the country in which the suit arose; if none such appears, the law of the defendant; and in the absence of specific law and usage, justice, equity, and good conscience alone.

Their Lordships cannot accept this view. In a case of *Daya Ram* v. *Sohel Singh*,[4] which related to proof of a Hindu custom, the Chief Court of the Punjab had to consider a similar question on the terms of s. 5 of the Punjab Laws Act, the words of which are more strictly in favour of the appellant's contention than those of the Regulation that governs this dispute. This contention was dealt with by Robertson, J. at p. 410 of the report in words which their Lordships think so aptly and expressly declare the true relation of the necessity of proof as between customary and established law that they may with advantage be reproduced. The learned judge said: 'In all cases it appears to me under this Act, it lies upon the person asserting that he is ruled in regard to a particular matter by custom, to prove that he is so governed, and not by personal law, and further, to prove what the particular custom is. There is no presumption created by the clause in favour of custom; on the contrary, it is only when the custom is established that it is to be the rule of decision. The Legislature did not show itself enamoured of custom rather than law, nor does it show any tendency to extend the 'principles' of custom to any matter to which a rule of custom is not clearly proved to apply. It is not the spirit of customary law, nor any theory of custom or deductions from other customs which is to be a rule of decision, but only 'any custom applicable to the parties concerned which is not . . .'; and it therefore appears to me clear that when either party to a suit sets up 'custom' as a rule of decision, it lies upon him to prove the custom which he seeks to apply; if he fails to do so, clause (b) of s. 5 of the Punjab Laws Act applies, and the rule of decision must be the personal law of the parties subject to the other provisions of the clause.'

The principle that underlies this statement is, in their Lordships' opinion, correct, and is applicable to the construction of the Regulation that governs the present case. It is therefore incumbent upon the plaintiff to allege and prove the custom on which he relies, and it becomes important to consider the nature and extent of the proof required. Their Lordships have carefully

4 (1906) PR No. 110.

considered the difficulty of applying all the strict rules that govern the establishment of custom in this country to circumstances which find no analogy here. Custom binding inheritance in a particular family has long been recognized in India (see *Soovendranath Roy* v. *Heeramonee Burmoneah*),[5] although such a custom is unknown to the law of this country, and is foreign to its spirit. Customs affecting descent in certain areas or customs affecting rights of inhabitants of a particular district are perhaps the nearest analogies in this country. But in England, if a custom were alleged as applicable to a particular district, and the evidence tendered in its support proved that the rights claimed had been enjoyed by people outside the district, the custom would fail. This principle, however, it seems to their Lordships, ought not to be applied in considering such a custom as the one claimed here, since, if the custom were in fact well established in one particular family, whether it were enjoyed or no by another family would not affect the question, since the custom might be independent in each case, and the evidence would not establish that the custom failed by reason of the inability to define the exact limits within which it was to be found when once it was established that, within certain and definite limits, it undoubtedly existed.

Nor are their Lordships prepared to accept without qualification the statement of the additional Judicial Commissioner, Mr H. N. Crouch, that it is necessary to reject as useless for proving the custom—

> [A]ll those instances where we have no evidence that the deceased left any estate at all, or where there is no evidence to show its nature or value, or the amount of liabilities against it, e.g., whether or not it consisted merely of a *jagir*, or *mafi* land, or of heirlooms, or of land heavily mortgaged, or of the family demesne; where there is no proof and no admission that the lady said to have been excluded had a legal claim to a share under the ordinary law; where, in case of a married lady, we have no evidence showing the actual amount of dowry received; where, in case of unmarried ladies, there is no proof that they knew of the custom and stood aside in obedience to it. And in all those cases where a witness states that he has himself excluded his own sisters, or nieces, our judgment as to the value of such statement as evidence of the custom having been enforced must be held in suspense until there is also evidence before us that the ladies had independent advice, and, with full and intelligent knowledge of the custom, voluntarily acquiesced in their exclusions.

An example of each of the conditions there laid down ought certainly to be established by some witness, but it is not, in their Lordships' opinion, necessary that all should be proved in every case, as this might greatly

5 (1868) 12 Moo IA 91.

weaken the evidence by tradition to which in a custom of the character under consideration great weight is due.

But, as pointed out by this Board in *Ramalakshmi Ammal* v. *Sivanantha Perumal Sethurayar*:[6]

> It is of the essence of special usages modifying the ordinary law of succession that they should be ancient and invariable: and it is further essential that they should be established to be so by clear and unambiguous evidence. It is only by means of such evidence that the courts can be assured of their existence, and that they possess the conditions of antiquity and certainty on which alone their legal title to recognition depends.

It is therefore necessary to define what is the custom, and then examine the evidence to see if it satisfies the conditions so laid down. It is urged against the appellant that he alleged the custom on which his case depends in three different forms: first, in the plaint filed on 12 July 1907, in which he asserted his rights as arising from current and immemorial custom of the dynasty of the parties; secondly, in an affidavit sworn by him on 10 July 1907, where he said that the custom was 'that a woman after her marriage loses all interest and right of inheritance in the property left by her relations (on the father's side)'; and finally in the plaint in the present proceedings, where the custom is asserted in these terms:

> But according to the custom regulating the inheritance by females in the family of the parties and amongst the respectable Balochis and Sardars, which is ancient and which is invariable, and has been acted upon from time immemorial, and which has obtained amongst Sunnis or Shias alike, a woman is entitled to her proper dowry according to the rank or status of the family, and she has no other rights of inheritance to the property of her paternal relations.

There certainly is a marked difference between these different customs, but their Lordships are not prepared to give this fact such weight as to crush the appellant's case, and they will assume that the custom upon which he relies is a custom by which, in the event of intestacy, daughters of the deceased are excluded in favour of their brothers, and sisters in favour of male paternal collaterals, and the question is, was such a custom proved?

A very large number of witnesses were called in its support, and a number of instances, amounting to sixty-one in all, were given as evidence of its operation. This evidence has been the subject of the most painstaking and careful analysis by both the courts, and has again been carefully considered by their Lordships with the assistance of the criticisms made,

6 (1872) 14 Moo IA 585.

both in the District Court and in the Court of the Judicial Commissioner. Upon the whole their Lordships think that this evidence fails to satisfy the necessary standard of proof and that upon this point the judgment of the court upon appeal must be accepted.

Their Lordships do not propose to examine again in detail each one of the instances mentioned, for there are one or two general observations which are, in their opinion, sufficient. The custom alleged, in its form most limited and best suited to the plaintiff's case, is a custom confined to the Talpur Mirs, the descendants of one Kaku Khan. These descendants are now represented by eight different families, namely, Sorabanis, Rustomanis, Bijranis, Shahdanis, Mahomedanis, Shahwanis, Jamanis, and Manikanis, of which the deceased belonged to the Shahdanis. Relevant and material instances are to be extracted from the descent of these families. The attempt to extend the custom to the 'respectable Balochis and Sardars' broke down, and it would in their Lordships' opinion, under any circumstance, have been unsafe to assume a custom applicable to a group of people so vaguely defined as those covered by the definition of 'respectable Balochis and Sardars.' Dealing, therefore, with the Talpur Mirs alone, their Lordships think the evidence is subject to the following comments:

In the first place, many of the instances relate to descendants of a ruling family and depend upon the eldest son inheriting to the exclusion of his brothers and sisters. Although it is true that the sisters are excluded, yet it is plain that we have not in these cases reached the custom on which the plaintiff relies, because in a ruling family an overriding custom has excluded all males as well as females in favour of the eldest male. Nine further cases relate to instances where the excluded daughters were unmarried and living with their brothers. These instances cannot be confidently relied upon. The position and relationship of the different members of the family must always be considered in determining whether claims are not met because the rights to which they relate do not exist, or whether they are put on one side because, in the circumstances, there is no need that they should be asserted. This is pointed out in the case of *Mirabivi* v. *Vellayanna*[7] by Turner, C. J. and Hutchins, J. It is there stated at p. 465:

> It must be admitted that instances have been adduced in which the claims of daughters and sisters to a share have been ignored, or they have been allotted maintenance, though the cases mentioned by the judge of a partition in the father's lifetime are not inconsistent with Mahommedan law. There are also cases in which married daughters have been treated as estranged from the family. But instances of this kind will be found to occur where there is no doubt that the family is governed

7 ILR 8 Mad 464.

by pure Mahommedan law. Indeed, in many parts of the country it is unusual for Mahommedan ladies to insist on their unquestioned rights. They will often prefer being maintained by their brothers to taking a separate share for themselves, and when they are married the marriage expenses and presents are often, by express or implied agreement, taken as equivalent to the share which they could claim. Moreover, Mahommedan females are so much under the influence of their male relations that the mere partition of the property among the males without reference to them cannot count for much.

With that statement their Lordships are in entire agreement.

In certain other instances there is no substantial evidence of property to be divided, and in the most recent cases of all there is only one witness who speaks in their support, although it is plain that there must have been others who could have spoken upon the matter. It ought not, of course, to be assumed that a custom fails because certain of the instances brought forward in its support may be referable to other causes than the custom relied upon; nor again, because in certain respects some of the witnesses may be found untrustworthy.

But there is one outstanding circumstance in the present case which their Lordships think demands attention. Mir Rustom Khan is the admitted head of the Rustomanis. He is a man of position and authority, and he says in plain terms that 'there is no such custom amongst our families by which daughters and sisters are excluded from inheritance. They get their share of inheritance according to Mahommedan law. [....]

In every case of this kind the burden of proof lies heavily upon the plaintiff, and, though his evidence may consist of a number of striking instances in support of his case, it receives a severe blow when prominent members of the families concerned deny that the custom exists.

There is also another piece of evidence which is of considerable value: this is to be found in the revenue records which relate to the descent of the property of Mir Ghulam Ali Khan, who died leaving three widows, one sister, two daughters, and a brother; one of these records, dated October, 1903, shows a clear division according to the Mahommedan law, and not according to any such custom as is alleged. There are no other revenue records produced, and it is said that the reason of their non-production is that they do not assist the defendants' case. But their Lordships think the omission is serious. The best evidence associated with any such custom as that alleged would be found in connection with the division of land, and these records would at least have established the fact that land was left, its extent and character, and would, were it the fact, make clear the point which the evidence leaves uncertain, that, in the division of this property, the women were excluded. [....]

The ground upon which their Lordships base their judgment does not include any such considerations: it is their opinion that, although there is much reason in history for the custom alleged, and some evidence by which it receives support, yet on the whole the evidence has fallen short of the standard to which it must attain in order to succeed in altering the devolution of property according to Mahommedan law to a devolution determined by a family custom, and they will accordingly humbly advise His Majesty that this appeal should be dismissed with costs.

◊ UPDATE ◊

1. *Application of custom in general*

In all parts of the subcontinent the decisions in the old cases of *Ghasiti* and *Abdul Hussain* [Cases 8 and 9], relating to custom and usage, can now be applied to the Muslims only subject to the provisions of the legislation regulating the application of Muslim law, viz., the Muslim Personal Law (Shariat) Application Act 1937 in India and Bangladesh and the Muslim Personal Law (Shariat) Application Act 1962 in Pakistan.

In India the scope of the Muslim Personal Law (Shariat) Application Act 1937 has been greatly extended by legislation in the three southern States. Being a central law, this Act could not have applied to agricultural lands which were at the time of its enactment, and remain, a State subject. Hence Section 2 of the Act, which made Muslim law applicable to the Muslims in all matters relating to family relations and inheritance, had exempted from its scope succession to agricultural lands. This exemption has now been done away with in Tamil Nadu, Andhra Pradesh and Kerala by State legislation, making custom and usage relating to inheritance in derogation of Muslim law unenforceable also in matters of succession to agricultural lands. See the Muslim Personal Law (Shariat) Application (Madras Amendment) Act 1949 [now in force in Tamil Nadu and Andhra Pradesh] and the Muslim Personal Law (Shariat) Application (Kerala Amendment) Act 1963.

For a case decided by the Supreme Court on the implications of the first of these amending Acts see *C Mohammad Yunus* v. *Syedunnisa* (1962) 1 SCR 67, in which the court pointed out the binding nature of the provision of the Act relating to the application of Muslim law by the courts in all matters mentioned in Section 2.

Section 3 of the Act of 1937 enables Muslims to ensure application of Muslim law in respect of adoption, wills and legacies by means of individual declarations to that effect. This provision of the Act remains unaffected by the South Indian amending laws.

In Pakistan, by virtue of a new Shariat Act no custom in derogation of Muslim law can now be pleaded by a Muslim in any matter relating to family relations (including adoption) and succession (including wills and legacies). See the Muslim Personal Law (Shariat) Application Act 1962, now read with the Enforcement of Shari'ah Act 1991.

2. *Specific Customs*

The rule stated in the old Privy Council decision in *Abdul Hussein* [Case 9], under which the plea of a custom excluding women from inheritance had failed merely for want of evidence, cannot be followed now anywhere in the subcontinent in view of the specific legislation directing the courts to apply Muslim law in matters of inheritance.

In India, in *Mohammad Sandhukhan* v. *Ratnam* AIR 1958 Mad 144 it was held by the Madras High Court that even if there is any room for applying custom, the courts would refuse to do so if the custom in question merely excludes women from inheritance.

In the Indian case of *Moulvi Mohammad* v. *Mohaboob Begum* AIR 1984 Mad 7 a custom allowing succession rights to an adopted child was upheld by the Madras High Court, holding that:

> The Shariat Act has ruled out custom or usage with reference to the enumerated subjects in section 2 thereof and enables the Muslims to rule out custom or usage with regard to three more subjects referred to in section 3 (1). Adoption as such is not one of the enumerated subjects in section 2. Adoption is not necessarily inheritance or succession, although it may lead to inheritance and succession. It is not the case of the petitioners that any declaration under section 3 (1) was made by anyone concerned in the instant case so as to rule out custom or usage on the question of adoption. Hence it cannot be said that there could not be a plea and proof of custom relating to adoption at all in the instant case, if in fact there was and is such a custom prevailing as claimed by the respondent. In the said circumstances it is possible to proceed on the basis that there can be a custom or usage having the force of law with regard to adoption.

In Pakistan, the custom of excluding women from inheritance continues to prevail in certain regions of the country—under various devices like family arrangement, ouster and adverse possession—in disregard of the provisions of the Muslim Personal Law (Shariat) Application Act 1962. In *Ghulam Ali* v. *Ghulam Sarwar Naqvi* PLD 1990 SC 1 the Supreme Court forcefully held that any such custom or practice is illegal and not enforceable by law:

> The Holy Prophet declared some important rights of females vis a vis males. It is against the spirit of those rights to hold that a brother can legally claim 'adverse possession' against his sister and much less 'ouster'. Under the new dispensation in Pakistan such a claim may not be entertainable at all without encountering jurisprudential hurdles… The females cannot be treated so in our system.

V. Marriage

10. Abdul Kadir v. Salima
(1886) 8 All 149 (FB)

Marriage defined—nature of dower—unpaid dower—restitution of Conjugal rights—Juristic conflict

A Hanafi husband brought a suit for restitution of conjugal rights. The defendant pleaded that the suit was not maintainable as the *maher* (dower) was not paid; whereupon the plaintiff deposited the whole amount in court. The wife also pleaded cruelty and divorce: both the allegations were found to be false.

Held that, as the wife had cohabited with her husband for three months after her marriage, and there was no evidence of demand by the wife of her unpaid dower, the husband was entitled to restitution.

This is a well-known case in the law of marriage, in which Mahmood J. made a number of observations, most of which have been incorporated in Muhammadan law as received in the subcontinent, but some have also been criticized and rejected in later decisions.

The observations may be summarized as follows:

(i) the nature of Islamic marriage;

(ii) the husband's liability to pay dower;

(iii) matrimonial rights of husband and wife, and

(iv) general rules for the guidance of the courts.

I. Marriage in Islam is a purely civil contract. This is discussed and criticized in *Outlines,* 85 seqq.

II. Dower is money or property promised by the husband to be paid to the wife in consideration of marriage. It is a token of love and respect, and not the price of connubial intercourse. The wife has the right to deny herself to the husband so long as the dower remains unpaid. But once the marriage has been duly consummated, her right is lost (Abū Yūsuf and Imām Muhammad, *contra* Abū Hanīfa). Criticized but followed by Sulaiman, CJ in *Anis Begam* v. *Muhammad Istafa* (1933) 55 All 743.

III. The mutual rights regarding consortium need not be specifically dealt with, as they can be understood and realized from the general discussion.

IV. As a general rule, an action for restitution of conjugal rights can be filed in India as a civil suit. For restitution, see generally *Outlines*, 115 seqq., and *Itwari* v. *Asghari*, Case 17, infra.

The plaintiff in this suit claimed restitution of conjugal rights. The parties to the suit were Sunni Muhammadans governed by the Hanafi law. The plaintiff was married to the defendant Salima on 5 March 1883, and her dower was fixed without any specification as to whether it was to be partly or wholly prompt or deferred. She cohabited with her husband, the plaintiff, up to 15 June 1883, when she went on a visit to her father, the defendant Chimman. On 28 June 1883 the plaintiff instituted the present suit on the allegation that he requested Chimman to allow Salima to return to cohabitation with him, but that Chimman 'flatly refused to comply with the plaintiff's request and obstructed him in bringing the defendant Salima with him'; that the defendant Salima had 'been won over by the defendant Chimman to his own side'; and that the plaintiff's wife, the defendant Salima, was 'not therefore willing to come with the plaintiff'. Upon these allegations the plaintiff prayed that 'the defendant Chimman be ordered to send the defendant Salima with the plaintiff, and not to interfere with the latter in bringing her with him, and the defendant Salima be also ordered to come with the plaintiff and live with him as his wife.'

To the suit so instituted two separate defences were made on one and the same day, 24 July 1883.

The defendant Chimman simply protested against being impleaded in the suit, stating that he 'never refused to send Salima to her husband's house,' that she was 'herself wise and major' and could form a judgment as to her own interests.'

The defendant Salima raised three main pleas in defence: First, that she had been irrevocably divorced by the plaintiff, and was therefore no longer his wife; secondly, that 'notwithstanding the divorce, the plaintiff had not paid the defendant's dower,' so that, 'even if the plaintiff had not repudiated the defendant, he was not competent to bring his suit so long as he did not satisfy her dower-debt'; and thirdly, that the plaintiff had treated her with cruelty, and she was therefore in fear of grave personal injury.

In this stage of the case the plaintiff deposited the whole dower-money in court on the 20 August 1883; and the court of first instance (Munsif of Mirzapur), having examined the evidence produced on either side, held that the allegations set up in defence were not proved; that the nature of dower not having been 'specified at the time of marriage, only a part of the dower becomes, under the Muhammadan law, payable on demand'; that 'before the institution of the suit, the dower was never demanded by the defendant';

that 'the defendant having insisted on payment of the dower, the plaintiff has paid the money into court'; and that such payment under the circumstances of the case entitled the plaintiff 'to succeed in his claim for bringing his wife to his house.'

Upon appeal by both the defendants, the lower appellate court (District Judge of Mirzapur), relying upon certain rulings, and without going into the merits of the case as to the pleas regarding divorce and cruelty, held that 'the whole of the dower is to be considered as prompt' under the Muhammadan law, and that 'payment into court after institution of the suit was insufficient, because the husband had no cause of action at the time when he brought his suit.' Upon this ground the District Judge, decreeing the appeal, dismissed the suit *in toto*.

The plaintiff appealed to the High Court, impugning the view of the Muhammadan law taken by the lower appellate court. The appeal came on for hearing before Oldfield and Mahmood, JJ., who, having regard to the rulings of the court in *Sheikh Abdool Shukkoar* v. *Raheem-un-nissa*,[2] *Wilayat Husain* v. *Allah Rakhi*,[3] and *Nazir Khan* v. *Umrao*,[4] referred to the Full Bench the question 'whether, under the circumstances of this case, the plaintiff had the right to maintain the suit.'

Petheram, C. J. observed while delivering the judgment:

This case was argued before the Full Bench on 26 March, 1885, when the Judges constituting the court were the same as now, except that Mr Justice Mahmood was officiating for Mr Justice Tyrrell. Mr Justice Mahmood has now left the court, but we have had the advantage of his written opinion, which we adopt and deliver as the judgment of the court.

Judgment [Mahmood, J, *adopted by Full Bench*][1]

The question raised by this reference is one not free from difficulty, arising partly from the manner in which the subject has been dealt with in the textbooks of Muhammadan law, and partly from the *ratio decidendi* adopted in some of the reported cases which I shall presently refer to and discuss. But before doing so, I consider it necessary to recapitulate the facts of this case, so far as they are required for the purposes of answering this reference.

[. . .]

The plaintiff has preferred this second appeal impugning the view of the Muhammadan law taken by the lower appellate Court, and the question

1 C. Petheram, CJ and Straight, Oldfield, Brodhurst, & Tyrrell, JJ.
2 NWPE, HR 1874, p. 94.
3 ILR 2 All 831.
4 *Weekly Notes*, 1882, p. 96.

raised by the contention of the parties is one the decision of which will affect the domestic family life of the Muhammadan community. It therefore falls essentially within the purview of s. 24 of the Bengal Civil Courts Act (VI of 1871), which binds us to adhere to the rules of Muhammadan law in determining such questions. The clause is a reproduction of s. 15, Bengal Regulation IV of 1793. Referring to that clause, the Lords of the Privy Council, in *Moonshee Buzloor Ruheem* v. *Shums-oon-nissa Begum*,[5] which was a suit for restitution of conjugal rights by a Muhammadan against his wife, made certain observations which furnish the guiding principle upon which such cases should be determined. After quoting certain passages from the judgment of the learned Judges of the Calcutta High Court their Lordships went on to say:

> 'The passages just quoted, if understood in their literal sense, imply that cases of this kind are to be decided without reference to the Muhammadan law, but according to what is termed "equity and good conscience", i.e., according to that which the Judge may think the principles of natural justice require to be done in the particular case. Their Lordships most emphatically dissent from that conclusion. It is, in their opinion, opposed to the whole policy of the law in British India, . . . and they can conceive nothing more likely to give just alarm to the Muhammadan community than to learn by a judicial decision, that their law, the application of which has been thus secured to them, is to be over-ridden upon a question which so materially concerns their domestic relations. The judges were not dealing with a case in which the Muhammadan law was in plain conflict with the general municipal law, or with the requirements of a more advanced and civilized society, as for instance if a Mussulman had insisted on the right to slay his wife taken in adultery. In the reports of our Ecclesiastical Courts there is no lack of cases in which a humane man, judging according to his own senses of what is just and fair, without reference to positive law, would let the wife go free; and yet, the proof falling short of legal cruelty, the Judge has felt constrained to order her to return to her husband' (pp. 614–15).

I have quoted the passage at such length, because it has come within my notice that vague and variable notions of the rule of 'justice, equity and good conscience' are sometimes regarded as affecting the administration of native laws in such matters to a degree not justified or necessitated by the general municipal law applicable to all persons, irrespective of their race or religion: and applying the observations of the Lords of the Privy Council to the present case, I have no doubt that this case must be decided according to the rules of Muhammadan law, the order of the court, whatever it may be, being, of course, subject to such rules as the exigencies of the general municipal law may require.

[5] 11 Moo IA 551.

In this view of the case the reference cannot, in my opinion, be satisfactorily answered without considering, first, the exact nature and effect of marriage under the Muhammadan law upon the contracting parties; secondly, the exact nature of the liability of the husband to pay the dower; thirdly, the matrimonial rights of the parties as to conjugal cohabitation; and fourthly, the rules of the general law as to the decree of court in such cases.

But, as preliminary to the consideration of these various points, I may observe that a suit for restitution of conjugal rights is a suit 'of a civil nature,' within the meaning of s. 11 of the Civil Procedure Code, and this view is supported by the terms of articles 34 and 35, sch. ii, Limitation Act (XV of 1877), and the provisions of s. 260 of the Code itself. To quote the language of the Privy Council in the case already referred to,

'upon authority, then, as well as principle, their Lordships have no doubt that the Mussulman husband may institute a suit in the Civil Courts of India for a declaration of his right to the possession of his wife, and for a sentence that she return to cohabitation; and that that suit must be determined according to the principles of the Muhammadan law' (p. 610).

What, then, are the rules of the Muhammadan law upon the first three points which I have already enumerated? I will deal with each of those points separately, and in doing so will refer to the important rulings which constitute the case law upon the subject.

In dealing with the first point, I adopt the language employed in the Tagore Law Lectures (1873) in saying that—

Marriage among Muhammadans is not a sacrament, but purely a civil contract; and though it is solemnized generally with recitation of certain verses from the Quran, yet the Muhammadan law does not positively prescribe any service peculiar to the occasion. That it is a civil contract is manifest from the various ways and circumstances in and under which marriages are contracted or presumed to have been contracted. And though a civil contract, it is not positively prescribed to be reduced to writing, but the validity and operation of the whole are made to depend upon the declaration or proposal of the one, and the acceptance or consent of the other, of the contracting parties, or of their natural and legal guardians before competent and sufficient witnesses; as also upon the restrictions imposed, and certain of the conditions, required to be abided by according to the peculiarity of the case (p. 291).

That this is an accurate summary of the Muhammadan law is shown by the best authorities, and Mr Baillie, at page 4 of his *Digest*, relying upon the texts of the *Kanz*, the *Kifayah*, and the *Inayah*, has well summarized the law:

Marriage is a contract which has for its design or object the right of enjoyment and the procreation of children. But it was also instituted for the solace of life, and is one of the prime or original necessities of man. It is therefore lawful in extreme old age after hope of offspring has ceased, and even in the last or death illness. The pillars of marriage, as of other contracts, are *Eejab-o-kubool*, or declaration and acceptance. The first speech, from whichever side it may proceed, is the declaration, and the other the acceptance.

The *Hedaya* lays down the same rule as to the constitution of the marriage contract, and Mr Hamilton has rightly translated the original text:

Marriage is contracted—that is to say, is effected and legally confirmed—by means of declaration and consent, both expressed in the preterite. [Arabic text: *Cases*, 108]

These authorities leave no doubt as to what constitutes marriage in law, and it follows that, the moment the legal contract is established, consequences flow from it naturally and imperatively as provided by the Muhammadan law. I have said enough as to the nature of the contract of marriage, and in describing its necessary legal effects I cannot do better than resort to the original text of the *Fatawa-i-Alamgiri* which Mr Baillie has translated, in the form of paraphrase, at page 13 of his *Digest*, but which I shall translate here literally, adopting Mr Baillie's phraseology as far as possible:

The legal effects of marriage are that it legalizes the enjoyment of either of them (husband and wife) with the other in the manner which in this matter is permitted by the law; and it subjects the wife to the power of restraint, that is, she becomes prohibited from going out and appearing in public; it renders her dower, maintenance, and raiment obligatory on him; and establishes on both sides the prohibitions of affinity and the rights of inheritance, and the obligatoriness of justness between the wives and their rights, and on her it imposes submission to him when summoned to the couch; and confers on him the power of correction when she is disobedient or rebellious, and enjoins upon him associating familiarly with her with kindness and courtesy. It renders unlawful the conjunction of two sisters (as wives) and of those who fall under the same category. [Arabic text: *Cases*, 109]

That this conception of the mutual rights and obligations arising from marriage between the husband and wife bears in all main features close similarity to the Roman law and other European systems which are derived from that law cannot, in my opinion, be doubted; and even regarding the power of correction, the English law seems to resemble the Muhammadan, for even under the former 'the old authorities say the husband may beat his wife;' and if in modern times the rigour of the law has been mitigated, it is because in England, as in this country, the criminal law has happily stepped in to give the wife personal security which the matrimonial law does not. To use the language of the Lords of the Privy Council in the case already cited:

> The Muhammadan law, on a question of what is legal cruelty between man and wife, would probably not differ materially from our own, of which one of the most recent expositions is the following: 'There must be actual violence of such a character as to endanger personal health or safety, or there must be a reasonable apprehension of it.' 'The court', as Lord Stowell said, in *Evans* v. *Evans*, 'has never been driven off this ground', (pp. 611–12).

Now the legal effects of marriage, as enumerated in the *Fatawa-i-Alamgiri*, come into operation as soon as the contract of marriage is completed by proposal and acceptance; their initiation is simultaneous, and there is no authority in the Muhammadan law for the proposition that any or all of them are dependent upon any condition precedent as to the payment of dower by the husband to the wife.

This leads me to the consideration of the second point, upon which the greatest stress has been laid in the argument at the bar. It was contended by the learned pleader for the respondent that, under the Muhammadan law, the wife's dower is regarded as nothing more or less than price for connubial intercourse, and that the right of cohabitation does not therefore accrue to the husband till he has paid the dower to the wife. The argument, so urged, renders it convenient to deal with the third point along with the second.

I have already shown that, under the Muhammadan law, the right of cohabitation comes into existence at the same time and by reason of the same incident of law as the right of dower. That the latter may modify and affect the former cannot be doubted: how it affects and modifies it is the main subject of this reference. Dower, under the Muhammadan law, is a sum of money or other property promised by the husband to be paid or delivered to the wife in consideration of the marriage, and even where no dower is expressly fixed or mentioned at the marriage ceremony, the law confers the right of dower upon the wife as a necessary effect of marriage. To use the language of the *Hedaya*:

> The payment of dower is enjoined by the law merely as a token of respect for its object (the woman), wherefore the mention of it is not absolutely essential to the validity of a marriage; and, for the same reason, a marriage is also valid, although the man were to engage in the contract on the special condition that there should be no dower (Hamilton's *Hedaya* by Grady, p. 44).

Even after the marriage the amount of dower may be increased by the husband during coverture (Baillie's *Digest*, p. 111); and indeed in this, as in some other respects, the dower of the Muhammadan law bears a strong resemblance to the *donatio propter nuptias* of the Romans which has subsisted in the English law under the name of marriage settlement. In this sense and in no other can dower under the Muhammadan law be regarded as the consideration for the connubial intercourse, and if the authors of the Arabic text-books of Muhammadan law have compared it to price in the contract of sale, it is simply because marriage is a civil contract under that law, and sale is the typical contract which Muhammadan jurists are accustomed to refer to in illustrating the incidents of other contracts by analogy. Such being the nature of the dower, the rules which regulate its payment are necessarily affected by the position of a married woman under the Muhammadan law. Under that law marriage does not make her property the property of the husband, nor does coverture impose any disability upon her as to freedom of contract. The marriage contract is easily dissoluble, and the freedom of the divorce and the rule of polygamy place a power in the hands of the husband which the Lawgiver intended to restrain by rendering the rules as to payments of dower stringent upon the husband. No limit as to the amount of dower has been imposed, and it may either be prompt, that is immediately payable upon demand, or deferred, that is payable upon the dissolution of marriage, whether by death or divorce. The dower may also be partly prompt and partly deferred; but when at the time of the marriage ceremony no specification in this respect is made, the whole dower is presumed to be prompt and due on demand [*Mirza Bedar Bakht Mahomed Ali Bahadoor* v. *Mirza Khurrum Bakht Yahya Ali Khan Bahadoor*[6]]. The question when such dower becomes payable was discussed by the Lords of the Privy Council in *Malleeka* v. *Jameela*[7] and in *Ranee Khajooroonissa* v. *Ranee Ryeesoonissa*[8] and in the former of these cases their Lordships approved the rule laid down by the Sadr Diwani Adalat of these provinces in *Nawab Buhadoor Jung Khan* v. *Uzeez Begum*,[9] wherein the court considered 'the nature of the exigible dower to be that of a debt payable generally on demand after the date of the contract, which forms the basis of the obligations, and payable at any period during the life of the husband, on which that demand shall be actually made, and therefore until the demand be actually made and refused, the ground of an action at law cannot properly be said to have arisen.' These rulings leave no doubt that although prompt dower may be demanded at any time after the marriage, the wife is under no obligation to make such demand at any specified time during coverture, and that it is only upon making such demand that it

6 2 Suth. PCJ 823.
7 LR Sup. Vol. IA 135; 11 BLR 375.
8 LR 2 IA 325; 5 BLR 84.
9 NWP SDAR 1843–6, p. 180.

becomes payable in the sense of performance being rendered in fulfilment of an obligation.

The right of dower confers another right upon the Muhammadan wife, and the nature of this second right is described in the *Hedaya* in a passage on which the learned pleader for the respondent has relied for his contention. The passage is to be found in Grady's edition of Hamilton's *Hedaya*, at page 54; but as the translation is not sufficiently close, and is moreover interpolated with paraphrases. I translate the original text here literally, since much depends upon the exact meaning of the passage:

It is the wife's right that she may deny herself to her husband until she receive the dower, and she may prevent him from taking her away (that is, travelling with her), so that her right in the return may be fixed in the same manner as that of the husband in the object of the return and become like sale. And it is not for the husband that he may prevent her from travelling or going out of his house and visiting her friends until he has paid the whole exigible dower, because the right of restraint is for securing fulfilment (of his right) to the rightful person, and he has not the right to securing fulfilment before rendering fulfilment (himself); and if the whole dower is deferred, it is not for her to deny herself because of her having dropped her right by deferring it, as in sale. And in this matter Abu Yusuf holds the contrary opinion. And if the husband has retired with her, the same would be the answer according to Abu Hanifa: but the two disciples have said she has not the right to deny herself, and the difference of opinion subsists where there is retirement with her consent; but if she was forced or an infant or insane, her right of denying herself does not drop according to the unanimous opinion of our doctors. [Arabic text: *Cases*, 112–13]

Another passage to be found in the *Dur-ru-l Mukhtar* has also been cited by the learned pleader for the respondent, and I translate it here before considering the exact effect of these authorities upon the present case:

It is the wife's right to prevent the husband from connubial intercourse, and that which is implied therein, and from journeying with her, even though after connubial intercourse and retirement to which she has consented, because all connubial intercourse has been contracted with her, and the rendering of some does not imperatively require the rendering of the rest. This right is for the purpose of obtaining what has been stated as prompt dower, whether wholly or partly. [Arabic text: *Cases*, 113]

Relying upon these passages, the learned pleader for the respondents contends that the right of cohabitation does not accrue to the husband at all until he has paid the prompt dower, and that, inasmuch as the plaintiff in the present case had not paid the dower to his wife, defendant No. 2, her refusal to cohabit with him did not afford a cause of action for a suit for restitution of conjugal rights. In support of this contention certain reported cases have been cited, which I wish to notice here. In *Sheikh Abdool*

Shukkoar v. *Raheem-oon-nissa*[10] it was held that a suit will not lie by a Muhammadan to enforce the return of his wife to his house, even after consummation with consent, until her prompt dower has been paid. The rule was followed to its fullest extent in *Wilayat Husain* v. *Allah Rakhi*[11] and in *Nasrat Husain* v. *Hamidan*,[12] and in the former of these cases it was held that a Muhammadan cannot maintain a suit against his wife for restitution of conjugal rights, even after such consummation with consent as is proved by cohabitation for five years, where the wife's dower is prompt and has not been paid. In *Eidan* v. *Mazhar Husain*,[13] where the suit prayed for restitution of conjugal rights, and the defendant in her written statement having claimed dower, the lower appellate Court, setting aside the decree of the first court, decreed the claim conditional upon payment of prompt dower, this court upheld the decree by a judgment which is silent upon the specific question whether the dower not having been paid before suit, the plaintiff had the right to come into court with such a prayer. In *Nazir Khan* v. *Umrao*,[14] however, a Division Bench of this court upheld the decree of the lower appellate court, which had dismissed the suit *in toto*, reversing the decree of the court of first instance, which had passed a decree in favour of the plaintiff (husband) conditional upon his paying the prompt dower. The ruling is in full accord with the *ratio decidendi* adopted in the case of *Sheikh Abdool Shukkoar*,[15] which appears to be the leading case upon the point under consideration, so far as this court is concerned. No ruling of any other High Court was cited at the hearing in support of the respondents' contention except the case of *Jaun Beebee* v. *Sheikh Munshee Beparee*[16] which does not appear to me to be decisive on either side of the contentions raised in the case. The ruling of this court in *Sheikh Abdool Shukkoar* v. *Raheem-oon-nissa* is, therefore, the only leading case upon the subject, but, with due deference, I am unable to agree in the rule there laid down.

The texts cited by the learned pleader for the respondents undoubtedly show, what is a well-recognized rule of the Muhammadan law of marriage, that the marriage contract having been completed and its legal effects having been established, the right of claiming prompt dower comes into existence in favour of the wife, and that she can use such a claim as a means of obtaining payment of the dower and as a defence for resisting a claim

10 NWP HCR 1874, p. 94.
11 ILR 2 All 831.
12 ILR 4 All 205.
13 ILR 1 All 483.
14 *Weekly Notes*, 1882, p. 96.
15 NWP HCR, 1874, p. 94.
16 WRCR 93.

for cohabitation on the part of the husband against her consent. And when I say this, I put the case in favour of the respondents in its strongest possible light, for even upon this question in cases where cohabitation has taken place, the conflict of authority is too great to render it an undoubted proposition of the Muhammadan law. The learned Judges in the case to which I have just referred seem to have appreciated this difficulty, but preferred to adopt the view of Imam Abu Hanifa in preference to the concurrent opinions of his two eminent disciples, Qazi Abu Yusuf and Imam Muhammad, notwithstanding the fact that a passage was cited to them from the *Durr-ul-Mukhtar* in support of the view that 'where on such a point there is a difference between Abu Hanifa and his disciples, the opinion of the latter should prevail.' Both Imam Abu Hanifa and Imam Muhammad were purely speculative jurisconsults, who spent their lives in extracting legal principles from the traditional sayings of the Prophet; but Qazi Abu Yusuf, whilst equally versed in traditional lore, had, in his position as Chief Justice of the Empire of the Khalifa Harun-ul-Rashid, the advantage of applying legal principles to the actual conditions of human life, and his *dicta* (especially in temporal matters) command such high respect in the interpretation of Muhammadan law, that whenever either Imam Abu Hanifa or Imam Muhammad agrees with him, his opinion is accepted by a well-understood rule of construction. But before proceeding any further, I wish to quote a passage from the celebrated *Fatawa Qazi Khan,* a text-book as high in authority as the *Durr-ul-Mukhtar:*

> A wife, having surrendered herself to her husband before the fulfilment (i.e., payment) of dower, subsequently denies herself (to him) for securing fulfilment of the dower. She has this right in the opinion of Abu Hanifa; but Abu Yusuf and Imam Muhammad maintain that she has not the right of prohibiting him from connubial intercourse, and doubts have arisen in regard to their opinions as to the power of preventing her from journeying. And according to the opinion of Abul Qasim As-Saffar it is her right that she may prevent him from taking her on a journey. [Arabic text: *Cases*, 115]

But the best summary of the law is to be found in the latest authoritative work on the Muhammadan law, the *Fatawa-i-Alamgiri* in a passage which Mr Baillie has translated somewhat briefly at pages 124–5 of his celebrated *Digest*. The passage being the most complete exposition of the law upon the subject, I translate it here myself as closely as possible, from the original text itself:

> In all places, when the husband has had connubial intercourse with her, or validly retired with her, the whole dower is confirmed. If she intends to deny herself to him for securing fulfilment (i.e. payment) of her exigible dower, it is her right to do so

according to Imam Abu Hanifa; but this is opposed to the opinions of his two disciples (Qazi Abu Yusuf and Imam Muhammad), and in like manner the husband cannot prevent her from going out or travelling or going on a voluntary pilgrimage, according to Abu Hanifa, except when she goes out in an indecent manner. As to her right to all this before she has surrendered herself (consummation), there is unanimity of opinion, as there is as to the rule when the husband has had connubial intercourse with her whilst she is a minor or has been forced or insane, in which cases her father might refuse to surrender her until the payment of her prompt dower—so in the *Itabiyyah*. And if the husband has had connubial intercourse with her or retired with her with her consent, it is her right to refuse herself to go on a journey until payment of her whole dower according to the written engagement, or the prompt part of it according to the custom of our country. This view is according to Abu Hanifa, but his two disciples maintain that she has no such right, and the Shaikh-ul-Imam, the jurisconsult, the pious Abul Qasim As-Saffar, was accustomed to decide according to Abu Hanifa, so far as going on a journey is concerned; but in the matter of refusing herself, he used to decide according to the opinions of the two disciples, and several of our learned doctors have approved of this distinction. [Arabic text: *Cases*, 116]

Having cited these various passages from text-books of the highest authority upon the Muhammadan law, I proceed to consider the exact effect they have upon the present case. And here I have to point out that in this case the court of first instance found that no demand for dower had been made by the wife (defendant No. 2) before the institution of the suit, and that she had already cohabited with her husband, the plaintiff, and there is no question that she had attained majority when she was married. These matters were not dealt with by the lower appellate Court, which decided the case upon the preliminary point, and they may be taken to be so for the purposes of this reference.

I have already said enough to show that the right of dower does not precede the right of cohabitation which the contract of marriage necessarily involves, but that the two rights come into existence simultaneously and by reason of the same incident of law. The right of the wife to claim maintenance from her husband arises in the same manner as one of the legal effects of marriage, and to say that any of those effects are not simultaneously created by the contract of marriage amounts, in my opinion, to a violation of the fundamental notions of jurisprudence regarding correlative rights and obligations arising from one and the same perfected legal relation. Indeed, so far as the question now under consideration is concerned, the rules of Muhammadan law leave no doubt when that system of law is consulted as a whole and not upon isolated points. The fact of the marriage gives birth to the right of cohabitation not only in favour of the husband but also in favour of the wife, and to say that the payment of dower is a condition precedent to the vestiture of the right, is to hold that a relationship, of which the rights and obligations are essentially correlative, may come into existence at one time for one party and another time for the other party. If the payment of dower were a condition precedent to the initiation of the right of cohabitation, a Muhammadan wife, having quarrelled with her husband, could not sue him for cohabitation till she had in a previous litigation sued and, obtaining a decree, realized her dower, because, *ex hypothesi*, her right of cohabitation with her husband would be dependent for its coming into existence upon the payment of her dower. Yet such is the logical result of the argument pressed upon us on behalf of the respondents. Such, however, is not the rule of the Muhammadan law, and even the passages which have been cited on behalf of the respondents do not support any such proposition. The passage in the *Hedaya*, which I have closely translated from the original Arabic text, no doubt entitles the wife to resist the claim of the husband for cohabitation with her by pleading the non-payment of her prompt dower, but it proceeds essentially upon the assumption that his right to put forward such a claim is antecedent to the plea. In the passage itself he is called 'the rightful person,' and the impediment to the enforcement of his right of cohabitation with his wife is stated to be the non-payment of her prompt dower, a rule which, having been borrowed from the Muhammadan law of sale, is based simply upon the analogy of the lien which the vendor possesses upon the goods for payment of the price before delivery. The rule is simply analogical, and giving to it its fullest scope, it falls far short of maintaining the proposition upon which the argument for the respondents rests. The passage from the *Durr-ul-Mukhtar*, following the analogy of sale even further, expressly lays down that the right of the wife to resist the husband's claim for cohabitation is intended to be for the purpose of realizing her prompt dower. The same is the effect of the passage which I have cited from the *Fatawa Qazi Khan* and the *Fatawa Alamgiri*, and the rule, as stated by the Muhammadan jurists, bears, in the eye of jurisprudence, the strongest possible analogy to the ordinary rule of the law of sale, which has been best stated in s. 95 of the Indian Contract Act (IX of 1872), namely, that 'unless a contrary intention appears by the contract, a seller has a lien on sold goods as long as they remain in his possession and the price or any part of it remains unpaid.' The same is the principle upon which, in the law of sale, the right of stoppage *in transitu* is based, and the lien which the vendor has amounts to nothing more or less than the definition given by Grose, J., in *Hammonds* v. *Barclay*,[17] that it is 'a right in one man to retain that which

[17] East 227.

is in his possession belonging to another till certain demands of him, the person in possession, are satisfied.' But this lien essentially presumes the right of ownership in the vendee, and terminates as soon as delivery has taken place. I have followed up the analogy of sale so far, because nearly the whole argument of the learned pleader for the respondents proceeded upon the circumstance that in the passages, which he cited, marriage has been compared to sale, dower to the price, and surrender of the wife to her husband to delivery of goods in the law of sale.

But to return to the passages which I have quoted from the *Fatawa Qazi Khan* and the *Fatawa Alamgiri*, it is apparent that the sole object of the rule which entitles the wife to resist cohabitation is to enable her to secure payment of her prompt dower. And it is equally apparent from those passages that the opinion of Imam Abu Hanifa is contradicted, not only by his two eminent disciples, Qazi Abu Yusuf and Imam Muhammad, but also by Shaikh Assaffar so far as the question of cohabitation is concerned. Imam Abu Hanifa and his two disciples are known in the Hanafi school of Muhammadan law as 'the three Masters,' and I take it as a general rule of interpreting that law, that whenever there is a difference of opinion, the opinion of the two will prevail against the opinion of the third. Now, bearing this in mind, it is clear that the two disciples of Imam Abu Hanifa, regarding the surrender of the wife to her husband as bearing analogy to delivery of goods in sale, held that the lien of the wife for her dower, as a plea for resisting cohabitation, ceased to exist after consummation. According to the ordinary rule of interpreting Muhammadan law, I adopt the opinion of the two disciples as representing the majority of 'the three Masters,' and hold that, after consummation of marriage, non-payment of dower, even though exigible, cannot be pleaded in defence of an action for restitution of conjugal rights; the rule so laid down having, of course, no effect upon the right of the wife to claim her dower in a separate action.

But the rule enunciated by me need not be applied in its fullest extent to the present case, because here, in the first place, it has not been found that the wife ever demanded her dower before the suit was filed, or that she declined to cohabit with her husband the plaintiff upon the ground that her dower had not been paid. She relied upon allegations of divorce and cruelty, both of which were found by the court of first instance to be untrue, and upon these findings I hold that she had no defence to the action. The plaintiff, as I have already shown, acquired by the very fact of the marriage the right of cohabitation; he was not bound to pay the dower before it was demanded, and upon the findings of the first court, the first intimation which he had of such demand was the written defence of his wife (defendant No. 2) in the course of this unfortunate litigation. And upon intimation of such a demand, he actually brought the money into court and deposited it for payment to his wife, the defendant No. 2, as her dower. Under such circumstances, the view of the learned District Judge, which follows the rulings to which he has referred, simply amounts to saying that the plaintiff must institute another suit like the present for enforcing the same remedy. I have already said that the present suit, bearing in mind the conjugal rights created by the Muhammadan law, was not premature, and the view of the learned District Judge can only have the effect of circuity of action in contravention of the maxim that it is to the benefit of the public that there should be an end to litigation.

This leads me to the consideration of the fourth point formulated by me at the outset, namely, the general law as to decrees in such cases. The question involves mixed considerations of substantive law and procedure, and the answer to it is fully furnished by the *dicta* of the Lords of the Privy Council in the case of *Munshee Buzloor Ruheem* v. *Shums-oon-Nissa Begum*,[18] to which reference has already been made. After giving a brief sketch of the matrimonial law of the Muhammadans, their Lordships went on to say:

> The Muhammadan wife, as has been shown above, has rights which the Christian—or at least the English—wife has not against her husband. An Indian court might well admit defences founded on the violation of those rights, and either refuse its assistance to the husband altogether, or grant it only upon terms of his securing the wife in the enjoyment of her personal safety and her other legal rights; or it might, on a sufficient case, exercise that jurisdiction which is attributed to the *Qazi*. Enough has been said to show that, in their Lordships' opinion, the determination of any suit of this kind requires careful consideration of the Muhammadan law, as well as strict proof of the facts to which it is to be applied (p. 612).

Abiding by this dictum, I have carefully considered the Muhammadan law as I have already stated, whilst the facts of the case must, for the purposes of this reference, be taken to be those found by the court of first instance. And upon this state of things I am of opinion that the decree passed by the court of first instance was right and proper. The question as to the form of decree in such cases and the manner in which it may be executed was discussed in a very learned judgment by Markby, J., in *Gatha Ram Mistree* v. *Moohita Kochin Atteah Doomoonee*[19] in which that learned Judge, after briefly reviewing the laws of other civilized countries, came to the conclusion that the Ecclesiastical Law of England was the only

[18] 11 Moo IA 551.
[19] 14 BLR 298.

system which justified the view that 'a Court could enforce the continuous performance of conjugal duties by unlimited fine and imprisonment;' but the learned Judge declined to follow that law in Indian cases, and held that the provisions of s. 200 of the old Civil Procedure Code (Act VIII of 1859) were not applicable to decrees for restitution of conjugal rights. The Legislature has, however, stepped in to remove doubts upon this point, and ss. 259 and 260 leave no doubt as to the manner in which a decree for recovery of a wife or for restitution of conjugal rights can be enforced under the present Code. The case before Mr Justice Markby was, however, one between Hindus, and all that he said in that case would not necessarily apply to a case between Muhammadans. Nor need the English law upon the subject be consulted, though I may observe that, judging by the ruling of Mr Justice Coleridge in *In re Cochrane*,[20] the rule of English law as to the husband's general power over the wife's personal liberty goes as far as any civilized law can go in the direction of subjecting the wife to the control of the husband. An account of that case is given by Mr Macqueen in his treatise on the *Rights and Liabilities of Husband and Wife*, and it appears that the order of the court in that case was very peremptory—'Let her be restored to her husband.' The rules of our law, however, necessitate no such course, and in passing decrees in suits for restitution of conjugal rights among Muhammadans, the *dictum* of the Privy Council already quoted furnishes the guiding principle. Courts of justice in India, in the exercise of their mixed jurisdiction as courts of equity and law, are at full liberty to pass conditional decrees to suit the exigencies of each particular case, upon the principles which have been so well stated by Mr Justice Story in his celebrated work on *Equity Jurisprudence*, 11th ed., ss. 27 and 28. So I understand the principle upon which the observations of the Lords of the Privy Council in the case to which I have so often referred were based, and I may with advantage cite another passage from that judgment:

> It seems to them clear that if cruelty in a degree rendering it unsafe for the wife to return to her husband's dominion were established, the court might refuse to send her back. It may be, too, that gross failure by the husband of the performance of the obligations which the marriage contract imposes on him for the benefit of the wife might, if properly proved, afford good grounds for refusing to him the assistance of the court. And, as their Lordships have already intimated, there may be cases in which the court would qualify its interference by imposing terms on the husband. But all these are questions to be carefully considered, and considered with some reference to Muhammadan law (pp. 615–16).

20 8 Dowlings' PC 630; 4 Jur. 534.

In the case in which their Lordships made these various observations the question of non-payment of dower as a defence to the action did not arise, nor do the facts of the case as found in the report show whether the dower was prompt or deferred, whether it had been demanded or not before institution of the suit, and of course there was nothing in the way of deposit by the husband of the amount of dower during the course of the trial in the court of first instance. These are the distinguishing features of this case; and if the distinction has any tendency to alter the principle, such tendency is entirely in favour of the plaintiff-appellant's case.

To return once more to the case of *Sheikh Abdool Shukkoar* v. *Raheem-oon-Nissa*;[21] which is the leading case upon the subject, I have to observe, with profound deference, that the *ratio decidendi* adopted in that case seems to me to proceed upon a misconception of the rule of Muhammadan law as to the exact time when the right of mutual cohabitation vests in the married parties, and also as to the exact nature of the husband's liability to payment of dower, and the exact scope of the right which a Muhammadan wife possesses to plead non-payment of dower in defence of a suit by her husband for restitution of conjugal rights. It is one thing to say that such a defence may be set up under certain conditions; it is a totally different thing to say that 'until the dower was paid no cause of action could accrue to the plaintiff.' The payment of dower not being a condition precedent to the vesting of the right of cohabitation, a suit for restitution of conjugal rights, whether by the husband or by the wife, would be maintainable upon refusal by the other to cohabit with him or her; and in the case of a suit by the husband, the defence of payment of dower could, at its best, operate in modification of the decree for restitution of conjugal rights by rendering the enforcement of it conditional upon payment of so much of the dower as may be regarded to be prompt. Such was actually the form of the decree which was upheld by this court in *Eidan* v. *Mazhar Husain*,[22] and a decree to the opposite effect was approved by another Bench of this court in *Nazar Khan* v. *Umrao*.[23]

Defences which do not go to the root of the action, but only operate in modification of the decree, are well known to our courts, and the principles upon which they are based are recognized by courts of equity both in England and in America under the general category of compensation or lien when pleaded by the defendant in resistance or modification of the plaintiff's claim. I have already said enough, with reference to the argument of the

21 NWP HCR 1874, p. 94.
22 ILR 1 All 483.
23 *Weekly Notes*, 1882, p. 96.

learned pleader for the respondents, to introduce an analogical comparison between the contract of sale and the contract of marriage under the Muhammadan law, and between the claim of a Muhammadan wife for her dower and a lien as understood in the law of sale.

A lien is not in strictness either a *jus in re* or a *jus ad rem*, but it is simply a right to possess and retain property until some charge attaching to it is paid or discharged.... It is often created and sustained in equity where it is unknown at law; as in cases of the sale of lands, where a lien exists for the unpaid purchase-money (Story, *Eq. Jur.*, 11th ed., s. 506).

So that, pushing the analogy of the law of sale to its fullest extent, the right of a Muhammadan wife to her dower is at best a lien upon his right to claim cohabitation, and I am unaware of any rule of Muhammadan law which would render such lien capable of being pleaded so as to defeat altogether the suit for restitution of conjugal rights.

There is one more consideration which I wish to add to the reasons which I have already given at such length in support of my view. The Muhammadan law of marriage recognizes nothing except right, in its legal sense, as the basis of legal relations and of those consequences which flow from them. And if the husband did not before payment of dower possess the right of cohabitation with his wife, it would follow as a necessary consequence in Muhammadan jurisprudence that, where the dower is prompt and cohabitation has taken place before the payment of such dower, the issue of such cohabitation would be illegitimate.

It would be easy to show that such would be the logical consequence in Muhammadan law of the reasoning pressed on behalf of the respondents; but I need not go further in considering this matter, as I have referred to it only because in the course of the argument it was said that, before payment of prompt dower, the cohabitation of a Muhammadan wife with her husband was simply a matter of concession and not of right as understood in that law.

For these reasons I would answer the question referred to the Full Bench in the affirmative, leaving it to the Bench that referred the case to deal with its other aspects. And I may add that I have considered it my duty to go so fully into this question out of respect for the rulings which were cited on behalf of the respondents, but in which I have been unable to concur, and also because such questions, which usually arise only among the poorer classes of the Muhammadan population, seldom come up to this court for adjudication, but of course affect domestic relations of the Muhammadan community at large.

11. RE ULLEE

(1885) 53 Law Times Reports, NS 711 [British case]

Mixed marriage—Christian and Muslim—legitimacy of offspring—custody of illegitimate children—discretion of the court—access

S., an Englishwoman, had married, according to the Islamic ritual, N., an Indian Muslim, he being already married. The children of this marriage had been recognized by N. as his children and his heirs according to Muhammadan law, and English guardians had been appointed to them by N.'s will in respect of money settled on them by the English Government. S. now moved that an order might be made giving her the custody of her children, as she admitted that her union with N. was not a marriage. and therefore contended that, as her children were illegitimate, she had the right to the custody of them.

Held, that, although the marriage was invalid according to the law of Christendom, the children were not necessarily illegitimate, as they had been recognized as legitimate by N., and by the Government, and were legitimate by Muhammadan law.

Held also, that, even if the children were illegitimate by international law, S. was not, according to English law, their lawful guardian, and was only granted the custody of them up to seven years of age, and that after that age the court would decide the right to custody according to what it thought best for the interests of the infants. In the present case, the court held that the children had passed from the control and custody of S. into that of the guardians appointed by N.'s will, that the application by S. must be refused, but that she was entitled to access.

The law as to polygamous marriages has undergone considerable change in recent years. In England it has been held in two recent cases that if a Hindu, having a lawfully married wife living in India, goes through the form of marriage at a registry office in England with an Englishwoman, such a marriage is a nullity and the English wife is entitled to a decree nisi: *Srini Vasan* v. *Srini Vasan,* [1946] Probate 67; and *Baindail* v. *Baindail*, [1945] 2 All E. R. 374, affirmed on appeal, [1946] Probate 122.

The Hindu marriage, which at the time of celebration was potentially polygamous in character, has thus been partially recognized by the law of England. There is therefore no reason why, by a parity of reasoning, the Muslim marriage, still potentially polygamous in character, should not so be recognized. It is therefore submitted that certain observations of Chitty J. and a part of his reasoning in *Re Ullee* would now be treated as overruled.

It may be pointed out that by a recent enactment, the Hindu marriage in India has been rendered strictly monogamous, Hindu Marriage Act

1955, Section 5 (a). Although the tendency in Islamic countries seems to be towards monogamy, in the subcontinent the *nikah* remains potentially polygamous in character: JND Anderson, *Islamic Law in the Modern World*, London, 1959. For a fuller discussion, see *Outlines,* 98 seqq.

[....][24]

12. Rex v. Hammersmith
(1917) KB 634

Husband and wife—mixed marriage—muslim domiciled in India and Christian woman—dissolution of marriage—'writing of divorcement'

A marriage solemnized in England between a Muslim domiciled in India and a Christian woman cannot be dissolved by the husband handing to the wife a 'writing of divorcement,' although that would be an appropriate mode of effecting the dissolution of a *nikah* marriage according to Muhammadan law.

For a full discussion see *Outlines*, 153 seqq., and 178.

On the recognition of polygamous marriages in criminal law, see *Cambridge Law Journal*, April 1963, 18–20.

[....][25]

◊ UPDATE ◊

1. *Nature of marriage*

The statement made in the case of *Abdul Kadir* v. *Salima* [Case 10] that marriage in Islam is 'a purely civil contract' is inaccurate. In *Sirajmohmedkhan* v. *Hafizunnisa* AIR 1981 SC 1972 the Indian Supreme Court has correctly described it as a 'sacrosanct contract'.

In *Noor Mohammad* v. *Mohammad Ziauddin* AIR 1992 MP 244 the Madhya Pradesh High Court has emphasized the religious sanctity of marriage among the Muslims of India.[26]

24 See text of the judgment of Chitty, J in *Cases*, 127–30.

25 Text of the judgment of V. Reading, CJ, and S. Eady, LJ, may be seen in *Cases*, 133–44.

26 The court cited my opinion on this point from my book *The Muslim Law of India*, 1st edition, Allahabad 1980, now 3rd ed., Butterworths, Delhi 2002.

2. *Bigamy*

The Muslim Family Laws Ordinance 1961 promulgated in the united Pakistan imposed restrictions on the Muslim husband's supposed freedom to contract a bigamous marriage (Section 6). The Ordinance has remained in force in Bangladesh where it was adapted to the local administrative system by the Muslim Family Laws (Amendment) Ordinance 1985.

As regards the scope and interpretation of the anti-bigamy provision under the Ordinance, reference may be made to Pakistan Supreme Court's decision in *Faheemuddin* v. *Sabeeha* PLD 1991 SC 1074.

In the Bangladesh case of *Makbul Ali* v. *Manwara Begum*, 39 DLR (1987) 181 it was clarified that the second wife of a bigamist husband cannot be prosecuted under the anti-bigamy provisions of the Ordinance of 1961.

While the Ordinance only puts certain restrictions on a Muslim husband's supposed right to contract a bigamous marriage, in *Jesmin Sultana* v. *Mohammad Elias* (1997) 17 BLD 4 the Dhaka court has recommended an outright prohibition of polygamy:

> We find that Section 6 of the Muslim Family Laws Ordinance 1961 is against the principles of Islamic law. We recommend that this Section be deleted and be substituted with a Section prohibiting polygamy.

In the Indian case of *Begum Subhanu* v. *Abdul Ghafoor* AIR 1987 SC 1103, a case where a Muslim wife had claimed separate maintenance on the ground of bigamy on her husband's part, the Supreme Court observed:

> From the point of view of the neglected wife… it will make no difference whether the woman intruding into her matrimonial life and taking her place in the matrimonial bed is another wife permitted under law to be married and not a mistress. The legal status of a woman to whom the husband has transferred his affections cannot lessen her distress and her feelings of neglect. In fact from one point of view the taking of another wife portends a more permanent destruction of her matrimonial life than the taking of a mistress.

In India the freedom of a married non-Muslim converting to Islam to contract another marriage without divorcing his first non-Muslim wife was examined in the leading case of *Sarla Mudgal* v. *Union of India* AIR 1995 SC 1531. The court declared such a marriage to be invalid and penal under Sections 494–5 of the Indian Penal code 1860. This decision was reaffirmed by the court in *Lily Thomas* v. *Union of India* (2000) 6 SCC 224, observing that:

> Even under Muslim law (right to) plurality of marriages is not unconditionally conferred upon the husband. It would, therefore, be doing injustice to Islamic law

to urge that the convert is entitled to practise bigamy notwithstanding the continuance of his marriage under the law to which he belonged before conversion. The progressive outlook and wider approach of Islamic law cannot be permitted to be squeezed and narrowed by unscrupulous litigants.

3. *Restitution of conjugal rights*

As regards the principles relating to restitution of conjugal rights stated in the old Allahabad decisions in *Anis Begum* and *Abdul Kadir* [Cases 3 & 10], the courts in the subcontinent do not recognize that a husband can ask for this relief as of right. The judicial trend everywhere now shows reluctance to grant the relief where it is resisted by the wife on any reasonable ground.

The ratio of the Allahabad ruling in *Itwari's* case [Case no. 17], regarding cruelty on the part of the husband as a valid defence in the hands of a wife where he seeks restitution of conjugal rights, was followed in *Raj Mohammad* v. *Saeeda Amina Begum* AIR 1976 Kant 201.

In a case of restitution of conjugal rights non-payment of prompt dower in terms of a marriage agreement is also a valid defence in the wife's hands. In the Indian case of *Rabia Khatoon v Mukhtar Ahmad* AIR 1966 All 548 it was held by the Allahabad High Court that where in a case of non-payment of prompt dower the wife refuses herself to the husband after an initial cohabitation, the court may pass a decree of restitution of conjugal rights subject to the condition of payment of the dower.[27]

4. *British cases*

The judgments of the British courts in *Re Ullee* and *Rex v Hammersmith* [Cases 11 & 12] deal with the application of Muslim law to the Muslims in the UK courts. These are actually rulings on Conflict of Laws and do not form part of the Muslim law as applicable in the subcontinent. On the points involved in these cases there is now a large body of recent judicial decisions.[28]

27 In my opinion the relief of restitution of conjugal right does not fit in Islam's scheme of matrimonial rights. See the arguments in my book *The Muslim Law of India*, 3rd ed., Butterworth, 2001, pp. 77–80. My viewpoint that every decree for restitution of conjugal right should be time-bound and after the expiry of the stipulated time should result into an automatic dissolution of the marriage has been referred to by the Delhi High Court in *Harvinder Kaur* v. *Harmandar Singh* AIR 1984 Del 66—TM.

28 A reference may be made to David Pearl & Werner Menski, *Muslim Family Law*, 3rd ed., Sweet and Maxwell, London 1998, Chapter 3: 'Muslim Law in Britain' and Chapter 4: Conflict of Laws'.

VI. Dower

13. Hamira Bibi v. Zubaida Bibi
(1916) 43 IA 294

Widow—unpaid dower—Widow in possession of property—lien—account of profits—right to interest as compensation

A Muslim widow lawfully in possession of her husband's estate in lieu of her dower cannot, in the absence of an agreement, be made to account for the profits of the estate without being allowed reasonable compensation for forbearing to enforce her right to the dower debt; this compensation can be allowed in the form of interest upon the dower.

In a suit by heirs of a deceased Muslim to recover their shares in the estate from a widow in possession and entitled to a lien for her dower, it was found that the annual profits were less than 6 per cent interest upon the dower debt. The Board affirmed the decree of the High Court declaring the plaintiffs severally entitled to recover their respective shares, but only upon payment of a quota of the dower proportionate to those shares.

Woomatool Fatima Begum v. *Meerunmun-nissa Khanum* (1868) 9 Suth WR 318 approved. See *Outlines,* 136 seqq., and *Mulla*, §§ 296–304.

Consolidated Appeals from two decrees of the High Court of Allahabad (11 August 1910), varying two decrees of the Subordinate Judge of Gorakhpur (15 September 1906).

The first respondent, defendant in both suits, was the widow of Inayat Ullah, who died in 1892. The suits were instituted in 1906 by the other heirs of Inayat Ullah to recover their shares in the estate, in the possession of which the first respondent had been allowed to remain in exercise of her lien for dower. The plaintiffs alleged that the dower had been satisfied out of the profits. The sole question was whether in accounting for the profits of the estate the widow was entitled to interest, claimed at 6 per cent, upon her dower debt. The facts are stated in the judgment.

The Subordinate Judge framed several issues, of which the following only were material to the appeal: (8) According to law and custom, is interest allowable upon dower debt?; (9) Is the defendant entitled to any, and what, damages by reason of non-payment of her dower debt?

The two suits were tried together. The Subordinate Judge held that the defendant was entitled to the interest claimed, and found that the net annual income received by her from the estate was less than the annual amount of interest due to her. As the plaintiffs had not offered to pay the whole of the dower debt, he dismissed the suits.

The plaintiffs in both suits appealed to the High Court, and the appeals were heard together by Sir John Stanley, CJ, Banerji and Karamat Husain, JJ. The last named learned judge in delivering the leading judgment held that the question of the payment of interest was not one regarding 'marriage,' and that consequently Mahommedan law was not made applicable by Act XII of 1887, s. 37, sub-s. 1; that the dower being a debt, the matter was not one within s. 37, sub-s. 2, of that Act, namely, a matter as to which no law was applicable and which had to be determined solely 'according to justice, equity and good conscience,' though, if it were, he deemed it unjust and inequitable that a widow should be held liable to account for the profits of the estate without being entitled to a reasonable rate of interest upon the dower. After considering the authorities, he held that the preponderance was in favour of allowing interest. On the further question whether the plaintiffs were entitled to recover their respective shares of the estate on payment of a proportionate part of the dower debt, the learned judge held that it was reasonable to direct that they should do so. The learned Chief Justice and Banerji J. delivered judgments concurring with that of Karamat Husain J. It was accordingly decreed that the decrees of the Subordinate Judge be set aside and decrees passed for possession provided that the respective plaintiffs paid the amounts named in the decrees within six months, but that in default of payment by any of the plaintiffs his suit should be dismissed. The appeal is reported at ILR 33 All 182.

Judgment [Parker, J.][1]

A short statement of the facts which have given rise to this litigation will explain the point for determination involved in these consolidated appeals.

One Shaikh Inayat Ullah, a Mahommedan inhabitant of the district of Gorakhpur, in the United Provinces of India, died in March, 1892, leaving him surviving a widow and daughter, named respectively Zubaida Bibi and Najm-un-nisa; a sister, Hamira Bibi; and two brothers, Khadim Hossain and Ihsan Ullah. All these persons became entitled under the Sunni law, to which Inayat Ullah was subject, to certain specific shares in his estate. Besides the widow's share of one-eighth, Zubaida was entitled to her unpaid dower. This has been found in a previous proceeding to have amounted to the large

1 With Parker, John Edge, & Syed Amir Ali, JJ.

sum of one lakh of rupees. The other heirs of Inayat Ullah, not being in a position apparently to pay this sum without alienating at least a considerable part of the estate, allowed the widow to take or remain in possession of the whole to satisfy her claim out of the rents and issues of the landed property. It is not clear whether the widow was let into possession in the lifetime of Inayat Ullah or after his death. But it is not disputed that since 1892 Zubaida has been in possession.

In 1902 the other heirs of Inayat Ullah brought a suit against her to recover possession of their shares. Their suit was dismissed on the ground that it was misconceived inasmuch as it was not a suit for the purpose of taking accounts, and thus ascertaining what portion of the dower debt was then unsatisfied. The present suits were instituted with that object on 15 March 1906, in the Court of the Subordinate Judge of Gorakhpur, one by Hamira Bibi and the other by the widow and sons of Khadim Hossain, who had died either before or after the suit of 1902. The reliefs prayed for in both suits were the same, namely, (*a*) for the taking of accounts; (*b*) for decree to plaintiffs of their respective shares in case the dower debt was found to be discharged; and (*c*) for an award to the plaintiffs of any sum found to have been received by her in excess of her dower. Zubaida in her defence among other pleas set up a claim for interest on her unpaid dower; she alleged that the income of the property was less than the interest she claimed; that, consequently, the debt was still unsatisfied, and that the plaintiffs were accordingly not entitled to recover possession of their shares in Inayat Ullah's estate.

The Subordinate Judge, who tried the case in the first instance, considered the defendant was entitled to interest at 6 per cent per annum on her dower; that the interest thus calculated exceeded the annual net income from the estate, and that, therefore, it was clear no portion of the debt was discharged. In the result he dismissed both suits. On appeal to the High Court at Allahabad, the learned judges took the same view as to the right of the widow, Zubaida, to receive interest; but they varied the decrees of the court of first instance with regard to the total dismissal of the suits; they made a declaration that the plaintiffs should recover possession of their respective shares in the estate provided they paid to the defendant their quota of the dower debt proportionate to such shares, which quota the learned judges specified.

From these decrees of the Allahabad High Court the plaintiffs have appealed to His Majesty in Council, and the sole question for determination is whether the defendant Zubaida is entitled to any interest or compensation in respect of her dower unpaid at the time of Inayat Ullah's death. The case has been elaborately argued on both sides and a large number of authorities have been cited. On behalf of the plaintiffs it has been argued with considerable force that the Mussulman law prohibits usury and usurious dealings between Moslems; that dower is a liability springing under the provisions of that law from the status of marriage; and that, therefore, all incidents and rights connected therewith must be subject to the Mussulman law. It was further contended that the Mahommedan widow's lien on the husband's estate for unpaid dower is the only creditor's lien which has been recognized and maintained intact by British courts of justice, and that it ought not to be extended beyond what the Mussulman law itself permits by allowing interest when it is not contracted for. On the other side it is argued that the Mahommedan law prohibiting usury has been repealed in India by Act XXVIII of 1855, and that consequently there is no bar to Mussulmans receiving or paying interest, and that the practice of receiving interest is common among them both in India and other countries. It is further urged that, in any event, the widow is entitled to some interest by way of damages for non-payment of dower at the due time.

In the view their Lordships take of the case it is unnecessary in their opinion to examine much of the argument addressed to the Board or to discuss the numerous cases cited at the Bar.

There is a conflict of judicial opinion in India on the question whether the Mussulman rule relating to usury was or was not abrogated by Act XXVIII of 1855. Sir Barnes Peacock CJ, sitting with Macpherson J., held in the case of *Ram Lal Mookerjee* v. *Haran Chandra Dhar*[2] that it was not. 'Hindu law,' he said, 'did certainly as between Hindus restrict the rate of interest to be charged; and I do not think that Act XXVIII of 1855 was ever intended to repeal the Hindu or Mahommedan law as to interest.' Then, after reciting the preamble of the Act, he added as follows: 'That Act' (meaning Act XXVIII of 1855) 'did no more than repeal the various Regulations and Acts which the English Government of India had passed on the subject of usury.' In a later case, *Mia Khan* v. *Bibi Bibijan*,[3] Phear J., sitting with Markby J., took a different view. In the ordinary course, on this difference of opinion arising between two Division Benches of the same court, the case should have been referred to a Full Bench. But Phear J. did not take that course and decided the point differently, holding that the Act of 1855 had abrogated the Mussulman law prohibiting usury. Their Lordships do not think it necessary to decide on the present occasion which view is right, nor do they think that Act XXXII of 1839 has any application.

Dower is an essential incident under the Mussulman law to the status of marriage; to such an extent this is so that when it is unspecified at the time

2 Beng. LR (OC) 130.

3 5 Beng. LR 500.

the marriage is contracted the law declares that it must be adjudged on definite principles. Regarded as a consideration for the marriage, it is, in theory, payable before consummation; but the law allows its division into two parts, one of which is called 'prompt', payable before the wife can be called upon to enter the conjugal domicile; the other 'deferred', payable on the dissolution of the contract by the death of either of the parties or by divorce. Naturally the idea of payment of interest on the deferred portion of the dower does not enter into the conception of the parties. But the dower ranks as a debt, and the wife is entitled, along with other creditors, to have it satisfied on the death of the husband out of his estate. Her right, however, is no greater than that of any other unsecured creditor, except that if she lawfully, with the express or implied consent of the husband, or his other heirs, obtains possession of the whole or part of his estate, to satisfy her claim with the rents and issues accruing therefrom, she is entitled to retain such possession until it is satisfied. This is called the widow's lien for dower, and this is the only creditor's lien of the Mussulman law which has received recognition in the British Indian courts and at this Board.

When a widow is allowed to take possession of her husband's estate in order to satisfy her dower debt with the income thereof, it is either on the basis of some definite understanding as to the conditions on which she should hold the property, or on no understanding. If there is an agreement, express or implied, that she should not be entitled to claim any sum in excess of her actual dower, she must abide by its terms. But where there is no such understanding, and a claim is made as in the present case, the question arises whether, on equitable considerations, she should not be allowed some reasonable compensation, not only for the labour and responsibility imposed on her for the proper preservation and management of the estate, but also for forbearing to insist on her strict legal right to exact payment of her dower on the death of her husband. Their Lordships think that she is so entitled, and obviously compensation for forbearance to enforce a money payment is best calculated on the basis of an equitable rate of interest. This appears to be consistent with the chapter on 'The Duties (*Adab*) of the *Kazi*' in the principal works on Mussulman law, which clearly shows that the rules of equity and equitable considerations commonly recognized in the Courts of Chancery in England are not foreign to the Mussulman system, but are in fact often referred to and invoked in the adjudication of cases.

In the case of *Woomatool Fatima Begum* v. *Meerunmun-nissa Khanum*[4] the plaintiff, who had held possession of her husband's estate under a lien

4 9 Suth. WR 318.

for dower, was dispossessed by a decree of the court. She then sued one of the heirs for a proportionate amount of her dower. Among other questions raised, the defendant claimed that the plaintiff must account for mesne profits during the period she held possession. Sir Barnes Peacock C. J., sitting with Jackson and Macpherson JJ., after remarking that the 'plaintiff does not ask to receive interest upon her dower, but she asks that she may not be compelled to account for the profits of the land during the term she held it in lieu of her dower, discussed various considerations which led him to think that it would be inequitable to make her account for the profits, except on the terms of allowing her reasonable interest on her dower debt. The annual rents and profits being less than such reasonable interest, the claim for mesne profits was disallowed. Their Lordships think that this was in accordance both with sound sense and with law.

In the present case the courts in India have allowed the defendant, on taking her accounts, 6 per cent per annum by way of equitable compensation. It was not contended that, if interest by way of compensation were allowed at all, this rate was too high under the circumstances. The contention was that no interest by way of compensation could be allowed at all.

Their Lordships are therefore of opinion that this appeal fails and should be dismissed with costs, and they will humbly advise His Majesty accordingly.

14. MAINA BIBI v. CHAUDRI VAKIL AHMAD (1924) 52 IA 145

Widow's unpaid dower—Nature of right—Res judicata—Decree against widow for possession after payment—failure to pay dower—subsequent suit by same plaintiffs

The Supreme Court of India has held that a Muslim widow in possession of her husband's estate in lieu of her claims for dower remaining unpaid, whether with the consent of the heirs or otherwise, is not entitled to priority as against his other unsecured creditors: *Kapore Chand* v. *Kader Unnissa* [1950] SCR 747.

The case law on the subject is considerable, and it is still not clear

(*a*) whether the right is transferable; and

(*b*) whether it is heritable.

The balance of authority appears on the whole to be in the negative on both the points, *Outlines,* 136 seqq.

Mulla, § 302, gives all the modern cases, but the statement of the law requires revision.

The widow of a deceased Muslim being in possession of his estate in lieu of her dower, heirs of the deceased obtained against her a decree that they should have possession of their shares of the estate upon payment of a proportionate part of the dower debt within six months, and that upon failure to pay their suit should be dismissed. After the six months had elapsed without the payment being made, the widow made by deed a gift of the estate and parted with possession of it to the donees. Several years after the first decree the same heirs sued the widow and the donees for possession of their shares:

Held, that the suit was not barred by *res judicata* owing to the earlier decree and that the plaintiffs were entitled to possession unconditionally, no opinion being expressed as to whether the representatives of the widow could in some other suit recover the unsatisfied portion of her dower debt.

Quaere, whether the widow could transfer her dower debt or her right to retain possession until the debt was discharged.

Judgment of the High Court affirmed.

Appeal (No. 79 of 1922) from a decree of the High Court (19 March 1919) affirming a decree of the Subordinate Judge of Allahabad (18 March 1916).

The facts, which appear more fully from the judgment of the Judicial Committee, were in short as follows:

A Muslim named Muin-ud-din died in 1890 possessed of immovable property, the subject of the present litigation. He was survived by his widow, the appellant Maina Bibi, who entered into possession of his property. In 1902 the plaintiffs, respondents in the present suit, sued the widow, claiming immediate possession of their shares of the estate. The widow pleaded that the estate was a gift to her by her husband, and alternatively that she was entitled to possession until her dower was paid. The trial judge in 1903 made a decree for possession on condition that the plaintiffs paid to the widow Rs 25,387 within six months, and the decree provided that in default of payment the suit should be dismissed. An appeal to the High Court was dismissed, the time for the payment being extended to 3 December 1906. The plaintiffs-respondents did not pay the money and the widow remained in possession.

In 1907 Maina Bibi executed two deeds of gift of her husband's estate in favour of the defendants-appellants, to whom she gave possession. The terms of the deeds appear from the judgment; by them the widow purported to convey an absolute title.

The plaintiffs-respondents filed the present suit in 1915 against the widow, Maina Bibi and her alienees, the defendants-appellants. The plaintiffs claimed that the widow could not according to Muhammadan law transfer the properties. They claimed possession unconditionally, or alternatively upon payment of the proportionate amount of the dower debt, after deducting the profits of the property.

The defendants pleaded, among other things, that the decree of 1902, affirmed in 1906, operated as res judicata; further that the claim was barred by limitation.

The Subordinate Judge held that the claim was not barred, and that the plaintiffs were entitled to possession of their shares without any condition as to payment.

Upon appeal to the High Court the decision was affirmed. The learned judges (Rafique and Lindsay JJ.) were of opinion that the decision in *Bachun* v. *Hamid Husain*[5] established that according to Muhammadan law a widow in possession of her husband's estate in lieu of her unpaid dower cannot alienate the estate. They held further that the former decree did not operate as *res judicata*, since the cause of action in the present suit was different.

Subbaiya v. *Maracayar*.[6] With regard to mesne profits and interest reference was made to *Hamira Bibi* v. *Zubaida Bibi*.[7]

Judgment [Atkinson, J.][8]

This is an appeal from a judgment and decree dated 12 March 1919, of the High Court at Allahabad affirming the decree of the Subordinate Judge of Allahabad, dated 18 March 1916. The main, if not indeed the determining, question for decision by the Board in this case is the proper construction and effect of a certain decree of the Subordinate Judge of Allahabad dated 28 November 1903, affirmed on 3 July 1906, by the High Court on appeal. This latter decree was made in a suit brought by the present respondents and others against the widow of the deceased owner of certain lands and premises described in the plaint in which she was then in lawful possession under a claim to hold the same until the dower-debt to which she was admittedly entitled should have been paid to her.

After the death on 6 May 1890, of this owner named Shaikh Muin-uddin, a considerable amount of litigation was set on foot between several

5 (1871) 14 Moo IA 377.
6 (1923) LR 50 IA 295, 299.
7 (1916) LR 43 IA 294.
8 With Syed Amir Ali, Dunedin and Salvesen, JJ.

persons claiming to be interested in or have claims upon his property. This litigation has been fully dealt with in the clear and admirable judgments delivered in this case by the Subordinate Judge and by the High Court respectively. It is only necessary, however, in this appeal to refer to such of the suits as bear directly upon the questions requiring decision by the Board. In addition, all these learned judges have in their judgments cited and criticized with acuteness a great many authorities, analysed the evidence, and dealt fully with the relevant facts proved. As their Lordships agree with them in the conclusions of law and fact at which they have arrived, it is scarcely necessary for the third time to cite and criticize more than one of these authorities, or to deal with the established facts in great detail. In their view the application of some few well-established principles of the Mahommedan law to the salient facts of the case will enable the appeal to be satisfactorily disposed of.

The widow of the above-mentioned owner of the property in suit, immediately on the death of her husband, admittedly took possession of his immovable property, including the property in suit, and procured her name to be entered on the registry as its possessor instead of his.

It appears to their Lordships that it will suffice to refer to only one of the authorities cited as to the rules of the Mahommedan law touching the rights and liabilities of Mahommedan ladies in relation to their claim for dower. That is *Bachun* v. *Hamid Husain*,[9] decided by this Board over fifty years ago, and accepted as a sound as well as a binding authority.

In that case a Mahommedan widow whose husband had died without issue was put into possession of her husband's estate as a co-heir and to secure her dower. The point in controversy was whether, having been so put into possession, she was entitled to retain it until her dower-debt was paid, to the exclusion of the other heirs of the deceased. It was held that she was so entitled. Sir Montagu Smith in delivering judgment said 'the claim of Musammat Bibi Bachun to hold the property to satisfy her dower cannot be founded upon an original hypothecation of the estate for her dower, for such a right does not arise by Mahommedan law as the consequence of any gift of dower, nor was there any agreement entered into on the part of the husband to pledge his estate for the dower. But the appellant, having obtained actual and lawful possession of the estates under a claim to hold them as heir and for her dower, their Lordships are of opinion that she is entitled to retain that possession until her dower is satisfied, and the respondents cannot recover possession unless that satisfaction has taken place. It is not necessary to say whether this right of the widow in possession

9 (1871) 14 Moo IA 377.

is a lien in the strict sense of the term, although the right is so stated in a judgment of the High Court in a case of *Ahmed Hossein* v. *Khadija*.[10] Whatever the right may be called, it appears to be founded on the power of widow as a creditor for her dower to hold the property of her husband of which she has lawfully, and without force or fraud, obtained the possession until her debt is satisfied, with the liability to account to those entitled to the property subject to the claim for the profits received. This seems to be the ground upon which the claim of the widow to retain the possession of the property was put in *Ameer-oon-nissa* v. *Moorad-oon-nissa*.[11]

That decision is well supported by many authorities. In the first-quoted sentences of his judgment Sir Montagu Smith alluded to a feature of the case with which he was dealing which distinguishes it from the case of mortgage, usufructuary or other. In the case of a mortgage the mortgagee takes and retains possession, under an agreement or arrangement made between him and the mortgagor. Any rights the mortgagee may get are conferred upon him by the mortgagor. In the present case, as well as in that dealt with by Sir Montagu Smith, neither the possession of the property nor the right to retain that possession when acquired is conferred upon the widow by the agreement or the bounty of her deceased husband. The possession of the property being once peaceably and lawfully acquired, the right of the widow to retain it till her dower-debt is paid is conferred upon her by the Mahommedan law. The husband, when he grants dower to his wife cannot, according to Sir Montagu Smith, by any original hypothecation of his property, secure to her the payment of it. But the original and intentional hypothecation of the mortgaged property to secure the repayment of the mortgage debt is the very essence of every mortgage, usufructuary or other. The difference between a usufructuary mortgage and an ordinary mortgage is not so much a difference in the kind of security created as in the method of enjoying it. In each case the property of the mortgagor is pledged to secure the debt, and when the amount secured is paid, the property pledged must be returned to the owner. The main difference between a usufructuary mortgage and an ordinary mortgage is that in the former it is part of the initial agreement by which the security is created that the mortgagee shall at once go into possession of the mortgaged property and apply the proceeds he may derive from the use and occupation of it to discharge the mortgage debt; while in the case of an ordinary mortgage of the usual sort it is in general not the initial intention of the parties that the mortgagee should go into possession of the property pledged immediately or at all, although he has power to do so if the interest on the

10 (1868) 10 Suth. WR 369.
11 6 Moo IA 211.

mortgage money be not paid. Should he go into possession, he must account for the receipts just as must the usufructuary mortgagee. The widow who holds possession of her husband's property until she has been paid her dower has no estate or interest in the property as has a mortgagee under an ordinary mortgage. Mr De Gruyther called the attention of the Board to s. 58, and following sections, of the Transfer of Property Act, and urged their Lordships to apply, by analogy, the principles embodied in those sections, at least in the case of usufructuary mortgages, to this case; but there are essential differences between the position of a Mahommedan widow entitled to dower, who, like the widow in the present case, enters upon her deceased husband's property lawfully and peaceably, and only claims to retain that possession till her dower-debt is satisfied, and the position and right of a mortgagee usufructuary or other to whom an owner pledges his property to secure the repayment of a debt. There is no real or true analogy between the two. It has been well said that there is nothing more misleading than a false analogy. Their Lordships are therefore of opinion that in a case such as the present it would be on their part rash, if not unwise, to attempt to apply either the provisions of those sections of the Transfer of Property Act or the principles these sections embody to the widows.

It is now necessary to turn to the examination of the pleadings filed in the suit of 1902, and the issues raised by them, with the view of ascertaining what was the res adjudicated upon in that case, and what was the effect upon the properties or other interests of the parties of the dismissal of that suit, or the non-payment by the plaintiff to the widow of the sum found to be due to her.

In the plaint in that suit the plaintiffs claimed, amongst other things, that it should be held that the defendant No. 1, Maina Bibi, the widow, was in possession of her late husband's estate in lieu of her dower-debt, and that if any portion of that debt still remained to be recovered from the said estate, then a decree for the possession of the said estate might be passed in her favour upon the condition of the payment of such a proportionate amount of that debt as might properly be chargeable against their share of the property. Musammat Maina Bibi, in answer to this claim, filed her written statement on 22 May 1902. She alleged, amongst other things: (1) that her dower-debt, still unpaid, amounted to the sum of Rs 51,000; (2) that her deceased husband had during his lifetime given to her his entire immovable property in lieu of her dower-debt and put her into possession and enjoyment of the same; and (3) that since she had been so put into this possession of the said property she had, without any objection from the plaintiffs or others, continued to hold that possession, as she was by every means entitled to do until the amount of her dower-debt had been fully paid. On these pleadings, issues were framed by the Subordinate Judge. The second of those issues ran thus: Was the property in suit given by the deceased Muin-ud-din by way of gift to the defendant No. 1 in satisfaction of her dower, and, if so, is the gift binding on the plaintiffs? His finding on this issue is to the effect that no evidence was offered by the defendant No. 1 on the point, although she had raised the plea in her written statement; and that at the hearing the widow's pleaders accepted the finding arrived at in an earlier suit, in which she was defendant, that she was, with the acquiescence of the heirs of her deceased husband, in possession of the property in suit in lieu of her dower. On the first issue the Subordinate Judge found that the amount of the widow's dower was, in fact, Rs 51,000, and that the plaintiffs in the suit had accepted that amount as accurate.

These findings were not questioned on the appeal taken to the High Court; but in subsequent litigation the widow persisted in putting forward the defence, thus practically abandoned and never proved, that a gift had been made to her by her deceased husband of all his property in lieu of her dower. No satisfactory evidence has ever been given to support it.

[....]

These pleas have been already dealt with. They are, in their Lordships' view, quite unsustainable. It was contended, as their Lordships understood, that Musammat Maina Bibi had by the deeds of 1907 assigned both her dower-debt and her right to hold possession of her husband's estate until that debt was paid. It is doubtful whether she could have done either of these things, but however that may be, it is clear she, in fact, never purported or attempted to do either of them. On the contrary, in those deeds she describes herself as the absolute owner of the property of her deceased husband, and purports to convey that absolute ownership to her donees. There is no ground for the contention, if it has been really put forward, that because these deeds fail to effect a transfer of the absolute interest with which they purport to deal they operate to transfer the widow's dower-debt and her right to hold possession of the lands till that debt is paid. By giving up the possession of the lands, as in her deeds she alleges she has done, she has undoubtedly lost her right to hold the possession of them. Their Lordships express no opinion on the point whether her representatives may not be entitled to recover the unsatisfied balance of the dower-debt. If she has that right this judgment does not alter it or interfere with its exercise in any way.

She and her advisers have, in their Lordships' opinion, taken an entirely erroneous view of the effect of the non-payment by the plaintiff in the suit of 1902 of the sum decreed to be due to her. That failure did not convert her into the absolute owner of the immovable property of her deceased husband, of which she had been in possession, nor did it confer upon her any proprietary interest in it or any right to dispose of it.

The judgment appealed from was, in their Lordships' opinion, for the above-mentioned reasons right, and should be affirmed, and this appeal be dismissed with costs, and they will humbly advise His Majesty accordingly.

◊ UPDATE ◊

1. *Concept of dower*

The exposition of the true concept and nature of dower found in the Allahabad High Court's decision in the *Abdul Kadir* v. *Salima* case of 1888 [Case no. 10] has been referred to in several Indian cases. In *Fuzlunbi* v. *K. Khader Vali* AIR 1980 SC 1730 the Supreme Court reproduced some passages from that case and from the Privy Council's judgment in *Hamira Bibi* of 1916 [Case 13].[12]

2. *Widow's dower*

In *Hussaini* v *Hussaini* AIR 1983 AP 225 it was held that the general law of limitation would not apply to a Muslim widow's case for realization of her dower if she has had a lien on the husband's property in lieu of her claim in accordance with Muslim law.

In *Ghouse Yar* v *Fatima* AIR 1988 AP 354 the court held that a widow's lien on the deceased husband's property in lieu of her unpaid dower will not get automatically transferred to the person to whom she may transfer her right to the dower.

The wisdom of the decision of Khaliquzzaman, J in *Kapore Chand's* case, referred to by Fyzee in his introductory remarks for *Maina Bibi's* case [Case no. 14] is open to doubt. Dower is not a 'debt' in the ordinary sense of the word. A deceased husband's life-partner cannot be equated with his ordinary creditors and must be given priority over them.[13]

3. *Divorced wife's dower*

In India, under the provisions of the Muslim Women (Protection of Rights on Divorce) Act 1986, Section 3 (1) a divorced woman is entitled, *inter alia*, to:

[12] The court cited my appreciation of the exposition of the law of dower in the old cases of 1888 and 1916 from my book *The Muslim Law of India*, 1st ed., LBC, Allahabad—TM, 1980.

[13] I have dissented from the *Kapore Chand* ruling on these lines with reference to some Islamic principles in my book *The Muslim Law of India*, 3rd ed., Butterworth, Delhi, 2002, pp. 130–2.

(c) an amount equal to the sum of *mahr* or dower agreed to be paid to her at the time of her marriage or at any time thereafter according to Muslim law.

And she can secure payment of all such dower—i.e., both prompt (if still unpaid) and deferred—by means of speedy proceedings in a magistrate's court—Section 3 (2) & (3).

4. *Interest on dower*

The Qur'an prohibits giving and taking of *riba* (usury) of all kinds and it is generally believed that the prohibition covers even bank interest. In the Pakistan case of *Mahmood-ur-Rahman* v. *Government of Pakistan* PLD 1992 FSC 1 the Federal Shariat Court decided that all forms of interest were absolutely prohibited in Islamic law. Accordingly, the court directed the government to amend its relevant laws in order to eliminate all such forms of interest. An appeal against this decision was rejected by the Pakistan Supreme Court in *Kaneez Fatima's* case PLD 1993 SC 901.

These rulings adversely affect the old Privy Council decision in *Hamira Bibi* [Case 13] providing for payment of interest on widow's unpaid dower.

VII. Dissolution of Marriage

15. MOONSHEE BUZUL-UL-RAHEEM v. LUTEFUT-OON-NISSA (1861) 8 Moore's IA 379

Ṭalāq (repudiation)—Khul' (dissolution of marriage at wife's instance)—Legal incidents

Muhammadan law recognizes two different kinds of dissolution of marriage; one is known as *ṭalāq* (*talak*), the other as *khul'* (*khoola*, *khula*). A divorce in the *ṭalāq* form is the arbitrary act of the husband, who may divorce his wife without proper cause; but in this form of divorce, the husband is liable to pay the *mahr* (dower, *dyn-mahr*).

In the *khul'* form the divorce takes place at the instance of the wife and with the consent of the husband, for which the wife as a rule gives some consideration to the husband. Non-payment of such consideration however does not render the divorce void.

There is a good deal of case law on the subject of *ṭalāq* and *khul'*, *Outlines*, 142 seqq. and 155 seqq., but it is now perfectly clear that in the forms known as *khul'* and *mubara'at* it is not absolutely essential for the wife to pay some compensation to the husband; and there is also no presumption that the husband has been released from the obligation to pay the wife's *mahr*. The best discussion is in *Tyabji*, § 167.

This suit was brought by the Respondent against the Appellant to recover *dyn-mahr* (marriage gift), secured by *kabeenamah* (deed of marriage settlement), by reason of the divorce of the Respondent from the Appellant.

It appeared from the evidence that in the year 1842 the Appellant, a Muslim, married the Respondent. On that occasion a marriage settlement was executed, by which the Appellant settled on the Respondent, by way of dower (*mahr*), Rs 10,000 and 1000 gold *mohurs*. In the early part of the year 1847, the Appellant also married one Shumsoonissa, a rich widow. From that time the Appellant did everything he could to get rid of the Respondent; treating her with great harshness, refusing to permit her to see her mother, denying her food and clothing adequate to her station, in the hope of inducing her to ask for a divorce by which she would forfeit her right in respect of her dower, and to force her to return the marriage settlement, which was at this time deposited with her mother for safe custody. The Respondent complained to her mother of the treatment she met with from her husband, and begged her to return the marriage settlement to him. In consequence of these complaints her mother, in the years 1848, 1849 and 1850 filed petitions in the Foujdary Court, complaining of the treatment to which her daughter was subjected at the hands of the Appellant, and praying for the interference of the court. Under one of these petitions she obtained an order for the Appellant to allow her to see her daughter. At the interview which ensued the Appellant, who was present, said to the mother, 'I have divorced her (the Respondent); you give up the paper and take your daughter'. The mother refused at this time to give up the marriage settlement; but subsequently, no redress having been obtained by the petitions, on the 24th of August, 1850, hearing from her daughter that her condition was becoming more miserable, sent that document to the Appellant. Having obtained the deed, the Appellant compelled the Respondent to execute an *ibra-namah* [deed of relinquishment] and a deed of divorce, after which he turned her out of his house at mid-night in a state of insensibility.

In consequence of this treatment the Respondent, on the 7th of September, 1850, filed a petition in the Foujdary Court, for the production of the deed of divorce and other documents. This petition was dismissed, on the ground that the Foujdary Court had no power to make an Order as to their genuineness.

Thereupon the Respondent filed a plaint *in forma pauperis*, in the Zillah Court of Twenty-four Pergunnahs, against the Appellant, in which she alleged that the Appellant had dissolved the marriage by divorcing her, and further stated that two instruments by which she was alleged to have given up her *dyn-mahr* were obtained from her by fraud and duress, and by the plaint sought to recover her dower of Rs 10,000, and 1000 gold *mohurs*, valued at Rs 16,000, making in the aggregate Rs 26,000.

The Appellant, by his answer, denied that he had divorced the Respondent by *ṭalāq*, that she left his house, having subsistence money of her *iddat*; and alleged that she had executed an *ibranamah* and had thereby released him from all claims in respect of her dower; and that, on the 24th of August, 1850, she had given him a *khoola* and executed a *khoolanamah,* by which the claim sought to be enforced by the plaint was barred.

The Respondent, in her replication asserted that the *ibranamah* set up by the answer was a fabrication, and that the execution of the *khoola-namah* had been obtained by duress, and she contended that the Appellant by pleading a *khoola* divorce had admitted the existence of a divorce, which was *ṭalāq*.

By a proceeding of the court, under sec. 10, Ben. Reg. XXVI of 1814, the following issues were fixed: On the perusal of the pleadings the chief points in dispute are these: First, had the Defendant divorced the female Plaintiff or not? Second, had the female Plaintiff, relinquishing her claim to the *kabeen*, executed or not the *ibranamah* of the 4th of *Bysack* [*Baisakh*, a month of Hindi calender], 1254, and the *khoolanamah* of the 9th *Bhadro* [another Hindi calender month], 1257? On the perusal of the replication, and the issues on merits, the issues on law are these: Although the divorce of the Defendant, and the execution of the *khoola-namah* by the female Plaintiff be not proved, still the Defendant states that he obtained the *khoolanamah*. Now, according to Mahommedan law, is it tenable or not as claimed by the female Plaintiff?

Evidence was entered into by both parties, and in support of the plea of the alleged *ibranamah*, an instrument was put in by the Defendant, purporting to have been executed by the Plaintiff. This instrument, after reciting that the Plaintiff had for a long time been passing her days in the greatest happiness and pleasure as a wife, and that her husband had in every way shown his love and affection towards her, went on to exonerate him from all liability in respect of her marriage portion, whatever the amount might be. It purported to be witnessed by nine persons of whom only one, Ahmed Hosein, was called as a witness, and he admitted that he himself did not see the document signed by the Plaintiff, but stated that he recognized her by her voice from behind a *purdah* (screen). In support of the *khoolanamah*, six witnesses were examined by the Defendant, of whom two only, Syud Mahommud and Syud Allee (*Ameen* of the Defendant's *Mudrissa*), deposed to having seen the Plaintiff execute it. Syud Mahommud, however, admitted that he did not know whether the Plaintiff signed it voluntarily or not, and both witnesses were contradicted as to the circumstances of the execution by the statement contained in the *khoola-namah*.

The court directed a *fatwa* by the Mahommedan Law Officer attached to the court. The case submitted to the *Moulvi* and his *fatwa* thereon was as follows:

'Luteefut-oon-Nissa Beebee claims her *dyn-mahr* money, stating that Moonshee Buzul-ul-Raheem married her on a *dyn-mahr* of the sum of Rs 10,000 and 1000 gold *mohurs*, and consummated the marriage, and they lived as husband and wife. Afterwards he, without fault, and without her pleasure, divorced her from himself. Therefore, she prefers the claim to the *dyn-mahr*. Moonshee Buzul-ul-Raheem states that he did not divorce her, and did not declare that he had divorced her; but that she had given him a *khoola*, and executed a *khoolanamah* accordingly. The wife says that the allegation of Moonshee aforesaid, to the effect that he got a *khoola*, is, conformably to Mahommedan law, a proof of the divorce. Under these circumstances, if the *talāk* and *khoolanamah* aforesaid are not established, still is the Moonshee liable by Mahommedan law for the *dyn-mahr* on his own allegation that he had received a *khoolanamah*?'—'Answer—The husband's statement of the *khoola* taking place, and of the wife's denial of it, are of two kinds; First, the man claims *khoola* in this manner, viz. 'I have entered into a *khoola* with my wife in lieu of so much property, and she has voluntarily agreed to it; I am, therefore, entitled to that much of the property.' The wife denies the *khoola*, and the man is unable to adduce proof of his claim. Under these circumstances, there shall be a divorce inferred in consequence of the husband's admission, but the claim to the property, that is to say, in lieu of the *khoola*, shall remain as it was, that is to say, it shall not be proved without the wife's admission, or testimony of witnesses; because the claim is based on two things; one, *ṭalāk*, which is to be proved by the admission of the husband, since he is competent to make the divorce, and it does not depend on the acknowledgment of the wife; and the other is the wife's liability to payment of the property in lieu of *khoola*, which cannot be proved unless the wife has agreed to it. The wife's agreement, however, is proved either by her own admission, or by evidence of witnesses. The second kind is this: the wife claims from the beginning, saying, 'My husband has divorced me after consummation of the marriage; I am, therefore, fully entitled to the whole *mahr* and *iddat* allowance.' The husband in answer, in order to repel the claim to *mahr* and *iddat* allowance, alleges execution of the *khoola*, stating that 'The wife has given me a *khoola;* my liability to her claim of the *mahr* and *iddat* allowance is extinct.' This second kind conforms to the question. The divorce on which the wife claims her *dyn-mahr* is irreversible divorce, and carries with it no property. This divorce, however, if proved, obliges the husband to pay the entire *mahr* and *iddat* allowance. The divorce which is dependent on the *khoola*, which the man alleges is quite a different one, and this divorce, if proved, extinguishes the *mahr*, as also the stipulation for the *iddat* allowance. Under these circumstances the allegation of *khoola* which the man makes can never be admission of or submission to the divorce alleged by the wife. So, if the wife's allegation be proved, the husband shall be fully liable for payment of the *mahr* and *iddat* allowance; and if the husband's allegation be proved, in that case the entire *mahr* and *nufka* (*nafaqa*, maintenance) to which he was liable will become extinct. If the allegation of neither be proved, then the *mahr* shall remain in force as it was, that is to say, it will not be extinguished. The difference between the two kinds is, that in the first kind the husband claims the *khoola*; and the object of his alleging the *khoola* is to claim the property in lieu of which divorce is made, and the wife denies this. Since the *khoola* is the same as that of an irreversible divorce, and, as the husband is competent to give a divorce, therefore, divorce, according to his admission, is established; but as the wife's liability to give property cannot be proved without her consent and acknowledgment, therefore, proof of the wife's liability depends entirely upon her own admission or evidence of witnesses. And, in the second kind, the wife claims *mahr* and *iddat* allowance against her husband on the ground of divorce being effected without property, and the husband denies the claim, and in order to render void the wife's claim, alleges that she, of her own accord, has relinquished the marriage and extinguished it, and mentioned this relinquishment as being the *khoola*. Under this circumstance, although the husband apparently claims the *khoola*, yet she is the Defendant, and denies it; for the object of the *khoola* is merely to rebut the claim of the *mahr*, and not to prove any property due by the wife, nor to prove the divorce which is included in the *khoola*. The allegation of this *khoola* can never prove the wife's claim, which rests on the *ṭalāk* without property, if the wife's claim, under on divorce without property, is not proved, and if the husband's allegations of *khoola* effected in lieu of property be not also proved. In that case, the wife's claim of *dyn-mahr* shall continue in force as before, and the husband's allegation of *khoola* shall be extinct. As proof of divorce depends on *khoola* being made, and as it is unnecessary for the husband to prove the divorce, and as he is not also required to prove the *khoola*, his object being to rebut the claim to the *mahr*, therefore, when *khoola*, which is the chief thing, is not proved, then *ṭalāk*, which is a branch of it, and is not the object sought for, shall not be established, because neither the husband nor wife claims this divorce. When divorce is not proved, in that case the liability of payment of the whole *mahr* and also the *iddat* allowance on the divorce, shall also not be established.

The cause was heard by the Principal Sudder Ameen (Baboo Lokenath Bose), who by his judgment found that the Respondent had failed to prove a simple divorce (*talāk*). The judge gave his reasons why he rejected both the *khul-nāmah* and the *ibrā-nāmah*, and passed a decree in favour of the Respondent.

From this decision the Appellant appealed to the Sudder Dewanny Adawlut at Calcutta. [....]

The Sudder Dewanny Adawlut ordered that a *Fatwa* should be given by the Mahommedan Law Officer of that court, on the following case submitted to him:

'The wife sues her husband on allegation of a divorce for her *dyn-mahr* (the marriage portion due), and the husband denying the divorce, in order to bar the marriage portion, pleads a *khoola* from his wife. By the Mahommedan law, an irreversible divorce is not established, nor is the *khoola* of the wife. Under these circumstances, is the mere allegation of *khoola* pleaded by the husband a real divorce sustainable or not; and is the wife entitled to claim the whole of the marriage portion, the same as would have been the case on proof of the divorce given on the part of the husband?'

The *fatwa* given was as follows:

'If the case be such as stated, then, by the mere allegation of *khoola* on the part of the husband, which is tantamount to a relinquishment of property, the divorce of his wife will be fully established, and the wife will be entitled to demand the whole of the *dyn-mahr* as in the case of a divorce by the husband being proved.'

The following authorities were referred to by the *Moulvi* in support of the *Fatwa: Fosool Emandee*, pp. 279, 481 (Calcutta Edit.); *Doorool-Mokhtar* and *Tahtanee*, pp. 190–1 (Egypt Edit.).

The hearing of the appeal by the Sudder Court took place before Abercrombie Dick, Henry T. Raikes and James Hard-wicke Patton, the judges of that court. The question as to the effect of pleading *khoola* by the Appellant was first argued and disposed of by the court. The material part of the judgment upon that point was in these terms:

'The question before the court is, whether the mere pleading of a *khoola* in defence, and inability to prove it, entitles the Plaintiff to claim immediate payment of dower, notwithstanding she has failed to prove such a divorce by her husband as would have entitled her. We are of opinion, that as Defendant has rested his defence on the *ibranamah* and *khoolanamah* it has that effect. The plea to exempt from payment of dower in virtue of a *khoolanamah* is an admission of such a divorce (that is, an irreversible divorce) as entitles a wife to claim immediate payment of dower; and the release from such liability is dependent on proof of the truth of the *khoolanamah* and the *ibranamah*, the burden of which lies on the Defendant, for it is a special plea. The Appellant's pleaders will, therefore, proceed to show that both those deeds have been duly proved.'

The evidence in support of the two instruments, the *ibranamah* and *khoolanamah* was then investigated, when the court finally decreed as follows:

'We are of opinion, after a careful consideration of the evidence adduced, and the circumstantial facts on record in the case, that the evidence for the genuineness of the *ibranamah* is utterly defective. Only one witness out of seven or eight has been produced to testify to it. It purports to have been executed by Plaintiff under the name of Wozerut-oon-Nissa, a name she declares she never bore, and there is no proof that she, Plaintiff, was so called. It sets forth that it was given out of love and affection for her husband, yet it bears the same date as his marriage with another lady, who had declared she would not enter his house until plaintiff was turned out of doors. In short, the terms of the deed, with the reasons for giving it, are altogether irreconciliable with the notorious conduct of the husband to the donor, and the known facts opposed to it. The recital of it in the *khoolanamah* by no means proves its due execution. The *khoolanamah* is certainly proved to have been witnessed according to forms prevalent among Mahommedans of rank; but there is a remarkable want of care evident on the part of the respectable witnesses who have testified to it, to ascertain that the act of the lady was free and unrestrained. Finally, the recorded fact that no fewer than six complaints of ill treatment by her husband had been presented to the Magistrate by the Plaintiff, from the date of the alleged *ibranamah* and the marriage with the second wife to the date of Plaintiff giving up her *kabeenamah* and executing the *khoolanamah*, is sufficient, together with the other circumstances above alluded to, to satisfy the court that the execution of the *khoolanamah* was not a voluntary unrestrained act. It is, therefore, a nullity.'

The Sudder Court by their decree dismissed the appeal with costs.

Judgment [Kingsdown, J.][1]

This suit was instituted in the Civil Court of the Twenty-four Pergunnahs by the Respondent, Luteefut-oon-Nissa, suing as a pauper against the Appellant, Moonshee Buzul-ul-Raheem, to whom she had been married, to recover her *dyn-mahr*, consisting of the sum of Rs 10,000 and of 1000 gold *mohurs* valued at Rs 16,000, amounting together to Rs 26.000.

This sum was payable by the Appellant to the Respondent in the event of the dissolution of the marriage, and she alleged in her plaint that the Appellant had dissolved the marriage by divorcing her. She further stated, that two instruments by which she was alleged to have given up her *dyn-mahr* had been obtained from her by the force or fraud of the Appellant, and were of no avail to bar her rights.

The Appellant, in his answer, denied the divorce as stated by the Respondent, but alleged that two instruments, one a *khoolanamah*, had been executed by her, by which she released her *dyn-mahr*, and which deeds he insisted were binding upon her.

The Zillah Judge was of opinion, that no divorce except by *khoola* had been proved by the Respondent, but he held that the plea of the Appellant admitted a divorce by *khoola*, and that the instruments set up by him as containing a release of the *dyn-mahr* were fraudulent and void, and that, therefore, the marriage being dissolved, the Respondent was entitled to recover her claim, and he decreed accordingly.

This decision by the Zillah Court was confirmed by the Sudder, and from the order of the Sudder the present appeal is brought.

Upon the facts, we think, that there is little doubt. The question is mainly one of Mahommedan law, and we should not lightly in such a case disturb the concurrent decision of two courts. But we are quite satisfied that the decision is conformable both to law and to justice.

It appears that by the Mahommedan law divorce may be made in either of two forms; *talāk* or *khoola*.

A divorce by *talak* is the mere arbitrary act of the husband, who may repudiate his wife at his own pleasure, with or without cause. But if he adopts that course he is liable to repay her dowry, or *dyn-mahr*, and, as it seems, to give up any jewels or paraphernalia belonging to her.

1 With Knight Bruce, Edward Ryan & Turner, JJ; Assessor: Lawrence Peel.

A divorce by *khoola* is a divorce with the consent, and at the instance of the wife, in which she gives or agrees to give a consideration to the husband for her release from the marriage tie. In such a case the terms of the bargain are matter of arrangement between the husband and wife, and the wife may, as the consideration, release her *dyn-mahr* and other rights, or make any other agreement for the benefit of the husband.

It seems, that according to existing usage, a divorce by *talāk* is not complete and irrevocable by a single declaration of the husband: but a divorce by *khoola* is at once complete and irrevocable from the moment when the husband repudiates the wife and the separation takes place. In these particulars the two modes of divorce differ.

But there is one condition which attends every divorce, in whichever way it takes place, namely, that the wife is to remain in seclusion for a period of some months after the divorce, in order that it may be seen whether she is pregnant by her husband, and she is entitled to a sum of money from her husband, called her *iddat*, for her maintenance during this period.

At the hearing of this case, two points were made by the Appellant's Counsel. They insisted, first, that the instruments releasing the Respondent's claim under her settlement were valid; and, secondly, that if the *khoolanamah* executed by the wife were laid out of the case, there was no evidence at all of divorce, and then the marriage was not shown to be dissolved; that the Respondent could not approbate and reprobate the same deed—insist that it was good for the purpose of establishing a divorce, and bad for the purpose of securing to the husband the price which he was to receive for consenting to it.

This objection, however plausible, is founded on a misconception of the real nature of the divorce. The divorce is the sole act of the husband, though granted at the instance of the wife, and purchased by her. The *khoolanamah* is a deed securing to the husband the stipulated consideration, but it does not constitute the divorce. It assumes it, and is founded upon it. The divorce is created by the husband's repudiation of the wife, and the consequent separation. The law might have provided that non-payment of the consideration should invalidate the divorce, but it is clear, as well from the opinion of the Law Officers of the Indian courts, as from the authorities cited at our Bar, that the law is otherwise.

The non-payment by the wife of the consideration for the divorce no more invalidates the divorce than in England the non-payment of the wife's marriage portion invalidates the marriage.

In this case the husband, while denying a divorce by *talāk*, not only did not deny but set up a divorce by *khoola*. He alleged distinctly, in his answer, that the Respondent took from him a *Furuckuttee* (*furqati*, which is a deed of divorcement), that she took from him also the subsistence money of her *iddat*, and gave him a receipt for it, and that she then quitted his house with the assent and under the care of her mother.

That a divorce, therefore, had taken place, was the common case of both parties, and the only question was, whether the husband could insist on receiving the consideration which he says that he had stipulated.

This must depend on the validity of the deeds which he sets up in bar of the Respondent's demand. The dissolution of the marriage being admitted, it is for the Appellant to make out that the Respondent has given up the rights which *prima facie* result from the dissolution, and upon this part of the case their Lordships have never felt the least doubt.

Two instruments are relied on by the Appellant: one an *ibranamah*, or instrument by which the wife is made, out of regard and affection for her husband, voluntarily to release to him all claim to her *dyn-mahr*. This instrument purports to have been made on the 16th of April, 1847. It states that the settlement by which the *dyn-mahr* is secured is in the possession, not of the wife, but of her mother; that the wife, therefore, cannot give up the instrument, and is not aware of what the *dyn-mahr* consists.

There is nothing like satisfactory proof that the Respondent ever gave her assent to this deed with a knowledge of its contents, and the admitted facts of the case make it in the highest degree improbable, almost impossible, that she should have done so.

At the time at which this instrument purports to have been made, the husband had married, or was on the point of marrying, a second wife, as by law he was entitled to do. The evidence of one of the witnesses states, that the marriage took place either in April, 1847, or in the following October; and from the time of the marriage, and indeed from the time when it was decided upon, their Lordships are quite satisfied from the evidence that the Appellant and the Respondent were equally desirous of a divorce. Indeed, it appears that the second wife stipulated as a condition of her consent to the marriage, that her husband should divorce his first wife. He had the power to do so by *ṭalāk*, but this would not answer his purpose; he desired to get rid of his wife, but to retain her dowry, and he prepared this deed in order that, having procured a release of the dowry, he might exercise his power of divorce. The mother of the wife, however, had possession of the settlement, and refused to give it up, and it seems to have been thought by the husband that it would be impossible for him to establish the *ibranamah* unless he could procure a confirmation of it, and a surrender of the settlement by the mother, and a divorce by *khoola*. For this purpose he had recourse to measures of great cruelty; he refused to permit the mother to see her daughter, and, by a long series of ill-usage, unless there be much exaggeration in the evidence, injured the health and even endangered the life of the respondent. The mother, after repeated applications to the Foujdary Court for the protection of her daughter, at last yielded, and gave up the settlement; under such circumstances the *khoolanamah* was obtained, which professed to confirm the *ibranamah*. The courts below have most properly held that instruments so obtained can have no legal effect. They can be of no more avail, when used as a defence against the claims of the wife, than they would have had if the husband were suing upon them as Plaintiff to enforce rights secured to him.

Their Lordships are quite satisfied that the judgment complained of is correct, and they will humbly advise Her Majesty to affirm it, with costs.

16. Sayeeda Khanam v. Muhammad Sami

PLD 1952 Lahore 113 (FB)

Divorce—'incompatibility' defined and explained—khul' and mubara'at—shiqaq—texts and commentaries considered

The question before the Full Bench was whether incompatibility of temperaments between the spouses constitutes a valid ground for dissolving the marriage at the suit of the wife.

The expression 'incompatibility of temperaments' in relation to the facts of a normal marriage involves a total lack of sympathy between the spouses and a resistance to mutual adaptation. It also involves a hatred or aversion on the part of one or both the parties to continue a happy and peaceful life. Particular instances of difference of opinion do not constitute necessarily the evidence of incompatibility. These differences must be regarded by the court individually and collectively before arriving at a decision. Upon such consideration, Cornelius CJ was not satisfied in this case that incompatibility existed.

The significance of the Quranic term *shiqāq* (breach or misunderstanding) was considered in relation to well known Traditions of the Prophet, and also *nushuz* and *i'raḍ*. The opinion of Ameer Ali was accepted that:

> Where there is nothing except incompatibility of temperaments, aversion, hatred and dislike, the marriage can only be dissolved by the method of mutual agreement.

Marriage may also be terminated unilaterally by the husband (*talāq*).

The *ḥakams* (arbitrators) are elders of the tribe or clan whose duties involve conciliation; but they have not the power to dissolve the marriage, except in the Mālikī school. In Hanafi law neither incompatibility of temperaments, nor aversion, nor dislike are sufficient grounds for a wife to obtain judicial rescission of her marriage.

This case represents the classical view of Hanafi jurists as understood in India. But a later Full Bench decision of the Lahore High Court, *Balqis Fatima* v. *Najm-ul-Ikram Qureshi* PLD 1959 Lahore 566, adopted the Mālikī view that in a fit case *hakams* (arbitrators) have the power to dissolve the marriage, as being closer to the teaching of the Qur'an and more conducive to amelioriating the lot of women at the present time. It is doubtful if this decision can be considered satisfactory unless legislative authority exists for the application of the Mālikī law to Hanafis; and this despite the fact that the end to be achieved is a worthy one. See *Outlines*, 168 seqq.

Judgment [Cornelius A., CJ]

This reference to a Full Bench involves the question whether incompatibility of temperaments between the spouses constitutes a valid ground for dissolution of a marriage under Muslim law, and has been made by Kayani J. in the case *Mst Sayeeda Khanam* v. *Muhammad Sami R. S. A.* 62 of 1950. The facts of the case, so far as they are necessary for the purposes of this judgment, are that the wife as plaintiff had sued for dissolution of her marriage with the defendant her husband on the grounds of failure to maintain her for a period exceeding two years' failure to discharge marital obligations without reasonable cause for a period exceeding three years, cruelty, false accusation of immorality, depriving her of her dower, obstructing her in the saying of her prayers, and, as to the clash of temperaments, that the defendant was of irritable nature and changing demeanour and given to imposing his will by force, and further that as a result of the difference in the temperaments of the spouses, the plaintiff had begun to hate the defendant. The trial court found that the plaintiff's case in respect of failure to maintain and failure to discharge marital obligations over the statutory periods had not been proved, and similarly, the charges of taking away of the plaintiff's dowry and of obstructing her in saying her prayers were unproved. As regards the question of conflict of temperaments, he thought much could have been said for the plaintiff's case, but she was put out of court as a result of the decision of a Division Bench of this Court in the case *Umar Bibi* v. *Muhammad Din* (AIR 1945 Lah 51), where it was held that a divorce cannot be granted with reference to a Muslim marriage, on the grounds of incompatibility of temperaments, dislike or hatred. The learned Subordinate Judge, however, found that there had been cruelty as well as the levelling of a false charge of immorality, and on these grounds, he granted the plaintiff a divorce. An imputation of adultery, known as *lian*, constitutes a ground for divorce under Muslim law. Cruelty is a valid ground for divorce under the statute law, *viz.,* the Dissolution of Muslim Marriages Act 1939, section 2, clause (*viii*). The findings in respect of cruelty were as follows. The plaintiff had undergone many privations and sufferings. Owing to a mishap to a member of the husband's family shortly after she entered it by marriage, she was described as *manhoos*. Her visits to her own relations were disapproved, and she was beaten whenever she stayed with her relations too long. Visits by her relations to her were also disapproved, and these led to the husband suspecting her of immorality. He carried this suspicion so far that he would not let her go to the kitchen, in case she might meet the cook there. When she protested against his accusations of immorality, he beat her. He did not care for her to look well, and therefore refused to allow her to wash and dress her hair. Once in the presence of one of her friends, he beat her with a broom.

On appeal to the District Judge, the decree awarded to the plaintiff was reversed. The learned District Judge on a revaluation of the oral evidence led in the case, including that for that of the plaintiff herself, came to the conclusion that no cruelty had been proved, and that the evidence for the plaintiff was rebutted by statements of the defendant's witnesses. As regards the disagreements between the spouses, the learned District Judge remarked concerning the plaintiff that 'the change in her circumstances seems to have turned her head and led her to believe that she is more than a match for her husband. She had declared concerning herself and her husband as follows: 'Our temperaments are so conflicting that it is impossible for us to pull together.'

With reference to this and to another statement by the plaintiff that she was a self-respecting woman, the learned District Judge remarked that this was, in his opinion, 'a misdescription of the temperament of a self-willed and self-opinionated woman'. He thought that she was anxious to get rid of her husband because she disliked him for various reasons and did not think he was up to her mark, but opined that so long as the husband chose to retain her and so long as he did not give her an excuse for seeking the cancellation of her marriage, the union must continue. With reference to the question of incompatibility of temperaments, the learned District Judge also referred to the Division Bench case of 1945, which has already been cited.

The plaintiff then instituted a second appeal in this court and in arguments before the learned Single Judge hearing the appeal, the question was raised that 'since even the District Judge has recognized that the temperaments of the plaintiff and the defendant were incompatible, this was enough to secure for the plaintiff a dissolution of her marriage'. Accepting this position, namely, that the District Judge had agreed that there was incompatibility of temperaments as between the parties, the learned Single Judge proceeded to refer to the Division Bench case of 1945 mentioned above and to a commentary on the *Sahih-ul-Bukhari* known as *Umdat-ul-Qari*, and expressed the opinion that if Muslim law recognizes '*shiqaq*' as an adequate ground for divorce, it falls within clause (*ix*) of section 2 of the Dissolution of Muslim Marriages Act 1939. This clause lays down that a woman married under Muslim Law shall be entitled to obtain a decree for the dissolution of her marriage on any (other) ground which is recognized as valid for the dissolution of marriages under Muslim law. In view of the Division Bench decision to the contrary effect, he directed that the case should be placed before the Chief Justice for reference to a larger Bench.

It is necessary first to consider the meaning to be given to the phrase, 'incompatibility of temperaments'. The expression is not a term of art, and learned counsel for the parties in the course of an exhaustive argument have been unable to furnish us with any authoritative judicial interpretation of the expression. In the ordinary dictionary meaning, 'incompatibility' may be rendered as 'incapacity for harmonious combination or association', 'incapacity for appearing or being thought of together or of entering into a system of theory or practice.' 'Temperament' may be defined as 'constitution or frame of mind', 'disposition', 'character of mind or mental reactions which are characteristic of an individual'. With reference to the parties to a marriage, the expression 'incompatibility of temperament must be understood in relation to the various forces acting on the couple which compel or induce them in the direction of harmonious and happy association. There are in favour of such a result, a considerable number of powerful factors. Besides the fact that the pair belong to opposite sexes and may be assumed to possess a normal desire for making a happy union of their lives, there are the various pressures which are exercised by their respective families and by society, and in addition, through the procreation of children, the forces which guide them in the direction of mutual adaptation are greatly reinforced by the affection which accompanies the raising of a family. Where, therefore, it is found that there is such a lack of agreement between the couple as to fall within the full meaning of the expression 'incompatibility of temperament', this must be traced to a total lack of sympathy between them, such as induces a resistance to mutual adaptation, despite the various influences guiding the couple in that direction. There should and must be basically hatred or aversion on the part of one or both of the parties to the marriage to produce such a result.

In view also of the fact that a married couple live in close association with each other, this utter lack of sympathy or aversion or hatred cannot fail to express itself in the behaviour of the couple towards each other. Indeed, the best evidence to establish incompatibility of temperament must necessarily be that afforded by instances of such behaviour. It is of course entirely insufficient, to establish incompatibility of temperament in a particular case, for one of the spouses to declare, as was done by the plaintiff in the present case, that their temperaments are completely conflicting and they cannot pull together. That however is not the only evidence on the subject in this case. There are a number of acts of alleged cruelty adduced by the plaintiff, in regard to which she has led evidence, and for the purpose of determining whether there is indeed incompatibility of temperament, it is open to us to take these various acts into account. They have already been mentioned above, and having regarded them both individually and collectively with care, I fail to see in them proof of such a degree of difference of dispositions or of reactions to particular incidents and influences, or even of lack of sympathy as would qualify for the description incompatibility of temperament. The instances are more readily traceable to bad manners, tendency to suspect the plaintiff's character, tendency to give expression to such suspicion, and tendency to use violence towards the wife, on the part of the husband. For the display of bad manners, the plaintiff was not at all responsible; she did not time her arrival in the family herself and, therefore, it cannot be said that her husband's description of *manhoos* [inauspicious] applied to her was his reaction to anything said or done by her. As regards the imputations of immorality, they arise out of visits by the plaintiff to her kitchen and to her relations, and here again, there is no question of reaction on the part of the husband to anything in the nature of a characteristic act by the plaintiff, and, therefore, it is impossible to infer any clash of disposition here, at the most, a defect of mentality in the husband may be deduced. To the same category belongs his refusal to allow her to dress and look well. There remain the allegations of beating, and this is also of unilateral effect indicating a fault in the nature of the husband. Therefore, I would be inclined to say that in the present case, the evidence is hardly adequate to draw a conclusion of incompatibility of temperament between the spouses. For that, it would be necessary, by means of inferences drawn from instances of behaviour as between the spouses, to gain an impression concerning the mental characteristics and the general disposition and frame of mind of each of the spouses, and thereafter to draw the conclusion that, having the minds that they possessed, it was impossible for them to adapt themselves to each other, and, therefore, they were incapable of living together in harmonious association. As I have remarked, the evidence on the record is insufficient for making such a survey and examination of the mentalities of the spouses in this case.

This finding does not, however, conclude the matter, for the learned Single Judge, in the referring order, has included also the matter of aversion and hatred as between the spouses, as constituting a breach upon which a claim for dissolution could be grounded. In the referring order, the learned Single Judge has placed considerable emphasis upon the Arabic word '*shiqaq*,' meaning a breach or separation into two from a condition of unity, as used in verse 35 of Chapter IV of the Holy Qur'an. Towards the close of the order, he has used words which convey the impression that, in his opinion, *shiqaq* by itself is an adequate ground for divorce in Muslim law. Elaborate arguments have been addressed to us on this point, and, speaking with great respect to the view of the learned Single Judge, it seems that the texts of revealed scripture do not support his view. Before proceeding to consider these texts, I may deal at this stage with a certain tradition reported by Bokhari, on which the learned counsel for the appellant relied strongly as an instance of divorce being decreed by the Holy Prophet in a case in which there was no more than aversion towards the husband on the part of the wife as a cause of action for seeking the separation. I reproduce the tradition from Al- Haj Maulana Fazlul Karim's translation of the *Mishkat-ul-Masabih*, a classified collection of Traditions. The Tradition appears at page 703 of Book II of this translation, which is entitled '*Al-Hadis*', is in the following words:

> Ibn Abbas reported that the wife of Sabet bin Qais came to the Holy Prophet and said: 'O Messenger of Allah! (As for) Sabet bin Qais, I do not blame him about (his) character and piety but I dislike infidelity over Islam. The Apostle of Allah asked: Can you not return his garden? Yes, said she. The Prophet said: Accept the garden and give her a single divorce.

It seems evident that this is a very condensed account of this authentic instance in which the Holy Prophet himself decreed a divorce between the parties to a marriage. A somewhat fuller account is given in the Commentary of Imam Razi on the Holy Qur'an, entitled *Tafsir-ul-Kabir*, Vol. II, and runs as follows:

> It has been reported that this verse (i.e. verse 35 of Chapter IV) was revealed respecting the case of Jamila daughter of Abdullah son of Ubayy and her husband Sabet son of Qais son of Shemas. The facts were that she hated him with intense hatred and he loved her with intense love. She came to the Holy Prophet and said: 'Effect separation between me and him as I hate him. I saw him, from the side of my veil, coming amongst people. He was of the shortest stature, the ugliest in face and blackest in complexion. I do not prefer infidelity (*Kufr*) after having accepted Islam.' Sabet addressed the prophet as follows: 'O Prophet of Allah, order her that she should return the garden I gave her.' The Holy Prophet said to

her: 'What have you to say?' She replied: 'I agree and I will give more.' Then the Holy Prophet said: 'No, only the garden.' Then the Holy Prophet said to Sabet: 'Take from her what you gave and clear her way.' Sabet did this and it was the first *khula* in Islam.

Strenuous efforts were made to employ this as an instance of divorce by judicial decree, where the woman sought separation, and had nothing to found the prayer upon beyond aversion for her husband. Accepting the facts, as stated by Imam Razi in elaboration of the authentic tradition, it becomes clear beyond doubt that the case is indeed one of *khula*, and not of divorce by a judicial decree. No more is needed beyond the opinion of the learned divine Imam Razi for reaching this conclusion, and it need only be added that nothing can be made of the fact that the Holy Prophet himself made a direction to the husband as to how he was to act in the circumstances; I would regard that as an act of creation and establishment of the institution of *khula* in Islam, for the guidance of all husbands similarly situated, rather than as a decree awarded by the Holy Prophet acting either in the capacity of a Judge or as Head of the State of Islam. For it is evident that as the case came before the Holy Prophet, on one side the wife expressed a desire for separation from her husband, not on any ground affecting his character or his devotion to religion, but because his physical appearance excited aversion in her mind. Immediately after the wife had spoken her mind, the husband put forward a claim for return of the garden which he had given her; it should be noticed that he did not protest against his wife's behaviour and, indeed, by asking for a consideration, he must be deemed to have expressed willingness that the marriage bond should be broken in return for an advantage to be received by him. It only remained for the Holy Prophet to discover whether there was agreement on the part of the wife to the proposition offered by the husband, and the tradition makes it clear that the Holy Prophet did so and, finding that there was a consensus between the parties, he gave a direction which stands as guidance for all other Muslim married couples for all time. If any authority be needed to exclude the possibility that the Holy Prophet was allowing a divorce to a woman plaintiff on the mere ground of her aversion for her husband, coupled with willingness to restore her dower to him, it may be found in the recorded Traditions of *Ahmad*, *Tirmizi* and *Abu Daud*, reproduced at page 702 of Book II of the compilation of *Al-Hadis*, referred to above. These Traditions are as under:

1. Saoban reported that the Messenger of Allah said: Whichever woman asks her husband for divorce without fault, the fragrance of paradise is unlawful for her.

2. Ibn Omar reported that the Apostle of Allah said: The most detestable of lawful things near Allah is divorce.

It will be noticed that in the authentic version of the tradition respecting Sabet-b-Qais and his wife, there is no reference to the physical appearance of the husband, and the wife is said to have declared clearly that she did not blame him for his character or his religious devotion, but she disliked infidelity after accepting Islam. If, then, it be contended that on the basis of the wife's aversion alone, the Holy Prophet decreed a divorce, on condition of return of dowry, there would be a patent inconsistency with the solemnly declared opinion of the Holy Prophet that a woman seeking divorce from her husband without fault will not enter Paradise. But, as has been seen already, this is not the most logical or natural interpretation to be placed upon the recorded tradition concerning Sabet-b-Qais, but, on the other hand, it should be regarded, as declared by the learned divine, Imam Razi, as an act of establishment by the Holy Prophet of the institution of *khula* in Islam. It is unnecessary to elaborate the differences between divorce by *khula* and divorce as sought by the plaintiff in the present case. In *khula*, the marriage is dissolved by an agreement between the parties for a consideration paid or to be paid by the wife to the husband, it being also a necessary condition that the desire for separation should come from the wife. Where the desire for separation is mutual, there too dissolution by mutual agreement for a consideration to be paid by the wife to the husband is lawful, but it is described in that case as *mubar'aat*. It has been held by the courts in India that for the purpose of dissolving a marriage under either of these modes, it is sufficient that the husband should propose to pronounce *ṭalāq* or otherwise to dissolve the marriage for a consideration and that the wife should accept the proposal; it is not necessary then that the word '*ṭalāq*' should be pronounced but the contract itself operates to dissolve the marriage. (*Muhammadan Law* by Tyabji, Third Edition, sections 162 and 163). I may refer also in this context to an observation in the learned work of Syed Ameer Ali on Mahommedan Law, Fifth Edition, Volume II, at page 507 in the Chapter entitled '*Khula* and *Mubaraat*'. The passage reads as follows:

> When the wife, owing to her aversion to the husband, or her unwillingness to fulfil the conjugal duties, is desirous of obtaining a divorce, she may obtain a release from the marital contract by giving up either her settled dower, or some other property; such a divorce is consequently called *khula*.

In order to differentiate between the separation in this form, and separation by decree of a court on one of the numerous grounds available under

Muslim law, I cannot do better than refer to another passage from the same learned treatise which occurs at the commencement of section 1 of Chapter XV, at page 519:

> According to the Sunni and Shiah schools, when the married parties have no tangible cause of complaint against each other, but a mutual aversion due to incompatibility of temper, want of sympathy, etc., they can dissolve the marriage-tie by mutual agreement. When the husband is guilty of conduct which makes the matrimonial life intolerable to the wife, when he neglects to perform the duties which the law imposes on him as obligations resulting from marriage, or when he fails to fulfil the engagements voluntarily entered into at the time of the matrimonial contract, she has the right of preferring a complaint before the *Kazi* or Judge and demanding a divorce from the court.

The words employed by the learned author are admirably precise and clear. It would appear, therefore, that unless the wife can adduce one or more instances of such behaviour, as will entitle her to present a prayer for dissolution thereon to the *Kazi*, if she finds the marriage tie intolerable for no more specific reason than that there is incompatibility of temperaments between the parties or that she has aversion for the husband, she must by the offer of consideration induce the husband to release her. Once the husband has agreed, the release takes effect, and it would seem that the husband would have a right of suit to recover the consideration in return for which he consented to the arrangement, should there be failure of payment on the part of the wife. The divorce, however, would take effect as soon as there was an agreement.

I propose now to consider in some detail, and I hope with proper respect, the words of revealed Scripture as contained in Chapter IV of the Holy Qur'an with respect to the subject of *shiqaq* as between the spouses. In this connection, I propose not to attempt an interpretation of verse 35 by itself but to take it in its context, along with other verses relevant to the same subject. In doing so, I believe myself to be following a practice which is sanctioned by learned Muslim divines. Thus, I observe that in his learned work entitled *The Religion of Islam* the late Maulana Muhammad Ali MA, LLB, when quoting verse 35 from Chapter IV, at page 673, reproduces immediately after, Verse 130 from the same Chapter. I propose to reproduce below four Verses from this Chapter, namely, Nos. 34, 35, 128, and 130, and will employ for the purpose the translation of Maulana Muhammad Ali:

> 34. Men are the maintainers of women, because Allah has made some of them to excel others and because they spend out of their property; the good women are therefore obedient, guarding the unseen as Allah has guarded; and (as to) those on whose part you fear desertion, admonish them, and leave them alone in the sleeping

places and beat them; then if they obey you do not seek a way against them; surely Allah is High, Great.

35. And if you fear a breach between the two, then appoint a Judge from his people and a Judge from her people; if they both desire agreement, Allah will effect harmony between them: surely Allah is Knowing, Aware.

128. And if a woman fears ill usage or desertion on the part of her husband, there is no blame on them, if they effect a reconciliation between them, and reconciliation is better; and avarice has been made to be present in the (people's) minds; and if you do good (to others) and guard (against evil), then surely Allah is aware of what you do.

130. And if they separate, Allah will render them both free from want out of His ampleness, and Allah is Ample-giving, Wise.

It is necessary, at the outset, to make some observations, themselves based on the footnotes contained in the same volume, regarding the precise meanings to be attached to two expressions occurring in these verses. Firstly, as to the word '*nushuz*' which occurs both in verse 35 and in verse 128 I would refer to footnote No. 632 at page 236 of the 1920 edition of Maulvi Muhammad Ali's translation of the Holy Qur'an. This occurs under verse 128 and I reproduce it below in full:

There are two words, *nushuz* and *i'rad*, used here. The former literally means rising. You say *nushizat-ul-mar'a* as meaning the wife was or became disobedient to her husband, and exalted herself against him, and resisted him and hated him and deserted him. And you say *nushiza-ba'liha 'alaiha* meaning her husband treated her unjustly and was unkind to her, or estranged himself from her, or disliked or hated her. *i'rad* is literally turning away, avoiding, shunning or leaving a thing. Hence I render the first word as ill-usage and the second as desertion, as order is generally indicative of the comparative strength of the significance in the absence of other considerations.

The second word requiring careful interpretation is the word '*hakama*' appearing in verse 35, where it is said that in case of *shiqaq*, you (that is to say, the State or its representative) should appoint *hakama*, one from his tribe and the other from her tribe. The expression '*hakama*' is the plural of the word '*hakam*' which has been rendered as 'judge' by Maulana Muhammad Ali. In other translations, it has been rendered as 'arbiter'. It seems to me, and here I speak with the greatest possible respect, that it is largely the result of employment of these two senses, viz., 'Judge' and 'arbiter' in the commentaries upon and the translations of this particular verse, which have introduced in a great number of minds the feeling that judicial functions were conferred by this verse upon the two persons whom the representative of the State was required to appoint for the purpose of enquiring' into the relationship between the spouses. Learned counsel appearing before the Bench have been good enough to procure dictionaries of the Arabic language, in which the radical and generic senses of all Arabic words have been expressed in English with great particularity. I may refer to one of these, viz., *Lane's Dictionary*, Volume I, page 616. The word '*hakam*', of which the plural is *'hakama'*, is stated to have the following as its primary meanings:

he prevented, restrained or withheld him from acting in an evil and corrupt manner, as also, from doing that which he desired.' Several derivatives are also defined and among these, mention may be made of the following: (1) '*Al-Hakam*' means the Judge, a name of God, a person of most advanced age. (2) '*Hakam*' means one who judges, decides judicially, etc., arbiter, umpire, one who exercises rule.'

Giving then the radical meaning to the word '*hakam*' and bearing in mind the possibility, nay the probability, that there could never be an intention of confusing jurisdictions, or providing more than one authority to be seized of a particular matter (in this case the question whether the spouses were to be separated) at the same time, I am of the opinion that the meaning of the word '*hakama*', which should be accepted for the purposes of placing a correct interpretation upon verse 35, is that which is in contradistinction with the judicial function. Having regard again to the organization of society, among the peoples to whom this Scripture was revealed, viz., on a tribal and family basis, it becomes reasonably possible that by *hakama* is meant persons from the tribes of the respective spouses who exercise authority over the members of their tribes in such a way that they are capable of restraining such persons from acting in any particular way, or from acting wrongly, and such persons could only be those who were acknowledged heads of the tribes, i.e., the legitimate chiefs or otherwise the elders of the tribes. The phenomenon is observable to this day in many parts of the western Punjab where tribal chiefs and elders still exercise almost undisputed sway over their people, and in fact exercise a benevolent and paternal rule, of which the benefits are numerous and whose passing is regarded by all enlightened persons with regret. If this differential sense be applied to the word '*hakama*', as employed in verse 35, it becomes possible to perceive the nature of the direction with clarity and without any possibility of causing confusion of jurisdictions.

With these preliminary remarks, I proceed to state what in my humble view is the intention of the verses which have been re-produced above. Verse 34 commences with a statement of the reasons for the superiority of men over women, and proceeds to enjoin obedience and right conduct upon good women. Then, it is prescribed, with reference to women who become rebellious to their husband's authority, that the husbands should admonish them and withdraw their company from them in the sense of refusing to cohabit with them and should beat them. The nature of the treatment enjoined indicates that the husband is not responsible, in any way, for the wife's behaviour, by any conduct on his part. If by these methods, obedience on the part of the wife is restored, then no further action is to be taken against her. But if a *shiqāq* (breach) be feared, then an elder holding authority is to be appointed from the tribe of each of the spouses.

Does the word *'shiqāq'* refer to any kind of breach? Obviously it cannot mean any slight or temporary difference, but must be confined to serious rifts calling for the intervention of tribal elders for the preservation of coherent society. Can it mean a breach from any cause, or is there emphasis upon the cause stated in the preceding verse (i.e., 34)? I incline strongly to the latter view, namely that the breach must be due to refusal by the wife to render obedience to her husband. For in such conduct, there is a breach of the bond of obedience by which the wife is bound to her husband, and on her part, there is also a breach of an underlying though unexpressed term of the contract of marriage, namely that she shall be obedient to her husband.

What the elders are to do, how they are to proceed, what powers they have of a procedural nature, and whether or not they have power to impose their decision upon the couple, is not stated, but the verse declares that if the spouses desire agreement, then Allah will effect harmony between them. In logical order, after verse 35 should be read verse 128, which deals with the converse problem, namely, that of a woman who is faced with unjust treatment or aversion on the part of her husband. In this case, there is no mention of reference to elders or otherwise, but the verse proceeds to say that reconciliation is the best course, and no blame will attach to the couple if they effect reconciliation; then follow certain rules of general guidance, which are intended, in the context, perhaps to minimize the danger that reconciliation may be frustrated by the parties being guided purely by their self-interest, such as that avarice is found in the minds of human beings, and that the people should do good to others and guard against evil. Noticeably, there is no reference here to *shiqāq* or breach between the spouses. Next in order should be read verse 130, which lays down clearly that if the spouses separate, Allah will render them both free from want out of His ampleness. When this verse is read in conjunction with the repeated injunctions in verses 35 and 128, that reconciliation and agreement is the better course, its effect may be appropriately understood to be that, having made every effort at restoring normal relations between themselves, then, if still the spouses cannot agree, and they separate, their action will not merit disapproval. As to how they are to separate, nothing is said in the verse, but there is no doubt of the various processes provided by the law of Islam in this respect, and these divide into three classes, namely, separation by divorce pronounced by the husband, separation by mutual agreement, and separation by judicial decree.

As has been seen, the opinion of the learned writer Syed Ameer Ali is that where there is nothing except incompatibility of temperament, aversion, hatred and dislike, the marriage can only be dissolved by the method of mutual agreement; it could of course also be dissolved by the husband acting unilaterally, but we are dealing with a case in which the husband is not willing to grant a divorce. The argument for separation by judicial decree is based upon the reading of verse 35 in Chapter IV, which, in my humble opinion, gives a wholly specialized character to the persons appointed by the *Qazi*, in accordance with the command contained in the verse, a character which the expression employed, namely, '*hakama*', does not necessarily convey. The matter has attracted the notice of learned commentators of the Holy Qur'an, and learned counsel for the parties have referred us to several of the commentaries on the subject. I propose to cite some of these commentaries below, but it is desirable that at this stage I should emphasize that, whatever be the conclusion as to the power which verse 35 in Chapter IV of the Holy Qur'an be held to confer upon the chiefs or elders who are appointed to enquire into the breach, there seems to be neither argument nor authority available for supposing that this power is to be exercised by the *Qazi*, in whose place the secular courts of Pakistan may be deemed to sit, particularly in a case where no such 'mediators' have been appointed. It is necessary to mention this, for the reason that, in the argument addressed to us on the part of the appellant, it seemed to be assumed to be sufficient for inducing the secular court to grant a decree in the present case to show that on a true interpretation of verse 35 in Chapter IV of the Holy Qur'an, the 'mediators' have this power. It is obvious that this proposition is incapable of acceptance.

The commentaries, from which I propose to quote, have already been considered and cited at some length in the learned judgment of Mr Justice Abdur Rahman in the case *Umar Bibi* v. *Muhammad Din*, cited above. I will, therefore, content myself with reproducing somewhat more fully a translation of Imam Razi's commentary at pages 223–4 of his book entitled *Tafsir-ul-Kabir*; this translation has been prepared at the request of the Bench by Mr Muhammad Shafi, learned counsel for the appellant. It is reproduced below:

Q. 7. Is it permissible for the *hakama* to issue an order binding on the spouses without their sanction or permission, for instance, to effect divorce or to direct the woman to free herself by paying something from her property?

A. With respect to this question, according to Shafei, there are two schools of thought. One is that the order of the *hakama* will be binding, and this view is held by Imam Malik and Imam Ishaq. The other school of thought is that it is not permissible for the 'arbiters' so to act, and this is the view of Abu Hanifa, who considers that this is a matter of delegation like other delegations.

Imam Shafei has reported a Tradition from Hazrat Ali and that has been reported by Ibn Sirin from Ubaida. It is to the effect that a man and a woman came to Hazrat Ali and each one of them was accompanied by a number of persons. Hazrat Ali ordered that one *hakam* should be appointed from the man's family and one from the family of the wife, and addressing the *hakama* he said: 'Do you know what your duties are? Your duty is to unite the couple if they can be united, and if you decide to separate, separate them.' The woman said she accepted what Allah had ordained whether the verdict be for or against her. But the husband said that he did not want separation. Hazrat Ali then said to the husband: 'You have uttered a lie. You should also have given the same undertaking as your wife.'

Imam Shafei has observed that in this tradition there is argument for both views. In support of one view is the declaration of Hazrat Ali that if they deemed it proper to unite the couple, they should do so, or they could separate them, and this is held as authority for saying that the verdict of the 'arbiters' prevails without the consent of the spouses. In support of the second opinion, it is urged that when the husband did not agree, Hazrat Ali hesitated, and when Hazrat Ali addressed the husband and said that he was wrong, his meaning was that the husband was not right in not doing the same thing as the wife had done.

In support of the first opinion, it is pointed out that Allah has called them, namely, the arbiters, *hakamain*, and *hakam* is the judge, and when Allah made him *hakam*, He clothed him with the authority of *hukam*. In support of the second opinion, it is said that when Allah called them *hakamain*, He did not give them any authority other than reconciliation and this demands that except reconciliation nothing is delegated to them.

The essence of the problem and the arguments which may be adduced in favour of each of the two conflicting views are set out in this passage with commendable perspicacity and fairness. I propose to refer briefly to the opinion expressed in the *Umdat-ul-Qari* and *Fath-ul-Bari* which are reproduced at pages 55 and 56 respectively of the judgment cited above. In the *Umdat-ul-Qari*, it is stated that there is a difference of opinion as to the procedure to be adopted where the *hakama* agree on separating the parties. Imam Malik, Imam Auzai and Imam Ishaq are of the opinion that the view of the *hakama* will be enforced independently of any authority and without the permission of the spouses. But the Kufis and Imam Shafei and Imam Ahmad Ibn-i-Hanbal are of the opinion that the *hakama* cannot act without the permission of the husband in whom the right to divorce vests if the husband refuses, then only the judge can effect a divorce. The Fath-ul-Bari on the same subject declares that if the *hakama* agree, their order will be enforced without delegation or reference, but if they agree that the spouses should be separated, there are two opinions as to the action which is to follow. Imam Malik, Imam Auzai and Imam Ishaq are of the view that the order can be enforced without delegation and without the permission of the spouses, but the Kufis, Imam Shafei and Imam Ahmad Ibn-i-Hanbal are of the view that the *hakam's* powers are dependent upon receiving such permission. It is common ground that the opinions of the four great Imams, Malik, Shafei, Abu Hanifa and Ahmad Ibn-i-Hanbal are entitled to a degree of respect beyond that due to any others. The consensus of opinion among them is clearly to the effect that the *hakama* may only act for the purpose of dissolving the marriage, provided the power is delegated to them by the husband. It is settled under Muslim law that the husband may, either in the contract of marriage or by agreement after marriage, delegate to his wife or to any other person his power to divorce the wife (Tyabji's *Muhammadan Law*, Third Edition, page 213). This being the case, there can be no doubt whatsoever that, if the husband delegates his power of divorce to the *hakama*, they may exercise it on a general review of the temperaments and characters of the spouses, without reference to any conduct on the part of the husband, or any other cause of action such as would have grounded a prayer by the wife before a *Qazi* for dissolution of her marriage. They are well equipped to make a thorough enquiry into the relation between the couple and the state of their minds at the time when enquiry is held; they are also, by virtue of their positions as elders of their respective tribes, in a position to estimate with a high degree of certainty whether reconciliation is at all possible. If, having done their best, to bring reconciliation (and this would appear to be the clear intention of verse 35 in Chapter IV of the Holy Qur'an), they form the opinion that reconciliation is impossible and separation is desirable, they may grant a divorce on behalf of the husband under the authority delegated to them. But this would be wholly different from a judicial decree of separation, which can only be given upon satisfactory proof regarding the occurrence of one or more of a specified number of acts by the husband, which are prescribed by the law of Islam as sufficient causes of action for such relief.

The existence of doubt among the principal Imams on this point is clear, and it is also clear that three of the four favour the view that the *hakama* cannot grant a divorce unless they be authorized to do so by the husband; where the husband does not agree, the matter is one for the jurisdiction of the judge. It is no doubt this circumstance which weighed with Mr. Justice Abdur Rahman in reaching the decision in the case *Umar Bibi* v. *Muhammad Din,* and, speaking with great respect both to his learning as well as to the views of the learned commentators, I also am of the same opinion, namely, that the view of Imam Abu Hanifa, Imam Shafei and Imam Ahmad Ibn-i-Hanbal is the correct one. Besides being eminently logical, it also has the merits that it avoids all confusions of powers and jurisdictions.

The same conclusion can also, in my opinion, be drawn from the consideration that in the favour of verses from the Holy Qur'an which have been cited above, the provisions for mediation is only made in the case where the wife, without cause furnished by her husband, becomes intolerant of his authority and refuses to perform her marital obligations. There is no such provision in the case where the wife fears unjust treatment, or hatred, avoidance or shunning amounting to desertion, on the part of her husband. The omission cannot be without significance. Where the wife is an injured party, there is first an injunction that an attempt at reconciliation should be made by the parties, having cleared their hearts of selfishness, and acting solely with a desire to do good and to avoid evil. There is then a reference to the permissibility of separation where reconciliation is not possible. How is separation to be effected in such a case surely, either by *khula* or by reference of the injury, as a justiciable issue, to the proper authority, for the wife cannot (except in the rare case of special delegation) divorce herself, and she has no power to compel the husband to divorce her. There must be some fault on the husband's part to justify recourse to the *Qazi*, for the seeking, by a woman, of divorce from her husband, without fault, is severely deprecated.

On the other hand, where the wife's determined disobedience and non-performance of her marital obligations is the cause of estrangement, there being no fault in the husband, he can very well deal with the case under his unilateral power of divorce, but it is enjoined that there should first be a reference to tribal elders. This would ensure not only the sanctity and preservation of marriages against the danger that divorces may be given too lightly, but also that marriages are not reduced to contracts of unwilling slavery for the wife. The need of reference to the judicial authority of the State does not arise for there is available the powerful influence of the tribal elders to ensure that everything is done by the parties which is necessary to bring about a proper and complete resolution of the difficulty. Delegation of the husband's power of divorcing his wife to the elders can likewise be ensured, if it should prove necessary.

In either case, there must be more than mere irreconcilability of dispo-sition, or mere hatred or dislike between the spouses to attract the application of these verses from the Holy Qur'an. These are, at the most, incidents of the psychology of the spouses in relation to each other. If the couple are incapable of mutual adjustment, that would show that they are psychologi-cally incapable of meeting on a common ground; that they are askew like the skew lines of the mathematician which never meet. If there is simple aversion or hatred between them, that amounts to no more than a state or feeling. For such a state of affairs, neither of the spouses need be worthy of blame. But the verses clearly do not apply unless there is some fault, in the nature of a wrong action or a wrongful act, on the part of the wife in the first case and of the husband in the second case.

I am accordingly of the opinion that, under Muslim law, such matters as incompatibility of temperaments, aversion, or dislike cannot form a ground for a wife to seek dissolution of her marriage, at the hands of a *Qazi* or a court, but they fall to be dealt with under the powers possessed by the husband as well as the wife under Muslim law as parties to the marriage contract.

17. Itwari v. Asghari

AIR 1960 Allahabad 684

Muhammadan law—marriage—husband taking second wife—suit for restitution of conjugal rights against first wife—discretion of court to grant relief—defence of cruelty—burden of proof—presumption—court will refuse decree if it is unjust and inequitable

In a suit for restitution of conjugal rights by a Muslim husband against the first wife after he has taken a second, if the court after a review of the evidence feels that the circumstances reveal that in taking a second wife the husband has been guilty of such conduct as to make it inequitable for the court to compel the first wife to live with him, it will refuse relief.

Muhammadan law as enforced in India has considered polygamy as an institution to be tolerated but not encouraged, and has not conferred upon the husband any fundamental right to compel the first wife to share his consortium with another woman in all circumstances. A Muslim husband has the legal right to take a second wife even while the first marriage subsists, but if he does so, and then seeks the assistance of the Civil Court to compel the first wife to live with him against her wishes on pain of severe penalties including attachment of property, she is entitled to raise the question whether the court, as a court of equity, ought to compel her to submit to cohabitation with such a husband. In that case the circumstances in which his second marriage took place are relevant and material in deciding whether his conduct in taking a second wife was in itself an act of cruelty to the first.

In considering the question of cruelty in any particular case, the court cannot ignore the prevailing social conditions, the circumstances of actual life and the change in the people's habits and modes of living.

The Muhammadan law is not very different from the English law on the question of cruelty.

The onus would be on the husband who takes a second wife to explain his action and prove that his taking a second wife involved no insult or cruelty to the first. But in the absence of cogent explanation the court will presume, under modern conditions, that the action of the husband in taking a second wife involved cruelty to the first and that it would be inequitable for the court to compel her against her wishes to live with such a husband.

Where the court finds that the husband never really cared for his first wife and filed his suit for restitution only to defeat her application for maintenance: *Held* that the suit was *mala fide* and should be dismissed.

This case is fully discussed in *Outlines*, 118.

Judgment [SS Dhawan, J.]

(1) This is a Muslim husband's appeal against the decision of the learned District Judge, Rampur, dismissing his suit for restitution of conjugal rights against his first wife who refused to return to him after he had taken a second wife and accused him of cruelty to her. The appellant Itwari was married to Smt Asghari about the year 1950 and lived with her for some time. Then things went wrong and the wife ultimately left him to live with her parents; but he took no steps to bring her back and married another woman.

The first wife filed an application for maintenance under Sec. 488, CrPC. Thereupon the husband filed a suit against her for restitution of conjugal rights. For some reasons he impleaded her father and two brothers as co-defendants. The wife contested the suit and alleged that she had been turned out by her husband who had formed an illicit union with another woman whom he subsequently married. She alleged that he had beaten her, deprived her of her ornaments and thus caused her physical and mental pain. He had also not paid her dower.

(2) The learned Munsif decreed the husband's suit and held that the wife had failed to prove that she was really ill-treated and that the husband had not been guilty of such cruelty as would disentitle him to a decree for restitution of conjugal rights against her. He held that the mere fact that the husband had taken a second wife raised no presumption that Smt. Asghari

had suffered inequitable treatment at his hands, and was influenced by the husband's explanation that he had not taken his second wife to live in his house with Smt. Asghari.

He also took the view that if the wife felt aggrieved by her husband's second marriage she should have obtained a decree for dissolution of marriage, and expressed surprise that she had not done so, thereby adopting the strange and inconsistent view that the husband's conduct in taking a second wife is a good ground for the first wife to sue for dissolution of her marriage and put an end to all the rights of the husband but no ground for contesting the husband's suit for assertion of the same rights under the same marriage.

The fact that the wife had taken things lying down weighed with the learned Munsif in disbelieving her allegation of cruelty against Itwari. He decreed the husband's suit and also passed an order directing Smt. Asghari's father and brother not to prevent her from going back to him.

(3) On appeal, the learned District Judge, Rampur, reversed the finding of the trial court and dismissed the husband's suit with costs. He was of the opinion that Itwari had filed his suit for restitution of conjugal rights only as a counter-blast to the wife's claim for maintenance under Sec. 488, CrPC and pointed out that, after the wife had left him and been living with her parents for so many years, he took no steps to get her back and that his long silence was an indication that he never really cared for her. He observed:

> In view of this circumstance I am prepared to believe Smt. Asghari's evidence that she was ill-treated and turned out by her husband and that the latter is now putting up a show to get her back only to escape from the liability to pay maintenance allowance.

He took the view that the wife who had been deserted and not taken care of by the husband for so many years would not find peace with him after another woman had already been installed as his wife. Accordingly he allowed the wife's appeal. Against this decision Itwari had come to this court in second appeal.

(4) Mr N. A. Kazmi, learned counsel for the appellant, urged the following arguments in support of the appeal. First, in a suit for restitution of conjugal rights the question whether the husband has: been guilty of such cruelty as will defeat his right to consortium is a mixed question of law and fact, and the High Court in second appeal can re-examine the evidence and form its own conclusion whether cruelty has been established against the husband.

Secondly, the mere fact that the husband had taken a second wife is no proof of cruelty as every Muslim has the right to take several wives up to a maximum of four and the view taken by the District Judge is wrong in law. Thirdly, to defeat a husband's suit for assertion of his conjugal rights there must be proof of cruelty of such a character as to render it unsafe for the wife to return to her husband's dominion. I shall now proceed to consider these contentions on merits.

(5) The first question is whether the conduct of the husband in taking a second wife is any ground for the first wife to refuse to live with him or for dismissing his suit for restitution of conjugal rights. Learned counsel for the husband vehemently argued that a Muslim husband has the right under his personal law to take a second wife even while the first marriage subsists. But this right is not in dispute in this case.

The question before the court is not whether the husband had the right to take a second wife but whether this court, as a court of equity, should lend its assistance to the husband by compelling the first wife, on pain of severe penalties, to live with him after he has taken a second wife in the circumstances in which he did.

(6) A marriage between Mohammedans is a civil contract and a suit for restitution of conjugal rights is nothing more than an enforcement of the right to consortium under this contract. The court assists the husband by an order compelling the wife to return to co-habitation with the husband. 'Disobedience to the order of the court would be enforceable by imprisonment of the wife or attachment of her property, or both', *Moonshee Buzloor Ruheem* v. *Shumsoonissa Begum*, 11 Moo IA 551 (609); *Abdul Kadir* v. *Salima*, ILR 8 All 149 (FB).

But a decree for specific performance of a contract is an equitable relief and it is within the discretion of the court to grant or refuse it in accordance with equitable principles. In *Abdul Kadir's Case*, ILR 8 All 149 (FB), it was held that in a suit for conjugal rights, the courts in India shall function as mixed Courts of Equity and be guided by principles of equity well established under English Jurisprudence. One of them is that the court shall take into consideration the conduct of the person who asks for specific performance.

If the court feels, on the evidence before it, that he has not come to the court with clean hands or that his own conduct as a party has been unworthy, or his suit has been filed with ulterior motives and not in good faith, or that it would be unjust to compel the wife to live with him, it may refuse him assistance altogether. The court will also be justified in refusing specific performance where the performance of the contract would involve some hardship on the defendant which he did not foresee, whereas its non-performance would involve no such hardship on the plaintiff.

(7) It follows, therefore, that, in a suit for restitution of conjugal rights by a Muslim husband against the first wife after he has taken a second, if

the court after a review of the evidence feels that the circumstances reveal that in taking a second wife the husband has been guilty of such conduct as to make it inequitable for the court to compel the first wife to live with him, it will refuse relief.

(8) The husband in the present case takes his stand on the right of every Muslim under his personal law to have several wives at a time up to a maximum of four. He contends that if the first wife is permitted to leave the husband merely because he has taken a second, this would be a virtual denial of his right. It is necessary to examine this argument.

(9) Muslim law permits polygamy but has never encouraged it. The sanction for polygamy among Muslims is traced to the Koran (Qur'an), IV, 3:

'If ye fear that ye cannot do justice between orphans, then marry what seems good to you of women, by twos, or threes, or fours or if ye fear that ye cannot be equitable, then only one, or what your right hand possesses.'

This injunction was really a restrictive measure and reduced the number of wives to four at a time; it imposed a ceiling on conjugal greed which prevailed among males on an extensive scale. The right to four wives appears to have been qualified by a 'better not' advice, and husbands were enjoined to restrict themselves to one wife if they could not be impartial between several wives—an impossible condition according to several Muslim jurists, who rely on it for their argument that Muslim law in practice discourages polygamy.

(10) A Muslim has the undisputed legal right to take as many as four wives at a time. But it does not follow that Muslim law in India gives no right to the first wife against a husband who takes a second wife, or that this law renders her helpless when faced with the prospect of sharing her husband's consortium with another woman. In India, a Muslim wife can divorce her husband, under his delegated power in the event of his taking a second wife, *Badu Mia* v. *Badrannessa,* 40 IC 803 (AIR 1919 Cal 511 (2)).

Again a Muslim wife can stipulate for the power to divorce herself in case of the husband availing himself of his legal right to take another wife *Sheikh Moh.* v. *Badrunnissa Bibee*, 7 Ben. LR App. 5 (sic), *Badarannissa Bibi* v. *Mafiattala,* 7 Ben. LR 442. In *Ayatunnessa Beebee* v. *Karam Ali*, ILR 36 Cal 23, it was held that a Muslim wife, who has the power given to her by the marriage contract to divorce herself in the event of the husband taking a second wife does not lose her option by failing to exercise it the very moment she knows that he has done so, for 'a second marriage is not a single but a continuing wrong to the first wife'.

The court significantly described a second marriage as a 'continuing wrong' to the first wife. The implications of these rights of the first wife are unmistakable. To say the least, a law cannot regard the husband's right to compel all his wives to submit to his consortium as fundamental and inviolate if it permits a wife to make a stipulation that she will break up her marriage on his taking a second wife. Further, the moral foundation of this right is considerably weakened if the law, while tolerating it, calls it 'a continuing wrong' to the first wife and permits her to stipulate that she will repudiate her marriage vows on the coming of a second wife.

If Muslim law had regarded a polygamous husband's right to consortium with the first wife as fundamental and inviolate, it would have banned such stipulations by the wife as against Muslim public policy. But it has done no such thing. On the contrary Muslim law has conferred upon the wife's stipulated right to dissolve her marriage on her husband taking a second wife a force overriding the sanctity of the first marriage itself.

If Mohammedan law permits and enforces such agreements it follows that it prefers the breaking up of the first marriage to compelling the first wife to share her husband with the second. The general law, too, recognizes the sanctity of such agreements, and it has been held that a contract restraining a Muslim husband from entering into a second marriage during the lifetime of the first is not void under Sec. 23 of the Contract Act which bans agreements in restraint of marriage.

(11) I am, therefore, of the opinion that Muslim law as enforced in India has considered polygamy as an institution to be tolerated but not encouraged, and has not conferred upon the husband any fundamental right to compel the first wife to share his consortium with another woman in all circumstances. A Muslim husband has the legal right to take a second wife even while the first marriage subsists, but if he does so, and then seeks the assistance of the Civil Court to compel the first wife to live with him against her wishes on pain of severe penalties including attachment of property, she is entitled to raise the question whether the court, as a court of equity, ought to compel her to submit to cohabitation with such a husband. In that case the circumstances in which his second marriage took place are relevant and material in deciding whether his conduct in taking a second wife was in itself an act of cruelty to the first.

(12) Mr Kazmi contended that the first wife is in no case entitled to consider the second marriage as an act of cruelty to her. I cannot agree. In *Shumsoonnissa Begum's* case, 11 Moo IA 551, the Privy Council observed that 'the Mohammedan law, on a question of what is legal cruelty between man and wife, would probably not differ materially from the English law'.

It follows that Indian law does not recognize various types of cruelty such as 'Muslim' cruelty, 'Christian' cruelty, 'Hindu' cruelty, and so on, and that the test of cruelty is based on universal and humanitarian standards that is to say, conduct of the husband which would cause such bodily or mental pain as to endanger the wife's safety or health.

(13) What the court will regard as cruel conduct depends upon the prevailing social conditions. Not so very long ago in England a husband could inflict corporal chastisement on the wife without causing comment. Principles governing legal cruelty are well established and it includes any conduct of such a character as to have caused danger to life, limb, or health (bodily or mental) or as to give a reasonable apprehension of such a danger, *Rayden on Divorce*, 5th edition, p. 80.

But in determining what constitutes cruelty, regard must be had to the circumstances of each particular case, keeping always in view the physical and mental condition of the parties and their character and social status, *Rayden on Divorce*, p. 80. In deciding what constitutes cruelty, the courts have always taken into consideration the prevailing social conditions, and the same test will apply in a case where the parties are Mohammedans. Muslim society has never remained static and to contend otherwise is to ignore the record of achievements of Muslim civilization and the rich development of Mohammedan jurisprudence in different countries. Muslim jurisprudence has always taken into account changes in social conditions in administering Mohammedan law.

Necessity and the wants of social life are the two all-important guiding principles recognized by Muhammadan jurisprudence in conformity to which laws should be applied to actual cases, subject only to this reservation, that rules which are covered by a clear text of the Qur'an or a precept of indisputable authority, or have been settled by agreement among the learned, must be enforced as we find them. It seems to me beyond question that, so long as this condition is borne in mind, the court in administering Muhammadan law is entitled to take into account the circumstances of actual life and the change in the people's habits, and modes of living: *Muhammadan Jurisprudence* by Sir Abdur Rahim, Tagore Law Lectures, 1908, p. 43.

(14) The most convincing proof of the impact of social changes on Muslim law is the passing of the Dissolution of Muslim Marriages Act 1939, by which the legislature enabled a Muslim wife to sue for the dissolution of her marriage on a number of grounds which were previously not available. One of them is the failure of the husband who has more wives than one to treat all of them equitably in accordance with the injunctions of the Qur'an.

It is but a short step from this principle to ask a husband who has taken it into his head to have a second wife during the subsistence of the first marriage to explain the reasons for this conduct and, in the absence of a convincing explanation, to conclude that there is little likelihood of the first wife receiving equitable treatment from him.

'By this Act the legislature has made a distinct endeavour to ameliorate the lot of the wife and we (the courts) must apply the law in consonance with the spirit of the legislature,' Sinha J. observed in *Mt. Sofia Begum* v. *Zaheer Hasan,* AIR 1947 All. 16. I respectfully agree, and would like to add that in considering the question of cruelty in any particular case, the court cannot ignore the prevailing social conditions, the circumstances of actual life and the change in the people's habits and modes of living.

(15) Today Muslim women move in society, and it is impossible for any Indian husband with several wives to cart all of them around. He must select one among them to share his social life, thus making impartial treatment in polygamy virtually impossible under modern conditions. Formerly, a Muslim husband could bring a second wife into the household without necessarily meaning any insult or cruelty to the wife. Occasionally, a second marriage took place with the consent or even at the suggestion of the first wife.

But social conditions and habits among Indian Mussalmans have changed considerably, and with it the conscience of the Muslim community. Today the importing of a second wife into the household ordinarily means a stinging insult to the first. It leads to the asking of awkward questions, the raising of unsympathetic eyebrows and the pointing of derisive fingers at the first wife, who is automatically degraded by society. All this is likely to prey upon her mind and health if she is compelled to live with her husband under the altered circumstances.

A husband who takes a second wife in these days will not be permitted to pretend that he did not realize the likely effect of his action on the feelings and health of the first wife. Under the law, the husband will be presumed to intend the natural consequences of his own conduct, *Simpson* v. *Simpson,* (1951) 1 All ER 955. Under the prevailing conditions the very act of taking a second wife, in the absence of a weighty and convincing explanation, raises a presumption of cruelty to the first. (The Calcutta High Court called it a 'continuing wrong'.)

The onus today would be on the husband who takes a second wife to explain his action and prove that his taking a second wife involved no insult or cruelty to the first. For example, he may rebut the presumption of cruelty by proving that his second marriage took place at the suggestion of the first wife or reveal some other relevant circumstances which will disprove cruelty. But in the absence of a cogent explanation the court will presume, under modern conditions, that the action of the husband in taking a second wife involved cruelty to the first and that it would be inequitable for the court to compel her against her wishes to live with such a husband.

(16) Mr Kazmi relied on an observation of the late Sir Dinshah Mulla in his *Principles of Mahommedan Law*, 14th edition, page 246, that: 'cruelty, when it is of such a character as to render it unsafe for the wife to return to her dominion, is a valid defence', to a suit for restitution of conjugal rights by the husband. Learned counsel argued that cruelty which would fall short of this standard is no defence. I do not read any such meaning in that eminent author's observation which is really borrowed from the judgment of the Privy Council in *Shumsoonnissa Begum's Case*, 11 Moo IA 551. But I have indicated that the Privy Council observed in that case that the Mohammedan law is not very different from the English law on the question of cruelty.

The court will grant the equitable relief of restitution in accordance with the social conscience of the Muslim community, though always regarding the fundamental principles of the Mohammedan law in the matter of marriage and other relations as sacrosanct. That law has always permitted and continues to permit a Mohammedan to marry several wives up to the limit of four. But the exercise of this right has never been encouraged and if the husband, after taking a second wife against the wishes of the first, also wants the assistance of the Civil Court to compel the first to live with him, the court will respect the sanctity of the second marriage, but it will not compel the first wife, against her wishes, to live with the husband under the altered circumstances and share his consortium with another woman if it concludes, on a review of the evidence, that it will be inequitable to compel her to do so.

(17) Counsel for the appellant argued vehemently that dismissal of the husband's suit against the first wife virtually means a denial of his right to marry a second time while the first marriage subsists. I do not agree. A Muslim husband has always the right to take a second wife. If he does so, he cannot be prosecuted for bigamy, the second marriage is valid, the children of the second wife are legitimate and he is entitled to the enjoyment of his rights (subject to his obligations) under the second marriage.

But it is not at all necessary for the enjoyment and consummation of his rights under the second marriage that he should apportion his consortium between two women. On the contrary, nothing is more likely to mar the conjugal bliss of his second marriage than that his new wife should be asked to share it with the old. The second wife is not likely to view with sympathy her husband's attempt to compel the old wife to return to his consortium and, to put it very mildly, the dismissal of the husband's suit for restitution against the first wife is not likely to break the second wife's heart.

Therefore, if, in his conjugal greed, the husband does not rest content with the enjoyment of his new connubial bliss but, like Oliver, asks for more and is refused relief by the court, he cannot complain that his rights under the first marriage have been impaired. The court will be justified in inquiring whether it will be equitable to compel his first wife to submit to his consortium in the altered circumstances.

(18) Even in the absence of satisfactory proof of the husband's cruelty, the court will not pass a decree for restitution in favour of the husband if, on the evidence, it feels that the circumstances are such that it will be unjust and inequitable to compel her to live with him. In *Hamid Hussain* v. *Kubra Begum*, ILR 40 All 332: (AIR 1918 All 235), a Division Bench of this court dismissed a husband's prayer for restitution on the grounds that the parties were on the worst of terms, that the real reason for the suit was the husband's desire to obtain possession of the wife's property and the court was of the opinion that by a return to her husband's custody the wife's health and safety would be endangered though there was no satisfactory evidence of physical cruelty.

In *Nawab Bibi* v. *Allah Ditta,* AIR 1924 Lah 188 (2), Shadi Lal C. J. and Zafar Ali J. refused relief to a husband who had been married as an infant to the wife when she was a minor but had not even cared to bring her to live with him even after she had attained the age of puberty. In *Khurshid Begum* v. *Abdul Rashid*, AIR 1926 Nag. 234, the court refused relief to a husband because it was of the opinion that the husband and wife had been 'on the worst of terms' for years and the suit had been brought in a struggle for the possession of property.

(19) These principles apply to the present case. The lower appellate court has found that the appellant never really cared for his first wife and filed his suit for restitution only to defeat her application for maintenance. In the circumstances, his suit was *mala fide* and rightly dismissed.

(20) Lastly, the Appellate Court, reversing the finding of the trial court, believed the wife's allegation of specific acts of cruelty committed by the husband and held that she had been deserted and neglected by the husband for so many years. In the circumstances, I concur in the opinion of the District Judge that it will be inequitable to compel the first wife to live with such a husband. The appeal is dismissed under O. 41, R. 11, CPC.

◊ UPDATE ◊

1. *Talaq by men*

The exposition of the laws on *talaq* (out of court divorce by husband) and *khula* (such a divorce at the instance of wife) as given in the old case of *Moonshi Buzloor Rahim* [Case 15] does not fully reflect the true law on these concepts as now restored by legislation or judicial decisions in several Muslim countries.[2]

In India the courts, gradually realizing that the concept of *talaq* has been very much misunderstood in the past, have made appreciable efforts to remove the misconceptions in this respect. In *Yusuf Rowthan* v. *Sworennma* AIR 1971 Ker 261, Justice VR Krishna Iyer observed:

It is a popular fallacy that a Muslim male enjoys under the Quranic law an unbridled authority to liquidate the marriage. The Holy Qur'an expressly forbids a man to seek pretexts for divorcing his wife so long as she remains faithful and obedient to him. Indeed a deeper study of the subject discloses a surprisingly rational, realistic and modern law of divorce.

In *Jiauddin Ahmad* v. *Anwara Begum* (1981) GLR 358 the Assam High Court said:

There has been a good deal of misconception of the institution of *talaq* under the Muslim law. Both from the Holy Qur'an and the *Hadith* it appears that, though divorce was permitted, yet the right could be exercised only under exceptional circumstances. There is a large and influential body of Muslim jurists who regard *talaq* emanating from the husband as really prohibited except for necessity and only with the sanction of a judge administering Muslim law.

When a deserted Muslim wife seeks a maintenance order under the Code of Criminal Procedure, in order to defeat her right the husband often pleads that he had orally divorced her on a past date. Without demanding proof of the same, the courts have so far been accepting the plea and expressing their inability to help the wives. In *Shamim Ara* v. *State of UP* AIR 2002 SC 2nd Suppl. 3551, the Supreme Court of India has now decided that this cannot be done any more and that in any such case the husband will have to establish by evidence that he had properly effected a *talaq*; without this his plea of *talaq* will not defeat the wife's claim to maintenance.

We are also of the opinion that the *talaq* to be effective has to be pronounced. The term 'pronounce' means to proclaim, to utter formally, to utter rhetorically, to

[2] See details in my book *Statutes of Personal Law in Islamic Countries*, 2nd ed., IIRC, Delhi, 1995, pp. 255–8.

declare, to utter, to articulate.... We are very clear in our mind that a mere plea taken in a written statement of a divorce having been pronounced some time in the past cannot by itself be treated as effecting *talaq* on the date of delivery of the written statement to the wife.

In Pakistan and Bangladesh instant *talaq* is no more possible and the cases of divorce are now regulated by Section 7 of the Muslim Family Laws Ordinance 1961 which subjects it to the true Islamic procedure for the same. In *Ghulam Fatima* v. *Abdul Qayyum* PLD 1981 SC 460, *Sheh Din* v. *State* PLD 1984 Lah 137, and many other rulings, the courts have interpreted this provision of the Ordinance, trying to restrict the misuse of the traditional law by the husbands.

2. *Khula by women*

The decision relating to *khula* given in 1952 in Pakistan by the Lahore High Court in *Sayeeda Khanam* v. *Muhammad Sami* [Case 16] is now to be read subject to the later Supreme Court rulings on that subject.

In *Khurshid Bibi* v. *Muhammad Amin* PLD 1967 SC 970 the Supreme Court gave a correct exposition of the law of *khula* holding that it is the wife's right not dependent on husband's consent. Referring to *Surah* II : 229 of the Holy Qur'an relating to *khula,* the court observed:

There are no words in this verse indicating that the consent of, or *talaq* by, the husband is necessary for *khula.* Where the husband disputes the right of the wife to obtain separation by *khula*, a third party must decide the matter, and it will have to be adjudicated upon by the *qazi*, and any other interpretation of the Quranic verse would deprive it of all efficacy as a charter granted to the wife.

The law of *khula* so clarified was reaffirmed in a number of later cases including *Akhlaq Ahmad* v. *Kishwar Sultana* PLD 1983 SC 169; *Abdul Rahim* v. *Shahida* PLD 1984 SC 329 and *Muhammad Siddique* v. *Kalsoom Bibi* 1984 SCMR 523.

In Bangladesh the law as laid down in *Khurshid Bibi's* case has remained in force after its separation from Pakistan.

3. *Talaq-e-tafwiz by women*

In India the wife's right to *talaq-e-tafwiz* (delegated divorce) has been explained by the Madhya Pradesh High Court in *Noor Mohammad* v. *Mohammad Jiauddin* AIR 1992 MP 244.[3]

3 The court cited with approval my exposition of the concept of *talaq-e-tafwiz* from my book *The Muslim Law of India*, 2nd ed., LBC, Allahabad 1982.

In Bangladesh in *Tahazzad Hossain Sikdar* v. *Hossneara Begum* PLD 1967 Dhaka 421 it was clarified that where one of the grounds for a *talaq-e-tafwiz* arrangement made in favour of a wife is non-payment of her prompt dower and she exercises her right on that ground, the husband cannot seek shelter under those old judicial decisions ruling that a wife who has initially agreed to the consummation of her marriage cannot refuse cohabitation any more on the ground of non-payment of her prompt dower.

4. *Maintenance of divorced women*

Section 488 of the old Criminal Procedure Code of the subcontinent (1898) contained an anti-vagrancy provision empowering magistrates to make temporary orders for payment of maintenance to destitute wives, children and parents, to last till the settlement of their claims by the civil courts under the personal laws applicable.

In India the new Criminal Procedure Code enforced in 1973 extended this relief to divorced wives. The question whether this extended provision could be applied to the Muslims in its entirety was considered and decided in the affirmative by the Supreme Court in *Bai Tahira* v. *Ali Hussain* AIR 1979 SC 362, *Fuzlunbi* v. *K Khadar Vali* AIR 1980 SC 1730 and *Zohra Khatoon* v *Mohammad Ibrahim* AIR 1981 SC 1243.[4]

Doubts were expressed in some quarters about the correctness of these rulings and the matter was referred to a larger Bench which re-affirmed their ratio in the clebrated case of *Mohammad Ahmad Khan* v. *Shah Bano Begum* AIR 1985 SC 985. Alluding in his judgment to some Qur'anic verses and relying on their non-traditional interpretation, Justice YV Chandrachud decided that:

> These *ayats* (verses) leave no doubt that the Qur'an imposes an obligation on the Muslim husband to make provision for or to provide maintenance to the divorced wife. The contrary argument does less than justice to the teachings of the Qur'an…there is no escape from the conclusion that a divorced Muslim wife is entitled to apply for maintenance under Section 125 [of the Code of Criminal Procedure 1973] and that *mahr* is not a sum which, under the Muslim personal law, is payable on divorce [full payment of dues 'payable on divorce' would absolve the husband of his liability to pay further maintenance under the Code].[5]

[4] The second of these cases cited my appraisal of the ruling in the first case from my book *The Muslim Law of India*, ibid.

[5] My views on the need for preventing misuse of Muslim law were elaborately cited in the *Shah Bano* judgment from my book *Muslim Personal Law: Role of the State in the Subcontinent*, 1st ed., Vikas, Delhi 1977 and from my journal *Islamic and Comparative Law Quarterly*, Vol. 1, 1981.

The *Shah Bano* judgment had led to a realization on the part of the Muslim religious leaders that their religious law on divorced women's rights needed codification. A popular movement followed and Parliament passed the Muslim Women (Protection of Rights on Divorce) Act 1986 providing for the enforcement of divorced Muslim women's rights to seek their unpaid dower and bridal property from the former husband as also maintenance from him, her own relatives and the State Wakf Board, through speedy proceedings before the magistrates.

In *Tamil Nadu Wakf Board* v. *Syed Fatima* AIR 1996 SC 2423 the Supreme Court clarified that a divorced Muslim woman can through a single application seek all the remedies available under the new Act of 1986 and claim maintenance from all those who under the Act are bound to provide the same one after the other.

A number of writ petitions had been filed in 1986–87 challenging the Constitutional validity of the Muslim Women (Protection of Rights on Divorce) Act 1986, on the plea that it had overruled the *Shah Bano* decision in an entirely un-Constitutional way. Interpreting the Act in tune with the *Shah Bano* ruling, the Supreme Court has now decided in *Danial Latifi* v. *Union of India* (2001) 7 SCC 740 that the Act is Constitutionally valid and has not superseded the ratio of the *Shah Bano* decision:

> While upholding the validity of the Act, we may sum up our conclusions. A Muslim husband is liable to make a reasonable and fair provision for the future of the divorced wife which obviously includes her maintenance as well. Such a reasonable and fair provision extending beyond the *iddat* period must be made by the husband within the *iddat* period in terms of Section 3(1) (a) of the Act.

In Bangladesh a decision very similar to the Indian Supreme Court's ruling in the *Shah Bano* case of 1985 was delivered in *Md. Hefzur Rahman* v. *Shamsun Nahar Begum* (1995) 15 BLD 34. Referring to the Qur'anic verses on *mata-e-ma'ruf* [II: 241], as was done in the Indian *Shah Bano* case, the court gave a ruling that a divorced Muslim woman will be entitled to get maintenance from her husband till she gets remarried:

> Considering all the aspects, we finally hold that a person after divorcing his wife is bound to maintain her on a reasonable scale beyond the period of *iddat* for an indefinite period, that is to say till she loses the status of a divorcee by remarrying another person.

VIII. Paternity and Legitimacy

18. Muhammad Allahdad v. Muhammad Ismail
(1888) 10 All 289 (FB)

Legitimacy—acknowledgment of sonship—conditions and incidents—practice

The rules of Muhammadan law relating to acknowledgment by a Muslim father of another as his son are rules of the substantive law of inheritance. Such acknowledgment, unless there are legal impediments, confers upon the person acknowledged the status of a legitimate son, and therefore, an heir.

Where there is no proof either of legitimacy or illegitimacy, and the marriage between the parents of the acknowledged son is not unlawful, the acknowledgment (*iqrar*) by the father affords a conclusive presumption that the son is legitimate and capable of inheriting from the father. Such a status, once conferred, cannot be destroyed subsequently either by the acknowledger or any other person.

This is the leading case on the subject. The case law on legitimacy and acknowledgment is enormous. A full discussion will be found in *Outlines*, 182 seqq.

This was an appeal under s. 10 of the Letters Patent from a judgment of Brodhurst J., dated the 22 March 1886, dissenting from the judgment of Petheram CJ, and affirming the decision of the Subordinate Judge of Meerut, who had dismissed the suit. The facts of the case are stated in the report of the case before the Division Bench and in the judgment of Straight J., now reported. For the purpose of making the arguments of counsel intelligible the following summary will be sufficient:

The parties were Sunnite Muslims. The suit was brought by Muhammad Allahdad Khan and Musammat Hakim-un-nissa (to whom Muhammad Allahdad Khan had sold his rights and interests in a portion of the property in dispute) against Muhammad Ismail Khan and his three sisters, and three other persons, for a declaration of right to and possession of two shares in certain villages left by Ghulam Ghaus Khan, father of the first four defendants, upon the ground that the first-mentioned plaintiff was the eldest son of Ghulam Ghaus Khan and brother of the defendants, and was therefore entitled to the shares, under the Muhammadan law, by right of succession. The defence of the first four defendants was to the effect that Allahdad Khan was only the step-son of Ghulam Ghaus Khan, having been born prior to the marriage of his mother, Moti Begam, with Ghulam Ghaus Khan. The case of the plaintiffs was that even if they failed to prove that Allahdad Khan was the son of Ghulam Ghaus Khan, yet Ghulam Ghaus Khan had, on various occasions, acknowledged him to be his son, and therefore, under the Muhammadan law, Allahdad Khan was entitled to inherit as the legitimate son of Ghulam Ghaus Khan. They filed certain letters and other documents in which the deceased expressly referred to Allahdad Khan as his son; and contended that these references amounted to acknowledgements of him as a son by the deceased, which, under the Muhammadan law, gave him the status of a legitimate son.

The defendants 5, 6, 7 held a lease of parts of the property in suit from the daughters of Ghulam Ghaus Khan. They filed a written statement of defence in the following terms:

> That defendants have taken the lease of the villages from the actual owners, and they have reason to believe that the plaintiff is not the legitimate son of Ghulam Ghaus Khan. Defendants have, year after year, paid in good faith the lease-money to the daughters of Ghulam Ghaus Khan, the owners of the property, from whom defendants have taken the lease. Defendants have been unnecessarily joined as parties to the suit.

No issue was fixed by the court of first instance with reference to this written statement. The issues which it framed were: '1. Whether Allahdad Khan, plaintiff, is a son of Ghulam Ghaus Khan? 2. Whether this suit is vitiated by the defect of champerty and ought for that reason to fail? 3. What amount of stamp duty ought, according to law, to have been paid on the deed to Hakim-un-nissa, and is it receivable in evidence in this suit? 4. Had Allahdad Khan, plaintiff, knowledge of the proceedings in the former suits while they were pending, and is his not being a party to them a bar to this suit? 5. What amount of debts, if any, due by Ghulam Ghaus Khan has been paid by Ismail Khan? 6. What sort of decree, if any, is the plaintiff entitled to?'

The court decided the first four of these issues only. After dealing at length with the first issue and deciding it against the plaintiffs, the Subordinate Judge observed that, in his view of the case, it was not necessary to determine the other issues.

The conclusions of the learned judges of the Division Bench hearing the appeal are thus summarized in the head-note of the report at ILR 8 All 235:

Held by Petheram CJ that the acknowledgment by the deceased of the plaintiff as his son in fact conferred upon the latter the status of a legitimate son capable of inheriting the deceased's estate, although the evidence showed that the deceased never treated him as a legitimate son or intended to give him the status of legitimacy. *Held* by Brodhurst J. that the documents above referred to did not show more than that the deceased regarded the plaintiff as his stepson: that the plaintiff was never called his son except by courtesy, and in the sense in which a European would ordinarily describe his stepson as his son: and that there was no sufficient evidence of acknowledgment from which an inference was fairly to be deduced that the deceased ever intended to recognize the plaintiff and give him the status of a son capable of inheriting.

The grounds on which the plaintiffs appealed from the judgment of Brodhurst J. were as follows:

1. Because the appellant is proved to be a legitimate son of Ghulam Ghaus Khan.

2. Because, under the Muhammadan law, the acknowledgments of Ghulam Ghaus Khan are sufficient to establish that the appellant is his legitimate son.

3. Because the onus of proof was on the respondent, and he has failed to discharge that onus.

Judgment-I [Straight, J.][1]

This is an appeal, under s. 10 of the Letters Patent, from a judgment of my brother Brodhurst, dated the 22nd March, 1886, affirming, in difference with the opinion of Petheram, CJ, a decree of the Subordinate Judge of Meerut of the 3rd of March, 1885. The suit to which the appeal relates was instituted by the plaintiff-appellant before us on the 13th of May, 1884, in the Court of the Subordinate Judge of Meerut, for a declaration of his right to and possession of his share of the property left by his deceased father, Ghulam Ghaus Khan, who died on the 6th of November, 1879. The defendants cited by him were Muhammad Ismail Khan, son, and Musammat Fidayat-un-nissa, Karamat-un-nissa, and Barkat-un-nissa, daughters of the said Ghulam Ghaus Khan, and four other persons, lessees or mortgagees in possession of portions of the property leased or mortgaged to them by the other defendants. The real contesting defendant was Muhammad Ismail Khan, and the single and substantial position taken up by him with which we are concerned is that the plaintiff was not a son of Ghulam Ghaus Khan, but that he was born of the body of one Musammat Moti Begam before her

[1] With John Edge, CJ and Straight & Mahmood, JJ.

marriage with Ghulam Ghaus Khan. The Subordinate Judge found that 'the weight of evidence on the record then proves that Allahdad is not really a son of Ghulam Ghaus Khan, and that he never really acknowledged him as such', and he accordingly dismissed the suit. The plaintiff then appealed to this Court, and the case came before a Division Bench consisting of Petheram, CJ, and Brodhurst, J. The former was of opinion that the evidence established that 'Allahdad Khan was the illegitimate son of Ghulam Ghaus Khan; that he was born before the marriage of Ghulam Ghaus Khan and Moti Begam; that it is proved by evidence, the truth of which is beyond doubt, that upon several occasions in 1861 and 1862 Ghulam Ghaus Khan did at that time acknowledge the plaintiff, Allahdad Khan, to be his son in fact, and that the case resolves itself into a pure question of law, namely, what, according to the Muhammadan law, is the effect of an acknowledgment by a Muhammadan that a particular person born of the acknowledger's wife before marriage is his son? How does such an acknowledgment affect the status of the person in reference to whom it is made?' Petheram, CJ, then proceeded to discuss three rulings of their Lordships of the Privy Council reported in 11 Moore's Indian Appeals, p. 74, LR 9 I A, p. 8, and LR 11 IA, p. 31, which in the result he took to be authorities for the proposition that 'an acknowledgment of children by a Muhammadan as his sons gives them the status of legitimacy'. Upon this view of the matter he would have reversed the decision of the Subordinate Judge and decreed the plaintiff's claim. Brodhurst, J., found: 'From the evidence and the whole circumstances of the case it is, I think, palpable that Allahdad was not the son of Ghulam Ghaus Khan; that he was not legitimated by Ghulam Ghaus, and that he well knew that he was at the highest nothing more than Ghulam Ghaus Khan's step-son, had never been called his son except by courtesy, and had no right to any share in his (Ghulam Ghaus's) property.' He also referred to the case in LR 11 IA, p. 31, and observed: 'I see nothing to lead me to believe that Ghulam Ghaus ever regarded Allahdad in any other light than that of a stepson: and applying the principle contained in the above remarks of their Lordships of the Privy Council to the present case, I find that there is no sufficient evidence of the acknowledgment by Ghulam Ghaus Khan of Allahdad Khan as his son from which an inference is fairly to be deduced that Ghulam Ghaus ever intended to recognize him and give him the status of a son capable of inheriting, and I would therefore dismiss the appeal with costs.' It is from this judgment of Brodhurst, J., that the appeal now before us has been preferred. The case was very ably argued at the hearing on both sides, and the delay in pronouncing judgment has occurred owing to the necessity that arose for consulting the original texts of the Muhammadan law and considering them in conjunction with the several rulings of their Lordships of the Privy Council to which Petheram, CJ, referred. The contentions for the appellant were—1st, that the evidence established Allahdad Khan, the plaintiff, to be the legitimate son of Ghulam Ghaus Khan; 2nd, that the acknowledgments proved to have been made by Ghulam Ghaus Khan of Allahdad Khan as his son were sufficient to confer on Allahdad Khan the status of a legitimate son. Upon the first of these two matters it is to be observed that while Petheram, CJ, on the one hand, was of opinion that the facts showed the plaintiff to be the illegitimate son of Ghulam Ghaus Khan, Brodhurst, J., on the other, considered that all they proved was that he was 'the son of Moti Begam by an unknown father.' To clear the way to a consideration of the second ground put forward for the plaintiff, which, in my judgment, raises the real and only question to be determined, I may at once conveniently state that, in my opinion, the finding of Petheram, CJ, that the plaintiff has proved himself to be the illegitimate son of Ghulam Ghaus Khan, cannot be sustained. For the purposes of this judgment it seems enough to say that the evidence does not establish to my satisfaction that he was born of the loins of Ghulam Ghaus Khan; that the facts go to show that Moti Begam was his mother, but that they do not suggest or prove any particular person to be his father. What the date of Moti Begam's admitted marriage with Ghulam Ghaus Khan is, is, it seems to me unproved. The dispositions of Muhammad Baz Khan and Sipahdar Khan, witnesses for the plaintiff, the former of whom is his connection by marriage, are, to my mind, of such a character as to make it unsafe to rely upon them, while the same remark applies to the statements of Faizullah Khan, Ilahi Bakhsh Khan, and Sirdar Khan called for the defendant, about whom the Subordinate Judge remarks: 'Their demeanour produced in my mind the impression that they were strong partisans who were prepared to swear anything and everything that they found would be favourable to the case for the defence.' The fact remains, and an important central fact it is, that at some time or another before the birth of the defendant Ismail Khan, Ghulam Ghaus Khan and Moti Begam had become man and wife; and this is common ground between the parties. Whether their marriage took place before or after the plaintiff's birth is, in my opinion, not established. The first contention for the plaintiff, therefore, must be decided adversely to him. Then arises the crucial and difficult point raised in the second contention on his behalf, namely, that the acknowledgments proved to have been made by Ghulam Ghaus Khan of the plaintiff as his son are sufficient to confer on him the status of a legitimate son, with the legal consequence of a right to inherit. This point involves two questions—1st, what, in fact, were the acknowledgments? 2nd, what is the legal effect, under the Muhammadan law, of such acknowledgments?

With regard to the first of these two matters, it is satisfactory to feel that the materials for determining it are mainly to be found in the shape of documents which, if their authenticity be established, speak for themselves without fear of falsehood. I have said nothing as yet and shall have little to say about the evidence of the plaintiff and the defendant Ismail Khan, because it is obvious to my mind that both of them have made many statements that are untrue—notably in the case of the plaintiff as to his ignorance of the litigation between Ismail Khan and his sisters and Musammat Nanhi and her children, upon which point the answers to interrogatories of Sheikh Wahid-ud-din, which I believe, contradict him, and in the case of the defendant as to his denials of the several letters, undoubtedly written by him to the plaintiff, in which he addressed him as 'brother' and spoke of Ghulam Ghaus Khan as 'the father'. Without particularizing further, it does not seem to me that any useful purpose would be served by my travelling in detail through the evidence of either of these persons, each of whom called the other as his witness. They are obviously bitterly hostile to one another, and it is clear that neither was over-scrupulous in what he swore to. So far as their testimony is concerned, I think that the one may be fairly set off against the other, as neither can be safely trusted. Before concluding my judgment, I shall later on have something to say with regard to the conduct of the plaintiff, upon which so much stress is laid by my brother Brodhurst and the Subordinate Judge, the materiality of which I need not discuss now.

I turn, then, to the documentary evidence for the plaintiff directly showing statements made by Ghulam Ghaus Khan that the plaintiff was his son and indicating treatment of him as such, which is as follows: [His Lordship proceeded to discuss the evidence in detail, and continued:]

To sum up the matter briefly, therefore, the case for the plaintiff consists of the direct acknowledgments and treatment of him as a son by Ghulam Ghaus Khan, as shown by the documents Nos 35A, 36, 37, 38, 39, and 40; his reputation and recognition as a son of Ghulam Ghaus Khan, as disclosed by the documents Nos 43, 44, 45, and 46 and the various letters written by the defendant to him upon which I have already commented. It seems to me, therefore, that the matter stands thus: The plaintiff is admittedly the son of Moti Begam, whose marriage to, or carnal intercourse with, any other man than Ghulam Ghaus Khan, is not attempted to be proved and who, at the time of her death in 1859, was admittedly the wife of Ghulam Ghaus Khan. How her connection with him originated, or what the date of her marriage to him was, there is no satisfactory evidence to show, but that she lived in his house for a long period of time, cohabiting with him and bearing him several children whose legitimacy is not disputed, is beyond question. The defendant in effect asks us to draw a sharp dividing line between the date of the birth of the plaintiff and of his own, and to find as a fact that no marriage was subsisting when the plaintiff was born, but that it had taken place when he was born. My answer to this proposition must be and is, that there is no evidence upon which I can safely rely to justify me in coming to any such finding, and if the defendant had to maintain the converse position to that now asserted by him, he would be in similar straits as the plaintiff to prove a marriage between Ghulam Ghaus Khan and his mother. That there was no legal obstacle to a marriage must be conceded, and though its date remains unestablished, I need for the purposes of my judgment say no more than this, that it may as well have taken place before as after the birth of the plaintiff.

Such being the material facts as to acknowledgment and treatment of the plaintiff by Ghulam Ghaus Khan, the next point to be determined is, what is the legal effect of such acknowledgments and treatment according to the Muhammadan law? If the rules of that law deal with such matters as questions of evidence, i.e., as mere adjective law, and simply lay down principles for guidance in forming presumptions or drawing inferences, then they would not come within the term 'Muhammadan law' as used in s. 24 of the Bengal Civil Courts Act, i.e., the substantive Muhammadan law regarding succession, inheritance, &c., and I should have to deal with the case according to the rules of evidence contained in the Evidence Act. Petheram, CJ, in his judgment has treated the decisions of their Lordships of the Privy Council to which he refers as enunciating rules of substantive law 'as laid down in the books,' but he adds, 'the law so laid down is not, in my opinion, in accordance with the custom of the people of this country.' With the most profound respect for so eminent an authority, I think this remark is somewhat misleading and calculated to create doubts and impressions that a close scrutiny of the matter does not warrant. There are many apparent anomalies in both the Hindu and Muhammadan law that strike the mind of an English lawyer with astonishment, if not dismay, as irreconcilable with the principles of the English statute and common law that he has been taught; and in India it is natural enough that among our High Court advocates and pleaders, who represent the progress of English thought and influence upon the more or less undigested mass of doctrines and principles to be found in the Mitakshara or the various sources whence the Muhammadan law is drawn, the discussion of questions such as we have here should be maintained on modern lines and according to what may fairly be called popular views. But so long as the rules of the Hindu and Muhammadan law stand with such expositions and rulings as have been made in regard to them by their Lordships of the Privy Council, so long are we, sitting as judges in this country, constrained by statute to find out what those rules are, and when we have ascertained them with precision to give effect to them. I have done my best to ascertain whether the rulings of their Lordships are in any way at variance with the practices recognized by the Muhammadan community, and I cannot discover that any custom has grown up or exists which overrides or alters those principles of Muhammadan substantive law which I shall presently state in detail. Let us, however, first look to what their Lordships of the Privy Council have said in *Lalli Begam's case*[2] to which Petheram, CJ, among others refers: 'Their Lordships, however, are relieved from a discussion of those authorities, inasmuch as the rule of the Muhammadan law has not been disputed at the Bar, viz., that the acknowledgment and recognition of children by a Muhammadan as his sons gives them the *status* of sons capable of inheriting as legitimate sons, unless certain conditions exist, which do not occur in this case. That rule of the Muhammadan law has not been questioned at the Bar.' The original case from which the appeal was preferred is to be found reported in the Punjab Record for 1875, at page 21 of the Civil Rulings, and from this it appears that Mr Boulnois, a Judge of the Chief Court, held in effect that 'the acknowledgment of a son renders that person the legitimate son of the acknowledger under Muhammadan law, although the person acknowledged was born out of wedlock'. This view may possibly seem to be in accordance with the often-quoted passage to be found in their Lordships' judgment in the case of *Ashruf-ood-Dowlah Ahmad Hossein Khan* v. *Hyder Hossein Khan*[3] commencing—'But the presumption of legitimacy from marriage follows the bed, &c.' Nevertheless, with the greatest deference, it seems to me that Mr Boulnois' proposition goes too far, and that it is not in harmony with the texts. I see nothing in their Lordships' judgment in *Lalli Begam's case*[4] to lead me to conclude that they accepted the rule of Muhammadan law in the terms stated by Mr Boulnois; indeed, they themselves formulated it in the manner already recited by me. This case of *Lalli Begam* is instructive not only from what their Lordships said as to this rule of the Muhammadan law, but from its result in that while the question as to whether Lalli Begam was married to the Nawab before the birth of the plaintiffs was left undetermined, it was nevertheless held that they had by acknowledgment and recognition by him as his sons acquired the *status* of sons and a title to inherit. Their Lordships remark: 'However, there is really no dispute about the law, and their Lordships in this case have not to lay down any new principles of law, but only to apply a well-established principle to the

2 LR 9 IA 8; ILR 8 Cal. 422.
3 11 Moo IA 94.
4 LR 9 IA 8; ILR 8 Cal 422.

facts.' That principle was embodied in the second question stated by them as arising for decision, viz., whether, no marriage between Lalli Begum and the Nawab being established, there is proof of an acknowledgment and recognition by the Nawab of the two plaintiffs as his sons which would give them the status of sons and a title to inherit.

Now I do not hesitate to say, having very carefully considered the language of their Lordships' judgment, that they unhesitatingly adopted the view that the rules of Muhammadan law relating to acknowledgment by a Muhammadan of another as his son or daughter, as the case may be, are rules of substantive law, and such an acknowledgment, if there is no legal impediment to it, confers a status of legitimacy just as, by the analogy of the Roman law, manumission of a slave conferred on him the status of a free man. Without further preface I proceed to state what the more important; authorities are, which, having given them my most careful consideration, I take as establishing two propositions: 1st, that proved acknowledgments by a Muhammadan of another person as his son or daughter, if none of the conditions in bar subsists, which will presently appear, confer on such person the status of a legitimate child with its legal consequences; 2nd, that such an acknowledgment once made cannot be recalled either by the acknowledger himself or any one claiming under him. I may remark that the following quotations are, as the names of the authors will show, from the highest sources known to the Muhammadan law:

(a) *Birjandi*[5]

The book on acknowledgment has been placed next to that of evidence, because an acknowledgment is a kind of information and as such like evidence. The reason why these two subjects precede the subjects of claims is that the ascertainment of evidence and acknowledgment occur in most cases before the claim. As a matter of language the word *ikrar* is derived either from *qarár* which means rest and confirmation, as if the acknowledger establishes by his acknowledgment a right against himself, or the word is derived from *qurrat-ul-ain*, that is, comfort of the eyes, because the person in whose favour an acknowledgment is made receives thereby comfort to his eyes, and thus the acknowledger comforts the eyes of the person in whose favour the acknowledgment is made.

An acknowledgment is giving information as to the right of a person enforceable against the acknowledger; that is, the person who gives such information. Some difficulty has arisen (in consequence of this definition) in the case of an acknowledgment by an agent appointed to conduct litigation and also in the case of an executor, inasmuch as in these cases the acknowledgment of these persons amounts to giving information as to the right of another person against the principal in the one case and the ward in the other.

5 Book on Acknowledgement, pp. 291–4.

The requirement of acknowledgment is that it should be indicative of that in respect of which the acknowledgment is made, not a mere allusion thereto. This means that it is indispensable that the acknowledgment should expressly state the subject of the acknowledgment as if it already exists, and that by the acknowledgment the proof thereof is expressed. It is not an effect of an acknowledgment that anything is for the first time founded or established, and it is on this account that when the person in whose favour the acknowledgment is made comes to know that the acknowledger was false in his acknowledgment, the subject of the acknowledgment is not lawful to such a person (as a matter between him and his Creator, the Almighty), since he would in such a case be taking the subject of acknowledgment without the real willingness of the acknowledger. But if the acknowledger has delivered the subject of acknowledgment willingly, then it is lawful and becomes like an investiture of ownership by the acknowledger, and as such on the footing of gift. This is so because ownership is established in favour of him for whom the acknowledgment is made, and this without any verification or acceptance on his part; but such ownership is nullified by his rejecting it, so that if he first verifies it and then rejects it, such rejection is not valid. So in the *Kafi*.

(ii) If a person acknowledges the sonship of a boy whose descent is unknown, and he is such that one like him can be born of one like the acknowledger, and the boy verifies the acknowledgment, his descent is established. This has accidentally been mentioned with reference to the sonship of a boy, because, even if the acknowledgment of a daughterhood is made in respect of a woman, the same rule applies. But it is essential that such sonship (or daughterhood) should be without an intermediary link: so much so that if an acknowledgment is made that the boy is the son's son of the acknowledger, the descent is not established, and this result is similar to that of acknowledging another to be a brother.

It is a condition precedent (to the validity of acknowledgment of parentage) that the descent of the acknowledged be unknown, because, if his descent is known, his sonship other than to his parent would be impossible. What is meant by a descent not being known is that it should be unknown in the town in which he resides, and this explanation is contained in the *Kifaya* that the trustworthy reference is to the place of birth. It is stated in the *Kenaya* that when a person regarding one whose descent is known says, 'This is my son, and when I die all my estate is his', then according to some of the jurists the acknowledged will be entitled to one-third of the estate by way of legacy, whilst according to other jurists he would not be entitled even to one-third: and this last doctrine seems to be most consistent with right principles.

The limitation that the acknowledged might have been born of the acknowledger means that the age of the acknowledger should exceed the age of the acknowledged at least by twelve years, and this because it is the minimum period of puberty for a youth; and this limitation is necessary because if the acknowledger had not attained puberty, the acknowledgment would be falsified obviously. It is also a condition that the acknowledged boy should verify the acknowledgment, because, if he does not verify, an impediment is created and his descent is not established by the mere acknowledgment, but requires proof. This, however, applies only to cases in which the boy acknowledged is capable of expressing himself; when he is too young to express himself, verification by him is not a condition. It is stated in the chapter on the manumission of slaves in the *Fatawa Kazi Khan* that some jurists have held that sonship is not established unless it is verified by the person in whose favour it is made. But the correct doctrine is that such a condition is not essential as above stated, and this is in conformity with the doctrine of the *Hedaya* and many other books.

(b) *'Aini*[6]

In the case of a man in sickness acknowledging a youth of unknown parentage it is a condition that such a youth might have been begotten by such an acknowledger, because, if the acknowledged is older in age, the obvious fact falsifies the acknowledgment. Indeed, *Malik* has gone the length of holding that even if notoriety contradicts the acknowledger, such as by indicating that he was an Indian whilst the acknowledged boy was a Persian, the latter's descent is not established. The restriction that the acknowledged youth should verify the acknowledger has been imposed because the rule as to a youth who can express himself is applicable owing to his being in his own competency, whilst, on the contrary, an infant is in the power of another, and as such descends to the footing of animals, and no importance is attached to his verification. But according to the three Masters (i.e., Imam Abu Hanifa, Imam Muhammad, and Kazi Abu Yusuf) the descent is established without any such verification if the acknowledged be below the age of discretion. The descent is established because it is one of the necessities of nature, and there can be no objection thereto, even though the acknowledger be in sickness at the time of the acknowledgment. The acknowledged youth will participate with the heirs in the inheritance, because such is one of the consequences of the proof of descent. The acknowledgment by such in respect of a child or parents or wife or a manumitted slave will hold good, because, since it does not involve attribution of descent to anyone else, the acknowledgment must be accepted.

(c) *Durr-ul-Mukhtar*[7]

(i) If a person makes an acknowledgment in favour of a stranger whose parentage is unknown and thereafter acknowledges him to be his son, and the latter verifies it whilst he is one of those who are fit to make such a verification, his descent is established with reference to the time of his being begotten.

(ii) If a person makes an acknowledgment in favour of a youth whose parentage is unknown either at his birthplace or in the town where he is, that the latter is his son, and the acknowledger and the acknowledged are such in age that the latter may be born of the former as a son, and the youth verifies it, he being capable of discretion (because otherwise his verification is not necessary as already stated), then his descent is established, though the acknowledger be in sickness: and when the descent is so established, the youth will participate with the other heirs.

6 *Sharh-i Kanz*, Vol. II, p. 162.
7 Chapter on Sick Person's Acknowledgment, pp. 603–4.

(d) *Al-Ashbahu Wan-Naza'ir*[8]

When the person in whose favour an acknowledgment is made falsifies the acknowledger, the acknowledgment is nullified, except in the case of acknowledgment as to the freedom of slaves, as to the parentage, and as to the rights arising out of manumission of slaves: so the rule has been laid down in the *Sharh-ul-Majma* on the ground that such acknowledgments are not susceptible of annulment.

(e) *Fatawa-i Alamgiri*[9]

(i) When a man acknowledges a son expressly or impliedly the negation thereof will not be valid thereafter, whether such acknowledgment is made at the time of the birth or afterwards. Express acknowledgment is when a man says 'The child is mine' or says 'This is my child'; and implied acknowledgment is that the man should remain silent when he is being congratulated upon the birth of the child, in which case he may be required to take an oath. So in the *Ghayat-ul-Bayan*.

(ii) If the husband is without penis and she is not aware of his condition and gives birth to a child and he claims him, then the *Kazi* is to hold his descent to be established; and if she thereafter comes to be aware of his condition and therefore claims separation, she is entitled to do so, because the child necessarily becomes his even without proof of sexual intercourse.

(iii) A man says in favour of a boy 'There is my son' and then he dies; thereafter the mother of the boy, she being a free woman, comes forth and says 'I am the wife of deceased.' Thereby she is the wife of the deceased, and both she and the boy inherit from him.

(iv) If a man has illicit intercourse with a woman, who then becomes pregnant, and afterwards marries her and she then gives birth to a child, if such child is born after expiration of six months or more, his descent is established. But if she gives birth within less than six months his descent is not established? unless he claims him and does *not* say that the child is the result of illicit intercourse. But if he says 'that the child is born of me by illicit intercourse, the descent is not established and he will not inherit from him. So in the *Yanabi*.

(f) *Fatawa Qadi Khan*[10]

(i) A man has married a woman by a defective marriage and thereafter he retires with her, and thereafter she gives birth to a child after expiration of six months; his descent is established from him. There is difference of opinion as to the exact fixation of this time, because the question is whether these six months are to be calculated from the date of the marriage or from the time of retirement. Abu Hanifa and Abu Yusuf (on whom be peace!) regard this from date of the marriage; but Muhammad regards the six months from the time of retirement, and this is the accepted doctrine. In the case of a valid marriage all the three Masters are agreed that the period is

8 Book on Acknowledgment, p. 422.
9 Vol. I, pp. 703, 710, 726–7.
10 Section on Rules of Paternity, pp. 421–4.

to be regarded from the time of the marriage. Some of the jurists have said that in the case of the valid marriage retirement is not a condition precedent, but that there must be a state of things when they might have had intercourse.

A man has had illicit intercourse with a woman and she is impregnated by him, and during her pregnancy he marries her and has not had sexual intercourse with her till she gives birth to a child; then they (*i.e.*, the three) have held that the marriage is valid, if she was not during her *iddat* in consequence of some one else and penitence is necessary for him; and the jurist Abul Layth holds that if she gives birth to the child after the expiration of six months or more from the time of the marriage, the marriage is lawful and the descent is established. But if she gives birth to the child in less than six months from the date of the marriage, the marriage is not established and the child will not inherit from him, *unless* the man says 'This is a son from me' and does not say 'This is the offspring of illegitimate intercourse'.

(ii) A man has married a woman and she gives birth to a child in less than six months. Muhammad maintains that the marriage is defective 'according to my views and those of Abu Yusuf'.

A *majbub* (eunuch) has married a woman who lived with him for a time and then gave birth to a child. Abu Yusuf in such a case holds that the son is his son and she is lawful to him.

(iii) A man has married a woman and has then divorced her at the time before intercourse, and she gives birth to a child at the end of six months from the time of the marriage. The child is his child, though Zufar holds a contrary view

[Arabic texts of extracts under (a) to (d): *Cases* 208–16]

From these passages it appears to me that the proposition stated by their Lordships of the Privy Council in *Lalli Begam's Case*, as not being questioned before them, but which has been questioned before us in this appeal, namely, that the acknowledgment of children by a Muhammadan as his sons gives them the status of sons capable of inheriting as legitimate sons, unless certain conditions exist, is established to be a distinct and specific rule of the substantive Muhammadan law relating to inheritance to which we are bound to give effect. Birth during wedlock, that is to say, legitimate birth, necessarily confers a right to inherit; illegitimate birth, that is, without wedlock subsisting between the father and mother at the date of the child's begetting, confers no such right. But where there is no proof of legitimate birth or illegitimate birth and the paternity of a child is unknown in the sense that no specific person is shown to have been his father, then his acknowledgment by another, who claims him as his son, according to the authorities I have quoted from, affords a conclusive presumption that the child acknowledged is the legitimate child of the acknowledger and places him in that category. In the present case we have the fact that Moti Begam, the undoubted mother of the plaintiff, admittedly at some time or other, when it was we have no reliable proof, became the wife of Ghulam Ghaus Khan, that the plaintiff was acknowledged as a son by Ghulam Ghaus Khan and treated by him as such, and the plaintiff accepted and described himself as holding that position. It seems to me, therefore, that the requirements of the rule of the Muhammadan law have been satisfied, and that the plaintiff has established his acknowledgment and recognition by Ghulam Ghaus Khan as a son which gave him the status of a son and a title to inherit. This being so, it remains to be seen whether such a status once conferred can be destroyed by any subsequent act of the acknowledger or those who claim through him? It is equally clear that it cannot, and in support of this view there are not only the authorities of the Muhammadan law which I have quoted, but a decision of their Lordships of the Privy Council reported in 11 Moore's Indian Appeals, p. 94, in which it was held 'that the denial of a son after an established acknowledgment, though supported by a deed of repudiation and disclaimer by the father, is untenable'. As it seems to us that there were distinct acknowledgments by Ghulam Ghaus Khan of the plaintiff in 1861, it becomes immaterial to consider whether Ghulam Ghaus Khan did or did not personally cause, or bring about, the entry which was made in the *wajib-ul-arz* of 12 September 1870, upon which so much stress was laid by the learned counsel for the defendant in the course of his argument: though, if it were necessary to do so, I should have said without hesitation that there is no evidence to show that it was the result of any act or declaration of his. From the same point of view it is unnecessary to discuss the conduct of the plaintiff in regard to the suit brought by the defendant in 1880 and his delay in coming into court with his present claim. None of these matters could alter or destroy his status as a son if once conferred by acknowledgment, and it would serve no useful purpose, and only lead me into greater length in a judgment already sufficiently prolix were I to explain my views in detail with regard to them.

For the reasons I have given I have come to the conclusion that this appeal must be decreed and the status of the appellant as the legitimate son of Ghulam Ghaus Khan, with the consequent right of inheriting a share in the deceased father's estate, be declared.

Then arises the question as to the precise form our order should take, and I much regret that upon this point I am at difference with the learned Chief Justice and my brother Mahmood. I feel sure that I must be wrong in my own view, and I have endeavoured to convince myself that I am, but I am unable to do so.

In determining what our order should be, it is necessary to examine the terms of ss. 562, 563, and 564 of the Civil Procedure Code; for if I understand the matter aright, those sections read together and in contrast to the provisions of ss. 565, 566, distinctly direct a court of appeal not to remand a case, unless it has been determined and disposed of by the court of first instance 'upon a preliminary point, so as to exclude any evidence of fact which appears to the appellate court essential for the determination of the rights of the parties, and the decision upon such preliminary point is reversed in appeal.'

The question here, then, is whether the Sub-Judge can be said to have disposed of this suit upon a preliminary point, to the exclusion of evidence of fact. In determining that question it is important to see, apart from the mere question of the status of the plaintiff, which, with the rest of the court, I am willing to treat as a preliminary point, and which the Sub-Judge has determined, what were the other issues raised? It will not be disputed that the first four issues settled by the Sub-Judge for trial, including that of status, have been disposed of by him. The fifth issue which he settled was this—'What amount of debts, if any, due by Ghulam Ghaus Khan has been paid by Ismail Khan?' That issue was fixed in reference to the seventh paragraph of the written statement in which Ismail Khan vaguely and without any particulars said: 'The plaintiff has in his petition of plaint referred to the balance of the mortgage money due by the ancestor, but he has not mentioned the large debt paid by the defendant: the latter, like the former, is also payable from the property.'

Now no one would deny, having regard to the Full Bench ruling of this court,[11] and according to the principles of the Muhammadan law of inheritance, that, so far as Ismail Khan was concerned, if he was in possession of the estate of Ghulam Ghaus Khan, and if he had paid the debts of Ghulam Ghaus Khan, he would be entitled to hold on to the possession of Allahdad Khan's share of that estate, so long as, and until, Allahdad Khan paid off his quota of the debts which Ismail Khan had paid: and this is not denied.

But in the plea taken by Ismail Khan which, I have said, is of the vaguest possible kind, no mention is made of any debts that were paid, and, for aught I know to the contrary, no such payments were ever made. An issue having been fixed by the Sub-Judge in reference to that question, there is not a pretence for suggesting, and Mr Conlan frankly admits that upon the face of this record there is not a particle of proof, to show that Ismail Khan ever paid a pice of the debts of the ancestors. Moreover, I have asked in vain to have pointed out to me any trace upon the record to indicate that, at any stage of the trial in the first court, the Subordinate Judge, either by order or expression of opinion, actually excluded or led the defendant Ismail Khan or his pleaders to believe that he would exclude, or that it was unnecessary to produce, evidence upon this point.

11 *Jafri Begam* v. *Amir Muhammad Khan*, ILR 7 All 822.

What, then, are the materials from which I am to infer that the court below disposed of this case upon a preliminary point, so as to exclude any evidence of fact which was necessary for the determination of the rights of the parties? Neither Mr Conlan nor any other person has satisfied me upon this point, and it appears to me that this being so, I am not justified, in reference to the language of ss. 562, 563, and 564 of the Code, and more especially to the prohibition contained in such last-mentioned section, to make the form of remand proposed by the rest of the court.

It is clear, and in accordance with many expressions of opinion by their Lordships of the Privy Council, the effect of which is embodied in those sections, that a court of appeal should not send a case back to a court of first instance in such a way as to open the door to one or both of the parties making a new case with fresh evidence—a most dangerous thing to do in this country. There is nothing whatever to show in the present instance that Ismail Khan was prevented from producing evidence or led to believe by the court of first instance that the evidence upon the question of payment of debts was unnecessary because it was going to decide the case upon a preliminary point. I do not think that we are entitled sitting here upon this point, and upon a mere speculation as to the possibility of Ismail Khan having had some claim to an equitable charge in respect of the debts of Ghulam Ghaus, paid by him, to remand the case back to the court of first instance generally, so as to allow of a third person, who has acquired his interest *pendente lite* and after the appeal was filed here, to open up this part of the defence *de novo* and call witnesses and give other proof which Ismail Khan never attempted to produce.

There was undoubtedly, and the learned Chief Justice has put his finger upon that, a defence set up by the three persons, lessees of the villages from Ismail Khan, against whom the relief sought is stated in the third paragraph of the plaint. It is true, no doubt, that if those lessees had proved the matter set out in their statement of defence, there might have been, *prima facie,* a good answer in point of law to the claim of the plaintiff. In respect of these defendants it may be said that no issue was specifically stated by the Sub-Judge in respect of their defence, and their answer to the plaintiff's claim, which would be direct notice to them to give their evidence in regard to it. That being so, I am disposed to assist them to this extent that, as the court of first instance failed to frame an issue with regard to these defendants, and as the determination of such an issue appears to me essential for the right decision of the case, I would remit an issue under s. 566 of the Code to the lower appellate court for determination.

The matter therefore stands thus: In my opinion, as regards Ismail Khan, we cannot remand the case under s. 562 of the Code, because it has not been disposed of upon a preliminary point so as to exclude, evidence of fact, and we should therefore proceed to dispose of it upon the evidence upon the record, if there is any. It is said for the plaintiff, and I see no reason to doubt it, that there is no evidence on the record of the payment of any debt of Ghulam Ghaus Khan by Ismail Khan, and therefore, in regard to that particular matter, we ought, in my opinion, to dispose of it at once, and, there being no evidence, to dispose of it adversely to Ismail Khan.

With regard to the second question, I would remand an issue to try the question as to whether the defendants, lessees, did pay to Ismail Khan the rent of such land under a *bona fide* belief that he was the true proprietor. The question of costs would have to be determined hereafter.

Judgment-II [Mahmood, J.]

I concur in what has fallen from my brother Straight as to the facts of the case, and also as to the rules of law applicable to those facts. But because, in the course of the elaborate argument which was addressed to us at the Bar, many suggestions were made as to the exact scope of the rule of Muhammadan law relating to the acknowledgment of parentage, and much was argued as to such acknowledgment being a substitute for adoption as recognized in other systems, such as the Roman or the Hindu law, I am anxious to specify my own views.

First, then, as to the facts of the case, for the reasons so exhaustively. stated by my brother Straight, I have no doubt that the following conclusions are justified by the evidence:

(1) That Moti Begam did not stand in any such position of relationship with Ghulam Ghaus as would render her marriage with him unlawful;

(2) that she is not proved to have been ever married to any person other than Ghulam Ghaus;

(3) that she was married to Ghulam Ghaus;

(4) that the exact date of her marriage with reference to the birth of the plaintiff Allahdad is unascertainable for want of trustworthy evidence;

(5) that she cohabited with Ghulam Ghaus for a considerable number of years and was treated by him as his lawful wife;

(6) that the plaintiff Allahdad was acknowledged and treated by Ghulam Ghaus as his son;

(7) that in such acknowledgment or treatment there was no express specification as to whether Allahdad was a step-son, a legitimate son, or an illegitimate son of Ghulam Ghaus;

(8) that similar acknowledgment or treatment was accorded to him by the defendant Ismail and the other children of Ghulam Ghaus by Moti Begam, and indeed by the rest of the family.

Such being the main conclusions as to the facts of the case, I am desirous of stating the propositions of the Muhammadan law applicable to these facts. My brother has so fully quoted the authorities of Muhammadan law that I am relieved of the necessity of repeating them, and need only refer to them for formulating my propositions.

The first and perhaps the most important question in the case is whether the rule as to the acknowledgment of parentage is a rule of the Muhammadan substantive law of inheritance or merely a rule of evidence. The question is important, because unless it is a 'question regarding succession, inheritance, marriage or caste, or any religious usage or institution', within the meaning of s. 24 of the Bengal Civil Courts Act (VI of 1871) which governs this case, we are scarcely at liberty to apply the Muhammadan law in its integrity to this case, and the alternative would be almost unavoidable, to apply to the question the rules of evidence, as to the admissions and presumption of legitimacy, contained in the Indian Evidence Act (I of 1872), by s. 2 of which enactment all other rules of evidence have been abolished.

Now, it cannot be denied that in all medieval systems of jurisprudence much confusion exists between rules of substantive law and rules of adjective law, that is, between rules which affect the merits and go *ad litis decisionem* and rules which regulate the remedy and, as rules of procedure, only go *ad litis ordinationem*. The Muhammadan system of jurisprudence is no exception to the general rule, and I have before now felt considerable difficulty in distinguishing the rules of the substantive law of Muhammadan inheritance from the rules of evidence. I allude in particular to the case of *Mazhar Ali* v. *Budh Singh*,[12] which related to the inheritance of a missing person, and in which, after much consideration, a Full Bench of this Court agreed in holding that the question there raised was a question of evidence and as such governed by ss. 107 and 108 of the Evidence Act.

Is the question now before us one of a similar character? In order to decide this question I have been at some pains to consult the original authorities of the Muhammadan law which my brother has already quoted, and I am responsible for the English translation of the original Arabic of those texts. The first of them is a passage from *Birjandi* which describes the exact place which *iqrar* or acknowledgment in general occupies in Muhammadan jurisprudence, and the passage leaves no doubt that the

12 ILR 7 All 297.

Muhammadan jurisconsults themselves do not treat the subject of acknowledgments as forming part of the rules of evidence, though they recognize the fact that acknowledgments resemble admissions. To use the language of *Birjandi*, 'an acknowledgment is giving information as to the right of a person enforcible against the acknowledger, that is, the person who gives such information,' and 'it is indispensable that the acknowledgment should expressly state the subject of the acknowledgment as if it already exists, and that by the acknowledgment the proof thereof is expressed.' The author then goes on to explain that 'it is not an effect of an acknowledgment that anything is for the first time founded or established'.

So far, it would seem at first sight that an *ikrar* or acknowledgment stands in the Muhammadan law much on the same footing as an ordinary admission as defined in s. 17 of the Evidence Act; and if the matter rested here, I confess I should have been inclined to regard the question as one appertaining to the province of the law of evidence. But acknowledgments of parentage under the Muhammadan law rest upon a footing higher than that of ordinary admissions as pure matters of evidence. The rules of the Muhammadan law applicable to such acknowledgments and the conditions under which such acknowledgments can be validly made are stated in the authoritative texts which my brother Straight has already quoted, and to those texts I wish to add a passage from the *Hedaya* which sums up the law upon the subject:

If a person acknowledge the parentage of a child who is able to give an account of himself, saying 'This is my son', and the ages of the parties be such as to admit of the one being the child of the other, and the parentage of the child be not well known to any person, and the child himself verify the acknowledgment, his parentage is established in the acknowledger, although he (the acknowledger) be sick; because the parentage in question is one of those things which affect the acknowledger himself only and no other person. It is made a condition, in this case, that the ages of the parties be such as to admit of the relation of parentage; for if it were otherwise, it is evident that the acknowledger has spoken falsely. It is also made a condition that the parentage of the boy be unknown; for if he be known to be the issue of some other than the acknowledger, it necessarily follows that the acknowledgment is null. It is also made a condition that the boy verify the acknowledgment; because he is considered as his own master, as he is supposed able to give an account of himself. It were otherwise if the boy could not explain his condition; for then the acknowledgment would have operated without his verification. It is to be observed that the acknowledgment, in this instance, is not rendered null by sickness, because parentage is an original and not a supervenient want. By the establishment of the parentage, therefore, the boy becomes one of the acknowledger's heirs in the same manner as any of his other heirs.' (Hamilton's *Hedaya* by Grady, p. 439.)

In commenting upon this passage of the *Hedaya,* the author of the *Kifaya* points out that the rule as to acknowledgment of parentage is based upon the words of the Koran [Qur'an], 'call them after their fathers';[13] and the author explains that such acknowledgment is sufficient, 'because the burden of the obligation in respect of the child rests especially on the father, and the latter's acknowledgment affects himself personally and is thus accepted without any verification by the mother'.[14] Another celebrated commentary on the *Hedaya*, the *Fath-ul-Qadir*, in explaining the rule contained in the above passage as to the condition that the acknowledged child should be of unknown parentage, goes on to say that the condition has been imposed, because otherwise the descent of the acknowledged child could not be established from the acknowledger since 'descent after it is established is not susceptible of the annulment'.[15]

The last point is important, and is to the same effect as the text from the *Ashbah* and the first text from Vol. I of the *Fatawa-i-Alamgiri*, both of which are quoted in my brother Straight's judgments. The same rule is stated in another portion of the *Fatawa-i-Alamgiri*; and to use the words of Mr Baillie's translation, 'descent, when once established, cannot be dissolved or cancelled, neither can it be transferred from one person to another' (*Baillie's Dig*., p. 408).

The passage from the *Ashbah*, however, throws the greatest light upon the nature of such acknowledgments and their effect under the Muhammadan law. The passage shows that whilst ordinary acknowledgments stand upon one footing an exception is made in favour of such acknowledgments as relate to matters of personal status, and that in such cases the law does not allow cancellation or annulment of the acknowledgment. This peculiarity of such acknowledgments, that is, the permanency of their effect when duly made, upon the personal status of the persons in respect of whom such acknowledgments are made, is in itself sufficient to justify the conclusion that the acknowledgment of parentage, though it has reference to evidential presumptions and other considerations, is in effect a rule of personal status in the eye of Muhammadan law; and I am fortified in this conclusion by the uniform practice of the courts in India and of the Privy Council in dealing with such questions as falling within the province of the Muhammadan law of inheritance and marriage.

13 Qur'an, XXXIII: 5. [Arabic text: *Cases*, 223]

14 Hidaya with its commentary *Al-Kifaya*, vol. III: Book on Acknowledgement, p. 581.

15 Book on Acknowledgment, Section on Sick Person's Acknowledgment, p. 611. [Arabic text: *Cases*, 224]

The various propositions of the Muhammadan law as they apply to the fact of this case and the steps of legal reasoning upon which those propositions proceed may now be stated.

The right of inheritance under the Muhammadan law is based upon three grounds described by Mr Baillie to be *nusub* [*nasab*, descent], which is *kurabat* [consanguinity], or kindred; special cause, which is marriage, that is, a valid marriage, for there are no mutual rights of inheritance by a marriage that is invalid or void, according to all, and *wula,* which is of two kinds, *wula* of emancipation and *wula* of *moowalat*, or mutual friendship. In this case we are concerned only with *nusub*, that is, relationship by consanguinity of descent, which in Muhammadan law means legitimate descent only, so far as inheritance from or through males is concerned, and marriage between the parents of the inheritor is a condition precedent to his legitimacy. 'The intercourse of a man with a woman who is neither his wife nor his slave is unlawful and prohibited absolutely. When there is neither the validity nor the semblance of either of these relations between the parties, their intercourse is termed *zina* and subjects them both to *hadd* or specific punishment, for vindicating the rights of Almighty God.' (Baillie's *Dig*., p. I). 'The offspring of a connection where the man has no right nor semblance of right in the woman, by marriage or slavery, is termed *wulud-ooz-zina*, or child of *zina*, and is necessarily illegitimate' (26, p. 3). The *Durr-ul-Mukhtar* states the acknowledged general rule that 'an illegitimate child as well as a child of curse or imprecation inherits only from the relations on the mother's side by reason of its being no residuary and having no father' (Tagore Law Lectures, 1873, p. 123). The same is the effect of the rule as stated in Rumsey's *Chart of Muhammadan Inheritance* (p. 342, 3rd ed.); and it is more fully expressed in *Aini*, where it is laid down that 'illegitimate children and children of curse do not inherit, except from the mother's side, because their parentage on the father's side is wanting; so they do not inherit from their putative fathers, but as their parentage on the mother's side is established, they, on account of such parentage, inherit only from their mothers and half brothers by the mother's side the legal shares and no more.' (Tagore Law Lectures, 1873, p. 123.) 'When a man has committed *zina* with a woman, and she is delivered of a son whom he claims, the descent of the son from the man is not established, but it is established from the woman by the birth' (Baillie's Dig., p. 411).

From these passages two points are perfectly clear, *viz., first*, that so far as inheritance from males or through males is concerned, the existence of legitimacy of descent or consanguinity is a condition precedent to the right of inheritance; and *secondly,* that such legitimacy depends upon a valid marriage or connection between the parents of the inheritor. Now, the

Muhammadan jurists themselves in dealing with the question of parentage, *nusub*, or relationship by consanguinity, recognize a distinction between cases in which inheritance is claimed from or through the father and inheritance claimed from or through the mother. 'Maternity admits of positive proof, because the separation of a child from its mother can be seen. Paternity does not admit of positive proof, because the connection of a child with its father is secret; but it may be established by the word of the father himself or by a subsisting *firash* (bed), that is, a legally constituted relation between him and the mother of the child' (Baillie's Dig., p. 389). And it may be taken as an undoubted proposition of the Muhammadan law of inheritance that in no case can an illegitimate child, that is, the offspring of *zina* or illicit intercourse, be entitled to inheritance from his father or through him, because he is regarded as *nullius filius*, that is, a person whose *nusub* or descent from the father is wanting.

I have already said that in the case of establishing descent from a mother and claiming inheritance from her, legitimacy is not a condition precedent to such right of inheritance; but in the case of inheritance from the father legitimacy is absolutely necessary before any such right can be claimed. The question then is, whether in cases like the present, where the paternity of a child, that is, his legitimate descent from his father, cannot be proved by establishing a marriage between his parents at the time of his conception or birth, the Muhammadan law recognizes any other method whereby such marriage and legitimate descent can be presumed, inferred, or held to be established as a matter of substantive law for purposes of inheritance.

In dealing with this part of the case much help is rendered by the case-law upon the subject. In *Khajah Hidayat Oolah* v. *Rai Jan Khanum*[16] the principle was laid down by the Lords of the Privy Council 'that, under the Muhammadan law, where a child has been born to a father of a mother where there has been not a mere casual concubinage, but a more permanent connection, and where there is no insurmountable obstacle to such a marriage, then, according to the Muhammadan law, the presumption is in favour of such marriage having taken place'; and their Lordships go on to add, 'that in considering this question of Muhammadan law we must, at least to a certain extent, be governed by the same principles of evidence which the Musalman lawyers themselves would apply to the consideration of such a question' (p. 318). The general effect of the ruling in that case is that continual cohabitation of the parents and acknowledgment of the child by the father is presumptive evidence of marriage between the parents and of the legitimacy of the offspring. Their Lordships had to deal with a similar

16 Moo IA 295.

question in *Mahomed Bauker Hoossain Khan* v. *Shurf-oon-nissa Begam*[17] in which their Lordships held, that although by the Muhammadan law the legitimacy of a child of Muhammadan parents may be presumed or inferred from circumstances, without any direct proof either of a marriage between the parents or of any formal act of legitimation, in the absence of evidence or circumstances sufficient to found such a presumption or inference, a claim by a party as a legitimate son to share in an intestate's estate should be dismissed. But whilst laying down this rule their Lordships went on to say:

> But in arriving at this conclusion, they wish to be distinctly understood as not denying or questioning the position that, according to the Muhammadan law, the law which regulates the rights of the parties before us, the legitimacy or legitimation of a child of Muhammadan parents may properly be presumed or inferred from circumstances without proof, or at least without any direct proof, either of a marriage between the parents or of any formal act of legitimation (p. 159).

The exact effect of these rulings was again considered by their Lordships in the important case of *Ashruf-ood-Dowlah Ahmed Hossein Khan* v. *Hyder Hossein Khan*,[18] where their Lordships observed:

> The presumption of legitimacy from marriage follows the bed, and whilst the marriage lasts, the child of the woman is taken to be the husband's child; but this presumption follows the bed, and is not antedated by relation. An ante-nuptial child is illegitimate. A child born out of wedlock is illegitimate; if acknowledged, he acquires the status of legitimacy. When, therefore, a child really illegitimate by birth becomes legitimated, it is by force of an acknowledgment express or implied, directly proved or presumed. These presumptions are inferences of facts. They are built on the foundations of the law, and do not widen the grounds of legitimacy by confounding concubinage and marriage. The child of marriage is legitimate as soon as born. The child of a concubine may become legitimate by treatment as legitimate. Such treatment would furnish evidence of acknowledgment. A court would not be justified, though dealing with this subject of legitimacy, in making any presumptions of fact which a rational view of the principles of evidence would exclude. The presumption in favour of marriage and legitimacy must rest on sufficient grounds, and cannot be permitted to override over-balancing proofs, whether direct or presumptive (pp. 113–14).

This passage, if taken as an abstract enunciation of the law, might lend colour to the contention that even a child whose illegitimacy is proved may be legitimated by an acknowledgment, and indeed it was upon this interpretation of that passage that a considerable portion of the argument on behalf of the plaintiffs-appellants proceeded. But the Lords of the Privy

17 Moo IA 136.
18 Moo IA 94.

Council themselves in *Muhammad Azmat Ali Khan* v. *Musammat Lalli Begam*[19] took occasion to explain the exact effect of that passage and went on to say:

These observations must be taken with a reference to the facts of that case, and in that case it appeared that there was a *Moottah* marriage after the birth of the child. There was no acknowledgment, and the treatment of the child was equivocal. Sometimes he was treated as son and at others not; and indeed by a deed executed by the father for that purpose he was distinctly repudiated by him as his son. In that case it was decided that in the absence of express acknowledgment, the evidence was insufficient either to raise the presumption of a marriage which in point of time would cover the birth of the child or of an acknowledgment. The facts and questions in that case were very complicated, and some of the passages in the judgment referred to by the Judge below can only be understood by referring to the question to which they were addressed (p. 19).

These observations are, in my opinion, an important limitation upon the interpretation of the passage on which so much reliance was placed at the Bar in the argument for the appellants. The general effect of the ruling in the case last cited is that, according to Muhammadan law, the acknowledgment and recognition of children by a father as his sons give them the status of sons capable of inheriting as legitimate sons, and this rule was affirmed again by the Privy Council in *Sadakat Hossein* v. *Syed Mahomed Yusuf*,[20] where their Lordships expressly refrained 'from offering any opinion upon the very important question of law' whether 'the offspring of an adulterous intercourse could be legitimated by any acknowledgment' (p. 36).

This last reservation is to my mind a most significant one, as showing that the passage which I have quoted from their Lordships' judgment in *Ashruf-ood-Dowlah Ahmed Hossein Khan* v. *Hyder Hossein Khan*[21] must not be understood loosely in the sense of being an abstract enunciation of the law applicable to all cases; for I cannot help feeling that if that passage were to be interpreted loosely and regardless of the facts of the case in which those observations were made, there would have been no necessity for reservation of opinion by their Lordships in the case of the acknowledgment of an offspring of an adulterous or even of an incestuous intercourse. Illegitimacy under the Muhammadan law, as indeed under other systems, arises from the absence of a lawful matrimonial relation between the parents of the child; and if illegitimacy which is proved and placed beyond doubt were no impediment to an acknowledgment, there would be no logical

19 LR 9 IA 8; ILR 8 Cal 422.

20 LR 11 IA 31; ILR 10 Cal 663.

21 11 Moo IA at, p. 113.

reason why the offspring of an adulterous or incestuous intercourse should not acquire the status of legitimate children when acknowledged by the father.

After having carefully considered the various rulings of the Lords of the Privy Council in the cases to which I have referred, I am of opinion that their Lordships never intended to go the length of laying down the rule that a child who is proved to be illegitimate, either in consequence of marriage between his parents being disproved, or being unlawful, could be legitimated by an acknowledgment. All the cases which their Lordships had before them were cases in which the question of marriage itself was a matter in dispute and involved in obscurity with reference to the legitimacy of the child. In other words, those cases were such as left either the fact or the exact time of the alleged marriage a matter of uncertainty, that is, neither proved nor disproved; and their Lordships in dealing with those cases applied the principles of the Muhammadan law of acknowledgment of parentage with reference to legitimacy for purposes of inheritance. Any other view of those cases would involve the proposition that their Lordships intended to go far beyond the authority of the Muhammadan law itself as to acknowledgments of parentage and legitimacy for purposes of inheritance.

Yet such was the effect of the argument addressed to us in support of the appeal, and indeed that argument went the length of contending that the Muhammadan law as to acknowledgment of parentage was nothing more or less than a substitute for affiliation by adoption as recognized by the Roman or the Hindu law, that is, an affiliation which has no reference either to the consanguinity of descent of the acknowledged child from the acknowledger or to the legitimacy of such descent. I have already said that this contention is not warranted by any of the rulings of the Lords of the Privy Council, and I now proceed to show that it is positively opposed to the rules of the Muhammadan law itself.

Not a single authority of that law has been quoted, and I am not aware of any, which would justify the conclusion that legitimacy of descent from a father is not an absolutely indispensable condition precedent to the very existence of the right of inheritance from the father, and I have already shown that children born of *zina* (which means fornication, adultery, or incest) can never be legitimated or entitled to inherit from their father. Nor can such children be made legitimate by any kind of acknowledgment where the illegitimacy is a proved and established fact. The Muhammadan law of acknowledgment of parentage with its legitimating effect has no reference whatsoever to cases in which the illegitimacy of the child is proved and established, either by reason of a lawful union between the parents of the child being impossible (as in the case of an incestuous intercourse or an adulterous connection), or by reason of marriage necessary to render the child legitimate being *disproved*. The doctrine relates only to cases where either the fact of the marriage itself or the exact time of its occurrence with reference to the legitimacy of the acknowledged child is not proved in the sense of the law as distinguished from disproved. In other words, the doctrine applies only to cases of uncertainty as to legitimacy, and in such cases acknowledgment has its effect, but that effect always proceeds upon the assumption of a lawful union between the parents of the acknowledged child. This is abundantly clear from the authorities from which my brother Straight has already quoted. Among those authorities the passages from the first volume of the *Fatawa Alamgiri* may at first sight contradict the view to which I have given expression, and I am therefore anxious to explain that those passages have no such effect. The first of those texts only shows that an acknowledgment of parentage when duly made cannot be negatived. The second text, which relates to the case of a *majbub*[22] acknowledging a child and such acknowledgment taking effect, notwithstanding the acknowledger's mutilated condition, proceeds upon the general principle of Muhammadan law against bastardizing children, and the words 'the child necessarily becomes his even without proof of sexual intercourse' which occur in the text must not be understood to mean anything beyond the rule that even in such a case acknowledgment of parentage obviates the necessity of ascertaining either the time or the extent of the mutilation of the acknowledger's person. The text assumes the existence of a valid marriage and the possibility of the acknowledged child's legitimate descent from the acknowledger, and I have no doubt that it would be misunderstanding the text if it were held to mean that even where there is a physical impossibility of the child's descent from the acknowledger, the child becomes of one who could not be his father. The reason of the rule relates not to any theory of adoption, but to the theory that an acknowledgment of parentage obviates any investigation as to the physical condition of the acknowledger's potency or impotency for procreating the offspring of a valid marriage. The same is the explanation of the latter part of the second text which my brother Straight has quoted from the *Fatawa Kazi Khan*.

The third text from the *Fatawa-i Alamgiri* requires no explanation, but the fourth text does require reference to show that it does not contradict the view which I have taken as to the assumption of legitimacy being a condition precedent to the validity of an acknowledgment of parentage. Now that text begins by assuming that the offspring was the result of an

22 From *jubb*, a eunuch. *Durr-ul-Mukhtar*, p. 267. See footnote at p. 27, Baillie's *Dig*.

illicit intercourse, but the birth of the child took place during lawful wedlock, and it was acknowledged by the father. Now, so far as my view that the assumption of a legitimate descent is a condition precedent to the validity of the acknowledgment of parentage is concerned, it is enough to point out that in the text itself the condition is imposed that the birth of the child should take place after the expiration of six months (the shortest period of gestation under the Muhammadan law) from the date of the marriage—a condition which proceeds upon the theory of the possibility of a legitimate birth. The same is the theory upon which the latter part of the text proceeds, although it relates to birth within six months of the marriage, because the implication there is that the acknowledgment of the father must be taken to involve the possibility of a legitimate intercourse between the parents of the acknowledged child at the time of his being begotten. The text would be misunderstood if not considered in the light of the circumstance that divorce under the Muhammadan law rests entirely with the husband, that it may under certain limitations be retracted by him, and that there may be a remarriage between the parties. It is no doubt in view of this circumstance that the Muhammadan jurists have placed acknowledgment of the parentage of a child by a man upon an exceptionally strong footing, as obviating the necessity of an investigation into facts which would otherwise be necessary to establish the legitimacy of the child, with reference to the marriage of his parents, the period of his conception, and the date of his birth. The principle of the Muhammadan law on this head is much the same as that adopted by the courts of justice in England, where the rule is represented by the maxim *semper praesumitur pro legitimatione puerorum*, or by a cognate rule *semper praesumitur pro matrimonio*, the authority of which was recognized in *Piers* v. *Piers*.[23] And it is important to observe that in the very text with which I am now dealing it is expressly indicated that an acknowledgment of parentage is ineffective if accompanied by an intimation that the acknowledged offspring was the result of an illicit intercourse. The words of the text are: 'if he says that the child is born of me by illicit intercourse, the descent is not established and he will not inherit from him,' and they leave no doubt in my mind that it is only by misapprehension of the principles of Muhammadan law that it can be held that a person proved to be a *walad-ooz-zina*, that is, the offspring of a fornication, adultery, or incest, can ever be legitimated by any kind of acknowledgment by the father. It is upon the same principles that the first and third texts from the *Fatawa Kazi Khan* quoted by my brother Straight must be explained, and the latter part of the first text, as also the third text, show that the matter

23 HL Cas 331.

as to the effect of acknowledgment of parentage, though a rule of substantive law, proceeds entirely upon an assumption of the possibility of legitimate descent of an acknowledged child from the acknowledger, and that the rule as to the effect of such acknowledgment does not extend to cases where such legitimate descent was impossible owing either to the impossibility of a valid marriage between the parents of the child, or owing to the existence of such a marriage being disproved by trustworthy evidence. And I have no doubt that I am representing the views of the Muhammadan jurists rightly when I say that there is no warrant in the principles of the Muhammadan law to justify the view that a child proved to be the offspring of fornication, adultery, or incest could be made legitimate by any act of acknowledgment by the father. I repeat that the rule is limited to cases of uncertainty of legitimate descent and proceeds entirely upon an assumption of legitimacy and the establishment of such legitimacy by the force of such acknowledgment.

I have dwelt upon this point at such length because the judgment of Petheram, CJ, now under appeal begins by saying:

> The evidence in this case proves, in my opinion, that the Plaintiff-appellant Allahdad was the illegitimate son of Ghulam Ghaus Khan. I also think upon the evidence that he was born before the marriage of Ghulam Ghaus Khan with Moti Begam, and therefore it has been established that he was, in the inception at all events, an illegitimate son of his father.

Similarly, my brother Brodhurst, in summing up the effect of the evidence in this case, went even further than Petheram, CJ, in saying:

> The following appear to be the established facts:—that Allahdad was not born in wedlock; that he was the son of Moti by an unknown father; that his mother was at the time of his birth and up to the time that she married Ghulam Ghaus a prostitute.

If I had taken the same view of the evidence as Petheram, CJ, or my brother Brodhurst, as to the parentage or birth of Allahdad, I should have found it impossible to have favoured his claim; but according to the view of the facts which my brother Straight has taken and in which I concur, the date of the marriage of Ghulam Ghaus with Moti Begam with reference to the birth of Allahdad is wholly uncertain owing to want of trustworthy evidence, and, indeed, it is not even established that he was the natural son of Ghulam Ghaus. But direct evidence of paternity is not to be expected in such a case any more than in a case where the question of alleged illegitimacy does not complicate the facts. Indeed, in the Muhammadan law, as in other systems of jurisprudence, direct proof of paternity is not required, and rules of presumption more or less stringent are adopted by various systems as furnishing the place of absolute proof of paternity which, *ex necessitate rei*, cannot be proved by positive and direct evidence, because, as the *Fatawa Alamgiri* puts it, 'the connection of a child with his father is secret,' as distinguished from 'maternity, which admits of positive proof, because the separation of a child from its mother can be seen'. To sum up the matter, I agree in the views of my brother Straight in holding that the entire question of the descent, birth, and legitimacy of Allahdad is involved in obscurity owing to the exact date of his mother's marriage with Ghulam Ghaus being unascertainable, and that, therefore, this case presents all those conditions to which the Muhammadan law as to the acknowledgment of parentage is most appropriately applicable; and further, as my learned brother has shown here, the requisite acknowledgment in words and by treatment was made by Ghulam Ghaus without any such intimation of Allahdad being the offspring of illicit intercourse as would vitiate the effect of the acknowledgment according to the texts which my learned brother has quoted.

Such being my view of the facts of the case, it is not necessary to enter into any elaborate discussion as to how far the provisions of s. 112 of the Indian Evidence Act (I of 1872), as to birth during wedlock being conclusive proof of legitimacy, would affect a case such as this. That section of course proceeds upon adopting the period of birth, as distinguished from conception, as the turning point of legitimacy. 'It is a peculiarity of the English law that it does not concern itself with the conception, but considers a child legitimate who is born of parents married before the time of his birth, though they were unmarried when he was begotten' (Lord Mackenzie's *Roman Law*, p. 130, 4th ed.).

That peculiarity of the English law has no doubt been imported into India by s. 112 of the Indian Evidence Act, and it may some day be a question of great difficulty to determine how far the provisions of that section are to be taken as trenching upon the Muhammadan law of marriage, parentage, legitimacy, and inheritance, which departments of law under other statutory provisions are to be adopted as the rule of decision by the courts in British India. Fortunately the difficulty does not arise in this case owing to the date of the marriage of Ghulam Ghaus with Moti Begam with reference to the birth of Allahdad being uncertain, and I need not therefore refer to the difficulty any further than by saying that there is enough authority in the texts of the Muhammadan law to show that, under that system of jurisprudence, questions of legitimacy are referred to the date of the conception of the child and not to the period of his birth.

Nor need I dwell much upon that part of the argument of the learned *Pandit* for the appellant which aimed at showing that the Muhammadan rule as to the acknowledgment of parentage is only a substitute for adoption as understood in the Hindu and the Roman system of jurisprudence, or that the rule of the Muhammadan law is the same as the Roman or the Scotch rule relating to the legitimation of children *per subsequens matrimonium*, that is, legitimation of ante-nuptial children whose illegitimacy is proved and admitted by subsequent marriage between the parents. So far as this argument refers to the Hindu law of adoption, I need only say, with reference to the numerous authorities which were considered by me in *Ganga Sahai* v. *Lekhraj Singh*,[24] that adoption under that system has no reference to the natural descent of the adopted child from the adoptive father; that adoption, at least in its principal form is established by a gift from the parents of the child to the adoptive parents; that the power of adoption itself is based upon religious considerations relating to the spiritual welfare of the adoptive father in the life to come after death; that the effect of such adoption takes away the adopted child from the family of his natural parents and affiliates him to the family of the adoptive father. Further, under that law only male children can be adopted for religious reasons, although no doubt secular considerations, such as the continuity of a family and devolution of inheritance, may form motives of adoption. None of these main elements of the theories upon which the Hindu law of adoption proceeds is common to the Muhammadan law, for there, as I have shown, acknowledgment of parentage proceeds upon the theory of actual descent of the acknowledged child (whether male or female) from the father who acknowledges it, and such descent being the result of a legitimate intercourse between the parents, and when either of these two essentials is disproved, the one by proving that the acknowledged child is the offspring of another man, the other by proving either that marriage between the acknowledger and the mother of the child was impossible or did not exist at the time which would make the child legitimate, the acknowledgment itself would be ineffective.

For similar reasons there is absolutely no analogy between the Roman law of adoption and the Muhammadan law of the acknowledgment of parentage. Under the Roman system adoption, whether in the form of *arrogatio* or in the later form of *adoptio* proper, was simply one of the methods of acquiring *patria potestas*, that is, the rights of control enjoyed by the head of a Roman family over his children, and it went through various stages of modification both as to the method by which it was acquired and as to its conditions and effects upon the adopted children. The history of the law and its rules have been well summarized by Mr Hunter in his work

24 ILR 9 All 253.

on *Roman Law* (pp. 58–66), and by Colquhoun in his work on *Roman Civil Law* (Vol. I, ss. 683–705, pp. 545–58). It is not necessary to enter into any detail of the reasons and rules which distinguish the Roman adoption from the Muhammadan law as to the acknowledgment of parentage, and it is enough to say that before the age of Islam adoption by a feigned parturition was common and well recognized among the ancient Arabs, that the cognate as well as the agnate rights were attributed to children so adopted, and that such adoption and its legal effects were abrogated by the express words of the Koran and have never since found a place in Muhammadan jurisprudence in connection with marriage, inheritance, or for any other legal purpose. (See Colquhoun's *Roman Civil Law*, s. 707, Vol. 1, p. 559.)

Then, so far as legitimation is concerned as a rule of the Roman law and of the Scotch law, I need only refer again to Colquhoun's *Roman Civil Law* (ss. 660, 666, 667, and 683) and to Lord Mackenzie's *Roman Law* (pp. 130–4), which describe the rules, conditions, and effect of legitimation under both those systems, and it only requires a comparison between those rules and the rules of the Muhammadan law as to acknowledgment of parentage to show that no analogy exists between the principles upon which those rules proceed and those upon which the Muhammadan rule of the acknowledgment of parentage is founded. Putting the matter shortly, the former two systems proceed upon the principle of legitimating children whose illegitimacy is proved and admitted, whilst the Muhammadan law relates only to cases of uncertainty and proceeds upon the assumption that the acknowledged child is not only the offspring of the acknowledger by blood, but also the issue of a lawful union between the acknowledger and the mother of the child. To illustrate this distinction I may refer to the rule adopted in Scotland and I may also say in France (Lord Mackenzie's *Roman Law*, pp. 132–3), as to the legitimation of ante-nuptial children by reason of a subsequent marriage between their *parents—per subsequens matrimonium*. In both those countries the marriage itself, subject to certain restrictions, has the legitimating effect. No such rule is known to the Muhammadan law, and we should really be introducing doctrines foreign to that system if, influenced by the analogies furnished by the Roman, the French, or the Scotch law of legitimation, we were to place acknowledgment of parentage under the Muhammadan law on the same footing as the rule of legitimation *per subsequens matrimonium* rests on in the foreign systems of law to which I have referred.

It is apparent from what I have said that I fully concur with my brother Straight as to the weight of evidence and the facts of this case, and that I have as a matter of law arrived at the same conclusion as he has arrived at with reference to the status of the plaintiff Allahdad to be that of a legitimate child of Ghulam Ghaus, and as such entitled to inherit from the latter and entitled to maintain the suit. But then comes a question upon which, unfortunately, I am unable to agree with my learned brother, namely, the question as to what order we should pass upon this appeal. The facts of the case and the pleadings of the parties show that this is one of those cases which fall within the purview of the Full Bench ruling of this court in *Jafri Begam* v. *Amir Muhammad Khan*[25] and of a Division Bench ruling in *Muhammad Awais* v. *Har Sahai*.[26] These rulings show that no absolute and unconditional decree should be passed for possession in favour of the plaintiff, if it is true that during his remaining out of possession debts due by the deceased Ghulam Ghaus Khan were lawfully paid by the heirs in possession. If such payment of debts be proved, the effect would be that the payment of a proportionate share of such debts would be a condition to which the decree in favour of the plaintiffs would be rendered subject with reference to the various equities that may arise in the case.

Have we, then, upon the record any material for framing such a decree? The learned counsel for the parties are agreed that there is no sufficient material upon the record to enable us to frame such a decree. All that is contended by the learned *Pandit* for the appellants is that, in the absence of such materials, it is the duty of this court as the court of appeal to decree the suit absolutely without any further remand for a proper trial of the points upon which the equities aforesaid would proceed. It is important to observe that not only the heirs of the deceased Ghulam Ghaus Khan, but also three lessees, were parties defendants to the suit, and it is clear that in a suit of this character, if the court below had framed adequate issues arising out of the proceedings of the parties and after taking evidence thereon had adjudicated upon those issues, we should have been bound by s. 564 of the Code of Civil Procedure to go ourselves into the merits of the evidence and to refrain from a remand such as s. 562 of the Code contemplates. But for the reasons stated by the learned Chief Justice such is not the case here; and agreeing with him in the interpretation of the law upon the subject of remand for new trials under s. 562 of the Court of Civil Procedure, I hold that all that the learned Judge of the lower court tried and decided in this case was the preliminary question of the plaintiff Allahdad's status to sue as the heir of the deceased Ghulam Ghaus, and that, by reason of the view taken by that Judge upon this point of status, the rest of the case was not tried upon the merits, and that, therefore, the case is a fit one for remand under s. 562 of the Code of Civil Procedure.

I agree with the learned Chief Justice in the order which he has made.

25 ILR 7 All 882.
26 ILR 7 All 719.

19. Sadik Husain v. Hashim Ali
(1916) 43 IA 212

Gift—Trust—Delivery of possession—Invalidity—Legitimacy—Acknowledgment of paternity

The Oudh Laws Act by s. 3 provides that Muhammadan law is to be applied to questions between Muslims regarding, *inter alia*, 'gifts'; that word includes gifts made through the medium of a trustee, and the necessity under Muhammadan law for delivery of possession in the case of a gift without consideration is not modified by the Transfer of Property Act (IV of 1882) although the gift is made by a registered trust deed.

An acknowledgment by a Muslim that a person is his son is substantive evidence that the person is his legitimate son; statements by a member of a Muslim family, in this case the widow of the alleged father, that a person is a son, or an heir, are evidence of family repute of legitimacy.

Having regard to the duty of official inquiry imposed by s. 62 of the Oudh Land Revenue Act (XVII. of 1876), statements in a petition signed by a *pardanishin* lady upon which mutation of names is ordered, are admissions by her to which weight should be attached.

The Judicial Committee will not in future read, or allow to be used, documents not endorsed by the trial judge, as required by the Code of Civil Procedure, 1908, Order XIII., r. 4.

Observations by their Lordships as to the dilatory character of the litigation, and as to the mischief of allowing witnesses to be recalled for cross-examination at protracted intervals.

See *Outlines,* 181, 184–5.

Consolidated Appeals from two decrees of the Court of the Judicial Commissioner (13 November 1911) partly reversing and partly modifying decrees of the Subordinate Judge of Lucknow (25 October 1909).

The facts and the nature of the litigation are stated in the judgment of their Lordships. Two questions arose upon the appeals—namely (1) whether a registered deed of settlement, dated 5 February 1895, executed by Nawab Zaigham-ud-Daula, deceased, in favour of his wife and sons, was a valid disposition of the properties therein comprised, and (2) whether one Sultan Mirza was a legitimate son of the said deceased Nawab.

The Subordinate Judge held that the settlement was invalid under Muhammadan law, and that the gifts to the settlor's sons were further invalid as being contingent gifts. He held that the onus of disproving the status of Sultan Mirza was upon the plaintiffs who alleged his illegitimacy, and that they had not satisfied that onus.

Upon appeal to the Court of the Judicial Commissioner, the learned judges held that the validity of the settlement did not depend upon Muhammadan law, since, in their opinion, trusts were not 'gifts' within the meaning of s. 3 of the Oudh Laws Act, 1876, but were governed by the Indian Trusts Act, 1882. They held that the settlement was valid under that Act and the Transfer of Property Act, 1882. They found that there had been a delivery to the trustees of the Calcutta property settled. Upon the legitimacy issue they found that Sultan Mirza was not a legitimate son of the Nawab. The appeal is reported at 14 Oudh Cases, 356.

Judgment [Atkinson, J.][27]

These are consolidated appeals from two decrees of the Court of the Judicial Commissioner of Oudh, Lucknow, both dated 13 November 1911, which reversed in part and modified in part two decrees, each dated 25 October 1909, of the Court of the Subordinate Judge of Lucknow.

The first of the two suits in which those last-mentioned decrees were made was instituted by Mirza Sadik Husain Khan, the appellant in both the present appeals, to enforce a mortgage dated 26 June 1900, executed in his favour by the third respondent in the first appeal, namely, Nawab Ummat-ul-Fatima, in her own right, and also as guardian of her two sons, then minors, the first and second respondents in the first appeal, to secure the repayment of Rs 20,000 admittedly advanced by the mortgagee to this lady, with interest at 1 per cent per mensem.

The second of these suits was instituted by the respondents Nawab Saiyed Hashim Ali Khan and Nawab Kasim Ali Khan, the latter by his guardian, against this same mortgagee and one Sultan Mirza, who claimed to be the step-brother of the plaintiffs. That suit was for a declaration that a mortgage dated 3 November 1900, made by the said Sultan Mirza of his share in all the family property in this mortgagee's favour, to secure the repayment of a sum of Rs 8000 with interest, was a nullity, on the ground that the said Sultan Mirza was not entitled to any share in the family property, first by reason of the provisions of a certain indenture dated 5 February 1895, hereafter dealt with, and secondly because he was not the legitimate son of his alleged father, the grantor in the said deed. This declaration is the only specific relief prayed for, but there is a prayer for general relief.

The litigation relates to the estate of Nawab Zaigham-ud-Daula, who was the son of the Prime Minister of the last King of Oudh, and a Mahommedan of the Shiah sect. He was admittedly regularly married twice. By his first wife, Badshah Begum, he had two sons and one daughter, all of whom predeceased him, and one daughter, Raushan Ara Begum, who survived

27 With Parker, John Edge & Syed Amir Ali, JJ.

him. By his second wife, the third respondent in the first appeal, married after the death of the first wife, he had two sons, the first and second respondents in that appeal. He died on 1 August 1898.

Both suits were tried by the same Subordinate Judge, who delivered separate judgments. The Court of the Judicial Commissioner dealt with both the appeals in one judgment.

The appellants and the respondents in both appeals agree in stating that the principal questions for decision are (1) whether the trust indenture of 5 February 1895, duly executed by the deceased Nawab and registered, was a valid disposition of the properties therein comprised, and, if so, whether the above-mentioned mortgages, so far as they purport to charge these properties, and the alleged share of Sultan Mirza in the family property respectively, are invalid; and (2) whether Sultan Mirza was shown to be the legitimate son of Zaigham-ud-Daula, the grantor in the trust deed. It was not, as their Lordships understood, disputed that the sum of Rs 20,000, purported to be secured by the first mortgage, was, in fact, advanced to the Nawab's widow; nor that it was borrowed for the purpose of being applied in payment of certain of the settlor's debts, in order to save some of the properties comprised in the trust deed from being sold at the suit of some unsatisfied creditors, nor that it was, in fact, so applied. No question was raised as to whether the first mortgage did not, under the circumstances, capture whatever interest the three respondents might have had in the entire immovable property of Zaigham-ud-Daula, however derived. Their Lordships therefore base their decision solely on the points raised by the parties and dealt with by the courts below.

It was contended in the second suit by Mirza Sadik Husain Khan, the mortgagee, that between the dates of the marriages of the Nawab with the two above-mentioned ladies he contracted a marriage in the muta form with an Abyssinian slave girl, named Zohra Kainam, who had been brought home by his father on the occasion of his making a pilgrimage to Mecca and subsequently given by the father to him, and that Sultan Mirza was the offspring of that union. The fact that such a marriage ever took place was denied by the plaintiffs in that suit, and a vast body of evidence, oral and documentary, was adduced by both sides on the issue of Sultan Mirza's legitimacy. [....]

These are no doubt very important points. Owing, however, to the conclusions at which their Lordships have arrived on the other points raised in the case, they do not find it necessary to express any opinion on these points, and therefore abstain from doing so. By s. 3 of the Oudh Laws Act (XVIII of 1876) it is enacted that between Mahomedans the Mahomedan law is to be applied to the many important matters therein enumerated, including, amongst others, 'wills, legacies, and gifts'. The Court of the Judicial Commissioner has held that the term 'gifts' as here used does not include gifts in trust. Their Lordships cannot adopt such a narrow construction of the term 'gifts' as would exclude any gift where the donor's bounty passes to his intended beneficiary through the medium of a trust, so that while a gift by A to C direct would be governed by the Mahommedan law, a gift by A to B in trust for C would be governed by some other law. So to hold would, they think, defeat the plain purpose and object of this section of the statute. The Mahommedan law in their view, therefore, applies to this deed; and the gift made by it, being voluntary, is void under that law, unless it was accompanied by a delivery of such possession as the subject of the gift is susceptible of. In *Chaudhri Mehdi Hasan* v. *Muhammad Hasan*[28] it is laid down by this Board that, according to Mahommedan law, a holder of property may in his lifetime give away the whole or part of it if he complies with certain forms, but that it is incumbent on those who seek to set up such a transaction to prove that those forms have been complied with, and this will be so whether the gift be made with or without consideration. If the latter, then unless it be accompanied by delivery of the thing given, so far as it is capable of delivery, it will be invalid. If the former, delivery of possession is not necessary, but actual payment of the consideration must be proved, and the bona fide intention of the donor to divest himself in praesenti of the property and to confer it upon the donee must also be proved. The case of *Ranee Khujooroonissa* v. *Roushun Jehan*[29] supports this statement of the law. [....]

There is nothing to show that the requirements of the Oudh Revenue Act of 1876 were not strictly complied with. In the absence of such evidence it must be assumed that they were complied with. These proceedings accordingly amount to something far more important and convincing than a mere admission by Fatima Begum of Sultan Mirza's legitimacy. They amount to the doing of an act by her by which an additional sharer in the property of the deceased is brought in and is given the right to receive portion of the income of that property. Further the act was accompanied by a statement explaining it and setting forth the grounds on which it was based, namely, the heirship, as a legitimate son, of Sultan Mirza. It would appear to their Lordships that the more probable inference to be drawn from this treatment of Sultan Mirza is that it is but a continuance of the recognition and treatment he received during the lifetime of the deceased Nawab, rather than an entire departure from the course previously pursued.

28 LR 33 IA 68, 76.
29 LR 3 IA 291.

It would be strange indeed if the ill-begotten child of a menial servant and a frail negress, never therefore owned as a son of the Nawab or treated by him as such, should be at once selected for such an honour. Moreover, it was not a barren honour, for, if Sultan Mirza speaks the truth, from the time of the mutation he and the other heirs 'have been realizing their shares of the profits separately'. He does not appear to have been contradicted or even cross-examined on this point, and the husband of Raushan Ara Begum, who is still alive, was not produced to prove that his wife, though excluded from all further participation in her father's assets by the trust deed, did not also receive her share of the income of these zamindari villages.

On 9 June 1899, Fatima Begum applied under s. 10 of Act VIII of 1890 to the District Judge of Lucknow to be appointed guardian of the persons and property of her two minor sons. The application purports to be signed by her in both her capacities and by the same pleader, Lochan Lal. It contains a final passage in the usual form to the effect that she knew of her own knowledge that the entire immovable property to which the minors are entitled was of the value therein stated in detail, and that they were in possession of this property, and that their relatives are, amongst others, Hasan Mirza, brother of the minors, born of a harem of Zaigham-ud-Daula, deceased. In the schedule to the application, also purporting to be signed by her, she sets out the shares of each of the properties contained in the trust deed belonging to the minors. Every item in this schedule is inconsistent with the provisions of the trust deed. [....]

The very first recital in this deed is that Zaigham-ud-Daula died a natural death in Lucknow on 1 August 1898, leaving him surviving his widow, the declarant, his two minor sons, and Nawab Sultan Mirza, his major son, and Raushan Ara Begum, his major daughter, as his heirs. It is further recited that the District Judge ordered the declarant to contract a debt of Rs 16,000 on the security of the property of the minors; and that, in compliance with that order and with a view to raise money to pay off the amount due on a certain decree named, she mortgaged her own share in these properties.

In their Lordships' view, the only reasonable inference to be drawn from these documents and proceedings is that Fatima Begum, if aware of the purport and contents of the trust deed, consistently treated it as invalid, and never, with full knowledge of its purport and effect, or, indeed, at all, elected to accept the provision made by it for her and her children as a satisfaction of the unpaid balance of her dower. If she was never fully informed of its purport and contents, any election by her to accept the provision made for herself and her children by it in discharge of the unpaid balance of her dower would, of course, be of no avail. If this be so, the mortgagee's rights cannot be affected, or his security invalidated, by any course of action she might have chosen to take after the execution of the mortgage.[...]

Their Lordships are therefore of opinion that, possession of the property mortgaged not having been proved to have been delivered, the gift is, according to the Mahomedan law applicable to the case, void, and that the mortgage sued upon is therefore a valid and a binding instrument and a good security.

The only question remaining for consideration is the legitimacy of Sultan Mirza. The burden of proving his illegitimacy rests, according to the pleadings in the first instance at all events, on the plaintiffs in the second suit. It would appear to their Lordships that a fallacy underlies some of the arguments addressed to them on behalf of the respondents on this point. It consists in assuming that the fact, even if true, that Sultan Mirza was treated by the Nawab, and especially by his family, with less care, kindness, consideration, and respect than the sons of the high-born ladies to whom the Nawab had been united by *nikkai* marriages, furnishes proof of Sultan Mirza's illegitimacy. Under the Mahommedan law, and indeed under the English law, the legitimate son of the most low-born, debased, and degraded woman to whom a man could be lawfully united has just the same proprietary right in his father's property as if his mother had been the most well-born and the purest. But it is rather against human nature to suppose that this equality before the law should secure equality of treatment in the domestic circle. It was also urged that the treatment which Sultan Mirza and his mother received in the Nawab's family was quite inconsistent with his position as the legitimate son of the Nawab and of her position as the legitimate wife, through a muta marriage, of the Nawab. The defect of that argument is that the position in the family of both Sultan Mirza and his mother, and the treatment both received, especially the latter, is still more inconsistent with her being, as the respondent alleged, the mistress of a menial servant, and he the offspring of their intercourse. Even while she was pregnant with child she was permitted privileges which it is almost impossible to believe would have been accorded to her if, her state being known, as it must have been, it was attributable to her improper intimacy with a menial servant. Sultan Mirza, when he grew up, turned out to be rather a *mauvais sujet*. His connection with theatres displeased the Nawab. His mother had eloped or disappeared. If he was the illegitimate son of the menial servant there was no reason why the Nawab should not have turned him adrift. On the contrary he kept him on in his (the Nawab's) home, undoubtedly associated, to some extent, with him, had him about his person, and, it is apparent on the evidence, had some regard for him. In their Lordships' view the reasonable inference from all the evidence on this point is that Sultan Mirza was, at all events, the son of Zaigham-ud-Daula and this negress.

The crucial question then is, Was he the Nawab's legitimate son? There is no question that Sultan Mirza was the son of this woman. That is admitted by all parties. Now four witnesses have proved distinctly that the Nawab acknowledged him to be his son. That *prima facie* means his legitimate son: *Fuzeelun Beebee* v. *Omdah Beebee*.[30]

The first of these witnesses, Nawab Faghfur Mirza, the son of Prince Mutaz-ud-Daula, belonging to the family of the Kings of Oudh, states that he knew Zaigham-ud-Daula for thirty to thirty-five years; that he knew Sultan Mirza and his mother; that he saw the Nawab and Sultan Mirza treating each other like father and son; that he went to see the deceased Nawab in his last illness, and then found Sultan Mirza attending him; that the Nawab had been displeased with Sultan Mirza because the latter had become addicted to singing and dancing, but that as far as the witness could judge the Nawab had forgiven him; that fifteen or sixteen years had elapsed since then; and that the Nawab on one occasion introduced Sultan Mirza to the witness as his son. The second witness, Khan Bahadur Shujaat Ali Khan, states that Zaigham-ud-Daula told him that the negress, Sultan Mirza's mother, was his *muta* wife, that he saw Sultan Mirza visiting the family in which Raushan Ara Begum lived at Murshidabad, and that this family treated him as a son, as did also Zaigham-ud-Daula himself. The third witness, Husain Ali Mirza, son of the Nawab Nazim of Bengal, states that Raushan Ara Begum was married to Mirza Kamyal Baksh, son of the late King of Oudh; that he knew Sultan Mirza; that he saw him with his father Zaigham-ud-Daula, who told the witness that Sultan Mirza was his son by a muta woman; and that he saw him once or twice visiting at Murshidabad during Zaigham-ud-Daula's lifetime. This witness was subjected to a cross-examination, presumably considered effective, as to the time of the day at which the deceased Nawab made this statement to him. The last of these witnesses is Munshi Salig Ram. He says that one day, about fourteen or sixteen years before he gave his evidence, he, jesting, asked Zaigham-ud-Daula whence he got this boy Sultan Mirza, and he replied that he was his son by an Abyssinian, his wife by muta, presented to him by his (the Nawab's) father; that he saw Sultan Mirza many times, and saw his father treat him as a relation, a son, or brother, and not as a servant.

The Subordinate Judge has criticized in detail the evidence in conflict with these statements, and shows conclusively, their Lordships think, that much weight cannot be attached to it. Putting aside Sultan Mirza's own

30 10 Suth. WR 469.

evidence, their Lordships cannot find anything in the case to discredit the evidence of the four witnesses above named. They have no interest to induce them to state what they do not believe to be true. The criticism passed upon their evidence was, first, that Sultan Mirza was only introduced to each of them once, and therefore their recollection is unreliable, as if it was to be expected that a father would naturally introduce a son to a friend as his son more than once; and, second, that they speak to what took place many years ago. They profess, however, to have a clear recollection of the events they depose to; and the Subordinate Judge, who had the advantage of seeing and hearing them, believed them.

Much reliance was placed upon two documents in addition to the trust deed, which, it was contended, contained a distinct repudiation by Zaigham-ud-Daula of Sultan Mirza's legitimacy, namely, the Tarikh Quaisara and the memorandum bearing date 15 February 1893. Both these documents were composed many years subsequent to the dates of the acknowledgments deposed to by the four witnesses mentioned. In the first he names his children by his first wife and those by Fatima Begum, and states that there can be no heirs to him but these; that these persons are the owners of and heirs of his property; and that if any other claimant comes forward his claim should be considered invalid by the Government. In the memorandum he states that, one of his sons by his first marriage having died, his three sons, one daughter, and his wife Fatima, five persons in all, are his heirs, and he proceeds to declare that besides these he has none, and that if any added person comes forward as his heir other than a son or daughter thereafter born to him by his wife Fatima Begum, his claims shall be considered false and unlawful. It is quite evident from these documents that Zaigham-ud-Daula was very apprehensive that some person would come forward claiming to be his heir, else it would be meaningless and purposeless to write thus. These apprehensions and fears would have been irrational if the person whose claim he desired to defeat was the well-known progeny of the negress and a menial servant. But his fears could easily be accounted for, if in fact he had had a son by a *muta* wife whom he had treated to some extent as a son, and who by reason of that treatment might be a formidable claimant, but yet whose claims he desired, not unnaturally perhaps, to discount. Their Lordships do not think that the evidence of the four witnesses above mentioned is rebutted or discredited by these documents.

If this be so, the rule of the Mahommedan law applicable to the case is well established: No statement made by one man that another (proved to be illegitimate) is his son can make that other legitimate, but where no proof of that kind has been given such a statement or acknowledgment is substantive evidence that the person so acknowledged is the legitimate son of the person who makes the statement provided his legitimacy be possible; *Muhammad Allahdad Khan* v. *Muhammad Ismail Khan*;[31] *Nawab Muhammad Azmat Ali Khan* v. *Lalli Begum*.[32]

It is also well established according to Mahommedan law that if a member of a family, such as Fatima Begum was of her husband's family, makes statements touching the sonship or heirship of a person, such as are contained in many of the written documents she has signed in reference to Sultan Mirza's heirship, those statements are good evidence of the family repute concerning him; *Anjuman Ara Begum* v. *Sadik Ali Khan*;[33] Baber *Ali Khan* v. *Anjuman Ara Begum*.[34]

On the whole case, therefore, their Lordships are of opinion that the decrees appealed from in these consolidated appeals are both erroneous and should be reversed, and the decrees of the Subordinate Judge in both should be restored, and that both appeals should be allowed with costs here and below, and they will humbly advise His Majesty accordingly. [...]

20. Habibur Rahman v. Altaf Ali
(1921) 48 IA 114

Legitimacy—acknowledgments—presumption—proof of illegitimacy—concurrent findings

Under Muhammadan law no statement made by a man that another, proved to be illegitimate, is his son can make that other legitimate. If an acknowledgment is of legitimate sonship, and that relationship is possible in fact and law, it gives rise to a rebuttable presumption that there was a marriage between the parents.

Where a trial judge bases his judgment upon a finding of fact and two of three judges constituting the appellate court agree with the finding and conclusion, the third judge arriving at the same result upon a different finding of fact, there are concurrent findings to which the rule of practice of the Board applies.

See *Outlines*, 185 seqq.

Appeal (No. 54 of 1920) from a judgment and decree of the High Court, Calcutta (1 August 1918) affirming a decree of that court in its original civil jurisdiction (14 May 1917).

The first appellant instituted a suit against the respondents claiming to be the sole heir of Nawab Sobhan of Bogra; the deceased Nawab was a

[31] ILR 10 Allah 289.
[32] ILR 9 IA 8.
[33] (1899) 2 Oudh Cases, 115, 123, 125.
[34] LR 30 IA 94, 103.

Sunnite Muslim. A second plaintiff to whom Habibur Rahman had transferred part of his claim was joined, but for convenience Habibur Rahman is hereinafter referred to as the appellant or the plaintiff.

The plaint alleged that the plaintiff was the son of the Nawab by his second wife, one Mozelle Cohen, a Jewess converted to Islam. The respondents by their defence denied that the Nawab and Mozelle Cohen were married and alleged that the plaintiff was an illegitimate son of the Nawab by Mozelle Cohen. After the hearing was commenced the plaint was amended by alleging that the Nawab had acknowledged the plaintiff as his son, and stating that if the marriage was not proved reliance would be placed upon the acknowledgment as establishing the plaintiff's legitimacy.

Three of the issues framed were: (1) Was Mozelle Cohen married to Sobhan? (2) If so, was Habibur the legitimate son of Sobhan and Mozelle Cohen? (6) Was there any acknowledgment as pleaded, if so, what is its legal effect?

The trial judge (Greaves J.) found upon the first issue that Mozelle Cohen was not married to the deceased Nawab, and on the second that Habibur Rahman was not their legitimate son. On the sixth issue he found that though the Nawab had not acknowledged Habibur Rahman as a son generally, he had done so on two occasions, but the learned judge said that he did not find that those acknowledgments were made with the intention of conferring legitimacy upon the plaintiff. Upon those findings, after a consideration of the law applicable, the suit was dismissed.

An appeal, heard by Sanderson CJ and Woodroffe and Chitty JJ., was unanimously dismissed. The Chief Justice and Chitty J., in separate judgments, each found that the alleged marriage was disproved, and held that that being the case the suit failed, since the plaintiff could not by any acknowledgment be rendered legitimate. Woodroffe J. held that no acknowledgment made with the intention of conferring legitimacy had been proved; he accordingly agreed that the appeal should be dismissed. The judgments, both at the trial and upon the appeal, are reported at ILR 46 C. 259.

Judgment [Lord Dunedin][35]

In this suit the plaintiff and appellant Habibur Rahman Chowdhury, claims a declaration that he is the legitimate son of the late Nawab of Bogra, who died intestate on 2 July 1915. The suit is opposed by the late Nawab's grandson, who is the son of a legitimate daughter, and by two nephews, the sons of an elder brother. The plaintiff is admittedly the natural son of the late Nawab, his mother having been a Jewess, Mozelle Cohen, who became

35 With Buckmaster, Shaw, John Edge & Syed Amir Ali, JJ.

a Mohammedan and cohabited with the Nawab. He was born in 1893. The Nawab had a daughter by the same lady in 1891. The Nawab's legitimate wife, the grandmother of the first defendant, died in 1890. The plaintiff based his claim on two grounds. He averred first that Mozelle was married to the Nawab. He further averred that on many occasions the Nawab had acknowledged him as his legitimate son. The defendants aver that no marriage ever took place. They also deny that any proper acknowledgment of legitimacy was made.

The case went to trial before Greaves J., and oral evidence was led and documentary evidence produced on both sides. Greaves J. held that no marriage was proved, but that, on the contrary, it was proved that Mozelle Cohen was no better than a prostitute and that no marriage ever did take place. He held that the Nawab did acknowledge the plaintiff as his legitimate son, but he held that in law, as the fact of no marriage was conclusively established, such acknowledgment would not confer the status of legitimacy. He therefore dismissed the suit.

Appeal was taken by the plaintiff. In the appellate Court the Chief Justice agreed with Greaves J. that the marriage was in fact disproved. Differing from Greaves J., he held that there was no proper acknowledgment of legitimacy, but, upon the assumption that there was, he agreed with Greaves J. on the law that such an acknowledgment, in the face of the disproof of the marriage, was of no avail.

Woodroffe J. thought that there was no acknowledgment of legitimacy and no affirmative proof of marriage, and therefore the plaintiff failed, but he did not go the length of holding that there had been disproof of marriage.

Chitty J. held that the marriage was disproved. That being so, he did not feel called upon to decide with certainty as to whether there was a good acknowledgment of legitimacy or not, though he indicated that the bias of opinion was that there was not.

The plaintiff is thus faced by two adverse concurrent findings of fact to the effect that the existence of a marriage is disproved. As, however, the junior counsel for the plaintiff urged that this was not so, it is well to make it clear as to what constitute concurrent findings.

The first issue as settled by the trial judge was, 'Was Mozelle Cohen married to Sobhan?' (the Nawab). His finding as to this was: 'I hold that upon the evidence the long connection of Sobhan and Mozelle was inconsistent with the relation of husband and wife, and that Mozelle is, upon the evidence, proved to be merely his concubine, and that Mozelle Cohen was not married to the deceased Nawab.'

The Chief Justice said: 'I think the learned judge was right in holding that Mozelle was never married to the late Nawab Sobhan; to put it in other words, in my judgment it has been proved that Mozelle was never married to the late Nawab'; and Chitty J. said: 'I do not believe that any marriage between Abdus Sobhan and Mozelle Cohen ever took place; in other words, I find the marriage disproved.' These two learned judges form a majority of the appellate court. That makes a concurrent finding, and it is not vitiated as such because, as here, the other judge in the appellate court does not come to the same conclusion in fact though coming to the same result in law arising from another fact. Of course, to be concurrent findings binding on this Board, the fact or facts found must be such as are necessary for the foundation of the proposition in law to be subsequently applied to them.

The senior counsel for the appellants was unable to deny that there were concurrent findings as to the non-existence of the marriage. His argument was directed to this, that, assuming he could show a good acknowledgment of legitimacy, that conferred the status of legitimacy and made it irrelevant to enter into any inquiry as to the fact of marriage.

The case might be disposed of by holding, as the majority of the learned judges of the appellate court did, that there was no proper acknowledgment of legitimacy. There is not, however, as to this a 'concurrent finding', for the learned trial judge thought otherwise, and it would be necessary to examine the evidence before coming to the above conclusion. Their Lordships do not think it necessary to embark on this inquiry. They will, without deciding, assume that there was a proper acknowledgment, for, as is to be presently explained, they are of opinion that such acknowledgment, in face of the fact that there was no marriage, is of no avail. Their Lordships consider that this result is reached on principle, and is concluded by authority.

Before discussing the subject, it is as well at once to lay down with precision the difference between legitimacy and legitimation. Legitimacy is a status which results from certain facts. Legitimation is a proceeding which creates a status which did not exist before. In the proper sense there is no legitimation under the Mohammedan law. Examples of it may be found in other systems. The adoption of the Roman and the Hindu law effected legitimacy. The same was done under the Canon law and the Scotch law in respect of what is known as legitimation *per subsequens matrimonium*. By the Mohammedan law a son to be legitimate must be the offspring of a man and his wife or of a man and his slave; any other offspring is the offspring of *zina*, that is, illicit connection, and cannot be legitimate. The term 'wife' necessarily connotes marriage; but, as marriage may be constituted without any ceremonial, the existence of a marriage in any particular case may be an open question. Direct proof may be available, but if there be no such, indirect proof may suffice. Now one of the ways of indirect proof is by an acknowledgment of legitimacy in favour of a son. This acknowledgment must be not merely of sonship, but must be made in such a way that it shows that the acknowledgor meant to accept the other not only as his son, but as his legitimate son. It must not be impossible upon the face of it; i.e., it must not be made when the ages are such that it is impossible in nature for the acknowledgor to be the father of the acknowledgee, or when the mother spoken to in an acknowledgment, being the wife of another, or within prohibited degrees of the acknowledgor, it would be apparent that the issue would be the issue of adultery or incest. The acknowledgment may be repudiated by the acknowledgee. But if none of these objections occurs, then the acknowledgment has more than a mere evidential value. It raises a presumption of marriage—a presumption which may be taken advantage of either by a wife-claimant or a son-claimant. Being, however, a presumption of fact, and not *juris et de jure*, it is, like every other presumption of fact, capable of being set aside by contrary proof. The result is that a claimant son who has in his favour a good acknowledgment of legitimacy is in this position: The marriage will be held proved and his legitimacy established unless the marriage is disproved. Until the claimant establishes his acknowledgment the onus is on him to prove a marriage. Once he establishes an acknowledgment, the onus is on those who deny a marriage to negative it in fact.

A large number of cases were cited to their Lordships which they think it unnecessary to discuss in detail. It is quite true that in the earlier of the series not only is stress laid on the fact that an acknowledgment of legitimacy has more than a mere evidential value, but also there are expressions used such as that by a proper acknowledgment the status of legitimacy is 'acquired'. Fastening on such expressions, the learned counsel for the appellants argued that to enter into an inquiry into the fact of marriage when a good acknowledgment had been made out was not only bad law but a sin against the rules of logic. The simple answer to this is that the phraseology of such expressions as cited above must not be pressed to disturb what is the ruling principle, and that principle is that in Mohammedan law such an acknowledgment is a declaration of legitimacy and not a legitimation. A declaration, though it cannot be withdrawn, may be contradicted, for it is only a statement: legitimation is an act, which being done cannot be undone. So the rules of logic remain untouched.

The whole question was thoroughly examined in a very learned judgment by Mahmood J. in the case of *Muhammad Allahdad Khan* v. *Muhammad Ismail Khan*;[36] and finally, in the case of *Sadik Husain Khan* v. *Hashim Ali*

36 ILR 10 All 289.

Khan and Others.[37] Lord Atkinson, delivering the judgment of the Board, said as follows: 'If this be so, the rule of the Mohammedan law applicable to the case is well established. No statement made by one man that another (proved to be illegitimate) is his son can make that other legitimate, but where no proof of that kind has been given such a statement or acknowledgment is substantive evidence that the person so acknowledged is the legitimate son of the person who makes the statement provided his legitimacy be possible.' That statement is, in their Lordships' view, clear and conclusive, and what they have said above is no more than an elaboration of what was there said.

Their Lordships will therefore humbly advise His Majesty to dismiss the appeal with costs.

◊ UPDATE ◊

1. *Acknowledgement of paternity*

The rules of Muslim law relating to acknowledgement of legitimacy of children as stated in the old decisions in *Abdool Razack*, *Muhammad Allahadad* and *Habibur Rahman* [Cases 6, 18 and 20] have been generally followed by the courts in all parts of the subcontinent. The Supreme Court of India reiterated these rules in the leading case of *Mohd Amin* v. *Vakil Ahmad* AIR 1952 SC 358.

2. *Application of Evidence Act*

In India Section 112 of the Indian Evidence Act, on the legitimacy of children, continues to apply to the Muslims. The provision, however, cannot be applied if the marriage of the child acknowledged was invalid under Muslim law. This was asserted in *AG Ramchandran* v. *Shamsunnisa* AIR 1977 Mad 182.

In *Dukhtar Jahan* v. *Mohammad Farooq* AIR 1987 SC 1049 the Supreme Court of India has held that the premature birth of a child does not by itself raise a presumption of illegitimacy.

In Pakistan, in *Hamida Begum* v. *Murad Begum* PLD 1975 SC 624 the Supreme Court decided that, notwithstanding Section 112 of the Evidence Act 1872, a child born within six months of marriage will not be legitimate unless the husband acknowledges it to be his child under the provisions of Muslim law.

37 LR 43 IA 212, 234.

IX. Guardianship

21. Skinner v. Orde
(1871) 14 MIA 309

Conversion to Islam—colourable conversion—guardianship

A child born in India whose father was a European British subject and a Christian, must be presumed to have the father's religion, and his corresponding civil and social status, and it is the duty of a guardian to bring up his ward in his father's religion.

An infant, the child of a Christian father and the issue of a Christian marriage, was left by the death of her father of very tender age and brought up by her mother as a Christian during her early youth. Her mother, after cohabiting with a man having a wife and professing the Christian religion became, with him, a Muslim for the purpose, as it appeared, of giving legal effect to a Muslim marriage between them. The alleged marriage was not proved to have been duly celebrated.

The infant after attaining the age of fourteen years and being with her mother, professed a desire to become a Muslim in religion and adopted the Muslim mode of life. The courts in India, having been applied to under the circumstances by her relatives to remove the infant from the custody of her mother, made an order under the provisions of the Acts Nos. XL of 1858 and IX of 1861 and placed the infant under a Christian guardian. Such order, on appeal, was confirmed by the Judicial Committee.

This case is fully discussed in *Outlines*. 61 seq.; see also pp. 58, 59, and 172 seqq.

Judgment [James, J.][1]

This is an appeal from an Order of the High Court of the North-West Provinces, in substance, confirming an order of the Judge of the Court of Meerut, removing an infant ward and her property from the custody and guardianship of her mother, the appellant, and the alleged second husband of that mother.

1 With Colvile, Mellish, Smith and Collier, JJ; Assessor: Lawrence Peel.

The application was made to the Judge under the provisions of the Indian Act, No. IX, 1861, which are as follows:

1. Any relative or friend of a minor who may desire to prefer any claim in respect of the custody or guardianship of such Minor, may make an application by petition, either in person or by a duly constituted Agent, to the principal Civil Court of original jurisdiction in the district, by which such application, if preferred in the form of a regular suit, would be cognizable, and shall set forth the grounds of his application in the petition. The court, if satisfied by an examination of the Petitioner, or his agent, if he appear by Agent, that there is ground for proceeding, shall give notice of the application to the person named in the petition as having the custody or being in the possession of the person of such minor, as well as to any other person to whom the court may think it proper that such notice should be given, and shall fix as early a day as may be convenient for the hearing of the petition, and the determination of the right to the custody or guardianship of such Minor.

2 The court may direct that the person having the custody or being in possession of the person of such minor shall produce him or her in court, or on any other place appointed by the court, on the day fixed for the hearing of the petition, or at any other time, and may make such order for the temporary custody and protection of such minor as may appear proper.

3. On the day appointed for the hearing of the petition, or as soon after as may be practicable, the court shall hear the statements of the parties, or their Agents, if they appear by Agents, and such evidence as they or their Agents may adduce, and thereupon shall proceed to make such Order as it shall think fit in respect to the custody or guardianship of such Minor and the costs of the case.

The Judge accordingly, after hearing the case presented to him, made an Order, removing the ward from the custody of her mother. An appeal from this Order was presented to the High Court, which court pronounced the final order now complained of. The Act, No. IX. of 1861, gives no further appeal, but on the statement made to this Tribunal that the question really involved the religious education of a ward, special leave was given by Her Majesty, on the recommendation of this Board, to prosecute the appeal now to be disposed of.

Several English cases have been cited to their Lordships, and one is referred to and relied on in the judgment of the Judge of the court of Meerut; and it is, obviously, of very great assistance to the Courts in India, and to this Board, to see how, in the exercise of a similar jurisdiction for the same object, the courts in this country have thought it best to act for the protection and welfare of infant wards. The course of decision in the English and Irish Courts of Chancery has been such as to lay it down as a matter of positive law of the court, that in the matter of religious education great, and in the absence of controlling circumstances, paramount, weight should be given to the expressed or implied wishes of the deceased father. It was contended with some plausibility before their Lordships, that this rule had its origin in the statutory power of English fathers to appoint guardians for their children.

However this may be, their Lordships do not think it necessary or desirable for the determination of this case, to refer to or rely on any such rule.

The Indian Act certainly does not expressly refer to any such right and appears to have had one object in contemplation, the protection of the infant ward, and to have given the Judge (subject, of course, to appeal) the power, and to have imposed on him the duty, of doing what, in his judgment, is best for the infant; and no other power or duty.

In India, however, all, or almost all, the great religious communities of the world exist, side by side, under the impartial rule of the British Government. While Brahmin, Buddhist, Christian, Mahommedan, Parsee, and Sikh are one nation, enjoying equal political rights and having perfect equality before the Tribunals, they co-exist as separate and very distinct communities, having distinct laws affecting every relation of life. The law of husband and wife, parent and child, the descent, devolution, and disposition of property are all different, depending, in each case, on the body to which the individual is deemed to belong; and the difference of religion pervades and governs all domestic usages and social relations.

From the very necessity of the case, a child in India, under ordinary circumstances, must be presumed to have his father's religion, and his corresponding civil and social status; and it is, therefore, ordinarily, and in the absence of controlling circumstances, the duty of a guardian to train his infant ward in such religion.

What are the facts of the present case? Beyond all question the Ward was the child of a Christian Father, the issue of a Christian marriage. She was left an infant of very tender years, her Father being one of the victims of the great outbreak and massacre at Delhi in the year 1857. She remained thenceforth under the protection of her mother, a lady, apparently, of ancestry not Christian, and with no great knowledge of Christian tenets, or attachment to Christian habits. But she was married to a Christian in a Christian Church, and does not appear to have professed any other faith, or to have reverted in costume or customs to her ancestral faith until the autumn of 1867. The child up to that time had certainly been brought up and, so far as she was educated at all, educated as a Christian girl, eating, drinking, and associating with her Christian cousins, and going to a school.

In the autumn of 1867 this occurred. The House of the widow became the house of one John Thomas John, a clerk of inferior grade in the Judge's court, and they lived and cohabited together as husband and wife, John Thomas John being already the husband in Christian marriage of a living Christian Wife. It is suggested that this union was sanctified and legalized in this way—that the widow became a Mahommedan, that John Thomas John became a Mahommedan, and that having thus qualified himself for the enjoyment of polygamous privileges, he contracted in Mahommedan form a valid Mahommedan marriage with the widow, the Appellant.

The High Court expressed doubts of the legality of this marriage; which their Lordships think they were well warranted in entertaining.

But however this may be, their Lordships can entertain no doubt, that when the connection between John Thomas John and the widow was formed, whether it was merely adulterous or under the cover of a Mahommedan marriage, the home was no longer a fit home for a Christian young girl; and if the matter had then been brought to the notice of the Judge, it would have been his plain duty, without delay, to find a more suitable home and guardianship than what had become, in fact, the home and guardianship of John Thomas John. The matter was not, however, brought so soon as it ought to have been to the attention of the Judge.

Some relatives interfered, in order that the child might be sent to a proper school—a proper Christian school; and John Thomas John and his alleged Wife, professing to yield to the suggestion, took the girl in June, 1869, up to Simla, with the avowed object of placing her in a Christian school there. They now represent that this project failed, by reason of the girl's refusal to go to school; and that she began to express a preference for the Mahommedan religion, and the Oriental mode of feminine life in seclusion behind the *purdah*; and that at some period (the time is not exactly fixed) a *moulavie* was introduced, who confirmed her in her resolution to become a Mahommedan. The young lady, who by this time had attained the age of fourteen years, or thereabout, made the following deposition:

I know Mr John. I first knew him when we came to Meerut, and for the past two years know him well. No one has ever persuaded me to be a Mussulmani. My own feelings alone have prompted me. I wish to remain a Mussulmani. I would not be persuaded to become a Christian, because it is from my own conviction that I am a Mussulmani. I am in the *purdah* by my own free will. I went up to Simla with my mother and Mr John. They wished me to go to school, and pressed me very much to go, but I would not consent. I heard of the marriage of my Mother to Mr John five or six days after it took place. I cannot say how long Mrs James Skinner has known of the marriage, but she must have known of it a long time, as they have lived together for two years, and it has been matter of notoriety. I believe all Mrs Skinner's family must have known of it. I wish to return to my Mother. I believe Mrs James Skinner to be a Mussulmani; Mrs Orde to be a Christian. To Counsel for Petitioners—My Mother can read very little—small storybooks; but she cannot read Persian, nor write at all. She can only read the Urdu in print, not the written character, excepting very good text-hand. I have read easy Books on religion in Urdu, but not studied them. I am studying the Koran with a teacher. There was a picture of my Father, and there were several other pictures; but as I had heard that it was strictly forbidden to keep pictures by our religion, I, therefore, destroyed them with my own hands. The picture was on paper in a frame with glass. It was destroyed soon after we returned from the Hills. I heard that to keep pictures was prohibited after my return from the hills, from a Preacher, a *moulavie*, who came to the house and preached a sermon. No one advised me otherwise. I had long thought of becoming a Mussulmani, but when I was young did not understand the different religions; when I returned from the hills I turned my attention to it, and had the preacher called to preach. Almost all my family are Christians. I have had no intercourse during the last six or seven months with any others who are Christians, but their family and Mrs Benu. Since I have been in their house I have not had any Letter of any kind from Mr John. I had some Letters from my cousin Sophy, who is in Calcutta, and Charlie, which were on my table. These I sent for. Two from Charlie I sent for the day before yesterday, which were old, and I tore them up; the other from Sophy I sent for yesterday, and showed it to Mrs. Aldwell. The two from Charlie I sent for by Achakrai, and the one from Sophy by my *Ayah*. To Counsel for Petitioners—I know Mrs Benu. I have seen her several times since I came from Simla. I know her to be a Christian.

This evidence was, with the consent of the Counsel on both sides, and also of the principal parties, though the questions and answers were put and given in the vernacular of the country, Urdu, recorded by the Court in English, and was read over to the witness in Urdu, and by her acknowledged to be correct.

The case of the Appellant, in fact, rested on this deposition. An eloquent appeal was made to their Lordships' feelings not to sanction such a violation of the young lady's present religious convictions and natural feelings as was involved in tearing her from her Mahommedan home and mother, and committing her to the care of a Christian strange schoolmistress, The Judges of the High Court, however, did not think that deposition sufficient to induce them to abstain from making in July, 1870, the Order for the appointment of the Guardian, which would have been the only possible Order that could have been made in 1867.

Their Lordships cannot dissent from that conclusion. It would be very easy, of course, for a Mother, under such circumstances, to procure from a young daughter the expression of a wish to remain with her and to become a Mahommedan like her, rather than continue a Christian and go to a strange school; and it is impossible, in their Lordships' judgment, to believe that in the interval which had occurred between the visit to Simla and the application to the court any such knowledge of the differences between the two religions had been acquired, or any such settled conscientious convictions had been formed, as to make it really likely that her moral and religious condition would be endangered by placing her where she should receive the secular and religious instruction and training which she ought to have long previously and without interruption enjoyed. Their Lordships are, therefore, of opinion, that the Order, in so far as it removed the Ward from her mother and alleged stepfather, and placed her under a Christian Guardian, was right, and that is really the only matter that has been brought before them.

Their Lordships will humbly report to Her Majesty that, in their opinion, the Order of the High Court ought to be affirmed, and this appeal dismissed with costs.

This recommendation of their Lordships is, of course, without prejudice to any application to be made by or on behalf of the Ward concerning her future position; and considering the present age of the young lady, their Lordships think it would be very proper for the court to ascertain for itself what her present opinions and wishes are, and what, having regard to those wishes and opinions, would in the present state of things be best for her.

Affirming the principle of the Order, their Lordships feel that it would be very difficult for an Appellate Tribunal in this country to interfere without injury, as to the details of the particular guardianship and scheme, which must so essentially be a matter of quasi parental discretion to be exercised on the spot by those best acquainted or best able to acquaint themselves, with all the circumstances, and their Lordships disclaim any desire so to interfere. But they suggest, for the consideration of the court in India in similar cases, that while selecting a school (such, for example, as Miss Scanlan's in this instance) it would be desirable, where practicable, to have some independent person as guardian, to whom the ward could apply, in whom the court and the ward could confide, and whose duty it would be to communicate to the court any matter which might arise.

22. Imambandi v. Mutsaddi (1918) 45 IA 73

Minors—guardianship—alienation by mother—invalidity—marriage—legitimacy—acknowledgments—admission of documents—Code of Civil Procedure (V of 1908), Order XIII., R.1

Under Muhammadan law a mother has no power as *de facto* guardian of her infant children to alienate or charge their immovable property.

During a father's life he is the legal guardian of his minor children, though the mother has rights as to their custody. After his death, his executor (in Hanafi law) is their legal guardian or, if there is no executor, their grandfather, or if he be dead, his executor. In the absence of any legal guardian the duty of appointing one devolves upon the judge as representing the Sovereign. If the mother is the father's executor, or has been appointed, she has the powers of a legal guardian, but those powers are subject to strict conditions as to immovables. If there is no legal guardian, the person in charge of a minor (such as the mother) has power as *de facto* guardian to incur debts, or to pledge the minor's goods and chattels, for the minor's imperative necessities (such as food, clothing or nursing), but has no power to deal with the immovable property.

Ayderman Kutti v. *Syed Ali* (1912) ILR 37 Mad 514 disapproved.

Clear and reliable evidence that a Muslim has acknowledged children as his legitimate issue raises a presumption of a valid marriage between him and the children's mother.

Rule as laid down in *Mahatala Bibee* v. *Prince Ahmed Haleem-ooz-Zaman* (1881) 10 Cal LR 293 applied. This case is the foundation for the modern law on the powers of the mother as guardian. The question is fully discussed in *Tyabji*, § 259, and *Outlines,* 194 seqq. and index.

Judgment [Syed Ameer Ali, J.][2]

This is an appeal from a judgment and decree of the High Court of Calcutta, dated 30 August 1911, which affirmed the decree of the Subordinate Judge of Saran awarding to the plaintiffs possession of a share in certain landed property situated in that district.

The property in suit belonged originally to one Ismail Ali Khan, a wealthy Mahommedan inhabitant of the sub-division of Siwan in the Saran district. The plaintiffs allege that on his death in March, 1906, he left him surviving three widows and several children, and that from one of these widows named Enayet-uz-Zohra, acting for herself and for her two minor children, they purchased the share in suit for the possession of which they brought the present action.

It appears that shortly after Ismail Ali Khan's death the contesting defendants 1 to 7 applied to the Revenue Courts for mutation of names (as proprietors) in the Collector's records, and, as usually happens in these cases in India, especially in Mahommedan families, immediately this application was made a claim was put forward on behalf of Enayet-uz-Zohra and her children that they were equally entitled with the other heirs of Ismail Ali Khan to have their names entered as co-sharers in the estate by right of inheritance, the allegation being that Zohra was one of his lawfully

2 With Shaw, John Edge, Walter Phillimore & Lawrence Jenkins, JJ.

wedded wives and that her children were his legitimate issue. The Revenue Courts rejected her claim, holding that it was not established to their satisfaction that she was Ismail Ali Khan's married wife or that the children were his lawful issue. They accordingly made an order directing the registration of the contesting defendants' names in succession to Ismail Ali Khan.

It should be mentioned here that the defendants 1 and 5 are admittedly Ismail Ali Khan's married wives, defendants 2, 3, and 4 are his issue by defendant 1, and defendants 6 and 7 his daughters by defendant 5.

The plaintiffs are dealers in hides, and also live at Siwan. There seems to have been litigation between them and Ismail Ali Khan in his lifetime, and since his death they seem to have espoused Zohra's cause. The deed executed by Zohra bears the date 10 June 1906, and purports to convey to the plaintiffs the shares of both herself and her minor children, and in the suit they are included as defendants 8 to 10. The reliefs sought are of a twofold character: first, a declaration of the title and status of the plaintiffs' vendors; and, secondly, a decree in favour of the plaintiffs for possession of the shares covered by the deed of sale.

The contesting defendants denied, as they had done in the Revenue Courts, that Zohra was one of Ismail Ali Khan's married wives or that her children were his legitimate issue, and they further contended that the shares the plaintiffs claimed to recover did not pass under the sale. The sixth issue framed by the Subordinate Judge seems to relate to this point.

The plaint was filed on 25 March 1909, but it does not appear to have been admitted until April 2. The contesting defendants filed their written statements in July, 1909; after that the case dragged its slow length along until 18 June 1910, when the actual trial began. In the interim, however, various interlocutory orders were made, including an order for the appointment of Zohra as guardian ad litem for her children (though her interest in the suit was clearly adverse to theirs). Admittedly she was never appointed under the Guardian and Wards Act (VIII of 1890) a guardian of their property. [....] Their Lordships are not satisfied that the books are not the genuine account-books of Ismail Ali Khan. What effect the absence in them of entries in Zohra's name may have in the consideration of the general evidence is another matter.

In the absence of any statutory provision making compulsory the registration of Mahommedan marriages, the Indian courts, in case of a dispute as to the factum of a marriage, are usually left to discover, or attempt to discover, the truth from a mass of conflicting and often very unsatisfactory evidence of witnesses. Such has been the burden cast on the courts in the present instance. The plaintiffs have endeavoured to prove in two ways that

Zohra was one of Ismail Ali Khan's wives, namely, first, by direct evidence of an actual marriage, and, secondly, by the acknowledgment by him of her children as his legitimate issue, and by the presumption of marriage arising from such acknowledgment. The defendants, on the other hand, tried to show that Zohra was a woman of loose character, with the object apparently of establishing that it was most unlikely a man in Ismail Ali Khan's position would marry such a person. They also called a number of witnesses, who are said to have been on terms of intimacy with him, to state that they never heard him speak of Zohra as his wife. Including the inference from the account-books, all the evidence on the defendants' side is purely and naturally negative. In their Lordships' opinion the oral testimony regarding the solemnization of a marriage accompanied by ostentatious ceremonies and high dower is by no means satisfactory, and if the case stood there the absence of Zohra's name in Ismail Ali Khan's account-books might have weighed heavily against her. But their Lordships find clear evidence of a reliable character regarding his acknowledgment of her children. Her case, therefore, comes within the rule of Mahommedan law to which Garth C. J. and Wilson J. gave expression in *Mahatala Bibee* v. *Prince Ahmed Haleem-ooz-Zaman*.[3]

In their Lordships' opinion the legal presumption arising in favour of Zohra from the acknowledgment of the children is not displaced by the mere inference the defendants seek to draw from the absence of entries in her favour in Ismail Ali Khan's account-books. Such absence is capable of explanation, and it is possible she could have explained it had her attention been called to the matter. One explanation, however, is on the surface: on the facts proved in the case it is quite clear that this lady's father, though belonging to the same clan as Ismail Ali Khan, was a man considerably inferior in social status; it is not at all unlikely that the deceased was not particularly proud of his connection with the daughter. This would explain both the absence of the entries and his reticence about her to ordinary acquaintances and even friends. On the whole case, their Lordships are of opinion that both Zohra and her children are entitled to their legal shares in the inheritance of Ismail Ali Khan. But the courts in India have awarded to the plaintiffs, on the basis of the deed of purchase from Zohra, a decree for possession of her share and the shares of defendants 9 and 10. And the question is whether they have acquired any title to the infants' shares under the sale by the mother. The defendants objected in the High Court to the decree of the Subordinate Judge On the ground that she had no power to convey her children's interest to the plaintiffs. The learned judges overruled

[3] 10 Cal LR 293.

the objection on the ground that the question did not arise in the present case. Their Lordships regret to have to differ from this view. This is an action in ejectment; the defendants are in possession; the plaintiffs, if they are to obtain possession of the minors' shares, must do so on the strength of their own title. It is essential, therefore, to consider whether the title they allege to have acquired under the conveyance by Zohra is well founded.

The question how far, or under what circumstances according to Mahommedan law, a mother's dealings with her minor child's property are binding on the infant has been frequently before the courts in India. The decisions, however, are by no means uniform, and betray two varying tendencies: one set of decisions purports to give such dealings a qualified force; the other declares them wholly void and ineffective. In the former class of cases the main test for determining the validity of the particular transaction has been the benefit resulting from it to the minor; in the latter, the admitted absence of authority or power on the part of the mother to alienate or incumber the minor's property.

In this conflict of opinion their Lordships think it desirable that a definite rule should, if possible, be laid down; and with this object they propose to review briefly the provisions and principles of the Mahommedan law, as they apprehend it, governing the subject.

It is perfectly clear that under the Mahommedan law the mother is entitled only to the custody of the person of her minor child up to a certain age according to the sex of the child. But she is not the natural guardian; the father alone, or, if he be dead, his executor (under the Sunni law), is the legal guardian. The mother has no larger powers to deal with her minor child's property than any outsider or non-relative who happens to have charge for the time being of the infant. The term '*de facto* guardian' that has been applied to these persons is misleading; it connotes the idea that people in charge of a child are by virtue of that fact invested with certain powers over the infant's property. This idea is quite erroneous: and the judgment of the Board in *Mata Din* v. *Ahmed Ali*[4] clearly indicated it. There an infant's share was sold by the elder brother in whose charge the child was, along with his own share, to pay a joint ancestral debt. The vendee at the time of the sale was in possession of the whole property under a mortgage executed by the ancestor. On attaining majority the younger brother, ignoring the sale, brought a suit against the vendee-mortgagee for the redemption of his own share. The defence set up was that the sale by the infant's *de facto* guardian, made for a valid necessity, was binding on the infant. The lower courts decreed the plaintiff's claim; on appeal to this

[4] LR 39 IA 49.

Board the arguments proceeded on the same lines as in the present case, though in reverse order.

Lord Robson, in delivering the judgment of the Board, observed as follows:

It is urged on behalf of the appellant that the elder brothers were de facto guardians of the respondent, and, as such, were entitled to sell his property, provided that the sale was in order to pay his debts and was therefore necessary in his interest. It is difficult to see how the situation of an unauthorized guardian is bettered by describing him as a '*de facto*' guardian. He may, by his de facto guardianship, assume important responsibilities in relation to the minor's property, but he cannot thereby clothe himself with legal power to sell it.

And he went on to add:

There has been much argument in this case in the courts below, and before their Lordships, as to whether, according to Mahommedan law, a sale by a *de facto* guardian, if made of necessity, or for the payment of an ancestral debt affecting the minor's property, and if beneficial to the minor, is altogether void or merely voidable. It is not necessary to decide that question in this case.

And he then proceeded to state the reasons why that was not considered necessary. This latter passage in Lord Robson's judgment has created the impression that their Lordships' decision was confined to the special facts of that case and left open the general question regarding the validity of alienations by unauthorized guardians of the property of minors.

As already observed, in the absence of the father, under the Sunni law, the guardianship vests in his executor. If the father dies without appointing an executor (*wasi*) and his father is alive, the guardianship of his minor children devolves on their grandfather. Should he also be dead, and have left an executor, it vests in him. In default of these de jure guardians, the duty of appointing a guardian for the protection and preservation of the infants' property devolves on the judge as the representative of the Sovereign: Baillie's *Digest* (ed. 1875) p. 689: Hamilton's *Hedaya*, vol. 4, bk. 52, c. 7, p. 555. No one else has any right or power to intermeddle with the property of a minor, except for certain specified purposes, the nature of which is clearly defined. But the powers of even the de jure guardians are confined within legal limits. For example, whilst an executor-guardian (*wasi*) may 'sell or purchase movables on account of the orphan under his charge either for an equivalent or at such a rate as to occasion an inconsiderable loss', dealings with his immovable property are subjected to strict conditions: Baillie's *Digest*, p. 687. The reason for the restrictions is thus given in the *Hedaya*, vol. 4, p. 553: 'The ground of this (the difference in the power of dealing with the two kinds of property) is that the sale of movable property is a species of conservation, as articles of that description are liable to decay, and the price is much more easily preserved than the article itself. With respect, on the contrary, to immovable property, it is in a state of conservation in its own nature whence it is unlawful to sell it—unless, however, it be evident that it will otherwise perish or be lost, in which case the sale of it is allowed.' In fact, the Mussulman law appears to draw a sharp distinction between movable and immovable property (*'aqar*) in respect of the powers of guardians, as will be seen from the following passage in Baillie's *Digest*, bk. 10, c. 8, p. 689: 'With regard to the executor of a mother or a brother—when a mother has died leaving property and a minor son, and having appointed an executor, or a brother has died leaving property and a minor brother, and having appointed an executor, the executor may lawfully sell anything but *'aqar* belonging to the estate of the deceased, but can neither sell the *'aqar*, nor lawfully buy anything for the minor but food and clothing, which are necessary for his preservation. The executor of a mother has no power to sell anything that a minor has inherited from his father, whether movable or immovable, and whether the property be involved in debt or free from it. But what he has inherited from herself when it is free from debts and legacies, the executor may sell what is movable, but he cannot sell *'aqar*. If the estate is involved in debt or legacies, and the debt is such as to absorb the whole, he may sell the whole, the sale of *'aqar* coming within his power: and if the debt does not absorb the whole, he may sell as much of it as is necessary to defray the debts, and as to his power to sell the surplus there is the same difference of opinion as has been stated above.'

When the mother is the father's executrix, or is appointed by the judge as guardian of the minors, she has all the powers of a de jure guardian. Without such derivative authority, if she assumes charge of their property of whatever description and purports to deal with it, she does so at her own risk, and her acts are like those of any other person who arrogates an authority which he does not legally possess. She may incur responsibilities, but can impose no obligations on the infant. This rule, however, is subject to certain exceptions provided for the protection of a minor child who has no de jure guardian. A fatherless child is designated in the law-books an 'infant-orphan' (*yeteem saghir*). The *Hedaya* classifies the acts that may have to be done for an infant under three heads. It says:

> Acts in regard to infant-orphans are of three descriptions, viz.: (1) Acts of guardianship, such as contracting an infant in marriage, or selling or buying goods for him, a power which belongs solely to the *wallee*, or natural guardian, whom the law has constituted the infant's substitute in those points; (2) acts arising from the wants

of an infant, such as buying or selling for him on occasions of need, or hiring a nurse for him, or the like, which power belongs to the maintainer of the infant, whether he be the brother, uncle, or (in the case of a foundling) the *mooltakit*, or taker-up, or the mother, provided she be the maintainer of the infant; and as these are empowered with respect to such acts, the *wallee*, or natural guardian, is also empowered with respect to them in a still superior degree; nor is it requisite, with respect to the guardian, that the infant be in his immediate protection; (3) *nafa' mahaz*, i.e.; acts which are purely advantageous to the infant, such as accepting presents or gifts, and keeping them for him, a power which may be exercised either by a *mooltakit*, a brother, or an uncle, and also by the infant himself, provided he be possessed of discretion, the intention being only to open a door to the infant's receiving benefactions of an advantageous nature (vol. 4, bk. 44, p. 124).

The examples given under the second head indicate the class of cases in which the acts of an unauthorized person who happens to have charge of a child are held to be binding on the infant's property. They also help to explain and illustrate the extent of such 'de facto guardian's' powers. The permissibility of these acts depends on the emergency which gives rise to the imperative necessity for incurring liabilities without which the life of the child or his perishable goods and chattels may run the risk of destruction. For instance, he may stand in immediate need of aliment, clothing, or nursing; these wants must be supplied forthwith. He may own 'slaves' or live-stock; food and fodder must be immediately procured. And these imperative wants may recur from time to time. Under such circumstances power is given to the lawful guardian to incur debts or to raise money on the pledge of the minor's goods and chattels (*mata'*) [*Majma'-ul-Anhar*, vol. 2, p. 571]. And this power, in the absence of a de jure guardian, the law extends to the person who happens to have charge of the child and of the child's property, though not a constituted or authorized guardian.

There is no reference to the pledge or sale of immovable property (*'aqar*), as the power of dealing with that class of property is confined to the de jure guardians, and is treated in the *Fatawa-i-Alamgiri* in a separate chapter: Baillie's *Mahommedan Law of Sale*, c. xvi.

It is to be observed that under the third 'description' of acts that may be needful for an infant, a person in charge of a child, although not a de jure guardian, may validly accept on behalf of his ward an unburdened bounty, it being an act 'purely advantageous' to the child, to use the expression of the *Hedaya*.

The reasoning on which it is sought to give to persons who happen to have charge of the person and property of a child, and are, therefore, called 'de facto guardians', the same powers as are possessed by de jure guardians is purely inferential. It proceeds on the analogy of a dealing by an outsider who purports to sell another's property without any authority from the real owner. Such a person in the Hanafi law is called a '*fazuli*', or, as Hamilton spells it, '*fazoolee*', which expression is defined by Richardson to mean a person 'busying himself in things not belonging to him, or acting without authority'. With the effect of the acts of a *fazuli* their Lordships will deal presently. Before doing so they wish to refer briefly to the state of the decisions in the Indian courts.

The Calcutta High Court, in sustaining transactions entered into by de facto guardians, has proceeded mainly on considerations of necessity for and benefit to the infant. The other High Courts, generally speaking, have cut the Gordian knot by holding that all such dealings with a minor's property were void.

Their Lordships do not feel called upon to examine in detail either set of decisions. But the last case on the subject in the Madras High Court requires their careful and respectful consideration: *Ayderman Kutti* v. *Syed Ali* [5] In their judgment in this case the learned judges have examined the law at considerable length, and their decision appears to divide itself into three broad propositions: first, that as regards the powers of guardians, de jure as well as de facto, the Mahommedan law recognizes no distinction as to the nature or kind of property, namely, whether it is immovable or movable; secondly, that in substance the powers of an unauthorized person who has charge of an infant are co-extensive with those of a lawfully constituted guardian, except in so far that the acts of the former are subject to considerations of necessity or benefit to the infant; and, thirdly (and this seems to form the essence of the judgment), that dealings by 'a de facto guardian' are neither void nor voidable, but are 'suspended' until the minor on attaining majority exercises his option of either ratifying the transaction or disavowing it.

With regard to the first of the above propositions, their Lordships have already indicated their views. In their opinion the Mahommedan law, for obvious reasons, makes a distinction, and a sharp distinction, between 'goods and chattels' (*mata*') and immovable property (*'aqar*) with regard to the powers of dealing by guardians.

The second proposition, speaking with respect, appears to their Lordships to lose sight of the fact that the acts of de jure guardians also are subject to the conditions of necessity for or benefit to the infant. So that, upon the reasoning of the Madras judgment, the powers of 'a de facto guardian' would, to all intents and purposes, be co-extensive with those of a de jure guardian. This conclusion would wipe out one of the most important

5 ILR 37 Mad 514.

safeguards provided by the Mahommedan law for the protection of the interests of infants. The learned judges say that

The law as regards the effect of dealings with a minor's property by a de facto guardian otherwise than in a case of absolute necessity or clear advantage to the minor is but a corollary of the general rule relating to sales, a person professing to deal with another's property, but without having legal authority to do so, i.e., by a *fazuli*, as he is technically called; such sales generally are treated as *mauquf*, or dependent.

Then, after referring to various authorities, they continue as follows:

The result of the above discussion is that, according to Muhammadan jurists, in cases of urgent and imperative necessity, such as those mentioned, the de facto guardian can alienate the property of the minor, no distinction being made between movable and immovable property.

It would have been an advantage to their Lordships if they had been placed in a position to judge for themselves, on the actual texts, the meaning of the Arabian text-writers and commentators. However, the *Hedaya* and the *Fatawa-i-Alamgiri* are recognized as standard authorities in India on the Hanafi branch of the Sunni law. Of the *Hedaya* there is a rendering in English made by Mr Hamilton under the orders of Warren Hastings; and a large part of the *Fatawa-i-Alamgiri*, paraphrased into English by Mr Neil Baillie, forms the works commonly known as Baillie's *Digest* (Hanafi law). Both Mr Hamilton and Mr Neil Baillie in their renderings have, with the object of elucidation, occasionally added phrases which do not exist in the original, but on the whole the English versions of the *Hedaya* and of the *Fatawa-i-Alamgiri* are valuable works on Mahommedan law.

The subject of sales by unauthorized persons is treated in the *Hedaya* in a separate section entitled 'of *Fazoolee Beea* [*fuzuli bai*], or the sale of the property of another without his consent' (vol. 2, bk. 16, p. 508). It says: 'If a person were to sell the property of another without his order the contract is complete, but it remains with the proprietor either to confirm or dissolve the sale as he pleases. Shâfei is of opinion that the contract, in this case, is not complete, because it has not issued from a lawful authority, for that is constituted only by property or permission, neither of which exists in this case.' It then proceeds to give the arguments of the Hanafi doctors in support of their view that the unauthorized contract is 'complete'. And then it adds: 'If the proprietor should die, then the consent of the heirs is of no efficacy in the confirmation of the *fazoolee* sale, in either case, that is, whether the price have been stipulated in money or in goods; because the contract rested entirely on the personal assent of the deceased.'

In other words, the so-called sale remains wholly ineffective until it receives the 'confirmation' of the owner, to whom alone belongs the power of 'confirming' it. If he dies before he has 'confirmed' it, the transaction falls to the ground, as the right to adopt the *fazuli's* act does not pass to his heirs.

In the *Fatawa-i-Alamgiri* the subject is treated under the designation of 'dependent sales' (vol. 3, p. 245; Baillie's *Mahommedan Law of Sale*, pp. 218–19):

> When a person sells the property of another, the sale is suspended, according to us [i.e., the Hanafis], for the sanction or ratification of the proprietor; and the existence of both the parties to the contract, and of the subject of sale, is a necessary condition to the validity of his sanction.... If the owner should die before sanctioning the sale, sanction by his heir would not suffice to give it operation. Sanction by an owner himself renders a sale operative.[6]

The word in the above passage translated as 'suspended' is derived from the same root as the word that has been translated in the heading as 'dependant', and in this connection really means 'is dependent upon'; also the words 'or ratification' have been introduced by Baillie by way of explanation. The word *ijazat* in the original is rightly rendered into 'sanction'.

The *Majma'-ul-Anhar* states the rule relating to a sale by a *fazuli* in similar terms; it says in substance that such a sale is 'established' (takes effect) on the sanction of the *malik* (owner), subject to four conditions, which it specifies. And then it adds significantly that according to Shâfei (the founder of the second great Sunni school of law) all dealings by an unauthorized person are absolutely void (*bâtil*) (vol. 2, p. 88).

In their Lordships' opinion the Hanafi doctrine relating to a sale by an unauthorized person remaining dependent on the sanction of the owner refers to a case where such owner is sui juris, possessed of the capacity to give the necessary sanction and to make the transaction operative. They do not find any reference in these doctrines relating to *fazuli* sales, so far as they appear in the *Hedaya* or the *Fatawa-i-Alamgiri*, to dealings with the property of minors by persons who happen to have charge of the infants and their property—in other words, the 'de facto guardians'.

The Hanafi doctrine about *fazuli* sales appears clearly to be based on the analogy of an agent who acts in a particular matter without authority, but whose act is subsequently adopted or ratified by the principal which has the

6 The 'Book on Sale' in the *Fatawa-i-Alamgiri* has been rendered into English by Baillie under the name of the *Mahommedan Law of Sale*.

effect of validating it from its inception. The idea of agency in relation to an infant is as foreign, their Lordships conceive, to Mahommedan law as to every other system.

In this connection it should be noted, that whilst chapter 12 deals exclusively with the effect of 'dependent sales', in chapter 16 the rules relating to the powers of guardians are discussed at considerable length: Baillie's *Mahommedan Law of Sale*, p. 243; *Fatawa-i-Alamgiri*, vol. 3, p. 229. The following rule lays down the conditions governing the sales by the executor (i.e., the appointed guardian) of the immovable property of an infant:

And, according to modern decisions, the sale of immovable estate by an executor is lawful only in one of the three cases following: that is, where there is a purchaser willing to give double its value, or the sale is necessary to meet the minor's emergencies, or there are debts of the deceased, and no other means of paying them: Baillie's *Mahommedan Law of Sale*, p. 247; *Fatawa-i-Alamgiri*, vol. 3, p. 233.

Having regard to the object in view, this dictum appears to their Lordships to apply to all forms of property which, like '*aqar*, combine both security and permanency. But it does not exclude the discretion of the judge to sanction any alteration of investment in the interests of the infant.

The following case affords a further illustration of the limitations on the powers of '*de facto* guardians':

A woman after the death of her husband sells property that belonged to him, supposing herself to be his executrix, and her husband having left minor children; she after some time declares that she was not the executrix, her assertion, however, is not to be credited as against the purchaser, but the sale remains in suspense till her children arrive at puberty. If they should admit that she was the executrix, the sale by her is lawful; but if they deny the fact, the sale is void; and though the purchaser should have manured the purchased land, he has no recourse for reimbursement against the woman. What has been said is on the supposition that the woman sues for a cancellation of the sale, on the ground that she was not the executrix; but if the minor sue on that ground, his claim is to be heard': *Baillie*, p. 249; *Fatawa-i-Alamgiri*, vol. 3, p. 234.

The rest of the passage is immaterial for the purposes of this judgment.

The above case shows that even where the mother believes she is vested with authority as her husband's executrix and in that belief purports to deal with the minor's property, a purchaser let into possession by her is liable to be ejected at the instance of the minor. Her own subsequent denial of authority does not affect the purchaser's position; but if the transaction is impugned by the rightful owner, namely, the infant, the onus is on the vendee to establish the foundation of his title, that is, that his vendor possessed in fact the authority under which she purported to act.

A further rule, which is given in the 'Book on Pledges' (Mortgages) (*Kitab-ur-Rahn*) of the *Fatawa-i-Alamgiri*, which does not appear to have been translated by Mr Baillie, is equally explicit. After stating the principle applicable to the powers of the father to pledge or mortgage his minor child's property, it goes on to say; 'the mother: if she pledges (mortgages) the property of her infant child, it is not lawful, unless she be the executrix [of the father] or be authorized therefor by the guardian of the minor; or the judge should grant her permission to pledge the infant's property. Then it is lawful; and the right to possession and user is established in the *murtahin* (pledgee or mortgagee) without power of sale': *Fatawa-i-Alamgiri*, vol. 5, p. 638.

It seems to their Lordships that the power to sell cannot be wider than the power to mortgage.

For the foregoing considerations their Lordships are of opinion that under the Mahommedan law a person who has charge of the person or property of a minor without being his legal guardian, and who may, therefore, be conveniently called a 'de facto guardian,' has no power to convey to another any right or interest in immovable property which the transferee can enforce against the infant; nor can such transferee, if let into possession of the property under such unauthorized transfer, resist an action in ejectment on behalf of the infant as a trespasser. It follows that, being himself without title, he cannot seek to recover property in the possession of another equally without title.

Their Lordships are accordingly of opinion that the decree of the High Court, in so far as it awards to the plaintiffs possession of the shares of the defendants 9 and 10, should be discharged, and, subject to this variation, it should be affirmed and the appeal be dismissed with costs. And their Lordships will humbly advise His Majesty accordingly.

Their Lordships cannot help deprecating the practice which seems to be growing in some of the Indian courts of referring largely to foreign decisions. However useful in the scientific study of comparative jurisprudence, reference to judgments of foreign courts, to which Indian practitioners cannot be expected to have access, based often on considerations and conditions totally differing from those applicable to or prevailing in India, is only likely to confuse the administration of justice.

◊ UPDATE ◊

1. *Natural guardians*

As regards the old Privy Council ruling of 1871 in *Skinner* v. *Orde* [Case 21], legal guardians embracing a new religion may still lose their right to guardianship in all parts of the subcontinent. Strangely, the Caste Disabilities Removal Act 1850, which protects legal rights of the converts, has never been used in this matter. On the contrary, in India the old legal position seems to have been formalized by a provision to that effect included in the Hindu Minority and Guardianship Act 1956 (Section 6).

In Pakistan and Bangladesh the Caste Disabilities Removal Act 1850 has been specifically made inapplicable to the Muslims. See the Caste Disabilities Removal (Amendment) Act 1963, in force in both the countries.

In Bangladesh, in the case of *Md Abu Baker Siddique* v. *SMA Baker* (1986) BLD 245 it was held that the old texts relating to custody of children are not binding on the courts and that such matters should be governed by the welfare of the child concerned. It was observed by the court:

> The court's power to determine the entitlement of a party to the *hizanat* is not limited to mere observance of age rules so as to exclude the consideration of the interest of the child which would, however, depend on the facts and circumstances of a given case.

2. *Age of majority*

The Indian Majority Act 1875—which regulates the age of majority except in matters of marriage, dower and adoption—has been amended in India to adopt eighteen years as the uniform age of majority. See the Indian Majority (Amendment) Act 1999. Muslim children who have attained the age of eighteen years can, therefore, lawfully deal with their own property.

3. *Custody of children*

The rules of Muslim law on the mother's right to the custody of her children have been explained in India in *Suharabi* v. *VD Muhammad* AIR 1988 Ker 30, *Farzanabi* v. *Ayub* AIR 1989 Bom 375 and *Irfan* v. *Mumtaz* AIR 1999 Bom 25.

In Bangladesh a leading case on the right of a mother to have the custody of her child is that of *Kazi Mohd Ilyas* 41 Dhaka Law Reports 616 (1989).

4. *Guardianship of property*

The rules of Muslim law on guardianship of property as explained in the old Privy Council ruling in *Imambandi* [Case 22] remain unchanged in the whole subcontinent. In India some of these have been reiterated by the Supreme Court in its decisions in *Mohammad Amin* v. *Vakil Ahmed* AIR 1952 SC 358 and *Syed Shah Ghulam Ghouse Mohiuddin* v. *Syed Shah Ahmad Mohinddin Kamisul Qadir* AIR 1971 SC 2148.

As regards gifts to a minor with delivery of possession to his mother, the rule of Muslim law as stated in the old ruling in *Sadik Hussain* [Case 19] remains generally in force in the subcontinent. The Supreme Court of India has examined it from different angles in *Mahboob* v. *Syed Ismail* AIR 1995 SC 1205 and *Maner* v. *Maner* (2000) 8 SCC 507.

5. *Maintenance of children*

Under Muslim law the primary liability to provide maintenance to children belongs to their father and he cannot shun it by deliberately depriving himself of all his property. In *Ibrahim Fathima* v. *Saleem* AIR 1980 Mad 82 the Madras High Court observed:

> Children's right to maintenance in a Muslim household always attaches to the father's property in such a way and in such a measure that it is not affected by any subsequent alienation by the father with notice of the charge or by an alienation which is gratuitous.

The Muslim Women (Protection of Rights on Divorce) Act 1986 includes a provision relating to maintenance of a divorced woman during the period in which she is feeding a child. Its faulty wording created an impression that it spoke of the maintenance of the child being fed by her. In *Noor Saba Khatoon* v. *Quasim* AIR 1997 SC 3280 the Supreme Court clarified that this provision in fact provides for the maintenance of the divorced woman herself by her former husband as long as she feeds his child. On the continued right of children to seek maintenance from their father under the Code of Criminal Procedure the court held that:

> The children of Muslim parents are entitled to claim maintenance under Section 125 CrPC for the period till they attain majority or are able to maintain themselves whichever is earlier, and in case of females till they get married, and this right is not restricted, affected or controlled by the divorcee wife's right to claim maintenance for maintaining the infant child/children in her custody for a period of two years from the date of birth of the child concerned under Section 3 (1) (b) of the 1986 Act.[7]

[7] The judgment cites my exposition of the law on this point from my book *Statute Law relating to Muslims in India*, Qazi Publications, Delhi 1995.

X. Illegitimate Child

23. Gohar Begam v. Suggi

1960(1) SCR 597

Habeas corpus—application for recovery of child—unmarried Muslim woman—Hindu father—duty of court—alternative remedy, if a bar—principles applicable—Criminal Procedure Code, 1898 (*V of* 1898), s. 491

An unmarried Hanafi mother of an illegitimate female child made an application under s. 491 of the Code of Criminal Procedure for the recovery of the child from the respondents.

Held, that under the Muhammadan law the mother of an illegitimate female infant child is entitled to its custody. The refusal to restore such a child to the custody of its mother would result in an illegal detention of the child within the meaning of s. 491 of the Criminal Procedure Code. A dispute as to the paternity of the child is irrelevant for the purpose of the application. The Supreme Court will interfere with the discretionary powers of the High Court if the discretion was not judicially exercised.

Held, also, that before making the order for the custody of the child the court is called upon to consider its welfare.

Held, further, that the fact that a person has a remedy under the Guardian and Wards Act is no justification for denying him the remedy under s. 491 of the Criminal Procedure Code.

Held, further, that in issuing writs of *habeas corpus* the courts have power in the case of an infant to direct its custody to be placed with a certain person.

See *Outlines*, 192 seq.

Judgment [Sarkar, J.]

The appellant is an unmarried Sunni Moslem woman. She has an infant female illegitimate child called Anjum. The appellant made an application to the High Court at Bombay under s. 491 of the Code of Criminal Procedure for the recovery of the custody of the child from the respondents. That application was refused. Hence this appeal.

The appellant's case is as follows: She is the daughter of one Panna Bai. The respondent Kaniz Begum is Panna Bai's sister. Kaniz Begum, whom it will be convenient to refer as the respondent, took the appellant over from Panna Bai and brought her up. Prior to 1951 the respondent had put her in the keeping of two persons and had thereby made pecuniary gain for herself. In 1951 the appellant met one Trivedi and since then she has been living continuously in his exclusive keeping. The appellant stayed with Trivedi at Jabalpur up to 1954. On 4 September 1952, the child Anjum was born to her by the said Trivedi. In November 1953 she bore another child to him of the name of Yusuf alias Babul. In 1954 the appellant with her said two children, her mother who had been living with her, and Trivedi left Jabalpur and came to live in Bombay. After coming to Bombay, Trivedi for sometime lived with his relatives as he could not find independent accommodation. During this time, the appellant with her children and mother stayed with the respondent who was then living in Bombay, but Trivedi used to visit the appellant daily at the residence of the respondent. In January 1956 the appellant bore a third child to Trivedi called Unus alias Chandu. After the birth of Unus, Trivedi took the appellant, her mother and the two younger children to a hill station near Bombay called Khandala, and the party stayed there for three or four months. At the time the appellant had gone to Kandala, the respondent went to Pakistan on a temporary visa and she took the child Anjum with her presumably with the consent of the appellant. After returning from Khandala, Trivedi was able to secure a flat for himself in Marine Drive, Bombay, and the appellant with her mother and two sons began to stay with him there. In April 1957 Trivedi moved into another flat in Warden Road, Bombay, with the appellant, her two younger children and mother, and has since then been living there with them. After the respondent returned from Pakistan with Anjum, the appellant who had then moved into the flat in Marine Drive, asked the respondent to send Anjum to her but the respondent refused to do so. Since then the respondent has been refusing to restore the custody of the child Anjum to the appellant.

In these circumstances, the appellant made her application under s. 491 of the Code of Criminal Procedure on 18 April 1958. [....]

The respondent opposed the application denying the correctness of some of the allegations made in the petition of the appellant. She denied that Trivedi was the father of the child Anjum and said that the father was a Shia Moslem called Samin Naqui. She said that the appellant's mother had given the appellant to her to bring up when very young as she had not the means to do so herself, and since then the appellant had been living with her all along and left her flat in company with Trivedi only during her temporary absence in Pakistan in 1956. She denied that she had made the appellant live in the keeping of any person as alleged by the latter. She contended that she had intended that the appellant would marry and live a clean and respectable life but other influences operated upon her and she went to live with Trivedi as his mistress. She denied that she had prevented the appellant access to the child Anjum as the latter stated. She contended that she was looking after the child Anjum with great care and solicitude, and had put her in a good school and kept a special Aya for her. She also said that she was well off and had enough means to look after the child well. She contended that it was not in the interest of the child to live with the appellant because she was living in the keeping of a man who might turn her out and she would then have to seek the protection of another man. She said that she had no child of her own and was fond of Anjum whom she had been treating as her own child.

The learned Judges of the High Court observed that the case raised various controversial questions, specially as to the paternity of the child, as to whether the respondent had made the appellant live in the keeping of different persons and also as to whether she had prevented the appellant from having access to the child. The learned Judges observed that it was not the function of a court in an application under s. 491 to record findings on such controversial facts and that, in these circumstances, the proper forum for the appellant was to move a civil court under the Guardian and Wards Act for the custody of the child. The learned Judges further observed that they were *prima facie* satisfied that the child was not illegally and improperly detained by the respondents. They therefore dismissed the appellant's application.

We are unable to appreciate the view of the learned Judges of the High Court. It seems to us that the controversial facts referred to by them were wholly irrelevant to the decision of the application. We have not been able to find one single fact relevant to the issue in this case which is in controversy. The facts, which are abundantly clear and beyond dispute are these. The child Anjum is the illegitimate daughter of the appellant who is a Muslim woman. The child was at the date of the application less than six years old and now she is just over seven years old. The appellant is a singing girl by profession and so is the respondent. The appellant stated in her affidavit that the respondent was in the keeping of a man and this the respondent has not denied. It is not the respondent's case that she is a married woman leading a respectable life. In fact she admits that she allowed Trivedi to live in her flat with the appellant as his mistress and took money from him for 'Lodging and Boarding Charges'. Trivedi has sworn an affidavit acknowledging the paternity of the child and undertaking to bring her up properly as his own child. He is a man of sufficient means and the appellant has been for a considerable time living with him as his mistress.

On these undisputed facts the position in law is perfectly clear. Under the Mohammedan law which applies to this case, the appellant is entitled to the custody of Anjum who is her illegitimate daughter, no matter who the father of Anjum is. The respondent has no legal right whatsoever to the custody of the child. Her refusal to make over the child to the appellant therefore resulted in an illegal detention of the child within the meaning of s. 491. This position is clearly recognized in the English cases concerning writs of *habeas corpus* for the production of infants. In *The Queen* v. *Clarke*[1] Lord Campbell, CJ, said at p. 193:

> But with respect to a child under guardianship for nurture, the child is supposed to be unlawfully imprisoned when unlawfully detained from the custody of the guardian; and when delivered to him, the child is supposed to be set at liberty.

The courts in our country have consistently taken the same view. For this purpose the Indian cases hereinafter cited may be referred to. The terms of s. 491 would clearly be applicable to the case and the appellant entitled to the order she asked.

We, therefore, think that the learned Judges of the High Court were clearly wrong in their view that the child Anjum was not being illegally or improperly detained. The learned Judges have not given any reason in support of their view and we are clear in our mind that that view is unsustainable in law.

Before making the order the court is certainly called upon to consider the welfare of the infant concerned. Now there is no reason to think that it is in the interest of the child Anjum to keep her with the respondent. In this connection it is relevant to state that at some stage of the proceedings in the High Court the parties appeared to have arrived at a settlement whereby it had been agreed that the child Anjum would be in the custody of the appellant and the respondent would have access to the child. The learned Judges of the High Court however were not prepared to make an order in terms of this settlement because, as they said, 'It did not appear to be in the interest and welfare of the minor.' Here again they give no reason for their view. Both parties belong to the community of singing girls. The atmosphere in the home of either is the same. The appellant as the mother can be expected to take better care of the child than the respondent. Trivedi has acknowledged the paternity of the child. So in law the child can claim to be maintained by him. She has no such right against the respondent.

1 (1857) 7 EL & BL 186: 119, ER 1217.

We have not been able to find a single reason how the interests of the child would be better served if she was left in the custody of the respondent and not with the appellant.

We further see no reason why the appellant should have been asked to proceed under the Guardian and Wards Act for recovering the custody of the child. She had of course the right to do so. But she had also a clear right to an order for the custody of the child under s. 491 of the Code. The fact that she had a right under the Guardians and Wards Act is no justification for denying her the right under s. 491. That is well established as will appear from the cases hereinafter cited.

The learned Advocate for the respondent said, we should not interfere with the order of the High Court as it was a discretionary order. The learned Judges however have not given any reason which led them to exercise their discretion in the way they did. We are not satisfied that the discretion was judicially exercised.

We are clear in our view that the judgment of the High Court was wrong and should be set aside.

It is further well established in England that in issuing a writ of *habeas corpus* a court has power in the case of an infant to direct its custody to be placed with a certain person. In *The King* v. *Greenhill*[2] Lord Denman, CJ, said:

> When an infant is brought before the court by *habeas corpus*, if he be of an age to exercise a choice, the court leaves him to elect where he will go. If he be not of that age, and a want of direction would only expose him to dangers or seductions the court must make an order for his being placed in the proper custody.

See also *The Queen* v. *Clarke*.[3] In Halsbury's *Laws of England*, Vol. IX, art. 1201 at p. 702 it is said:

> Where, as frequently occurs in the case of infants, conflicting claims for the custody of the same individual are raised, such claims may be enquired into on the return to a writ of *habeas corpus,* and the custody awarded to the proper person.

Section 491 is expressly concerned with the directions of the nature of a *habeas corpus*. The English principles applicable to the issue of a writ of *habeas corpus*, therefore, apply here. In fact the courts in our country have always exercised the power to direct under s. 491 in a fit case that the custody of an infant be delivered to the applicant: see *Rama lyer* v. *Nataraja lyer*,[4]

2 (1836) 4 AD & E 624, 640; III ER 922, 927.
3 (1857) 7 EL & BL 186; 119 ER 1217.
4 AIR 1948 Mad 294.

Zara Bibi v. *Abdul Razzak*,[5] and *Subbuswami Goundan* v. *Kamakshi Ammal*.[6] If the courts did not have this power, the remedy under s. 491 would in the case of infants often become infructuous.

We, therefore, set aside the judgment and order of the High Court and direct the respondents other than the State of Bombay to make over the custody of the child Anjum to the appellant. Let the child be produced by the respondents before the Registrar, Appellate Side, High Court of Bombay, and the Registrar will then make over custody to the appellant. The passport in respect of the child Anjum deposited in this court by the respondents may be made over to the Advocate on record for the appellant. The injunction restraining the removal of the child Anjum outside Greater Bombay will continue till she is delivered to the appellant.

◊ UPDATE ◊

1. *Mother-Child relation*

Unlike the Shia Ithna Ashari law, the Hanafi law recognizes a direct relationship between a mother and her children without regard to their legal status as to 'legitimacy'. This very humane law was taken note of in *Gohar Begum* [Case 23] decided in 1960 by the Indian Supreme Court.

2. *Statutory law*

A similar rule relating to guardianship of illegitimate children has been incorporated in the Hindu Minority and Guardianship Act 1996, Section 6, saying that the mother of an illegitimate male or female child is its first natural guardian.

3. *Pre-marital pregnancy*

The Supreme Court of India has held that the fact of pre-marital pregnancy of a woman, if known to the husband at the time of marriage and not then objected to by him, cannot later be raised as a ground to challenge the validity of marriage. *Amina* v. *Hasan Kaya* (2003) 6 scc 93.

5 (1910) 12 Bom LR 891.
6 (1930) ILR 53 Mad 72.

XI. Gifts

24. Moonshee Buzloor Ruheem v. Shumsoonnissa Begum
(1867) 11 Moo IA 551

Gift by pardanashīn woman—proof required—bēnāmī transactions—cruelty as between husband and wife—restitution of conjugal rights—'justice, equity and good conscience'

A *pardanashīn* lady is entitled to the protection which, according to the authorities, the law gives to her in India.[1]

In a suit by a wife a Muslim woman against her husband to recover the value of Company's paper and real and personal estate, the plaint alleged, that such paper being her separate property, had been, as she lived in seclusion, endorsed and handed over to her by her husband for the purpose of receiving the interest thereon. The defence of the husband was, that he had purchased such paper from his wife, and on the endorsement and delivery had paid the full value to his wife, who had appropriated the proceeds to her own use.

Held, upon a review of the evidence, that although the wife failed to prove affirmatively the precise case alleged by her in the plaint, the husband was bound to show something more than the mere indorsement and delivery of the Company's paper, and that from the relations subsisting between the parties, the *onus probandi* was upon him to establish; first, that the transaction which he set up was a *bona fide* sale; and second, that he gave full value for the Company's paper so received from his wife.

Held further, that in the absence of proof of the husband having the means of purchasing the Company's paper, he being at the time in embarrassed

[1] According to Wilson's *Glossary, parda* is a veil, screen or curtain, especially one which excludes the women of the family from the gaze of men; and a *pardanashin* (or *-nishin)* lit., 'seated behind the curtain', is a compound word applicable to a respectable female (Hindu as well as Muslim) who observes the rule of seclusion, and who is on that account excused from personal appearance in a Court of justice, H. H. Wilson, *A Glossary of Judicial and Revenue Terms*, enlarged and edited by A. C. Ganguli and N. D. Basu, Eastern Law House, Calcutta, 1940. See also *Wilson*, 54; *Tyabji*, § 359A; *Outlines,* 215.

circumstances, and the condition of the wife, a *pardanashīn* lady, that no purchase had taken place, and that the transaction was fraudulent as against her.

Although the habit of holding land *benami* is prevalent in India, such fact does not justify the court in making every presumption of such holding against apparent ownership.

A suit for restitution of conjugal rights will lie in a civil court by a Muslim husband to enforce his marital rights.

By the Muhammadan law such a suit is in the nature of a suit for specific performance, being founded on a contract of marriage, the Muhammadan law regarding it as a civil contract, and the court will enforce all the obligations which flow from such a contract.

If, however, there be cruelty to a degree rendering it unsafe for the wife to return to her husband's dominion, the court will refuse to send her back to his house; so also, if there be a gross failure by the husband of the performance of obligations which the marriage contract imposes on him for the benefit of the wife, it affords sufficient ground for refusing him relief in such a suit.

From the frame of the pleadings and issues, the question of cruelty was not properly entered into, but in the circumstances of the conduct of the husband towards his wife, the Judicial Committee declined to direct the wife to be sent back to her husband, and remitted the cause back to the court below for a new trial, with liberty to frame issues and take evidence as to the specific acts of cruelty.

Judgment [James W. Colvile, J.][2]

The Appellant, in three of the four appeals of which their lordships have now to dispose, is Moonshee Buzloor Ruheem, a Bengal *zemindar*. The Respondent, in all four appeals, is his Wife, Shumsoonnissa Begum. Her Father, Moonshee Hossain Ali, died in the year 1837, possessed of considerable wealth. His co-heirs, according to Mahommedan law, were his three Widows, Ashruffnissa, Oomdatunnissa, and the Respondent's Mother, Komerunnissa; two Daughters, viz., the Respondent and a posthumous child, named Nujmunnissa, and his nephew, Booali. His estate was divisible amongst these persons, in twenty-four parts or shares, of which the Respondent and her sister each took eight. The settlement of his affairs, however, occasioned a good deal of litigation, and the Respondent did not obtain full possession of her share until November, 1847.

She had previously, and in the month of April or May of that year, being

2 With E.V. Williams & Torin Kindersley, JJ, and Assessor Lawrence Peel.

then a Widow, with five children by her first Husband, become the Wife of the Appellant, Moonshee Buzloor Ruheem. By him she has had one Daughter. In July, 1853, in consequence of the death of her sister, Nujmunnissa, which took place in August, 1849, and of the compromise of a suit with that Lady's Husband, she received a large accession of fortune. Her cohabitation with the Moonshee continued until the 28th of December, 1855; when, on a complaint of her of ill-usage on his part, she was allowed by the Magistrate of the Twenty-four Pergunnahs to leave his house. They have since lived separately, and the present litigation dates from that time.

On the 8th of April, 1856, she instituted against her Husband a suit for the recovery of her property which, she alleged, he had detained or made away with. On the same day he commenced against her and one of her sons-in-law a suit, of which the object was, to enforce his marital rights, by compelling her to return to his house and control. These suits, in the argument before us, were called, respectively, the 'Property suit' and the 'Restitution suit'—a nomenclature which it may be convenient to adopt.

The property suit was originally brought against the husband alone [....]

The restitution suit was tried by the Principal Sudder Ameen of the Twenty-four Pergunnahs, who, by his decree, dated the 28th of December, 1860, dismissed it with costs. On appeal, the High Court of Calcutta confirmed that decision by its decree of the 25th of July, 1863. The Moonshee has appealed against both these decrees.

His remaining appeal is against a decree of the High Court, made on the 13th of February, 1863, in another suit instituted against him by his wife. [....]

Having thus stated the general history and scope of this unfortunate and complex litigation, their Lordships will proceed to deal first with the appeals in the property suit. The Respondent having preferred no appeal against the decree of the High Court, her claims, in respect of the moveable property, must be taken to be now reduced to one for the Government securities, to the amount of Rs 234,800, which the Moonshee has been ordered to restore or replace. And their Lordships will begin by considering, whether the decrees under appeal can be supported against him in that respect.

That all these securities came to her hands whilst she was an inmate of his *zenanah*; that they all passed from her to him; that some of them remain in his possession; and that others have been traced to his creditors—is incontestable. That she came to his house a wealthy woman, and left it almost destitute, admits of no doubt. And it can scarcely be denied that transactions of this nature and magnitude between Husband and Wife, with such a result, require a full and clear explanation on the part of the former, supported by such evidence as shall satisfy a court of justice that they were conducted fairly and properly, and with a due regard to the rights and interests of the Wife. Her case is, that the securities were entrusted to him for a particular purpose, viz., that of receiving the interest on them for her, and that though they may have been indorsed, she never meant to transfer the property in them. His case is, that he purchased them from her on several occasions, and that on their indorsement and delivery he paid her the full value for them. The principle of the judgments of the courts below seems to be, that although the Wife may have failed to establish affirmatively the precise case alleged by her, her Husband, having admitted the receipt of the securities from her, was bound to show something more than mere indorsement and delivery; that the relation of the parties being what it was, it lay upon him to prove that the transactions which he set up were *bonâ fide* sales and purchases, and that he actually gave full value for what he received from her. Their Lordships are clearly of opinion, that this is a sound principle, and in accordance with the long-established practice of the courts in India. The Attorney-General, indeed, argued that a distinction is to be drawn in this respect between a Mahommedan and a Hindoo woman; nay, that in all that concerns her power over her property, the former is by law more independent than an English woman of her Husband. It is no doubt true that a Mussulman woman, when married, retains dominion over her own property, and is free from the control of her Husband in its disposition; but the Hindoo law is equally indulgent in that respect to the Hindoo Wife. It may also be granted that in other respects the Mahommedan law is more favourable than the Hindoo law to women and their rights, and does not insist so strongly on their necessary dependence upon and subjection to, the stronger sex. But it would be unsafe to draw from the letter of a law, which, with the religion on which it is chiefly founded, is spread over a large portion of the globe, any inference as to the capacity for business of a woman of a particular race or country. In India the Mussulman woman of rank like the Hindoo, is shut up in the *zenanah*, and has no communication, except from behind the *purdah*, or screen, with any male persons, save a few privileged relatives or dependants; the culture of the one is not, generally speaking, higher than that of the other, and they may be taken to be equally liable to the pressure and influence which a Husband may be presumed to be likely to exercise over a Wife living in such a state of seclusion. Their Lordships must, therefore, hold that this lady is entitled to the protection which, according to the authorities, the law gives to a *purdah-nusheen*, and that the burden of proving the reality and *bonâ fides* of the purchases pleaded by her Husband was properly thrown on him. They will proceed to consider whether the courts below were right in holding that he has failed to prove his case. [....]

Both the courts below have, however, disbelieved these witnesses and have cast discredit on the books, as being unlike those which were likely to be kept in order to record the transactions of a person in the Appellant's position. The Zillah Judge, obviously a gentleman of experience and ability, appears to have tried the cause very carefully; and their Lordships cannot but feel the difficulty of holding against his judgment—confirmed, as it is, by that of the High Court—that either the witnesses or the books, considered by themselves, are trustworthy. In what degree, then, do the other facts and proceedings proved in the cause tend to confirm or to cast doubt upon their testimony? [....]

Now, as that answer was filed long before any disagreement had arisen between the Appellant and Respondent, it can hardly be doubted that, if not actually prepared under his direction, it was at least filed with his concurrence. And it is to be observed that this statement is by no means consistent with the case now made by him of sales out and out to him, in order to raise money to meet the Respondent's debts and other necessary expenses.

That case suggests the questions so much insisted upon in the courts below, viz. first, why should the Appellant wish to purchase these large amounts of Company's paper, and how was he able to pay for them? and secondly, why should the Respondent wish to sell her Company's paper, and how has she disposed of the proceeds of it? What answer does the evidence give to these questions?

The Appellant is no doubt shown to be a *zemindar* possessed of considerable estates. But the evidence tends to show that, at the time of his marriage, and at the date of the earlier, at least, of these transactions, he was, like many landed proprietors, an embarrassed man. He and his Brother owed large sums to one Ramchand Mookerjea, and to Ashotosh Day, and Promothonauth Day. These were secured by bond and by judgments confessed, probably on warrant of attorney, in the Supreme Court, of which one bore date the 27th of March, 1845, and was for C. Rs 148,000, and the other, dated the 30th of June, 1846, was for C. Rs 100,000. The precise amounts due on these judgments debts are not shown, but it is pretty clear that neither judgment, at the time of the earlier transfers of the Respondent's papers, was satisfied. It is admitted by the Appellant that most of the Company's paper, which, he says, he purchased on the 27th of May and 12th of June, 1848, were, on the 6th of July, transferred by him to Ashotosh Day, in payment of one of these debts. He and his brother were also at this time, bound, under an Order of the Supreme Court of the 12th of April, 1848, to pay into court the sum of Rs 62,000. It is not credible that a person under these liabilities should be purchasing Government securities, bearing a rate of interest considerably lower than that at which his debts were running on—securities which, if the necessity for selling them existed, might have been sold through a broker in the market.

Again, the Appellant's case is, that the Respondent, when she married him, was herself in debt; that she afterwards required large sums for the marriages of her children and other family ceremonies; that she sold her Government securities in order to meet these necessities, and applied the proceeds in meeting them. He is driven to this allegation, because, as it is clear that she carried nothing with her out of his house, it would be still more difficult to support a theory that the money remained with her in some other form of investment. It is to be observed, however, that some of his own witnesses assign a different motive for the sale. Some of them say that she sold in order to get rid of difficulties caused by the Company's papers standing in the name of a *purdah-nusheen*. Others say, as she says herself in her answer in the execution suit, that she was afraid of being cheated by her agents. That the Respondent, during her seven or eight years of cohabitation with the Appellant, must have incurred considerable expenses in respect of her children by the first marriage, and for other family purposes, is pretty certain; but that she should have expended upwards of two lacs of rupees, the proceeds of these Company's papers over and above the other property, which, at one time, she unquestionably possessed, is not very credible. It is to be remembered also that, on the assumption of the courts below, she had the interest of these Company's papers wherewith to meet her necessary expenses. It is inconceivable that if these very large sums had been expended in the payment of debts, and for the other purposes alleged, the Appellant should not have been able to give better proof of the fact. It may suit his present purpose to profess that he had little personal connection with the management of her affairs; but the evidence, and in particular his petitions of the 27th of October, 1854, and the 4th of December, 1855, are strong to show that this was not the case. He there represents himself as active in the management of her property and interests.

The first of these documents is, in various particulars, strangely inconsistent with the case which the Appellant now sets up. He is there defending himself from a charge, made before the Magistrate, of having confined his Wife, and having refused to give up to her not merely the Company's papers derived from Nujmunnissa, which, according to his case, would then be still in her possession, but also Company's papers to the amount of Rs 80,000 or 90,000, which, according to his present case, he had long before 1854 purchased from her; yet he does not say a word of this purchase. He covers the whole charge with the general answer, 'The entire property of Shumsoonnissa Begum being her own property, and my entire property being mine, what ground could there exist between her and me that I should confine her?'

We have hitherto considered the evidence with reference to the alleged sales of the Government securities generally. Some parts of it, however, suggest considerations which apply exclusively to the alleged transactions of 1855 and the transfer of the papers for Rs 114,300. It may be, that the means of the Appellant to make these alleged purchases had then been further diminished by the litigation in which he appears to have been engaged with his first Wife, and by the decree which she obtained against him. On the other hand, he may have been in more prosperous circumstances than he was in 1848. But if he, so late as the months of March and July, 1855, paid to the Respondent the value of these papers, it is almost incredible that he should not be able to give some better explanation how she disbursed those large sums between those dates and the following December, when she left his house destitute. Again, his petition of June, 1854, discloses a state of things which is far more consistent with the Respondent's case, that she made over to him these Company's papers in 1853, as soon as she received them, than with his, that they were not transferred to him until 1855. It shows that in June, 1854, a petition had been presented to the Magistrate, complaining of his ill-treatment of his Wife. He, no doubt, denied the charge, and treated it as emanating, not from his Wife, but from discharged servants; and the Magistrate then considered that the charge was unfounded. But when light is thrown upon this transaction by what subsequently happened, by his ill-usage of the Respondent, which is proved, and by her release from the house by the Magistrate, on the subsequent petition of 1855, it is difficult to resist the conclusion, that the quarrel between the Husband and Wife had begun in 1854 (the date to which her plaint assigns its commencement), or, at all events, that in July 1855, there must have been a state of feeling between them which would make a voluntary sale of her property to him a most improbable transaction. If he did, so shortly before their final separation, obtain a transfer of those securities to himself, the burden of showing that he did so righteously is assuredly made heavier.

Again, the evidence of ill-usage which has been given in this suit seems to have a further bearing upon the issue between the parties which is now under consideration. We have not now to consider, whether what he did was within, or in excess of, the marital powers of a Mussulman Husband. It is sufficient to say that very harsh treatment, and a restraint from which the Magistrate saw fit to release her, are proved, and that she left the house in circumstances to which no native woman of her rank, who was not suffering under a sense of intolerable wrong, would have exposed herself. Now, what was the cause of this grave quarrel? Her account of it is more probable than his, if indeed he has given any. It seems more likely that he should have attempted by harsh measures to frighten her out of a just demand, than that he should have met, in that way, one which was without foundation. Her conduct, too, if the quarrel had begun in 1854, has ever since been consistent; his, as has been shown above, has been inconsistent.

It would, doubtless, have been more satisfactory if the Respondent had thought fit to support her claim by her own testimony. Her abstaining from so doing certainly affords an objection to her case deserving of serious consideration; and their Lordships do not think that it is altogether removed by the suggestion of the strong repugnance felt by native females in the Respondent's position to taking such a step. But the objection, though it may weaken, does not destroy the case made by the Respondent; and their Lordships are of opinion, that, whatever weight may be due to it, it is quite insufficient to affect the conclusions in her favour to be drawn from the facts and circumstances of the case, which have been already adverted to.

The admission of the Tutor, a witness produced on the part of the Respondent, to the effect that on the transfer to which he speaks he saw money pass, is also a circumstance in the Appellant's favour But, if the witness has spoken the truth about the money, it is to be remembered that the transaction to which he speaks was that of the 27th of May, 1848, when it may have been desired to make a colourable sale for the purpose of defeating the execution in the manner shortly afterwards attempted.

Their Lordships, then, after carefully weighing the evidence and considering the able arguments addressed to them, have come to the conclusion, that the burden of proving *bona fide* purchases of these Company's papers was properly thrown on the Appellant; that he has failed to do so, and that no ground has been shown for disturbing the concurrent judgments of both the courts below on this part of the case. [....]

The substantial issue on this part of the case is one between the Respondent and Jodonath Bose; it is obvious, therefore, that the principle upon which, on the trial of the issue already considered, the burden of proof was shifted from the Plaintiff to the Defendant, is not necessarily applicable to the trial of this issue. The Respondent comes into court seeking to be relieved from the effect of her own conveyances, the execution of which she does not dispute, against one who, if not an absolute stranger, stands in no fiduciary relation to her; and it lies upon her to establish her right to that relief. Has she done so?

She has proved that Jodonath Bose is the servant of her husband. She has produced three witnesses, Gholam Arub, Gholam Ruhman, and Sheik Takee, to prove that her Husband is the person who is really in the possession, or in the receipt of the rents and profits of the property. But nothing can be less satisfactory than the testimony of these witnesses, of whom the first is her Manager; the second, a tailor; and the third, a menial servant; none of them having any connection with the lands.

The evidence of possession given on the other side, by Ryots and others, may not be altogether trustworthy; but, such as it is, it outweighs the loose statements of these three witnesses. Some of the inferences to be drawn from the conveyances from her to her husband are also favourable to the Respondent's case; but these apply only to that portion of the property claimed, which consists of her original share in the Dum-Dum garden.

It may be conceded that the conveyances from her to her Husband in 1848, considered with the light reflected on them from other parts of this case, and in particular from the proceedings in the execution suit, could not stand. It may also be conceded that if the question were between her and her Husband, he ought not to be permitted to say that she is bound by her fraudulent conveyance, since she may be presumed to have executed it under his influence or pressure. And if the property had passed directly from him to his dependant, the presumption that the latter is a mere Trustee for him might be stronger than it is.

But what are the facts proved? This portion of the property in dispute passed apparently by sale from Moonshee Buzloor Ruheem to Dilrus Begum. It remained with her for nearly five years; was sold, ostensibly at least, by her to Jeegree Khanum, from whom two months later it passed to Jodonath Bose. These intermediate conveyances are treated in the courts below, and in the argument before their Lordships, as mere 'circuity of fraud': and it has been argued that we have no proof who Dilrus Begum and Jeegree Khanum are, or, indeed, that there ever were such persons. But what proof, on the part of the Respondent, is there to support these arguments? On the other side, there are witnesses who state, that Dilrus Begum was the Wife of the Nawab of Chitpore, a well-known person, and that *Jeegree Khanum* was a Wife or concubine of apparently the same person. The conveyance to Dilrus Begum was by English deed, prepared and executed in the office of a respectable English Attorney, acting apparently for the purchaser. That circumstance afforded the means of investigating that transaction. But no attempt has been made to do so. Again, that Dilrus Begum was a real personage, not necessarily connected with the Appellant, the Moonshee, is placed almost beyond a doubt by the undisputed fact that in 1843, several years before the second marriage of the

Respondent, the six shares of this garden had been conveyed to her by Boodi and Ashruffnissa. What, again, was the motive for this 'circuity of fraud'? If Dilrus Begum held five years' benamee from the Moonshee, why raise suspicion by transferring the property from her to his known dependant, Jodonath Bose? Sir Roundell Palmer insisted strongly on the fluctuations in the amounts of the purchase-money for which the different instruments purported to convey the same property, as a badge of fraud. The first transaction, which we may admit to have been fictitious, expresses a consideration which, on a comparison with the price for which the six shares were sold in 1843, seems to be below the real value of the property. Tried by that test, the sum of Rs 4000, for which it was conveyed to Dilrus Begum, would be about the true value. This fact, taken by itself, tends to support the reality of the sales to Dilrus Begum. Again, if she sold for Rs 6000, property which had cost her Rs 7000, the difference is not greater than might be accounted for by the necessities of the Vendor, or by a diminution in the value of the property in the period during which it remained in her hands. The further reduction of the price to Rs 4000, in the sale to Jodonath Bose, is certainly a more suspicious circumstance. It is not, however, one which seems to go very far to supply any defect of proof on the part of the Respondent. It is not impossible that Jeegree Khanum may have found that she had made a bad bargain, or that Jodonath Bose may have made an extremely good one. On the other hand, if the transactions were fictitious, and the price cost the professed purchaser nothing, it is not easy to see why an adequate consideration was not expressed in the conveyance. There seems to have been no inquiry or cross-examination on this point in the courts below.

Again, what is the case proved in respect of the conveyances from the Respondent herself to Jodonath Bose? [....]

On the whole, then, their Lordships are of opinion, that the Respondent has failed to show a sufficient title to recover any of the shares in these gardens from the Appellant, *Jodonath Bose*. The habit of holding land *benamee* is inveterate in India; but that does not justify the courts in making every presumption against apparent ownership. This principle was enforced by this Committee in a recent case.[3] Their Lordships do not deny that in this particular case the connection of Jodonath Bose with the other Appellant, the proved conduct of the latter towards his Wife, and other circumstances, threw some cloud of suspicion over the title to these parcels of land. But such suspicions are not proof. Their Lordships think that the Judges of both courts below have given too much weight to them; that they have not

3 *Sreemanchunder Dey* v. *Gopaulchunder Chuckerbutty*, *ante*, p. 28.

sufficiently considered in what degree the burden of proof lay upon the Respondent; and that when the proofs which she ought to have given and might have given were defective, they have allowed the deficiency to be supplied by presumptions and inferences which the facts do not altogether warrant. Their Lordships cannot, therefore, recommend Her Majesty to confirm this portion of the decrees in the 'Property suit.'

As the third suit also concerns property, and the point raised by the appeal in it is very short, their Lordships think it will be convenient to dispose of it before they proceed to consider the appeal in the 'Restitution suit.' [....]

The High Court has reversed this decision, for the following reasons: They hold with him that the omission to include this item in the first suit was an oversight; that she knew of the existence of this paper before she brought her first suit, and might have included it therein; and that the real question to be decided was, whether that omission, neglect, or oversight was sufficient to bar her present claims under the law fairly applied. This question they decide in the negative, on the ground that it was clear she was not actuated by any fraudulent or dishonest motive; that the stamp paid on the first suit would have covered also this paper; that she cannot have omitted this claim in order to bring the case within the cognizance of a particular court; and that although it may be desirable for the ends of justice that the various items claimed by a Plaintiff should form the subject of one single action, yet there was nothing in the law to make it imperative upon her to include every item of such a claim as hers in a single suit.

To these reasons their Lordships cannot assent. If the words of a law are clear and positive, they cannot be controlled by any consideration of the motives of the party to whom it is to be applied, nor limited by what the Judges who apply it may suppose to have been the reasons for enacting it. The words of this law are—'If a Plaintiff relinquish or omit to sue for any portion of his claims.' It plainly includes accidental or involuntary omissions as well as acts of deliberate relinquishment. In their Lordships' opinion, the only ground on which (if at all) the judgment of the High Court could be supported, is that which is somewhat doubtingly expressed by the judges in the following sentence: 'Nor do we think that, under the circumstances of the case, the Plaintiff may not fairly plead that she has a distinct and separate cause of action for the recovery of this piece of paper made over to the Defendant on a particular date.' Their Lordships think that the correct test in all cases of this kind is, whether the claim in the new suit is, in fact, founded on a cause of action distinct from that which was the foundation of the former suit, and they have accordingly considered whether the present suit can be maintained on that ground. But the cause of action in the former suit of the Respondent seems to them to be the refusal by the Husband to restore, or his misappropriation of, the Wife's property, which she says she intrusted to him. There is nothing to distinguish the deposit of this particular Company's paper from the deposit of those which she deposited with it, and has recovered in the former suit. It was a mere item of her demand, and is admitted on the face of her present plaint to have been omitted from it, for no other reason than the very insufficient one before mentioned. If she was justified in instituting a separate subsequent suit for this particular Company's paper for Rs 10,000, she could have been equally justified in making each one of the Company's papers which are comprised in the 'Property suit' successively the subject of an independent suit. Their Lordships are of opinion, that the ruling of the Zillah Judge on this point was correct, and that the suit was properly dismissed. This being their view, it is unnecessary to say anything on the question of limitation. They are disposed, however, to think that the claim being founded on an alleged breach of trust, was not, as pleaded, subject to limitation, either under the old law or under Act, No. XIV of 1859, which, the suit having been commenced in December, 1861, seems to be the law applicable to it. If the Plaintiff had failed to prove a breach of trust, but had established some other title to relief, the question of limitation might have arisen. But this could only happen upon a trial of the suit on its merits.

Their Lordships will now address themselves to the novel and difficult questions raised by the appeal in the 'Restitution suit.'

The first is, that which has been strenuously argued at the Bar, though it does not appear to have been raised in the courts below, or even in the Respondent's case, viz., whether any suit by a Mussulman husband will lie in the Civil Courts of India to enforce his marital rights under the Mahommedan law, by compelling his wife, against her will (she being a free agent and not detained by others), to return to cohabitation with him. If the law which regulates the relations of the parties gives to one of them a right, and that right be denied, the denial is a wrong; and unless the contrary be shown by authority, or by strong arguments, it must be presumed that for that wrong there must be a remedy in a court of justice. Of authority negativing the jurisdiction there is none. It has been argued that the proper remedy, if there be one, is the denial of maintenance to the rebellious wife, or, at most, a suit for damages; because a suit to compel the wife to return to her husband, though obviously a more complete remedy than either of them, is in the nature of a suit for specific performance; and being founded on the contract of marriage, which the Mahommedan law regards as a civil contract, the court entertaining the suit must be prepared to enforce all the obligations, however minute, which, according to that law, flow from the contract, whichever party has a right to insist upon them. And referring to the definition of some of those obligations, as given with somewhat prurient particularity in certain Mahommedan treatises, the learned Counsel argued that it was impossible for courts constituted like those of British India to exercise such a jurisdiction. It may be admitted that the courts of India would properly decline to entertain such questions; although amongst the *Wahabees* of Central Arabia, or other communities in which the Mahommedan law is observed in its utmost strictness, the Magistrate might perhaps take cognizance of them. But this admission is not decisive of the question. The Canonists lay down many things concerning the relative duties of man and Wife which the Christian courts, at least of our Country, feel compelled to leave as duties of imperfect obligation. They do not, therefore, refuse to enforce the broad duty of cohabitation. In the words of Lord Stowell, quoted by Mr Attorney-General, 'They are content to take the Wife to the Husband's door and to leave her there.'

But how does this question stand upon the authorities? In the case of *Ardaseer Cursetjee* v. *Perozeboye* (6 Moore's Ind. App. Cases 390), in which it was here decided, that a suit for restitution of conjugal rights between Parsees, and *a fortiori,* one between Hindoos and Mahommedans, did not lie on the Ecclesiastical side of the Presidency Courts, Dr Lushington, in delivering the judgment of the Committee, says

> The Civil Courts in India can bend their administration of justice to the laws of the various suitors who seek their aid. They can administer Mahommedan law to Mahommedans, Hindoo law to Hindoos; but the Ecclesiastical law has no such flexibility.

And after ruling that the court below had not the jurisdiction which it claimed, he adds:

> But we should much regret if there were no court and no law whereby a remedy could be administered to the evils which must be incidental to married life amongst them (the Parsees). We do not pretend to know what may be the duties and obligations attending upon the matrimonial union between the *Parsees*, nor what remedies may exist for the violation of them; but we conceive that there must be some laws, or some customs having the effect of laws, which apply to the married state of persons of this description.

And he afterwards observes, 'Such remedies (the remedies afforded by their own usages) we conceive that the Supreme Court on the civil side might administer; or at least remedies as nearly approaching to them as circumstances would allow.' It maybe said that those dicta, though proceeding from so high an authority, are extrajudicial, and merely indicate an opinion that suits of this kind might possibly be entertained by the Civil Courts of

India. The Attorney-General, however, has cited positive authorities which support the jurisdiction, and shows the principles upon which it ought to be exercised. There are the cases of *Maulvi Abdul Wahab* v. *Mussumat Hingu*, decided in 1832, and reported in 5 Ben. Sud. Dew. Ad. Rep. p. 200; of *Mussumaut Ameena* v. *Kuttoo Khan,* decided in 1841 and reported in 7 *Ben.* Sud. Dew. Ad. Rep. p. 27; and the case of *Kulleemooddeen* v. *Sona Chand Bibi,* decided in 1848 and reported in the Reports of the Bengal *Sudder* Court for that year, at p. 795. In the last of these cases the suit was dismissed on the ground that the marriage was not proved, but the jurisdiction was not questioned. The second case may be distinguishable from the present on the ground that the Wife was of tender years, and under the control of the co-Defendants in the suit. But in the first case the Wife was clearly of full age, and a free agent. The co-Defendant in the suit, though charged with harbouring her, had little more control over her than the co-Defendant in the present case had over the Respondent. The suit, which went through three courts, was resisted by the wife on grounds personal to herself; and it was finally decided that, according to the Mahommedan law, by which the question was to be decided, the Plaintiff had a right to the possession of his Wife, and she was compelled to return to him. It does not very clearly appear by what process the judgment in this case, or in that of *Mussumat Ameena* v. *Kuttoo Khan* was to be enforced. From some passages it might be inferred that in the event of disobedience the Wife was to be given bodily into her Husband's hands. Whether this could be done under the new Act of Procedure, which now regulates the Civil Courts of India, may well be doubted. Disobedience to the Order of a court directing the Wife to return to cohabitation would seem to fall within the 200th section of the Code, and to be enforceable only by imprisonment, or attachment of property, or both.

Upon authority, then, as well as principle, their Lordships have no doubt that the Mussulman husband may institute a suit in the Civil Courts of India, for a declaration of his right to the possession of his wife, and for a sentence that she return to cohabitation; and that that suit must be determined according to the principles of the Mahommedan law. The latter proposition follows not merely from the imperative words of Ben. Reg. IV of 1793, sec. 15, but from the nature of the thing. For since the rights and duties resulting from the contract of marriage vary in different communities; so, especially in India, where there is no general marriage law, they can be only ascertained by reference to the particular law of the contracting parties.

The matrimonial law of the Mahommedans, like that of every ancient community, favours the stronger sex. The husband can dissolve the tie at his will, subject to the condition of paying the wife her dower and other allowances; but she cannot separate herself from him except under the arrangement called *kolah* [*khula*], which is made upon terms to which both are assenting parties, and operates in law as the divorce of the wife by the husband.[4] It cannot, we think, be doubted that, whilst the tie subsists, his power over her is considerable. The cases already cited are to the effect that he may compel her to return to his House, if she has left it. We do not find this expressed in the *Hedaya*, which speaks only of her forfeiting her right to maintenance if she be disobedient or refractory, or go abroad without her Husband's, consent, until she return and make submission (Vol. I. Book IV, ch. xv. p. 394); but it seems implied throughout, that she, from the time she enters his house, is under restraint, and can only leave it legitimately by his permission, or upon a legal divorce or separation, made with his consent. In fact, the principle of keeping a man's *hareem* in seclusion and under his control, is so essential a part of the framework of Oriental society, that it is naturally assumed and taken for granted by the Musulman expounder of the law.

On the other hand, the law assures to the Wife considerable rights as against her Husband. She may insist on maintenance according to her rank and his ability; and if he fails to give it, she may enforce that right before the *Kazee* (*Hedaya*, Vol. I. Book IV. chap. xv. sec. 1. pp. 393, 394). If he has power to keep her within the *Zenanah*, and to prevent access to her, subject to certain qualifications, he is bound to provide her with a separate apartment, exclusively appropriated to her use (*ib*. p. 402). As to personal violence, there are certainly passages in the *Hedaya* which, founded on a text in the Koran, imply that the Husband may use it for correction; but this right of corporal chastisement is expressly said to 'be restricted to the condition of safety;' and it may be questioned whether these authorities go the full length of the *Futwa* at p. 14 of the record (see *Hedaya*, Vol. II. Book VII. ch. vi. pp. 75–81). The Mahommedan law, on a question of what is legal cruelty between Man and Wife, would probably not differ materially from our own, of which one of the most recent expositions is the following: 'There must be actual violence of such a character as to endanger personal health or safety; or there must be a reasonable apprehension of it.' 'The court,' as Lord *Stowell* said, in *Evans* v. *Evans*,[5] 'has never been driven off this ground.'

If, however, it be granted that, according to Mahommedan law, the husband may sue to enforce his right to the custody of his wife's person;

4 See *Moonshee Buzul-ul-Raheem* v. *Luteefut-oon-nissa*, 8 Moore's Ind. App. Cases, 379.

5 Hagg. Con. Rep., 37, *et seq.*

and that, if her defence be cruelty, she must prove cruelty of the kind just described, it by no means follows, that she has not other defences to the suit which would not be admitted by our Ecclesiastical Courts in a suit for the restitution of conjugal rights. The marriage tie amongst Mahommedans is not so indissoluble as it is amongst Christians. The Mahommedan wife, as has been shown above, has rights which the Christian—or at least the English—Wife has not against her Husband. An Indian court might well admit defences founded on the violation of those rights, and either refuse its assistance to the Husband altogether, or grant it only upon terms of his securing the Wife in the enjoyment of her personal safety, and her other legal rights; or it might, on a sufficient case, exercise that jurisdiction which is attributed to the *Kazee* by the *Futwa* (if the law, indeed, warrants such a jurisdiction), of selecting a proper place of residence for the Wife, other than her husband's house.

Enough has been said to show that, in their Lordships' opinion, the determination of any suit of this kind requires careful consideration of the Mahommedan law, as well as strict proof of the facts to which it is to be applied. Has the present case been so tried and determined in the courts below? Their Lordships are constrained to say, that this has not been the case. In the first place, they think that the *ratio decidendi* adopted by the judges of both courts is erroneous. The Principal Sudder Ameen held, that oppression had been proved (the correctness of his conclusion will be hereafter considered). He did not then proceed to consider, whether the oppression was so far beyond the bounds of marital authority, under the Mahommedan law, as to constitute an answer to the suit. He seemed to think that, oppression once proved, the case was taken out of the Mahommedan law, and was to be decided on what the court, upon general principles, might deem to be expedient for the security of the wife's person. He then proceeded to argue, apparently without the slightest foundation of proof, that the wife, having been ill-treated, had probably been unfaithful, and that if she were restored to her husband, he was not unlikely to revenge himself by taking her life. He afterwards argued, with more reason, upon the danger of restoring her to one who had been decreed liable to pay her a very large sum of money.

The facts upon which the judges of the High Court proceeded were, that the Magistrate had seen fit to release the Respondent from her husband's house, and that a decree had passed against him for having made away with her property for a large sum, of which they overstated the amount. They appear to have considered that, according to the Mahommedan law, these facts were not an answer to the suit; and they then say, 'This being so, are we required to decide this case in conformity with the principles of the

Mahommedan law? Are we to compel the Defendant to return to her husband, convinced as we are that she should not be forced to return? If, under the Mahommedan law, no Wife can separate herself from her Husband under any circumstances whatsoever, the law is clearly repugnant to natural justice, and we are not bound to follow it. The Mahommedan law giving no relief to a woman, be the conduct of the Husband ever so bad, it is a case to be disposed of by equity and good conscience. And on these principles we have no hesitation in saying, that the grounds upon which the Defendant has separated from her husband justify her in that step.'

The passages just quoted, if understood in their literal sense, imply that cases of this kind are to be decided without reference to the Mahommedan law, but according to what is termed, 'equity and good conscience,' i.e., according to that which the judge may think the principles of natural justice require to be done in the particular case.

Their Lordships most emphatically dissent from that conclusion. It is, in their opinion, opposed to the whole policy of the law in British India, and particularly to the enactment already referred to (Reg. IV. of 1793, sec. 15), which directs, that in suits regarding marriage and caste, and all religious usages and institutions, the Mahommedan laws with respect to Mahommedans, and the Hindoo laws with regard to Hindoos, are to be considered as the general rules by which judges are to form their decisions; and they can conceive nothing more likely to give just alarm to the Mahommedan community than to learn by a judicial decision, that their law, the application of which has been thus secured to them, is to be overridden upon a question which so materially concerns their domestic relations. The judges were not dealing with a case in which the Mahommedan law was in plain conflict with the general Municipal law, or with the requirements of a more advanced and civilized society—as, for instance, if a Mussulman had insisted on the right to slay his wife taken in adultery. In the reports of our ecclesiastical courts there is no lack of cases in which a humane man, judging according to his own sense of what is just and fair, without reference to positive law, would let the wife go free; and yet, the proof falling short of legal cruelty, the Judge has felt constrained to order her to return to her husband.

In what they have just said their Lordships must be taken to object only to the general supersession of the Mahommedan law as the *ratio decidendi* in cases of this description, which seems to them to be implied in the judgments under review.

They do not mean to lay down that it was sufficient for the decision of the case to show that, according to the Mahommedan law, the husband has a right to the custody of his wife, or that there was no answer to his suit unless it could be shown that the wife had been separated from him either by *talak* [*talaq*] or *kolah* [*khula*], either of which would dissolve the *vinculum*. This assumption, which seems to have been made by the Judges of the High Court, is, their Lordships think, erroneous. It seems to them clear, that if cruelty in a degree rendering it unsafe for the Wife to return to her husband's dominion were established, the court might refuse to send her back. It may be, too, that gross failure by the husband of the performance of the obligations which the marriage contract imposes on him for the benefit of the Wife, might if properly proved, afford good grounds for refusing to him the assistance of the court. And, as their Lordships have already intimated, there may be cases in which the court would qualify its interference by imposing terms on the Husband. But all these are questions to be carefully considered, and considered with some reference to Mahommedan law.

Before, however, any of these principles can be applied, the facts to which they are to be applied must be established by legal proof; and this, their Lordships are of opinion, has not been done in the present case. Besides the evidence on the futile and now abandoned issue about freemasonry, there is little evidence in the cause.

The Zillah Judge's judgment in the 'Property suit' was put in evidence. The fact, therefore, that the Appellant had been decreed liable to make good a large sum of money to the Respondent in respect of the property which he had misappropriated was established; but the proof of personal cruelty rests almost entirely on the proceeding of the Magistrate. That proceeding is neither one *inter partes* nor even a conviction of the Appellant upon a criminal charge. It was treated by the Nizamut Adawlut as being the record of an act done by a Police Officer, and not the judicial proceeding of a Magistrate. It is, therefore, difficult to see how, in strictness, it can be evidence at all against the Appellant; but at most it proves only that the Magistrate set the lady free from what he considered improper restraint.

To establish a case of cruelty as a defence to the suit, the Respondent might have called the Magistrate, if then still in India, to speak to the state in which he found her when he set her free. She might also have given such evidence of her treatment as she adduced in the 'Property suit', but which, whatever were her reasons for it, she did not adduce in this suit. And lastly, she might have given her own testimony, which it is most desirable to have on such an issue. She has failed to do any of these things; and it is impossible to say that the courts below had before them in proof, the facts from which any court could infer that a defence on the ground of cruelty had been established.

From what has been said, it must be obvious, that their Lordships are not prepared to affirm the decrees under appeal in this suit. They do not, however, feel themselves in a condition to make a final decree, which would put an end to this painful litigation. They will not visit upon the Respondent the mismanagement of her cause by sending her back at once to her husband. Enough has been shown to render it doubtful, whether she can be restored to his *zenanah* with safety, at least whilst the relation of debtor and creditor continues to subsist between them, unless proper security for her protection is taken. It may ultimately turn out that she ought not to be sent back at all. Their Lordships must, therefore, unwillingly recommend that this cause be remitted to the High Court, with directions to put the same in a course of retrial, and with power, if necessary, to amend the issues or frame new ones. If cruelty be relied upon as a defence, there should be a distinct issue as to the fact of cruelty.

Their Lordships, however, cannot help suggesting, for the consideration of the parties, that it is for the interest, the happiness, and the respectability of both to settle the questions still open between them by amicable arrangement rather than by further litigation. They have surely friends who might effect such an arrangement between them.

Their Lordships have now only to recapitulate the several recommendations which they will humbly make to Her Majesty on these appeals. These are—

First; that the appeal of the Appellant, Moonshee Buzloor Ruheem, in the 'Property suit', be dismissed, except so far as it relates to his liability to pay the mesne profits of the shares in the Dum Dum and Narain Mundul gardens jointly with the Appellant, Jodonath Bose; that the appeal of the last-named Appellant in the same suit be allowed; and that the decree of the High Court be amended, by omitting so much thereof as relates to the shares in those gardens, and by directing, in lieu thereof, that that portion of the Respondept's claim be dismissed with costs, and that the said decree be in all other respects confirmed.

Secondly; that in suit, No. 256 of 1862, the decree of the High Court be reversed, and that, in lieu thereof, the decree of the Zillah Judge dismissing the Respondent's suit, with costs, be affirmed, with the costs of the appeal in the High Court.

Thirdly; that in the 'Restitution suit' the decrees of the High Court and of the Principal Sudder Ameen be reversed, and the cause be remitted to the High Court, with directions to have the same retried on fresh evidence, and with power to amend the issues, or to frame new issues, if they shall see fit to do so. [....]

25. Ranee Khujooroonnissa v. Mussamut Roushun Jehan (1876) 3 IA 291

Will—deed of gift—compromise—presumption of marriage

D. H., a Muslim, died in 1841, and his eldest son *E.*, possessed himself of all his property by virtue of a deed of gift and will dated in 1839. In 1852 the widow of a younger son, as guardian of the Respondent, her infant daughter, sued *E.* to set aside both deed and will, and to recover the property; but after a judgment was obtained she withdrew from the suit on terms of a compromise filed therein.

In 1860, the Respondent and her husband sued *E.*, now represented by the above-named Appellant, to set aside this compromise on the ground of minority, fraud, and collusion, for a review of the above-mentioned judgment, and to recover over and above the property comprised in the suit in which that judgment was given; first, a share derived by her father from his pre-deceased brother; second, a share in right of her grandmother *L.*, whom she alleged to have been a wife of *D. H.*; third, a share of property recovered by *E.* by decree of the Privy Council:

Held, that, the compromise being set aside on the issues found, both parties were remitted to their original rights, including the right of appeal from the above judgment.

It appearing that the deed of gift by *D. H.*, purporting to give to *E.* one-third of his property, was without consideration, and was unaccompanied by delivery of possession, and was only intended to operate after *D. H.'s* death, *Held*, that this was an evasion of Muhammadan law, which prevents a testator from interfering by will with the course of devolution of property among the heirs, and that the deed was invalid.

The will having declared *E.* the executor and representative of *D. H.*, there followed this passage: 'I divide the remaining two thirds now under my possession, uninterfered and unconcerned by anyone else, into three portions. One portion to be laid out as the executor may think proper for the testator's welfare hereafter, by charity and pilgrimage, and to keep up the family usage, namely, the expenses of the mosque and *tazeeadaree* of the sacred martyrs, and for the comfort of the travellers, the surplus amount to be appropriated by himself, the executor.' Then it goes on to say that from the other two thirds, 'he shall keep everyone by his good conduct and affection contented and satisfied. It is also necessary for all persons having rights, heirs, and friends connected with me to obey the said executor and consider him my representative.' Then further: 'None of the heirs have power to sell or divide the landed property mentioned in the will.'

Held, that this will in its general scope was in contravention of the Muhammadan law. The devise of one portion, considering the vague character of it, and that the beneficial interest is left to *E.*, after he has devoted what he may deem sufficient to indefinite pious uses, was in reality an attempt to give under colour of a religious bequest an interest in one third to *E.*, in contravention of Muhammadan law.

It appearing that the son of *L.* had always been treated by *D. H.* and all the members of the family as a legitimate son, a presumption arose that *L.* was *D. H.'s* wife, which was strengthened rather than rebutted by the evidence.

The passage at p. 308, below, dealing with the difference between the law of wills and the law of gifts is often cited and discussed, *Ameer Ali*, i, 33 seq.; *Tyabji*, Index; *Outlines,* 208.

This appeal was preferred from a judgment of a Divisional Bench of the Bengal High Court dated the 6th of January, 1866, which affirmed a judgment of the Judge of Purneah in Bengal (28 March 1865), and modified another judgment of the same Judge (6 April 1865), passed in the same suit and relating to other issues, and also, by special leave of the Judicial Committee, from an order of the same Bench passed on an application for review.

The present suit was instituted by the Respondent to get rid of an alleged compromise or former litigation as not binding on her, and to assert her claim as the only child of one Nuzeeroodeen Hossein to 14-16ths of the estate, to which he at the time of his death was entitled as one of the heirs of his father, Deedar Hossein, of his mother, Bibee Loodhun, and of his brother, Edoo Hossein.

Enayut Hossein, the Defendant in the court below, who died pending the appeal, which was prosecuted by his widow above-named, did not dispute the Respondent's status as the only child of her father, or that such father was one of the sons and heirs-at-law of Deedar Hossein; but he set up a deed and will from his own father, Deedar Hossein, in favour of himself as the eldest son, under which he contended that the younger children, including Nuzeeroodeen, were only entitled to maintenance allowances, and not to a share of the estate, and that they had assented to and taken that provision.

He also alleged that a former suit, the nature of which is sufficiently described in the judgment of their Lordships, brought by Respondent's mother, as her guardian, to assert the same right, had been settled with the guardian and withdrawn, so as to bar the present suit.

As to the claim to a share of Loodhun's estate, he also contended that Loodhun was not a married wife of Deedar Hossein, and therefore not an heir; and as to the claim to a share of Edoo Hossein's estate he contended that Edoo had survived Nuzeeroodeen, by reason of which, according to Mahommedan law, the Respondent could take nothing which had belonged to Edoo.

The Judge held in the first-mentioned judgment (March 28) that the Respondent was not bound by the alleged compromise, and was entitled to what she claimed in respect of her father's original share of his father's estate. He gave her a decree for the same which was affirmed by the Divisional Bench.

In the second judgment of the Judge (April 6) he held that Loodhun was not proved to be a wife of Deedar Hossein, and that Edoo had survived *Nuzeeroodeen* and consequently rejected Respondent's claims *pro tanto*, as also to a share of certain interests which had been recovered by *Enayut Hossein* in litigation.

The Divisional Bench reversed the Judge's findings on these points, and held Respondent entitled also to those portions of her claim.

Judgment [Robert P. Collier][6]

This case, which fills a great mass of printed paper, and has occupied much time, finally resolves itself into a few points not attended with any very great difficulty. In order to make those points intelligible, a short history of the whole case appears to be necessary. Rajah Deedar Hossein died in 1841, possessed of half of the large zemindary of Soorjapore., He left five sons and five daughters. According to the contention of the one side he left five widows; according to the contention of the other side he left one wife and four concubines. Enayut Hossein, his eldest son, possessed himself of all the property of the deceased Rajah by virtue of two documents which he set up, and which will have to be referred to subsequently, one being a deed of gift as it is called, and the other a will, both dated the 18th of November, 1839, about two years before the death of the Rajah.

The first document purported to convey to Enayut one-third of the zemindary. The will may be shortly described as giving to Enayut Hossein a third of what remained, burdened with a trust of a somewhat indefinite character for pious uses, but with a bequest of the residue after those pious uses had been satisfied to the beneficial use of Enayut himself. Enayut was put into possession of the whole of the landed property, and it was directed that the other children were not to be enabled to sell or dispose of their shares in any way. Enayut was to pay them certain annuities, which he does not appear to have done, and it was only of the personal property that a division

6 With J.W. Colvile & M.E. Smith, JJ.

was directed in accordance with the Mahommedan law. By virtue of these documents *Enayut* took possession of the property of his father, and appears to have reduced the other members of the family to a state of poverty. He struggled for some time to obtain mutation of names, in pursuance of these documents. The mutation was opposed by other members of the family, but was finally obtained in 1844 upon Enayut giving security. After that time some abortive suits were instituted by different members of the family in *forma pauperis*; but the first proceeding necessary to notice at all at length, is a suit instituted by Khoobunissa, who was the widow of Nuzeeroodeen, the third son of Rajah Deedar Hossein, in 1852, as guardian and protector of her infant daughter Roushun Jehan (the present Plaintiff), to set aside both the deed and the will, and to obtain possession on behalf of her daughter of a fourteen annas share (the daughter's share) of the property of *Nuzeeroodeen*. She appears to have also brought a suit for the other two annas on her own behalf.

This suit came to be heard before Mr Loch, who was the Judge at Purneah in 1855. His decision was to the effect that both the documents, the deed and the will, were in fact executed by the Rajah Deedar; that the deed was valid, but that the will was invalid because it had not obtained the consent of the heirs other than Enayut, which according to his view of the will was necessary by the Mahommedan law. Enayut Hossein appealed against that decision, and Khoobunissa would have had an undoubted right to her cross appeal but for what subsequently transpired. Pending this suit, which was decided in 1855, Enayut Hossein had instituted a cross suit against Khoobunissa for the purpose of carrying into effect an alleged compromise to which he said she was a party, he alleging that she had received some Rs 31,000, and had executed a document compromising the suit in his favour. This she denied. Issues were raised upon it, and this case came on for trial in August, 1856, rather more than a year after the other decision. But on the 30th of August of that year a compromise, which in some respects may be undoubtedly called a real compromise, was come to. Khoobunissa then filed a document, in which she declared that she would not any longer contest the questions between her and Enayut Hossein; that she had received certain money from him, and agreed altogether to his terms, and in that document there was a statement that her daughter Roushun Jehan assented to this compromise. Roushun Jehan was also represented as a party to the transaction, and as asserting herself to be of age. That compromise was given effect to by Mr Loch; it was also given effect to by the Sudder Dewanny Adawlut Court, which dismissed the appeal, and gave a decree in the terms of it in December, 1856.

Roushun Jehan, the present Plaintiff, in 1859 married Syud Ahmed Reza, a member of the other branch of the family, who possessed the half of the pergunnah Soorjapore other than that which was held by Deedar Hossein; and in 1860 she filed a suit, in which she asserted that she was no party to and had no knowledge of the compromise between *Enayut* and her mother, and that it was effected by fraud and collusion on the part of both of them. She prayed that that compromise might be set aside, and she prayed in substance for a review of the judgment of Mr Loch, so far as it was against her. She made also three further claims; the first to a share derived by her father from his brother Edoo Hossein, who had died before him; the second to a share in right of her grandmother, Bibee Loodhun, whom she alleged to have been a wife of Deedar Hossein. She thirdly claimed that there should be added to the whole zemindary property a portion which Enayut Hossein had recovered by a decree of this Board against the *Rezas*, in respect of the right of his grandmother Ranee Sumree. It may be as well at once to dismiss this part of the case, by stating that it is not now denied on the part of Enayut that he recovered this sum, not in his own right, but as a trustee for all the other members of the family.

This suit appears to have been deplorably dealt with in the inferior courts of India. It came first before Mr Beaufort, who framed a certain number of issues, and proceeded as far as deciding the issues in bar. Then it came before Mr *Birch*, who upset all that Mr Beaufort had done, and dismissed the suit altogether in a summary manner, on the ground that the cause of action was not stated with sufficient precision. The High Court set this mistake right by remanding the cause to be retried; whereupon it came before Mr *Simson*, who had succeeded Mr Birch. Mr Simson, who seems to have very imperfectly apprehended the nature of the suit, framed an issue, which by no means decided it, and after his trial (if it can be so called) of the case, it came before the High Court again, and was again remanded. This occurred in January or February, 1864, when a very careful and luminous judgment was given by the Chief Justice Sir Barnes Peacock and another member of the court, which it is now necessary more particularly to refer to. The High Court, after stating that the case had not been properly tried or even apprehended, remanded it for the following issues to be tried, in addition to the one laid down by Mr Simson, which was as to the validity of the deed. [....]

All the first ten issues which related to the validity of the compromise in the suit which was heard before Mr Loch, and came before the Sudder Dewanny Adawlut, were decided by the Judge, Mr Muspratt, before whom this case came on its remand, in favour of the Plaintiff. With respect to the latter issues, the Judge found against the Plaintiff upon the question of Edoo Hossein surviving his brother Nuzeeroodeen, her father, and he found against her on the question of her right to succeed to any portion of the property of her grandmother Bibee Loodhun. The case came on appeal before the High Court, who gave a very elaborate judgment in January, 1866. The High Court agreed with the learned Judge of the Zillah Court in his finding on all the ten issues relating to the compromise, and there being two concurrent findings upon these issues, which are questions of fact, their Lordships are by no means disposed to disturb them. Indeed, it has scarcely been argued that, giving effect to the rule on this subject, they should be disturbed.

The High Court next came to the conclusion that the compromise being set aside, owing to fraud and collusion on the part of Enayut Hossein, Enayut Hossein's right of appeal against Mr *Loch's* judgment was not revived, whereas the right of appeal on the part of the Plaintiff Roushun Jehan was revived. From that finding their Lordships differ. It appears to them that the effect of setting aside the compromise was to remit both parties to their original rights, and that if the Plaintiff is to be allowed to be heard to appeal against so much of the decision of Mr Loch as is against her, Enayut Hossein ought to be heard to appeal against so much of the decision as is against him. The High Court further affirm the decision of Mr Loch on the subject of the will, which was in favour of the Plaintiff, but they reverse his decision so far as it concerns the deed, which was against her. Further, they reverse the decision of Mr Muspratt upon the two questions of the right of the Plaintiff to succeed to Edoo Hossein, and her right to succeed to her grandmother. The case, therefore, reduces itself to four questions,—first, the validity of the deed; secondly, the validity of the will; thirdly, the survivorship between Edoo and Nuzeeroodeen; and, fourthly, the Plaintiff's right to succeed to her grandmother.

The policy of the Mahommedan law appears to be to prevent a testator interfering by will with the course of the devolution of property according to law among his heirs, although he may give a specified portion, as much as a third, to a stranger. But it also appears that a holder of property may, to a certain extent, defeat the policy of the law by giving in his lifetime the whole or any part of his property to one of his sons, provided he complies with certain forms. It is incumbent, however, upon those who seek to set up a proceeding of this sort, to show very clearly that the forms of the Mahommedan law, whereby its policy is defeated, have been complied with. There is no question of the execution by Rajah Deedar Hossein of this deed giving one third to his son Enayut on the 10th of November, 1839. The deed was either—to use English expressions—a deed of gift simply, or a deed of gift for a consideration. If it was simply a deed of gift without consideration, it was invalid unless accompanied by a delivery of the thing given, as far as that thing is capable of delivery, or, in other words, by what is termed in the books a seisin on the part of the donee. In their Lordships' judgment there was no delivery of this kind. Even assuming that although the estate was under attachment, a sufficient seisin in it remained to the donor which he could impart to the donee, still it appears by the evidence of Mr Perry, which is treated as trustworthy on both sides, that in point of fact Rajah Deedar Hossein remained in receipt of the rents and profits of the property until his death. Therefore if the deed were a mere deed of gift there was not that delivery of possession which was necessary: to give it effect by Mahommedan law. A question which was touched upon, though not much argued, viz. whether the doctrine of Mahommedan law relating to 'confusion of gifts' applied, appears not to arise, as there was no delivery of possession.

But it was contended that this was a deed of gift for a consideration, and therefore that the delivery of possession was not necessary It was, however, conceded that in order to make the deed valid in this view of the case, two conditions at all events must concur, viz., an actual payment of the consideration on the part of the donee, and a *bona fide* intention on the part of the donor to divest himself *in presenti* of the property, and to confer it upon the donee. Undoubtedly, the adequacy of the consideration is not the question. A consideration may be perfectly valid which is wholly inadequate in amount when compared with the thing given. Some of the cases have gone so far as to say that even a gift of a ring may be a sufficient consideration; but whatever its amount, it must be actually and *bona fide* paid.

Upon the subject of consideration there is the evidence of Mr *Perry*, who was present at the time of the execution of the document, who says that the Rajah admitted that at some previous time he had received the consideration. [....]

Taking into consideration all these circumstances, their Lordships have come to the conclusion that the transaction set up on behalf of the Defendants was not a real one, that no real consideration passed, that there was no intention on the part of the Rajah to part with the property at once to his son, but that both father and son were endeavouring to evade the Mahommedan law, by representing that to be a present transfer of property which was intended only to operate after the father's death. Their Lordships therefore agree with the High Court in their view of the effect of the deed.

The next question arises as to the will. It was found as a fact by Mr Loch that the heirs had not consented to this will; and with that finding their Lordships are satisfied. But it was argued by Mr Cowie, first, that the will did not require confirmation; secondly, that at all events so much of it as gave one-third to Enayut Hossein for pious uses was not in contravention of Mahommedan law, and was therefore valid without confirmation. The effect of the will is, in the first place, to declare Enayut Hossein the executor and representative of *Deedar*, and to direct him to look after the zemindary, and so forth. Then follows this passage: 'I divide the remaining two-thirds now under my possession, uninterfered and unconcerned by anyone else, into three portions. One portion to be laid out as the executor may think proper for the testator's welfare hereafter, by charity and pilgrimage, and keep up the family usage, namely, the expenses of the mosque and *tazeeadaree* of the sacred martyrs, and for the comfort of the travellers, the surplus amount to be appropriated by himself, the executor.' Then it goes on to say, from the other two-thirds 'he shall keep everyone by his good conduct and affection contented and satisfied. It is also necessary for all persons having rights, heirs, and friends connected with me to obey the said executor and consider him my representative.' Then further: 'None of the heirs have power to sell or divide the landed property mentioned in the will.' This will, in its general scope, appears to their Lordships to be in contravention of Mahommedan law. With respect to the limited contention, that it may be supported with respect to the devise of the one-third share, it appears further to their Lordships that that devise, considering the vague character of it and that the beneficial interest is left to Enayut Hossein after he has devoted what he may deem sufficient to certain indefinite pious uses, is in reality an attempt to give, under colour of a religious bequest, an interest in one-third to Enayut Hossein, in contravention of Mahommedan law. [....]

Under these circumstances, whatever might have been their Lordships' view if the case had come before them as a tribunal of first instance, they do not think that sufficient ground has been shown for reversing the decision of the High Court.

There remains the question of the right of the Plaintiff to succeed to *Bibee* Loodhun, and that depends upon whether Bibee Loodhun was merely a concubine or a wife. It is an undisputed fact that Nuzeeroodeen, the son of Bibee Loodhun, was treated by his father and by all the members of the family as a legitimate son. It is not that he was on any particular occasions recognized by his father, but that he always appears to have been treated on the same footing as the other legitimate sons. This of itself appears to their Lordships to raise some presumption that his mother was his father's wife. That such a presumption arises under such circumstances appears to have been laid down in a case which has been referred to, Khajah Hidayut *Oollah* v. *Rai Jan Khanum*,[7] in which Dr Lushington, who delivered the

[7] 3 Moore's Ind. Ap. Ca. 295.

judgment of this Board, makes this observation;[8] 'The effect of that appears to be, that where a child has been born to a father, of a mother where there has been not a mere casual concubinage, but a more permanent connection, and where there is no insurmountable obstacle to such a marriage, then, according to the Mahommedan law, the presumption is in favour of such marriage having taken place.' In this case there is no evidence that Bebee Loodhun was a woman of bad character, or that her connection was merely casual. She appears to have lived in the house at all events up to the death of the Rajah.

The same doctrine was laid down rather more strongly in a recent case, which came before this Board on the 20th of March, 1873. In the case of *Newab Mulka Jehan Sahiba* v. *Mahomed Ushkurree Khan*, a case from Oudh, and a Sheeah case, their Lordships say: 'This treatment of the daughter by the Appellants'—that is to say, the treatment of the daughter as a member of the family,—'affords a strong presumption in favour of the right of her mother to inherit from her.' The question there was whether the mother, who was said to be a slave girl, inherited from her daughter, whom she survived, the same question which would have arisen in this case if Bibee Loodhun had survived her son Nuzeeroodeen. Their Lordships go on to say, after noticing various acts of acknowledgment of the legitimacy of the child: 'After these acknowledgments, Mulka Jehan and the Appellants who act with her ought in their Lordships' view to have been prepared with strong and conclusive evidence to rebut the presumption raised by their own acts and conduct; and in the absence of such evidence, they think the presumption must prevail.'

It appears to their Lordships, therefore, that the undoubted acknowledgment by the father and by the whole family of the legitimacy of Nuzeeroodeen raises some presumption of the marriage of his mother. But it is said that that presumption is rebutted. The evidence chiefly relied upon for that purpose is the will of the Rajah, in which undoubtedly there is this expression: 'For the maintenance of four female servants monthly, 75; annually 900,' and Bibee Loodhun does appear to have been one of those female servants there mentioned. At the same time, it is to be observed, this expression occurs only in the schedule; whereas in a part of the will preceding that schedule there is this expression: 'The shares of the executor and of the sons, daughters, and wives of the testator and other claimants from the estate fixed annually at,' so and so; and the subsequent provision for the maintenance of every female servant appears to be an expansion of that paragraph in which they are spoken of as wives.

8 p. 318.

But further; there is the undoubted acknowledgment by Enayut Hossein himself of *Bibee Loodhun* being a wife, inasmuch as when Khyroonissa the principal wife brings a suit against him, Enayut Hossein objects, on the ground that Bibee Loodhun, one of the other wives, is not joined.

Under these circumstances, it appears to their Lordships that there is evidence not only from the acknowledgment of Nuzeeroodeen's legitimacy by the family, but from the admission of Enayut Hossein, that Bibee *Loodhun* was a wife, and not merely a servant. It is indeed alleged that she was what is called a temporary wife, and among the Sheeah sect there appears to be a power of taking a mere temporary wife. But it is to be observed that there is no evidence of her marriage being what is called a temporary marriage, and indeed the witnesses who seek to impugn the marriage on the part of the Defendant speak of Bibee Loodhun not as a temporary wife but as a mere servant. The question, therefore, seems to be not whether she was a temporary wife in the sense attached to that term in Mahommedan treatises, but whether she was a wife or whether she was a mere servant. On the whole, their Lordships concur with the finding of the High Court. The evidence preponderates that she was a wife and not as a mere servant, though no doubt a wife of an inferior order.

A question further arose as to the amount of the share which the Plaintiff would be entitled to, assuming that Bibee Loodhun was a wife, and it would certainly seem that her share would only be a fifth of an eighth, that is, a fortieth share; whereas she appears to have received something more by the decree of the court. But it is to be observed that this in a great measure is a matter of detail, and possibly a clerical error or miscalculation, which might have been set right on an application to the High Court, and that in fact the High Court did invite applications for the purpose of remedying errors of this kind.

The result is, that with the exception of the slight variation of amount in the case of the claim of Mussamut Bibee Loodhun, their Lordships will humbly advise Her Majesty to affirm the decree of the High Court, and to dismiss this appeal with costs.

26. Mahomed Buksh v. Hosseini Bibi
(1888) 15 IA 81

Gift—proof required for forgery—undue influence—'improvident act' of pardanashin—musha'—persuasion

In this case it was held upon the evidence, overruling the judgment of the High Court, that a *hibanama* which the plaint alleged to be a forgery was a genuine document and that it was executed by a *pardanashin* lady who well knew what she was doing and was bound thereby.

Where a plaintiff sues alleging that a deed purporting to be executed by herself is a forgery, the court ought not to admit the inconsistent issue whether it was executed under undue influence.

But where the issue of undue influence is rightly raised, the court should consider (1) whether the transaction is a thing which a right-minded person could be expected to do; (2) whether it was improvident; (3) whether legal advice if wanting was necessary; (4) whether the transaction originated with the donor.

Where one of three Muslim co-sharers gives his share before division to either of the other two, such gift is not invalidated by the doctrine of *musha'*.

Where a gift is public and authorizes the donee to take possession, which is in fact taken subsequently, the gift is not invalidated because the donor was not at the time in possession, and did not, therefore, at the time transfer it.

See *Mulla*, § 146, ill. (b); *Outlines*, 219, 231.

Appeal by special leave from a decree of the High Court (Bengal) (12 September 1884), reversing a decree of the Subordinate Judge of Gaya (7 October 1882), which had dismissed the suit.

The suit was instituted by Shahzadi Bibi, who died shortly afterwards, to recover possession of a one-sixth share of the estate of Omda Bibi (the deceased wife of the Appellant, Mahomed Buksh Khan), on the allegation that a *hibanama*, or deed of gift, dated the 30th of May, 1881, and purporting to be executed by Shahzadi Bibi, in favour of Omda Bibi's infant children, was a forged document.

The Subordinate Judge found all the issues in the Appellants' favour, and dismissed the suit with costs. He found that the document was genuine and *bona fide*, executed and delivered with the consent of Shahzadi Bibi.

The High Court expressed themselves in this way: 'On the whole, we are not satisfied that the deed was ever executed, or, even if it was, that Shahzadi understood its content, and was a free agent at the time of the transaction.'

Judgment [Macnaghten, J.][9]

In this case the suit is brought to recover property contained in a *hibbanama* or deed of gift bearing date the 30th of May, 1881, and purporting to be executed by a widow lady named *Shahzadi Bibi*, who is dead. The persons to whom the *hibbanama* purports to convey the property are grandchildren of Shahzadi, the infant children of her daughter Omda, who had died a very

9 With Hobhouse, Barnes Peacock & R. Coutch, JJ.

short time before. The ground of action alleged by the plaint is that the *hibbanama* was a fabricated document, and that the alleged signature of Shahzadi was a forgery.

To understand the story and the position of the parties, it is necessary to give a short sketch of the pedigree of the family. Shahzadi Bibi was the daughter of Sikundar Ali and Hesamut Bibi; she had two brothers, Nawab Ali and Mannujan. Nawab Ali married a person of the name of Hedayat. Shahzadi Bibi herself married one *Nubi Buksh.* By him she had only two children, both daughters, Omda Bibi and Hosseini Bibi. Omda Bibi married Mahomed Buksh Khan, and by him had nine children, who are the infant Appellants. *Hosseini* married Rubidad Khan. Mahomed Buksh Khan was the son of Jehangir Buksh Khan. Jehangir married a person of the name of Mahamdu. Mahamdu's mother was Hasan Bibi. Jehangir's mother was *Rousham Bibi*, who also appears to have been the mother of Nubi Buksh and the sister of a lady called Daem Bibi, who was grandmother or in the position of grandmother, to Shahzadi.

It appears that from Daem Bibi, Shahzadi derived a property consisting of some twenty-two villages. In 1876, being then the wife of Nubi Buksh, but living apart from her husband, and apparently not being on good terms with him, she determined to make over this property to her daughter Omda Bibi. Her general *mokhtar* at that time was Mahadeo Lal. He seems to have remonstrated against the gift, and to have informed her husband, who also remonstrated. The lady, however, was firm in her purpose, and on the 9th of September, 1876, she executed a *hibbanama* granting this property to her daughter.

Now there is no question as to the genuineness of that document. It is executed by Shahzadi, by the pen of Mahadeo Lal, her general *mokhtar*; but she also authenticates it by writing upon it some words in Hindi '*likha-se-janoge*,' which are said to mean, 'From what is written you will know'. Among the attesting witnesses were Jehangir Buksh Khan, Jewan Lal, Mahadeo Lal, and Dost Mahomed Khan, who were examined in this suit in connection with the execution of the *hibbanama* of the 30th of May, 1881. It is not unimportant to observe that it appears by the attestation of the *hibbanama* of 1876 that Dost Mahomed Khan was the person who then identified Shahzadi Bibi, which confirms his statement in this case that he was in the habit of appearing before her.

After that deed was executed disputes arose between Nubi Buksh Khan and Shahzadi. [....]

At the end of 1879, or the beginning of 1880, Nubi Buksh died. On his death fresh disputes arose in the family. They were ultimately settled by a deed of compromise bearing date the 14th of February, 1880. From that time until the present quarrel the parties appear to have lived on good terms. [....]

On the 22nd of September, 1881, Shahzadi filed her plaint in this suit. The only ground of action alleged in the plaint is, that the *hibbanama* of the 10th of May, 1881, was a fabricated document, and that her alleged signature was a forgery. On the 12th of October, 1881, Shahzadi died. The proceedings were continued by her daughter Hosseini Bibi, and her father and mother Sikundar Ali and Hesamut Bibi. On the 16th of March, 1882, issues were settled. Amongst the issues was this: '2nd. Whether the *hibbanama* on behalf of Shahzadi Bibi is genuine and valid and executed with her knowledge and consent, or whether it was manufactured without her knowledge and consent, or whether it was executed under undue influence?' In their Lordships' opinion the latter part of that issue ought not to have been admitted. It was absolutely inconsistent with the case made by Plaintiff. It only becomes possible on the assumption that the alleged cause of action is unfounded. There was another issue which also was only admissible on that assumption, namely: '3rd. Whether in case the said *hibbanama* is proved to be genuine it is invalid on any ground according to Mahommedan law.'

The questions therefore which had to be decided by the court, and which have now to be considered by their Lordships, are three: First, was the deed really executed by Shahzadi? Secondly, if so, are there any circumstances which go to prove that it ought not to be held binding upon her? and thirdly, is the gift valid under Mahommedan law?

Now to take the first question: Was the deed really executed by Shahzadi? It purports to be executed by her by the pen of Mahadeo Lal, who was no doubt for a considerable time her general *mokhtar*. It purports to bear as her signature the Hindi words which admittedly she wrote on the deed of the 9th of September, 1876, by way of authenticating that document. Her execution is attested by no less than twenty-one witnesses, nine of whom, as well as the writer, have been examined in support of the deed. She was a *pardanashin* lady. There were women inside, and they of course, according to the evidence could have seen her execute the deed. Three swear they saw the execution. Two whose presence is deposed to by several witnesses swear that they were not even in Madarpore. Their evidence however is not believed by either court. Of the male witnesses, three, and three only, according to the evidence, could have seen the deed executed—Nawab Ali, who died before the hearing, Mannujan, and Dost Mahomed. The others attest the deed on Shahzadi's admission. In the afternoon of the day on which the deed is alleged to have been executed, the sub-registrar came over and took her acknowledgment. The sub-registrar is stated by the Subordinate Judge to be 'a respectable and learned person.' He deposes that he knew Shahzadi's voice, and that she acknowledged the deed before him.

The Subordinate Judge, who had the advantage of seeing the witnesses, unhesitatingly came to the conclusion that the deed was genuine. He relied principally on the evidence of Mannujan, Mahadeo Lal, and Manwar Ali, the sub-registrar. The High Court came to a different conclusion. They say: 'We think that a large amount of suspicion attaches to this evidence, and we are not satisfied that the deed was really executed by Shahzadi.' Their Lordships cannot consider the judgment of the High Court satisfactory. The learned Judges suspect everybody; they suspect everything. Everyone who took an intelligent part in the transaction, the dead as well as the living—Shahzadi's relations as well as her son-in-law's dependents; even the sub-registrar of the district who attended only in the discharge of his official duties—one and all are alike involved in general and indiscriminate suspicion.

The learned judges say that they cannot but regard Jehangir Buksh Khan as the prime mover in the matter; and they add, 'We cannot help suspecting that this witness had a good deal more to do with the preparation, execution, and registration of this deed than he has chosen to tell the court.' In their Lordships' opinion this witness seems to have answered fairly every question that was put to him, and if his evidence be true, and there is nothing to contradict it, his connection with the transaction was of the slightest. According to his statement, he was summoned by a letter from *Shahzadi* to come over and witness the execution of the deed. He came over in the early morning; he spoke to Shahzadi, and she spoke to him. She acknowledged that she had executed the deed, and he attested it. Then he mounted his horse and rode away, and that appears to be the only connection he had with the transaction, except that he is the father of Mahomed Buksh Khan, and Mahadeo Lal was his general *mokhtar*.

The learned judges also mention as a matter of suspicion that no independent person seems to have been called in to attest that deed, and that no independent person has deposed in favour of its execution. The latter conclusion is not quite accurate. The sub-registrar, whether he is to be believed or not, was unquestionably an independent person, and had no connection whatever with either side. It is somewhat difficult to understand what is meant by the objection that no independent person was called into attest the deed. It has not been suggested that any member of the family or any person who would naturally have been present if the deed were genuine was absent on the occasion when it is said to have been executed. Every member of the family with whom we are acquainted, with the exception of Hosseini Bibi and her husband, was present and attested the deed. It would not have been very natural that Hosseini or her husband should have been called in to attest a deed which disappointed their hopes or at any rate defeated their chance of succession. But, in point of fact, according to the statement of Rubidad Khan, Hosseini Bibi was incapacitated by illness from going to Madarpore. It is stated that she did not go there until the chehloom. Rubidad Khan also states that he was not there; that he was present at the burial, but that from the time of the burial till the chehloom he did not go to Madarpore. It is difficult to see what advantage would have been gained by summoning an independent person to attest the deed. The lady was a *pardanashin* lady. A stranger would not have been admitted to her presence. The attestation of a stranger who could not have seen her write and who could not have known her voice would have carried the matter very little further.

Then there are three minor matters of suspicion on which the learned Judges comment. They say the draft of the deed was not produced. It is difficult to see what light that draft could have thrown upon the transaction. At any rate, it was not called for. It is said that two letters which are mentioned in the evidence as having been sent by Shahzadi to summon Mahadeo Lal and Jehangir Buksh Khan were also not produced. They were not called for either. The Plaintiffs seem to have been satisfied with a statement of what was contained in those letters by the recipient of the one and the writer of the other. Of course, if the deed was forged, notwithstanding the publicity connected with it, there could have been no difficulty in forging *Shahzadi's* signature to a letter.

The learned judges also observe that it is a remarkable circumstance that none of the female witnesses who were behind the *purda* make any direct statement on the point of Shahzadi's writing the words in Hindi. They merely state, say the Judges, in general terms that *Shahzadi* executed the deed. That observation also does not appear to be quite accurate. The three ladies who were behind the *purda*, and who gave evidence for the Defendants, Malik Jehan Bibi, Hasan, and Mahamdu, state that the deed was executed by *Shahzadi* in their presence. One—and one only—of those ladies was cross-examined upon the point, and her statement in cross-examination is very positive. That is Mahamdu. She says, 'The females had witnessed it in my presence. First the females witnessed it and then the males. The signature of *Shahzadi Bibi* was put in my presence. Shahzadi Bibi ordered Mahadeo Lal to sign for her, and then he signed for her. After that she wrote below it two or four letters in Hindi which she knew.' Mahamdu seems to have been the first witness who was examined on behalf of the Defendants—certainly the first or second—the other two were not cross-examined upon the point. Their cross-examination appears to have been entirely directed to irrelevant objects.

'Another very suspicious circumstance' in the opinion of the learned Judges is this, that the Hindi words written, or said to have been written, on the deed by Shahzadi Bibi with the object of authenticating it are identically the same, letter for letter, as those which are found on the *hibbanama* of 1876. They add, 'The fact of these Hindi words corresponding so exactly with those on the deed of 1876, which was apparently not in Shahzadi's possession or produced before her at the time of execution, does certainly raise the suspicion that they were not really written by her but had been copied by some other person from the former deed.'

Now it is material to mention a circumstance which in that passage appears to have been overlooked, namely, that those words occur not once only, but twice. They were written in the morning, and they were written again in the evening when the sub-registrar came over to take Shahzadi's acknowledgment. The sub-registrar states that he knew Shahzadi's voice; he states that he read the deed to her. Then he goes on to say—'I asked whether she had executed the deed of gift or not? She said that she had executed it, and it might be registered. On the back of the deed of gift I, at that time, wrote out the registration with my own hand. After that I asked the Mussumat who knew her. The Mussumat said that Nawab Ali Khan and Mannujan Khan, who are her full brothers, knew her. I then asked both of them, and they said that they knew her. After that I wrote out in the deed the identification by both. After that I pointed out to *Nawab Ali Khan* the place where he should sign for Shahzadi Bibi, and also the place where they should affix their own signatures. After that Mahadeo Lal, mokhtar signed for Shahzadi Bibi by his own pen, and she also wrote 'You will know from what is written.' Nawab Ali Khan and Mannujan Khan affixed their signatures. After the signature affixed by Mahadeo Lal, Shahzadi Bibi affixed her signature. I did not make any objection to what Shahzadi Bibi wrote because on other occasions also when I had taken her admission and made registration she used to write so much, and I knew that she knew to write so much.' Therefore whether the first signature—that is the Hindi words—be genuine or not, it is quite plain that these same words were added again in the evening when the sub-registrar went over to take Shahzadi's acknowledgment. If the learned judges of the High Court are right, who was the forger? None of the ladies could write; that is clear. Jehan Lal, the writer of the deed, was not present at the time; he only came up just as the sub-registrar was going away. The only males who, according to the evidence, saw the lady on that occasion were her brother Nawab Ali, and Mannujan. Mannujan cannot write. So that the words must either have been written by

Nawab Ali or by the lady herself. There is not the slightest ground to suspect Nawab Ali of any fraud or forgery, and therefore it appears to be the necessary conclusion that the words must have been written by the lady herself.

When the cloud of suspicion in which the High Court has enveloped the transaction has been cleared away, the evidence in favour of the genuineness of the deed is absolutely overwhelming. There is no evidence whatever on the other side.

There is nothing but Shahzadi's assertion that she did not execute the deed—an assertion in which no doubt she persisted from the time she complained to the Magistrate down to the time of her death.

Their Lordships think that the Subordinate Judge was right in relying on the evidence of the sub-registrar and of Mahadeo Lal the *mokhtar*, with whose character the Subordinate Judge also seems to have been acquainted. He says he 'holds a diploma, and is a respectable person in his community, and the court has never seen any act of his by which it can suspect him.' Mannujan broke down on cross-examination. The Subordinate Judge attributes his confusion entirely to illness, and apparently the civil surgeon and assistant civil surgeon of the district certified to that effect. Be that as it may, their Lordships think that it would not be safe to rely on Mannujan's evidence, except so far as it is corroborated by other witnesses, and they consider that more reliance is to be placed on the fact that the signature of Shahzadi was identified by her brother Nawab Ali, who seems to have been in a superior position to Mannujan. He was a person of education, and appears to have been trusted by other members of the family. The mother, Hesamut, employed him to receive for her the allowance which her husband was condemned to pay, and she says 'I was on good terms with Nawab Khan. There was no misunderstanding between us at any time. I had confidence in him.' Certainly if this deed was a forgery he must have known all about it, but what possible reason can there be to suspect him of having been a party to such a gross fraud? In their Lordships' opinion there is none. It is not necessary to go further into the evidence. It is sufficient to say that their Lordships have come to the same conclusion as the Subordinate Judge, that the deed was really executed by Shahzadi.

Then comes the question, was the deed executed under such circumstances that it ought not to be allowed to stand? Duress and coercion may be laid out of consideration. The witnesses who spoke to anything of that kind were discredited by both courts. But there remains the more subtle form of undue influence. Their Lordships desire not to say a word which could interfere with the settled principles on which the court acts in considering the deeds of *purdanashin* ladies or could tend to lessen the protection which it is the duty of the court to throw around those who are unable to protect themselves. They do not forget that this lady was a *purdanashin* lady. They do not forget that at the time of the execution of the deed she was living in more than ordinary seclusion; that she was in very deep distress; and that she was surrounded by the members of that branch of the family to which the objects of her bounty more immediately belonged. But bearing all these things in mind, and reviewing the whole evidence, they come to the conclusion that the lady knew perfectly well what she was doing, and that in every sense the act was her own act.

Where undue influence is alleged it is necessary to examine very closely all the circumstances of the case. The principles are always the same though the circumstances differ, and, as a general rule, the same questions arise. The first and practically perhaps the most important question is, was the transaction a righteous transaction, that is, was it a thing which a right-minded person might be expected to do? Can there be any doubt about the answer to that question? Shahzadi made a settlement on Omda. Omda was her favourite daughter, and had a large family. By an untoward and unlooked-for event a share of Omda's fortune which was principally derived from that settlement devolves on Shahzadi. To her the acquisition of property by her daughter's untimely death seems to have been an odious and repulsive thing, and she determines as soon as possible to give it back to her daughter's orphan children. Was there anything unnatural in that? It appears to their Lordships to have been a most natural act, and one which a right-minded person would be disposed to do.

Then there comes the question—was it an improvident act? That is to say, does it show so much improvidence as to suggest the idea that the lady was not mistress of herself and not in a state of mind to weigh what she was doing? Upon that Mr Doyne made some forcible observations. He said that by the earlier *hibbanama* this lady had stripped herself of all that she possessed; that she had reduced herself to penury; that then by accident a portion of the property came back to her, and he insisted that it was an improvident act on her part to divest herself immediately of that pittance when she had nothing else to live upon. Now that case is not made by the evidence. There does not appear from first to last any complaint on the part of the lady that she was reduced to poverty. Nor was her position that of a pauper. She had a house of her own; she had servants; she comes in a *dooli*; so far as the evidence goes she had enough for her wants, and her wants as a widow were probably very small. It does not therefore appear to have been a transaction so improvident as to show that it was not her own act.

Then was it a matter requiring a legal adviser? What could have been simpler than what she desired to do? She was not apportioning her property among the members of her family; she was not determining how much she could spare, but when property came to her by this sad accident, she says, 'I will have none of it.' What could a legal adviser have told her? If he had advised her to wait till she left the house where Mahomed Khan was; if he had told her to place herself between two fires, and allow Rubidad Khan on the one hand and Mahomed on the other to urge the claims of their respective children she would not have benefited much by the advice.

Lastly, did the intention of making the gift originate with *Shahzadi?* Upon that there is positive evidence, and there is negative evidence. The positive evidence is very strong, but the negative evidence appears to be stronger still. Mahadeo Lal, who was unquestionably her general *mokhtar* as long as she had any property to deal with, and who was employed by her to prepare this deed, says: 'I went to Shahzadi Bibi at the deori for condolement', and then Shahzadi Bibi told me this: 'I at first gave my property in writing to my daughter *Omda Bibi*, but now owing to her death one-sixth share devolves upon me. As I have no hope of living long I do not like to take the estate of Omda Bibi. I wish to give that share to her sons and daughter. Please write out a draft of *hibbanama*.' In cross-examination he says even more positively that it was her own doing, and that he prepared the *hibbanama* by her own direction.

Then Mahamdu says this in cross-examination: 'Shahzadi Bibi herself commenced to talk about the *hibba*. I do not recollect how many days after going to Madarpore conversation took place about the *hibba*. But she had spoken of it after ten or fifteen days. Shahzadi Bibi first spoke about the *hibba*, to me and other females. Shahzadi Bibi said: "I had already given in writing during the lifetime of my daughter. Now she is dead, and a share has devolved upon me. How can I snatch it from grandsons and granddaughters? The children have become motherless. I will again give them in writing." We told her: "It is your pleasure. You have got a share; you may do with it whatever you like." There is not a scrap of evidence to show that the idea was suggested to her by Mahomed Buksh Khan or anyone else. And it is a circumstance not to be overlooked that Mahomed Buksh Khan did not obtain any benefit personally for himself.

But the negative evidence is still stronger. No case of undue influence was set up by Shahzadi. The plaint is based on forgery and forgery alone. The question of undue influence was introduced for the first time in the issues; but although it was introduced then, it was not accepted by the family. We find that on the application for registration, which took place a few days after the issues were settled—the date is the 23rd of March,

1882—the sole averment still is that the deed was a forgery. It is somewhat singular that, although the ladies who were examined as witnesses for the Defendants were the first witnesses who were examined, and they stated that Shahzadi executed the deed of her own free will and without undue influence, the ladies on the other side who came forward a month afterwards to give evidence preferred to state what both courts have held to be absolutely untrue, namely, that they were not present at Madarpore at all; they preferred stating that to admitting that they were present, and trying to make out a case of undue influence, which they must have known then would have been fatal to the deed if it could be proved.

Their Lordships therefore hold that the suggestion of undue influence is not proved.

There remains the question whether the gift was good by Mahommedan law. On that two points were made. In the first place it was said to be open to objection on the Mahommedan doctrine of *mooshâá*, which appears to be this: that a gift of an undivided share in a subject capable of division is not good because it would lead to confusion. But it appears to be settled by Mahommedan law that if there are two sharers of property, one may give his share to the other before division. That seems to be established by a passage in Macnaghten's *Precedents*, Case XIII, which was adopted in the case to which Mr Mayne referred, of *Ameena Bibi* v. *Zeifa Bibee*.[10]

Now, if one of two sharers may give his share to the other, supposing there are three sharers, what is there to prevent one of the three giving his share to either of the other two? Mr Doyne was asked what confusion that would introduce. Mr Doyne took refuge in the doctrine itself, which he said was a very refined doctrine. To extend it to this case would be a refinement on a refinement, amounting in their Lordships' opinion almost to a *reductio ad absurdum*.

The other point was that the gift was invalid because possession was not given. That subject was considered in a case which came before this Board in 1884, *Kali Das Mullick* v. *Kanhya Lal Pundit*.[11] There it is stated that the principle on which the rule rests has nothing to do with feudal rules, and that the European analogy is rather to be found in the cases relating to voluntary contracts or transfers, where, if the donor has not done all he could to perfect his contemplated gift, he cannot be compelled to do more. In this case it appears to their Lordships that the lady did all she could to perfect the contemplated gift, and that nothing more was required from her. The gift was attended with the utmost publicity, the *hibbanama* itself authorizes the donees to take possession, and it appears that in fact they did

10 3 Suth. WR 37.

11 Law Rep. 11 Ind. Ap. 218.

take possession. Their Lordships hold under these circumstances that there can be no objection to the gift on the ground that *Shahzadi* had not possession, and that she herself did not give possession at the time. That view seems to be supported by a passage in Macnaghten's *Precedents*, Case X., where the question was: If property left by two brothers devolve on the widows, 'Are the widows entitled to dispose of their late husband's property by gift, and if they have a right to do so, is the deed of gift executed by them in favour of one of the husband's heirs available in law?' Then it is stated that, 'Although the widows at the time of the execution of the deed of gift were not seized of the property, yet if agreeably to their desire, the donee, in pursuance of a judicial decree, became subsequently seized thereof, the fact of the donors having been out of possession at the time of making the gift is not sufficient to invalidate it.'

Their Lordships, therefore, are of opinion that the appeal ought to be allowed, and that the decree of the High Court ought to be reversed and the decree of the Subordinate Judge restored, and they will humbly advise Her Majesty accordingly. The Respondents will pay the costs of the appeal, and the costs in the High Court. The deposit of £300, which was made by the Appellants, will be returned.

27. Farid-un-Nisa v. Mukhtar Ahmad
(1925) 52 IA 342

Pardanashin woman—wakfnama—validity—onus of proof

A Muslim woman who was illiterate and *pardanashin* executed a deed by which she gave her whole property in wakf, reserving a small monthly stipend to herself and to her husband and who was an invalid, and also the right for her life to use a house, the *mutawallis* agreeing to pay the stipends and to keep the house in repair. In a suit to cancel the deed and to recover possession:

Held, upon the evidence, that the defendant *mutawallis* had not discharged the onus upon them, which was to prove that the actual import of the *wakfnama* had been brought home to the mind of the grantor, and that therefore it was not binding upon her.

Consideration of the nature and extent of the onus of proof as appearing from various decisions of the Judicial Committee.

The observations of Lord Sumner, beginning from p. 332, on the onus of proof in cases relating to *pardanashin* women are authoritative and are often cited. For a full discussion see *Tyabji*, § 359A. A good selection of cases on *pardanashins* will be found in Mulla, *Transfer of Property Act*, comment to Section 126. See also 'The Impact of English Law on the

Shariat in India' by Asaf A. A. Fyzee, *Revue Égyptienne de Droit International*, xviii (1962), 1, 11 seqq., esp. 14.

Appeal (No. 118 of 1923) from a decree of the Court of the Judicial Commissioner [of Oudh] (January 14,1921) reversing a decree of the Subordinate Judge of Bara Banki (30 April 1918).

The suit was brought by the appellant, a Muslim *pardanashin* woman, for cancellation of a deed of wakf executed by her, and for possession of the property; the defendants (respondents) were the *mutawallis* under the deed.

On appeal to the Court of the Judicial Committee that decree was set aside, and the suit was dismissed.

Judgment [Sumner, J.][12]

The plaintiff-appellant, having sued to recover possession of a residence and agricultural land at or near Ahmadpur, the Subordinate Judge of Bara Banki passed a decree in her favour against two of the defendants, who are now respondents to this appeal. In the Court of the Judicial Commissioner of Oudh this decree was set aside and the suit was dismissed. The plaintiff had executed a *wakfnama*, covering the property and appointing the respondents *mutawallis* of the wakf, and accordingly the claim is in substance to set the deed aside.

At the time of the execution the plaintiff was a married woman, illiterate, childless and *pardanashin*. She and her husband, Sheikh Karim-ud-din, were Mahommedans. Most of the property in question had been given to her upon her marriage by her maternal grandfather, but the residence, known as the mahal, and some sir land, both in the village of Ahmadpur, came to her by inheritance. Since her marriage she had lived there continuously, and, although during the earlier part of their married life her husband was generally absent on Government service, he had retired and for some years had resided entirely at Ahmadpur. He suffered from an incurable disease, had become nearly blind, and was otherwise crippled and incapable, but his mind was not in any way affected.

The defendants, the *mutawallis*, who were in possession, relied upon the wakfnama as their title. Its gist was to divest the plaintiff of the whole of her property, which became vested in them, but it reserved to her a life stipend of Rs 34 per mensem, and another of Rs 33 per mensem to her husband, and also gave her the right to continue to reside in 'the mahal' for life, the *mutawallis* being bound to keep it in repair, as well as to pay the stipends. They were two brothers, sons of a sister of the plaintiff's

12 With Blanesburgh, John Edge, Syed Amir Ali & Salvesen, JJ.

husband, to whom he was much attached. Their Lordships do not think it is sufficiently made out that they or either of them had acted as men of business for the appellant, and they put this point aside, but she was on friendly terms with them. It is said that she was at enmity with her own relations, for reasons that do not appear to reflect on her. At any rate, she virtually lived apart from and saw little of them, nor had she, in fact, any support or advice from their side.

Very shortly after the marriage the management of the property was assumed by the plaintiff's husband, her father, who had previously managed it, being now dead, and he continued to manage it as long as he lived. He employed the necessary karindas and others for the purpose, and directed the disposition of the rents and profits. Over and above his salary he was himself a man of little or no means. His wife never took part in the management, nor was she shown to have had any business knowledge or experience. From time to time, under the direction of her husband, she executed *muktarnamas* and other documents for estate purposes, but she relied on him entirely as to their necessity and purport. Sums for her personal and household purposes were paid to her with fair regularity, and they seem to have been, though modest, probably sufficient; but she did not direct the whole even of the household expenditure, and her own outlays were on various occasions criticized by her husband and even censured as improvident. There is this to be said for him, that the estate was encumbered and, when he took up the management, much embarrassed, but in time he considerably improved its position. The *wakfnama* enumerates sundry charges outstanding upon it, amounting in all to about Rs 12,800, with an annual interest of Rs 730, for the service and discharge of which the *mutawallis* were to provide, and the total value of the property, when settled by the deed, was from Rs 40,000 to Rs 50,000, and the income about Rs 2500.

The respondents recognized that the burden of proof was on them: *Tacoordeen Tewarry's Case*;[13] and they accordingly set about to prove her intelligent execution of the deed, its contents having been read and explained to her both upon and after execution. It was not, however, contended that she had had any legal advice about it or any consultation with her own relations. She, on the other hand, raised two answers; the first, that she executed it under actual undue influence of her husband, which dominated her choice and will, and the second, that, when she executed it, she had had no explanation of its nature and contents, but throughout believed it to be an instrument needed for the routine management of the estate, such as she had constantly executed before. A contention, that she had never executed

13 (1874) LR IIA 206.

it and that the thumb mark which it bears is not hers, has not been persisted in.

The probabilities are not unequally balanced. She was a conforming and sincere Mahommedan, though not shown to have been of any exceptional piety. Her husband was a leper, and, even if he lived, as she says she was sure that he would, his management of the estate, at any rate, was nearing its end. The estate was no easy matter to deal with, and the assurance of an income, similar to that which she had hitherto enjoyed, and the continued use of her old home for life, might seem to be a desirable arrangement. She had nothing against the young men who were named as *mutawallis*. They were well known to her, and, as to her own people, it is not pretended that she felt either duty or inclination towards them. A gift of her property to God, with a modest provision for herself and her husband during life was no bad thing, even though she herself was only about thirty years of age.

On the other hand, her husband had been manager of his wife's property so long that he might quite probably regard it as his own, and certainly he so treated it. He, at least, could not have failed to foresee his death at no distant date, as actually befell within the year. He had no great opinion of his wife's prudence or moderation, and the idea that her property might pass away from him and his must have been repulsive to him. Security for his own last days and a provision for his widow, coupled with some acquisition of merit by the performance of a pious act, must have made the idea of a wakf attractive to him. Though burdened with religious obligations, the property would, at any rate, be kept in his family.

There is a third probability. It is that the appellant may have been fully acquainted with the scope of the deed, have fully concurred in the creation of the wakf for which it provided, and have executed the *wakfnama* freely and with understanding, but have changed her mind, for, after a few months of widowhood and pilgrimage, she married again.

After the fullest examination of the evidence, voluminous even for a case of this kind, their Lordships are of opinion that the *wakfnama* was not executed under actual undue influence of the husband, and that, both before its execution and also shortly after its execution, when it came to be registered, its contents were read over to the appellant and were to some extent explained to her. In what terms that explanation was given the evidence does not show, and its sufficiency becomes the real issue on the appeal.

As for the case of actual undue influence, the husband was not present when the deed was registered, and there is nothing but mere suggestion derived from the character of the transaction and his marital relation to her to show that, when it was executed, his will operated on hers at all. In her evidence she declared with spirit that, had she known what the real import of the deed was, she would have refused entreaties and defied threats, and would never have given the smallest portion of her property to him or his relations. There is a ring of truth about this, which must prevail over the ingenious suggestion that, in the circumstances of the case, she must be deemed, all unknown to herself, to have been chronically under the hypnotic suggestion or control of her husband, while believing and even glorying in her fancied independence.

Again, their Lordships are not prepared to reject the evidence that the *wakfnama* was explained to the lady before it was executed. It was open to much criticism, and the learned Subordinate Judge refused to believe it, but the evidence had been recorded by his predecessor and he had not seen the witnesses. Their Lordships agree with the learned judges of the Judicial Commissioner's Court that there is no sufficient ground for its rejection. Taking it, however, as it stands, the question remains whether it goes far enough to satisfy the burthen of proof which rests on the respondents.

The deed was registered on 3 November 1914. A month or six weeks previously the appellant's husband, Karim-ud-din, being unable to write or read, sent for his nephew, a young man named Jamal-ud-din, and dictated to him a *wakfnama* word by word. This took five or six hours. The appellant was not present, and Karim-ud-din sent the young man into the house to ask her what salaries she wished to have inserted in the deed. To this she replied by asking whether Karim-ud-din was getting him to write the draft. All this, which is deposed to by Jamal-ud-din, a witness called by the respondents, seems to point to some previous communication on the subject between the husband and the wife, but what it was is not known.

During the previous three years the plaintiff had spoken on several occasions of creating some wakf, but full details of her scheme were never given, and once at least she was dissuaded from doing anything at all. Such details as are given show that her ideas then differed substantially from the scheme of the *wakfnama* which was ultimately executed. When Jamal-ud-din told her that a draft was being prepared she proceeded to say (i) that the salaries for herself and her husband were to be within Rs 100 per mensem; (ii) that certain other things were to be provided for in the deed—namely, that the *rajabi* and *maulud*, which she had celebrated, were to continue to be celebrated as before, that at Moharram *majlis* and *sabils* were to be continued, that other ritual acts should also be performed, and that a masjid at Ahmadpur, which her mother's father had built and she herself had always caused to be cleaned and repaired, should be cleaned and repaired as before; (iii) that a plot of land, which she had given to a certain Kabir-ud-din for a house, should not be included in the *wakfnama* at all.

All this Jamal-ud-din says that he reported to Karim-ud-din, who agreed to the provisions required. He was then sent back to the appellant to ask whether some provision should be made for payment to the *mutawalli*, to which she replied that one-third of the Rs 100 provided for her husband and herself should be paid to him as his pension. Jamal-ud-din then completed his task and, as far as he remembers, the draft then provided for all the matters which the appellant had required. He placed it in her custody, and to her question replied that all her requirements had been provided for. He did not see the plaintiff again till after the registration of the *wakfnama*, nor did he see the draft again either. In fact, it was never put in evidence, nor did any witness prove that the draft, as it left the hand of Jamal-ud-din, was ever compared with the fair copy which the plaintiff ultimately executed. The evidence is merely that one, Mustafa Husain, a brother-in-law of the defendants, engaged a person named Wazir-ud-din to make a fair copy of this draft, because he could write a good hand, and, on getting the draft from the plaintiff, read it over, and he says, apparently from memory two years after-wards, that this draft and the draft ultimately executed were the same, except for the mention of a debt to Wazir-ud-din of Rs 400 for procuring the necessary stamped paper, a matter only arranged after Jamal-ud-din's draft was prepared.

All this is absolutely denied by the plaintiff, but, as the whole of her evidence cannot be true, and as the evidence given by Jamal-ud-din and Mustafa Husain is confirmed by other witnesses, their Lordships accept this story generally.

The form of the deed itself thereupon becomes of some importance. It is lucidly and logically drafted, with much more of a lawyer's phraseology and orderly arrangement and much less of a layman's irrelevance and colloquialism, than such deeds in India often contain. It differs, however, from the account given by Jamal-ud-din in several particulars, and no one suggests that, between the time when he gave her his draft and the time when Wazir-ud-din read over his fair copy to her before she executed it, she was ever told of any departure from the terms in which her wishes had originally been expressed.

The following differences are material. Clause 2 states that the plaintiff appoints the first defendant 'whom I have brought up and treated as my son' to the office of *mutawalli*, and continues 'from to-day I have put Mukhtar Ahmad and Iftikhar Ahmad in possession of the said property as *mutawallis*.' As a matter of fact, this admittedly was an afterthought. Mukhtar Ahmad, the first defendant, on hearing of the wakf (though not from the plaintiff), said that, as he was busy, he wished his younger brother Iftikhar to be joined as a *mutawalli*. Accordingly this was done, and as, by a subsequent clause,

No. 12, each *mutawalli* was to have Rs 33 per mensem, the sum of Rs 100, which the plaintiff had fixed to cover the stipends had in view, her husband, and the one *mutawalli*, whom alone she of herself, now became an aggregate of monthly stipends of Rs 133.

Clause 20 specified how 'the *mutawalli*' was to expend the surplus income, after payment of Government revenue, the expenses mentioned, and all other necessary expenses as to the management. He was to do so 'after taking into consideration the then existing circumstances of the wakf property and as to what sum is reasonable to spend, when and on one or more of the following purposes'—twelve in number. These purposes, except 'repairs of the mosque in Ahmadpur,' are expressed in general terms. The last sweeps in 'other expenses on pious objects, which may come up.' Subsequent provisions give further powers 'beside these expenses…to spend money or [query "on"] anything without the permission of the authority for the time being having power to interfere with the affairs of the wakf,' and 'if any of the objects mentioned in cl. 20 is void in law the *mutawalli* shall spend the money on any other legal object' (cl. 21). Among the twelve objects particularly named there occur quite generally some of the pious purposes named by the appellant to Jamal-ud-din, though one is omitted. In no case is there mention of the continuance of those ceremonies, which the appellant herself had performed. The objects supported by the *mutawalli* under these denominations might in his discretion be wholly divorced from those which the plaintiff had prescribed, and might be entirely unconnected with her or her place of residence in Ahmadpur. The question at once arises, 'Was the appellant ever really made aware of these discrepancies, and did she assent to them?'

As a formally valid instrument the *wakfnama* itself is not impugned, and their Lordships therefore do not criticize it. The real question is, whether the appellant was so made cognizant of its contents and purport that it can be said, that the respondents have discharged the onus of showing that she understood it so as to make it her deed.

The law of India contains well-known principles for the protection of persons, who transfer their property to their own disadvantage, when they have not the usual means of fully understanding the nature and effect of what they are doing. In this it has only given the special development, which Indian social usages make necessary, to the general rules of English law, which protect persons, whose disabilities make them dependent upon or subject them to the influence of others, even though nothing in the nature of deception or coercion may have occurred. This is part of the law relating to personal capacity to make binding transfers or settlements of property of any kind. That the instrument here is a *wakfnama* is a mere accident, and the general and well-settled law of wakf is not in question. The case of an illiterate *pardanashin* lady, denuding herself of a large proportion of her property without professional or independent advice, is one on which there is much authority. Independent legal advice is not in itself essential: *Kali Buksh Singh's Case.*[14] After all, advice, if given, might have been bad advice, or the settlor might have insisted on disregarding it. The real point is, that the disposition made must be substantially understood and must really be the mental act, as its execution is the physical act, of the person who makes it: *Wajid Khan's Case*;[15] *Sunitabala Debi's Case.*[16] The appellant clearly had no such advice, nor is it contended that she had. If, however, the settlor's freedom and comprehension can be otherwise established, or if, as is the respondents' case here, the scheme and substance of the deed were themselves originally and clearly conceived and desired by the settlor, and were then substantially embodied in the deed, there would be nothing further to be gained by independent advice. If the settlor really understands and means to make the transfer, it is not required that some one should have tried to persuade her to the contrary. Again, the question arises how the state of the settlor's mind is to be proved. That the parties to prove it are the parties who set up and rely on the deed is clear. They must satisfy the court that the deed has been explained to and understood by the party thus under disability, either before execution or after it, under circumstances which establish adoption of it with full knowledge and comprehension: *Sudisht Lal's Case*;[17] *Shambati Koeri's Case*;[18] *Sajjad Husain's Case.*[19] Further, the whole doctrine involves the view that mere execution by such a person, although unaccompanied by duress, protest or obvious signs of misunderstanding or want of comprehension, is in itself no real proof of a true understanding mind in the executant. Evidence to establish such comprehension is most obviously found in proof that the deed was read over to the settlor and, where necessary, explained. If it is in a language which she does not understand, it must, of course, be translated, and it is to be remembered that the clearness of the meaning of the deed will suffer in the process. The extent and character of the explanation required must depend on the circumstances. Length, intricacy, the number and complexity of the dispositions, or the unfamiliarity of the subject matter, are all reasons for requiring an increased amount and efficiency of explanation. Thus a matter

[14] (1913) LR 41 IA 23.
[15] (1891) LR 18 IA 144, 148.
[16] (1919) LR 46 IA 272, 278.
[17] (1881) LR 8 IA 39, 43.
[18] (1902) LR 29 IA 127, 131.
[19] (1912) LR 39 IA 156.

not likely to attract the attention of the executant in itself ought not to be relied on as binding, unless her attention has been directly drawn to it: *Sham Koer's Case*.[20] So if the deed, as presented for execution, differs substantially, either by way of addition or of omission, from the scheme and details which the intending settlor has previously laid down, the discrepancy ought to be clearly pointed out and its nature and effect should be fully described, unless, which must be rare, the difference is so obvious that even a person in the settlor's position must perceive and appreciate it for herself. If the description and explanation have been partial or erroneous, or have not been given at all, the question will then arise, as it arises where there has been no independent legal advice, whether, if proper information had been given, it would have affected the mind of the executant in completing the deed. On the other hand, the doctrine cannot be pushed so far as to demand the impossible. The mere declaration by the settlor, subsequently made, that she had not understood what she was doing, obviously is not in itself conclusive. It must be a question whether, having regard to the proved personality of the settlor, the nature of the settlement, the circumstances under which it was executed, and the whole history of the parties, it is reasonably established that the deed executed was the free and intelligent act of the settlor or not. If the answer is in the affirmative, those relying on the deed have discharged the onus which rests upon them. Of course fraud, duress and actual undue influence are separate matters.

In the present case it is quite clear that certain matters were not brought to the appellant's notice before the deed was executed, or at all. Not only was a second *mutawalli* with an additional salary introduced into the draft which was executed, but it made no provision for the settlor's desires as to the maintenance and repair of the mosque in Ahmadpur and as to the various religious ceremonies mentioned by her to Jamal-ud-din, beyond including them among the objects on which the *mutawallis* might expend the wakf funds, if and so far as they thought proper. As the deed stands, the *mutawallis* could decline to continue any of the special pious observances which the appellant desired to continue, and could leave her to maintain them herself out of her diminished income, and to die in the knowledge that, with her, these objects would have no one left to care for them.

Their Lordships cannot regard these matters as insignificant or such as the plaintiff could reasonably be supposed not to insist upon. She was a woman of property, who had lived all her married life in her own family house, hard by, as it would seem, to the mosque erected by her relations.

20 (1902) LR 29 IA 132, 137.

Hers had been a lonely and restricted existence. Karim-ud-din, as a husband, was in many respects a very disappointing person. His own means were small, and for many years his official duties caused him to reside at a distance. She was herself piously disposed, and it was eminently natural in such a woman under such circumstances that she should attach importance to the instructions which she gave to her husband through Jamal-ud-din. Her piety may well have manifested itself primarily in her care for the mosque, which her family had founded, and for the celebration of the observances to which she herself had diligently attended. If she had really appreciated that in none of these cases was that perpetual continuance assured, which was evidently dear to her mind, their Lordships are far from being satisfied that she would have patiently submitted to her disappointment and have accepted intelligently and without a word the surrender of her own preferences to the discretion of the *mutawallis*. The only prudent and probable conclusion is that, as the words were read over to her, she failed, very naturally, to observe the change. She would hear mention of the mosque and of nearly all the ceremonies by name, and would easily miss the difference between the inclusion of these objects in the powers of the *mutawallis* and the prescription of these objects as obligatory charities to be maintained by the *mutawallis* in any event. They are confirmed in this view by observing that, until a late stage in the argument before the Board, this precise discrepancy between the first draft of the *wakfnama* and its ultimate form had not attracted the attention of anybody, either in the courts below or on this appeal. No doubt, where so many other points were in contest, this one might well pass unobserved, but this circumstance only makes it the more likely that the appellant could not herself detect what has, in fact, eluded the vigilance of counsel and judges during two protracted hearings. It is not proved when or by whom the original draft was remodelled. There is no evidence that Wazir-ud-din so much as knew that the appellant had given any particular instructions before the scheme was put into writing, and he could not draw the appellant's special attention to something that he never knew. Upon the story told by the respondent's witnesses there never was any chance that those, who explained the deed, should point out these matters, and it is certainly not enough to say that, if the appellant cared about them, she should herself have asked about them, especially as the form of the deed was such as might well have misled her into taking it for a provision of all that she desired. From this point of view the appellant's subsequent action does not assist the respondents. Registration and mutation were promptly asked for by those interested in supporting the deed, and the plaintiff herself attended the proceedings without protest. These circumstances are in themselves very favourable to the respondents' case, but the registering officer, who says that he read and explained the deed to her, knew as little of the above-mentioned discrepancies as did Wazir-ud-din, and the appellant's answers are quite consistent with her being in ignorance of a change, of which no one had informed her. As the respondents have to bear the onus of bringing home to her mind the actual import of the deed, they cannot rely on the fact that the appellant's own evidence is untrustworthy, for it is by the evidence of their own witnesses alone that this defect is established, and by that evidence they must stand. The conclusion that they have failed to discharge the burthen of proof is one arrived at not out of any consideration for this lady in particular, but in defence of those strict rules which have been laid down for the protection of the defenceless in India, and it is a matter of obligation upon their Lordships to be strict and unwavering about it.

They will humbly advise His Majesty that the appeal should be allowed, and that the decree passed by the learned Subordinate Judge should be restored with costs here and in both courts below.

◊ UPDATE ◊

1. *Parda custom*

The custom of *parda* (veil), though fast dying out in the urban society in South Asia, remains prevalent among certain sections of the people in all parts of the subcontinent. It is in fact a local custom not confined to the followers of any particular community.

The observance of *parda* as a religious obligation is now a controversial issue. In India in the context of Muslim religion it has been examined in some election cases including *Nirmal* v. *CEO* AIR 1961 Cal 289 and *M. Peeran Saheb* AIR 1988 AP 377. In the former case it was observed in respect of the position of the practice of *parda* in Islam:

> There is no express injunction about keeping *parda*. Moderation of social intercourse of the two sexes is advocated and it has been laid down that women should cast down their looks and not diplay their ornament in public. The annotators hold that there is no absolute injunction for covering the face or the hands. What have been laid down are questions of prudence and general deportment. The matter, therefore, rests not on religion but on social practice.

Reference was made in the judgement approvingly, to the government counsel's argument that frequent appearance of the pictures of the then Iranian Queen Farah Diba in the world-press went against plea that *parda* was incumbent on all Muslim women.

2. *Pardanashin women*

As regards the need for special legal protection of *pardanashin* (veiled) women in matters of property transactions as stated in the old judicial rulings of *Moonshee Buzloor Raheem*, *Mahomed Buksh* and *Farid-un-Nisa* [Cases 24, 26 and 27], it has been reasserted in several cases of recent times in all parts of the subcontinent.

In *Kharbuja Kuer* v. *Jangbahadur Rai* AIR 1963 SC 1203 the Indian Supreme Court observed:

> In India *pardanashin* ladies have been given a special protection in view of the social conditions of the times. They are presumed to have an imperfect knowledge of the world, as by the *parda* system they are practically excluded from social intercourse and communion with the outside world.

The law on this point was examined at length by the Orissa High Court in *Kishore Ray Thakur Bije* v. *Basnati Kumar Das* AIR 1994 113.

In Pakistan, the Supreme Court has dealt with the law for *pardanashin* women in *Jannat Bibi* v. *Sikandar* PLD 1990 SC 642 and *Irshad Hussain* v. *Ijaz Hussain* PLD 1994 SC 326.

3. *Gifting property in Muslim law*

The basic features of the law of gift as explained in the case of *Rani Khajooroonissa* [Case 25] have been re-sated in India in *Hafiz Abdul Basit* v. *Hafiz Ahmad* AIR 1973 Del 280, *Rashid* v. *Batulan* AIR 1882 All 111 and *Imbichimoidinkutty* v. *Pathumuni* AIR 1989 Ker 148.

Section 129 of the Transfer of Property Act 1882 protects the Muslim law of gifts. On its continued enforcement in India see *Chota Uddandla* v. *Masthan Bi* AIR 1975 AP 271.

The essential requirements for making a gift under Muslim law have been reaffirmed by the Indian Supreme Court in *Mahboob Sahab* v. *Syed Ismail* AIR 1995 SC 1205.

XII. Life Interests

28. Umjad Ally Khan v. Mohumdee Begum
(1867) 11 Moore's IA 517

Gift of government promissory notes by father to son—absolute ownership transferred—reservation of recurring income only—Ithnā 'Asharī Shiite school

A gift *inter vivos* of government promissory notes (negotiable securities) by a father to his only son (Shiite Muslims) accompanied by delivery of possession and a transfer into the son's name without any reservation of the dominion over the corpus by the donor except a stipulation for the right to the accruing interest on the notes during the donor's life to be applied by him to certain religious and charitable purposes, is a valid gift by the Muhammadan law of the Ithnā 'Asharī school and creates a trust on the donee to pay the interest to the donor during his life.

Whether the non-assent of the heirs vitiates the will of a Muslim made in favour of one heir to the prejudice of the other heirs. *Quaere*?

The law of succession, *ab intestato*, applies only to the assets which constitute the succession.

The classic discussion of life interests will be found in *Tyabji*, §§ 443, 443A, 444, 444A. Tyabji's views as to the distinction between *'ayn* and *manāfi'* (corpus and usufruct) have now been accepted by the Privy Council; and life interests in a variety of forms are fully established. *Anjuman Ara v. Nawab Asif Kader* (Case 30, below); *Outlines*, § 46.

Judgment [Edward V. Williams][1]

This is an appeal, under an order made on a special application to Her Majesty, for leave to appeal against so much of the decree of Mr Campbell, made by him when Judicial Commissioner of Oudh, as reverses or varies a decree of Mr Fraser, the Civil Judge of Lucknow, in favour of the

[1] With J.W. Colvile & Bolt, JJ, and Assessor Lawrence Peel.

Appellant. The suit in which Mr Fraser's decree was made was brought by the Respondents, Mohumdee Begum and Nawab Begum, as Daughters and co-heirs of the deceased *Nawab*, against the Appellant as the Son and the Administrator of his Father's estate, under Act, No. XXVII of 1860, against the Widow of their Father and two Sisters of the Plaintiff, also co-heirs; and, lastly, against certain other persons described as nominal Defendants whom it is unnecessary here to name or further to describe.

The suit was in the nature of an administration suit; it sought a discovery of a portion of the assets alleged to be withheld, and an account, and a division of the assets amongst the heirs according to the Mahommedan law. The deceased and his family were Mahommedans, and followers of the *Sheah* school. The Widow of the deceased instituted also a distinct and separate suit against the heirs, claiming her dower according to a settlement of it upon her by her Husband, and claiming, in addition to it, a large sum of money by gift from her Husband during his lifetime. Her claim to one-eighth of the clear assets seems not to have been disputed. The Appellant claimed a large portion of the property, consisting of promissory notes of the Government, commonly called Company's paper, amounting to Rs 735,300, as his property by gift from his Father in the lifetime of the latter, the validity of which gift was disputed by the Respondents, the Plaintiffs in the suit, as well as by the Widow, a co-Defendant. [...]

The matters to be determined on this appeal are three in number, and are: First, the validity of the gift to the Appellant of the Company's paper, amounting to Rs 735,300; secondly, the appointment of a stranger to be and act as co-Trustee with the Appellant in the trust as to the family, religious, or charitable fund called *Rud Muzalim*, and the direction to settle a scheme for the administration of that fund; and, thirdly, the reservation of his judgment, indefinitely, by the Judicial Commissioner, on the right of the Appellant, as declared by Mr Fraser in his decree, in respect of the landed property adjudged to the Appellant by that last-mentioned decision.

The first in order of these matters involves an important point of Mahommedan law relating to gifts, *inter vivos*.

If the gift be sustained as a valid gift, *inter vivos*, it will be unnecessary to review the evidence as to the genuineness of certain documents propounded by the Appellant, and said to constitute a valid testament by the Mahommedan law, or to consider in any way the validity or effect of those documents.

The effect of the non-assent of co-heirs to a bequest to an heir by a Mahommedan of the *Sheah* sect becomes also immaterial as a subject of inquiry here, if the gift be valid as a gift *inter vivos*.

Before the validity of this gift, as one *inter vivos*, is determined, it must first be considered by their Lordships what the real nature of the transfer was. The legal title in the promissory notes was undoubtedly in the Appellant, in his Father's lifetime, by virtue of an act of the Father.

But though the transfer of a legal title will satisfy that provision of the Mahommedan law which relates to the point of seisin, in its legal and technical sense, yet that alone will not suffice where no intention exists to transfer the beneficial ownership, either present or future. The facts relating to the gift have been most carefully investigated by Mr Fraser, the Civil Judge. The Judicial Commissioner, paying a just tribute of commendation to Mr Fraser on his accurate investigation of the facts, expresses no dissent from his conclusion as to them, but reverses his decision as to this gift as erroneous in point of law. Mr Fraser's observations as to the mode of dealing amongst natives living amongst themselves as a family, in a state of family union, and dealing in this state with the proceeds of property standing in the names of separate members of the family, to whom it has been transferred by the parent and head of the family, and on the deference to his wishes and arrangements, and acquiescence in them commonly exhibited, are forcible as arguments to exclude the notion of fraudulent concealment or design in a transfer circumstanced as the present. They strengthen the probability of an intended transfer of property in the lifetime of the Donor, with a reservation of the use or proceeds of the money transferred during the lifetime of the Donor only.

In consequence of the tendency amongst natives to disguise their ownership under *benamee* transfers of property, a natural suspicion arises often that such is the design when the transaction is really fair and open, and the apparent and real title are entirely consistent. The transaction questioned in this case, though between natives, differs in no respect as to the manner of dealing with the property in question (Company's paper in the hands of the Government Agent at Calcutta at the time of and after the gift), from the mode in which a European Father and Son, designing to make between themselves a similar disposition of the like property, giving the paper to the Son with a reservation of the interest to the Father for life, might have dealt with it so as completely to effectuate their intention. There is no evidence of any attempt or design to conceal from the Government Agent, or from others, the origin of the property, its source, transfer, or continuing state of enjoyment. Mr Fraser accordingly, and very reasonably, negatives any fraud in the transactions as to these notes, and Mr Campbell, though he treats the case as one undeserving of support in a court of justice, proceeds not on actual fraud, but on his views of the policy of the law, and treats the transaction as fradulent in contemplation of law, and done in evasion of its provisions, which limit the testamentary power of a Mahommedan and aim in some degree at equality of division amongst the descendants *ab intestato*.

Everything which took place in respect of these notes at the Government Agent's Office was perfectly consistent with the Appellant's real title in them. It is true his case is stated higher in his pleadings than the real title warrants; but the case, as stated, includes the real title, and is only the common error which is so frequently observed in the cases of Natives in India, where their legal advisers, from ignorance or foolish craft, misstate a good case, and place it on false grounds. This was not an absolute transfer of the whole property, including all future interest, beneficial as well as legal; nor was it a *benamee* transaction. A mere *benamee*, or *ism furzee* title, is simply a nominal title without interest. It may, or may not, be fraudulent in design. Such a disposition by a Donor, where the transfer of the property, from its very nature, effected a legal transfer of it, would be simply the creation of a trust in his favour, and would, of course, leave the disposition *ab intestato* undisturbed. But such was not the intention here, and such is not the nature of the disposition. The object of the disposition is correctly stated by Mr Fraser to have been to give the Son a larger share of the Father's property than would come to him by succession *ab intestato*. Mr Campbell, the Judicial Commissioner, treats that intention and act as evasive of the testamentary law of Mahommedans and as inconsistent with their law of gifts.

Upon the first ground of decision it is to be observed, that in the absence of immoral, or illegal purposes accompanying and prompting an act of disposition of property, a disposition which the law admits cannot be evasive of the law. The law of succession *ab intestato* applies only to the assets which constitute the succession. If the law allows alienation so as to defeat a succession, the question, whether a subject or property is part of the assets or not, raises simply the question, whether the transfer of it is legally complete. The design to alter, and so in one sense to defeat, the disposition of property, is simply a design to conform to the law, whilst working out an unforbidden design. The other view of the subject, that this is an incomplete gift by the Mahommedan law, is one which presents more difficulty, and will be presently considered. On moral grounds the transaction cannot be impeached. It seems to have proceeded simply from the cause assigned for it in Mr Fraser's judgment, viz., a desire to maintain the dignity of the eldest branch of the family; neither can the policy of the law be invoked, for the reason above assigned, that the policy of the law is to be collected from its whole body, and not from a detached portion of it; so that if the law suffers a Father by an act, *inter vivos*, to alter his succession, his exercise of that power cannot be deemed a fraud upon the law.

It remains to be considered whether a real transfer of property by a Donor in his lifetime under the Mahommedan law, reserving not the dominion over the corpus of the property, nor any share of dominion over the corpus, but simply stipulating for and obtaining a right to the recurring produce during his lifetime, is an incomplete gift by the Mahommedan law. The text of the *Hedaya* seems to include the very proposition and to negative it. The thing to be returned is not identical, but something different. See *Hedaya*, tit. 'Gifts,' Vol. III. Book xxx. p. 294, where the objection being raised that a participation of property in the thing given invalidates a gift, the answer is, 'The Donor is subjected to a participation in a thing which is not the subject of his grant, namely, the use [of the whole indivisible article] for his gift related to the substance of the article, not to the use of it.' Again, if the agreement for the reservation of the interest to the Father for his life be treated as a repugnant condition, repugnant to the whole enjoyment by the donee, here the Mahommedan law defeats not the grant, but the condition. *Hedaya*, tit. 'Gifts,' Vol. III. Book xxx. p. 307. But as this arrangement between the Father and the Son is founded on a valid consideration, the Son's undertaking is valid, and could be enforced against him in the courts of India as an agreement raising a trust, and constituting a valid obligation to make a return of the proceeds during the time stipulated. The intention of the parties, therefore, is not found to violate any provision of the *Hedaya*, and the transfer is complete. The Mahommedan law authority whom Mr Campbell consulted, supported it. His opinion is treated somewhat lightly as a nude opinion, unsupported by authority; but it is to be observed, that unless some authority had been cited to show the transaction invalid, effect should have been given to the manifest intention of the parties. [....]

Their Lordships think, that a valid gift, *inter vivos*, as to the Company's paper, was effected by the Nawab in his lifetime in favour of his Son, the Appellant, and, therefore, they deem it unnecessary to consider the question as to the genuineness of the documents set forth as constituting his will, or to consider, whether the non-assent of the heirs does or does not vitiate the will of a Mahommedan of the Sheah school in favour of an heir. They will humbly advise Her Majesty to reverse the decision of the Judicial Commissioner of Oudh, except as to appointment of a co-trustee, and to affirm the decision of the Civil Judge, with that variation.

29. Sardar Nawazish Ali v. Sardar Ali Raza
(1948) 75 IA 62

Ithnā' Asharī Shiite will—successive life estates—power of appointment to surviving devisee—validity—Oudh Estates Act (*I of* 1869)

The main question in this appeal was whether a power of appointment given to a life tenant was valid according to the Ithnā 'Asharī Shiite law. The rule laid down in this case was: Where an Ithnā 'Asharī Shiite testator bequeaths his property to *A*, *B*, and *C* successively, and then provides that the last surviving devisee should have the power to nominate his successor from among the descendants of the three life tenants, such a power was not known to any school of Muhammadan law as received in India. A full discussion will be found in *Outlines*, 246 seqq.

Consolidated Appeals (No. 18 of 1945) from a judgment and decree of the Chief Court (12 January 1943) [of Oudh] which modified a decree of that court in its original civil jurisdiction (30 October 1937).

The following facts are taken from the judgment of the Judicial Committee. Sardar Nawazish Ali Khan will be referred to hereinafter as 'the appellant,' and Sardar Ali Raza Khan as 'the respondent'. The family to which the parties belonged were Shia Muhammadans of the Ithnā 'Asharī sect, governed by the Imamia law. The litigation which led up to these appeals arose out of the wills of Nawab Sir Nawazish Ali Khan and Nawab Nasir Ali Khan, who were related to the parties to these appeals as shown in the pedigree following:

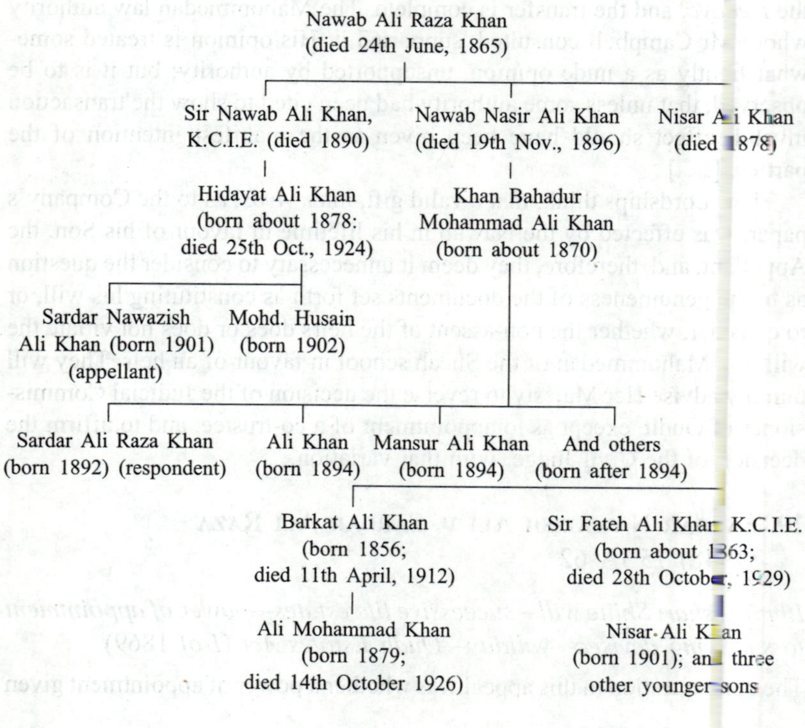

The estates the title to which was contested in these appeals were an estate in Oudh (hereinafter called 'the Oudh estate') known as the Nawabganj Aliabad estate, in the Bahraich district, which was granted to Nawab Ali Raza Khan, and was shown as No. 151 in List I of the lists in the Schedule to the Oudh Estates Act, 1869, and No. 39 in List V, so that under s. 8 of that Act the intestate succession was regulated by the rule of primogeniture and in accordance with the scheme laid down in s. 22 of the Act. Secondly, an estate in the Punjab called the Rakh Juliana estate (hereinafter called 'the Juliana estate') which was granted by the Government of India to Nawazish Ali Khan.

Both those estates were owned by Nawazish Ali Khan. He transferred the Juliana estate to his brother Nasir Ali Khan in his lifetime. By his will, dated 14 February 1882, he bequeathed the Oudh estate to his said brother under the power conferred by s. 11 of the Oudh Estates Act, 1869, which enabled him to make such a bequest notwithstanding that under his family law he could only bequeath one-third of his property. At the date of his death in 1890 Nawazish Ali Khan had a son, Hidayat Ali Khan, who would have succeeded to the Oudh estate under the Act of 1869 if Nawazish Ali Khan had died intestate. That was relevant in connetion with the descent of the Oudh estate.

On 15 July 1896, Nasir Ali Khan executed two wills, one disposing of the Oudh estate, and the other of the Juliana estate and another estate in the Punjab. It was common ground that the heirs assented to the wills. Those wills were in substantially the same form. It will be sufficient to quote the material provisions of the will with regard to the Oudh estate:

Now, under s. 11 of Act 1 of 1869, I, by means of this will, do hereby appoint Nawab Fateh Ali Khan son of my late brother Nawab Nisar Ali Khan, my executor and successor of all this Taluqdari estate with all the rights and interest aforesaid and do hereby authorize the executor that whatever Taluqdari powers over the above-mentioned *ilaqa* and over all the properties movable and immovable I the said declarant have, my devisee, to wit, Nawab Fateh Ali Khan, after my lifetime shall have like myself the very same powers including the power of possession and enjoyment as owner provided he be alive. Similarly after the lifetime of the devisee Nawab Fateh Ali Khan my son Nawab Mohammad Ali Khan shall, if alive, be his successor. He shall also have the very same powers as have been bestowed on Nawab Fateh Ali Khan by means of this deed of will. After the lifetime of my son Nawab Mohammad Ali Khan, Nawab Hidayat Ali Khan son of the late Sir Nawab Haji Nawazish Ali Khan Saheb shall be his successor provided he be alive. After all these three successors the fit amongst the descendants of the successors shall succeed. The last devisee shall have power to nominate as his successor anyone whom he might consider fit from amongst the descendants of each of the three successors and if the last devisee die without nominating a successor the male descendants of each of the three successors shall have power to appoint as successor whomsoever they consider fit and superior amongst themselves. The line of successors shall continue according to this very rule. In the event of disagreement the Government shall have power to appoint as successor anyone amongst the descendants of each of the three successors whom it considers the fittest. And if anyone amongst our family claims maintenance contrary to the wishes of the Taluqdars, to wit, my successors, he shall in no way be entitled as of right to get maintenance. The successors shall have power to give or not maintenance in the event of good conduct and obedience.

On the death of Nawab Nasir Ali Khan on 19 November 1896 (before the birth of the appellant), Fateh Ali Khan entered into possession of both properties. On his death, on 28 October 1923, his son Nisar Ali Khan took possession thereof. Hidayat Ali Khan died in 1924. On 9 December 1925, Mohammad Ali Khan (who will be referred to hereinafter as 'Mohammad') instituted a suit claiming both the properties. This litigation was eventually taken in appeal to the Privy Council (*Nisar Ali Khan* v. *Mohammad Ali Khan*[2]) where it was decided that Fateh Ali Khan and Mohammad took life estates under the wills. The Privy Council refused to consider what would happen after Mohammad's death.

As a result of that litigation Mohammad got possession of the Oudh estate and the Juliana estate. By a document dated 30 June 1934 Mohammad, after reciting the wills of Nasir Ali Khan, declared as follows:

Whereas according to the decision of the Privy Council, I the declarant also in accordance with the said will, have been in possession of the property left by the late Nawab Nasir Ali Khan and on account of the death of the late Sardar Hidayat Ali Khan Saheb, son of the late Haji Sir Nawazish Ali Khan, I, the declarant, in accordance with the will am the last legatee and am in every manner subject to the said will, entitled and competent to nominate successor; whereas I the declarant have reached my full age and consider it proper and necessary to abide by the said will executed by the late Nawab Nasir Ali Khan in order to remove future domestic disputes. I the declarant therefore, in my unimpaired five senses, without repugnance and force, nominate as successor Nawabzada Nawazish Ali Khan son of late Sardar Hidayat Ali Khan, for this reason that although, by the grace of God, each of the three legatees mentioned in the will dated 15 July 1896, has male issues still, among all of them the said Nawabzada Nawazish Ali Khan is in every way fit to be preferred for succession.... The said Nawabzada Nawazish Ali Khan shall also be bound to continue to pay to the descendants of the family of Nawab Nasir Ali Khan and Nawab Nawazish Ali Khan, deceased, subject to (their) obedience, maintenance at the scale mentioned in s. 25. Act I of 1869.

Therefore I have with my own will and consent executed this document appointing successor according to the provision of schedule 1, Article 7 of the Stamp Act by way of appointment in execution of a power so that it may serve as an

2 (1932) LR 59 IA 268.

authority and be of use when needed—Dated 30 June 1934. The scribe of the deed is Syed Hidayet Husain, Vakil, Said Wara, Bahraich.

Mohammad died on 3 February 1935, and on his death the appellant obtained possession of both estates. On 25 September 1935, the respondent instituted in the Chief Court of Oudh against the appellant the suit out of which these appeals arose. By his plaint the respondent claimed a decree for possession of the Oudh estate, the Juliana estate and other estates with which this appeal was not concerned, and consequential relief.

Both the courts in India held that the power of appointment given by the wills of Nasir Ali Khan was valid according to Shia law but its purported exercise in favour of the appellant, who was not born in the lifetime of the testator, was invalid under the personal law so far as the Juliana estate was concerned but valid so far as the Oudh estate was concerned under the Oudh Estates Acts. Both courts held that the document of 30 June 1934, executed by Mohammad, was a will. The trial judge held that it gave to the appellant one third of the Juliana estate to which Mohammad was entitled as heir at law of Nasir Ali Khan. The Chief Court in appeal held that the will was not intended to affect, and did not affect, property of which the testator Mohammad was the absolute owner. With regard to the relief claimed in the suit the trial judge dismissed the suit of the respondent on the ground that it was a suit in ejectment and the respondent had not proved his title to the whole of the property claimed. In appeal the Chief Court varied the decree of the lower court by giving the respondent a decree for possession of one-fifth of the Juliana estate, the proportion of the estate to which he was entitled as one of the heirs of Mohammad.

Judgment [John Beaumont][3]

[....]

The questions which were argued on this appeal were: (1) Is it competent for a Shia Mohammadan governed by Imamia law by will to leave property to a person for his life and after his death to such members of a class as such person may appoint? Or, to state the question in more general terms, does Shia law recognize powers of appointment of a character with which English law is familiar? (2) If the answer to the first question is in the affirmative, can such power be exercised in favour of a person not born in the lifetime of the testator though born before the power is exercised? (3) Is the document executed by Mohammad on 30 June 1934, a will? If so, does it comprise property of which Mohammad was absolute owner? (4) What relief, if any, is the respondent (plaintiff in the action) entitled to?

3 With Uthwatt & Oaksey JJ.

A question was raised, but not seriously pressed, on the construction of the wills of Nasir Ali Khan. It was suggested that the power to appoint a successor was given to the last of the three named tenants for life, namely, Hidayat Ali Khan. Their Lordships feel no doubt that the courts in India were right in holding that the power was given to the last survivor of the three life tenants, and in the events which happened the power, if validly created, was vested in Mohammad.

The first question arising in this appeal, as to the validity of the power of appointment conferred by the wills of Nasir Ali Khan, is one of general importance in Islamic law. Both the courts in India based their opinion that such a power is valid under Muslim law on the decision of the Privy Council in *Bai Motivahoo* v. *Bai Mamoobai*.[4] In that case the Board upheld a power of appointment conferred by the will of a Hindu, holding that the question for consideration was whether there was anything against public convenience, anything generally mischievous or anything against the general principles of Hindu law, in allowing such a power. Applying a similar test in the present case, the courts in India held that a power of appointment can be conferred under Muslim law. Their Lordships are not satisfied that this is the correct test to apply in a case relating to the will of a Muslim. The origin of testamentary capacity in the case of Muslims is quite different from that in the case of Hindus. The Hindu texts make no reference to wills, and this is natural since the formal state of Hindu society in ancient times was the joint family, and on the death of a member the property in which he had an interest passed by survivorship to the other members of the family. It was only after partition and the acquisition of self-acquired property became common that the necessity to make wills arose, and testamentary power amongst Hindus has been based on long usage and judicial decision (see *Tagore's case*[5]). On the other hand, wills have been recognized under Muslim law from the earliest times. 'Wills are declared to be lawful in the Quran and the traditions, and all our doctors, moreover, have concurred in this opinion' (Hamilton's *Hedaya*, Vol. 4, p. 468). It would, however, appear that the Prophet was not in favour of unlimited testamentary power. It is recorded in the *Hedaya* (Vol. 4, p. 469) that he said to a follower when asked his opinion, 'You may leave a third of your property by will: but a third part, to be disposed of by will is a great portion; and it is better you should leave your heirs rich than in a state of poverty, which might oblige them to beg of others'; and at p. 472 of the same volume there is a saying attributed to the Prophet, 'God has allotted to every heir his particular right.'

4 LR 24 IA 93.
5 (1872) LR, IA Supp. 67.

Their Lordships have not been referred to, and are not aware of, any work on Mahommedan law, or any judicial decision in support of the view that powers of appointment, so special a feature of English law, are recognized in Muslim law. The matter seems never to have been discussed. In such circumstances, and at this date, to add to the testamentary capacity of Muslims the right to create powers of appointment might seem to encroach on the sphere of the legislature.

Their Lordships, however, would be very reluctant to differ from the courts in India solely on the ground of lack of precedent, and they propose, therefore, to consider the question whether the grant of such a power of appointment as was contained in the wills of Nasir Ali Khan conflicts with the general principles of Muslim law. The Chief Court in appeal took the view that under the wills of Nasir Ali Khan the estate vested after his death in the three successive tenants for life; that on the exercise of the power of appointment it would pass immediately to the appointee; that there was no period during which the estate would be in abeyance; and that the rights of the heirs of the testator were not affected or prejudiced. In their Lordships' opinion this view of the matter introduces into Muslim law legal terms and conceptions of ownership, familiar enough in English law, but wholly alien to Muslim law. In general, Muslim law draws no distinction between real and personal property, and their Lordships know of no authoritative work on Muslim law, whether the *Hedaya*, or Baillie or more modern works, and no decision of this Board which affirms that Muslim law recognizes the splitting up of ownership of land into estates, distinguished in point of quality like legal and equitable estates, or in point of duration like estates in fee simple, in tail, for life, or in remainder. What Muslim law does recognize and insist on, is the distinction between the corpus of the property itself (*ayn*) and the usufruct in the property (*manafi*). Over the corpus of property the law recognizes only absolute dominion, heritable, and unrestricted in point of time; and where a gift of the corpus seeks to impose a condition inconsistent with such absolute dominion the condition is rejected as repugnant; but interests limited in point of time can be created in the usufruct of the property and the dominion over the corpus takes effect subject to any such limited interests.

If a person bequeath the service of his slave, or the use of his house, either for a definite or an indefinite period, such bequest is valid; because as an endowment with usufruct, either gratuitous or for an equivalent, is valid during life, it is consequently so after death; and also, because men have occasion to make bequests of this nature as well as bequests of actual property. So likewise, if a person bequeath the wages of his slave, or the rent of his house, for a definite or indefinite term, it is valid, for the same reason. In both cases, moreover, it is necessary to consign over the house or the slave to the legatee, provided they do not exceed the third of the property, in order that he may enjoy the wages or service of the slave, or the rent or use of the house during the term prescribed, and afterwards restore it to the heirs. (*Hedaya*, Vol. 4, p. 527, chap. 5, entitled 'Of Usufructuary Will.')

This distinction runs all through the Muslim law of gifts—gifts of the corpus (*hiba*), gifts of the usufruct (*ariya*) and usufructuary bequests. No doubt where the use of a house is given to a man for his life he may, not inaptly, be termed a tenant for life, and the owner of the house, waiting to enjoy it until the termination of the limited interest, may be said, not inaccurately, to possess a vested remainder. But though the same terms may be used in English and Muslim law, to describe much the same things, the two systems of law are based on quite different conceptions of ownership. English law recognizes ownership of land limited in duration; Muslim law admits only ownership unlimited in duration, but recognizes interests of limited duration in the use of property.

There is a full discussion of the law on this subject in the judgment of Sir Wazir Hasan as reported in *Amjad Khan* v. *Ashraf Khan*.[6] That case challenged the doctrine accepted by Hanafi lawyers that a gift to 'A' for life conferred an absolute interest on 'A'; a doctrine based on a saying of the Prophet (*Hedaya*, Bk. III, p. 309).

An *amree* ['*umra*] or life grant is lawful to the grantee during his life and descends to his heirs. The meaning of *amree* is a gift of a house (for example) during the life of the donee, on condition of its being returned upon his death. An *amree* is nothing but a gift and a condition and the condition is invalid: but a gift is not rendered null by involving an invalid condition.

Sir Wazir Hasan in his judgment examined the appropriate texts and all the relevant decisions of the Privy Council. He pointed out the distinction in Muslim law between the corpus and the usufruct, between the thing itself and the use of the thing. On the construction of the deed which was in question in the case before him, he came to the conclusion that the donor intended to confer on his wife not the corpus, but a life interest only, that such life interest could take effect as a gift of the use of the property and not as part of the property itself, and that there was nothing in Muslim law which compelled him to hold that the intended gift of a life estate conferred an absolute interest on the donee. This case was taken in appeal to the Privy Council.[7] The Board agreed with Sir Wazir Hasan on the construction of the deed in question that only a life interest was intended, and held that if

6 (1929) ILR 4 Luck 305.
7 (1929) LR 56 IA 213.

the wife took only a life interest, it came to an end on her death, and the appellant, who was her heir, took nothing, and if the life interest was bad the wife took no interest at all and the appellant was in no better case. There is also a discussion of the basis on which a life interest under Hanafi law can be supported in the 3rd edition of Tyabji's *Muhammadan Law* at p. 487 et seq. That book, as the work of an author still living, cannot be cited as an authority, but their Lordships have derived assistance from the discussion.

Limited interests have long been recognized under Shia law. The object of '*Habs*' is 'the empowering of a person to receive the profit or usufruct of a thing with a reservation of the owner's right of property in it... I have bestowed on thee this mansion... for thy life or my life or for a fixed period' is binding by seisin on the part of the donee. (Bail: II. 226.) See also *Banoo Begum* v. *Mir Abed Ali*.[8] Their Lordships think that there is no difference between the several schools of Muslim law in their fundamental conception of property and ownership. A limited interest takes effect out of the usufruct under any of the schools. Their Lordships feel no doubt that in dealing with a gift under Muslim law, the first duty of the court is to construe the gift. If it is a gift of the corpus, then any condition which derogates from absolute dominion over the subject of the gift will be rejected as repugnant; but if on construction the gift is held to be one of a limited interest the gift can take effect out of the usufruct, leaving the ownership of the corpus unaffected except to the extent to which its enjoyment is postponed for the duration of the limited interest.

It remains to construe the wills of Nasir Ali Khan and to apply to them the rules of Muslim law. On the death of the first life tenant his son and heir claimed that the gift to his father was of the corpus, relying on the use of the word 'owner' (*malik*), and that all subsequent limitations were repugnant and void. This argument failed in all the courts, and it was held that the will created three successive life interests. As the will contained no gift of the corpus, that descended to the heirs of the testator subject to the interests of the life tenants in the usufruct. On the death of the surviving tenant for life, two alternative constructions of the wills have been suggested. First that the person to take under the power of appointment was to take absolutely. Secondly that the sentence in the wills 'the line of successors shall continue according to this very rule' means that the person to take under the power was to take for life and to possess a power of appointing a successor similar to that given to the survivor of the three tenants for life named in the wills, and that this arrangement was to continue for ever. If this be the meaning of the wills the power, if valid, would operate

8 (1907) ILR 32 B 172, 179.

on the usufruct, but the question would arise whether under Shia law as administered in India and in the light of public policy it is competent for a testator to provide in perpetuity for a succession of tenants for life not born in his lifetime taking under successive powers of appointment. Their Lordships do not find it necessary to decide this question, because they are satisfied that the first suggested construction of the wills is the right one, and that the person nominated under the power was to take an absolute interest. The words of the sentence quoted above are vague and not capable, their Lordships think, of bearing the extended meaning sought to be attributed to them. They appear to be words of emphasis and repetition merely. The testator is saying that the line of succession which he has laid down, namely to three successive tenants for life and then to the successor appointed under the power, is the line which is to continue from his death. If the successor is to take absolutely, the power operates on the corpus, and in their Lordships' view is clearly inconsistent with principles of Muslim law. It would interfere with the Muslim law of succession, and would involve that the heirs took the corpus of the property for a term, not merely of limited, but of uncertain, duration. The Chief Court found some support for its view that the power of appointment was valid in analogies drawn from wakfs. In their Lordships' opinion no such analogy exists in a case like the present, which is not founded on trust. In wakfs the property is vested either notionally in Almighty God, or in the wakif or his heirs, and all beneficial interests take effect out of the usufruct. For the above reasons their Lordships hold that the power of appointment contained in the wills of Nasir Ali Khan is invalid under Muslim law.

The next question for consideration is as to the nature and effect of the document of 30 June 1934, executed by Mohammad, which both courts in India held to be a will. No doubt in point of form it might be a will. But it is to be noticed that it purports only to exercise the power conferred by the wills of Nasir Ali Khan and to dispose of the property subject to the power. It contains no appointment of an executor, no gift of any property belonging to the testator, and no suggestion of revocability; it was stamped under an article of the Stamp Act relating to appointments made by any writing not being a will, and it is called a deed at the end of the document. In all the circumstances their Lordships think that the document was a deed and not a will. But if it be a will, their Lordships agree with the lower appellate court that the document did not pass property which Mohammad took as heir of his father. It was one thing to choose the appellant, who was the senior male member of the senior branch of the family, to succeed to the leadership of the family and to the family estates, but quite another thing to decide that the appellant was better suited than Mohammad's own children to inherit Mohammad's own property. There is nothing to show that Mohammad ever considered that question. This disposes of the appeal of the appellant relating to the Juliana estate, which belongs to the heirs of Mohammad under his personal law.

The cross-appeal of the respondent relates to the Oudh estate. The courts in India were of opinion that, apart from Muslim law, a power of appointment can be created under the wide power of disposition conferred by s. 11 of the Oudh Estates Act, 1869, which applies to all Taluqdaris, Hindu as well as Muslim. As against this view the respondent points out that neither the Act of 1869 nor the amending Act of 1910 mentions powers of appointment, and that ss. 78 and 79 of the Succession Act, 1865, which relate to powers of appointment, are not included amongst the sections incorporated in the Act of 1869. Their Lordships do not find it necessary to decide this question, because they are satisfied for the reasons now stated to be that if a power of appointment can be created under the Oudh Estates Act, the power sought to be conferred by the wills of Nasir Ali Khan does not fall within the Acts. The position is as follows. Estates in List V descend on intestacy under the law of primogeniture in accordance with the scheme laid down in s. 22 of the Act of 1869. Under s. 11 of the Act the holder of such an estate might, however, dispose of the estate, either in his lifetime or by will. The estate in the hands of a person taking it by such a disposition only remained under the Act (so as to be capable of being dealt with or pass under the Act and not under the personal law) if the transferee was a person who would have succeeded according to the provisions of the Act, if the transferee had died intestate. This was provided for by ss. 14 and 15 of the Act of 1869, which were (so far as material) as follows:

14. If any Taluqdar or grantee or his heirs or legatee hereafter transfer or bequeath the whole or any portion of his estate to another Taluqdar or grantee or to such a younger son as is referred to in section thirteen, clause two, or to a person who would have succeeded according to the provisions of this Act to the estate or to a portion thereof if the transferee or testator had died without having made the transfer and intestate, the transferee or legatee and his heirs and legatees shall have the same rights and powers in regard to the property, to which he or they may have become entitled under or by virtue of such transfer or bequest, and shall hold the same subject to the same conditions and to the same rules of succession as the transferor or testator.

15. If any Taluqdar or grantee or his heirs or legatee shall hereafter transfer or bequeath to any person not being a Taluqdar or grantee the whole or any portion of his estate, and such person would not have succeeded according to the provisions of this Act to the estate or to a portion thereof if the transferor or testator had died without having made the transfer and intestate, the transfer of and succession to the property so transferred or bequeathed shall be regulated by the rules which would

govern the transfer of, and succession to, such property if the transferee or legatee had bought the same from a person not being a Taluqdar or grantee.

It was held by the Judicial Commissioners of Oudh in *Rae Jagatpal Singh* v. *Thakurain Balraj Kunwar*[9] that any person mentioned in s. 22 as a possible heir might be said to be 'a person who would have succeeded according to the provisions of the Act to the estate.' On this construction of the Act, Nasir Ali Khan would have had power to dispose of the estate under s. 11 of the Act. But it was decided by the Privy Council in *Thakurain Balraj Kunwar* v. *Rae Jagatpal Singh*[10] that on the true construction of s. 14 of the Act of 1869, the expression 'a person who would have succeeded according to the provisions of the Act' is equivalent to 'the person or one of the persons to whom the estate would have descended according to the provisions of the special clause of s. 22 applicable to the particular case'; and does not include any person mentioned in s. 22 as a possible heir in a line of succession not applicable to the particular case. It was admitted in the Chief Court on appeal and before the Board that, as a result of this decision, the Oudh estate was taken out of the Oudh Estates Act, 1869, by the will of Sir Nawazish Ali Khan. He gave the estate by will to Nasir Ali Khan. Nasir Ali Khan was the brother of Sir Nawazish Ali Khan and Sir Nawazish Ali Khan left a son surviving him. Accordingly, Nasir Ali Khan was not the person to whom the estate would have descended if the testator had died intestate.

The position when the amending Act was passed was that under the will of Nasir Ali Khan there were three successive tenants for life with a purported power of appointment in the survivor which was invalid under the personal law, and subject thereto the estate was vested in Mohammad as the heir of Nasir Ali Khan. Then came the amending Act which by s. 7 substituted a new section for s. 14 of the Act of 1869, the effect of which was to restore the law to the state in which it was supposed to have been before the decision of the Judicial Committee in *Thakurain Balraj Kunwar's Case.*[11] By s. 21, s. 7 was made retrospective, but with this important reservation: 'nothing contained in the said section shall affect suits pending at the commencement of this Act, or shall be deemed to vest in or confer upon any person any right or title to any estate or any portion thereof, or any interest therein which is, at the commencement of this Act, vested in any other person, who would have been entitled to retain the same if this Act had not been passed, and the right or title of such other person shall not be affected by anything contained in the said section.' Assuming that

9 (1900) 3 OC 120.
10 (1904) LR 31 IA 132.
11 LR 31 IA 132.

the effect of the retrospective operation of s. 7 of the Act of 1910 was to bring the Oudh estate again within the purview of the Act of 1869, so that the estate would descend according to the rule of primogeniture and not under the personal law, it is clear that to impose on the interest of Mohammad a valid power of appointment the exercise of which would deprive him of his estate and which might be exercised by himself or others as future events might determine, would vest in other persons a right and title to the estate vested in him at the commencement of the Act of 1910. Their Lordships, therefore, are of opinion that the power of appointment contained in the Oudh will of Nasir Ali Khan was inoperative in relation to the Oudh estate.

As the power of appointment was invalid and ineffective as to both the Juliana estate and the Oudh estate, it is unnecessary to consider whether it could be exercised in favour of a person not born in the lifetime of the creator of the power.

The question then arises: to what relief is the respondent entitled? With regard to the Juliana estate the respondent claimed the whole estate for himself, relying on a custom which he failed to prove. Their Lordships agree with the courts in India that it would be wrong to grant to the respondent an order for possession on behalf of himself and his co-heirs. The suit was neither framed nor fought as a representative suit. The Chief Court, as already noted, granted the respondent a decree for possession of one-fifth of the estate, a decree which their Lordships think would be difficult to enforce, and which ought not to be enforced, because, as appears from the judgment of the Chief Court, the respondent has sold his share in the Juliana estate. Their Lordships, however, think that the position can be dealt with by a declaratory order under s. 42 of the Specific Relief Act.

With regard to the Oudh estate, the respondent contended before the Board that it passed under the Oudh Estates Act, 1869, to himself as the eldest son of his father under the rule of primogeniture established by the Act. It appears that in the appeal to the Chief Court the respondent contended that the estate passed under the personal law and not under the Act, the argument being directed against the view which had prevailed in the trial court that under the Act, though not under the personal law, the power of appointment could be exercised in favour of a person unborn in the life-time of the testator. Before this Board the appellant contended that the Oudh estate did not pass under the Act, but the argument advanced on his behalf failed to satisfy their Lordships that this was the effect of ss. 7 and 21. The question is of interest to the appellant only as bearing on the proper form of order and their Lordships do not feel called on to express a considered opinion as to the construction of the Act which would affect other parties. Their Lordships think that as between the parties to this appeal the respondent has shown his right to possession of the Oudh estate and an order can be made accordingly for possession of that estate, but such order will be without prejudice to any claim the heirs of Mohammad under the personal law, other than the respondent, may choose to make.

Their Lordships, therefore, will humbly advise His Majesty that the appeal of the appellant be dismissed, that the cross-appeal of the respondent so far as it relates to the Oudh estate be allowed, and that the decree passed by the Chief Court in appeal on 12 January 1943, be set aside and that the decree passed by the said court on its original side, dated 30 October 1937, also be set aside; that there be a declaration that the power of appointment given by the two wills of Nasir Ali Khan to Mohammad as the survivor of the successors appointed by those wills was invalid both in respect of the Juliana estate and in respect of the Oudh estate; and that the Juliana estate descended on the death of Mohammad to his heirs according to his personal law; that in respect of the Oudh estate there be an order that the appellant deliver up possession to the respondent, but that such order be without prejudice to any claim which the heirs of Mohammad under his personal law, other than the respondent, may choose to make to the Oudh estate.

[....]

30. Anjuman Ara v. Nawab Asif Kader
(1953) 2 Cal 109[12]

Life estates, if permissible—distinction between life-grant of corpus and of usufruct—strict proof of custom—scope of resulting trust—Indian Trusts Act (II of 1882), s. 83

In the Muhammadan law of gifts corpus must be distinguished from usufruct. Life-grants are not common in Muhammadan law; therefore the deed of gift must be carefully scrutinized as a whole.

I. If there is an absolute gift of the corpus, no questions arise and the gift will take effect.

II. If there is a limited grant,

(a) of the corpus, any restrictive conditions will be deemed to be void and the deed will take effect as an absolute grant;

(b) but if it is of the usufruct, then the grant is valid.

This case dealt with the Ithnā 'Asharī Shiite law. It was followed by *Shaik Mastan Bi* v. *Shaik Bikari Sahab* AIR 1958 Andhra Pradesh 751, which dealt with Hanafi law, *Outlines*, 248 seqq.

12 Chunder and P. N. Mookerjee, JJ.

Judgment [P. N. Mookerjee]

These two regular appeals arise out of a single suit for declaration of the plaintiff-respondent's title to certain G. P. notes of the face value of Rs 105,000 and the accrued interest thereon. In the suit there was a triangular contest between the plaintiff and the two sets of contesting defendants. In this contest the plaintiff has succeeded before the trial court and hence the present two appeals by the unsuccessful defendants.

The plaintiff who styles himself as the Nawab Bahadur of Murshidabad claims to be the sole heir of the last Nawab Nazim of Bengal, Bihar and Orissa and sets up his title to the disputed G. P. notes and interest on two counts, namely, (i) as the sole heir to the last Nawab Nazim, to whose estate, according to this contention, the said notes reverted, upon the death of the recorded holders thereof, namely, the seven daughters of the said Nawab Nazim, in whose names they were first acquired out of the Nawab Nazim's funds, but who had merely life-estates or life interests therein, and (ii) as the sole heir to the late Nawab Nazim and thus the head of the Nizamat, in which capacity—so runs this alternative contention—the plaintiff Nawab is entitled, by reason of a Nizamat family custom to usage, to the notes in question and the accumulated interest thereof 'in supersession of and in priority over' the claims of the heirs of the said seven daughters, even assuming that these ladies had absolute beneficial interest in the said notes, etc., which were, according to the common case of the plaintiff under both the above contentions, held by the Government, defendants nos 1 and 2, merely as trustees.

The suit was instituted in September, 1943 and therein the plaintiff Nawab impleaded as defendants the Province of Bengal, the Governor-General of India, and the heirs of the seven daughters of the late Nawab Nazim to whom reference has been made above. Of these defendants all except the heirs of the daughter Wahidunnessa alias Sahebzadi Begum appeared in the suit and filed written statements which were, broadly speaking, of three different types. The Governor-General and the Provincial Government, who were the first two defendants in the suit and who will be referred to at places in this judgment as the Government defendants, denied the plaintiff's allegation that they were trustees in respect of the suit properties, claimed the same as Government properties and also pleaded *inter alia* the bar of limitation to all adverse claims against them in respect of the said properties. (The Judge deals with the claims of defendants 3, 4, 7 series, and 9 series.)

There thus arose a triangular contest, the plaintiff's claim of title to the suit properties being resisted by the two sets of contesting defendants, namely, defendants nos 1 and 2, or, the Government defendants, and defendants nos 3 and 4 and 7 series and 9 series who all fought *inter se* on the question of title, the first or the former set, viz., the Government defendants, claiming the suit notes etc., as stated before, as Government properties and the other set, representing the several branches of four of the Nawab Nazim's seven daughters, who were the recorded holders of the same, claiming title in themselves and in the other heirs of the said seven ladies. In this contest, as already stated, the plaintiff succeeded before the trial court and hence the present appeals by the two sets of unsuccessful contesting defendants.

It is necessary now to narrate in some fuller detail the cases of the respective parties, and it will be convenient also to set out in the sequence the relevant findings of the learned Subordinate Judge and the points urged by the two sets of appellants in support of their respective appeals.

Upon certain simple allegations the plaint sets out two alternative cases in support of the plaintiff Nawab's claim of title to the disputed properties, viz., the suit notes and the accumulated interest. The primary allegation is that, from out of the Nizamat Deposit Fund, held by the Government or the first two defendants for the benefit of the last Nawab Nazim of Bengal, Bihar and Orissa and 'his heirs and the members of his family', a sum of Rs 20,000 was 'settled for life' upon each of his seven daughters, in the plaint, out of which sum again an amount of Rs 5000 was paid to each of the said seven daughters at their respective marriages and the balance, namely Rs 15,000 in the case of each of the said seven ladies, was invested in their names in G. P. notes which were held by the Government or the Government defendants as trustees for them during their respective lives and thereafter for the benefit of the late Nawab Nazim's heir and the plaintiff as such heir was entitled to the said G. P. Notes and the accumulated interest thereon, the respective funds, Rs 15,000 in each case, invested as aforesaid, having reverted to the late Nawab Nazim's estate upon the death of each of his said seven daughters. The alternative case pleaded anticipated a possible claim by the said ladies' heirs that the investments made were not merely for their respective lives but for their absolute benefit so that no question of any reversion or reverter could arise and the suit properties descended, upon the said ladies' death, to their respective natural heirs in absolute right, and the plaint proceeded to answer in advance this possible adverse claim or contention by asserting that, even to the absolute properties of the late Nawab Nazim's daughters, the plaintiff Nawab, as the head of the Nizamat family, was entitled 'in supersession of and priority over the claims' of the said daughters' heirs 'under customs and usages obtaining in the Nizamat family'.

The plaintiff's claim was opposed by the two sets of contesting defendants and, to his two alternative cases, made in the plaint, the Government defendants nos 1 and 2 pleaded *inter alia* by way of rejoincer that the Nizamat Deposit Fund was a part of the Government revenue and Government money, the said fund was not the property of the Nawab Nazim nor was it held by the Government for the said Nawab's benefit nor for the benefit of his heirs or the members of his family. They also denied the story of a trust, as set up in the plaint, and took further defences under the law of limitation and the proviso to s. 42 of the Specific Relief Act. It was, however, admitted by them, and here they supported the plaintiff, that the seven daughters of the late Nawab Nazim, named in the plaint, had mere life-interests in the disputed Government securities so that, upon their death, their heirs acquired no rights whatsoever in the said securities or their usufruct.

The daughters' heirs who resisted the plaintiff's claim denied *inter alia* the plaint allegation that the seven ladies had mere life-interests in the disputed securities and contested further the plaintiff's story of Nizamat family customs and usages upon which the latter's alternative case was sought to be founded in the plaint. The maintainability of the suit was also questioned by them in their written statements though they did not in terms refer to s. 42 of the Specific Relief Act. They, however, agreed with the plaintiff that the Government or the Government defendants were mere trustees in respect of the suit securities although the trust they pleaded was not the same as set up in the plaint. As a matter of fact, these contesting defendants differed from both the plaintiff and the Government defendants in that they asserted a title to the suit properties upon the footing that the seven daughters of the late Nawab Nazim, in whose names the disputed securities stood, and in whose names the disputed investments had been originally made, were absolute beneficial owners of the same, the Government merely holding them as trustees for them, that is, for the said seven ladies during their respective lives and for their respective heirs thereafter, so that upon the ladies' death their heirs became entitled to the suit properties.

The controversies between the parties, as above indicated, thus inevitably led to a triangular contest and the contentions which were urged by them in support of their respective cases before the learned Subordinate Judge—and in this court too—were manifold and gave rise to diverse complex problems. Indeed, the arguments embraced a wide field and, at times, not without justification, touched upon wider aspects of the points at issue than were ultimately found necessary for the purpose of this case. The learned Subordinate Judge found *inter alia*—

(a) that the suit was maintainable and not barred under s. 42 of the Specific Relief Act;

(b) that there was a trust in respect of the suit properties and the Government or the Government defendants were trustees in respect thereof and the suit was not barred by limitation;

(c) that the Nizamat Deposit Fund was not public money or Government money but was money held by the Government as trustees for the late Nawab Nazim and his heirs;

(d) that each of the seven daughters of the late Nawab Nazim got absolutely—the gift or grant in each case, though, *prima facie*, that is, purporting to be, and being also, as a mere matter of construction, only for the donee's or the grantee's life, was in law absolute—the sum of Rs [illegible]0,000 out of the said fund and the investments in the G. P. notes in suit were held by the Government as trustees for the said daughters so that, in the absence of the Nizamat family customs and usages, pleaded in the plaint, they would enure to the benefit of the said daughters' natural heirs; and

(e) that the said customs and usages had been proved, thus entitling the plaintiff Nawab to the suit properties in preference to the said natural heirs.

The learned Subordinate Judge also expressed the view that, if the gifts or grants to the late Nawab Nazim's seven daughters were for life only, upon the death of each of them the money invested on her account would 'go back to the fund from which it came', that is, to the Nizamat Deposit Fund, and it would return and be treated as a part of the parent fund, in which case also the plaintiff as the head of the Nizamat family and as the legal heir to the last Nawab Nazim of Bengal' would be entitled to it. [...]

F.A. No. 41 of 1946

We now turn first to the earlier appeal, F. A. No. 41 of 1946, where, as already stated, the ladies' heirs who contested the suit in the trial court are the appellants. From what we have said above, the contest between the parties in this appeal resolves itself into two broad questions, namely (1) whether, in or in respect of the G. P. notes in suit, the late Nawab Nazim's seven daughters had absolute interests or merely the right to enjoy the interest or usufruct thereof during their respective lives; and (2) whether the so-called overriding customs and usages, pleaded in the plaint, have been proved. The first of the above two questions demands careful consideration of the true construction of the document exhibit B4 which together with exhibits B2, B6 and B7 constitute the relevant grant and where, for our present purpose, all the relevant terms of the different gifts or grants, made to the Nawab Nazim's daughters are to be found, and a proper determination of the true nature of the said gifts and of the legal effect of the same; the second question requires a just assessment of the legal values of the instances of succession to females' properties, proved or sought to be proved by the contending parties in support of their respective cases, regarding the disputed usages and customs. On either of these two questions we are taking a view different from the learned Subordinate Judge's but, that notwithstanding, his final conclusion on this part of the case remains—as was also sufficiently indicated by him in his alternative finding—wholly unshaken and his decision of the issue of title in the plaintiff's favour definitely survives.

The appellants argue that exhibit B4, on its true construction, represents an absolute grant or gift to the seven ladies and their other two sisters, therein referred to as 'the daughters of the Nawab Nazim', Rs 20,000 each, the grant being contained in the opening paragraph, the succeeding para. 2 merely indicating the grantor's desire as to the mode or manner of enjoyment of the grant by the grantee and so not affecting its absolute character, or, at the most, imposing a condition or restriction upon the same, such condition or restriction being, in law, necessarily invalid, and the last part, namely, para. 3, just referring in that context to further or other provisions which might be thought or rendered necessary for the grantees and/or their heirs upon or by reason of the Nawab Nazim's death. Alternatively, it is also argued that, even assuming that, purely as a matter of construction of exhibit B4, the gifts or grants to the ladies limited to their lives, para. 2 being the really operative or effective part on the question of the grant, that would be tantamount to the conferment of life-estates on the said grantees in the G. P. notes in suit, and, life-estates being unknown in Mahommedan law, under which—so runs the further argument—such estates automatically enlarge into absolute estates, the interest of the several grantees in the respective G. P. notes was absolute in the eye of law. In either view, therefore,—so contend the appellants—the seven daughters of the late Nawab Nazim had full and absolute right, title and interest in the suit properties and, upon their death, the said properties devolved on their respective natural heirs, there being no contrary usage or custom in the Nizamat family to affect such devolution.

On the question of construction of exhibit B4 the learned Subordinate Judge rejected the appellants' contention—and his said finding is supported by all the appearing respondents—but he agreed with them in their view of the law, and accepted their alternative argument under this head, that the limited interests or life-estates, created by exhibit B4, became automatically enlarged into absolute interests or estates by the operation of the special rule of Mahommedan law. As, however, the learned Subordinate Judge found in favour of the plaintiff on the question of the Nizamat family custom or usage he eventually decreed the plaintiff's suit.

The propriety of the learned Judge's view that in Mahommedan law a life-grant is unknown and that it automatically enlarges into an absolute grant in favour of the grantee is assailed before us by the contesting respondents and both Mr Gupta and the learned Senior Government Pleader—whatever their differences in the other appeal, F. A. No. 42 of 1946—agree in resisting the appellants' argument that exhibit B4 contains absolute grants in favour of the grantees either as a matter of construction or as a matter of law.

[....]

...Of this para. 2 the language is clear enough to show that, in the several sums of Rs 15,000 each, the grantor's real intention was to give the grantees the benefit of the investment thereof in Government securities during their respective lives or, in other words, only the enjoyment of their usufruct till their respective deaths, and this notwithstanding the grant or payment—cash down—of the other part of the total gift (Rs 20,000), namely, Rs 5000 to each of them for her marriage expenses, and, notwithstanding, further, the common sanction for both the parts (Rs 5000 and Rs 15,000) making up the total grant (Rs 20,000), as recorded in the opening paragraph of the document. The language, used in para. 2, is inconsistent with the idea of any absolute grant of the several sums of Rs 15,000 each and it plainly discloses direct grants of the usufruct—and that alone and no more—to the several grantees during their respective lives. It also appears to us that the concluding paragraph of exhibit B4 which contemplated, upon the Nawab Nazim's demise, fresh consideration of the question of provision for his daughters and their children has no real bearing on the determination of the nature of the grant, as contained in the earlier part of the document, and if it has any such bearing that will rather support the limited character of the grants and will not in any way affect or alter the view we have taken above of the nature thereof. We are thus unable to persuade ourselves that, as a matter of construction, exhibit B4 conferred any absolute right on the grantees in or in respect of the several investments of Rs 15,000 each in Government securities or any absolute right in the said several sums of Rs 15,000 each, subject merely to the restriction on the manner or mode of enjoyment thereof that they were to be 'invested in Government securities in the names of trustees for "the benefit of the bride," that is, the grantee, "during her lifetime"'. We are also unable to find any ambiguity in the terms of exhibit B4 and we are not prepared to hold that the fact that life-grants or 'life-estates' are not so familiar in Mahommedan law [vide *Mst. Humeeda* v. *Mst. Budlun*,[13] *Abdul Wahid Khan* v. *Mst. Nuran Bibi*[14] and *Abdul Gafur*

13 (1872) 17 WR 525 (PC).
14 (1885) LR 12 IA 91.

and ors. v. *Nizamudin and ors.*[15] which we shall duly consider and explain in the course of this judgment] or the fact that, in the case of some of the grantees under exhibit B4, their heirs or creditors managed to get the invested amount or amounts (vide exhibits 2, 3 and 4) would affect the position or alter the conclusion that the grants, evidenced by that document (exhibit B4), in respect of the several sums of Rs 15,000 or the corresponding investments in Government securities were, as a matter of construction, limited to the lives of the respective grantees, or, would warrant the conclusion that such grants were absolute in character.

We hold, therefore, that exhibit B4, properly read, discloses only several life grants—or, more precisely, life-grants *simpliciter* and those again only in the usufruct—in favour of the Nawab Nazim's daughters in respect of the Government securities, referred to therein, and we reject the appellants' argument to the contrary on this question of construction.

This brings us to the other argument of the appellants on this part of their case, namely, the special argument, founded on the supposed rule of Mahommedan law that, in that system of jurisprudence, life-grants are unknown and they automatically enlarge into absolute grants. Mr Sarkar has contended that, even conceding that, as a pure matter of language or construction, the grants, referable to or found in exhibit B4, would not enure beyond the lives of the original grantees, namely, the daughters of the late Nawab Nazim, that construction must yield to the special rule of Mahommedan law, just above stated, so that, as a matter of law, exhibit B4 must be construed to have conferred upon the several grantees absolute interests in the several investments of Rs 15,000 each.

It thus becomes necessary to examine whether there exists in Mahommedan law any such rule as is contended for by the appellants' learned counsel. That question is one of some difficulty, and upon it judges have not always spoken with a uniform voice. There are, however, two decisions of the Judicial Committee which plainly negative the appellants' contention. In the first of these two decisions, *Amjad Khan* v. *Ashraf Khan*,[16] their Lordships rejected the theory of automatic enlargement and, in the other, *Sardar Nawazish Ali Khan* v. *Sardar Ali Raza Khan*,[17] not only was the earlier decision reaffirmed but the validity of life-grants in Mahommedan law was also, in general, affirmed and expressly recognized. In this latter case such grants were found to be quite sustainable in law where they could be held to operate—not upon the corpus but only upon the usufruct. In the face of these two authorities it is difficult to accept the appellants' submission and uphold the supposed

15 (1892) LR 9 IA 170.
16 (1929) LR 56 IA 213; [1929] AIR (PC) 149; 33 CWN 753.
17 (1948) LR 75 IA 62; [1948] AIR (PC) 134; 52 CWN 789.

rule of Mahommedan law on which reliance was placed on their behalf and to give effect to it in the present case, particularly when it is clear that the life-grants, with which we are here concerned, on their own language and as found above by us, relate exclusively and that, too, directly and specifically, to the benefits of the several investments in Government securities, that is, to the enjoyment of the usufruct thereof and are thus life-grants in the usufruct and not of the corpus.

If we are right in holding that the grants to the Nawab Nazim's daughters were, as a matter of construction, life-grants, that is, grants limited to their respective lives, the appellants are in the same predicament as the claimants before the Judicial Committee in *Amjad Khan* v. *Ashraf Khan*. If the grants were valid they ended with the grantees' lives and passed no interest to the appellants who are merely claimants under them: and, if invalid, they conferred no benefit on the grantees themselves and, necessarily, therefore, nothing on their heirs, the appellants before us, the latter claiming no higher title. In either view, therefore, the appellants can derive no assistance from exhibit B4 and can claim no interest in the suit properties. And, in our opinion, the decision of the Judicial Committee in *Amjad Khan's Case* is a direct authority against the theory of automatic enlargement, so much pressed by the appellants' learned counsel, and is a clear answer to his clients' claim and it definitely concludes them in the matter.

It is true that, in some of the earlier decisions in this country, e.g., the three Bombay cases in *Nizamudin* v. *Abdul Gafur*,[18] *Abdoola* v. *Mahomed*[19] and *Mir Akbar Ali* v. *Mir Abdool Ali*,[20] and possibly also the decision of this court, in *Mahomed Shah* v. *Official Trustee of Bengal*,[21] the view was taken that in Mahommedan law the grantee under a life-grant got an absolute estate, but this paradox was effectively resolved and the underlying theory exploded by the Privy Council in *Amjad Khan's Case*. We are unable to hold that in this last mentioned authority the question of automatic enlargement of life-grants in Mahommedan law was left open by the Judicial Committee. If that were so, the appeal before their Lordships could not have been decided. What was left open was the other question, namely, whether life-grants were valid in Mahommedan law, and the case was decided upon the view that, if the life-grant to Musammat Waziran was valid, it ended with the lady's death, and left nothing for the appellants who were claiming under her, and, if it was invalid, it conferred no benefit on the grantee herself and, necessarily, therefore, nothing on the appellants who were no more than claimants under

[18] (1888) ILR 13 Bom 264.
[19] (1905) 7 Bom LR 306.
[20] (1907) 9 Bom. LR 295.
[21] (1909) ILR 36 Cal 431.

her. If the theory of automatic enlargement had not been rejected by the Judicial Committee this latter conclusion would not have been made and, if the earlier decisions, cited above, were right, *Amjad Khan's Case* would have been quite differently decided. Those earlier decisions must, therefore, be deemed to have been overruled by the Privy Council in *Amjad Khan's Case* and they can no longer be held to be good law in this country and the appellants' argument, based on them, cannot be accepted.

On the effect of the decision of the Judicial Committee in *Amjad Khan's Case* our attention was drawn to the views of Ragnekar, J., in the two Bombay cases in *Rasoolbibi* v. *Usuf Ajam*[22] and in *Bai Saroobai* v. *Hussein Somji*,[23] but with all respect to the learned Judge we are unable to hold that, in *Amjad Ali's Case*, the Privy Council did not reject the theory of automatic enlargement of Mahommedan life-grants into absolute grants and did not overrule the earlier decisions in this country upholding the validity of that theory. For reasons already given, we would much prefer the views of the other learned Judges (Beaumont, C. J., as he then was, and Divatia, J.) who decided the said two Bombay cases and, in our opinion, as already stated, the authority of those earlier decisions can no longer be invoked to support the appellants' contention on this part of the case.

We are also of the view that the life-grants in the present case were perfectly valid in law. As we have said above, those grants related exclusively and specifically to the usufruct of the several investments in Government securities. They were thus—and this also we have already held-life grants in the 'usufruct' only and not grants of the 'corpus'. Such life—grants are nowhere forbidden in Mahommedan law. On the other hand the validity of such grants has been expressly upheld by the Judicial Committee in *Nawazish Ali Khan's Case* and the authority of this decision sufficiently protects the life-grants in the present case.

It seems to us further that in *Nawazish Ali Khan's Case*[24] the Judicial Committee clearly approved the view of Wazir Hasan, A. J. C, in *Amjad Khan* v. *Ashraf Khan*,[25] that life-grants simpliciter, that is, where they are not in the form of gifts subject to conditions—were valid in Mahommedan law and were supportable on the theory that they operated on the 'usufruct' and not on the 'corpus'. This appears to be sufficiently indicated when we find the following passage at p. 78 of the Report, namely—

Sir Wazir Hasan in his judgment examined the appropriate texts and all the relevant decisions of the Privy Council. He pointed out the distinction in Muslim law

22 (1933) ILR 57 Bom 737; [1933] AIR (Bom) 324.
23 (1936) 38 Bom LR 903 (FB); [1936] AfR (Bom 330 (FB).
24 *Supra* (75 IA 62).
25 (1925) AIR (Oudh) 568; p. 365, case I.

between the corpus and the usufruct, between the thing itself and the use of the things.

And it receives further confirmation when, lower down, their Lordships, while holding that there is no difference between the several schools of Muslim law in their fundamental 'conception of property and ownership' observed that 'limited interests have long been recognized under Shia law' and affirmed the validity of a grant quoted from Baillie in these terms: I have bestowed on thee this mansion…or thy life or my life or for a fixed period.

(Baillie, II, 226) [*vide* p. 79 of the Report] and also cited with approval the decision of Jenkins, C. J. and Heaton, J., in *Banoo Begum* v. *Mir Abed Ali*[26] where 'life estates' in Shia law were expressly recognized. The above discussion and particularly the form of the illustration, quoted from Baillie and approved by their Lordships in *Nawazish Ali Khan's Case*[27] at p. 79 of the Report, sufficiently shows that, according to the Judicial Committee, life-grants simpliciter were not invalid in Mahommedan law and it was only when such a grant was sought to be created by the device of a gift subject to a condition that the life-estate failed as such and got enlarged into an absolute estate, the law invalidating by its own force the attached condition.

To appreciate the true legal position it is necessary to remember that 'life-estate', that is, life-grant of a property which is usually called a life-estate is not regarded in Mahommedan law as an estate or interest in the corpus. That law recognizes only one kind of estate, namely, full ownership in the corpus. The corpus means the 'article', 'the thing', or 'the substance', It is distinct from the usufruct which means the 'use' of the 'article' or the produce of 'the thing'. A gift of the corpus connotes and comprehends the entire bundle of rights in 'the thing' or 'the substance', in other words, full rights over the 'article' or complete dominion over 'the substance'. The test is this complete dominion over 'the substance'. That dominion is absolute and indivisible. It permits no slicing and tolerates no obstacle or restriction. Grant of full dominion over the corpus may, however, be accompanied by a gift of the use or usufruct to another, that is, a condition or limitation as regards the usufruct, and both the grant and the condition will be valid. Limited interests—short of complete ownership—may also be created but not in the form of a gift of the corpus subject to a condition affecting the same—'the thing' or 'the substance'. Any such interest—whether limited 'in point of quality or in point of duration'—is, in Mahommedan law, different from the corpus and takes effect out of the usufruct.

26 (1907) ILR 32 Bom 172.
27 *Supra*, note 17.

In the Mahommedan law, therefore, as already stated, there is a clear distinction between the corpus or 'the substance' and the usufruct. Over the corpus that law recognizes only absolute, complete and indivisible ownership and there it countenances no detraction or limitation. In the usufruct however, limited interests can be created and the limitation may well be in point of time or duration, e.g. for life or for a fixed period. Limited interests are thus recognized in Mahommedan law—though not in the corpus but only in the usufruct—and where the grant is of a limited character—but not a grant of the corpus subject to condition—it takes effect out of the usufruct and is not regarded as a grant of the corpus at all but only as a grant of or in the usufruct. A grant of the corpus must be absolute and any condition or restriction derogatory to the grant and affecting the corpus must be disregarded and if a limited grant is sought to be made by such a device it leads to the same result, namely, that the condition or restriction is swept aside and the grant takes effect as an absolute grant, that being the only valid grant which can be made of the corpus. A grant of the corpus may, however, be validly made, accompanied by conditions or restrictions, relating to the usufruct, and it takes effect subject to those conditions: (vide *Nawab Umjad Ally Khan* v. *Mussammat Mohumdee Begum*,[28] which, though a Shia case, states the general Mahommedan law on the point, as explained in *Mohammad Abdul Ghani* v. *Fakhr Jahan Begum*,[29] a case under the Sunni or the Hanafi law. And as already said a limited grant—not in the form of a gift subject to a condition affecting 'the thing' as the substance as distinguished from its use or usufruct—would be valid and would take effect out of the usufruct.

The above principles are sufficiently recognized in *Nawazish Ali Khan's Case*,[30] and there is enough indication in that judgment that the whole discussion of this branch of the law proceeds on that basis, and they explain their Lordships' final conclusion on this part of the case, appearing at p. 351, above, that—

> In dealing with a gift under Muslim law, the first duty of the court is to construe the gift. If it is a gift of the corpus then any condition which derogates from absolute dominion over the subject of the gift will be rejected as repugnant; but if upon construction the gift is held to be one of a limited interest the gift can take effect out of the usufruct, leaving the ownership of the corpus unaffected except to the extent to which its enjoyment is postponed for the duration of the limited interest.

The passage quoted clearly supports the view we have taken above of the effect of this decision of the Judicial Committee and we hold, therefore,

28 (1867) II MIA 517.
29 (1922) LR 49 IA 195, 203.
30 *Supra*, note 17.

that the question of validity of life-grants, with which we are here concerned, must be answered in the affirmative.

We have practically held that, on the question of life-grants in Mahommedan law and their legal effect, the two decisions of the Privy Council, cited above, are settled law. But even so, any discussion of that subject would be incomplete without a reference to the two earlier decisions in this country, reported in *Amjad Khan* v. *Ashraf Khan*,[31] and *Achiruddin Ahmed* v. *Sakina Bewa*.[32] The first of the above two cases which went up on appeal to the Privy Council in *Amjad Khan's Case* has already been alluded to by us in the course of our discussion of the other Privy Council case of *Nawazish Ali Khan's Case*, and it has been pointed out that, in this latter case, the view of Wazir Hasan, A. J. C., in the Oudh case cited, on the validity and effect of life grants in Mahommedan law, was approvingly referred to by their Lordships of the Judicial Committee. The judgment of the other learned Judge (Ashworth, A. J. C.) who differed from his colleague on the question of law (including the question of construction of the deed there under consideration) does not appear to have found favour with the Privy Council either in *Amjad Khan's Case* or in *Nawazish Ali Khan's Case*[33] and must, therefore, be rejected. In his discussion of the law Sir Wazir Hasan reviewed all the relevant texts and came to the conclusion that a life-grant—not in the form of a gift: subject to a condition—was valid in Mahommedan law. The same view was held by this court in the case of *Achiruddin Ahmed* v. *Sakina Bewa*, above cited, where Chakravartti J., (as he then was), after an elaborate discussion of the texts from various authorities and reference apparently to Sir Wazir Hasan's judgment in the Oudh case, referred to above with evident approval (vide 50 C.W.N. at p. 73), reached a similar conclusion and, although it may be doubted whether the learned Judge was right in his reading of the earlier decision of this court in *Mahomed Shah* v. *Official Trustee of Bengal*[34] there can be no question that he took the correct view on the question of validity of life-grants in Mahomedan law. As we agree with the two learned Judges (Sir Wazir Hasan and Chakravartti JJ.,) In their interpretation of the relevant texts and as the same has apparently been approved by the Judicial Committee in *Nawazish Ali Khan's Case* we would end our discussion on this general question of Mahommedan law with a brief examination of the Privy Council cases, relied on by Mr Sarkar as supporting the appellants' contention.

31 *Supra*, note 16, p. 365.
32 (1945) 50 CWN 59.
33 *Supra*, note 17.
34 *Supra*, note 21.

The three Privy Council cases, to which our attention was particularly drawn by Mr Sarkar, and which are often cited as authorities against the validity of life-grants, or life estates, as they are usually called in Mahommedan law, are *Musammat Humeeda* v. *Mussamat Budlun*, *Abdul Wahid* v. *Mussammat Nuran Bibi and Abdul Gafur v. Nizamudin*,[35] already cited in an earlier part of this judgment. In our opinion, however, none of these cases supports the extreme proposition, canvassed by the appellants before us, or repudiates the view we have taken above of the nature and effect of life-grants in Mahommedan law. Nowhere in the cases cited has it been held that life-grants are necessarily invalid in Mahommedan law or that such grants are wholly unknown in that system of jurisprudence and they automatically enlarge into absolute grants. They merely point out that such grants are not very familiar amongst Mahommedans and in interpreting Mahommedan grants this aspect ought to be borne in mind so that, in cases of ambiguity in the matter of construction, courts should lean in favour of the view that absolute interest was intended to be conferred upon the grantee. The guarded language, employed in the Weekly Reporter case, suggests this, and this interpretation is amply borne out by the actual decision in that case and in the other two which quoted the same with approval and applied it to aid the construction of the two deeds, a 'compromise' in one case and a *wakfnāma* (will) in the other. That this is the true position appears plain when we examine the three cases in their proper perspective.

In *Mussamat Humeeda's Case* their Lordships were construing an arrangement between a Mahommedan lady and her son and, in the course of their judgment, they observed as follows:

> Upon what grounds then ought it to be held that what the son gave up, he gave up for only the life of his mother, retaining the legal reversion in himself? The creation of such a life-estate does not seem to be consistent with Mahommedan usage.

That, by their above observations, their Lordships did not mean to lay down that life-estates were absolutely unknown or forbidden or invalid in Mahommedan law becomes quite evident when we turn to the sentence next succeeding, namely, 'and there ought to be very clear proof of so unusual a transaction.' The line, just quoted, would have been wholly irrelevant—and unnecessary too—if no life-estates were, in their Lordships' opinion, at all permissible in the Mahommedan system of jurisprudence. We get further confirmation of this view when, lower down, we find the Board speaking of life-estates as 'transactions so improbable amongst Mahommedans' and of the evidence in the case as 'too weak to prove (such) a transaction', and,

35 *Supra,* notes 13–15.

in our opinion, no general argument of the invalidity of life-grants in Mahommedan law can be founded on their Lordships' pronouncement in *Humeeda's Case*.[36] That case, as we have already said, only enjoins that in construing Mahommedan deeds due weight should be given to the unfamiliarity of such transactions amongst Mahommedans.

The case of *Abdul Wahid*[37] referred with approval to the above observations in *Mst Humeeda's Case* and applied the principle of that decision to construe with its aid a Mahommedan compromise upon the broad view that the creation of a life-estate was an unusual transaction amongst the members of that community, it being not apparently consistent with their usage and so 'there ought to be clear proof' of such a transaction. Not the slightest departure was made from the law, as laid down in Mst *Humeeda's Case*, but the same was only fully accepted and applied to a similar situation, and it seems to us that *Abdul Wahid's Case* merely emphasized once again the unusual nature of the transaction and the need of very clear proof of it but did not negative its validity absolutely and under all circumstances.

There remains now the decision, reported in *Abdul Gafur and others* v. *Nizamudin and others*.[38] This case also hardly aids the appellants. The *wakfnama* here purported to settle certain properties on the executants' wives and children, etc., subject to an express limitation that none of them would have the power to alienate the said properties by sale, gift or mortgage. Clearly, therefore, it purported to make gifts subject to conditions or limitations in the shape of restraints against alienation. Such conditions or limitations were admittedly void in Mahommedan law and it was, accordingly, so held by their Lordships. Before their Lordships, however, an argument appears to have been made that the deed ought to be read as creating, in substance, successive life-estates or a series of life-rents, and, while dealing with that argument, their Lordships indicated the true approach in the matter of construction of Mahommedan deeds by referring to Mst *Humeeda's Case* and thereby drawing attention to the unusual nature of such transactions amongst Mahommedans and, the context and the reference to *Humeeda's Case* make it plain that their Lordships were not adding anything to the exposition of the law, as made by that earlier pronouncement, or laying down any new or different principle.

It is clear also from what has been stated above that *Abdul Gafur's Case*[39] was not a case of life-estate simpliciter but was a case of gifts subject to

36 *Supra,* note 13.
37 *Supra,* note 14
38 *Supra,* note 15.
39 *Supra* loc. cit.

conditions or limitations which were admittedly void in Mahommedan law. That was how the case was treated by their Lordships of the Judicial Committee at p. 178 of the Report where they made the following significant observations, namely:

Even if Tahirabibi had expressly consented to accept the will, she would not have been the owner of a life-estate, but a full-owner, with a prohibition against alienation, which, being void in law, could not affect either herself or her creditors.

The passage quoted also shows that their Lordships were making a distinction between the grant of a life-estate as such and a gift subject to a condition and were certainly not pronouncing against the validity of the former. Substantially similar was the position in *Abdul Wahid's Case*, too, where apart from the fact, already stated, that the disputed compromise was held to be similar to the one in Mst *Humeeda's Case* and to confer upon the grantee not a limited estate for life but an absolute estate on similar principles of construction, there was, strictly speaking, no life-grant simpliciter but a grant subject to an express condition, clearly affecting the corpus. In such circumstances, neither of the above two Privy Council decisions can be regarded as any authority against the validity of life-grants in Mahommedan law, particularly when *Humeeda's Case*; which apparently recognized the possibility of such grants, was approvingly cited by their Lordships in both the above cases and was, as a matter of fact, relied on by them as the law on the subject.

Mr Sarkar also referred in passing to two other decisions of the Judicial Committee, both reported in LR 8 IA, one at p. 25 and the other at p. 117. The first case *Haji Mahommed Faiz Ahmed Khan* v. *Haji Ghulam Ahmed Khan*,[40] turned on the construction of an instrument in which the executant, after making an absolute gift of certain villages in favour of his sister-in-law, went on to add the following:

I do declare and record that the aforesaid sister-in-law may manage the said villages for herself and apply their income to meet her necessary expenses and to pay the Government revenue.

On the strength of the above clause it was contended before the Privy Council that the transaction was not a gift, not even a life-grant, but an *ariat* or loan. This was rejected by their Lordships who, after referring to several other parts of the instrument in question and various features of the disputed transaction, held that the clause quoted was 'descriptive of the motive or consideration of the gift' and was ineffectual to control the operation of

40 (1881) LR 8 IA 25.

technical words of gift. There is nothing in this judgment against the validity of life-grants in Mahommedan law and, indeed, no such question appears to have been raised before their Lordships and, as already stated, there was no contention that the transaction represented a 'gift for life'. We may add also that, on our construction of exhibit B4, there is, in the present case, no absolute gift, followed by a qualifying or 'descriptive' clause, and para. 2 of that document (exhibit B4) contains the grant and is not a subsidiary clause and, accordingly, this case of *Haji Mahammed Faiz Ahmed Khan*[41] cannot aid the appellants on the question of construction either. In the other case *Prince Suleman Kadr* v. *Darab Ali Khan*[42] the question of validity of life-grants in Mahommedan law was expressly left open. Possibly, also this case, too, was the case of a gift subject to a condition and, accordingly, the condition appeared to their Lordships to be void. No other conclusion seems possible as, the parties in the case apparently belonging to the Shia school, it is difficult to believe that their Lordships would have pronounced a life-grant invalid. This disposes of all the cases cited on behalf of the appellants, in support of their present contention.

In the light of what we have stated so far, the true approach when a Mahommedan grant falls for consideration is first to construe the deed as a whole, bearing in mind that life-grants are not very familiar in Mahommedan law. If, upon such construction, the grant is held to be an absolute grant, no further question arises. If, however, the grant is found to be a limited grant, the direct or the immediate subject-matter of the gift has to be ascertained. If it is the corpus, as explained above, any restrictive condition affecting the same will be invalid and the grant will have effect as an absolute grant. If, on the other hand, the direct or the immediate subject-matter of the grant be the limited interest and not the corpus, the grant takes effect out of the usufruct as a valid limited grant. In this view of the matter we hold that the disputed life-grants in the present case were valid as such and did not enlarge into any absolute grant in favour of the grantees.

Pertinently also we may point out that, amongst Shias in this country, life-grants have long been recognized as valid, *Banoo Begum* v. *Mir Abed Ali*,[43] cited with approval by the Privy Council in *Nawazish Ali Khan's Case*.[44] It is undisputed, that the late Nawab Nazim or, for the matter of that, the Nizamat family—and all his descendants who are parties to the present suit—professed and profess the Shia faith, and so no difficulty arises in

41 Ibid.
42 (1881) LR 8 IA 117.
43 Supra, *note 26.*
44 Supra, *note 17.*

giving effect to the disputed grants which we have found to be limited to the lives of the respective grantees as such limited or life-grants. In this view, too, the appellants' alternative argument must fail. We, accordingly, reject the same.

It follows then that the learned Subordinate Judge's ultimate finding on this point in the appellants' favour is incorrect. It is, accordingly, reversed, the necessary consequence being that the appellants' claim of title to the suit properties—and with it the main purpose of this appeal—fails.

The above discussion really makes it unnecessary for us to consider the question of family usage or custom, alternatively relied on by the plaintiff on this part of the case. As, however, that question has been argued before us in great detail by the contesting parties, we shall record our views upon the same. Upon this point, too, we are unable to agree with the learned Subordinate Judge notwithstanding Mr Gupta's very elaborate arguments in support of the same. We find no evidence, at any rate no reliable evidence, of any such custom or usage in the matter of succession to properties of daughters of the Nizamat family. The instances, cited on the plaintiff's behalf, all relate to properties of Begums of the Nizamat family, that is, of females, married into the Nizamat household, and not of daughters of the said family who, as such daughters, particularly when they are married daughters, as in the case now before us, occupy quite a different position in relation to the same. It has not been proved that, to the properties of any deceased daughter, much less a deceased married daughter of the Nizamat family as such, the Nawab succeeded in preference to the lady's natural heirs. Rather, the evidence on record shows that at least in the case of some of the Nawab's daughters their properties passed upon their death to their heir or devises under will or even to their creditors. Mr Gupta's argument that that evidence is confined to cases of testate succession and is thus not opposed to the custom, pleaded in the plaint, which, according to him, refers only to cases of intestate succession, these alone being relevant in the present dispute between the parties, though plausible as an explanation and certainly ingenious, can hardly be accepted in the circumstances of this case. In any event, even upon that argument, the plaintiff's position would be no better. There is practically nothing in the present records pointing to the Nawab's succession to properties left by a daughter of the Nizamat family, and, in the absence of any sufficient evidence in that behalf, a finding in the plaintiff's favour on this question of custom would not be justified. This is apart from the other objection—not wholly without force—that, of this limited custom, so strongly relied on by Mr Gupta in this appeal, there is no proper or sufficient pleading in the plaintiff's plaint In support of his finding that the custom has been proved, the learned Subordinate Judge has referred to the judgment of this court in the case of *Booa Russoolee* v. *Nowab Nazim of Bengal*; and to a passage from the appellate judgment of the Judicial Committee in that very case, *Oomrao Begum* v. *Nawab Nazim of Bengal*, which he has quoted and used as an authoritative judicial recognition of such custom—of its validity and application as well—and, indeed, his decision on this point is largely founded upon the same and certain other passages, culled from the proceedings of the commissioners, appointed under the Nawab Nazim's Debts Act, which we shall presently examine.

The *Weekly Reporter* case—of which the High Court judgment is in *Booa Russoolee* v. *The Nawab Nazim of Bengal*[45] and the Privy Council's in *Oomrao Begum* v. *Nawab Nazim of Bengal*[46]—arose out of certain disputes between the then Nawab Nazim of Bengal who was the plaintiff there and the widows, mother and daughters of one Syed Mehdi Ally Khan who were impleaded by him as defendants. Those disputes centred upon the title to a certain zemindari, alleged to have been left by one Amirunnessa alias Doolhin Begum, the widow of Nawab Ali Jah, deceased, a grand-uncle of the plaintiff and who preceded him as Nawab Nazim', vide *Oomrao Begum* v. *Nawab Nazim of Bengal*.[47] In support of his claim to the said zemindari the plaintiff Nawab there pleaded *inter alia* and relied upon a family custom entitling him to succeed to the Begum's properties upon the latter's death in preference to their natural heirs and also upon a *ladavinama* or deed of disclaimer, executed in his favour by the defendants' predecessor Mehdi Ally Khan and his wife Azizunnessa, defendant no. 4 in the suit. Both courts in this country accepted the *ladavinama* as a genuine document but, while the learned trial judge held:

> That in consequence of it the defendants as heirs of Mehdi Ally could not claim a right to succeed to the (suit) property and consequently that it was unnecessary to come to any finding as to the custom set up by the Nawab under which he claimed the right to succeed to the property of the Begum

The High Court, on appeal, having found for the Nawab upon the question of the custom, treating the *ladavinama* as strong evidence in support of it, apparently considered it unnecessary to come to any definite decision as to the effect of the *ladavinama*. Upon further appeal, the Privy Council held that the *ladavee* or *ladavinama* was founded upon a valuable consideration and that the defendants were bound by it, their Lordships observing in the

45 (1869) 11 WR 382.
46 (1875) 24 WR 28.
47 (1875) 24 WR 28, 29 PC.

course of their judgment that the *ladavinama* was binding upon the heirs of Mehdi Ally and precluded them from setting up a claim to the property, in any view of the case Mehdi Ally and his heirs could not assert any title to the property without setting aside the *ladavinama*.

Their Lordships also made it clear that, having regard to their opinion as to the legal effect of the *ladavinama*, it was not necessary to decide whether, upon the death of the Begum, her property went over to the Nizamat according to usage, as stated in the *ladavinama*.

It further appears from the Report that the passage, quoted by the learned Subordinate Judge from 24 WR page 29, namely, the plaintiff (the Nawab Nazim of Bengal, Bihar and Orissa), according to the long established custom of his family, recognized by the Government of India on various previous occasions of the demise of Begums of his house succeeded as her heir to the said zemindari and treated by him as a part of the Privy Council decision, occurs in the recital portion of their Lordships' judgment where the plaintiff's case is stated and an extract from the plaint is given and forms no part of their decision or findings on any issue between the parties.

The above discussion makes it plain that neither the High Court decision nor the Privy Council judgment, to which reference has been made above, can be of any real assistance to the present plaintiff. Clearly, the question of the family custom was left open by the Judicial Committee and the passage from the Report on which the learned Subordinate Judge has relied upon a misconception that it was a part of their decision was not really so. To this passage the learned Subordinate Judge has attributed a far greater sanctity than it really deserves and this misplaced emphasis has led him to an obvious error. The passage quoted may, at the most, be used by the plaintiff as an ancient assertion, made about a century back, that, according to the long established custom of his family, the Nawab Nazim was entitled to the properties of deceased Begums of his house but, whatever effect be given to this assertion, it cannot go far enough to assist the plaintiff-respondent in his claim of title to the disputed properties. We have made it clear in an earlier part of this judgment that, in relation to the Nizamat family, a daughter as such—and the more so when she is a married daughter—stands in an essentially different position from a Begum of the house, and a Nizamat family custom which only entitles the Nawab to succeed to the Begum's properties would not necessarily be available to him for claiming title to the properties of a deceased daughter—far less of a deceased married daughter—of the Nizamat family as such.

[. . .]

◊ UPDATE ◊

1. *Life interests*

The validity of life interests of various kinds under the Shia school of Muslim law, examined in the old Privy Council ruling in *Umjad Ally* [Case 28] and the post-independence Indian decisions in *Nawazish Ali* and *Anjuman Ara* [Cases 29 and 30], is now well established in all parts of the subcontinent. These rulings have been followed also in some later cases decided under the Hanafi law.

Some recent Indian cases on life interests are *Beepathumma* v. *Rowther* AIR 1977 Ker 54, *Hayara* v. *Sait* AIR 1977 Mad 374 and *Jameela* v. *Ismail* AIR 1979 Mad 193.

2. *Gift to unborn child*

As to the validity of gifts in favour of unborn children to take effect at the expiry of a life interest, the late Justice M. Hidayatullah has strongly pleaded in favour of the same.[48]

3. *Family settlements*

The controversy whether relinquishment of *spes successionis* for a consideration as part of a family settlement would be valid and enforceable, on which various High Courts had expressed different opinions, was set at rest in India by the Supreme Court in favour of its legal validity—*Ghulam Abbas* v. *Qayyum Ali* AIR 1973 SC 554. Justice MH Beg observed:

> It may be mentioned here that Muslim jurisprudence, where theology and moral concepts are found sometimes mingled with secular utilitarian legal principles, contains a very elaborate theory of acts which are good (because they proceed from '*husn*'), those which are bad (because they exhibit '*qubh*'), and those which are neutral per se. It classifies them according to varying degrees of approval or disapproval attached to them.... The renunciation of a supposed right, based upon an expectancy, could not, by any test found there, be considered 'prohibited'. The binding force in future of such a renunciation would, even according to strict Muslim jurisprudence, depend upon the attendant circumstances and the whole course of conduct of which it forms a part. In other words, the principle of an equitable estoppel, far from being opposed to any principle of Muslim law, will be found, on investigation, to be completely in consonance with it.[49]

48 See his article 'Muslim Law: A Suggested Reform' in my book *Family Law and Social Change* [festschrift for Asaf A. A. Fyzee NM Tripathi], Bombay 1975, pp. 17–23

49 I have dissented from Justice Beg's ruling. My comments may be seen in the *Annual Survey of Indian Law*, IX: 1973 (ILI), pp. 212–14.

XIII. Wakfs

31. Vidya Varuthi v. Balusami Ayyar
(1921) 48 IA 302

Religious endowments, Hindu and Muslim—math and wakf—gift to idol, Muslim institution of wakf—compared with English 'trust'—managers of such endowments, not 'trustees'

The endowments of a Hindu *math* are not 'conveyed in trust,' nor is the head of the *math* a 'trustee' with regard to them, save as to specific property proved to have been vested in him for a specific object.

Consequently, art. 134 of Sch. I. of the Indian Limitation Act, 1908, which contains the expressions above quoted, does not apply where the head of a *math* has granted a permanent lease of part of its property not proved to be vested in him subject to a specific trust.

Semble, the same rule applies to the endowments of Muhammadan religious institutions, and to alienations by *sajjādanashīn* or *mutawallī*.

The observations of Ameer Ali in this case on the nature of religious endowments in Hindu and Muhammadan law, as distinct from a trust in English law, and on the nature of a *khānqāh* and *sajjādanashīn*, are often cited (pp. 311–15, 319, 322). *Tyabji*, 541 seqq., points out how the headnote in *Muhammad Rustam Ali* v. *Mushtaq Husain* (1920) 47 IA 224 is wrong and misleading. See also *Outlines*, 270 seqq., 274.

Appeal (No. 48 of 1919) from a judgment and decree (19 October 1916) of the High Court Madras reversing a decree of the temporary Subordinate Judge of Ramnad.

The suit was instituted in 1913 by the present respondents for possession of land in Madura forming part of the endowments of a *math* situated in Mysore State. The defendants were the present appellant, the head of the *math* (referred to as the *pandara sannadhi* or *matathipathi*), certain lessees from him, who were in possession, and others. The plaintiffs claimed under a permanent lease granted to them in 1891 by a former head of the *math*. They also claimed that they had acquired a good title under the

Indian Limitation Act; they relied on arts. 134 and 144 of the Schedule and s. 28.[1]

Both courts in India held that the lease of 1891 was not made for necessity, and that the land in suit was part of the general endowment of the *math*, not being subject to any specific trust. The Subordinate Judge dismissed the suit. He held that the head of the *math* was not a 'trustee' of its endowed property, and that consequently art. 134 of Sch. I did not apply. He was also of opinion that there had not been adverse possession so as to bring art. 144 into operation. The High Court allowed an appeal. A decree was made declaring that the first plaintiff was a permanent lessee of the land in suit and for possession and mesne profits. The judgment was delivered by Burn J. (Sudasiva Ayyar, J. agreeing). The learned judge was of opinion that expressions in the judgment of the Board in *Ram Parkash Das* v. *Anand Das*[2] constrained the court to hold that the head of the *math* was a trustee of the properties, and that consequently art. 134 applied. The appeal to the High Court is reported at ILR 40 Mad. 745.

In appeal the Primary Council reversed the decree of the High Court and restored the subordinate court's order.

Judgment [Syed Ameer Ali][3]

[....]

The suit that has given rise to this appeal relates to certain lands lying in the town of Madura in the Madras Presidency which admittedly belong to an old *math* situated within the Mysore State. The origin, development, and *raison d'etre* of these *maths* have been discussed in a number of cases decided in the Madras High Court to some of which their Lordships propose to refer in the course of this judgment. In their general characteristics they are almost identical with similar institutions in Northern India and in the Bombay Presidency. The heads of these foundations bear different designations in respect of the rights and incidents attached to the office; the difference arises from the customs and usages of each institution. The superior of this particular *math* has been called in these proceedings *matathipathi* and sometimes *pandara sannadhi*, which their Lordships

[1] Indian Limitation Act, 1908, Sch. I., art. 134, provides that for a suit to 'recover possession of immovable property conveyed or bequeathed in trust or mortgaged and afterwards transferred by the trustee or mortgagee for a valuable consideration', the period of limitation shall be 12 years from 'the date of the transfer'. By s. 28: 'At the determination of the period hereby limited to any person for instituting a suit for possession of any property, his right to such property shall be extinguished.'

[2] (1916) LR 43 IA 73, 76, 90.

[3] With Buckmaster, Dunedin & Shaw, JJ.

understand connote the same idea of headship. At the time this action was brought, the 26th defendant held the office of *matathipathi*. He has since died and the present appellant is the head of the institution. In 1891 one Srinivasa was the *matathipathi* and he on March 17 of that year granted to the 2nd plaintiff, a near relative, a permanent lease of the lands in suit, on a small quit rent of Rs 24 a year. Shortly after the grant of the lease Srinivasa died, and was succeeded by one Samudra, who held the office until 1906. On his death the now deceased defendant No. 26 became the head. In 1902 the 2nd plaintiff sub-leased the lands to the 1st and 2nd defendants for a period of ten years.

Since 1905 the *math* has been under the management of the Mysore State under a power of attorney, executed at first by the *matathipathi* Samudra and afterwards by his successor, in favour of the Dewan and his successors in office. About the same time the 2nd plaintiff conjointly with his son (the 3rd plaintiff) assigned their right and interest in the lands in suit to the 1st plaintiff. It is in evidence and, so far as appears from the judgments of the two courts in India, does not appear to be contradicted, that it was only in 1908 that the representative of the Dewan acting under the power granted by the *matathipathi* became aware of the transaction of 1891 under which the plaintiffs claim title. The sublease created in 1902 by the 2nd plaintiff in favour of the 1st and 2nd defendants was to have expired in 1912. But before its expiry they obtained a lease for 17 years from the representative of the Dewan. They are now in possession of the lands in suit under this lease. The plaintiffs are and were at the time they brought their suit on 5 March 1913, in the Court of the Subordinate Judge of Madura, admittedly out of possession. The present action is for declaration of title and for ejectment and possession, principally directed against the *matathipathi* as the head of the math and the 1st and 2nd defendants lessees holding possessions under him. The other defendants have been joined as parties apparently in consequence of certain rights they possess or exercise under those defendants.

The plaintiffs base their title on two grounds: First, that the permanent lease under which they claim was created under circumstances that would bind not only the grantor but all his successors; and secondly, that even if the lease was not valid they had acquired a title under the Indian Limitation Act.

Their case throughout has been that Srinivasa was a 'trustee' and that all his sucessors are 'trustees', that the lands were granted on a 'specific' trust, and that consequently under art. 134 of Sch. I. of the Indian Limitation Act (IX of 1908) they have acquired a good title against the *math*. The *matathipathi* controverted both allegations. He denied that the alienation by

Srinivasa was of such a character as would bind the *math*; he further denied that he and his predecessors were 'trustees' of the *math* or that the 2nd plaintiff or his assignee had acquired any right to the *math* lands by adverse possession. On these contentions, two points arose for determination which are embodied in the first two issues.

They thus concur with the first court that there was no 'specific trust' which was the foundation of the plaintiff's case. But after examining some of the judgments of their own court, they apparently felt constrained to hold that the decision of this Board in *Ram Parkash Das* v. *Anand Das*[4] had crystallized the law on the subject, and definitely declared the *mahant* to be a 'trustee.' It is to be observed that in that case the decision related to the office of *mahant*, but in the course of their judgment their Lordships conceived it desirable to indicate *inter alia* what upon the evidence of the usages and customs applicable to the institution with which they were dealing, and similar institutions, were the duties and obligations attached to the office of superior; and they used the term 'trustee' in a general sense, as in previous decisions of the Board, by way of compendious expression to convey a general conception of those obligations. They did not attempt to define the term or to hold that the word in its specific sense is applicable to the laws and usages of the country. As pointed out by their predecessors in *Greedharee Doss* v. *Nundokissore Doss*:[5] 'The only law as to these *mahants* and their functions and duties is to be found in custom and practice, which is to be proved by testimony.' Generally speaking, however, the duties and obligations resting on the superior indicated in *Ram Parkash Das* v. *Anand Das* do not seem to vary. In this particular institution the position of the *matathipathi* in relation to the math was clearly established by testimony and concurrently found by both courts. But the learned judges misapprehended their Lordships' judgment and proceeded to hold that as Srinivasa who granted the permanent lease was a 'trustee', his act fell under art. 134. To this article their Lordships will presently refer. Before doing so, however, they consider it necessary to observe that there are two systems of law in force in India, both self-contained and both wholly independent of each other, and wholly independent of foreign and outside legal conceptions. In each there are well-recognized rules relating to their religious and charitable institutions. From the year 1774 the Legislature, British and Indian, has affirmed time after time the absolute enjoyment of their laws and customs so far as they are not in conflict with the statutory laws, by Hindus and Mahommedans. It would, in their Lordships' opinion, be a serious inroad into their rights if the rules of the Hindu and Mahommedan laws were

4 LR 43 IA 73.
5 (1867) 11 Moo IA 405, 428.

to be construed with the light of legal conceptions borrowed from abroad, unless perhaps where they are absolutely, so to speak, *in pari materia.* The vice of this method of construction by analogy is well illustrated in the case of *Vidyapurna* v. *Vidyanidhi*,[6] where a *mahant's* position was attempted to be explained by comparing it with that of a bishop and of a beneficed clergyman in England under the ecclesiastical law. It was criticized, and rightly, in their Lordships' opinion, in the subsequent case, which arose also in the Madras High Court, of *Kailasam Pillai* v. *Nataraja Thambiran.*[7] To this judgment their Lordships will have to refer further later on.

It is also to be remembered that a 'trust' in the sense in which the expression is used in English law, is unknown in the Hindu system, pure and simple (J. G. Ghose, *Hindu Law*, p. 276). Hindu piety found expression in gifts to idols and images consecrated and installed in temples, to religious institutions of every kind, and for all purposes considered meritorious in the Hindu social and religious system; to *brahmans, goswamis, sanyasis*, etc. When the gift was to a holy person, it carried with it in terms or by usage and custom certain obligations. Under the Hindu law the image of a deity of the Hindu pantheon is, as has been aptly called, a 'juristic entity', vested with the capacity of receiving gifts and holding property. Religious institutions, known under different names, are regarded as possessing the same 'juristic' capacity, and gifts are made to them *eo nomine*. In many cases in Southern India, especially where the diffusion of Aryan Brahmanism was essential for bringing the Dravidian peoples under the religious rule of the Hindu system, colleges and monasteries under the names of math were founded under spiritual teachers of recognized sanctity. These men had and have ample discretion in the application of the funds of the institution, but always subject to certain obligations and duties, equally governed by custom and usage. When the gift is directly to an idol or a temple, the seisin to complete the gift is necessarily effected by human agency. Called by whatever name, he is only the manager and custodian of the idol or the institution. In almost every case he is given the right to a part of the usufruct, the mode of enjoyment and the amount of the usufruct depending again on usage and custom. In no case was the property conveyed to or vested in him, nor is he a 'trustee' in the English sense of the term, although in view of the obligations and duties resting on him, he is answerable as a trustee in the general sense for maladministration.

The conception of a trust apart from a gift was introduced in India with the establishment of Moslem rule. And it is for this reason that in many documents of later times in parts of the country where Mahommedan

6 ILR 27 Mad 435.
7 ILR 33 Mad 265.

influence has been predominant, such as Upper India and the Carnatic, the expression wakf is used to express dedication.

But the Mahommedan law relating to trusts differs fundamentally from the English law. It owes its origin to a rule laid down by the Prophet of Islam; and means 'the tying up of property in the ownership of God the Almighty and the devotion of the profits for the benefit of human beings'. When once it is declared that a particular property is wakf, or any such expression is used as implies wakf, or the tenor of the document shows, as in the case of *Jewan Doss Sahu* v. *Shah Kubeeruddin*[8] that a dedication to pious or charitable purposes is meant, the right of the *wakif* is extinguished and the ownership is transferred to the Almighty. The donor may name any meritorious object as the recipient of the benefit. The manager of the wakf is the *mutawalli*, the governor, superintendent, or curator. In *Jewan Doss Sahu's Case* the Judicial Committee call him 'procurator.' That case related to a *khankah*, a Mahomedan institution analogous in many respects to a math where Hindu religious instruction is dispensed. The head of these *khankahs*, which exist in large numbers in India, is called a *sajjadanishin*. He is the teacher of religious doctrines and rules of life, and the manager of the institution and the administrator of its charities, and has in most cases a larger interest in the usufruct than an ordinary *mutawalli*. But neither the *sajjadanishin* nor the *mutawalli* has any right in the property belonging to the wakf; the property is not vested in him and he is not a 'trustee' in the technical sense.

It was in view of this fundamental difference between the juridical conceptions on which the English law relating to trusts is based and those which form the foundations of the Hindu and the Mahommedan systems that the Indian Legislature in enacting the Indian Trusts Act (II of 1882) deliberately exempted from its scope the rules of law applicable to wakf and Hindu religious endowments. Sect. 1 of that Act, after declaring when it was to come into force and the areas over which it should extend 'in the first instance', lays down: 'but nothing herein contained affects the rules of Mahommedan law as to wakf, or the mutual relations of the members of an undivided family as determined by any customary or personal law or applies to public or private religious or charitable endowments.'

[....]

Sect. 3 of the Act gives a definition of the word 'trust' in terms familiar to English lawyers. It says: 'A "trust" is an obligation annexed to the ownership of property, and arising out of a confidence reposed in an

8 (1840) 2 Moo IA 390.

accepted by the owner, or declared and accepted by him, for the benefit of another, or of another and the owner; the person who reposes or declares the confidence is called the "author of the trust"; the person who accepts the confidence is called the "trustee"; the person for whose benefit the confidence is accepted is called the "beneficiary"; the subject-matter of the trust is called "trust-property" or "trust-money"; the "beneficial interest" or "interest" of the beneficiary is his right against the trustee as owner of the trust-property; and the instrument, if any, by which the trust is declared is called the "instrument of trust".'

In this connection it may be observed that in the case of *Muhammad Rustam Ali* v. *Mushtaq Husain*[9] the dedication was of specific property created by an instrument called a 'trustee-*nama*'. Lord Buckmaster, delivering the judgment of the Board, dealt thus with the objection as to the validity of the document: 'It is argued', said the noble lord, 'that the "trustee-*nama*" must have dealt with an interest in immovable property, for otherwise the trustees could have no right to maintain the suit; and such an argument at first sight makes a strong appeal to those who are accustomed to administer the English law with regard to trustees. It needs, however, but a slight examination to show that the argument depends for its validity upon the assumption that the trustees of the *wakfnama* in the present case stand in the same relation to the trust that trustees to whom property had been validly assigned would stand over here. Such is not the case. The *wakfnama* itself does not purport to assign property to trustees.'

In 1810 in the Bengal Presidency, and in 1817 in the Madras Presidency, the British Government had assumed control of all the public endowments and benefactions, Hindu and Mahommedan, and placed them under the charge of the respective Boards of Revenue.

[....]

Art. 134 is, as pointed out in *Abhiram Goswami's Case*,[10] controlled by s. 10 of the Limitation Act, which runs thus: 'Notwithstanding anything hereinbefore contained, no suit against a person in whom property has become vested in trust for any specific purpose, or against his legal representatives or assigns (not being assigns for valuable consideration), for the purpose of following in his or their hands such property, or the proceeds thereof, or for an account of such property or proceeds, shall be barred by any length of time.' The language of s. 10 gives the clue to the meaning

9 (1920) LR 47 IA 224.
10 (1909) LR 36 IA 148.

and applicability of art. 134. It clearly shows that the article refers to cases of specific trust, and relates to property 'conveyed in trust'. Neither under the Hindu law nor in the Mahommedan system is any property 'conveyed' to a *shebait* or a *mutawalli*, in the case of a dedication. Nor is any property vested in him; whatever property he holds for the idol or the institution he holds as manager with certain beneficial interests regulated by custom and usage. Under the Mahommedan law, the moment a wakf is created all rights of property pass out of the *wakif*, and vest in God Almighty. The curator, whether called *mutawalli* or *sajjadanishin*, or by any other name, is merely a manager. He is certainly not a 'trustee' as understood in the English system. [....]

From the above review of the general law relating to Hindu and Mahommedan pious institutions it would *prima facie* follow that an alienation by a manager or superior by whatever name called cannot be treated as the act of a 'trustee' to whom property has been 'conveyed in trust' and who by virtue thereof has the capacity vested in him which is possessed by a 'trustee' in the English law. Of course, a Hindu or a Mahommedan may 'convey in trust' a specific property to a particular individual for a specific and definite purpose, and place himself expressly under the English law when the person to whom the legal ownership is transferred would become a trustee in the specific sense of the term.

But the respondents rely on three decisions of the Indian courts in support of their contention that persons holding properties generally for Hindu and Mahommedan religious purposes are to be treated as 'trustees'. (The Board deal with decisions relating to Hindu shrines.)

The second decision relied upon in support of the respondents' contention is the case of *Behari Lall* v. *Muhammad Muttaki*,[11] which related to a Mahommedan shrine. The origin and history of these shrines or *durgahs*, as they are called, is described compendiously in the judgment in *Piran Bibi* v. *Abdul Karim*:[12] 'The *sajjadanishin* has certain spiritual functions to perform. He is not only a *mutawalli*, but also a spiritual preceptor. He is the curator of the durgah where his ancestor is buried, and in him is supposed to continue the spiritual line (*silsila*). As is well known, these durghas are the tombs of celebrated dervishes, who in their lifetime were regarded as saints. Some of these men had established *khankahs* where they lived and their disciples congregated. Many of them never rose to the importance of a *khankah*, and when they died their mausolea became shrines or *durgahs*. These dervishes professed esoteric doctrines and distinc

11 ILR 20 All 482.
12 (1891) ILR 19 Cal 203, 220, 222.

systems of initiation.... The preceptor is called the *pir*, the disciple the *murid*. On the death of the *pir* his successor assumes the privilege of initiating the disciples into the mysteries of dervishism or sufism. This privilege of initiation, of making *murids*, of imparting to them spiritual knowledge, is one of the functions which the *sajjadanishin* performs or is supposed to perform. The endowment is maintained by grants of land to the shrines by pious Moslems. The head of the institution, like that of a *khankah*, is called a *sajjadanishin*. The governance (*towliat*) of the endowment is in his hands; he is a *mutawalli*, with the duty of imparting spiritual instruction to those who seek it. The property of the "shrine" is wakf "tied up in the ownership of God".' The appointment of the *sajjadanishin* is regulated by usage and practice. This is referred to in the same judgment: 'Upon the death of the last incumbent, generally on the day of what is called the *saium* or *teja* ceremony (performed on the third day after his decease), the *fakirs* and *murids* of the *durgah*, assisted by the heads of neighbouring durgahs, instal a competent person on the *guddi*; generally the person chosen is the son of the deceased or somebody nominated by him, for his nomination is supposed to carry the guarantee that the nominee knows the precepts which he is to communicate to the disciples. In some instances the nomination takes the shape of a formal installation by the electoral body, so to speak, during the lifetime of the incumbent.'

The duties in connection with the 'shrine', apart from giving spiritual instruction, consist in the due observance of the annual ceremonies at the tomb of the saint, the distribution of charity at fasts and festivals, the celebration of the birthday of the Prophet, and the performance of other rites and ceremonials prescribed either by the religious law or by usage and practice. Ordinarily speaking, the *sajjadanishin* has a larger right in the surplus income than a *mutawalli*, for so long as he does not spend it in wicked living or in objects wholly alien to his office, he, like the *mahant* of a Hindu *math*, has full power of disposition over it.

In *Behari Lall* v. *Muhammad Muttaki*,[13] the plaintiff as *sajjadanishin* sued to set aside certain mortgages executed by his predecessor in office, and dated his cause of action from the time he was appointed as *sajjadanishin*. The learned judges, on a misconception of the rules of the Mahommedan law and of the judgment of their Lordships in *Jewan Doss Sahoo* v. *Shah Kubeeruddeen*,[14] held that the *sajjadanashin* was a 'trustee' One judge held that the suit was barred either under Art. 134 or Art. 144; the two others held that Art. 134 was applicable as the mortgages were created by a

13 ILR 20 All 482.
14 2 Moo. IA 390.

'trustee'. Their Lordships have to differ from that conclusion. In their opinion this case was not, in view of the considerations set forth above, correctly decided.

[....]

32. Abul Fata v. Russomoy Dhur Chowdhury (1894) 22 IA 76

Wakf—perpetual family settlement—illusory gift to the poor

Held, that under Muhammadan law a perpetual family settlement expressly made as wakf is not legal merely because there is an ultimate but illusory gift to the poor.

Meer Mahomed Israil Khan v. *Sashti Churn Ghose*[16] and *Bikani Mia* v. *Shuk Lal Poddar*[17] overruled.

For a full discussion see *Tyabji*, 592 and Index; *Outlines,* 290 seqq. Ameer Ali's criticism, somewhat verbose and lacking in method, is also valuable, i. 295 seqq.

Appeal from a decree of the High Court in Bengal (24 February 1891), reversing a decree of the Subordinate Judge of Sylhet (18 April 1889), and dismissing the appellants' suit with costs.

Judgment [Hobhouse, J.][15]

The object of this suit is to establish as a valid *wakfnama* a settlement of property effected by deed dated the 21st of December, 1868. The settlors were two brothers called Abdur Rahman and Abdool Kadir, Mahommedan gentlemen belonging to the Hanafi sect of the Sunnis. The Plaintiffs, now Appellants, are sons of Abdur Rahman, to whom interests are given by the settlement. The Defendants, a hundred and more in number, are the settlors themselves, and persons claiming interests in portions of the settled property by virtue of transactions with Abdur Rahman subsequently to the date of the settlement. Some of these claimants are Respondents to the present appeal.

The Subordinate Judge of Sylhet held that the settlement was valid as a *wakfnama*, and gave the Plaintiffs a decree on that footing. On appeal the High Court took a different view, and dismissed the suit. The great mass of the record relates to subordinate disputes—what parcels of property fall within the settlement, and what inferences are to be drawn from the way

15 With Watson, Shand & Richard Couch, JJ.
16 ILR (1892) 19 Cal 412.
17 ILR (1892) 20 Cal 116.

in which the settlors dealt with the property after the settlement. But the only question argued here has been the nature of the settlement itself; for in the view taken by their Lordships all others are immaterial.

[....]

The settlement begins thus: 'Committing ourselves to the mercy and kindness of the Great God...we...have made this permanent wakf according to Mahomedan law'.... Then are stated various incidents and duties attaching to the office of *mutawalli*, amongst which occur the following:

> It will be competent for us the *matwalis* [*mutawalli*] and our successor *matwalis* to enhance or reduce the allowances of the persons for whose benefit the wakf is made, who are now living, or who may hereafter be born, in consideration of course of their position and circumstances and the state of the income of the wakf properties. It will be competent for us the present *matwalis* and the *matwalis* who will be appointed after us, to use the wakf properties as security and to grant *putni*, *durputni* and permanent and temporary *ijara* settlements in respect of them, and with the money to be received as salami for the aforesaid settlements, to purchase some other properties and to exchange any of the lands of this wakf with some other lands, and to include the lands so acquired by purchase or in exchange in the wakf, and to spend the profit of the same towards the expenses of the wakf, and to keep the surplus profit in stock in the *tehbil*, and to try always to increase the wakf properties and the amount in cash. Whatever properties may be acquired by us the *matwalis* and our successor *matwalis*, after execution of this document, shall be included in this wakf. We the *matwalis* and the *matwalis* who will be appointed in our place hereafter shall have no power to make gift of any property in favour of relatives or strangers.

It is provided that future *mutawallis* shall always be chosen from the male issue of the settlors, or if they fail, from their relatives. Provisions are made to prevent any of the persons for whose benefit the wakf is made from claiming anything as of right, and from calling for accounts, and from alienating his interest or subjecting it to attachment. And towards the end of the deed its object is again stated:

> The object of this wakf of properties is that the properties may be protected against all risks, the name and the prestige of the family maintained, and the profits of these properties appropriated towards the maintenance of the name and prestige of the family, the support of the persons for whose benefit the wakf is made, and religious, purposes *&c*.

Such is the instrument which is propounded as a *wakfnama*. The motives stated are, regard for the family name, and preservation of the property in the family. Every specific trust is for some member of the family. The family is to be aggrandized by accumulations of surpluses, and apparently by absorption into the settlement of after-acquired properties; and no person is to have any right of calling the managers to account. These possessions are to be secured for ever for the enjoyment of the family, so far as the settlors could accomplish such a result, by provisions that nobody's share shall be alienated, or be attached for his debts. There is no reference to religion unless it be the invocation of the Deity to perpetuate the family name and to preserve their property, and the casual mention of unspecified religious purposes, &c., at the end of the sentence last quoted. There is a gift to the poor and to widows and orphans, but they are to take nothing, not even surplus income, until the total extinction of the blood of the settlors, whether lineal or collateral.

It seems that in the High Court the learned Advocate-General contended for the plaintiffs that a gift to the donors' descendants without any mention of the poor might be supported as a wakf; and even that the Mahommedan law intends that perpetual family settlements may be made in the name of religious trusts. In the case of *Ahsanulla Chowdhry* v. *Amarchand Kundu*[18] this Board said: 'They have not been referred to, nor can they find any authority showing that, according to Mahommedan law, a gift is good as a wakf unless there is a substantial dedication of the property to charitable uses at some period of time or other.' The Board proceeded to affirm the decision of the High Court of Calcutta, who held that a small part of the property had been well devoted to charity, but that as to the bulk of it the settlement was, notwithstanding some expressions importing a wakf, in substance nothing but a family settlement in perpetuity, and as such contrary to Mahommedan law. The principle of this decision has been quoted and approved in a subsequent case: *Abdul Gafur* v. *Nizamudin.*[19] This is a sufficient answer to the arguments used in the High Court.

Their Lordships, however, cannot now say that they have not been referred to any authority for the contrary opinion; for Mr Branson has cited to them two cases in which there are very elaborate judgments delivered in the Calcutta High Court by the learned Judge Mr Ameer Ali. Those judgments are in accordance with the opinion expressed by him in his Tagore Lectures, and if their Lordships have rightly apprehended them, they do go the whole length of the Advocate-General's argument. One is in the case of *Meer Mahomed Israil Khan* v. *Sashti Churn Ghose*,[20] where there

18 Law Rep. 17 IA 37.
19 Law Rep. 19 IA 170.
20 Ind. LR 19 Cal 412.

were some immediate gifts to the poor, and the gift was upheld, and no further appeal was presented. The other case is that of *Bikani Mia* v. *Shuk Lal Poddar*,[21] where there was no gift to the poor till after the failure of the settlor's family. It was heard by a Full Bench of five Judges, who decided that the deed was invalid, Ameer Ali J. dissenting.

The opinion of that learned Mahommedan lawyer is founded, as their Lordships understand it, upon texts of an abstract character, and upon precedents very imperfectly stated. For instance, he quotes a precept of the Prophet Mohammed himself, to the effect that 'A pious offering to one's family, to provide against their getting into want, is more pious than giving alms to beggars. The most excellent of *sadakah* is that which a man bestows upon his family.' And by way of precedent he refers to the gift of a house in wakf or *sadakah*, of which the revenues were to be received by the descendants of the donor Arkan [Arqam].[22] His other old authorities are of the same kind.

[....]

Having examined the authorities cited, their Lordships find a great preponderance against the contentions of the Appellants. Some authorities go so far as to hold that for a valid wakf the property should be solely dedicated to pious uses. On that point, however, this Board in *Ahsanulla Chowdhry's case*[23] adopted the opinion of Kemp J., to the effect that provisions for the family out of the grantor's property may be consistent with the gift of it as wakf. In favour of the view now urged for the Appellants there is the judicial opinion of Ameer Ali J. in *Bikani Mia's Case*,[24] dissenting from the rest of the court; a dictum of Sir *Raymond West* in the Bombay High Court in the case of *Fatma Bibi* v. *Advocate-General of Bombay*,[25] and a decision of Farran J. in the same court in the case of *Amrutlal Kalidas* v. *Shaik Husain*.[26] The weight of Ameer Ali J.'s opinion on this subordinate point is somewhat lessened by his support of the gift under consideration on the very broad grounds which their Lordships have considered to be untenable. The *dictum* of Sir R. West is mentioned in *Ahsanulla Chowdhry's Case*. *Farran*, J. had before him a case very closely resembling the present one. He described the settlement as 'a perpetuity of the worst and most pernicious kind, and would be invalid on that ground

21 ILR 20 Cal 116.
22 ILR 20 Cal 140.
23 Law Rep. 17 IA 28.
24 ILR 20 Cal 116.
25 ILR 6 Bom 53.
26 ILR 11 Bom 492.

unless it can be supported as a *wakfnama*';[27] and he thought that the authority of the *Hedaya* is against it; but he adopted the principle stated by Sir R. West, which he treated as a decision, and he supported the gift on the strength of the ultimate trust for the poor.

Their Lordships cannot assent to these conclusions. They make words of more regard than things, and form more than substance. In their judgment the Calcutta High Court have in this case rightly decided that there is no substantial gift to the poor. A gift may be illusory whether from its small amount or from its uncertainty and remoteness. If a man were to settle a crore of rupees, and provide ten for the poor, that would be at once recognized as illusory. It is equally illusory to make a provision for the poor under which they are not entitled to receive a rupee till after the total extinction of a family; possibly not for hundreds of years; possibly not until the property had vanished away under the wasting agencies of litigation or malfeasance or misfortune; certainly not as long as there exists on the earth one of those objects whom the donors really cared to maintain in a high position. Their Lordships agree that the poor have been put into this settlement merely to give it a colour of piety, and so to legalize arrangements meant to serve for the aggrandizement of a family.

They will humbly advise Her Majesty to dismiss this appeal with costs.

◊ UPDATE ◊

1. *Wakfs and their mutawallis*

The relevance of the old Privy Council decision in *Vidyaviruthi* v. *Balusami Ayyar* (Case 31), which was not a case under Muslim law, lies in Syed Ameer Ali's exposition of the concept and attributes of wakfs in Muslim law. These are now very well understood in the subcontinent. See the Indian Supreme Court's judgments in *Garib Das* v. *Munshi Hamid* AIR 1970 SC 1035 and *Wali Mohammad* v. *Rahmat Bee* 1999 SC 1136.

On the recognition of 'wakf by user' a recent Indian decision is *Syed Badruddin* v. *Karnataka Wakf Board* AIR 1995 Kant 151.

In *Mohammad Zainulabidin* v. *SA Modideen* AIR 1990 SC 507 the Supreme Court of India has observed that there is no general inhibition in Muslim law against a woman acting as the *mutawalli* of a wakf:

> It appears that the defendants were carrying a mistaken impression all along that females under Muslim law were not entitled to any right of management or possession in a *dragah.*

27 ILR 11 Bom 497.

The administration of wakfs is now governed in India by the new Wakf Act of 1995, which has replaced the old Wakf Act of 1954.

2. *Family wakfs*

The *Abul Fata* case [Case 32] has now no more than a historical value. Its dictum had been superseded by the Mussalman Wakf Validating Act 1913, which remains in force in all parts of the subcontinent.

In the leading case of *Fazlul Rabbi Pradhan* v. *State of West Bengal* AIR 1965 SC 1722 the Indian Supreme Court observed:

> The intention of the Wakf Validating Act was not to give a new meaning to the word 'charity' which in commonplace is a word denoting a giving to someone in necessitious circumstances and in law a giving for public good. A private gift to one's own self or kith and kin may be meritorious and pious but is not a charity in the legal sense and the courts in India have never regarded such gifts for religious or charitable purposes even under the Mahommedan law.

The income from family wakfs is regarded in India as an asset liable to wealth tax. See *Ahmed GH Ariff* v. *Commissioner of Wealth Tax* AIR 1971 SC 1691.

For the working of the Mussalman Wakf Validating Act of 1913 in Pakistan see *Ghulam Shabbir* v. *Nur Begum* PLD 1977 SC 75.

Notably, family wakfs have now been either abolished or subjected to severe restrictions in many Muslim countries.[28]

XIV. Mosques

33. Mahomed Ismail v. Ahmed Moolla
(1916) 43 IA 127

Mosque—scheme of management—guiding principle—interests of institution—intention of founder—'Kazi', definition and functions

In settling a scheme of management, under the Code of Civil Procedure, 1882, s. 539, for a Mahommedan public trust, religious or charitable, such as a mosque, the court has a complete discretion; it may defer to the wishes of the founder so far as they are conformable to changed conditions and circumstances, but its primary duty is to consider the interests of the general body of the public for whose benefit the trust was created; it may vary any rule of management which it finds either not practicable or not in the best interest of the institution.

The *Kazi* (cadi) and his functions defined (p. 134); *Outlines,* 306, 3 9 seqq.; Kādī, *Shorter Encyclopaedia of Islam* (Brill, 1953), 201.

Consolidated Appeals from two decrees of the Chief Court of Lower Burma in its appellate jurisdiction (29 May 1912) reversing a decree of that court (25 April 1910).

The first five appellants filed a plaint in the Chief Court under s. 539 of the Code of Civil Procedure, 1882, for the settlement of a scheme of management of a Sunni Mahommedan mosque at Rangoon. The appellants represented the Randher Vora community, namely, residents who originally came from Randher, a village near Surat, and their descendants. This class is referred to as the Randherias. The respondents in the first appeal represented the general Sunni Mahommedan community of Rangoon. The respondents in the second appeal represented the worshippers, other than Randherias, who, or whose predecessors, came from the Surat district. The following issue was ordered to be tried in the suit: Have all Sunni Mahommedans of Rangoon, or the Surati Vora community, other than the Randher Sunni Vora Jamat, any voice in the management of the jama masjid?

Robinson J. made a decree declaring that the deed of trust dated 16 March 1872, by which the management was vested in the Randher Sunni Vora community was good and valid, and ordered that a scheme of management should be submitted. The learned judge held that the five Randheria purchasers under the deeds of 1871 became absolute owners free from any trust, and that the deed of 16 March 1872, created a new and valid trust. He was further of opinion that the intention of the founder (who came from Randher) could be inferred from the facts that he had handed over the management to three Randherias, and that for a period of about sixty years the management and control had been exclusively in the hands of Randherias.

Both sets of respondents appealed. The appeals were heard by the Chief Judge (Sir Charles E. Fox) and Hartnoll J. The learned judges reversed the judgment of Robinson J. They held that the lands granted in 1862 were subject to a trust to build a mosque for the free use of all persons professing the Sunni sect of the Mahommedan religion, that the grants of 1871 were subject to the same trust, and that the deed of 16 March 1872, was invalid. It was accordingly declared that all Sunni Mahommedans were entitled to a voice in the management, and that the right was not confined to the Randher Sunni Vora Jamat.

Judgment [Syed Ameer Ali][1]

The suit which gives rise to these consolidated appeals was brought in the Chief Court of Lower Burma in its original civil jurisdiction, under the provisions of s. 539 of Act XIV of 1882, for the appointment of trustees and the settlement of a scheme of management in respect of a mosque situated in the city of Rangoon. The plaintiffs in the action are five Mahommedan worshippers at the mosque, who trace their origin to a place called Randher, said to be a suburb of the city of Surat in the Bombay Presidency, and in the earlier stages of these proceedings they appear to have claimed it as a Randheria mosque. It is, however, conceded now that it is a public mosque dedicated to the performance of religious worship by all Sunni Mahommedans without restriction as to place of origin, and that it is commonly known as the Sunni Jama Masjid.

To explain the contest between the parties it is necessary to give a short summary of the circumstances that have led to this unfortunate litigation. Like many other places in Burma, Rangoon is inhabited by a large number of Mahommedan emigrants from various parts of India who have domiciled themselves in the country for purposes of trade, and are generally known by the names of the towns or villages whence they originally came. For example, the plaintiffs, as already stated, derive their origin from Randher and, therefore, call themselves Randherias; whilst the larger community of Suratis or Soortees come either from the city or district of Surat. It is

1 With Viscount Haldane, John Edge & Lawrence Jenkins, JJ.

necessary to bear this in mind, as the mosque in question is sometimes called the Surati Mosque. The Randherias, though trying to differentiate themselves from the others, form in reality a section of the Surati community. They are mostly Voras, and they all profess the Sunni doctrines. [...]

The land on which the mosque was first built appears to have been afterwards added to by purchases made by Moolla Hashim or by his fellow townsmen, who made the same over to him as the custodian of the mosque. In 1862 one Moolla Ibrahim, a brother of Moolla Hashim, and two persons, of the names of Golam Moideen Moollah and Cassim Azim, obtained from the Government a grant in respect of certain other plots on the express trust 'to build and maintain thereon a mosque or place of worship for and to the use of all persons professing the Sunni sect of the Mahommedan religion'. These lands were also added or attached to the existing mosque, and shops were built there to yield an income for its maintenance.

In 1864 Moolla Hashim went on a pilgrimage to Mecca, leaving the management of the mosque in the hands of Moolla Ibrahim and the two persons already mentioned. He returned to Rangoon in 1866, but never resumed his management of the mosque. At this time the person in charge was one Mohammed Hashim Mehtar, who also is said to have been a native of Randher.

In 1870 the Government, finding that no mosque had been built on the lands granted in 1862, and that on the contrary shops had been erected thereon, issued a notice on the grantees to show cause why those lands should not be resumed. A meeting was thereupon held, apparently at the instance of the Randherias, of all the Sunni Mahommedans entitled to worship at the mosque, and it was decided to buy outright from the Government the land and build on it a proper masonry structure suitable to the growing needs of the community. Although there is some dispute with regard to the contributions of the general body of Sunnis apart from the Randherias, it may be taken as fairly uncontroverted that the bulk of the fund was subscribed by the Randheria section of the worshippers. The conveyance was taken in the names of five persons, named respectively Dooplay, Ariff, Pattal, Mohammed Hashim, and Ebrahim Ali Moolla, and these men in 1872, whilst the masonry mosque was in course of building, purported to create a new dedication.

The trust deed bears date 16 March 1872, and after reciting that it was made between the persons named above of the one part, and one Mohammed Hashim, representing the general Sunni Mussulman community, of the other part, proceeds to declare that 'the pieces or parcels of land upon a certain portion of which the Sunni Jamat Masjid is erected or is in the course of being built, together with the godowns attached thereto, are solely dedicated for the purpose of divine worship'. It then goes on to provide *inter alia* that its management shall remain exclusively in the hands of the Randheria Jamat (people or assembly).

The five persons in whose names the conveyance stood and who had executed the trust deed appear to have carried on the management for several years; in course of time some dropped out and others came in as trustees. How these men were placed in charge of the management of the mosque is not clear, for apparently no meeting of the Randheria Punchayet was held until 1894, and none between 1894 and 1906, nor in fact had the Randherias any 'organized association' with written rules for the purpose of giving effect to the wishes of their section of the community.

Matters remained in this condition until 1908, when disputes arose regarding the validity of the election of one Hashim Yacub Ally as a trustee in place of another Randheria, who had died the year before. It was in consequence of the quarrels among the Randherias themselves in connection with the election or appointment of this man that the present suit was launched in the Chief Court of Lower Burma. The original defendants to the action were four persons who were actually managing the mosque as trustees, but the validity of whose appointment as such was impugned by the plaintiffs. In addition three others were joined as defendants ostensibly to represent the Randheria section, but in reality, as the trustee defendants charge, to represent the plaintiffs' faction.

On the institution of the suit notices were issued by the court under s. 30 of the Civil Procedure Code to all persons entitled to worship at the mosque. Thereupon defendants 12 and 13, representing the general body of Sunni worshippers, and defendants 8 to 11, claiming to represent the Surati community, and 14 to 17 the other Randherias, appeared and applied to be joined as parties. Each set of defendants has filed a separate defence. Although the trustee defendants deny the plaintiffs' allegation that the mosque in question is a Randheria mosque, and affirm the validity of their and Hashim Yacub Ally's appointment as trustees, they associate themselves with the plaintiffs and their Randheria co-defendants in claiming that the right of management of the mosque belongs exclusively to their party. And they ask that the scheme, if any is to be framed, should be framed on that basis.

The defendants 12 and 13, who represent the general body of worshippers, controvert in substance the right of the Randherias to a monopoly of the management as opposed to the whole nature of the trust; and they claim that as the mosque is dedicated to the performance of public worship by all Mahommedans of the Sunni persuasion, now that a scheme is proposed to be settled under the direction of the court they should be allowed a voice in its administration.

The suit proceeded to trial before Robinson J., and the whole dispute centred round two points, namely (1) the effect of the trust deed of 1872, and (2) whether the Randherias should or should not have the sole and exclusive charge and management of the mosque.

The Randherias rested their case on the trust deed of 1872; they contended that it created a new trust and that the founders, namely, the five persons in whose names the land had been purchased from the Government, were entitled to provide that the management should remain exclusively in the hands of their own section of the community. The learned trial judge states their contentions in the following terms: 'It is urged that the original mosque was created by a Randheria; that the original grant was revoked and the lands sold outright to Randherias; that they thus became the creators of the trust and were at liberty to make any lawful condition they pleased as to the management of the trust.' And his decision is expressed in these words: 'The position in 1871, then, was that the five vendees became the absolute and untrammelled owners of these two plots and could do with them as they pleased.... They became the owners of the mosque, shops, and lands, and created a trust of them. It was undoubtedly open to them to manage the trust themselves or to lay down the manner in which it was to be managed, and this they did in exhibit C.' He accordingly came to the conclusion that the Randheria party were exclusively entitled to the management of the mosque.

On appeal by the respondents in the first and second appeals respectively, the learned judges of the Chief Court, differing from the trial judge, held in substance that the lands which were purchased by or in the names of the five persons in 1871 were acquired by them as trustees for the purposes of the existing mosque and subject to the trust therefor, and that nothing that took place in 1871 or 1872 had the effect of cancelling, or could in law cancel, the original trust; and that as the original trust was for the benefit of all persons 'professing the Sunni sect of the Mahommedan religion', they thought that 'all Sunni Mahommedans were entitled to a voice in the control of the Jama Masjid of Rangoon.'

The plaintiffs and the trustee defendants have appealed to His Majesty in Council, and the same contention that was put forward in the courts below, based on the document of 1872, has been urged on their behalf. It has further been contended that under the Mahommedan law the court has no discretion in the matter and that it must give effect to the rule laid down by the founder in all matters relating to the appointment and succession of trustees or *mutwallees*. Their Lordships cannot help thinking that the extreme proposition urged on behalf of the appellants is based on a misconception. The Mussulman law, like the English law, draws a wide distinction between public and private trusts. Generally speaking, in case of a wakf or trust created for specific individuals or a determinate body of individuals, the *Kazi*, whose place in the British Indian system is taken by the civil Court, has in carrying the trust into execution to give effect so far as possible to the expressed wishes of the founder. With respect, however, to public religious or charitable trusts, of which a public mosque is a common and well-known example, the *Kazi's* discretion is very wide. He may not depart from the intentions of the founder or from any rule fixed by him as to the objects of the benefaction; but as regards management which must be governed by circumstances he has complete discretion. He may defer to the wishes of the founder so far as they are conformable to changed conditions and circumstances, but his primary duty is to consider the interests of the general body of the public for whose benefit the trust is created. He may in his judicial discretion vary any rule of management which he may find either not practicable or not in the best interests of the institution.

Illustrations of this rule are to be found in almost every work on Mussulman law. And the authorities lay down that, 'were the *wakif* (the founder) to make a condition that the King or *Kazi* should not interfere in the management of the wakf, still the *Kazi* will have his superintendence over it, for his supervision is above everything.'...

In their Lordships' opinion, the real point in issue in the case, owing probably to the nature of the pleadings, has to some extent been missed by the courts in India. It has been treated as a question involving the determination of conflicting rights rather than a consideration of the best method for fully and effectively carrying out the purpose for which the trust was created. [....]

In giving effect to the provisions of the section and in appointing new trustees and settling a scheme, the court is entitled to take into consideration not merely the wishes of the founder, so far as they can be ascertained, but also the past history of the institution, and the way in which the management has been carried on heretofore, in conjunction with other existing conditions that may have grown up since its foundation. It has also the power of giving any directions and laying down any rules which might facilitate the work of management, and, if necessary, the appointment of trustees in the future....

The present case, however, in their Lordships' opinion, illustrates the mischief of leaving the power of appointing or electing trustees in the hands of an indeterminate and necessarily fluctuating body of people, whether they call themselves Punchayet or jamat. In order to avoid so far as possible a recurrence of the trouble that has brought about this long-drawn litigation, their Lordships think it desirable, in the interests of the institution which form the primary matter for consideration, that the appointment of future trustees should be entrusted to a committee of the worshippers the composition of which should be in the discretion of the judge, with due regard to local conditions and needs, subject to the provision that, so long as circumstances do not vary, a majority of such committee should be Randherias; and that in settling the scheme the judge should lay down rules for their guidance in the discharge of any supervisitorial functions that it may appear necessary to confide to them and for filling up vacancies on their body subject to his control.

Their Lordships are accordingly of opinion that the orders of the courts of India should be discharged and that the case should be remitted with the following declaration and directions to the Chief Court of Lower Burma to deal finally with the matter: that, all other conditions being equal, the Randheria section of the worshippers are preferably entitled to manage and act as trustees of the Sunni Jama Masjid of Rangoon; that the appointment of future trustees should be entrusted to a committee of the worshippers, the composition of which committee should be in the discretion of the court, with due regard to local needs and conditions, subject to the provision that, so long as circumstances do not vary, a majority of such committee should be Randherias; and that in settling the scheme the court should lay down rules for the guidance of the committee in the discharge of any supervisitorial functions that it may appear necessary to confide to them, and for filling up vacancies on their body subject to its control. [....]

34. QUEEN-EMPRESS v. RAMZAN
(1885) 7 All 461 (FB)

Hanafi mosque—judicial notice to be taken of Muhammadan law—disturbance in prayers—Indian Penal Code, 1860, Secs. 72, 296

A *masjid* (mosque) was used by the members of a sect of Muslims called the Hanafis, according to whose tenets the word *āmīn* should be spoken in a low tone of voice. While the Hanafis were at prayers, a Muslim of another sect, entered the *masjid* and in the course of the prayers, according to the tenets of his sect, called out *āmīn* in a loud tone of voice. For this act he was convicted of voluntarily disturbing an assembly engaged in religious worship, an offence punishable under s. 296 of the Penal Code.

The Full Bench (Mahmood, J., dissenting) ordered the case to be retried and directed that, in so trying it, the Magistrate should have regard to the following questions, namely: (1) Was there an assembly lawfully engaged in the performance of religious worship? (2) Was such assembly in fact disturbed by the accused? (3) Was such disturbance caused by acts and conduct on the part of the accused by which he intended to cause such disturbance, or which acts and conduct at the time of such acts and conduct he knew or believed to be likely to cause disturbance?

Held by Mahmood, J., that the act of the accused having presumably taken place during the interval when the prayers were not going on, the assembly was not at that time 'engaged in the performance of religious worship' and was not 'disturbed' within the meaning at s. 296 of the Penal Code; that in reference to the terms of s. 39 of the Code the accused did not disturb the assembly 'voluntarily'; that he was justified by the Muhammadan ecclesiastical law in entering the mosque, joining the congregation and in saying the word *āmīn* loudly if he thought fit; and that his conduct fell within the purview of s. 79 of the Penal Code and was therefore not an offence under s. 296.

Also per Mahmood, J., having regard to the guarantee given by the Legislature in s. 24 of Act VI of 1871 (Bengal Civil Courts Act) that the Muhammadan law shall be administered in all questions regarding 'any religious usage or institution', the court was bound by s. 57 (1) of Act 1 of 1872 (Evidence Act) to take judicial notice of the Muhammadan ecclesiastical law, and the rules of that law need not be proved by specific evidence.

This is a leading case on the subject of prayer in mosques and the dissenting opinion of Mahmood J. has come to be regarded as the foundation for many subsequent decisions. *Outlines,* 311 seqq.; *Shorter Encyclopaedia of Islam* (Brill, 1953), 330 seqq. [....]

This was an application to the High Court for the exercise of its powers of revision under s. 439 of the Criminal Procedure Code. It appeared that the applicants, Ramzan, Muhammad Husain, and Abdul Rahman, were convicted by the Cantonment Magistrate of Benares, Major R. Annesley, by an order dated the 25 September 1884, of an offence under s. 296, Indian Penal Code. [....]

A Revision application came for hearing before Brodhurst, J., by whom it was referred to a Divisional Bench. On the application coming before Oldfield and Mahmood, JJ., the learned Judges referred to the Full Bench the question 'whether the facts proved in this case amount to an offence under s. 296 of the Indian Penal Code.' [....]

On the 14th March the following opinion was delivered by Mahmood, J., on the question referred to the Full Bench.

Opinion [Mahmood, J.][2]

This case originally came on for hearing in the Single Bench before my brother Brodhurst, and, in view of the peculiarities of the question with

2 With W. C. Petheram, CJ, and Straight, Oldfield & Brodhurst, JJ.

regard to the right of worshipping in mosques possessed by Muhammadans, my learned brother referred the case to a Division Bench, of which, at his suggestion, and with the approval of the learned Chief Justice, I was to be a member. The case was accordingly heard by a Bench consisting of my brother Oldfield and myself; and, in consideration of the fact that the main object of the application for revision obviously was to obtain an authoritative ruling upon the question, and also because the applicant's counsel informed us that the applicants, having paid the fines inflicted upon them, were not undergoing the alternative sentence of imprisonment, we referred the case to the Full Bench, before which the case was re-argued by Mr Amir-ud-din on behalf of the applicants, and the learned Public Prosecutor on behalf of the Crown. Upon that occasion, after having fully heard the arguments on either side, I was unable to form any opinion such as could be made the basis of any order in the case, and being desirous of consulting the original authorities of Muhammadan law, I wished to reserve my order to enable me to prepare a judgment in writing, as the question raised by the reference seemed to be far from simple, specially as, in my opinion, it turned upon a very minute point of the Muhammadan ecclesiastical law. The learned Chief Justice and my learned brethren, however, were able on that occasion to form an opinion in the case and made an order remanding the case for retrial on certain issues. My brother Straight, whilst consenting to the order of retrial, was inclined to the opinion that the evidence on the record was sufficient to justify the conviction. I was, however, unfortunately not able to concur in, or dissent from the order for the simple reason that I had formed no definite opinion in the absence of the authorities of Muhammadan law, which had not been cited on either side.

Under these circumstances, it has devolved upon me now to deliver my judgment in the case, and I regret that the conclusion at which I have arrived is different from that at which the learned Chief Justice and the rest of the court have done. In view of this circumstance, and also because facts similar to those that exist in this case have before now been made the subject of criminal prosecutions in cases which have ultimately come up to this court in revision, I wish to explain my reasons fully.

The facts of the case itself are very simple. The mosque in question in this case is situated in muhalla Maddanpura, in the city of Benares, and it was built by one Ali Muhammad *alias* Allu, who is stated by the prosecution to have followed the doctrines of Imam Abu Hanifa, and was therefore a Hanafi. The prosecutor, Abdulla, is a brother-in-law of the founder of the mosque, his sister having been married to Allu, and the principal accused, Ramzan, is the son-in-law of Allu, and also otherwise related to him. The other two accused, Muhammad Husain and Abdul Rahman, are persons holding religious views similar to those held by Ramzan.

It appears that on the 22nd of August, 1884, the three accused joined the congregation in the mosque, and during the prayer said the word *āmīn* aloud. This appears to have led to a discussion as to whether it was right to say the word aloud in prayers, and a heated argument took place, resulting in the accused being turned out of the mosque with the help of the police, and the prosecutor prohibiting them from coming to the mosque again unless they renounced the rite of saying *āmīn* aloud in prayers.

On the 1st of September, 1884, Abdulla and some other persons presented an application to the Magistrate, describing the occurrence of the 22nd August, and asking for the interference of the Magisterial authorities, on the ground that breach of the peace was likely to take place by reason of the accused insisting upon saying the word *āmīn* aloud in prayers. No definite action appears to have been taken by the Magisterial authorities on that application beyond sending it for inquiry to the City Inspector of Police, and matters seemed to have stood thus, when, on the 20th of September, 1884, Abdulla by himself filed another petition, complaining of the accused, and charging them with 'the offence of insulting the religion of the Hanafia Musalmans' under ss. 297, 298, and 352 of the Indian Penal Code. The Magistrate, after having examined the prosecutor and the witnesses for the prosecution, framed charges against the accused under s. 296 of the Indian Penal Code, and after having taken the evidence on behalf of the defence, convicted them under that section, and sentenced them to pay a fine of Rs 25 each, or in default to undergo rigorous imprisonment for one month.

The accused have applied for revision to this court under s. 439 of the Criminal Procedure Code, on the ground that 'to pronounce the word *āmīn* in a loud tone during the prayers is not an offence punishable under s. 296 of the Indian Penal Code.'

The question so raised seems to me to involve mixed considerations of the meaning of the Indian Penal Code and the Muhammadan ecclesiastical law; for, according to my view, the application of the former depends upon the interpretation of the latter in connection with this case. But before discussing this question, I wish to express my views with reference to the observation which was made in the course of the argument, that this court is not bound to consider the Muhammadan ecclesiastical law in such cases without having the rules of that law proved by specific evidence like any other fact in a litigation. I am unable to accept this view, because, if it is conceded that the decision of this case depends (as I shall presently endeavour to show it does depend) upon the interpretation of the Muhammadan ecclesiastical law, it is to my mind the duty of this court, and of all courts subordinate to it, to take judicial notice of such law. I hold that cl. (1) of s. 57 of the Evidence Act (I of 1872) fully covers the Muhammadan ecclesiastical law in such cases, because, whenever a question of civil right or the lawfulness of an act arises in a judicial proceeding, even a Criminal Court is bound, *ex necessitate,* to resort to the civil branch of the law; and, in a case like the present, the question being the right of a Muhammadan to pray in a mosque according to his tenets, the question of legality or illegality would fall under the purview of the express guarantee given by the Legislature in s. 24 of the Bengal Civil Courts Act (VI of 1871), that the Muhammadan law shall be administered with reference to all questions regarding 'any religious usage or institution'. That the application of some of the sections of the Indian Penal Code depends almost entirely upon the correct interpretation of the rules of civil law, cannot, in my opinion, be doubted; and if it is so, the present case is only another illustration of this principle. Indeed, I am prepared to go the length of saying that, but for this principle, the rules of the Penal Code would in many cases operate as a great injustice, and acts fully justified by the civil law would constitute offences under that Code. I hold therefore that in a case like the present, the provisions of s. 56 of the Evidence Act fully relieve the parties from the necessity of proving the Muhammadan ecclesiastical law upon the subject, that that law is not to be placed upon the same footing with reference to this matter as any foreign law of which judicial notice cannot be taken by the courts in British India; and it follows that I can refer to the Muhammadan ecclesiastical law for the purposes of this case, notwithstanding the absence of any specific evidence on the record regarding its rules.

Now, before going further, I wish to observe that the main allegations on behalf of the prosecution, contained in the petition of the 1st September, 1884, and in that of the 20th September, 1884, relate to the conduct of the accused in saying the word *āmīn* aloud during prayers in the mosque; that in the evidence for the prosecution itself the loud utterance of that word is the gravamen of the accusation; that the Magistrate framed charges under s. 296, Indian Penal Code, with reference to that matter alone, disregarding the other sections of the Indian Penal Code cited on behalf of the prosecution; and that his judgment entirely proceeds upon the view that the loud utterance of the word *āmīn* during prayers constitutes a criminal offence under the circumstances of this case. It is true that in the evidence for the prosecution there were vague allegations as to other facts which might possibly have furnished basis for charging the accused under some other sections of the Indian Penal Code; but, as a matter of fact, the Magistrate did not charge or try the accused under any other section, and at all events we in the Full Bench are not concerned with the whole case.

Holding these views, I feel myself called upon, sitting as a Judge in the Full Bench to which the reference has been made solely as to s. 296 of the Indian Penal Code, to consider the case for the purpose of answering the reference only in that aspect, leaving it to the referring Bench to decide questions which may possibly arise in the case beyond the scope of the question referred.

But before discussing the various elements of the offence described in the section, I think it necessary to consider whether the saying of *āmīn* aloud in prayers is not an act which falls within the purview of s. 79 of the Indian Penal Code, which lays down the elementary proposition of the criminal law that 'nothing is an offence which is done by any person who is justified by law, or who by reason of a mistake of fact and not by reason of a mistake of law in good faith believes himself to be justified by law in doing it'.

The word *āmīn* is of Semitic origin, being used both in Arabic and Hebrew, and has been adopted in prayers by Muhammadans as much as by Christians. The word does not occur in the Qur'an, but, in conformity with the *Sunna,* or the practice of the Prophet, it is regarded by Muhammadans as an essential part of the prayers, as a word representing earnestness in devotion. The word is pronounced at the end of the first chapter of the Qur'an, which consists of the following prayers:—'Praise be to God, the Lord of all creatures; the most merciful, the King of the day of judgment. Thee do we worship, and of Thee do we beg assistance. Direct us in the right way, in the way of those to whom Thou has been gracious; not of those against whom Thou art incensed, nor of those who go astray.'

In order to understand the exact difficulty which has arisen in this case with reference to the word *āmīn*, it is necessary to bear in mind that Muhammadanism, like other religions, is divided into various sects or schools of doctrine, differing from each other either in matters of principle or in matters of detail as to the minor points of ritual. 'The Musalmans who assume to themselves the distinction of orthodox, are such as maintain the most obvious interpretation of the Qur'an and the obligatory force of the Traditions in opposition to the innovations of the sectaries, whence they are termed Sunnis or Traditionists... and it is their opinion alone which is admitted to have any weight in the determinations of jurisprudence.' These four schools or sects, of which this concise account has been given by Mr Hamilton in the Preliminary Discourse of his translation of the *Hedaya*, were founded by the four orthodox Imams, namely, Abu Hanifa, Malik, Shafe'i and Hanbal, all of whom flourished within the first two centuries of the Muhammadan era, or the eighth century of the Christian era. To use the language of Mr Hamilton again: 'The word orthodox as here used is confined purely to a justness of thinking in spiritual matters, concerning which the opinions of those four sects perfectly coincide, the differences among them relating solely to their expositions of the temporal law.'

I have mentioned all this in order to render intelligible what I am going to say presently regarding the Muhammadan ecclesiastical law with reference to pronouncing the word *āmīn* in prayers. All parties concerned in this case admittedly belong to the Sunni persuasion, and the mosque in question belongs also to the Sunni section of the Muhammadan population. It is an indisputable matter of the Muhammadan ecclesiastical law that the word *āmīn* should be pronounced in prayers after the *Sura-i-Fateha* or the first chapter of the Quran, and that the only difference of opinion among the four Imams is, whether it should be pronounced aloud or in a low voice. The *Hedaya*, which is the most celebrated text-book of the Hanafi school of law, lays down the rule in the following terms: 'When the *Imam* (leader in prayers) has said "nor of those who go astray", he should say *āmīn*, and so should those who are following him in the prayers; because the Prophet has said that "when the *Imam* says *āmīn*, you must say *āmīn* too",... and it must be said in a low voice, because such is the tradition stated by Ibn-i-Masud, and also because the word is the prayer, and should therefore be pronounced in a low voice,' That this doctrine is the result of weighing the authority of conflicting traditions is apparent from the commentary on the above passage of the *Hedaya* by Ibn-i-Humam, a celebrated author of the Hanafi school. These traditions are collected in the celebrated collections of Traditions (*Sihah*) of *Bukhari* and *Muslim*, both equally acknowledged as accurate traditionists by all the schools of the Sunni Muhammadans. From the same traditions the followers of Imam Shafai have evolved the doctrine that *āmīn* should be pronounced aloud, and the views of that school are best stated by Nawawi, a commentator on *Sāhih Muslim*. The followers of the other two Imams, namely, Malik and Hanbal, also maintain that the word *āmīn* should be pronounced aloud. But it is not necessary to cite authorities for this proposition, because their followers do not exist in British India. From what I have already said, it is clear that the doctrines of all the four Imams are regarded by Sunni Muhammadans as orthodox, and that the differences of opinion which exist between them are pure matters of detail. Indeed, in the greatest mosque in the world, namely, the *Kaaba* itself, the followers of all the four Imams are at full liberty to pray according to their own tenets. The Shafeis, as is apparent from the texts which I have already quoted, pronounce the word *āmīn* aloud in prayers, and to this no objection is or can be made on the ground that the practice is heterodox from a Sunni point of view. Indeed, the prosecutor in this very case, in his petition of the 20th September, 1884, after stating that the orthodox Muhammadans are the followers of the four Imams, goes on to say that 'if the defendants had been the followers of anyone of the four Imams, the complainant, who is a Hanafi, and other Muhammadans would not have shrunk from associating with them,' and the ground of the complaint is stated in the petition to be that the defendants 'are not the followers of any of the four Imams', that 'they intend to set up a new form of worship for themselves'; that 'they are therefore no longer Muhammadans'; and by saying the word *āmīn* aloud they 'have been guilty of the offence of insulting the religion of the Hanafi Musalmans.' Now, unless these allegations are substantiated, I am of opinion that there can be no case against the accused under s. 296 of the Indian Penal Code. The prosecutor states himself and the founder of the mosque to be a Hanafi, that is, the follower of Imam Abu Hanifa's doctrines. One of the highest authorities of that school is the *Durr-i-Mukhtar* in which the strongest text is to be found against saying *āmīn* aloud; but the text itself falls far short of substantiating the rule of ecclesiastical law, upon establishing which the case for the prosecution in my opinion depends. The text is as follows:

> It is in accord with the practice of the Prophet to say *āmīn* in a low voice, but the departure from such practice does not necessitate invalidity (of the prayer), nor a mistake, but it is only a detriment.

Even this passage only relates to the efficacy or validity of the prayer of the person who says *āmīn* aloud or in a low tone. There is absolutely no authority in the Hanafi or any other of the three orthodox schools of Muhammadan ecclesiastical law which goes to maintain the proposition that if any person in the congregation says the word *āmīn* aloud at the end of the *Sura-i-Fateha*, the utterance of the word causes the smallest injury, in the religious sense, to the prayers of any other person in the congregation, who, according to his tenets, does not say that word aloud. It is a matter of notoriety that in all the Muhammadan countries like Turkey, Egypt, and Arabia itself, Hanafis and Shafeis go to the same mosque, and form members of the same congregation, and, whilst the Hanafis say the word *āmīn* in a low voice, the Shafias pronounce it aloud. To say that the utterance of the word *āmīn* aloud, after the Imam has recited the *Sura-i-Fateha* causes a disturbance in the prayers of a congregation, some or many of whom say the word in a low tone, is to contradict the express provisions of the Muhammadan ecclesiastical law as explained by all the four orthodox Imams. I now pass to the next step in the case, namely, whether the accused in this case had the legal right to enter into and worship in the mosque with the congregation according to their own tenets. There is absolutely no evidence in the case to substantiate the accusation brought by the prosecutor against them that they are 'no longer Muhammadans'. They call themselves

'Muhammadi', which is the Arabic for 'Muhammadan', and although the prosecutor brands them as Wahabis, there is nothing to prove that they belong to any heterodox sect. Indeed, the only tangible ground upon which the prosecutor objects to their worshipping in the mosque and calls them Wahabis is their saying the *āmīn* aloud—a practice which, as I said before, is commended by three out of the four orthodox Imams of the Sunni persuasion, and which, according to the doctrine of Imam Abu Hanifa himself, does not vitiate the prayers. Now, it is a fundamental principle of the Muhammadan law of wakf, too well known to require the citation of authorities, that when a mosque is built and consecrated by public worship, it ceases to be the property of the builder and vests in God (to use the language of the *Hedaya*) 'in such a manner as subjects it to the rules of Divine property, whence the appropriator's right in it is extinguished and it becomes a property of God by the advantage of it resulting to his creatures.' A mosque once so consecrated cannot in any case revert to the founder, and every Muhammadan has the legal right to enter it, and perform devotions according to his own tenets so long as the form of worship is in accord with the recognized rules of Muhammadan ecclesiastical law. The defendants therefore were fully justified by law in entering the mosque in question and in joining the congregation, and they were strictly within their legal rights, according to the orthodox rule of the Muhammadan ecclesiastical law, in saying the word *āmīn* aloud.

I now proceed to consider whether, under the circumstances of this case, the prosecution have succeeded in substantiating an offence under s 296 of the Indian Penal Code.

The following seem to me to be the constituents of the *corpus delicti*:

(1) That the assembly was lawfully 'engaged in the performance of religious worship'.

(2) That the accused caused a 'disturbance' to such assembly.

(3) That they caused such disturbance 'voluntarily'.

In regard to the first point, there can be no doubt, and indeed there is no question, that the mosque being public, the congregation was lawfully assembled there for the purposes of religious worship.

The second question is not so simple, because the word disturbance is not defined in the Indian Penal Code. But I think I may adopt the language of Shaw, C. J., in an American case cited by Mr Bishop in his treatise on *Criminal Law*:

What shall constitute an interruption and disturbance of a public meeting or assembly cannot easily be brought within a definition applicable to all cases; it must depend somewhat on the nature and character of each particular kind of meeting, and the purposes for which it is held, and much also on the usage and practice governing such meetings. As the law has not defined what shall be deemed an interruption and disturbance, it must be decided as a question of fact in each particular case; and, although it may not be easy to define it beforehand, there is commonly no great difficulty in ascertaining what is a lawful disturbance in a given case.—(Bishop on *Criminal Law,* 6th ed., vol. 2, p. 308.)

In illustrating this, the learned author, after giving some examples of what would cause a disturbance, goes on to say: 'Again, among one class of religionists a solemn *amen* would be permissible, where among another class it would not be' (p. 310). In the present case I have already said enough to show that whilst the Hanafis, who evidently form the majority of the congregation of this mosque, prefer to say *āmīn* in a low voice, there is nothing in their tenets which would vitiate their prayers if any person among the congregation prefers the other equally orthodox tenet of pronouncing the word aloud. There is no allegation on behalf of the prosecution that the accused either uttered the word irreverently or at an improper juncture of the prayers, or otherwise than in the conscientious performance of their devotions. Nor is there any allegation to the effect that the accused pronounced the word *āmīn* in a loud tone with any intention of disturbing the assembly. The rest of the evidence for the prosecution only goes to show that the accused, being earnest believers in the doctrine of saying *āmīn* aloud, entered into a somewhat heated discussion with the other worshippers and employed the word *kafir* (unbeliever) to those who did not accept their doctrine upon the point. Purely as a question of the weight of evidence, I hold that such a discussion could not have taken place during the prayers, because the Muhammadan ritual absolutely prohibits the utterance of any words other than those of the prayers during the *namaz* or divine service. The prosecution itself makes no such allegation, and if the discussion took place before or after the service, though in the mosque itself, I hold that even if the discussion be regarded as a disturbance, it would not fall under the purview of s. 296, Indian Penal Code. This view of the law is in accord with that adopted by Abbott, C. J., in *Williams* v. *Glenister*, cited in *Russell on Crimes*, vol. 1, p. 417. In that case the person accused of having molested a religious assembly in a church had, notwithstanding the prohibition of the minister, stood up in his pew and read a notice 'after the Nicene Creed had been read, and whilst the minister was walking from the communion table to the vestry room, and whilst no part of the service was actually going on.' It was held that such act, having been done during an interval when no part of the service was in the course of being performed, and the party apparently supposing that he had a right to give the notice, he was not criminally liable.

The case, however, being based upon a statute is only analogically applicable to the present case, and I cite it simply to put my interpretation upon the phrase 'engaged in the performance of religious worship' as used in s. 296 of the Indian Penal Code. As to the merits of the present case itself upon this particular point, I have to observe that a Muhammadan mosque is in many respects different, so far as I know, from an ordinary Christian church; because it is not only a place for divine worship, but also intended for religious and moral teaching and discussion, and it is not unusual that, in places where the Muhammadan community is still flourishing, a library and a school form part of the mosque. I cannot therefore hold that to carry on religious discussion in a mosque, even though the majority of the people present at the time do not approve of such discussion, constitutes a criminal offence. There may indeed be circumstances which may render such discussion liable to cause breach of the peace; but in that case the law has provided other remedies, and, concerned as I am in the Full Bench only with s. 296 of the Indian Penal Code, I will simply say that the remedy does not fall under that section. The third point relates to the meaning of the word 'voluntarily' as used in s. 296 of the Indian Penal Code, and upon this point s. 39 of the Code provides an explanation in express language. I am of opinion that the evidence in this case does not prove that the accused uttered the word *āmīn* aloud with the intention of disturbing the rest of the congregation, though after the occurrence of the 22 August 1884, they might have known that the prosecutor and his friends would object to their saying the word aloud. But the question is not of any great consequence under my view of the case; because the accused being fully entitled by law to enter the mosque, to join the congregation, and to say the word *āmīn* aloud, they were justified by law to exercise their right of worship within the meaning of s. 79 of the Indian Penal Code.

At the hearing of the case before the Full Bench, the learned Public Prosecutor laid considerable stress upon the argument that to justify a conviction under s. 296, Indian Penal Code, it is of no consequence whether the act which causes the disturbance is in itself lawful or unlawful: that the mere fact of the disturbance being caused to the religious assembly is sufficient to constitute the offence, specially as the accused in this case had reason to believe that saying the word *āmīn* might be objectionable to the prosecutor and his party, and might cause breach of the peace. I am unable to accept this view of the law, for, to use the words of Field, J., in *Beatty* v. *Gillbanks* [LR 9 QBD 308], 'it amounts to this, that a man may be convicted for doing a lawful act if he knows that his doing it may cause another to do an unlawful act. There is no authority for such a proposition.' Not only do I hold that s. 79 of the Code furnishes a full answer to the argument; but that such a principle would place the minority at the mercy of the majority, and would, in a case like this, deprive them of the right of worship which the law distinctly confers upon them. Indeed if such a view were adopted, it would open the door for wrongful prosecution of innocent persons, who in the exercise of their lawful rights of worship resort to mosques for devotion. Such indeed may be the case here, because there is enough in the evidence for the defence to raise a suspicion that the saying of *āmin* aloud has been made a pretext for the prosecution with the object of preventing the accused from resorting to the mosque for worship, and thus to debar them from asking the prosecutor to render accounts of the disbursement of the income of the property belonging to the mosque, of which he states himself to be the *mutawalli* or superintendent. The witnesses for the defence, who are themselves Hanafis, have solemnly deposed that they do not object to *āmīn* being pronounced aloud in prayers, and their statements deserve weight, being in perfect accord with the doctrines of Imam Abu Hanifa himself.

Having taken this view of the case, I regret I am unable to concur in the order of retrial passed by the learned Chief Justice and my learned brethren, and I would return the case to the referring Bench with a negative answer to the question referred.

35. MOHAMMAD WASI v. BACHCHAN SAHIB (1955) 2 All 128 (FB)

Mosque—suit by Sunnites—perpetual injunction refused for not performing gahwara (Shiite) ceremonies in the mosque—nature of ceremonies permissible

1. A mosque once dedicated is open for worship to all Muslims.

2. It cannot be reserved for any particular denomination.

3. No person can claim that the form of congregational prayer said in a mosque be altered to suit him.

4. Every Muslim is entitled to go and say his prayers in any mosque in his own form of prayers and ritual, provided he does not disturb the other devotees. [This is the actual practice, daily, in the Omayyad Mosque, Damascus.]

5. The objects of the dedication of a mosque cannot be altered after the dedication is completed and acted upon. Nor can the beneficiaries be changed or limited.

6. A Muslim has a cause of action if he is deprived of his right to say his prayers in a mosque, or is prevented from doing so.

It may be mentioned in passing that this case refers to the right of entry for the purpose of saying prayers; it is absolutely clear in Islam that every human being regardless of caste or creed is entitled to enter a mosque at any time because it is the house of God.

For a discussion of the cases see *Outlines*, 312 seqq. Tyabji (Faiz B.) J. has made certain reservations as to clause 2. above, *Akbarally A. Adamji Peerbhoy* v. *Mahomedally Adamji Peerbhoy*, AIR 1932 Bom 356, cited in this case at p. 138. His treatment of the subject is valuable, *Tyabji*, §§ 514–19.

Judgment [Malik CJ][3]

[Since] this appeal... involves a general question of importance affecting the Shias and Sunnis, two sects of the Muslim community, it was ordered to be heard by a Bench of three Judges.

The two plaintiffs belong to the Sunni sect and are residents of Qasba Mahmudabad, District Sitapur. They brought a suit in their representative capacity... on behalf of the Sunnis of Qasba Mahmudabad against the first five defendants in their representative capacity as representing the Shia Muslims of the same Qasba. In paragraph 6 of the plaint it was said that as all the Sunni Muslims of Mahmudabad have the right to get a permanent injunction issued, the plaintiffs under Order I, rule 8 of the Civil Procedure Code seek permission to file the suit on behalf of all the Sunnis of Qasba Mahmudabad and, as all the Shias of Mahmudabad are prepared to contest the suit, permission is sought to file the suit against the defendants on behalf of all the Shia Muslims of Qasba Mahmudabad.'

When notice of the suit was issued, defendants 6 to 19 who are Sunni Muslims applied that they did not wish to be associated with the plaintiffs, nor did they want the plaintiffs to represent them, and they were, therefore, impleaded as defendants to the action.

There is a mosque situated near the railway station in Qasba Mahmudabad. The plaintiffs' contention was that it was constructed by a Sunni Musalman, that the *Azan* and the prayers had all along been said in the Sunni form and that the Shia Musalmans had nothing to do with this mosque, nor did they say their prayers in it, but with the aid of the police the Shia Musalmans had started forcibly decorating *tabut* and *gahwara* inside the mosque after doing *matam* etc., that according to the belief of the Sunni Musalmans, the said action was 'against *Shariyat* and it insults, debases and injures their feelings.' It was said that the Shia Musalmans had no right to have the *tabut* or the *gahwara* decorated inside the mosque or take it out in a procession from there after doing *matam*, etc. It was, therefore, prayed that a permanent injunction be issued against them. [....]

3 With Bhargava & Hari Shanker, JJ.

The relief claimed in the plaint was as follows:

That a permanent injunction be issued to the effect that the Shia Muslims of Qasba Mahmudabad should not decorate *tabut* or *gahwara* in the said mosque and take out their procession from the said mosque, nor should they do *matam* therein.

[....]

The Sunni defendants 6 to 19 supported the Shia defendants and pleaded that they consider *tazias* and *taziadari* as part of Islamic religion, that they join and participate in the Gahwara procession and they have no objection to the said acts being done as before. According to them the plaintiffs were a troublesome group who believed in creating disputes between different communities and they realize subscriptions for the purpose of litigation and misappropriate a part of it. It was pointed out that besides this mosque there were other mosques in Mahmudabad from which *tazias* were taken out and *Gahwara* processions, etc., were formed and decorated.

The Shia defendants denied that the mosque had been constructed by a Sunni. They claimed that they had been saying their prayers in the said mosque and that the decoration of *gahwara* and *matam*, etc., had been performed in the mosque for a long time and the procession was taken out from there and it was recently that the plaintiffs had started creating trouble. It was also pleaded that a large number of Sunnis believed in *taziadari* and they took part in the functions; that the mosque was originally constructed by one Ramzani Halwai who had built an Imambara and a Kachcha Idgah and he used to do *taziadari* in honour of Hazrat Imam Husain. The Rajas of Mahmudabad (who admittedly belong to the Shia sect) had, it was said, rebuilt the mosque, when it had fallen down, and had been responsible for its upkeep and maintenance. [....]

The fact remains that while a section of the Muslims abhor and condemn such practices, another section, though numerically less but probably equally well established, consider them meritorious. It is also a fact that even a fair number of Sunnis take part in *tazias* and *taziadari* and in the *gahwara* procession. As always happens, with the passing of time, the scriptures are differently interpreted by learned men and, if they can influence a sufficient number to form a nucleus, a new sect grows up and often there is bitter ill-feeling between the members of one sect and another, each condemning the other for what it considers to be a heretical or wrong interpretation of the sacred scripture. This happened among Christians, and in the middle ages there were widespread persecutions of Catholics by the Protestants and also of the Protestants by the Catholics. Protestants and Catholics have however separate churches of their own and the problem that has, therefore, arisen in some parts of India, as regards the use of mosques by different sects of Muslims, did not arise among Christians about the use of churches.

Chaudhri Niamat Ullah has put forward before us a very short and simple argument. His contention is that a mosque is the property of God primarily dedicated for saying of prayers. No Muslim can be excluded from saying his prayers in a mosque and no objection can be taken to his saying prayers therein so long as he says his prayers according to the well recognized ecclesiastical rules of Muslim faith. He has contended that, that being the primary object, besides the five prayers prescribed—the first (*fajr*) before dawn, the second (*zohar*) after mid-day, the third (*asr*) in the afternoon, the fourth (*maghrib*) after sunset and the fifth (*isha*) before midnight—a Muslim can say prayers at anytime during the day and night, and the mosque must therefore be available to him whenever he wants it for the purpose of saying his prayers, that anything else done in the mosque is by leave and licence, and that a mosque cannot be put to any other use if a Muslim objects to it on the ground that it interferes with his right to say his prayers.

[. . . .]

Learned counsel for the appellant has cited a number of authorities to establish his contention that a mosque is dedicated for the purpose of prayer alone, that other use is by leave and licence and that no one can claim a right to use it for any other purpose except for saying of prayers. He has relied on Tyabji's *Muhammadan Law*, sections 514 to 516. These sections, however, deal with the completion of a dedication. According to them the first public prayer said on the land or within the building completes a dedication for a mosque. It is also made clear that there can be no power of revocation once a mosque is dedicated and there can be no reservation of rights by the *waqif*, nor can a mosque be dedicated with an effective reservation for a particular sect or class of people. In *Akbarally A. Adamji Peerbhoy* v; *Mahomedally Adamji Peerbhoy*,[4] Tyabji J., observed at page 362:

> It has been laid down as a principle in a decision of great authority that a mosque must be a mosque for all; that it must be a building dedicated to God and not a building dedicated to God with a reservation that it should be used only by persons holding particular views of the ritual; that it is a place where all Muhammadans are entitled to go and perform their devotions as of right according to their conscience:

The learned Judge, however, made certain observations which we consider significant, He said:

4 AIR 1932 Bom 356.

However, I feel great difficulty in seeing how it can be given effect to in British India, where each community is free to govern itself by its own customs and usages, and its own interpretation of the Quran and of the fundamental rules of Islam; and the court does not lay down what shall be considered the true interpretation where rival interpretations have been adopted.

If the argument of learned counsel is given its full effect it can lead to a tyranny of the majority by a few. The Muslims of a locality may have a mosque built for prayers and make elaborate arrangement for *taziadari* or similar rituals in which they may have great faith. Any Muslim can then come forward and claim that nothing but prayers shall be said in the mosque and it shall not be used for any other purpose as he wants to say his prayers at any time he likes within twenty-four hours and the rituals would disturb his prayers.

In a country like India, where people are free to follow their own faith, according to their own belief, the policy of live and let live must govern the relationship between followers of various religions or sects, so long as it does not conflict against the rules of public morality or decency. It is not open to a member of a particular sect to claim that the others should not follow their faith according to their belief because it offends against his susceptibilities. We had recently a case from Amethi in which the Muslims had objected to the blowing of conch-shells on the ground that it was intimately connected with idol worship which was repugnant to Muslim sentiment.[5] It appears to us, therefore, that the only way of ensuring peace and religious freedom to all would be by laying down that the practices followed peacefully and without objection for years at a place of worship should not be disturbed on the ground that it was being objected to by some people because they claimed that it was repugnant to the true tenets of their faith.

A Muslim has no doubt a right to say his prayers in a mosque and he cannot be kept out of it. There are certain prayers which are said in a gathering and in that sense they may be called congregational prayers. In every mosque these prayers are said at particular hours and Chaudhri Niamat Ullah has urged, and probably rightly, that any of the five prayers said in a congregation cannot be repeated on the same day for the benefit of those who come late or who want to say the prayers in a different way. He had relied on a decision of the Patna High Court in *Hakim Khalil Ahmad* v. *Malik Israfi*.[6] In that case, in an old mosque built by the Sunnis, the Qadianis had been saying their prayers for a number of years. The learned Judges held that the plaintiffs who were Qadianis could not get a decree

5 See *Ahmad Ali* v. *Babu Ram* 1954 AWR 525.
6 (1917) PLR 37 IC 302.

that they were entitled to abstain from joining in the ordinary devotion at the mosque and to appoint an Imam of their own to lead the prayers after the usual daily prayers had been concluded.

It may be that nothing can be done in a mosque at a time when the five daily prayers are said, so as to disturb the saying of those prayers. Besides the five daily prayers a Muslim can say other prayers at any time of the day and night. These can be said at any place which is clean. The right that a Muslim has is merely to say his prayers, and if he is excluded or if he is disturbed or not allowed to say his prayers at the time he has been usually saying them in the mosque, he may have a just grievance.... In the absence of proof that the plaintiffs' rights were affected they cannot be said to have any cause of action for the suit.

There is another ground on which the suit must fail. It is clear from the judgment of the learned Civil Judge that the Sunni Muslims are bringing this mosque to various uses, which are summarized at page 180 of the paper book, as for (1) holding of *Sayums*, (2) holding discourses by *Maulanas*, (3) taking out *Jaloos Mahamdi* procession, (4) holding of *Milads*, (5) holding of *Jalsa Anna Fund*, and. (6) the reception of the *Maulanas* who went to deliver lectures at Mahmudabad. Since they are bringing the mosque to all these uses, they cannot claim that Shias and other Sunnis who believe in *taziadari* cannot bring the building to such use on the ground that the mosque is dedicated only for the purpose of saying prayers.

There is yet another ground why the suit must fail. The plaintiffs have confined the relief in the plaint to an injunction against Shias, while a large section of Sunnis also believe in *taziadari*, and if the suit is decreed they would be free to do *taziadari* while Shias will be forbidden from doing it. [....]

We have the findings of the lower appellate court that for more than forty years the ceremonies objected to have been performed in the mosque; that Shias and some Sunnis have been taking part in it; that the original founder himself believed in *taziadari* and that the mosque was never reserved for Sunnis alone. In these circumstances, if, by reason of the bitterness of feeling that has recently developed due to *madh-e-sahaba*[7] and *tabarra*[8]

7 Formal praise and salutations given to the First Four Companions (Abū Bakr, 'Umar, 'Uthmān, and 'Ali) by the Sunnites. These are known as the Orthodox (or Rightly Guided) Caliphs.

8 Literally, 'declaring oneself free from the responsibility of accepting someone as Caliph/Imām'. The word is used by Shiites in two senses. In the theological sense it is a dogmatic repudiation of the Sunnite Caliphs; but in actual practice especially in Northern India, it is the ritual ceremony of cursing the first three Caliphs namely, Abū Bakr, 'Umar, 'Uthman. This deplorable practice, formerly quite common in India, is now rapidly being given up by many enlightened Shiite orders, families and individuals.

controversy in Lucknow, a section of Sunnis have become more sensitive and want to exclude a considerable section of Muslims of the locality from doing what they have been doing peacefully and without objection for the last forty years or more, the court would be well justified in not using its discretion in favour of the plaintiffs. These observations would be enough to dispose of this appeal, but as a number of cases have been cited we may briefly deal with them.

A Hanafi Muslim says the word '*Amen*' at the end of his prayer silently or under his breath, while Wahabis say it loudly. A Wahabi Muslim for saying '*Amen*' in a loud voice was prosecuted under sections 79 and 296 of the Indian Penal Code (Act no. 45 of 1860). He was convicted by the lower court. There was an appeal to the High Court. The case was referred to a Full Bench and the Chief Justice and three other Judges sent the case back for a retrial to find out whether the accused had caused any disturbance at the time of saying of the prayers. See *Queen-Empress* v. *Ramzan*.[9] Mahmood, J. wrote a dissentient judgment in which he said:

> As to the merits of the present case itself upon this particular point, I have to observe that a Muhammadan mosque is in many respects different, so far as I know, from an ordinary Christian church; because it is not only a place for divine worship, but also intended for religious and moral teaching and discussion, and it is not unusual that in places where the Muhammadan community is still flourishing, a library and a school form part of the mosque.

I cannot, therefore, hold that to carry on religious discussion in a mosque, even though the majority of the people present at the time do not approve of such discussion, constitutes a criminal offence.

Learned counsel for the appellants has relied on *Ata-Ullah* v. *Azim-Ullah*.[10] As a result of the prosecution of Wahabis for saying 'Amen' in a loud voice, some Wahabis filed a suit for a declaration that they were entitled to pray and perform their religious devotion according to their own beliefs. The case was again referred to a Full Bench in which the learned Chief Justice made it clear that a mosque which is dedicated to God cannot be limited in its dedication to any particular sect or sects of Muslims and that every Muslim has a right to say his prayers according to the well recognized rules of Muhammadan ecclesiastical law.

The next case was *Jangu* v. *Ahmad Ullah*.[11] In this case also the dispute related to the saying of the word '*Amen*' in a loud voice at the end of the prayers by the Wahabis and they asked for a declaration from a civil court.

9 (1885) ILR 7 All 461.
10 (1890) ILR 12 All 494.
11 ILR 13 All 419.

The right was recognized, but it was made clear that they could not say '*Amen*' *mala fide* in such a loud voice as to disturb others.

The other case relied upon is *Sifat Ali Khan* v. *Ali Mian*.[12] This was a case in which the plaintiffs sued for a declaration that they were the *mutwallis* and *imams* of a certain mosque and that they had for more than 25 years been saying *namaz* as members of the Ahmadi or Qadiani sect and that the defendants who were non-Qadianis had on no account any right to offer their prayers in congregation led by some other *imam*. The case came up to this court in second appeal and it was held that the plaintiffs had failed to prove that they were the *mutwallis* and *imams* of the mosque or that they had any right to lead the prayers.

The next case relied on is *Syed Ahmad* v. *Hafiz Zahid Husain*[13] In that case a school or *maktab* was held within the compound of an ancient mosque built nearly 300 years before. Those in charge of the management of the school wanted to have a *pakka* building for that purpose and a suit was filed on behalf of the mosque and it was held that the mosque was dedicated for a specific purpose and every Muslim, of whatever locality and belonging to whichever sect of Muslims, had a right to say his prayers therein, and that the local Muslim population could not claim any special beneficial interest in themselves and could not, therefore, utilize the mosque property for building a school on a part of its ground. If we may say so, with respect, we accept both the propositions laid down in this judgment that a mosque is dedicated for worship and is open to all Muslims, local and others, and that the local Muslims cannot have a right to use it for any other purpose however meritorious or beneficial it may be to them.

In *Muthala Kandi Katturi Koya Molla* v. *Palli Veetil Abu Baker*[14] it was held by a Bench of the Madras High Court that every Muhammadan worshipper has the right both to offer prayer and to recite the Koran as a part of his right of worship in a mosque, but he cannot claim the right to use the mosque for the purpose of collecting subscriptions or distributing sweetmeats.

From all the authorities cited above it would appear that it is now well-settled that

(I) a mosque is dedicated for the purpose that any Muslim belonging to any sect can go and say prayers therein;

(2) it cannot be reserved for Muslims of any particular denomination or sect;

12 AIR 1933 All 284.
13 AIR 1934 All 792.
14 (1912) ILR 17 Mad 386.

(3) no one can claim to have the form of congregational prayer usually said in a mosque altered to suit him;

(4) even though the congregational prayers are said in a mosque in a particular form, any Muslim belonging to any other sect can go into a mosque and say his prayers at the back of the congregation in the manner followed by him so long as he does not do anything *mala fide* to disturb the others;

(5) the object of the dedication can neither be altered nor the beneficiaries limited or changed: and

(6) a Muslim will have a cause of action if he is deprived of his right to say prayers in a mosque or is prevented from doing so.

Accepting all these propositions the plaintiffs' suit must fail by reason of the fact that they are not able to prove that their right to say prayers has in any way been affected by reason of the action of Shia defendants. Secondly, it must fail because the nature of the relief claimed by them is defective. Thirdly, it must fail on the ground that, though the plaintiffs are objecting to certain functions and ceremonies held in the mosque at the instance of the defendants, they themselves have been performing other ceremonies which may be equally objectionable to others. And, lastly, it must fail because from the evidence it is clear that the mosque has been used for *taziadari*, etc. from its very inception; that *Gahwara* ceremonies have been performed therein for the last forty years or more and that Shias as also some Sunnis, have been taking part in it. In these circumstances if the defendants were not doing anything against public morality or decency, the plaintiffs cannot be allowed to claim the grant of a discretionary relief that the Shias and others be not allowed to follow the tenets of their faith in their own way without let or hindrance by others.

The result, therefore, is that this appeal fails and is dismissed with costs.

◊ UPDATE ◊

1. *Kazis, courts and mosques*

Justice Syed Ameer Ali's observation in the old Privy Council ruling in *Mahomed Ismail* [Case 33], that playing the role of the *kazi* under Muslim law the civil courts can interfere to ensure proper management of the mosques, finds its echo in the general trends relating to mosque administration in all parts of the subcontinent. The traditional role of the *kazi* in this respect is now effectively played by the State authorities and not too infrequently also by the courts. There is now a heap of legislation and a spate of judicial decisions relating to management of wakfs, including the mosques, in all three countries of the subcontinent.

2. *Status of mosques*

Considering the legal status of mosques in the *Ayodhya Reference* case—*M. Ismail Faruqi* v. *Union of India* AIR 1995 SC 605—the Indian Supreme Court has observed that the mosque is 'not an essential part of the practice of the religion of Islam'. The observation does not seem to be in accord with the Islamic religious principles. The court also referred in its judgment to an old opinion of the Lahore High Court approved by the Privy Council in the *Masjid Shahidganj* case (AIR 1940 PC 116) that 'the view that once consecrated a mosque always remains a place of worship as a mosque is not the Mohammedan law of India as approved by the courts'.

3. *Sectarian mosques*

The dispute referred to in the old Allahabad decision in *Queen Empress* v. *Ramzan* [Case 34] relates to the practice of *amin bil-jehr* in group prayers offered in the mosques, on which there has been a difference of opinion among the Muslims. When the *imam* (prayer-leader) loudly recites the opening chapter of the Qur'an, at the end of it those praying behind him are to utter the word '*amin*' (amen). The controversy is on whether this to be done quietly or in a loud voice. In the older days those who believed that it was to be said quietly sometimes made it a prestige issue and would not let the others say it loudly. Such religious trifles of the bygone age do not exist now anywhere and nobody now objects to the utterance of *amin* in a loud voice in the mosques.

The dictum of *Mohammad Wasi* v. *Bachchan Sahib* [Case 35] about the non-sectarian nature of mosques was reaffirmed in India in *Shah Abdul Baqi* v. *State of UP* AIR 1988 All 1.

4. *Use of amplifiers in mosques*

In the Indian case of *Navin Kumar* v. *Municipal Corporation of Bombay* AIR 1989 Bom 88 it was held that use of amplifiers in the mosques can be restricted by the State in public interest:

> Congregational prayers are a beautiful feature of the Muslim religion, and one remembers with pleasure the romantic sound of an early morning *moazzin* from the turrets of an upcountry mosque on a misty morning. But to transform it into a noisy fanfare is neither artistic nor necessary. I find nowhere that the religion of the Muslims enjoins it... May be that what is sought to be propagated in this instance is not profane music but a call to the faithful for offering their daily prayers but the objection remains.

XV. Pre-emption

36. Gobind Dayal v. Inayatullah
(1885) 7 All 775 (FB)

Pre-emption—Muhammadan vendor and pre-emptor and Hindu purchaser—Act VI of 1871 (Bengal Civil Courts Act), s. 24—'religious usage or institution'—principles of inheritance[1]—interpretation of Muhammadan law—'tricks and artifices' of the ancient law not permissible—'parties'

Held by the Full Bench that in a case of pre-emption where the pre-emptor and vendor are Muslims and the vendee a non-Muslim, the Muhammadan law is to be applied to the matter, in advertence to the terms of s. 24 of the Bengal Civil Courts Act (VI of 1871). *Sheikh Kudratulla* v. *Mahini Mohan Shaha*[2] dissented from.

Per Petheram, C. J., and Oldfield, J., that, by the provisions of s. 24 of the Bengal Civil Courts Act the court was not bound to administer the Muhammadan law in claims for pre-emption; but on grounds of equity that law had always been administered in respect of such claims as between Muslims, and it would not be equitable that persons who were not Muslims but who had dealt with Muslims in respect of property, knowing the conditions and obligations under which the property was held, should merely by reason that they were not themselves subject to the Muhammadan law be permitted to evade those conditions and obligations.

Per Mahmood, J., that by a liberal construction the rule of the Muhammadan law as to pre-emption is a 'religious usage or institution' within the meaning of s. 24 of the Bengal Civil Courts Act, and as such is binding on the courts.

Also *per* Mahmood, J., that the word 'parties' as used in s. 24 of the Bengal Civil Courts Act does not mean the parties to an action, but must

[1] The remarks of Mahmood J. are strictly obiter, but these are of great value (p. 782 of the Report).

[2] 4 BLR 134.

be interpreted with the reference to the inception of the right to be adjudicated upon.

Also *per* Mahmood, J.—The right of pre-emption is not a right of repurchase either from the vendor or from the vendee, involving any new contract of sale; it is simply a right of *substitution* entitling the pre-emptor, by reason of a legal incident to which the sale itself was subject, to stand in the shoes of the vendee in respect of all the rights and obligations arising from the sale under which he has derived his title.

The history and nature of the right of pre-emption is discussed by Mahmood, J. This case is discussed in *Outlines,* 326 seqq.

The suits in which these appeals arose were suits to enforce the right of pre-emption. The pre-emptor and vendor were in each case Muhammadans, and the vendees were Hindus. The right in each case was based upon the Muhammadan law, the plaintiff in the one claiming 'by virtue of his being a co-sharer in the right and property sold and also by right of vicinage', and in the other as 'a partner in the property the subject of sale'. In each case, the court of first instance dismissed the suit, being of opinion that the right of pre-emption could not be enforced by a Muhammadan against a non-Muhammadan vendee. The lower appellate courts, being of the contrary opinion, reversed the decrees and remanded the cases for disposal on the merits. The defendants in each case appealed to the High Court from the order of remand.

The appeals came for hearing before Straight and Mahmood, JJ., who referred the following question raised by them to the Full Bench:

> In a case of pre-emption where the pre-emptor and vendor are Muhammadans and the vendee a non-Muhammadan, is the Muhammadan law of pre-emption to be applied to the matter in advertence to the terms of s. 24 of Act VI of 1871?

Judgment [Mahmood, J.][3]

These two connected appeals have been referred together to the Full Bench as presenting the same question for determination by the court, and I have been requested by my learned brethren to deliver my judgment first. The question is exactly the same as that which was raised in *Sheikh Kudratulla* v. *Mahini Mohan Shaha.*[4] The order of reference in F. A. from Order No. 135 of 1883, after alluding to certain rulings of this court and of the Calcutta Court, and considering the great importance of the points of law involved, refers to the Full Bench the following question: 'In a case of pre-emption, where the pre-emptor and the vendor are Muhammadans and the vendee

3 With Petheram, CJ and Oldfield, Brodhurst and Duthoit, JJ.

4 4 BLR 134.

a non-Muhammadan, is the Muhammadan law of pre-emption to be applied to the matter, in advertence to the terms of s. 24 of Act VI of 1871?' This question presents itself to my mind in two aspects. The first is, whether s. 24 of the Bengal Civil Courts Act renders it imperative on this court and the courts subordinate to it to administer the Muhammadan law in cases of this nature? The second is, what is the Muhammadan law of pre-emption in regard to the point before us?

The first of these questions depends upon the construction to be placed on s. 24 of the Bengal Civil Courts Act (VI of 1871). In discussing this, I shall be within the recognized rules of interpretation in reviewing shortly the history of the particular section in question. It is not a new provision of the law. The principle which it embodies was recognized by the British rule at the outset of its authority in this country. The history of the recognition of this principle has been accurately traced by a learned Judge of the Indian Bench, Mr. Justice Field, at pages 169–71 of his valuable work on the Regulations of the Bengal Code. The legislation there described began with the Regulation of the 21 August 1772, which laid down the exact scope of the application of the Hindu and Muhammadan laws, and the omission to provide for cases which did not fall within the rule was supplied by the Regulation of the 5 July 1781, which directed that 'in all cases for which no specific directions are hereby given, the judges do act according to justice, equity, and good conscience.' The latter part of the rule was reproduced in s. 21 of Regulation III of 1793, and the former part of the rule was re-enacted in s. 15 of Regulation IV of 1793, which laid down that 'in suits regarding succession, inheritance, marriage, and caste, and all religious usages and institutions, the Muhammadan laws with respect to Muhammadans, and the Hindu laws with regard to Hindus, are to be considered as the general rules by which the judges are to form their decisions. To the two-fold rule so laid down, addition was soon after made by Regulation VIII of 1795, which enacted that 'in cases in which the plaintiff shall be of a different religious persuasion from the defendant, the decision is to be regulated by the law of the religion of the latter, excepting where Europeans or other persons, not being either Muhammadans or Hindus, shall be defendants, in which cases the law of the plaintiff is to be made the rule of decision in all plaints and actions of a civil nature.' The principle of applying the native laws according to the religious persuasions of the parties to the suit, and, with reference to the accident of their being arrayed as parties-plaintiffs or parties-defendants in the litigation, is an illustration of the simplicity which marks some of our oldest legislative enactments. The principle must have given rise, not only to confusion, but in some cases to positive injustice; whilst in cases where every one of the persons arrayed as parties to the suit belonged to a different persuasion, the application of the rule must have been impracticable. The experience of some years seems to have brought this difficulty into prominence, for we find that the next important piece of legislation on the subject was Regulation VII of 1832, s. 9, of which, while affirming the rules to which reference has already been made, added a new proposition as an injunction to the courts administering justice under the East India Company. The section ran thus: 'It is hereby declared, however, that the above rules are intended and shall be held to apply to such persons only as shall be *bona fide* professors of those religions at the time of the application of the law of the case, and were designed for the protection of the rights of such persons—not for the deprivation of the rights of others. Whenever, therefore, in any civil suit, the parties to such suit may be of different persuasions, when one party shall be of the Hindu and the other of the Muhammadan persuasion; or where one or more of the parties to the suit shall not be either of the Muhammadan or the Hindu persuasion, the laws of those religions shall not be permitted to operate to deprive such party or parties of any property to which, but for the operation of those laws, they would have been entitled. In all such cases, the decision shall be governed by the principles of justice, equity, and good conscience, it being clearly understood, however, that this provision shall not be considered as justifying the introduction of the English or any foreign law, or the application to such cases of any rules not sanctioned by those principles.'

Such was the law at the time when the celebrated case of *Sheikh Kuaratulla* v. *Mahini Mohan Shaha*[5] was decided by the Full Bench of the Calcutta High Court. Since that time, however, the provisions which I have referred to have been repealed by the Bengal Civil Courts Act (VI of 1871), and the question is now governed by s. 24 of that Act, which provides that 'where in any suit or proceeding it is necessary for any court under this Act to decide any question regarding succession, inheritance, marriage or caste, or any religious usage or institution, the Muhammadan law in cases where the parties are Muhammadans, and the Hindu law in cases where the parties are Hindus, shall form the rule of decision, except in so far as such law has, by legislative enactment, been altered or abolished. In cases not provided for by the former part of this section, or by any other law for the time being in force, the court shall act according to justice, equity, and good conscience.' It is this section with which we are directly concerned in the present case, and I have referred to the old Regulations because, without reference to them, the law in its existing form can scarcely be properly interpreted.

5 4 BLR 134.

The question then arises: Is pre-emption a 'religious usage or institution' within the meaning of the section? It cannot come within any of the other matters enumerated. A similar question was considered by a Full Bench of this court in connection, not with the subject of pre-emption, but with that of gift under the Muhammadan law. This was in the case of *Shumsh-ool-nissa* v. *Zohra Bibi*,[6] in which the court was divided in opinion, Spankie, J., differing from the other three judges, Stuart, C. J., Pearson and Jardine, JJ. The majority of the court were of opinion that, under s. 24 of Act VI of 1871, the Muhammadan law is not strictly applicable to questions relating to gifts, but it is equitable as between Muhammadans to apply that law to such questions. I shall presently refer to the dissentient judgment of Spankie, J., for whose opinion upon such questions I have always entertained the greatest respect. Shortly after this, the Full Bench case of *Chundo* v. *Hakeem Alim-ood-deen*,[7] was decided. That repeats the same principle, but is still more to the point, because it relates to pre-emption, and the majority of the court held that under s. 24 of Act VI of 1871, the Muhammadan law is not strictly applicable in suits for pre-emption between Muhammadans not based on local custom or contract, but it is equitable in such suits to apply that law. Here again Spankie, J., adhering to the opinion formerly expressed by him, dissented from the opinion of the majority of this court.

Now, as to the two Full Bench cases, the opinion of the majority of this court in regard to gift and pre-emption was that, although the court was, as a matter of fact, bound to apply the rules of Muhammadan law, it was so bound not by the strict terms of the first part of s. 24, but by the rule of justice, equity, and conscience, referred to in the second part. Spankie, J., on the other hand, held that the law of pre-emption, as of gift, must be applied under the first part of the section, being included under the head of 'religious usage or institution'. In other words, the majority thought that they might properly let their notions of justice, equity, and good conscience prevail over those of the Muhammadan law, while Spankie, J., held that the court was absolutely bound to follow that law. With all due respect to the majority in that case, I cannot help observing that the view expressed by Spankie, J., is the only one which could be accepted by a Muhammadan lawyer sitting here as a Judge. That learned Judge did not consider the question in any limited or superficial manner. He carefully and thoroughly dealt with the circumstances under which the Muhammadan law is binding upon the courts, and referred to the opinions expressed by Muhammadan writers, and, among others, to a work by my father, Syed Ahmed Khan Bahadur. He observed: 'It is contended that we cannot connect "religious

6 NWP HCR 1874, p. 2.
7 NWP HCR 1874, p. 28.

usage or institution" with cases of gift, and that it would be straining the ordinary acceptation of the meaning of the words to do so. But I am not satisfied that this is the case. "Usage" ordinarily means use or long continued use, custom, practice. "Institution" means the act of establishing, establishment, that which is appointed, prescribed or followed by authority, and intended to be permanent. One of the four senses in which the word "institution" is used technically extends to laws, rites, and ceremonies, which are enjoined by authority as permanent rules of conduct or of government. So far, then, as the ordinary meaning of the word goes, I do not see anything anomalous in the suggestion that judicial questions regarding gifts may be determined according to religious usage, which includes prescription as well as custom. So if laws have been enjoined by authority to govern questions of gift and were intended to be permanent, the word "institution" may not be misapplied. It is to be remembered that Hindu and Muhammadan laws are so intimately connected with religion that they cannot readily be dissevered from it. As long as the religions last, the laws founded on them last. Mr Baillie has noticed this, and he remarks that Muhammadans in the provinces are more in the habit of regulating their dealings with each other by their own law, and to disregard it would be inconsistent with justice, equity, and good conscience; and, this being so, he assumed that the Judges have been obliged to extend the operation of the Muhammadan law beyond the cases to which it is strictly applicable under the Regulations. He quotes Macnaghten in his preface to the *Principles of Muhammadan Law*, as having arranged the order of cases in which this law has been applied by our courts.' The learned Judge then proceeds to consider the cases in which Baillie holds that the Muhammadan law perforce applies. Then he goes on to say: 'Questions then, of gifts, pre-emption, & c., if not governed by Muhammadan law as expressed clearly in the text of the Quran, are controlled by religious usages founded on, or institutions enjoined by, the oral law or sayings of the Prophet.' And in conclusion: 'I am of opinion that the proper answer to the reference is that the suit giving rise to it should be determined by that law (i.e., the Muhammadan law), and without reference to the principles of justice, equity, and good conscience.'

Now, although the decision of the majority in that case is binding upon me, I regard the question as virtually reopened by this case, and I must therefore confess that I am unable to agree with it, and my reasons are these: In the first place, the Muhammadan law of gift or pre-emption either is or is not law in the proper sense, by which I mean a rule of conduct binding upon the subjects of the State, and upon the courts which the State has established. No doubt the opinion of the learned Judges leads to the same result. They also apply the Muhammadan law, not as a law, but only as a rule enjoined by equity. In my view, equity cannot, so to speak, invent rules by which rights are to be determined: it must follow and be guided by rules which are law in the strict sense. This is implied by the maxim *aequitas sequitur legem*; and the *lex* to be followed must mean the law of the land in which equity is administered, and not any foreign law or any system not obligatory on the courts. If it is supposed that equity can, in some unexplained manner, evolve rules as to gift or pre-emption without any example or analogy in the rules of law, I do not understand how the maxim is to be applied. No equity, for instance, could invent rules on the subject of inheritance or limitation and apply them to the determination of rights. Further, if the view of the majority of the court in the cases referred to were correct, the first part of s. 24 would be superfluous. It would be easy to apply their reasoning in regard to gift and pre-emption, to marriage and inheritance, and the other matters mentioned in the section, by simply following the rule of justice, equity, and good conscience provided by the latter part of the section, and by saying that the Hindu and Muhammadan laws were therefore to govern them.

Upon the present occasion it is unnecessary to consider whether 'gift' can properly be described as a 'religious usage or institution' within the meaning of s. 24. I am here concerned only with the question whether pre-emption can be so described. My own opinion is that it can, and although I cannot add much to the reasons given by Spankie, J., I may observe that pre-emption is closely connected with the Muhammadan law of inheritance. That law was founded by the Prophet upon republican principles, at a time when the modern democratic conception of equality and division of property was unknown even in the most advanced countries of Europe. It provides that, upon the death of an owner, his property is to be divided into numerous fractions, according to extremely rigid rules, so rigid as to practically exclude all power of testamentary disposition, and to prevent any diversion of the property made even with the consent of the heirs, unless that consent is given after the owner's death, when the reason is, not that the testator had power to defeat the law of inheritance, but that the heirs, having become owners of the property, could deal with it as they liked, and could therefore ratify the act of their ancestor. No Muhammadan is allowed to make a will in favour of any of his heirs, and a bequest to a stranger is allowed only to the extent of one-third of the property. Under these circumstances, to allow the Muhammadan law of inheritance, and to disallow the Muhammadan law of pre-emption, would be to carry out the law in an imperfect manner; for the latter is in reality the proper complement of the former, and one department of the law cannot be administered without taking cognizance of the other. Among Aryan systems, which favour the notion of the inchoate rights of heirs, the rule of primogeniture the *jus representationis*, and the exclusion of females from inheritance, except in special cases, the property is not so completely split up on the owner's death; but, under the Muhammadan system, upon a man's death, not only his children are entitled to succeed to his property, but also his wife, mother, father, and other heirs, according to well-defined rules; and I myself know of a case in which, after a Muhammadan's death, his property was divided into twenty-three shares, each heir having a separate share in every parcel. If such a law of inheritance were not mitigated by the law of pre-emption, the result would be serious inconvenience, and possibly even disturbance. It is hardly necessary to add that the *zenana* system, which the Muhammadans regard as based upon religious texts, and which emphatically prohibits invasion of the privacy of a domestic habitation, lends an importance to the pre-emptive right, even when claimed *ex jure vicinitatis,* which it would not perhaps have otherwise possessed. This would go some way to support Mr Justice Spankie's conclusions; but the point is perhaps not one of much practical importance, because, whatever view may be taken as to the right of pre-emption, all are agreed that it must be enforced by the courts. I need only refer to one more case on this part of the subject—*Ibrahim Saib* v. *Muni Mir Uddin Saib*,[8] decided by the Madras High Court, in which Holloway, J., stated the question to be 'Whether a Muhammadan can exercise the right derived from neighbourhood (*ex jure vicinitatis*) to insist upon the sale by a Hindu being made to him instead of to another Muhammadan.' I concur in the conclusion arrived at by Holloway, J., in that case, so far as that conclusion simply answered in the negative the specific questions enumerated by the learned Judge. But unless the Civil Courts Act in the Madras Presidency as to the administration of the Muhammadan law is very different to that which is in force in these Provinces, I am bound to say that there is much in his mode of treating the Muhammadan law of pre-emption, in which I am unable to concur.

So far I have been considering the question whether the Muhammadan rule of pre-emption can, at least by a liberal construction, be described as a 'religious usage or institution' within the meaning of the Bengal Civil Courts Act. Before leaving s. 24, I wish to refer to the word parties, which occurs in it. And upon this point much of what I have already said as to the provisions of the old Regulations applies also to the interpretation of this section. I do not understand the word to mean the parties to an action, but it must be interpreted with reference to the inception of the right

8 (1870) 6 Mad HC Rep. 26.

involved in the action. Any other interpretation would render the section impracticable, if not meaningless. Who are necessary parties to an action is a matter governed by the rules of procedure, and in a country like India, where personal laws prevail, it is not an uncommon occurrence that everyone of the persons arrayed as parties to the suit belongs to a different race and religion. In such a case, it would be impossible to administer any particular law if the word 'parties' in the section mean 'parties to the suit'. This is obviously the only interpretation which can apply to the administration of Muhammadan law of inheritance and succession by our courts. Indeed, cases are readily conceivable in which none of the parties to the suit are Muhammadans, but in which their right, having been derived by transfer or otherwise from Muhammadans, the Muhammadan law would be the sole rule of decision, because the inception of the rights to be adjudicated upon took place under that law. This can be best illustrated by supposing the case of a Muhammadan who dies leaving a widow, a son, and a daughter, each one of whom conveys his or her share, by gift or sale in the estate of the deceased, to a Hindu, a Christian, and a Parsi, respectively. It is to my mind obvious that in a suit between these various transferees, involving the ascertainment of the extent of the right of each person, the Muhammadan law would, under the former part of s. 24 of the Bengal Civil Courts Act, be the only possible guide for decision, and that law would apply in its strictest force, notwithstanding the circumstance that none of the parties to the suit belonged to the Muhammadan persuasion. There is no reason for not applying the same principle to the cases to which this reference relates; and it follows that the circumstance that some of the parties to these suits are Hindus, would not, *ipso facto*, render the Muhammadan law of pre-emption inapplicable, but that the question must be decided with reference to the rules governing the inception of the pre-emptive right claimed in these two cases. This leads me to another aspect of the question. To the cases out of which this reference has arisen, both Hindus and Muhammadans are parties, and the standing Full Bench rulings of this court, already referred to lay down the rule that the Muhammadan law of pre-emption is to be administered, not as a law by which the courts are bound, but only on the general principles of justice, equity, and good conscience. And if this is so even in cases where all the parties are Muhammadans, it follows *a fortiori* that in cases like the present, where some of the parties are Hindus, the same principle would apply; and thus the question whether the Hindu law recognizes any rules of pre-emption naturally assumes sufficiently great importance to justify my dwelling upon it at some length; for, no rule of equity can either invent the law of pre-emption or administer it to people who never had such a law. And, in view of this circumstance, I will deal with the matter under three heads; *first,* the history of the law of pre-emption, and its introduction into India; *secondly*, the manner in which it has been administered by the British Courts; and *thirdly*, the Muhammadan texts upon which my conclusions are founded.

Upon the first point, I desire to cite a passage from the introduction of Sir W. Macnaghten's *Principles and Precedents of Muhammadan Law* (p. 14). He says: 'Sales of land and other immovable property are clogged with an incumbrance, which is not, however, peculiar to this Code. I allude to the law of pre-emption. This confers the privilege on a partner or a neighbour to preclude any stranger from coming in as a purchaser, provided the same price be offered as that which the vendor has declared himself willing to receive for the property to be disposed of.' Then, after discussing the question whether pre-emption prevailed originally among the Hindus, he goes on to say: 'I have found in the *Maha Nirvana Tantra*, a work which chiefly treats of mythology, a passage which would seem to imply that pre-emption is recognized as a legal provision according to the notions of the Hindus. But it remains yet to be decided whether this shall be held to be practical law or not.'

Adopting the authority of these eminent Sanskritists, there is no doubt in my mind that the question which Sir William Macnaghten regarded as open to doubt is in reality not so, and that there has never been such a right as that of pre-emption recognized by the Hindu law, though I cannot forget that the rule of that law which prohibits any member of a joint undivided family from selling his share in the joint property without the consent of his co-parceners, aims at a result not dissimilar to that which the Muhammadan law of pre-emption is intended to achieve. The fact that some of the parties concerned in the present cases are Hindus, need not therefore in itself complicate the question as to the applicability of the Muhammadan law, nor create any such difficulty as would otherwise have arisen with regard to the question how the rule of pre-emption is to be administered according to justice, equity, and good conscience, in a case where, some parties being Hindus and the other Muhammadans, the law of each provided different rules for the enforcement of the pre-emptive right.

I now turn to the case-law upon the subject.

[. . . .]

These cases leave no doubt in my mind that the courts have never recognized the rule of pre-emption as a part of the Hindu law.

The law of pre-emption is essentially a part of Muhammadan jurisprudence. It was introduced into India by Muhammadan judges who were bound to administer the Muhammadan law. Under their administration it became, and remained for centuries, the common law of the country, and was applied universally both to Muhammadans and Hindus, because in this respect the Muhammadan law makes no distinction between persons of different races or creeds. 'A Musalman and a *Zimmee* being equally affected by principles on which *shafa* [shuf'a] or right of pre-emption is established, and equally concerned in its operation, are therefore on an equal footing in all cases regarding the privilege of *shafa*.' (Hamilton's *Hedaya*, vol. III, p. 592). What was the effect of this? In course of time, pre-emption became adopted by the Hindus as a custom. I may here refer to an official paper printed in the *Revenue Reporter,* Vol. V, at p. 150, in which it is said that the rule of pre-emption has been adopted as a custom almost universally throughout these Provinces, even by villages which are purely Hindu. I have already in *Zamir Husain* v. *Daulat Ram*,[9] and in the recent case of *Sheoratan Kuar* v. *Mahipal Kuar*,[10] explained my views as to the manner in which this custom has been adopted by the Hindu community.

Now, there can be no question that the Muhammadan law of pre-emption must be administered in cases in which all the parties concerned are Muhammadans. The question is, whether it should be administered in cases in which only the vendee is a Hindu. Before expressing my own view of the matter, I think it will be useful to review the case-law on the subject, and to ascertain how it stands at present. The most important of the cases is that of *Sheikh Kudratulla* v. *Mahini Mohan Shaha.*[11] It was there ruled by a majority of the Judges of the Calcutta High Court (Peacock, C. J., and Kemp and Mitter, JJ.), that a Hindu purchaser is not bound by the Muhammadan law of pre-emption in favour of a Muhammadan co-parcener, nor is he bound by the Muhammadan law of pre-emption on the ground of vicinage, because the right of pre-emption in a Muhammadan does not depend on any defect of title on the part of his Muhammadan co-parcener to sell except subject to his right of pre-emption, but upon a rule of Muhammadan law which is not binding on the court, nor on any purchaser other than a Muhammadan. The minority (Norman and Macpherson, JJ.), on the other hand, held that whenever a Muhammadan co-sharer or neighbour has a right of pre-emption, when property is sold by his neighbour or co-sharer, also a Musalman, his right is not defeated by the mere fact that the purchaser is a Hindu. The ruling of the majority of the court was adopted by a Division Bench of this court in *Moti Chand* v. *Mahomed Hossein Khan.*[12] These two cases are clear authorities against the opinion which I

9 ILR 5 All 110.
10 ILR 7 All 258.
11 4 BLR 134.
12 NWP HCR 1875, p. 147.

hold. Upon the converse of the proposition which they laid down, I may refer to a case in which the pre-emptor was a Muhammadan, the vendor a Hindu, and the vendee a Muhammadan. This was the Full Bench case of *Chundo* v. *Hakeem Alim-ood-deen*,[13] in which it was ruled (Spankie J., dissenting), that the application of Muhammadan law in a suit for pre-emption between a Muhammadan claimant of pre-emption and a Muhammadan vendee on the basis of that law, is not precluded by the fact of the *vendor* not being a Muhammadan. The rule so laid down was the only one which could be adopted consistently with the principle on which the two last mentioned cases were decided. But it was subsequently and formally overruled, in the Full Bench case of *Dwarka Das* v. *Husain Bakhsh*,[14] in which it was held (Stuart, C. J., and Pearson, J., dissenting) that where the vendor is a Hindu, a suit to enforce a right of pre-emption founded upon Muhammadan law is not maintainable. In this case, the majority of the court followed in principle the judgment of Couch, C. J., in *Poorno Singh* v. *Hurrychurn Surmah*,[15] where it was held, that the right of pre-emption arises from a rule of law by which the owner of the land is bound, and that it is essential that the *vendor* should be subject to that rule of law.

I have read these cases carefully, and it appears to me impossible to reconcile them. The most important of them are *Sheikh Kudratulla* v. *Mahini Mohan Shaha*,[16] and *Dwarka Das* v. *Husain Bakhsh*,[17] in which a Full Bench of the Calcutta High Court and a Full Bench of this court respectively laid down two propositions, one being, so to say, the converse of the other. Bearing in mind the rules of the Muhammadan law of pre-emption, it seems to me impossible to hold that both of these decisions can be right. I know that, as a matter of pure logic, it does not follow, because a proposition is true, that its converse must be true also; and it is obvious that, as a matter of pure reasoning, if a Muhammadan pre-emptor cannot enforce pre-emption against a Hindu purchaser, the vendor being a Muhammadan, it does not necessarily follow that a Muhammadan can enforce pre-emption where the vendor is a Hindu and the purchaser a Muhammadan. But the exigencies of the definite rules of the Muhammadan law of pre-emption happen to be such as to render it essential that the various propositions relating to the subject should be governed by a common principle and therefore be consistent with each other. I may illustrate my meaning by supposing concrete cases.

13 NWP HCR 1874, p. 28.
14 ILR 1 All 564.
15 10 BLR 117.
16 4 BLR 134.
17 *Supra*, note 12.

In all cases of pre-emption there are three parties to be considered—the pre-emptor, the vendor, and the purchaser. And so far as the question now under consideration is concerned, different cases may be imagined by supposing all, or one, or two of these three parties to be Hindus or Muhammadans. The simplest and ordinary case is where all the three parties concerned are Muhammadans, and in such circumstances it is obvious, as was indeed admitted by Mitter, J., and the learned judges who agreed with him in the case of *Sheikh Kudratulla* v. *Mahini Mohan Shaha*,[18] that the Muhammadan law would apply—a proposition which, as a matter of law, though not of logic, necessarily implies a negative answer where all the parties to a pre-emptive suit are Hindus. Nor can there be any difficulty in holding that, for similar reasons, the same negative answer must be given in a case in which, the pre-emptor being a Muhammadan, both the vendor and the vendee are Hindus; or conversely, where the pre-emptor being a Hindu, both the vendor and vendee are Muhammadans. And to carry the reasoning further, the same negative answer must be given where, both the pre-emptor and the vendor being Hindus, the only party who is Muhammadan is the vendee. Nor would anyone maintain that the Muhammadan law would govern a pre-emptive suit in which the pre-emptor and the vendee are both Hindus, and only the vendor is a Muhammadan. Indeed, I am not aware of a single case in which the Muhammadan law, as such, has been held applicable in any of such circumstances. The reason of the negative answer is that, although the Muhammadan law of pre-emption makes no distinction of race or creed, that law, from being the common law of the land applicable alike to Hindus and Muhammadans, has been reduced to the status of being a personal law of the latter, who alone can enforce the rights or incur the obligations created by that personal law. Rights derived from members of that community, whether by Hindus or by other non-Muhammadans, would, of course, be governed by the Muhammadan law, because, as I have already explained, the inception of the right and not the array of the parties to the suit must be the turning point of the decision within the meaning of s. 24 of the Civil Courts Act. But because a Hindu is not under that section subject to the Muhammadan law of pre-emption, he cannot avail himself of any pre-emptive right which that law creates only in favour of those who are subject to its behests. And the reason is simple. The rights and obligations created by that law, as indeed by every other system with which I am acquainted, must necessarily be reciprocal. Then, if a Hindu cannot as a pre-emptor avail himself of the Muhammadan law of pre-emption in a case where the vendor is a Muhammadan and the

18 4 BLR 134.

purchaser is a Hindu, what reason is there for holding that a Muhammadan pre-emptor *can* enforce the pre-emptive right where the vendor is a Hindu and the purchaser a Muhammadan? The question was discussed by this court in the Full Bench case of *Chundo* v. *Hakeem Alim-ood-deen*,[19] and the majority of the court gave an affirmative answer upon a reasoning which must necessarily lead to the conclusion that an affirmative answer should also be given to the proposition which, as I have just stated, can only be answered in the *negative.* Indeed, the untenability of the proposition, as already pointed out, was not long afterwards enunciated by the majority of the Full Bench of this court in *Dwarka Das* v. *Husain Bakhsh*, which furnishes an answer in the negative, perfectly consistent with my own view—an answer which gives full effect to an important portion of the reasoning adopted by Mitter, J., in *Sheikh Kudratulla* v. *Mahini Mohan Shaha*,[20] though it controverts the conclusion at which the learned Judge arrived. He says (p. 147):

> If we decide this case against the Hindu purchaser, and thereby deprive him of a property which has already become his by the law of his country, we must bear in mind that we have already decided that, so far as he is concerned, he will never be able to enforce any right of pre-emption even though a Muhammadan should choose to purchase a part of his family-house from one of his co-parceners. So long as this country was under the Muhammadan Government, the right of pre-emption was extended to all classes of persons without any distinction of creed, colour or birth, inasmuch as no such distinction was recognized in that respect by the Muhammadan law, which was in fact the law of the land. Now that the Muhammadan law has ceased to be the law of the country, it seems to me to be manifestly unjust and inequitable that we should enforce the Muhammadan law of pre-emption against a Hindu, without giving him the benefit of that law in other cases in which he would like to stand in the position of a pre-emptor.

I have said enough to show that with a great deal of the reasoning upon which this passage proceeds I entirely concur. But I reject the conclusion, because the necessary steps leading to it are based upon what I may respectfully call fallacies as to the rules of the Muhammadan law of pre-emption. These I shall presently discuss at some length; but I may here make some observations with reference to the illustration given in the passage, namely, the case of a Hindu co-parcener selling his share in his family-house to a Muhammadan. I should unhesitatingly say, in such a case, that the sale was subject to the incidents of the Hindu law which governed the rights of the vendor, that if that law provided a rule of pre-emption, the rule should

19 NWP HCR 1874, p. 28.
20 BLR 134.

be enforced against the Muhammadan purchaser, whether his law recognized it or not. In such a case there can be no question of the Muhammadan being deprived of a 'property which has already become his by the laws of his country'. He bought it subject to the rules which governed it in the hands of his vendor, from whom he has derived his title, and the circumstance that he is not a Hindu will not save him from the incidents of the Hindu law. Indeed, in the case supposed, as the law stands, the Muhammadan purchaser would no doubt be free from a pre-emptive claim at the instance of his Hindu vendor's co-parceners. But he would be free only because the Hindu law provides no pre-emptive right. He would, however, be liable to something worse, by reason of that law which governed the property in the hands of his vendor. The sale might be avoided at the instance of the Hindu co-parcener, if the subject of the sale was a share in joint property. And if it can be shown that property in the hands of a Muhammadan is 'in principle' as much subject to the pre-emptive claim of his Muhammadan co-parcener or neighbour as the marital estate in the hands of a Hindu widow, or the share of a member of a Hindu joint family, is subject to its own restrictions or qualifications as to sale, it seems to me that the enforcement of the Muhammadan rule of pre-emption against the Hindu purchaser from a Muhammadan would be anything but 'manifestly unjust and inequitable'. And once this proposition is established, it will be obvious that all the exigencies of Mr Justice Mitter's reasoning, contained in the passage cited, are satisfied by the *ratio decidendi* in *Dwarka Das* v. *Husain Bakhsh*,[21] wherein the majority of the Full Bench of this court declined to enforce the Muhammadan rule of pre-emption in a case in which the vendor was a Hindu, although the pre-emptor and the purchaser were both Muhammadans. For if the *ratio decidendi* of that ruling is correct, the matter stands thus: Property in the hands of a Muhammadan is subject to the pre-emptive claim of his Muhammadan co-parcener or neighbour; property in the hands of a Hindu is not so subject to the Muhammadan rule of pre-emption. The Muhammadan can claim the benefit of the law of pre-emption. The Hindu cannot claim the benefit of that law. These propositions, which seem to me to be intelligible, consistent, and equitable, would meet all the objections which Mitter, J., contemplated; and, if they are correct, there can be no question of either the Hindu or the Muhammadan being 'deprived' of his right by reason of the law of the other. The pre-emptive rights and obligations between Muhammadan co-parceners and neighbours being mutual, the principle of the maxim *qui sentit commodum sentire debet et onus* applies, but it would not apply in the case of a Hindu

21 ILR 1 All 564.

where no such reciprocity exists. And if the Hindu purchaser is to be affected by the Muhammadan pre-emptive claim, it would be on the principle of a cognate maxim that land passes with its burdens, *terra transit cum onere*, and there would be no violation of the notions of justice, equity, and good conscience.

This, however, begs the whole question, and having already supposed the various cases in which it would arise on account of the difference in religion of the partners in a pre-emptive case, the only case which remains to be conceived is one in which the pre-emptor and the vendor are both Muhammadans, and the only non-Muhammadan among the parties is the vendee. This is the case now before us, and to the question whether the Muhammadan law of pre-emption is applicable to such a case, my answer is in the affirmative. But because the authority of Sir Barnes Peacock and Mr Justice Dwarka Nath Mitter demands the highest respect from me, as from every one else connected with the administration of justice in British India, I feel myself bound, in differing with them, to explain my reasons fully by reference to original texts of the Muhammadan law of pre-emption, which I cannot help feeling would have led those eminent judges to a different conclusion had the texts been accessible in the English language. I make this observation because Sir Barnes Peacock at the beginning of his judgment in the celebrated case of *Sheikh Kudratulla* v. *Mahini Mohan Shaha*,[22] used expressions which leave no doubt that, even after the case had been argued before him in the full bench, his Lordship was inclined to form an opinion similar to that which I have formed in this case, and that he adopted the opposite view in consequence of the opinion which had been 'so forcibly and clearly expressed by Mr Justice Mitter'. And because the judgment of that learned Judge in the most exhaustive and powerful manner presents the opposite view to that which I hold in this case, the best way in which I can justify my own opinion is to examine the reasoning leading to the conclusions which he and the majority of the court adopted in that case.

Dealing thus with the question now before us, I may remark, in the first place, that I entirely agree with Mr Justice Dwarka Nath Mitter in holding that the answer to the question depends upon the nature of the right of pre-emption under the Muhammadan law. I also concur generally in the following remarks (p. 140): 'If that right is founded on an antecedent defect in the title of the vendor, that is to say, on a legal disability on his part to sell his property to a stranger, without giving an opportunity to his co-parceners and neighbours to purchase in the first instance, those co-parceners

22 BLR 134.

and neighbours are fully entitled to ask the Hindu purchaser to surrender the property, for although as a Hindu he is not necessarily bound by the Muhammadan law, he was at any rate bound by the rule of justice, equity, and good conscience, to inquire into the title of his vendor; and that very rule also requires that we should not permit him to retain a property which his vendor had no power to sell. If, on the contrary, it can be shown that there was no such defect in the title of the vendor, or, in other words, that he was under no such disability, even under the Muhammadan law itself, it would follow, as a matter of course, that there was no defect in the title of the purchaser at the time of its creation.' Further on he says: 'Now, so far as I can judge of the Muhammadan law of pre-emption from the materials within my reach, it appears to me perfectly clear that a right of pre-emption is nothing more than a mere right of repurchase, not from the vendor, but from the vendee, who is treated for all interests and purposes as the full legal owner of the property which is the subject-matter of that right.' In this passage, Mitter, J. referred to the materials upon which he based his conclusion, and he proceeds to quote passages from those materials. On this point I have to say that those materials appear to me to be in several respects inadequate. They are to be found in the *Hedaya,* or rather in the translation of the *Hedaya* made by Mr Hamilton about a century ago, under the orders of the Governor-General, Warren Hastings. It was not, however, a translation of the original Arabic text, but of a Persian translation. For that work gratitude is due to Mr Hamilton, but at the same time I am afraid it has been sometimes the source of mistakes by our courts in the administration of the Muhammadan law. Mitter, J. says that he is satisfied by certain passages in this work, that the conclusions at which he arrived were consistent with the Muhammadan law of pre-emption. I need not quote any more passages from the learned judgment, as I purpose to analyse all the main arguments adopted by the majority—Peacock, C. J., Kemp and Mitter, J. J. The first pro-position which those learned Judges laid down was, that the right of pre-emption under the Muhammadan law does not exist before actual sale, because, on the one hand, the pre-emptor has no right of prohibiting the sale, and, on the other hand, the vendor is not bound to offer the property for purchase to the pre-emptor before selling it to the stranger; and they held their view to be supported by the circumstance that the pre-emptor cannot before such sale relinquish his pre-emptive right, nor could the absence of his consent vitiate the sale. Upon this reasoning they held that a Muhammadan owner of property was subject to no legal disability arising out of pre-emption, but was free to sell it regardless of that right. They then proceeded to lay down the second main proposition that a sale, in respect of which pre-emption might be claimed, passed full ownership to the vendee, and did not involve 'any defect of title', because it could not be regarded as an infringement of a pre-existing pre-emptive right. From this the learned Judges concluded that the right of pre-emption under the Muhammadan law was 'a mere right of re-purchase, not from the vendor, but from the vendee,' which right could not be enforced by a Muhammadan pre-emptor against a Hindu *vendee*, because the property, even in the hands of the Muhammadan vendor, not being subject to the pre-emptive right at the time when the title of the Hindu vendee was created by the sale, the right could not run with the land nor follow it in the hands of a stranger, not subject to the Muhammadan law. These are the main conclusions at which the learned Judges arrived, and the rest of their reasoning seeks to support those conclusions by the argument that, under the Muhammadan law, the right of pre-emption is a right 'feeble' and 'defective', because, according to the rules of that law it can be easily defeated by devices which Mitter, J. designated as 'tricks and artifices'.

I believe in giving this analysis I have exhausted all the arguments which the learned Judges employed in arriving at the view to which I am opposed. But if it can be shown from the original texts of the Muhammadan law itself that the main propositions upon which the whole argument proceeds are in themselves erroneous, I think I shall have justified my view. First, then as to the nature of the right. I remember the salutary warning of the Roman jurist Javolenus (whom Creasy, CJ, has quoted in his work on *International Law*), that the task of laying down definitions is not only 'the most laborious, but also the most perilous'. The exigencies of this case, however, require that I should endeavour to define the right of pre-emption as prescribed by the Muhammadan law; and I think I am strictly within the authorities of that law when I say that pre-emption is a right which the owner of certain immovable property possesses, as such, for the quiet enjoyment of that immovable property, to obtain, in substitution for the buyer, proprietary possession of certain other immovable property, not his own, on such terms as those on which such latter immovable property is sold to another person. I could easily support every word of this definition by original Arabic texts of the Muhammadan law itself, but I will confine myself only to such texts as bear immediately upon the main propositions involved in this case. I may, however, observe that the nature of the right, as appears from the definition which I have given, partakes strongly of the nature of an easement,—the 'dominant tenement' and the '*servient* tenement' of the law of easement being terms extremely analogous to what I may respectively call the 'pre-emptive tenement' and the 'pre-emptional tenement' of the Muhammadan law of pre-emption. Indeed, the analogy goes further, for I shall presently show that the right of pre-emption, like an easement, exists before the injury to that right can give birth to a cause of action for a suit, sale in the one case corresponding to the invasion of the easement in the other. In short, I maintain that, under the Muhammadan law, the rule of pre-emption, proceeding upon a principle analogous to the maxim *sic utere tuo ut alienum non laedas*, creates what I may call a legal servitude running with the land; and the fact that that law has ceased to become the general law of the land cannot alter the nature of the servitude, but only render its enforcement dependent upon the religion of the party who claims the servitude and of the party who owns the property subject to that servitude.

Now, the main authority upon which the learned Judges relied for the view that the right of pre-emption does not exist before sale, is a passage in Mr Hamilton's *Hedaya* to be found at page 568, Vol. III, of his translation. The translation is at its best a very loose one when compared with the original Arabic text, which I shall literally translate here:

> Pre-emption becomes obligatory (i.e., enforceable) by a contract of sale, which means after the sale. Not that sale is the cause (of pre-emption), for the cause is conjunction (of the properties) as we have already mentioned. And the reason in the matter is, that pre-emption becomes obligatory when the seller has turned away from (i.e., wishes to get rid of) the ownership of his house, and the sale makes this apparent. Hence, proof of sale is sufficient as against him even to the extent of the pre-emptor taking it (the house) when the seller acknowledges the sale, although the buyer contradicts him.

The meaning to be evolved from the passage is obviously different from the interpretation which can be placed upon Mr Hamilton's translation, which indeed seems to me to have misled Mitter, J., and the other learned Judges who agreed with him. The Arabic word *tajibu* which occurs in this and other passages, and which Mr Hamilton translated as 'established', really means 'becomes obligatory, necessary or enforceable' as a term of law, and I cannot help feeling that if the passage had been accurately translated by Mr Hamilton, the majority of the Eull Bench in *Sheikh Kudratulla's Case* might possibly have arrived at a very different conclusion. It is unnecessary to quote any more passages from the original Arabic text of the *Hedaya*, which distinctly go to show that the cause or foundation of the right of pre-emption is the conjunction of the pre-emptive tenement with the pre-emptional tenement, that its object is to obviate the inconvenience or disturbance which would arise by the introduction of strangers, that the right exists antecedently to sale, and that sale is a condition precedent, not to the existence of the right, but only to its enforceability. Mr Hamilton's translation is sufficiently accurate to indicate these conclusions, and I shall therefore pass on to other books as high in authority as the *Hedaya* itself. Here is a short text from the *Durr-ul-Mukhtar*:

The cause of pre-emption is the contiguousness of the pre-emptor's property with the purchased property, whether by co-parcenership or vicinage.[23]

Again, a more explicit passage is to be found in *'Aini*, a commentary upon the *Kanz*:

The author says 'by sale', which must be referred to his expression, 'pre-emption becomes obligatory'. This would indicate that the cause of the obligatoriness of pre-emption is sale, that is the sale of the pre-emptional house, and some have held this very opinion. The correct opinion, however, is that the cause of pre-emption is the conjunction of the properties in a necessary manner, and sale is a condition (of pre-emption). From this it follows that pre-emption becomes enforceable by sale, that is, after its coming into existence.[24]

All the different views on the subject entertained by Muhammadan jurists, who were only too fond of the medieval schoolmen's method of arguing such questions, are to be found in *Birjandi,* a well-known commentary on the Muhammadan law:

Be it known that the language of the author implies that the cause of the obligatoriness of pre-emption is the conjunction of the pre-emptor's property with the subject of the sale in some way or other, and this is the opinion adopted by the *Mashaikh* (elders) in general. Khassaf says that pre-emption becomes enforceable by sale, then by demand, and therefore both become the cause; but as to this it may be said that when pre-emption is established by sale, there is no meaning in establishing it a second time by demand. Sheikh Abubakr Razi used to maintain that pre-emption becomes enforceable by sale, the right of taking possession is established by demand, and ownership (of the pre-emptor) is established either by decree or by mutual consent. Sheikh-ul-Islam held that co-parcenership, together with sale, constitutes the reason of the enforceability of pre-emption, and it is emphasized by demand, and ownership is established either by decree or by mutual consent, and so it is laid down in the *Zakhira.*[25]

These texts leave no doubt in my mind that the 'cause' or foundation of pre-emption is 'conjunction' of the pre-emptor's property with that of the vendor, and, inasmuch as such conjunction existed before the sale, it follows that the pre-emptive right originates antecedently to the sale in respect of which it may be exercised. For example, when two Muhammadans own

23 p. 697.
24 *Aini*, *Sharh Kanz*, Vol. II, p. 238.
25 *Birjandi*, p. 201.

shares in a house, the share of each may in turn be regarded as dominant or servient to the other for purposes of pre-emption, because the conjunction of the properties of the two owners being a circumstance common to both, alternately entitles the other to claim pre-emption when the proper occasion arises, that is, when either transfers his share by sale. The analogy of a non-apparent easement again suggests itself. It is true, as Mitter, J. says, that neither can prevent the other from selling his share to whomsoever he pleases, because the Muhammadan law 'nowhere recognizes any right of *veto* in the pre-emptor,' nor does it impose any 'positive legal disability' on the vendor in this respect. This, no doubt, at first sight suggests a distinction in principle between pre-emption and non-apparent easement, such as a right annexed to *A's* house to prevent *B* from building on his own land. But the distinction, so far as the question of the origin of right is concerned, is in reality not one of principle, but of detail, arising from the difference in the nature of the occasion demanding the exercise of the right. In the one case, that occasion is sale; in the other, it is building. Now, it is true that in the one case the pre-emptor cannot prevent his co-parcener from selling his property to a stranger, whilst in the case supposed, *A* could prevent *B* from building on his land. But the reason of the distinction is not that the right of the one did not exist before the sale, and the right of the other did exist before the building. The reason is this. The object of the non-apparent easement possessed by *A* is the beneficial enjoyment of his own property, and definite infringement of that right is ascertained when *B* takes any definite action to build upon his land, a state of things which would be sufficient to afford a cause of action in favour of *A,* seeking preventive relief or other assertion of his right of easement. But in the case of pre-emption, the object of the right is to prevent the intrusion, not of all purchasers in general, but only of such as are objectionable from the pre-emptor's point of view. Again, the right (unlike the right of veto possessed by members of a joint Hindu family with respect to the sale of his share by any one of them) is not free from definite qualifications, among which the most important is that the pre-emptor complaining of the intrusion of the purchaser should place himself absolutely in the position of the purchaser with reference to the terms of the contract of sale, such as the amount and payment of the price, & c. It is obvious, then, that before a pre-emptor can make up his mind to assert his pre-emptive right, he must, *ex necessitate rei*, know definitely who the purchaser is, and under what terms he has purchased the property, because it may well be that, on the one hand, he may have no objection to such purchaser, and on the other hand, even if he does object, he may not be in a position to pay the price which the purchaser has paid. No such considerations exist in the case of the right of easement which I have supposed by way of illustration. And it follows that before a sale is actually completed, the pre-emptor is not, *ex necessitate rei*, in a position to have definite information as to whether the proper occasion has arisen for the exercise of his already existing pre-emptive right. This is the reason why the law gives him no right of vetoing the sale. But the reason falls far short of showing that his right of pre-emption was wholly non-existent at the time of the sale, when the title of the purchaser was created. From what I have already said, it is perfectly clear to me that any action on the part of the pre-emptor before the sale would be premature, whether such action consisted of vetoing or consenting to a sale which has not yet been effected, and of which the terms and the purchaser have not yet been ascertained, in the sense of creating the legal rights and obligations which render a sale an accomplished fact in law. I have already said that, unlike the veto possessed by a member of a joint Hindu family, the right of pre-emption does not prohibit sale in general, regardless of the purchaser, of the amount of the price, and other terms of the contract of sale; and because the right is in its very nature incapable of being asserted or exercised till these matters are definitely ascertained, it follows that a sale, irrespective of the pre-emptor's consent, is not void in law. The pre-emptive right may or may not be asserted or enforced; and it would be absurd to say that that which is only possible should, by a retrospective effect, vitiate that which is certain, namely the sale. This is the manner in which the jurists of the Muhammadan law have dealt with this point of the rule of pre-emption, and it is upon very similar grounds that they hold the pre-emptor incapable of relinquishing his pre-emptive right in respect of a sale which has not yet taken place. They would say (and there is ample authority for this statement) that the identity of the purchaser, the amount of the price, and other terms of the sale, the certainty of which is essential, not to the existence, but to the exercise of the pre-emptive right, being still undefined by a legal relation between the vendor and the vendee, the pre-emptor had no means of knowing for certain whether he should or should not give up an ascertained legal right, and therefore the relinquishment of pre-emption before sale is void. Whatever the merits of this reasoning from a jurisprudential point of view may be, I confess I fail to see how it supports the view that the right of pre-emption does not exist as a restriction or qualification of the right of sale possessed by the owner of property subject to pre-emption. It is indeed not an absolutely unqualified disability, for it does not absolutely prohibit sale without the consent of the pre-emptor. But that it amounts to a qualified disability, distinctly operating in derogation of the vendor's absolute rights to sell the property, and thus affects his title, which would otherwise amount to absolute dominion, cannot, in my opinion, be doubted. That the results of such restrictions or qualifications are dependent for their enforcement upon the occurrence of the actual sale, is a circumstance which, in my opinion, does not affect the question relating to the inception of the right of pre-emption.

But, in opposition to this view, Mitter, J., and the learned Judges who concurred with him, relied upon the argument that 'there is nothing whatever in the Muhammadan law which imposes upon anyone the obligation of making the first offer to his neighbour, nor is there anything to show that the right of pre-emption is based upon any such obligation, the non-fulfilment of which would prevent the stranger from acquiring a complete and valid title to the property by virtue of his purchase'. In dealing with this argument, I must, in the first place, observe that one of the greatest difficulties in the administration of the Muhammadan law, as indeed of all ancient systems, lies in distinguishing moral from legal obligations. The Muhammadan law, having been evolved from the Quran and the sayings of the Prophet, naturally presents such difficulties, and the question whether the vendor is bound to offer the property to his co-parcener before selling it to a stranger, is an illustration of what I mean—a difficulty which was felt at an early stage by the Muhammadan jurists themselves. The following is a text from *Aini*, a commentary upon the *Kanz*, a well-known book on Muhammadan jurisprudence:

A co-parcener is one whose share has not been divided in the property sold. This is universally agreed upon, because it has been related by Jabir that the Prophet decreed pre-emption in respect of every joint undivided property, whether a grove or a house, saying: 'It is not lawful for anyone to sell till he has informed his co-parcener, who may take or leave it as he wishes; and if he has sold without such information; the co-parcener has a preferential right to the share.'[26]

This Tradition has been related by *Muslim, Abu Daud* and *Nasai* (1) Two other Traditions to the same effect are also to be found in *Muslim*, which is one of the books of acknowledged authority on *Hadis* or traditions. I will, however, quote only one of them, as it brings into prominence the difficulty with which I am now dealing:

It is related by Jabir that the Prophet said: 'Pre-emption exists in all joint properties, whether land, or house, or grove. It is not proper for him (the owner) to sell till he has offered it to his co-parcener, who may take it or reject it; and if the vendor fails to do this, his co-parcener has the preferential right to it until he is informed.'[27]

26 *Aini, Sharh Kanz*, Vol. II, p. 238.
27 *Muslim* Vol. II, p. 32.

Both these Traditions have much the same effect, but in the first of them the Arabic word *lā yabillu* occurs, which I have rendered by 'not lawful'; whilst in the second the phrase employed is *lā yaslubu,* which I have translated as meaning not proper. The importance which the Muhammadan jurists, in laying down legal principles, attached to the exact words in the sayings of the Prophet, at once gave rise to the question whether the injunction as to the vendor's giving notice to the pre-emptor and offering to him the property for purchase, was a mere moral behest or creates a legal obligation. I have already shown how Muhammadan jurists dealt with the right of pre-emption, and the method of arguing which they adopted had no doubt considerable influence in the interpretation of these two traditions. The difference of phraseology which I have already indicated, enabled them to put such an interpretation as would render the traditions consistent with the rule that the absence of the pre-emptor's consent does not vitiate the sale—the rule which had been unanimously adopted by the jurists. This is best shown by *Nawawi*, a celebrated commentary on *Muslim,* in which these traditions occur. The author explains the traditions in the following manner:

> The saying of the Prophet to the effect that it is not for him (the vendor) to sell until he has apprised his co-parcener is, in the opinion of our doctors, taken to refer to the moral propriety of giving notice and to the objectionableness of sale before such notice—an objectionableness which arises from impropriety. It does not, however, mean that such sale is absolutely prohibited, and this is the manner in which they have interpreted the *Hadis* (sayings of the Prophet), because it may be rightly affirmed of that which is morally objectionable, that it is not lawful, and thus the expression 'lawful' comes to mean permissible, which implies that both sides (positive and negative) are on an equal footing, whilst that which is 'morally objectionable' cannot be said to be permissible, both sides of which are equal, but, on the contrary, the 'morally objectionable' is that the rejection of which prevails (over its adoption).[28]

It is not necessary to pursue any further the syllogistic manner in which such questions were dealt with by Muhammadan jurists. I may, however, say that the ultimate reason which prevented them from interpreting these traditions in the sense of creating a legal obligation imposed upon the vendor was that, the language of the tradition being capable of two interpretations, they adopted the more lenient one, acting upon the presumption that a legal obligation does not exist till expressly provided, and that all contracts are lawful unless expressly prohibited by law. The law, therefore, as it stands, does not oblige the vendor to give notice of the projected sale to the pre-emptor, nor does it vitiate a sale executed without

28 *Nawawi, Sharh Muslim*, Vol. II, p. 32.

his permission. I am not at liberty to interpret the sayings of the Prophet in a sense other than that adopted by the recognized authorities on Muhammadan jurisprudence. But it is perfectly clear from these traditions that the very conception of pre-emption in Muhammadan law necessarily involves the existence of the right before the sale in respect of which it may be exercised. All that the interpretation of the Muhammadan jurists goes to show is, that the sale is not vitiated by the absence of the pre-emptor's consent—an interpretation which, whilst it is perfectly consistent with the rest of their method of reasoning in dealing with pre-emption, again falls short of establishing the proposition that the right is not antecedent in existence to the sale complained of by the pre-emptors.

I have now to deal with the argument that the right of pre-emption under the Muhammadan law is 'a mere right of repurchase, not from the vendor, but from the vendee'. I trust what I have already said goes far to show that this conclusion cannot be right. If by the expression repurchase is meant the institution of a new contract of sale other than that entered into by the vendor and the vendee, the hypothesis becomes obviously erroneous, because the entire argument, that the vendor of a pre-emptional tenement conveys an absolute ownership to the vendee unhampered by any defect of title arising out of pre-emption, applies as much to a Muhammadan as to a Hindu vendee. And if the right of pre-emption is only a right of repurchase, and if the right is to be enforced, not as a rule of law, but only by reason of the rule of justice, equity, and good conscience, I fail to see, even in a case where all the parties are Muhammadans, where the equity lies in forcing a man to sell that which is absolutely his own to a man who had no right in connection with it at the time when the title of the *vendee* was created. Equity is higher than the considerations of race and creed, nor will it allow parties to impose upon each other rules not sanctioned by the law. And if its rules prohibit a Hindu purchaser from being deprived of property of which he is the absolute owner, that same rule should, by ordinary legal analogy, benefit also a Muhammadan purchaser of property whose title is, *ex hypothesi*, as absolute and as free from defect as that of the Hindu vendee. Further, if pre-emption is only a right of repurchase from the vendee who, *ex hypothesi*, has, under the sale, derived an absolute title, unhampered by the pre-emptive right, there is no reason which would prevent the vendee from insisting that the terms of the new sale should be other than those under which he himself purchased. That this would be the necessary consequence of the hypothesis, seems to me to be as clear as the proposition that every absolute owner is at full liberty to sell or not to sell his property, and that if he chooses to sell it he can make his own terms as to the bargain of sale. That such a result is not only not warranted by the Muhammadan law of pre-emption, but would positively strike at the very root of the right itself, seems to me to be too obvious to require any explanation. But the Muhammadan law of pre-emption involves no such anomalous inconsistencies of reasoning, because the right of pre-emption is not a right of repurchase either from the vendor or from the vendee, involving any new contract of sale; but it is simply a right of substitution, entitling the pre-emptor, by reason of a legal incident to which the sale itself was subject, to stand in the shoes of the vendee in respect of all the rights and obligations arising from the sale under which he has derived his title. It is, in effect, as if in a sale-deed the vendee's name were rubbed out and the pre-emptor's name inserted in its place. Otherwise, because every sale of a pre-emptional tenement renders the right of pre-emption enforceable in respect thereto, every successful pre-emptor obtaining possession of the property, by the so-called repurchase from the vendee, would be subject to another pre-emptive claim, dating, not from the original sale, but from such repurchase—a state of things most easily conceivable where the new claimant is a pre-emptor of a higher degree than the pre-emptor who has already succeeded. The result would be that pre-emptive litigation could never end.

I could go on at much greater length to show that the hypothesis that pre-emption is only 'a right of repurchase from the vendee', would involve even greater anomalies inconsistent with the fundamental rules of the right of pre-emption. But I need not pursue the argument any further, because it seems to me that the general principles of jurisprudence suggest the same conclusions as those at which I have arrived. I take it as a fundamental principle that no state of things can give rise to cause of action, such as can be sued upon in a court of justice, unless there is a right and an infringement of that right—the right being necessarily antecedent to the injury. My conceptions of jurisprudence prevent me from conceiving any kind of right of which both the inception and the infringement depend upon one and the same incident. And it would be absurd to conceive a right of which the infringement takes place before the inception of the right itself. And if I am right so far, how would the right of pre-emption stand these tests, if it be taken not to exist before the sale in respect of which it is to be exercised? The injury to the right is the *intrusion* of a stranger under a sale, and the whole *object* of the right is to prevent such intrusion. And how could such intrusion be legally prevented if the right did not exist before the intrusion? Similar difficulties will arise if it be assumed that the point of the inception of the pre-emptive right is not sale, but *talab*, that is, demand of pre-emption by the pre-emptor. There can be no legal demand of a right which does not exist, nor could refusal by the vendee to surrender the pre-emptional property constitute any legal injury where no legal right existed.

But apart from the reasoning suggested by the analogy of jurisprudential conceptions, it seems to me that, if it is once conceded that the sole object of the pre-emptive right is to prevent the intrusion of strangers objectionable to the pre-emptor, it follows, I should say as a matter of 'common sense', that if a Muhammadan pre-emptor can by the exercise of his pre-emptive right prevent the intrusion of another Muhammadan, he should, *a fortiori*, be able to do so in the case of a purchaser who belongs to a different race and creed, for, *caeteris paribus,* it may be taken that a non-Muhammadan purchaser under such conditions would be more objectionable to the Muhammadan pre-emptor, and would demand a more strenuous exercise of the pre-emptive right.

Besides these arguments there is much on the subject of conflict of laws in the judgments delivered by Norman and Macpherson, JJ., in *Sheikh Kudratulla* v. *Mahini Mohan Shaha,*[29] which I might adopt in support of my view. But it is unnecessary to repeat the arguments which those learned Judges have already expressed with such force and lucidity. It, however, remains for me to deal with the reasoning adopted by Mitter, J. as to pre-emption being a right 'feeble and defective', because, on the one hand, it is lost if not immediately asserted, and, on the other hand, it can be defeated by 'tricks and artifices'. If feeble and defective only means that the right of pre-emption is transitory in the sense of requiring immediate assertion, I can understand the phrase. But I do not understand how the transitory character of the right can affect the question whether or not it should be enforced against a Muhammadan vendee and not against a non-Muhammadan. So far as this particular point is concerned, it seems enough to say that, if the right is legally enforceable against the one, it should be enforceable against the other. On the other hand, in one sense, full ownership itself may be called transitory, because, if *A,* being the owner of *X,* allows *B* to sell it to C, *A* being present at the time of the sale, his mission to assert his title to *X* would, in effect, by the doctrine of estoppel, defeat his right in *X.* Pre-emption is feeble in a sense not dissimilar in principle to the illustration which I have given. The object of the Muhammadan law in rendering the immediate demand of pre-emption a condition precedent to the exercise of the right, is to render it obligatory upon the pre-emptor to give the earliest possible notice to the vendee not to rely upon his purchase for making improvements, &c., or otherwise dealing with the purchased property. The rule is a very salutary restriction of right, which might otherwise be very capriciously enforced under a system of law which recognized no rule as to the limitation period for enforcing claims. Indeed,

29 4 BLR 134.

the rule rests much upon the same considerations as the doctrine of notice and the principle of acquiescence amounting to estoppel in equity jurisprudence. But such restrictions do not derogate from the right of pre-emption any more than another equitable rule of the same right, that the pre-emptor, in enforcing his right, cannot break up the bargain of sale by pre-empting only a portion of the property sold to one purchaser. The law of pre-emption is full of equitable considerations of this nature, but it is scarcely necessary to pursue the argument any further.

This brings me to the last point. Considerable portions of the judgments in *Sheikh Kudratulla's Case* are devoted to showing that the right of pre-emption can be defeated by what Mitter, J., calls: 'tricks and artifices', which Peacock, CJ, held are recognized and allowed by Muhammadan law; and from this it is inferred (though I confess, with due respect, I am not able to follow the reasoning) that the right is not enforceable against a Hindu purchaser, though enforceable against a Muhammadan. If any question of the 'tricks and artifices' referred to were involved in this case, I should have a good deal to say on the subject, but here I need only say once more that in dealing with questions of Muhammadan law, the distinction between moral behests and legal duties on the one hand, and between rules of substantive law and procedure on the other, must always be borne in mind. And I think I may safely say that most if not all the notions about the efficacy of these 'tricks and devices' arise from overlooking these distinctions. Peacock, CJ, says (p. 173): 'The Muhammadan law, as has been already shown by Mr Justice Kemp and Mr Justice Mitter, admits of all kinds of devices for the purpose of frustrating its own law. If there is a *bona fide* sale between a Muhammadan vendor and a Hindu purchaser, and they come forward and declare that which is not true, and say that it was not a sale intended to operate, but was a fictitious device, their words must be accepted according to the Muhammadan law, and the truth of the assertion cannot be disputed. They would be bound by the untruth which the vendor and the purchaser declare for the purpose of evading the right of pre-emption. Can we say that if they will state an untruth, the Hindu shall remain in possession of the property which he has purchased; but if they will not declare that which is untrue, there is an equity to take the property away from the purchaser?' The argument is consistent with certain passages in the text-books, which his Lordship went on to cite. But without attempting to explain the real reasons upon which those passages proceed, the argument may be fully answered by saying that in the case supposed, the question whether there has been a *bona fide* sale or not is not a question of substantive law, but a mere question of fact, to be ascertained by the rules of that department of procedure which consists of the rules of evidence; and that we are no more bound to follow the Muhammadan law of evidence in a pre-emptive suit than in a suit involving questions of succession or inheritance. The Muhammadan law of evidence, like other old systems, contains numerous rules which arose either from imperfect notions as to the distinction between the weight and admissibility of evidence, or from the rules of procedure, or from the political exigencies of the Muhammadan people, when those rules were formulated. The rule whether upon any particular point in a pre-emptive suit the statement of the pre-emptor, the vendor, or the vendee is to be believed, is an illustration of the former part of this proposition, and the latter part may be exemplified by the disability imposed upon non-Muhammadans to give evidence against a Muhammadan in a court of justice, the reason being stated to be 'that they have no power or authority over the Moslems, and are suspected of inventing falsehoods against them.' But the Muhammadan law of evidence is not the law of British India, and, whatever force the argument of Peacock, C. J., might have had in 1869, when his judgment was delivered, it can have no application now. For if it was intended as an enunciation of the Muhammadan law of evidence, since that time a Code of Evidence has been passed providing its own rules for ascertaining facts, and s. 2 of the enactment (Act I of 1872) has abolished all other rules of evidence. Similarly, it will be found upon close examination of the other devices to defeat pre-emption, referred to in the *Hedaya* and in Baillie's *Digest,* on which the learned Judges of the Calcutta Court relied, that they owe their origin to extremely technical rules of the Muhammadan law of contract, procedure or evidence, in none of which departments of law are we bound by these technicalities. The Muhammadan substantive law, in matters governed by it, cannot, of course, be administered without ascertaining the facts to which it is to be applied. But how those facts are to be ascertained, is a matter relating to the remedy, *ad litis ordinationem*, for which the courts in British India have their own rules. And there is in principle no more reason for saying that in a pre-emptive suit the questions, whether a valid *bona fide* sale has taken place or not, and if so, for what price, are governed by the Muhammadan law, than there would be for saying that when a decree is passed under the Muhammadan law for dower or inheritance, the process for executing that decree is to be regulated by the rules of procedure provided by that law. And, speaking generally, I may say that if it is once conceded that the technicalities of the Muhammadan law of contract, procedure or evidence are not binding upon us, it will be found that no 'tricks and artifices' can defeat the pre-emptive right in our courts. Such devices are held to be abominable even where the technicalities of Muhammadan adjective law might give them some plausible effect; and this is the prevalent doctrine, notwithstanding the opinion of Kazi Abu Yusuf, to be found in the passage from the *Hedaya*, to which Kemp, J., has referred. The opinion of Imam Muhammad, given in that same passage, condemns all devices; but there being no such questions in this case, I need not discuss the matter any further. But I wish to add that I have considered it my duty to deal with this reference at such elaborate length, not only out of respect for the eminent authorities with whom I have ventured to differ in arriving at my conclusions, but also because the rapid rise in the value of landed property in British India has gone far to extend the exercise of the pre-emptive right and to enhance its importance by confirming it as an incident of the proprietary tenure. Moreover, the right, though it no doubt operates as a restriction of the principle of free sale, and thus tends to diminish the market-value of property, must have enough to recommend itself, for even in some of the most civilized parts of Germany a similar right (*retrakt-recht*) is still maintained, either as a custom or as a rule of law. And if such is the case in a country where distinctions of race, caste, or creed do not prevail, it seems to me that the right must not be lightly dealt with in a country like India, where the population presents quite the opposite state of things, and where the intrusion of a stranger as a co-sharer must not only give rise to inconvenience but disturb domestic comfort, if not, as in some cases, lead to breach of the public peace.

My answer to this reference is in the affirmative.

◊ UPDATE ◊

1. *Validity of pre-emption laws*

Justice Syed Mahmood's judgment in the old Allahabad case of *Gobind Dayal* [Case 36] remains the bible on the law of pre-emption, to whatever extent it remains in force in various parts of the subcontinent.

The Hanafi law allowing pre-emption on the grounds of *khilt* (participation in appendages) and *jiwar* (neighbourhood), suffered a setback in India when the Supreme Court declared the customary and statutory laws allowing pre-emption on these grounds *ultra vires* the Constitution—*Bhau Ram* v. *Baijnath* AIR 1962 SC 1476; *Santram* v. *Labh Singh* AIR 1965 SC 314.[30]

The Supreme Court rulings were specifically followed in respect of Muslim law in *Mahfooz Ali* v. *Ali Hasan* AIR 1980 All 5. This development

30 A study of the impact of these cases on the Muslim law of pre-emption is found in my book *Islamic Law in Modern India*, ILI, Delhi, 1972. Later development may be seen in my book *the Muslim Law of India*, 3rd ed, Butterworth, Delhi 2001—TM.

brought the Hanafi law on a par with the other schools of Muslim law prevailing in India under which pre-emption is allowed on the ground of *jiwar* (neighbourhood) only, and not on any other ground. To this extent the Muslim law of pre-emption remains intact in India.

2. *Pre-emption by co-sharer*

The Supreme Court of India has ruled that a right of pre-emption would arise only where full ownership of an immovable property is sold and not when only some of the rights in the property are alienated—*Munnilal* v. *Bishwanath* AIR 1968 SC 450.

In a recent decision the Supreme Court has applied the Muslim law of pre-emption to co-sharers of property—*Matto Devi* v. *Damodar Lal* (2001) 6 SCC 330.

3. *Law in Pakistan*

The Hanafi law of pre-emption remains in force in Pakistan and the procedures and processes for exercising the right have been examined and explained in a number of recent cases. See *Government of NWFP* v. *Said Kamal Shah* PLD 1986 SC 360; *Sikandar* v. *Mohammad Ayub* PLD 1991 SC 1040.

XVI. Administration of Estates

37. JAFRI BEGAM v. AMIR MUHAMMAD
(1885) 7 All 822 (FB)

Inheritance—devolution not suspended till payment of deceased ancestor's debts—decree in respect of deceased Muslim's debts passed against heir in possession of estate—decree not binding on other heirs not parties thereto and not in possession, so as to convey their interests to auction-purchaser in execution—recovery of possession by other heirs contingent on payment of proportionate shares of debt for which decree was passed

Upon the death of a Muslim intestate who leaves unpaid debts, whether large or small with reference to the value of his estate, the ownership of such estate devolves immediately on his heirs, and such devolution is not contingent upon, and suspended till, the payment of such debts.

A decree relative to his debts, passed in a contentious or non-contentious suit against only such heirs of a deceased Muslim debtor as are in possession of the whole or part of his estate, does not bind the other heirs who by reason of absence or other cause are out of possession, so as to convey to the auction-purchaser, in execution of such a decree, the rights and interests of such heirs as were not parties to the decree.

In execution of a decree for a debt due by a Muslim intestate, which was passed against such of the heirs of the deceased as were in possession of the debtor's estate, the decree-holder put up for sale and purchased certain property which formed part of the said estate. One of the heirs who was out of possession, and who was not a party to these proceedings, brought a suit against the decree-holder for recovery of a share of the property sold in execution of the decree, by right of inheritance.

Held that the plaintiff was not entitled to recover, from the auction-purchaser in execution of the decree, possession of his share in the property sold, without such recovery of possession being rendered contingent upon payment by him of his proportionate share of the ancestor's debt for which the decree was passed, and in satisfaction whereof the sale took place.

Although criticized in some respects, this is the leading case on the subject of administration and has been often cited in cases and textbooks, *Tyabji*, Index; *Outlines*, 326 seqq.; *Bishan Singh* v. *Khazan Singh* AIR 1958 SC 838 at 841.

The case came on for hearing before Straight and Mahmood, JJ., who referred the following questions to the Full Bench:

(1) Upon the death of a Muhammadan intestate who leaves unpaid debts, whether large or small with reference to the value of his estate, does the ownership of such estate devolve immediately on his heirs, or is such devolution contingent upon, and suspended till, payment of such debts?

(2) Does a decree, relative to his debts, passed in a contentious or non-contentious suit against only such heirs of a deceased Muhammadan debtor as are in possession of the whole or part of his estate, bind the other heirs who, by reason of absence or other cause, are out of possession, so as to convey to the auction-purchaser, in execution of such a decree, the rights and interests even of such heirs as were no parties to the decree?

(3) If not, can such heirs as were no parties to the decree recover from the auction-purchaser, in execution of such decree, possession of their shares in the property sold, without such recovery of possession being rendered contingent upon payment by them of their proportionate shares of the ancestor's debts for which the decree was passed, and in satisfaction whereof the sale took place?

This last question was amended by the Full Bench to read as follows: 'If not, is the plaintiff in this case entitled to recover from the auction-purchaser in execution of such decree, possession of his share in the property sold, without such recovery of possession being rendered contingent upon payment by him of his proportionate share of the ancestor's debts for which the decree was passed, and in satisfaction whereof the sale took place?'

The following judgments were delivered by the Full Bench:

Petheram, CJ, Straight, Oldfield, and Brodhurst, JJ: Our answer to the first question referred to us in this case is in the affirmative, to the second question in the negative, and to the third question (as amended) also in the negative.

Judgment [Syed Mahmood, J.][1]

In this case I agree generally with the answers given by the learned Chief Justice and my learned brethren to the three questions referred to the Full Bench; but I do not intend on this occasion to state the grounds upon which

[1] With W.C. Petheram, CJ and Straight, Oldfield & Brodhurst, JJ. Mahmood, J. first gave a brief judgment and later his detailed reasons.

my conclusions are based. One reason why I refrain from doing so is that one of the greatest difficulties in the way of the courts established in British India is the paucity of textbooks on Muhammadan law written in English which are sufficiently accurate to be safe guides in the administration of those branches of that law which, by s. 24 of the Bengal Civil Courts Act (VI of 1871), we are bound to administer. The only means of information consists of books of reference which are either incomprehensive compilations or abbreviated translations and, in some cases, translations of translations. Another difficulty is that the language of the highest courts in India is not the language of the people, and consequently the vast majority of advocates who appear in those courts are those who must speak English and who, as a matter of fact, are not likely to refer to the original Arabic authorities. For these reasons, I confess, I fully expected that the judgment of the court would have been reserved in such a case.

As the learned Chief Justice rightly observed during the argument, there is 'no magic in Muhammadan law'. There is, of course, no magic in that system any more than in any other. The Muhammadan law is only a part of the general system of jurisprudence, and whatever is true as a matter of general principle would be true of any particular legal system worthy of the name, so long as its rules are accurately ascertained.

My difficulty in the present case does not arise from anything intrinsically abstruse in the three questions referred to the Full Bench, but from the fact that some of the highest tribunals in India have repeatedly expressed views upon the subject which, according to the conclusions arrived at by us today, directly contradict some of the principles of Muhammadan jurisprudence. I make this observation with due respect, and do so because it was for this reason only that my brother Straight and I made the reference. Speaking for myself, I should not otherwise have thought it necessary to refer the case to the Full Bench. And this being so, I should be sorry if anything said by me in this case merely added one more to the rulings to be found in the Reports; and I reserve the grounds of my conclusion, in the hope that I may, perhaps, be able to make my judgment of such a nature as might, in some measure, help to remove what I may respectfully call the existing cloud of judicial exposition upon these important questions. For this reason, I should have been glad to hear in the argument at the Bar some reference to the Arabic texts of the Muhammadan law; but under the circumstances, and considering that the learned Chief Justice and my learned brethren have been anxious to deliver their judgments at once, the only course open to me is that I must search out these texts for myself, and as that will require some time, I must, of necessity, reserve the reasons of my judgment till such time as the exigencies of the business of the court allow.

Detailed Reasons

When this case was argued before the Full Bench, I mentioned the reasons why I did not on that occasion set forth the exact grounds upon which I concurred in the conclusion at which the learned Chief Justice and the rest of the court had arrived. I was anxious, as I said then, to support my conclusions by citing original authorities of Muhammadan law—a course which I considered especially necessary in view of the long conflict of decisions which exists in the Reports upon the subject to which this reference relates. The exigencies of the business of the court have not allowed me, before now, to consult the original authorities of the Muhammadan law to which I wished to refer, and it has therefore devolved upon me to deliver my judgment now, although the rest of the Bench have already delivered their judgments.

Before, however, citing the original authorities of the Muhammadan law, I wish to consider briefly the various rulings to be found in the Reports, and which constitute the case-law upon the subject. I shall, in dealing with this part of the judgment, refer only to the most important cases which have been cited, as in the order of reference I have already summarized nearly all the cases.

The first question referred to us does not appear to have arisen simply and directly in any case to be found in the Reports, though it formed a necessary step of the *ratio decidendi* of some of the rulings which have been cited, and in this sense it was discussed and decided. Under this class of cases, the first authorities to which I wish to refer are the case of *Wahidunnissa* v. *Shubrattun*,[2] and another case very similar in principle, namely, *Bazayet Hossein* v. *Dooli Chund*.[3] The first of these was decided by the Calcutta High Court, and the second by the Privy Council. The principle which they lay down is, that the creditors of a deceased Muhammadan cannot follow his estate into the hands of a *bona fide* transferee for valuable consideration. Their effect is best described in the words used by their Lordships of the Privy Council in the latter of the two cases to which I have referred. Their Lordships say:

> At that time, if Najmooddin were the legitimate son of the deceased—and it has now been decided that he was—he had the right to convey his own share of the inheritance, and was able to pass a good title to the alienee notwithstanding any debts which might be due from his deceased father. For that position the case of *Wahidunnissa* v. *Shubrattun* was cited as an authority. In that case, the share of an heir was seized and sold in execution of a decree against the heir, in his individual,

2 6 BLR 54.
3 ILR 4 Cal 402.

and not in his representative, capacity, and it was held that the purchaser had a right to hold the property against a creditor of the ancestor who had obtained a decree for the debt before the seizure in execution. In that case, the creditor was a widow of a deceased Muhammadan, and her claim was in respect of dower. The principle of that case is applicable to the present, and the ruling is quite in accordance with the English law applicable to heirs and devisees as to real estate, and to executors as regards personalty.

Such being the effect of these cases, I am of opinion that the ruling of the Privy Council cannot be understood without holding that, upon the death of a Muhammadan owner, the inheritance vests immediately in his heirs, and is not suspended by reason of debts being due from the estate of the deceased. It is true that the present question was not then raised in an unmixed and direct form, for there were considerations as to third parties being *bona fide* transferees for value, which to some extent contributed to the decision. But no considerations arising from any doctrine of equity relating to 'notice' and *bona fide* transferees for value, could render the title of a transferee from a Muhammadan heir valid, where such transfer was made before the liquidation of the ancestor's debts, and if such liquidation were the turning point of the devolution of the inheritance. The Privy Council ruling is therefore a clear authority in support of my view, and indeed I may go the length of saying that no other view can reconcile the ruling with the undoubted principles of law and equity in such cases. But a short time before the Privy Council delivered their judgment, the same question regarding the devolution of inheritance was raised, but again indirectly, in the Calcutta High Court in *Assamathem Nessa Bibi* v. *Roy Lutchmeeput Singh*.[4] That was a Full Bench case in which two of the learned Judges dissented from the opinion of the majority. That opinion was stated by Garth, C. J., but it bears upon the second only of the points before us in the present case. The judgment of the minority was delivered by Markby, J., who considered the question of the devolution of Muhammadan inheritance as a necessary step to the conclusions at which he arrived. The learned Judge, relying upon certain passages in the *Hedaya*, held it to be clear that the estate of an intestate descends entire, together with all the debts due from and owing to the deceased; that it is therefore, to use a convenient expression adopted by lawyers, a 'universal succession'; that 'there ought, according to the Muhammadan law, to be in every case of death something very similar to what we should call an administration of the estate by a court of justice'; that, under the strict Muhammadan law, the personal liability of the individual heirs was 'something quite distinct from the liability of

4 ILR 4 Cal 142.

the estate'; that it was unimportant to determine whether such personal liability was *proportione haereditaria* or *proportione emolumenti*; but that 'the liability of the estate remained, if the creditors chose to resort to that remedy, until the debts had been completely liquidated.' And pursuing this argument, the learned Judge went on to say: 'If this be so, it follows, I think, that on the decease of a Muhammadan, neither his estate vested immediately in his heirs, nor did his heirs become immediately liable for his debts. Until the heirs came forward to take possession, the succession was vacant (*haereditas jacens*). But by a fiction the deceased owner was supposed during this interval to be represented by the estate itself (*quia creditum est haereditatem dominam esse et defuncti locum obtinere*). It is particularly to be observed, however, that it was the deceased owner, and not the heirs, who were thus represented (*personae vicem sustinet non haeredis futuri sed defuncti*).' This view was not adopted by the majority of the court, though their judgment mainly proceeds upon another ground, to which I shall refer in dealing with the second point before us.

I now pass to the passages of the *Hedaya* upon which Markby, J. based his opinion. I have carefully considered them, and I have come to the conclusion that they do not substantiate the conclusions at which that learned Judge arrived. In the first place, it must be remembered that the work to which he was referring is merely a translation of a translation leaving room for the remark of Mr Almaric Rumsey, that it is 'much to be desired that a new translation should be made of the *Hedaya*, this time from the original Arabic, and not from the intermediate Persian.' I agree in the observation, especially as the English terms employed in Mr Hamilton's translation are frequently not the equivalents of the original Arabic terms, and are not used with the degree of definiteness essential for a book on law. In the second place, to use the words of Mr Rumsey again, the law of inheritance is 'a branch of jurisprudence which the *Hedaya* does not formally discuss, but only mentions incidentally here and there.' Moreover—and this is the most important point—most of the passages relied upon by Markby, J., relate, not to substantive law, but to procedure, and in particular to the duties of the *Kazi* in matters connected with partition, compromise, composition, and other similar subjects; whilst some of the passages do not appear to me to apply to the question—I mean the passage in Vol. II of Mr Hamilton's *Hedaya*, to be found at p. 599, which belongs to the chapter 'Of bail in which two are concerned', and at pp. 530 and 539 of Vol. IV. The other passages in the *Hedaya* relied upon by Markby, J., I shall presently consider in discussing the second question referred to us.

I now proceed to cite the original authorities of Muhammadan law in support of my view. It is well known that the Muhammadan law of inheritance is based upon a passage in the fourth chapter of the Qur'an, which in Sale's translation is thus rendered:

God hath thus commanded you concerning your children: A male shall have as much as the share of two females, but if they be females only, and above two in number, they shall have two-thirds part of what the deceased shall leave; and if there be but one, she shall have the half. And the parents of the deceased shall have each of them a sixth part of what he shall leave, if he have a child; but if he have no child, and his parents be his heirs, then his mother shall have the third part. And if he have brethren, his mother shall have a sixth part, after the legacies which he shall bequeath and his debts be paid. Ye know not whether your parents or your children be of greater use unto you. This is an ordinance from God, and God is knowing and wise. Moreover, ye may claim half of what your wives shall leave, if they have no issue; but if they have issue, then ye shall have the fourth part of what they shall leave, after the legacies which they shall bequeath, and the debts be paid. They also shall have the fourth part of what ye shall leave, in case ye have no issue; but if he have issue, then they shall have one-eighth part of what ye shall leave, after the legacies which ye shall bequeath, and your debts be paid. And if a man or woman's substance be inherited by a distant relation, and he or she have a brother or sister, each of them two shall have a sixth part of the estate. But if there be more than this number, they shall be equal sharers in a third part, after payment of the legacies which shall be bequeathed and the debts, without prejudice to the heirs.

In reading this passage, I have emphasized the words after the legacies which he shall bequeath and his debts be paid, and also other phrases to the same effect, which have been repeated after each part of the passage describing the shares to be allotted to the heirs. These phrases gave rise to two difficulties in the minds of the Muhammadan jurists. The first was, whether the circumstance that legacies were mentioned before debts gave the former precedence over the latter in the administration of the estate of deceased persons; and the second was, whether the word after related to the devolution of inheritance, or to the ascertainment of the extent of the shares to be allotted to the various heirs. There is much learned discussion upon both these points in the Arabic works; but with the former of these points we are not concerned in this case; and in regard to the latter, I will content myself with the explanation of *Baizawi*, one of the greatest commentators on the Qur'an, whose views have been universally adopted by Muhammadan jurists. He says:

The words after the legacies which he shall bequeath or debts relate to that which precedes relating to the distribution of all the inheritance; that is, these are to be the shares of the heirs out of that which remains from legacies or debts.[5]

5 Al-Baidawi on Qur'an, IV:12. [Arabic text: *Cases*, 471]

The meaning of the explanation is, that the word after, as used in the Qur'an, simply refers to the balance of the estate after the payment of debts and legacies, but does not affect the question of devolution. That this is the interpretation accepted by the Muhammadan jurists in general is best shown by a passage in *Al-Sirajiyyah*, a treatise of the highest authority on the Muhammadan law of inheritance, which Sir William Jones translated about a century ago; and in citing the passage I cannot do better than adopt his words: 'Our learned in the law (to whom God be merciful) say: There belong to the property of a person deceased four successive duties to be performed by the Magistrate—first, his funeral ceremony and burial, without superfluity of expense yet without deficiency; next, the discharge of his just debts from the whole of his remaining effects; then the payment of his legacies out of a third of what remains after his debts are paid; and lastly, the distribution of the residue among his successors, according to the Divine Book, to the Traditions, and to the Assent of the Learned'—(Jones's *Works*, Vol. III, p. 517). I have quoted this passage to show the priority possessed by the three charges to which the estate is subject when inherited by heirs. This order of priority is, as is obvious from the passage, merely a direction as to the administration of the estate, and has no bearing upon the question of the exact point of time when inheritance devolves upon the heirs. When they inherit the property, they take it, of course, subject to these three prior charges, as they would subject to mortgages—the difference being (as pointed out by the Privy Council in the case which I have already cited) that an incumbrance by way of mortgage follows the property even in the hands of *bona fide* purchasers for value, with or without notice of the prior incumbrance; whilst the three charges on the estate of a deceased Muhammadan as described in *Al-Sirajiyyah* cannot do so. It is one thing to say that these three charges take precedence of the inheritance, in the administration of the estate and its distribution among heirs, and it is another thing to say that the inheritance itself does not open up until those charges are satisfied. And it is obvious that all the arguments adopted by Markby, J., as to debts, would, according to his hypothesis, necessarily apply also to funeral expenses and legacies, which, like debts of the deceased, are charges upon his estate. But I am unaware of any rule of Muhammadan law which would render such charges, or even mortgages, an impediment to the devolution of property on the heirs by inheritance. Funeral expenses, debts, and legacies, or any one or more of them, may indeed absorb the estate of the deceased, defeating every succeeding charge; and it is obvious that if nothing is left for the heirs they can take nothing. But this is a proposition widely different from saying that the devolution of inheritance is suspended till the various charges are satisfied. Indeed, upon this point, the books of

Muhammadan jurisprudence leave no doubt. The author of the *Ashbah*, a most celebrated book on maxims, lays down the maxim: 'Nothing enters the proprietorship of man without his option (consent), except inherited property'; and the following explanation follows as a commentary:

They (the Doctors of Law) have differed as to the time of the devolution of inheritance. The learned men of Irak maintain the last part of the ancestor's life, and the learned men of Balkh (maintain that it is) the moment of death.[6]

These authorities leave no doubt in my mind that the devolution of inheritance takes place immediately upon the death of the ancestor from whom the property is inherited. But I wish further to adopt certain tests to confirm my view. The first of them is an absolutely universal rule of the law of Muhammadan inheritance itself. The *jus representationis* being absolutely foreign to the Muhammadan law of inheritance, the question of the devolution of inheritance rests entirely upon the exact point of time when the person through whom the heir claims died—the order of deaths being the sole guide in such questions.

The rule of 'perfect' exclusion from inheritance—to use the language of *Al-Sirajiyyah*—'is grounded on two principles; one of which is, that whoever is related to the deceased through any person, shall not inherit while that person is living; as a son's son with the son; except the mother's children, for they inherit with her, since she has no title to the whole inheritance; the second principle is, that the nearest of blood must take.' To illustrate the principles, I adopt the language of Sir William Macnaghten: 'The son of a person deceased shall not represent such person, if he died before his father. He shall not stand in the same place as the deceased would have done had he been living, but shall be excluded from the inheritance if he have a paternal uncle. For instance, A, B, and C, are grandfather, father, and son. The father B dies in the life-time of the grandfather A. In this case, the son C shall not take *jure representationis*, but the estate will go to the other sons of A.' Now, in the above illustration, if we suppose that A died leaving both B and C, but B died before the debts and legacies were satisfied, the question would arise whether C would take a share along with his uncles, the other sons of A. The answer to the question depends absolutely upon the answer to the question whether immediately upon the death of A any share in the inheritance devolved upon *B*, for, if it did not, then C can have no vested interest in the inheritance. According to the views of Markby, J., upon the death of A 'neither his estate vested immediately in his heirs, nor did his heirs become immediately liable to his debts'; for

6 [Arabic text: *Cases*, 473].

'until the heirs came forward to take possession, the succession was vacant'. And, according to this hypothesis, C could take no share, because the debts and legacies of A not having been paid before the death of B, no share of the inheritance vested in him, and his son C could take no share along with his paternal uncles. That this would be the necessary result of the reasoning of Markby, J., seems to me to be obvious; but it is equally obvious that the Muhammadan rules of inheritance furnish quite the opposite answer. The law upon the subject has been well summarized by Sir William Macnaghten, and I adopt his words because they are in perfect accord with the rules contained in *Al-Sirajiyyah, Sharifiyyah*, and other authoritative Arabic treatises on the Muhammadan law of inheritance:

Where a person dies and leaves heirs, some of whom die prior to any distribution of the estate, the survivors are said to have *vested* interests in the inheritance; in which case the rule is, that the property of the first deceased must be apportioned among his several heirs living at the time of his death; and it must be supposed that they received their respective shares accordingly.

Mr Baillie, proceeding even more closely upon the Arabic texts, has enunciated the same rule in his work on Muhammadan inheritance: 'When some of the portions have become inheritances by the death of the parties entitled to them, before the estate has been actually divided among them . . . the rule is to arrange the original estate on the principles already explained, and to assign to each original heir his or her share, and then to arrange his or her estate, that is, his or her share of the original estate, on the same principles.' It is clear from these passages that in the case supposed by me, C would take the share in the estate of A, a proposition which directly contradicts the conclusions at which Markby, J., arrived. Indeed, I may go the length of saying that some) of the most important and undoubted rules of Muhammadan inheritance would become meaningless if any event other than the ancestor's death were to be considered as the point of the devolution of inheritance upon heirs.

It is scarcely necessary for me to pursue the argument much further; I will, however, take a few illustrations to justify the proposition which I have just laid down. Take the case of missing persons under the Muhammadan law of inheritance. Not long ago, in the case of *Mazhar Ali* v. *Budh Singh*[7] I had occasion to discuss the matter at full length, and here I will only say that the inheritance to his estate opens up at the moment when, by a legal presumption, he is taken to be dead, and all the arguments of the Muhammadan jurists make the presumption of the death of the missing person as the turning point of the devolution of inheritance on his heirs. To use the

[7] ILR 7 All 297.

words of Mr Almaric Rumsey in his work on Muhammadan inheritance, it must be remembered that 'the lost or missing person is deemed to die, not at the date at which he has become such, but at the precise time at which the declaration of his death is made; consequently his relations dying before that time cannot inherit from him.' Now, taking the case of persons dying by a common calamity, it will be found that the rules of Muhammadan inheritance again treat death as the turning point of the devolution. I will show this by citing a passage from Baillie's *Digest*, as it is taken from the text of the *Fatawa-i-Alamgiri*:

> Where several persons have been drowned or burnt together, and it is not known which of them died first, we treat them all as having died together. The property of each will accordingly go to his own heirs, and none of them can be heirs to another, unless it is known in what order they died, when those who died last will inherit to those who died before them. And the rule is the same when several are killed together by the falling of a wall, or in the field of battle, and it is not known which of them died first.

I might go further, and show that all the rules relating to the inheritance by or from posthumous children, proceeding upon the analogy of the rules relating to missing persons, render death as the only turning point of the devolution of inheritance. But I will take a case having even a more directly analogical bearing upon the point now under consideration. It needs no citation of authorities to say that, under the Muhammadan law, no property or right can be transferred or relinquished by the person entitled thereto, unless it is vested in him; that no valid will can be made in favour of an heir; that, even in favour of a stranger, a bequest can hold good only to the extent of a third of the property of the testator remaining after payment of his funeral expenses and debts; and that a bequest, notwithstanding these limitations, may be validated, and take effect with the consent of the testator's heirs. I have mentioned these rules as a statement of the premises from which I shall draw my conclusion. The question then arises, when should the consent of the heirs be given in order to render effective a will which exceeds the limitations imposed upon the testamentary power by the Muhammadan law? The answer is furnished by a passage of the *Hedaya*, which I will translate here from the original Arabic, although a paraphrase of the passage exists in Mr Hamilton's translations (Vol. IV, p. 470):

> Their (the heirs') consent during his (the testator's) life-time is not acceptable, for the reason that it would be previous to the establishment of their right. As their right is established upon the death (of the testator), therefore it is for them (i.e. they are at liberty) to reject it after his death, because it would then be after the establishment of their right, and therefore it is not for them to recede from it. [Arabic text: *Cases*, 476]

This is the prevalent doctrine of the school of Imam Abu Hanifa which governs this case. But some of the jurists of the same school, whilst doubting the reasoning, have adopted the same doctrine on the ground that, although a testamentary disposition in contravention of the limitations of law would, in itself, be illegal, yet effect would be given to it, because the consent of the heirs given after the death of the testator amounts to dealing with their own property, so that not the testamentary disposition, but the consent of the heirs, takes legal effect. This is shown by a passage in the *Fatawa Kazi Khan*:

As Sheikh-ul-Imam al-Ali-us-Safdi has said, that the answer of Abu Hanifa is difficult. He has allowed composition (regarding legacies) on the ground that the property in reality belongs to the heir on account of the extinction of the ownership of the deceased, and on account of its transfer to the heir, and it remains as if it was the property of the deceased for the needs of the deceased. Therefore before it was so employed for the needs of the deceased, it becomes the property of the heir, and when the purposes of the deceased are not attained, the property remains in the ownership of the heir. [Arabic text: *Cases*, 476–77]

In these passages there is not the slightest indication that the payment of funeral expenses, debts, or legacies, is a condition precedent to the vesting of the inheritance. These, of course, are charges upon the estate of the deceased in the sense in which I have already explained them; and I may concede that no distribution of the assets of a deceased Muhammadan's estate among his heirs can be made irrespective of those charges. But this has no bearing upon the question of the devolution of inheritance—a question which rests upon a reasoning analogical in principle to that which relates to the vesting of legacies considered by me not long ago in *Bachman* v. *Bachman*.[8] The inheritance of an heir, like a legacy, may be absolutely defeated if the debts of the deceased at the time of the administration of his estate are found to absorb the whole of his property. But this has no more bearing upon the question of the devolution of inheritance than upon the vesting of legacies, and I may say that in neither case is distribution or division of the estate a condition precedent to the vesting of the right. In the case of legacies, the terms of a will might, of course, affect the ordinary rule, and division may possibly be made a condition precedent to the vesting of the legacy. But I need not resort to analogies, for the texts of the Muhammadan law leave no doubt that distribution of the estate, or the payment of debts of the deceased, is not a condition precedent to the devolution of inheritance. Here is a passage from *Fatawa Kazi Khan:*

8 ILR 6 All 583.

A man died, and his heirs, by mutual consent, divided the inheritance among themselves, and then one of them, on his own behalf, brought a claim for debt due by the deceased. His claim will be entertained because debt neither prevents the establishment of the heir's proprietorship nor division (of the inheritance). [Arabic text: *Cases*, 477]

If it were necessary to carry the argument further, I might cite many passages even from the Muhammadan law of slavery (which, happily for mankind, is no longer the law of British India), which would support my view. It is, however, sufficient to say here that *'itq* or manumission of slaves is a power which can be exercised only by the full owner of the slave, and if the slave forms part of the inheritance, the heir can emancipate him, and the emancipation will take effect even though such manumission took place before payment of the debts of the deceased from whom the slave was inherited, the reason of the rule being, as stated by *Kazi Khan*, that the ownership of the heir was complete at the time of the manumission. [Arabic text: *Cases*, 478]

There is one more point to be considered in connection with the first question referred to us in this case. I hope I have said enough to show that the existence of debts due by the deceased does not affect the period of devolution of inheritance; but the point remains whether the extent or amount of the debts affects the question. Some of the passages quoted from Mr Hamilton's *Hedaya* in the Full Bench case of *Hamir Singh* v. *Musammat Zakia*[9] would go to indicate an affirmative answer. But the translation is only a loose paraphrase of the original Arabic, and is liable to convey a wrong meaning. What is meant by the heirs to an insolvent estate being prevented from inheriting, simply refers to the rule that nothing will be left for them to inherit if the liabilities of the deceased swallow up the whole estate. It is only in this sense that Mr Hamilton's translation can be understood, when it says that 'the circumstance of a small debt attaching to the estate of a deceased person does not prevent the heirs from inheriting, whereas if the estate were completely involved in debt they would be prevented.'—(*Hedaya*, Bk. XXVI.) I do not think it necessary to translate these passages in the *Hedaya* because, after what I have already said, it seems enough to add that the existence of debts, whether large or small, is quite immaterial. Whatever their extent, nature or amount may be, the property of the deceased is liable to their payment, and their extent regulates the balance of the estate only but does not affect its devolution.

The second point in F.A. No. 70 is similar to that raised in F.A. No. 50, and I have dwelt upon the first question at such length because it seems to

9 ILR 1 All 57.

me that the answer to the second question may be regarded as a corollary to the answer to the first. I have considered the passages of the *Hedaya* referred to in the Full Bench case of *Hamir Singh* v. *Musammat Zakia*,[10] and those cited by Garth, C. J. and Markby, J., in *Assamathem Nessa Bibi* v. *Roy Lutchmeeput Singh*. These passages have been understood by those learned Judges as governing the decision of cases like the present. I have also consulted other original authorities, such as *Fatawa Kazi Khan, Durrul Mukhtar, Shami,* and *Fathul Kadir*. All these books possess high authority, and no doubt there are passages to be found in them, as in the *Hedaya*, which attach significance to such questions as the following: whether the heir is in possession, whether he is in possession of the whole or only a part of the estate, the amount of the assets in his hands, whether the suit was contentious or non-contentious, whether the decree was passed *ex-parte* or in the presence of the defendant, and these points the authorities treat as regulating or at least affecting the binding effect of the decree upon those heirs who, being either out of possession or absent, are no parties to the litigation. On the other hand, there are passages to show that the decree will bind only the share of the defendant heir, or only so much of the property of the deceased as is in the hands of such defendant; whilst other passages lay down the rule that, even where no property belonging to the deceased has come to the hands of the heirs, the creditor of the deceased must sue them in order to obtain a decree, which might be executed against any such property of the deceased as may be subsequently discovered.

The rule is thus laid down in *Fatawa Kazi Khan:*

> If the debtor has died without leaving any property in the hands of the heir, even then the heir will be (impleaded as) defendant for the claimant of the debt (that is, the creditor), and evidence will be taken and decree will be passed as to the debt, in order that the creditor may take any assets of the deceased which may be discovered. [Arabic text: *Cases*, 479]

This rule is the same as that laid down by Morgan, CJ, and Ross, J., in *Madho Ram* v. *Dilbur Mahul*,[11] and, although the case related to the estate of a deceased Muhammadan, those learned Judges decided it without any reference to the Muhammadan law, and treated the question as simply a matter of procedure, Again, according to the authorities of the Muhammadan law, to which I have referred, the power of one or more heirs to represent absent heirs in a litigation is regulated by the consideration whether the litigant-heir appears in the suit as plaintiff or as defendant; and the power of representation is materially affected by the position of the

10 ILR 4 Cal 142.

11 NWP HCR 1870, p. 449.

litigant-heir as party to the suit. Further, there is authority for the proposition that a decree passed against the heir in possession as representing the whole estate of the deceased in the litigation may, under certain circumstances, be set aside at the instance of the absent heir to the extent of his share and that, when this is done, the matter should be adjudicated upon *de novo*, involving the production of evidence by the plaintiff again, in order to justify the correctness of the former decision. I do not consider it necessary to cite the original texts which go to maintain these propositions, because I am satisfied that these rules of law are provisions which go only to the remedy, *ad litis ordinationem*, being matters purely of procedure as to array of parties, production of evidence, *res judicata,* and review of judgment, &c. Indeed, they are treated as such in the text-books of the Muhammadan law itself, and are *in pari materia* with some of the most important provisions of our Civil Procedure Code. They are not matters of substantive law; they do not constitute rules of inheritance; and the courts in British India are no more bound by them than by any such rules of evidence or limitation as the Muhammadan law may provide, for the simple reason that they fall outside the purview of s. 24 of the Bengal Civil Courts Act, which enumerates the matters in which we are bound to administer the Muhammadan law. Under the opposite view, these rules would be in the anomalous position of conflicting with the provisions of the Civil Procedure Code upon the same subjects, and at the same time be equally binding upon the courts. But for the reasons which I have already stated, I do not think any such conflict arises out of the present state of the law in British India. Upon the death of a Muhammadan owner, his property, as I have already shown, immediately devolves upon his heirs, in specific shares; and if there are any claims against the estate, and they are litigated, the matter passes into the region of procedure, and must be regulated according to the law which governs the action of the court. The plaintiff must go to the court having jurisdiction, and institute his suit within limitation, impleading all the heirs against whose shares he seeks to enforce his claim; and if he omits to implead any of the heirs, the decree would be ineffective as regards the share of those who were no parties to the litigation. The maxim of law, that a matter adjudicated upon between one set of parties in no wise prejudices another set of parties, is, of course, the foundation of one of the rules of *res judicata,* which itself is subject to strict limitation, as shown by s. 13 of the Civil Procedure Code; whilst even Explanation V of that section cannot be applied, unless the especial provisions of s. 30 of the Code are applicable, and have been duly applied by the court in allowing one party to sue or defend on behalf of all in the same interest. There is, however, no such question in these cases, and to hold that a decree obtained by a creditor of the deceased against some of his heirs, will bind also those heirs who were no parties to the suit, amounts to giving a judgment *inter partes*, or rather a judgment in *personam,* the binding effect of a judgment *in rem*, which the law limits to cases provided for by s. 41 of the Evidence Act.

But our law warrants no such course, and the reason seems to me to be obvious. Muhammadan heirs are independent owners of their specific shares, and if they take their shares subject to the charge of the debts of the deceased, their liability is in proportion to the extent of their shares. And once this is conceded, the maxim *res inter alios acta alteri nocere non debet* would apply without any such qualifications as might possibly be made in the case of Hindu co-heirs in a joint family. Now, putting aside questions of fraud or collusion between the creditors of the deceased and the heir in possession, it may well be that such heir, though defending the suit, is incompetent to contest the claim, or, by reason of not being acquainted with the facts of the case, or not possessing evidence, cannot properly resist the claim. There seems no reason why, in such a case, those should be bound by the decree who were no parties to the litigation, and had no opportunity of defending themselves against the creditor's claim by putting forward their own case.

This leads me to the considerations of the various rulings having a bearing upon the question now under consideration. In the case of *Assamathem Nessa Bibi* v. *Roy Lutchmeeput Singh*[12] the judgment of Markby, J. proceeds considerably upon the inferences which he drew from cases relating to the joint Hindu family, and the power of one member to represent the whole of the joint estate in litigation. I have already suggested that there are such essential distinctions between the Hindu law relating to a joint family and the Muhammadan law of inheritance that it would be unsafe to draw any conclusion by analogical reasoning. On the other hand, it is obvious that the conclusion at which that learned Judge arrived as to the power of the heir in possession to represent the estate in litigation, was materially induced by the opinion which he formed regarding the devolution of Muhammadan inheritance, which he discussed as the first point in the case. Now, I am unable to agree fully in the judgment of Garth, CJ, in which Kemp and Jackson, JJ. concurred. There is much in the *ratio decidendi* with which I entirely agree, and there is no doubt that the distinction which the judgment draws between a decree passed by consent and a decree passed in a contested suit, is borne out by certain passages of the *Hedaya*, to which the learned Chief Justice referred. But, with due deference, I am unable to adopt

12 ILR 4 Cal 142.

the distinction, because, as I have already pointed out, those passages lay down rules of procedure which are not binding upon us, which are in many important respects inconsistent with the rules of the Civil Procedure Code, and, at all events, we can scarcely adopt some of them with consistency, unless we are prepared to adopt also other rules of the Muhammadan law of procedure which are complements of the rules so adopted. According to our own rules of procedure, there is no distinction between the binding effect of a decree passed by consent, and a decree passed in a contested suit. Both render the matter *res judicata*, and neither can bind those persons who were no parties to the litigation. There were, of course, reasons arising from the exigencies of life (such as the difficulty of communication and travelling) which induced Muhammadan jurists in the middle ages to frame rules of procedure in many essentials different from those which regulate the procedure of our courts. But those conditions of life no longer exist: the law of British India has framed its own rules of procedure; and bearing in mind the analogy of the principle by which not the *lex loci contractus* but the *lex fori* regulates all matters going to the remedy, *ad litis ordinationem*, I would reject the rules of the Muhammadan law of procedure in connection with the binding effect of decrees upon absent heirs. And it follows that a decree obtained in a litigation to which the absent heirs or those who were out of possession were no parties cannot be executed against them or against their shares in the inherited property. Indeed, such was the view adopted by Garth, CJ, himself in an earlier case—*Hendry* v. *Mutty Lall Dhur*,[13] with which I entirely concur, and which is in accord with the Full Bench ruling of this court in *Hamir Singh* v. *Musammat Zakia*.[14]

There is, however, one more important case, and the latest ruling upon the subject, which I must consider. This is the case of *Muttyjan* v. *Ahmed Ally*,[15] in which Morris, J., with the concurrence of O'Kinealy, J., went the length of laying down the broad rule, that when the creditor of a deceased Muhammadan sues the heir in possession, and obtains a decree against the assets of the deceased, such a suit is to be looked upon as an administration-suit, and those heirs of the deceased who have not been made parties cannot, in the absence of fraud, claim anything but what remains after the debts of the testator have been paid.

For this view of the law the learned Judges relied upon certain rulings, two of them being decisions of the Privy Council. I have consulted these cases, but I confess, with due respect, that I am unable to see how they support the broad rule of law laid down in that case. It seems to me that

13 ILR 2 Cal 395.
14 ILR 1 All 57.
15 ILR 8 Cal 370.

the nature of an administration-suit is essentially different from an ordinary suit for money brought by a creditor of a deceased person against his heir. I need only refer to s. 213 and to Nos. 105, 130, and 131 of the fourth schedule, read with s. 644 of the Civil Procedure Code, to explain my conception of the nature of an administration-suit. It appears to me that if every suit to recover a debt from the heir of a deceased debtor, irrespective of the form in which it has been instituted, is to be regarded as an administration-suit, any suit for money or any claim, however small, by tradesmen may be so considered, creating anomalies and difficulties upon which I need not, however, dwell. The rest of the rule laid down by Morris, J., is met by what I have already said, and seems to me to be contradicted by the rulings of Garth, CJ, in the two cases to which I have already referred. My answer to the second question referred to us is, therefore, entirely in the negative, and I give the answer, holding that it is unaffected by the question whether the decree is passed by consent or in a contentious suit, whether the heir is in possession of the whole or only a part of the estate of the deceased, or whether he is present or absent, in possession or out of possession. The same answer applies to the point referred in the connected case F.A. No. 50 of 1883.

The third question referred to us in this case does not depend upon any rule peculiar to the Muhammadan law; but upon the general principles of equity. The first point involved in the question is, whether in a case such as that contemplated, any equity exists in favour of the auction-purchaser, entitling him to retain the property till the plaintiff recoups him to the extent of his share of the ancestor's debts liquidated by the proceeds of the auction-sale. If so, then the second point is, whether effect can be given to that equity by a decree in this case. In my opinion both points must be answered in the affirmative.

The general principles of equity in such cases are to be found in ss. 696, 707, and 238a of Story's celebrated work *Equity Jurisprudence*, where illustrations are given of the general maxim, that he who seeks the aid of equity must do equity. For instance, as the learned author puts it: 'in many cases where the instrument is declared void by positive law, and also where it is held void or voidable upon other principles, courts of equity will impose terms upon the party, if the circumstances of the case require it.' Such seems to be the principle which underlies the judgment of a Division Bench of this court in *Mirza Pana Ali* v. *Saiad Sadik Hossein*,[16] in which, although the learned Judges held a deed of sale, whereby the mother of a Muhammadan minor had sold his share in the estate of his deceased father, to be invalid,

16 NWP HCR 1875, p. 201.

they dismissed his claim to recover possession of the share from the purchasers, who had redeemed a mortgage existing on the estate created by his father, because the plaintiff did not tender payment of his share of the mortgage debt. The learned Judges, however, do not appear, from the report of the case, to have considered the question whether in such a case a conditional decree could not be passed. The question, however, was decided by a Full Bench of this court in *Hamir Singh* v. *Musammat Zakia*,[17] in which it was held that in such a case a decree might be passed for possession in favour of the plaintiff, 'but it is only equitable to require that the recovery of her share should be contingent on the payment by her of her share of the debts, for the satisfaction of which the sale was effected.' The same rule was adopted by a Division Bench of this court in *Gulshere Khan* v. *Naubey Khan*.[18] In both these cases the sale was a private alienation, whilst in the present case the sale took place in execution of a decree to which the plaintiff was no party. But in my opinion this distinction does not alter the principle which enables courts of equity to exercise a vast and flexible jurisdiction for adapting their decrees to the requirements of each case. 'Some modifications of the rights of both parties may be required, some restraints on one side or on the other, or perhaps on both sides, some adjustments involving reciprocal obligations or duties; some compensatory or preliminary or concurrent proceedings to fix, contract, or equalize rights; some qualifications or conditions, present or future, temporary or permanent, to be annexed to the exercise of rights or the redress of injuries. In all these cases, courts of common law cannot grant the desired relief.... But Courts of Equity are not so restrained. They may adjust their decrees so as to meet most, if not all, of these exigencies, and they may vary, qualify, restrain, and model the remedy so as to suit it in mutual and adverse claims, controlling equities, and the real and substantial rights of all the parties' (Story's *Equity Jurisprudence*, ss. 27, 28). And, applying these principles to the present case, my answer to the third question is, that the plaintiff cannot obtain a decree for possession of his share of the property in suit without such decree being rendered contingent upon payment by him of such proportion of the purchase-money as would represent his proportionate share of the liability to the ancestor's debts liquidated by the proceeds of the auction-sale.

I wish to add that I have considered it my duty to consider this case at such length because of the conflict of decision existing in the Reports, which has thrown much doubt upon important rules of law governing the inher-

17 ILR 1 All 57.

18 *Weekly Notes*, 1881, p. 20.

itance of a population nearly as large as the whole of the German-speaking population of Europe.

38. Abdul Majeeth v. Krishnamachariar (1916) 40 Madras 243

Administration suit—private sale by one of several heirs of a deceased Muslim in possession of the estate—for discharging a debt binding on the estate—not binding on co-heirs or other creditors of the deceased

When one of the co-heirs of a deceased Muslim in possession of the whole or part of the estate of the deceased sells property in his possession forming part of the estate for discharging the debts of the deceased, such sale is not binding on the other co-heirs or creditors of the deceased.

Fathummabi v. *Vittil Ummachabi* (1903) ILR 26 Mad 734, overruled. *Hasan Ali* v. *Mehdi Husain* (1877) ILR 1 All 533, dissented from.

Quaere:—Whether a decree against one of the heirs of a deceased Muslim binds the others?

See *Outlines*, 376; *Tyabji*, § 571.

Judgment [Abdur Rahim][19]

The question referred to us is in these words: 'When one of the co-heirs of a deceased Muhammadan, in possession of the whole estate of the deceased or of any part of it, sells property in his possession forming part of the estate for discharging the debts of the deceased, is such sale binding on the other co-heirs or creditors of the deceased and, if so, to what extent?' The answer must be in the negative.

On the death of a Muhammadan, the inheritance vests in his heirs according to their respective shares, although in the administration of the estate the funeral expenses, debts and legacies must be paid first and it is only the residue that is available for distribution among the heirs. It is not correct to say that the devolution of the estate on the heirs does not take place or is postponed until the funeral expenses and the debts and legacies have been paid. This is evident from the following facts: if an heir designated by the law dies after the death of the propositus, his share descends on his own heirs and does not lapse to the general estate. Each heir is entitled to the income that has accrued since the testator's death, in proportion to his share, and he can transfer his share by sale or gift, subject, it may be, as to the latter form of disposition to such restrictions as are imposed by the doctrine of *musha'*.

19 With Spencer and Srinivasa Ayyangar, JJ.

The theory of Muhammadan jurisprudence, on which the right of succession and inheritance is based, is that even after death, the deceased's rights in his properties still inhere in him, to the extent necessary for meeting the funeral charges and the legal obligations and liabilities incurred in his life time and also for carrying out his wishes, as expressed in his last will and testament, within the limits laid down by the law. A deceased person is classed among persons of defective capacity and his rights and obligations are considered not merely with reference to matters pertaining to this world but also with respect to his spiritual concerns. The payment of his funeral expenses and debts is described as his last need. And as for testamentary bequests, it is stated that, according to strict juristic theory, they should not be lawful at all but have been sanctioned in order that the testator might make up for his shortcomings in life by making gifts to deserving objects.

It is argued that, as soon as a man is seized with 'death illness' (i.e., illness which results in his death), the right of succession of his relatives comes into existence, although it remains in an inchoate state, that is, in the nature of a *spes successionis* until death actually takes place, and the heirs entitled to succession are not ascertained until then. It is upon this theory that the right to bequeath by will is treated as a concession to the deceased and is limited to one-third of his possessions. The result is, on the death of a person his estate is to be divided in this way, one portion for the deceased himself equivalent to so much of the estate as is necessary and sufficient for meeting his funeral expenses, debts, obligations and bequests, the last not exceeding one-third of the estate, and what remains is to be distributed among the heirs according to their respective shares. Funeral expenses, debts and legacies are given preference because they are allowed by virtue of the rights of the deceased.

As far back as 1878, the Judicial Committee in *Bazayet Hossein* v. *Dooli Chund*,[20] held that an heir-at-law was entitled to alienate his share in spite of the fact that there were debts of the deceased still outstanding, and it would not have been possible to hold this if the inheritance did not devolve on the heir on the death of the propositus. Mr Justice Mahmood in *Jafri Begum* v. *Amir Muhammad Khan*[21] has fully discussed the question and I do not think it would be of any use to add anything more to his reasoning. As regards the nature of the tenure of the co-heirs' shares, the heirs of a deceased Muhammadan take their shares in severalty, their rights being analogous to those of tenants-in-common, and not of

20 (1879) ILR 4 Cal 402 (PC).
21 (1885) ILR 7 All 822 (FB).

members of a joint Hindu family: see *Abdul Khader* v. *Chidambaram Chettiyar*.[22]

There cannot be the slightest doubt therefore upon the principles of Muhammadan law and also upon the authorities that one heir has no right to deal with the shares of the other heirs. In the Muhammadan system such a tenure of property is called *shirkat* which literally means 'participation' and, in law, 'joint rights', and which is translated as 'partnership' by Mr Hamilton in his translation of the *Hedaya*.

[....]

This is absolutely clear authority in proof of the position that one heir has no authority, in law, to deal with the shares of his co-heirs. In the face of it it is not necessary to refer to other original text-books. It is stated, however, in *Pathummabi* v. *Vittil Ummachabi*[23] that, 'if the creditor of the deceased can seek his relief against one of several co-heirs in a case where all the effects of the deceased are in the hands of that heir, it can make no difference whether the heir meets the demand by a *bona fide* voluntary sale, or the property is brought to sale in execution of a decree obtained against him.' To the same effect is a decision of the Allahabad High Court in *Hasan Ali* v. *Mehdi Husain*.[24] The statement in *Pathummabi* v. *Vittil Ummachabi*[25] was purely by way of *obiter dictum* and, with all respect to the learned Judges, they failed to bear in mind, that the provision of the Muhammadan law that a decree against one heir in possession of all the effects of the deceased is binding on all if obtained after contest, is part of the processual law of that system and is not based on the ground that a single heir, if he happens to be in possession of the estate of the deceased, represents the rest of the heirs for the purposes of administration generally. The ground on which a decree against one of the heirs, in such circumstances, is treated as *res judicata* is, as stated in the books, that the decree in such cases is, in law, against the deceased and not against the particular heir who is made defendant in the suit.

In the *Hedaya* the matter is discussed in the chapter relating to the duties of the *kazi* and in some other text-books in the chapter dealing with claims, in which chapters the rules of procedure of the Muhammadan system are mostly laid down. In dealing with the question whether, when one of the heirs obtains a decree for the recovery of the property of the deceased in

22 (1909) ILR 32 Mad 276.
23 (1903) ILR 26 Mad 734.
24 (1877) ILR 1 All 533.
25 (1903) ILR 26 Mad 734.

possession of a third person, more than his share in that property should be made over to him in execution of the decree, it is stated that all the three doctors, that is, Abu Hanifa and his two disciples, agree that the decree enures not only in favour of the heir who actually is the plaintiff but also of the heir who did not join on account of absence from the country, though there is a difference of opinion as to whether the decree-holder shall be given possession of more than his share. This is how the principle is enunciated in the *Hedaya* (Grady, page 349):

'for any one of the heirs of a deceased person stands as litigant on the part of all the others with respect to anything due to or by the deceased, whether it be debt or substance; since the decree of the *kazi*, in such case, is in reality either in favour of or against a deceased; and any one of the heirs may stand as his representative with respect to such decree.'

The qualifying words 'with respect to such decree' which I have italicized are a material part of the proposition, and negative, by implication, the suggestion that, apart from a decree of court, a single heir represents the entire estate of the deceased and can deal with the shares of the co-heirs without their consent. In other textbooks of Muhammadan law, such as *Bahr-ur-Ra'iq* and *Al-Majallah* the same proposition is laid down under the heading of 'Claims'. Nowhere have I found any general statement that apart from representation in suits, one heir is entitled by his acts to bind the shares of the others. The dictum to the contrary, therefore, in *Pathummabi* v. *Vittil Ummachabi*[26] and the decision in *Hasan Ali* v. *Mehdi Husain*[27] seem to be without sufficient authority and inconsistent with clear statements of the law in books of authority.

There are a number of rulings, especially of the Calcutta High Court, in which the rule of Muhammadan law as to one heir representing the other co-heirs in suits, has been adopted. [....]

It is not necessary for us to pronounce any definite opinion upon this class of cases which deal with the question how far a decree against one of the heirs of a deceased Muhammadan binds the others and under what circumstances.

So far as voluntary alienations are concerned, which alone form the subject matter of reference, the Muhammadan law is clear that one of the heirs of a deceased person is not competent to bind the other heirs by his acts.

26 (1903) ILR 26 Mad 734.
27 (1877) ILR 1 All 533.

◊ UPDATE ◊

1. *Jafri Begum's case*

The judgment of Justice Syed Mahmood of the Allahabad High Court in *Jafri Begum* [Case 37], relating to administration of estates of deceased Muslims continues to be seen as a masterpiece of judicial exposition in all parts of the subcontinent.

In India the *Jafri Begum* ruling has been referred to and followed in some decisions of the Supreme Court—*Ebrahim* v. *Tek Chand* AIR 1953 SC 298; *Vecail* v. *Pathumma* AIR 1991 SC 720.

2. *Fyzee's quaere*

As regards the *quaere* put by Fyzee in his head-note to *Abdul Majeeth* [Case 38], it seems to have been answered under a decision handed down by the apex court in India soon after the publication of the original edition of this book.

In *Mohd Sulaiman* v. *NC Mohammad Ismail* (1966) SCR 937 the Supreme Court of India held that the ordinary rule that a decree against some of the heirs cannot bind those who were not made parties to the suit will not apply where the plaintiff had made a careful and bona fide enquiry as to who might be interested in the property. The court observed:

> A creditor of a Muslim dying intestate may sue all the heirs of the deceased, and where the estate has not been distributed between the heirs, he may execute the decree against the property as a whole without regard to the extent of the liability of the heirs *inter se*. The creditor is, however, not bound to sue all the heirs: the creditor may sue some only of the heirs and obtain a decree against those heirs, and liability for satisfaction of the decree may be enforced against individual heirs in the property held by them proportionate to their shares in the estate.

XVII. Inheritance

39. Rajah Deedar Hossein v. Ranee Zuhoor-oon Nissa (1841) 2 Moore's IA 441

While the majority of Muslims in India are Sunnite, Shiites will be governed by their own school of law.

Tyabji, § 6A; *Outlines*, 74 seqq.

Judgment [Baron Parke][1]

[....]

Their Lordships have now to pronounce their opinion upon an appeal from a final decree upon a review, of the Sudder Dewanny Adawlut of Bengal, pronounced on the 12th August 1822. The case was argued before us on three days. We have fully considered it, and are prepared to advise Her Majesty to affirm that decree.

The suit was instituted in January 1815 for the recovery of the moiety of the *Zemindary* of Pergunnah Soorjapore, to which the Appellant claimed to be entitled on the death of his brother Akbar, who died on 28th September 1813, leaving the Respondent his widow and three children. This *Zemindary* had formerly belonged to the Appellant's father, Fookur-ood-deen Hossein, who died in the possession of it in December 1793. After his death this Appellant and his brother, then minors, were in joint possession of the *Zemindary*, and so continued after their majority in 1799 or 1800 until the demise of Akbar.

The Respondent was put into possession by the collector after some proceedings instituted by the Appellant to prevent it; and the Appellant was put to commence his action, which he did in the Provincial Court of Moorshedabad in January 1814.

[....]

[1] With Brougham, Baron Parke, Bosanquet, Erskine & Lushington, JJ and Assessor Edward H. East.

Their Lordships feel no difficulty in concurring with the great majority of the judges in the opinion that the deeds of gift, under which the Respondent claims, are fabricated, and that the *Wusseeyut* and *Ikrar-namah* are open to so much suspicion, that the claim of the Appellant, so far as it is founded upon or confirmed by them, must fail. The absence of the original *Wusseeyut* from the place where it ought to have been if it had been a genuine instrument, its non-production, the conflicting accounts given of its contents, and the failure of the Appellant to bring it forward at an earlier period, and particularly in opposing registration of the Respondent's deed before the collector, when it would at all events have prevented that officer from letting the Respondent into possession—leave little doubt in the minds of their Lordships that the instrument was never executed by the deceased Rajah now that the evidence is insufficient to support it. If the *wusseeyut* was forged, the *ikrar-namah,* which recites it, must have been forged also. But without going so far, it is enough to say that the nature of the evidence in support of it, and the conduct of the Appellant in not producing this instrument before the collector, leave their Lordships in so much uncertainty as to its authenticity, that they consider that they ought not to attach any weight to it as supporting the Appellant's claim.

Two grounds therefore on which the Appellant has rested his claim having failed, it now becomes necessary to dispose of the third, that principally insisted upon in the argument before us, viz., the supposed family custom that the *Zemindary* had never been separated, but devolved entire on every succession, and that such custom was still in force....

Their Lordships, therefore, have arrived at the conclusion that on the death of Akbar his interest in the *Zemindary* devolved, according to the Mahommedan law of succession, to several heirs.

The only remaining question is, whether the law of succession is to be that which prevails amongst the Soonees or Sheeahs, the rule as to each sect being different, and both the litigant parties belonging to the latter. If the law of the *Sheeah* sect is to prevail, the Plaintiff has no title, as a brother cannot succeed.

By Regulation IV of 1793, sec. xv, it is provided that 'in suits regarding succession, inheritance, marriage and caste, and all religious usages and institutions, Mahommedan laws with respect to Mahommedans, and Hindoo laws with regard to Hindoos, are to be considered as the general rules by which judges are to form their decisions.' According to the true construction of this Regulation, in the absence of any judicial decisions or established practice limiting or controlling its meaning, the Mahommedan law of succession applicable to each sect ought to prevail as to litigants of that sect. It is not said that one uniform law should be adopted in all cases affecting

Mahommedans, but that the Mahommedan law, whatever it is, shall be adopted. If each sect has its own rule according to the Mahommedan law, that rule should be followed with respect to litigants of that sect. Such is the natural construction of this Regulation, and it accords with the just and equitable principle upon which it was founded, and gives effect to the usages of each religion, which it was evidently its object to preserve unchanged; we feel no doubt, therefore, that we ought to interpret the Regulation of 1793, to adopt the usage or law of each sect, unless there be a course of judicial decision or established practice to the contrary.

As to judicial decision there is none: and the only precedent bearing upon this question is in favour of the application of the *Sheeah* law. It is the case of *Wujih-on-Nissa Khanum* v. *Mirza Husun Ali*[2] in which it was proposed by the court as a question to the Mahommedan law-officers, what would be the distribution according to the law of either sect; and their direction implies that the *Soonee* law was not the established rule of decision in all cases in our courts of justice. As to the practice, we have availed ourselves of the means of consulting several gentlemen of great experience in the administration of justice in the Indian courts, and we cannot find that there is any course of practice with respect to all Mahommedan successions at variance with this construction. It is true that the Soonee law has generally prevailed, because the great majority of the Indian Mahommedans are *Soonees,* there being very few families of the Sheeah sect, except those of the reigning princes, which will account for the prevalence of the Soonee doctrines in the courts, but there is no practice which excludes the application of the *Sheeah* law to the rights of persons professing the tenets of that sect. The natural and equitable construction of the Regulations must therefore prevail.

For these reasons, the advice which their Lordships will give to Her Majesty is, that the judgment of the Sudder Dewanny Adawlut must be affirmed; and their Lordships do not think it right to make any alteration in that part of the decree which relates to costs.

[....]

40. Nawab Sultan Mariam Begum v. Nawab Saheb Mirza (1889) 16 IA 175

Construction—contract—issue and heirs—treaty between sovereign powers—perpetual pension—Islamic law displaced

By deed in 1838 the King of Oudh declared his intention to provide pensions

2 1 Mac, 266.

for various members of his family including Malka Jahan and her son, and to their heirs in perpetuity.

By treaty in 1842 between the King and the Government of India an additional pension was provided for Malka Jahan and her heirs:

Held that, the words 'issue' and 'heirs' having been used in the deed as convertible terms, the intention of the King must be construed to be that, on the death of any pensioner leaving issue, his heirs according to the Muhammadan law of inheritance should receive payment of the pension in the proportion regulated by that law.

Held, further, that by the treaty of 1842 the devolution of Malka Jahan's pension was not to be altered, and accordingly the rules of Muhammadan law must be observed.

A grant of pensions in perpetuity, though invalid by the ordinary Muhammadan law, takes effect under a treaty between sovereign powers.

This important case has not been dealt with sufficiently in any textbook to my knowledge. Wilson and Mulla omit it. Tyabji mentions it in the Index of Cases in the third edition (1940), but the printer has omitted the reference, and I have not been able to trace it.

The case has been discussed fully in my article 'The Impact of English Law on the Shariat in India', *Revue Egyptienne de Droit International*, xviii, 1962, I, 15–16.

It is an important principle, laid down in 1889 by the Privy Council, that a treaty between two sovereign powers displaces if necessary the personal law of the parties, notwithstanding the fact that the law is part and parcel of the religion of the particular community, *Outlines*, 386, note (*u*).

[. . . .][3]

41. Mitar Sen v. Maqbul Hasan
(1930) 57 IA 313

Caste Disabilities Removal Act (XXI of 1850), s. 1—scope of Act—descendants of Muslim converted from Hinduism—claim by Hindu collaterals

The Caste Disabilities Removal Act, 1850, s. 1, applies only to protect the actual person who either renounces his religion, or has been excluded from the communion of any religion, or has been deprived of caste.

3 Judgment by Barnes Peacock, J, with Watson and Richard Couch, JJ. Text of the judgment, not reproduced here, may be seen in *Cases*, 495–9.

Consequently, where the property of a Muslim converted from Hinduism has passed according to Muhammadan law to his descendants, Hindu collaterals cannot claim by virtue of the Act to succeed under Hindu law.

Bhagwant Singh v. *Kallu* (1888) ILR 11 All 100, overruled. *Vaithilinga* v. *Ayyathurci* (1917) ILR 40 Mad 1118, approved. Decree of the Chief Court, ILR 3 Luck 154 affirmed.

See *Tyabji*, 57 and Index; *Outlines,* 77 (iii) and (iv).

Appeal (No. 123 of 1928) from a decree of the Chief Court of Oudh (2 December 1927) affirming a decree of the Additional Subordinate Judge of Faizabad.

The question for determination in the appeal was whether by virtue of the Caste Disabilities Act 1850, a Hindu in the province of Oudh has a right to inherit according to Hindu law the estate of a Shiite Muslim who was descended from a Shiite Muslim, but had become a convert to Islam in 1843.

Judgment [Atkin, J.][4]

This is a case which involves a question of the inheritance of a property in Oudh, and it involves an important question as to the position of heirs of an ancestor who renounced his original religion of Hinduism and became a Mahommedan. The ancestor in question was a man named Jagardeo Singh who was, in 1843, at the date of his conversion to Mahommedanism a member of an undivided Hindu family tracing their descent, so far as is necessary to this case, from a common ancestor, Sangram Shah. Jagardeo Singh, as stated, was converted to Mahommedanism in 1843 and he died in 1844. He left two sons and two daughters, or at any rate he had two sons and two daughters, and one of the sons, who is the grandfather of the present defendants, was Agha Hasan Khan, who married and had a daughter, who married and whose children are the three defendants, 1, 2 and 3, in this case. On the death of the widow of Agha Hasan Khan the three children came into possession of the property which had belonged to Jagardeo Singh and had descended in that way to their grandfather. The property is claimed in this action by one Mitar Sen Singh, who is a descendant in the sixth generation of Babu Sangram Shah and would be the proper heir and would succeed to this property in accordance with Hindu law, on the footing that a custom prevailed in the family, as is alleged, which excludes females from inheritance. That custom has not gone to proof in this particular case. Its existence has been assumed for the purpose of the case, and their Lordships will so deal with the matter.

4 With Macmillan, John Wallis, George Lowndes and Binod Mitter, JJ.

The plaintiff founds his claim upon the Caste Disabilities Removal Act, Act XXI of 1850, which applied to Oudh at this time. It is important to bear in mind the words of the Act. It first of all recites s. 11 of Ben. Reg. VII of 1832. Then it says:

Whenever in any civil suit the parties to such suit may be of different persuasions, when one party shall be of the Hindu and the other of the Muhammadan persuasion, or where one or more of the parties to the suit shall not be either of the Muhammadan or the Hindu persuasions, the laws of those religions shall not be permitted to operate to deprive such party or parties of any property to which, but for the operation of such laws, they would have been entitled; and whereas it will be beneficial to extend the principle of that enactment throughout the territories subject to the government of the East India Company; it is enacted as follows.

The enacting part is contained in one clause, s. 1:

So much of any law or usage now in force within the territories subject to the government of the East India Company as inflicts on any person forfeiture of rights or property, or may be held in any way to impair or affect any right of inheritance, by reason of his or her renouncing, or having been excluded from the communion of any religion, or being deprived of caste, shall cease to be enforced as law in the courts of the East India Company, and in the courts established by Royal Charter within the said territories.

It has to be remembered that the law of succession in the case of a Hindu or a Mahommedan depends upon their own personal law: it depends upon the law of their religion, and there can be no question but that in this case, apart from the operation of this Act, inasmuch as the father of these children was in fact a Mahommedan, these children would be the proper heirs according to Mahommedan law and, even if there was a custom which excluded the daughters, nevertheless the Mahommedan law would in itself prevent a Hindu from succeeding as heir; and therefore, if the personal law of Agha Hasan Khan, the grandfather of these children, prevailed, then the plaintiff would have failed to establish his case. That is the only point which their Lordships have to determine, and therefore the plaintiff relies upon this Act and says that Jagardeo Singh renounced his religion but nevertheless the plaintiff was not to have his rights of inheritance impaired by reason of Jagardeo Singh having renounced the Hindu religion, and he claims therefore that, as he was a Hindu, he was entitled to establish his right of inheritance in accordance with the Hindu law.

There have been, no doubt, two conflicting lines of decisions on the construction of this Act. One has taken the wide view which is sought to be put upon this Act by the plaintiff in this case, and it cannot be better stated than in the judgment of Sir John Edge, then Chief Justice of Allahabad, in the case of *Bhagwant Singh* v. *Kallu*.[5] One passage only need be referred to in order to show how the broad construction relied upon by the plaintiff is expressed. Sir John Edge says:

The latter portion of the section, in my opinion, protects any person from having any right of inheritance affected by reason of any person having renounced his religion or having been excluded from caste.

The consequence of that would be that the plaintiff in this case would succeed in establishing his claim. It would have very far, reaching consequences if one tried to apply that principle to ordinary cases, because it would apparently mean that, if a Hindu becomes a Mahommedan, then the descendants of that Mahommedan throughout the ensuing generations, without any limit, would always derive their succession under the Hindu law of succession and not under the Mahommedan law of succession. It is unnecessary for their Lordships to discuss the far reaching effects of that decision. On the other hand, there has been another line of decisions which is exemplified by the case of *Vaithilinga* v. *Ayyathorai*[6] which takes the narrower view, the view which, in their Lordships' opinion is the correct view—namely, that this section in terms only applies to protect the actual person who either renounces his religion or has been excluded from the communion of any religion or has been deprived of caste. It is intended to protect such a person from losing any right of property or of succeeding as heir. It appears to their Lordships that when the Act is looked at that is the only reasonable construction that can be put upon it. The first limb of this section says 'So much of any law…as inflicts on any person forfeiture of rights or property', and Sir John Edge himself took the view that that part of the clause only applied to the person who renounced; the second limb proceeds 'or may be held in any way to impair or affect any right of inheritance by reason of his or her renouncing'. Now it is perfectly true that the words 'his or her' are not so easy to apply, because there is not a person expressed in the Act who is represented by 'his or her', but it seems to their Lordships to be plain that the words 'or may be held in any way to impair or affect any right of inheritance by reason of his or her renouncing' should be read 'any right of inheritance of any person reason of his or her renouncing'. The clause is given a simple meaning by this construction and their Lordships think that that is the correct view. In other words, when once a person has changed his religion and changed his personal law, that law

5 (1888) ILR 11 All 100, 104.
6 (1917) ILR 40 Mad 1118.

will govern the rights of succession of his children. It may, of course, work hardly to some extent upon expectant heirs, especially if the expectant heirs are the children and perhaps the unconverted children of the ancestor who does in fact change his religion, but, after all, it inflicts no more hardship in their case than in any other case where the ancestor has changed the law of succession, as, for instance, by acquiring a different domicil, and their Lordships do not find it necessary to consider any questions of hardship that may arise. They will certainly, in their Lordships' view, be outweighed by the immense difficulties that would follow if the wider view were to prevail. Their Lordships are definitely of opinion that the construction which was adopted by Sir John Edge was not the right construction and that case and any cases that followed it must be overruled so far as the construction of this Act is concerned.

Their Lordships, therefore, think that the opinion of the Chief Court and the judgment of the Chief Judge were perfectly correct. The reasoning appears to their Lordships to be well founded and they have come to the conclusion that this appeal must be dismissed with costs, and they will humbly advise His Majesty accordingly.

◊ UPDATE ◊

1. *School-wise application of Muslim law*

The old Privy Council ruling in *Rajeh Deedar Hossein* [Case 39] was not important in respect of the substantive law of inheritance. Its significance lay in the ruling that each 'sect' of the Muslims was to be governed by its own school of Islamic law in matters of personal law. This legal position remains in force in all parts of the subcontinent in respect of the un-codified law and ordinarily the courts apply to a case the Muslim law of the school to which the parties may belong.

The major Muslim-law statutes of the subcontinent, however, uniformly apply to all Muslims without regard to their different schools of law. See, eg, the Dissolution of Muslim Marriages Act 1939 (India-Pakistan-Bangladesh), the Muslim Family Laws Ordinance 1961 (Pakistan-Bangladesh) and the Muslim Women (Protection of Rights on Divorce) Act 1986 (India).

2. *Application of special laws*

As regards the old Privy Council judgment in *Nawab Sultan* v. *Saheb Mirza* [Case 40] on displacement of the Islamic law of inheritance by the ruler of a princely state, some of the old laws relating to the erstwhile princely states remain in force in India, including the Oudh Estates Act 1869.

In *Mohammad Ismail* v. *Sabir* AIR 1962 SC 1722 the Supreme Court of India allowed the provisions of the Oudh Estates Act 1869 to override those of the Mussalman Wakf Validating Act 1913.

The local tenancy laws in many Indian States have their own provisions relating to succession to agricultural lands, which apply also to the Muslims. In *Jamil Ahmad* v. *5th ADJ Moradabad* (2001) 8 SCC 599 the Supreme Court affirmed the application of such provisions in the tenancy laws of Uttar Pradesh to the local Muslims.

3. *Effect of conversion*

The Caste Disabilities Removal Act 1850, on which was based the Privy Council ruling in *Mittar Sen* [Case 41], has been indirectly amended in India by the Hindu Succession Act 1956 to make it partly inapplicable to those governed by that Act [Section 26].

In Pakistan and Bangladesh, the Caste Disabilities Removal Act 1850 is now inapplicable to the Muslims-as provided in the Caste Disabilities (Amendment) Act 1963.

4. *Orphaned grandchildren*

Section 4 of the Pakistan Muslim Family Laws Ordinance 1961, now in force in Pakistan and Bangladesh, had amended the law of inheritance so as provide shares in the estates of deceased persons to their predeceased children.

Section 4 of the Muslim Family Laws Ordinance was challenged in Pakistan before the Federal Shariat Court in *Federation of Pakistan* v. *Farishta* PLD 1981 SC 120. Since under the Constitution 'Muslim personal law' was kept out of the purview of the Shariat Court's power to test the conformity of the law to the Qur'an and *Sunnah*, the court refused the relief sought-holding that the term covered also statutory amendments of Muslim personal law.

5. *Inheritance cases*

It has been held in an Indian case that the widow of a deceased Muslim if related to him also by consanguinity may inherit from him in both the capacities—*Damodar* v. *Shahjadibi* AIR 1970 Cal 387.

A recent decision of the Indian Supreme Court shows how the property of a deceased Muslim woman leaving behind as her only heirs a sister and two daughters is to be distributed—*Newannes* v. *Shaikh Mohamad* AIR 1996 SC 702.

XVIII. Customary Law

42 Advocate General v. Muhammad Husen Huseni

(1866) 12 Bom HC Reports 323 [known as the *Aga Khan case*]

Khojas—whether Sunnites or Shiites (Ismā'īlī)—rights of dissident minorities—Sunnites—Shia Imami Ismailis—the Aga Khan—Khoja community of Bombay—History of the earliest divisions in Islam—Tragedy of Karbala—difference between Shiites and Sunnites—Ismailis, 'Ubaydullāh, founder of the Fatimid dynasty in Egypt—tenets of the Ismaili Khojas—Ḥasan b. Ṣabbāḥ—Mongol Invasion—Āghā Khān—Khojas—Split in the community—The Dasavatār—Khojas are Isma'ili. Shiites—definition—excommunication

The most important point decided in this case was that the followers of the Aga Khan are not Sunnites; and later, in 1909, it was held that the Isma'ilis are distinct from the Shiites of the Ithnā 'Ashari school, *Haji Bibi* v. *H. H. Sir Sultan Mahomed Shah* (1908) 11 *Bombay Law Reporter* 407.

The Aga Khan case lays down several propositions which are strictly not germane to our purpose, but which are sufficiently dealt with by *Tyabji* in § 481, especially pp. 596 seqq. For a modem discussion see *Outlines,* 66 seqq. and *Nur Ali* v. *Malka Sultana,* PLD 1961 (WP) Lahore 431.

Generally, see *'Ismā'īlīya'*, *Shorter Encyclopaedia of Islām,* (Brill, Leiden, 1953), 179.

Judgment [Arnould, J.][1]

[. . . .]

The 5th clause of the prayer is the most important. It in effect raises that question with which the evidence in this suit has been principally concerned, as to what in their origin were the religious tenets of the Khoja community, and what from the beginning has been the nature of their relations, spiritual

1 Full text of the elaborate judgment, of which only some extracts are being given here, may be seen in *Cases*, 1st ed., 1965, pp. 504–49.

or temporal, with the ancestors of the first defendant, Aga Khan, who on his part alleges that he is, and that his ancestors in a long line of hereditary descent have successively been, the *Imams* or spiritual chiefs of the Shia Imami Ismailis.

On the one hand the relators and plaintiffs contend that Pīr Sadrdin (whom both sides admit to have originally converted the Khojas from Hinduism to some form of Muhammadanism) was a Sunni; that the Khoja community has ever since its first conversion been and now is Sunni; and that no persons calling themselves Khojas who are not Sunnis, are entitled to be considered members of the Khoja community, or to have any share or interest in the public property of the Khoja community or any voice in the management thereof.

On the other side it is maintained by the first defendant, and by the other defendants, who are in the same interest with him, that Pīr Sadrdin was not a Sunni, but a Shia of the Imami Ismaili persuasion; that he was a *Dai*, or missionary, of one of the direct lineal ancestors of the first defendant—the Imam or spiritual chief for the time then being of the Imami Ismailis; that from the time of the first conversion till now the Khoja community has been and still is (with the exception of the relators and plaintiffs and those comparatively few families among the Bombay Khojas who adhere to them) of the Shia Imami Ismaili persuasion; that the said community (except as aforesaid) always has been bound in close ties of spiritual allegiance to the ancestors of the first defendant, Aga Khan, the hereditary chiefs or Imams of the Ismailis whom the Khoja community always have regarded and (except as above) still regard as their *Murshids* or spiritual heads.

It is to the issue thus raised that the great mass of the voluminous evidence taken in this suit was directed. It was expressly admitted by Mr Anstey, the very learned and able leading counsel for the relators and plaintiffs, that the determination of this issue would, in effect, dispose of the whole of the present suit.

'If the Khojas', he said, 'are proved in their origin to have been Sunnis, the relators and plaintiffs must succeed: if they are proved to have been originally Shias or Shia Imami Ismailis, or in any way non-Sunnis, then the defendants must succeed.' [....]

As to the great question in the present suit, that upon the determination of which, as already intimated, the decision of the controversy between these litigants, in my judgment, really turns—the question, namely, whether the Khojas are, and from the first have been Sunnis or non-Sunnis, subordinate to the Imam of the Ismailis as their spiritual head or not so subordinate—this does not appear to have been a question upon which Sir Erskine

Perry was called upon to pronounce; it is one, certainly, upon which he has not pronounced any adjudication whatever.

Sir Erskine Perry declared, upon the evidence before him, that certain property and certain privileges belonged to the Khoja community, but he did not decide, nor is there anything to show he ever was called upon to decide, what are the conditions of full membership in the Khoja community—whether the circumstance of being a non-Sunni (as the relators and plaintiffs contend), or of being a Sunni and as such disowning spiritual allegiance to the hereditary Imam of the Ismailis (as the first defendant and those who join with him contend), is to exclude from caste membership in the Khoja community, and to disentitle a man from sharing or having an interest in the public property of the community, or a voice in the management thereof.

The principal question, then, in the present suit, viz., aye or no, were the Khojas, in their origin as a separate religious community Sunnis or non-Sunnis—Sunni or Shia Imami Ismaili—bound or not bound by ties of spiritual allegiances to the Imams of the Imami Ismailis—this question is quite untouched by any previous judicial decision.

It is a historical question, to be decided by evidence as to matter of fact, and is quite as much within the competency of the equity side of the late Supreme Court, in the exercise of what is technically called its charitable jurisdiction, as any other question of fact arising out of the caste disputes of the Khoja community.

The cases in which similar questions have been entertained by English Courts of Equity are well known, and were copiously referred to at the bar. They are that class of cases of which the case of Lady Hewley's Charities, reported as *Shore* v. *Wilson*,[2] is probably the most familiar, and which all proceed upon and illustrate the now well-established principle that, when Courts of Equity, in the exercise of their so-termed charitable jurisdiction, are called upon to adjudicate between the conflicting claims of dissident parties in communities held together or distinguished by some religious profession or denomination, the rights of the litigants will be regulated by reference to what upon inquiry turn out to have been the religious tenets and opinions held by the community in its origin or at its foundation.

A minority, however numerically small, holding fast by these opinions, will be entitled to prevail against a majority, however numerically large, which can be shown to have receded from or renounced them.

The Khoja community is a community of this kind. The fact of a man being a Khoja indicates that he holds by some form or other of religious belief. What that form of religious belief was at the origin of the Khojas

2 9 Cl. and Fin. 855.

as a separate and distinct community is, therefore, a question of fact which, if disputed, must be determined by evidence in a Court of Equity, when asked, in the exercise of what is called its charitable jurisdiction, to decide on the relative rights of the dissident bodies within the same sect.

[....]

The clear conclusion at which I have arrived upon a full consideration of the evidence before me is this—that the Khojas never were Sunnis but that from the beginning they have been and (with the exception of the relators and plaintiffs and their followers in Bombay) still are Shias of the Imami Ismaili persuasion.

And this in effect disposes of the whole case against the relators and plaintiffs. Fully conceding to Mr Scoble the authority of the cases and dicta he cited on this point, it appears to me that they are not applicable to the present case. This is not a case in which the plaintiff has mistaken his remedy, but one in which he has failed in his proof. The relators and plaintiffs in this case are quite right in the standpoint they have assumed, viz., that the Khoja sect is a community held together and distinguished by certain religious opinions. Where they have failed, is in proving that these religious opinions are those of the Sunni Mahommedans. The court is now in a position to give an adequate description of the Khoja sect; it is a sect of people whose ancestors were Hindus in origin, which was converted to and has throughout abided in the faith of the Shia Imami Ismailis, and which has always been and still is bound by ties of spiritual allegiance to the hereditary Imams of the Ismailis.

In order to enjoy the full privileges of membership in the Khoja community, all the terms of the above description must be complied with; a person more especially who is not a Shia of the Imami Ismaili persuasion is, to use with a reversed application the language of the 5th paragraph of the prayer, 'not entitled unto, nor ought he to have any share or interest in' the public property of the Khoja community 'or any voice in the management thereof'.

[....]

◊ UPDATE ◊

1. *Status of Khoja Muslims*

The old Privy Council judgment in the *Aga Khan* case of 1866 [Case 42] contains a detailed account of the history and religious beliefs of the Shias in general and of the Isma'ili sect. It has now no more than a historical importance, and has hence been pruned in this edition. It is now well established in law that the Khojas are neither Sunni nor Ithna Ashari Shia and belong to the *Nizari* division of the *Isma'ili* sect of Islam.

As regards application of Muslim law, the Khojas are now to be governed by Muslim law as much as any other sect or group of Muslims. Old case law cannot supersede clear provisions of the Muslim Personal Law (Shariat) Application Act 1937 (in force in India and Bangladesh) and the Muslim Personal Law (Shariat) Application Act 1962 (in force in Pakistan).

A recent decision of the Indian Supreme Court relating to the Khojas is *Noorbanu* v. *D C G, Evacuee Property* AIR 1965 SC 1953.

2. *Khoja code of conduct*

A *Dastur-ul-Amal* (Code of Conduct), approved by the Agha Khan in 1967, has the force of law for the community and contains a number of personal law provisions. In some respects it was amended in 1996.[3]

[3] Extracts from the Khoja Code of 1967 may be seen in my book *Statute Law relating to Muslims in India*, Razi Publication, Delhi, 1995, pp. 209–13. See also my article 'Recent Religious Reform of Khoja Isma'ili Personal Law: An Appraisal', *Islamic and Comparative Law Quarterly, XII:* 1992, pp. 55–75.

XIX. Wills

43. Mirza Kurratulain v. Nawab Nuzhat-ud-Dowla (1905) 32 IA 244

Civil Procedure Code, s. 13—*effect of order of probate of Muslim will—Testamentary powers of Muslim—res judicata—estoppel—Act V of* 1881

In a suit by the heirs of a Muslim testatrix against the Administrator-General and the respondent for an account against the latter of her estate as having been obtained by him by undue influence and while he was in a fiduciary relation to her, it appeared that the will had been established and probate issued on the application of the Administrator-General acting under an indemnity from the respondent, opposed by the heirs as caveators, and that the will contained a confirmation of transactions between the respondent and the testatrix, and in particular of a release to him alleged to have been executed by her.

Held, that the appellants were not estopped by the probate or the proceedings which led to it from denying the validity of this confirmation and release. It was admitted that apart from the will those transactions and release could not be supported and, the probate proceedings not having been put in evidence, there was no sufficient evidence of the issues relating thereto and raised in this case having been directly and substantially in issue in those proceedings within the meaning of s. 13 of the Civil Procedure Code.

Held, further, that the provisions of the Probate and Administration Act (V of 1881) did not create an estoppel. In the case of a Muslim, whose testamentary power only extended to one-third of the estate, the two-thirds claimed adversely to the will by the heirs could not be affected by the terms of the will or by the effect of probate.

This case is fully discussed by *Tyabji*, 732, 734, 737, 739, 74[illegible].

Appeal from a decree of the High Court in Bengal (6 August 1903) reversing a decree of the Subordinate Judge of the 24 Pergunnahs ([illegible] March 1901) and dismissing the suit with costs.

Judgment [Arthur Wilson][1]

This is an appeal from a judgment and decree of the High Court in Calcutta dated 6 August 1908, which reversed the previous judgment and decree of the Subordinate Judge of the 24 Pergunnahs dated 4 March 1901.

The controversy between the parties relates to the estate of a Mahommedan lady known as Khas Mahal, who was the principal widow of the late ex-King of Oudh, and who died on 1 April 1894. About the facts which have to be considered there is no longer any controversy. The respondent, shortly known as Peara Saheb, was a distant relation of the ex-Queen. About the year 1881 he entered her service, in which he continued to the date of her death. He acquired her confidence in the highest degree, and became the head of her household and the manager of all her affairs. While occupying that position he received from her by way of gifts a large amount of property, in fact, substantially the whole of the property possessed by her which yielded any income.

On 12 November 1891, the lady executed a deed of release in the following terms:

> I, of my free will and accord and without inducement and temptation exercised by anybody, do declare that Nawab Peara Saheb, who is a near relation of mine, has pleased me with his good behaviour and services; and (his services) have afforded me much relief. The gift of things which I have from time to time made to him from the time of his connexion with the management of my affairs down to the present time have been made out of my natural affection for him and in recognition of his good and loyal services; and the cash and the things which I have given him have not been kept with him by way of deposit or trust or given as loan, and I and my heirs and representatives neither at present have, nor in future shall have, any right to get the same back or make demand for them. I further declare that the account of the cash and things and kind that up to the time of execution of this deed have been made over to him, for my own personal use, is not to be rendered or made up by him, and that I have kept with myself alone accounts and *tahbil*[2] of all kinds, and that I look after my *jumma kharach* (income and expenses) personally, and keep the account thereof with myself. The items which he has applied to his own uses, or which are with him, are those very items which I have out of my affection for him and in recognition of his services given him and allowed him to make use of after due deliberation. If I or after me my heirs and representatives prefer claim or demand against him in respect of the gifts and accounts, and *tahbil* and things and cash given, then it shall be considered null and void according to *Shara* (Mahommedan law) common usage and law. These words have therefore been written in the shape of

[1] With Davey and Robertson, JJ.

[2] Probably *tehsil* (custody, bailment).

a deed of release and acquittance and *safinama*, and after the completion of the necessary formalities delivered to him, so that it may serve him the purposes of an authority.

On 30 June 1893, the lady made her will, by which she appointed the Administrator-General of Bengal to be her executor if he should be willing to act, and if that officer should decline to act she appointed Peara Saheb.

I have from time to time made gifts of money and cash to the said Nawab Peara Saheb, and on the 12th day of November, 1891, I executed a safinama in his favour which has been duly registered. I have also by a deed of trust, dated the 1?th day of February, 1893, duly registered, dedicated certain property therein described for religious and charitable purposes. I confirm these transactions.

The respondent's influence over the lady continued unabated down to her death, and there is no evidence that at any time during the course of her dealings with him she had the advantage of any separate and independent advice. From the evidence in this case he appears to have taken a prominent part in arranging the provisions of the will, and to have given instructions to the attorney who drafted it.

When the lady died she left surviving her as her sole heirs (according to the Shiah law by which the family was governed) two grandchildren. Their title as heirs was denied by the lady herself in her will, and after her death was persistently contested by those who were interested in denying that title. Their right of inheritance has, however, been finally established.

Soon after the death of the testator the Administrator-General, having been put in motion by Peara Saheb and acting under an indemnity from him, applied in the High Court for probate of the will. The grandchildren as heirs entered a caveat. Their right to appear as caveators was disputed, but was ultimately established.

The proceedings with reference to the probate then went forward, and on 2 July 1900, the learned judge who heard the case pronounced in favour of the will. The probate accordingly issued, dated 30 August 1900. It further appears that there was an appeal against that decision, and that the appeal was dismissed.

While the probate proceedings were pending, the present suit was instituted on 26 March 1897, in the Court of the Subordinate Judge of the 24 Pergunnahs. The plaintiffs were the two grandchildren of the testatrix and another person to whom they had assigned a portion of their interest. The first plaintiff is now represented by the first group of appellants, and the other plaintiffs are appellants. The defendants to the suit were Peara Saheb (respondent in this appeal) and the Administrator-General. The plaint stated the confidential relations which had existed between Peara Saheb and the lady, and alleged that Peara Saheb had misused his position of confidence, and thereby become possessed of the bulk of her property; and the material part of the prayer was to the effect that Peara Saheb should be compelled to account for the property which had thus come into his hands, and should be declared to be a trustee for the plaintiffs. The written statement of Peara Saheb denied the case alleged in the plaint. Issues were settled of which it is only necessary to notice, for the present purpose, the 7th, 8th, and 9th:

7. Is the deed of release relied upon by defendant No. 1 genuine? Was the said defendant the confidential agent of, or in a fiduciary relation to, the late Khas Mahal as alleged in the plaint? Is the release bad on the ground of undue influence? Is it a fact that any of the properties in suit were obtained by undue influence or while defendant was in a fiduciary relation from Khas Mahal? Does the release bar the present plaintiffs?

8. Is defendant liable to render an account? If so, to what extent and in respect of what properties?

9. What properties, if any, belonging to deceased Khas Mahal were removed or received by defendant No. 1 or otherwise came into his possession either with or without her consent, and is he liable to render an account in respect of the same or of any and, if so, for what portion thereof, and to restore any, if so, for what portion thereof?

The Subordinate Judge delivered his judgment on 4 March 1901. He held that Peara Saheb had occupied a position of confidence, and had obtained the property in question by the exercise of undue influence, and that the alleged release was not genuine and not binding.

Before the time at which this judgment of the Subordinate Judge was delivered, the decision of the High Court establishing the will had been passed. It was necessary for him, therefore, to consider the effect of that decision upon the case before him. His view was that 'the judgment of the High Court in the probate case conclusively proves that the Administrator-General is the executor under the will of Khas Mahal. It does not conclusively prove that all statements in the will are true.' And he held that the statements relating to the transactions with Peara Saheb and the release to him were not true. In the result he made a decree in favour of the plaintiffs.

On appeal to the High Court, that court on 6 August 1903, held that the probate proceedings were conclusive of the questions arising in the present case. The learned judges said:

The will was strongly contested by the present plaintiffs Nos 1 and 2 when probate was applied for by the Administrator-General of Bengal, and the probate proceedings were pending during the trial of the present case in the court below, judgment being delivered on the 2nd of July, 1900, and probate issuing on the 30th of August in the same year. The decree now appealed against is dated the 4th of March 1901. The Administrator-General of Bengal applied for probate on the 14th of May 1894, and a caveat was entered by the plaintiffs Nos 1 and 2 shortly afterwards. In the probate suit substantially the same issues were raised as in the present case. The caveators set up that Khas Mahal was physically and mentally incapable of giving instructions for the will or of understanding the will, that she was unable to understand the nature of the dispositions contained in the will by reason of her feebleness of body and mind, and that the will was prepared and executed under the undue influence of the defendant Peara.

Sale J. sitting on the Original Side of the High Court held, however, that the caveators had absolutely failed to make out their case. He was satisfied that the lady did give instructions for her will, that she thoroughly understood its contents and executed it as a free agent, and not under the influence or ascendancy of Peara, and with full testamentary capacity, and probate was accordingly granted. The present plaintiffs Nos 1 and 2 appealed against that decision, but the appeal was dismissed with costs, There was no further appeal from that decision.

We must take it, then, for the purpose of the present discussion, that the lady thoroughly understood the purpose and effect of her will and that it was her voluntary act, and that she was of full testamentary capacity to make the will, and in that will she expressly confirms this release.

They therefore reversed the decision of the first court, and dismissed the suit with costs. Against that decision of the High Court the present appeal has been brought.

In the course of the argument before their Lordships the questions for decision became greatly simplified. It was admitted on behalf of the respondent that, apart from the will, the release and the other transactions between Peara Saheb and the lady could not have been supported. It was not disputed—indeed it could hardly have been disputed—that, upon the evidence in the present case and apart from the alleged effect of the probate and the proceedings which led up to it, the respondent could not have relied upon the confirmation of the earlier transactions contained in the will. The appeal was resisted solely upon the legal ground that the appellants are estopped by the probate, or by the proceedings which led to the issue of the probate, from denying the validity of the confirmation which the will purports to contain of the transactions between Peara Saheb and the testatrix during her lifetime, and particularly of the release alleged to have been executed by her. The correctness of that contention is what their Lordships have to consider.

[. . . .]

But their Lordships think that the contention of the respondent under s. 13 fails upon another and a simpler ground. The respondent is relying upon a bare legal difficulty to resist a case to which there is no substantial answer on the merits. He says that the questions now in issue were formerly in issue in the probate proceedings. How can their Lordships tell that? Those proceedings are not in evidence, as they ought to have been in order to support such a case. There is a petition for probate and the probate itself. There is mention of a caveat and of an affidavit in support of it. There are two judgments delivered at different stages, and there is mention of a decision on appeal. One of the judgments of the learned judge shows clearly enough what he understood to be the questions for decision, but that is not enough. Their Lordships cannot give effect to the estoppel contended for unless they can say for themselves that the matters now in issue were in issue in the probate proceedings. Whether any issues were settled in those proceedings or the points in dispute were otherwise formulated does not appear, nor do the terms of any decrees or orders made therein. Their Lordships, therefore, think that the alleged estoppel under s. 13 fails, because in the absence of the probate proceedings there is no sufficient evidence to support it.

The second ground of estoppel rests, not upon the probate proceedings or any issues raised and decided in the course of them, but upon the effect of the probate itself. This gives rise to a question of some general importance, and for the purpose of determining it, it seems to make no difference whether probate has been obtained in common form and ex parte or after opposition.

The question thus arising seems to depend upon the terms of the Probate and Administration Act (V of 1881). Sec. 4 of that Act says that 'the executor or administrator, as the case may be, of a deceased person is his legal representative for all purposes, and all the property of the deceased person vests in him as such.'

Sec. 88 gives to the executor or administrator power to sue in respect of causes of action that survive the deceased and to recover debts; s. 90 gives an executor or administrator large, but not unlimited, powers of disposition; s. 12 says that probate when granted establishes the will from the death of the testator; and s. 59 says that—

> Probate or letters of administration shall have effect over all the property, movable or immovable, of the deceased... and shall be conclusive as to the representative title against all debtors of the deceased, and all persons holding property which belongs to him, and shall afford full indemnity to all debtors paying their debts, and all persons delivering up such property to the person to whom such probate or letters of administration shall have been granted.

The title thus conferred upon every executor who has obtained probate is obviously convenient, as tending to facilitate the administration of the estate of the deceased and the adjustment of the rights of all parties connected with it. But in the case of every Mahommedan will it establishes a somewhat peculiar state of things.

A Mahommedan testator has not an unlimited power of disposition by will: he can only deal with one-third of his property; the remaining two-thirds pass to his heirs whatever the terms of the will may be. Thus the executor, when he has realized the estate, is a bare trustee for the heirs as to two-thirds, and an active trustee as to one-third for the purposes of the will; and of these trusts one is created by the Act and the probate irrespective of the will, the other by the will established by the probate. There are thus two trusts for different sets of persons of different properties and based upon different titles. And this state of things does not arise from any accidental conflict of laws such as gave rise to a somewhat similar complication in the case of *Concha* v. *Concha*,[3] but by the deliberate action of the Legislature. In giving effect to a system of so peculiar a nature as that described, their Lordships think it necessary to proceed with great caution.

The Act in question applies only to persons to whom the Indian Succession Act (X of 1865) did not extend—that is to say, Hindus, Mahommedans, and Buddhists. And, though the sections relating to probate in the Probate and Administration Act are substantially taken from the corresponding sections in the Succession Act, it must be observed that the last-mentioned Act, while to a large extent embodying the rules of the English law, yet departed in many particulars from those rules, and was not only made applicable to persons of European descent, or those to whom the system derived from the ecclesiastical courts might naturally be applied, but was made the law for all persons in British India other than Hindus, Mahommedans, and Buddhists, including, for instance, the Parsees, who form so important a part of the community in some districts of India.

Testamentary jurisdiction was first given to the Supreme Courts by their original charters—that in Bengal dated in 1774 being the first. And it was then given as a branch of ecclesiastical jurisdiction, and was to be administered according to the ecclesiastical law as in force in the Diocese of London. In the course of the series of events by which the British territories in India grew from a group of trading settlements into an empire, various branches of jurisdiction, which sprang originally from an ecclesiastical origin, have come to be applied by a number of legislative acts to new territories and new classes of persons, and administered by new tribunals. And in the progress of this development the ecclesiastical origin of such jurisdiction has been completely discarded, and the Legislature has gradually evolved an independent system of its own, largely suggested, no

[3] 11 AC 541.

doubt, by English law, but also differing much from that law, and purporting to be a self-contained system. Even in the case of the High Courts, the successors of the Supreme Courts (which alone possessed ecclesiastical jurisdiction), the testamentary jurisdiction which the charters purport to confer upon them is not given as a branch of ecclesiastical jurisdiction, and is not made dependent upon the law administered by English courts.

From an early date the Supreme Courts granted probates of Hindu and Mahommedan wills. The practice varied greatly from time to time, and it was never perhaps very satisfactorily determined upon what basis the jurisdiction rested. It was, however, established that such probates might issue. But the Supreme Courts never applied the English rule as to the necessity for probate to Hindu or Mahommedan wills, nor did they attribute to such probates when granted the English doctrines as to the operation of probate. Under that system a Hindu or Mahommedan executor took no title to property merely as such by virtue of the probate. In the case of Mahommedan executors such a title was created for the first time by the Probate and Administration Act.

These considerations seem to their Lordships strong enough to show that the effect of probate of a Mahomedan will granted after the Probate and Administration Act must be that which is given by the terms of the Act itself, neither more nor less. What, then, is the effect of the Act? Sec. 4, supplemented by Sec. 88, vests the whole property of the testator in the executor. Sec. 59 makes the probate conclusive as to his representative title against debtors of the deceased and persons holding property of his, and gives a complete indemnity to those who pay debts or deliver up property to the executor holding the probate. Those enactments appear to their Lordships incapable of being applied so as to give to the probate in the present case the effect contended for. The appellants do not in this action contest the title of the executor, though they show that, as to two-thirds of the estate, he is a mere trustee for them. They are not debtors of the estate, nor possessed of property belonging to it. They are not interested under the will, nor do they (necessarily) contest the validity of the will as a beneficial disposition to the legatees, and other persons claiming under it, of that part of the property of the testatrix which she could dispose of by will. But they say that they are entitled to two third parts of all the property of the testatrix which was not effectually disposed of by her in her lifetime. It is now admitted that the release was ineffectual for that purpose, and, if so, the money and other property in the hands of Peara Saheb was in the disposition of the testatrix at the time of her death. As she could not dispose of more than one third part of it by her will, the confirmation of the release could not confirm Peara Saheb's title in more than that one-third, and the appellants are entitled to the other two-thirds. The controversy is between the heirs claiming adversely to the will and a person who claims a beneficial interest under the will, and the provisions of the Act which have been cited seem to their Lordships to create no estoppel in such a case. They are, therefore, unable to concur with the learned judges of the High Court in thinking that the suit ought to be dismissed.

It remains to consider what the decree ought to be.... In the course of the argument before their Lordships the learned counsel for the appellants admitted that his clients were interested in the estate to the extent of two-thirds only, and intimated that they would be content with a decree upon this footing.

Their Lordships are satisfied that no injustice can have been done by the Subordinate Judge by reason of the principle upon which he proceeded in framing his decree, but they think, for the reason just stated, that the present appellants can claim only two-thirds of the amount awarded by the first court.

[....]

◊ UPDATE ◊

1. *Need for probate*

The Probate and Administration Act 1881, on which was based *Mirza Kurratulain's* case of 1905 [Case 43], was later incorporated into the Indian Succession Act 1925.

Under the Indian Succession Act 1925, the provisions of which only selectively apply to the Muslims, a probate is not necessary for the will of a Muslim. See Sections 211(1), 212(2), 213(2) and 217 to 218 of the Act. The dictum of *Kurratulain's* case is, therefore, relevant only for a case where a probate has been voluntarily obtained for the will of a Muslim.

2. *Bequeathable third*

The rule of Muslim law under which no Muslim can bequeath more than a third of his heritable property remains in force in all parts of the subcontinent.

In India this rule of Muslim law does not apply to a Muslim governed by the Special Marriage Act 1954, which ousts the application of the Muslim law of inheritance and replaces it with the parallel provisions of the Indian Succession Act 1925. Even in such a case the requirement of probate, from which the Indian Succession Act 1925 exempts the Muslims, does not become compulsorily applicable to them.

See *in re Alma Latifi* 1961 BLR 940.

Glossary*

adab-ul-kadi, adab al-qadi	rules of judicial administration
ain, ‘ain, ayn	corpus of property
akar, ‘aqar	immovable property
amana	trust
amen, amin	amen
aulad	children, descendants
azan, adhan	call from mosque for prayer
benami	anonymous/pseudonymous
dai, daee, da‘i	head of a religious group, esp. Isma‘ilis
dargah, durgah	shrine, mausoleum of a saint
dharmashatras	Hindu religious/legal books
dyn-mohr, dain mahr	dower debt
fateha, sura fateha	first chapter of Qur’an
fatwa	juristic opinion/verdict
fazuli, fazoolee, fuduli	unauthorized
fiqh, fiqah	Islamic jurisprudence
firash	bed
gaddi, guddi	headship of a religious group/institution
gahwara	a Shia ceremony
had, hadd, hodood	punishment for crime prescribed by Qur’an
hadith, hadees, ahadith	Prophet’s teachings
hakam, hukam, hakama	arbitrators, arbiters
hiba, hebah	gift
hibanama, heba-nama	gift deed
hila	legal excuse, trick, artifice

* Arabic/Persian/Urdu/Hindi expressions—singular, plural—as differently spelt in court-judgments, with their correct spellings and meanings.

ibranamah	release-deed
iddat, 'iddat' iddah	'no-remarriage' period after dissolution of marriage
ijma	consensus of jurists
ikrar, iqrar	acknowledgment
irad, iraz	desertion
jamat, jama'at	group, community, community-organization
jamatkhana	community centre
kabeenamah, kabin-nama	marriage agreement
kalma, kalmia	basic oath of belief in Islam
kazi, cadi, qadi	judge
khandan	family
khanqah	Muslim monastery
khoola, kolah, khul	divorce at wife's instance
khoolanamah, khula-nama	deed of divorce at wife's instance
kitabi, kitabia, kitabiyya	follower of a scriptural religion
koran, Quran	Qur'an—the holy book of Islam
lathi	staff
maher, mahr	dower
majbub	eunuch
manafe, manafi	usufruct
manhoos	inauspicious
mapillahs	a Muslim sect in South India
masjid	mosque
mata, muta, mut'a	compensation for divorce
matam	mourning
math	Hindu monastery
matwali, mutawalli	trustee of a wakf
moottah, mut'a	term marriage
mubarat, mubara'at	divorce by mutual consent
mufassil, mufassal	administrative division, district
mujtahid	Shia jurist
mooltakit, multaqit	care-taker of a fondling
murshed, murshid	spiritual guide
murtad, murtadd	apostate
musha, moosha	undivided share in property

nasab	lineage
nass, nusus	binding injunction of Qur'an
nikah, nikii, nikahi	marriage, marital ceremony, by marriage
nimmaz, namaz	Islamic prayer
nushuz	disobedience
parda, purda	veil
pardanashin	women in veil
punchayet panchayat	community tribunal
pundit	Hindu cleric
qaraba, qurba, qarabatdar	relatives
rahen, rahn	mortgage
sahih, sihah	authentic *Hadith* collections
sajjadanashin	trustee of a monastery
shiqaq, sheqaq	marital discord
shirkat, shirakat	partnership
silsilla, silsila	line of spiritual succession
tabut, taboot	coffin
tahbil, tahvil	custody, bailment
takiah, taqiyya	a Shia practice
talak, talaq	divorce
talaknama	written divorce
talaq-e-tafwiz	divorce by wife under delegated authority
taluqdar	land-holder
taqlid, taqleed	blindly following old jurists
tazia, taziadari	artificial coffin, a Muharram practice
towliat, tawliyat, tawliah	custody/management of wakfs
wakf, wakaf, waqf, awqaf	Muslim religious endlowment
wala, mowla	acquired relations
walad-ooz-zina, walad al-zina	bastard
wasika, wathiqa	royal/government grant
zamindar, zamindary	feudal lords, their estate
zillah, zila	district
zimmi, zimmee, dhimmi	non-Muslim subject in a Muslim state
zina, zena, zenakari	fornication, unlawful sex

Index of Statutes*

I. SUBCONTINENT

* Consolidated and classified list of statutes referred to in the original and the present editions of *Cases*.

II. INDIA

III. PAKISTAN

IV. BANGLADESH

Index of Cases*

I. SUBCONTINENT

* Consolidated and classified list of court rulings dealt with in the original and added to the present editions of *Cases*. Old rulings referred to inside the texts of the judgments included in the original edition of *Cases* are not listed here.

II. INDIA

III. PAKISTAN

IV. BANGLADESH

V. UK

Subject Index*

* References under *Cases* are to serial number of cases dealt with in the original and retained in the present editions. References under *Introduction* and *Updates* are to page numbers of the present edition.